Where to Sta
the guide to acces
in the UK and Ireland

Published by RADAR PROMOTIONS LTD for

THE ROYAL ASSOCIATION
FOR DISABILITY AND REHABILITATION

12 City Forum , 250 City Road
London EC1V 8AF

☎ 020 7250 3222
Fax 020 7250 0212
Minicom 020 7250 4119

Sponsored by

Directgov
Public services all in one place
www.direct.gov.uk

Get the most from London Underground

There is a range of guides and maps to help you plan your journeys by public transport in London, whatever your needs.

The information includes location of lifts, car parks, toilets and taxi ranks. The formats available include large print, Braille and audio translation. Large print and tactile maps are also available for some stations.

To request a copy:

- By phone: **020 7222 1234**
- By textphone: **020 7918 3015**

You can also plan your journey by logging on to
tfl.gov.uk/journeyplanner

For detailed information on accessibility at individual stations, log on to:
www.directenquiries.com

Contents

Head of Publishing
Peter Gaskell

Production Co-ordinator
Lucy Kearney

Design & Production
James Kerr

Design provided by
Impromptu Publishing Ltd
2nd floor, Century House
11 St Peter's Square
Manchester M2 3DN
Tel: 0161 236 9526
Fax: 0161 247 7978
info@impromptupublishing.com
www.impromptupublishing.com

Printed by
Brentwood

Cover photography: Arundel © Britain on View. South East Tourism- Simon Kreitem. Holkham Hall © Britain on View. Ballintoy © Britain on view. London © Britain on View

Discover caravanning.
Access all areas.
Have you considered touring caravan holidays as a great way to get out and about? You'll be able to access some of the most beautiful areas of Britain & Ireland and if you're more adventurous you could travel abroad, too.
Starting anything new is always a bit daunting, so it's good to know The Caravan Club are there to talk to for advice and encouragement.
No-one has more experience than The Club in all aspects of caravanning and touring – and members get all the help they need absolutely free.
The Club also offers the largest network of UK Sites in glorious locations and there are Club Resident Wardens on hand to welcome you.
With over 100 Club Sites having disabled facilities including toilets and showers, and almost 70 achieving Mobility 1 rating under the National Accessibility Scheme, The Carav Club strives to provide accessibility for all.
Whatever holiday experience you're looking for you'll find a Club Site to suit you including over 40 Sites open all year round.
Whichever Site you choose, you can be assured of excellent facilities, a friendly welcome, and consistently high standards.
THE CARAVAN CLUB
Touring Britain & Ireland
Call today for your FREE Touring Britain & Ireland brochure on 0800 328 6655 quoting RAD09 or visit www.caravanclub.co.uk

Introduction

Welcome to the 2009 edition of RADAR's guide to holiday opportunities for disabled people. The aim of this book is to give information on the accessibility and facilities of holiday accommodation for disabled guests in Britain and Ireland.

A major role of this guide is to help overcome the barrier of lack of information that still exists, despite increased provision. By highlighting what accommodation is out there, we hope to widen the choices available to disabled people and their families.

Although more accommodation providers have detailed access information on their websites it can be difficult to find that information. In printed mainstream material the information is even sparser. RADAR's guide bridges that gap.

The accommodation listed will not all be suitable for everyone. The entries seek to give information on the accessibility of the accommodation and the services available – they are not constrained by an external definition of what is accessible.

Neither are they recommendations – RADAR does not approve holiday accommodation. It organises and passes on information that can be used as a base from which choices can be made. While every effort has been made to provide accurate information, RADAR cannot be held responsible for any inaccuracy or complaint arising from either editorial or advertising in this guide.

The guide also contains information on many other organisations that can help disabled people and their families to plan a holiday. And of course the information it contains will also be of interest and use to disabled people who need to travel on business and those who book accommodation on their behalf.

As ever, RADAR would like to thank all those who have provided information or supported the guide through advertising this year. We are particularly grateful for the comments and suggestions from readers. While it has not been possible to incorporate all of them, have all been welcome and considered.

RADAR
October 2008

RADAR - for a just and equal society whose strength is human difference.

RADAR is the UK's leading national pan-disability organisation, run by and working for disabled people with a membership of 400 disability groups and organisations as well as individuals. RADAR acts with independence to fast track the expectations of disabled people to policy makers. It pioneers upbeat campaigns to stimulate changes in attitudes and behaviour.

RADAR was formed in 1977 and since then has been instrumental in influencing major policy changes including the Disability Discrimination Acts of 1995 and 2005.

We work with organisations of all types in order to achieve change through partnerships and coalitions. RADAR itself is an organisation of disabled people. That is to say that constitutionally the majority of our governing board of trustees must be disabled people. Currently, 70 per cent of our trustees are disabled.

Our Vision

RADAR's vision is of a just and equal society whose strength is human difference.

To this end, our mission is to support individuals, networks and policy-makers to do things differently. For the next three years we have selected three objectives. These are: freedom and choice in relationships, family and home – a strong home base with independent living support; an end to disability-related poverty – careers not just jobs, equal pay, the chance to build a pension and savings; and more people with ill-health, injury or disability in leadership positions.

For information on all RADAR's campaigns and activities contact:

RADAR, 12 City Forum, 250 City Road, London EC1V 8AF.
Telephone: 020 7250 3222
Text: 020 7250 4119
Fax: 020 7250 0212
Email: radar@radar.org.uk
Website: www.radar.org.uk

Planning & booking a holiday in Britain

In this guide you will find information to help you plan a holiday or a business trip. It is important to remember that this information is intended for people with a wide range of experiences of disability. Therefore not all of it will be relevant to everyone.

Although there is an increasing amount of holiday accommodation that is basically accessible for some disabled people, there are still few ordinary establishments that offer personal assistance or extensive facilities. It is therefore essential to ensure, before making a booking anywhere, that your individual requirements can be met. This may involve giving the owners or managers of accommodation detailed information about the effects of your impairment or condition and any specific facilities you might require.

If the suitability of the accommodation appears doubtful, it may be advisable to book elsewhere rather than arrive and discover that the facilities are inaccessible or unsuitable for you in some other way.

Before you book a holiday

- **Decide on the type of holiday you want** - this will include whether you will be on your own, with your family or friends or wish to join an organised group. It will also include whether you want meals provided or to stay in self-catering accommodation and which general area you would like to visit. These are matters of personal preference and individual cicumstances. It is worth thinking through your preferences before considering how your chosen holiday can work in relation to your impairment.

- **Find out as much as possible about the area you wish to visit** - local general tourist publications will often give some information on the suitability of an area and sometimes more specific information for disabled visitors. Tourist organisations and travel companies have duties to make reasonable adjustments to their services, so they should be able to provide information in the format that you ask for. Access guides exist for a number of areas and these and other useful publications to local areas are included in the regional sections of this guide. Some publications giving national information which may be useful to disabled holiday-makers are listed from page 45.

- **Plan ahead and book early.**

Booking the holiday

- **Consider whether you want to tell people about your disability/condition and its effects –** you are the expert on this. The more information that you give on your requirements, the more probable it is that the provider will be able to meet them to your satisfaction. On the other hand, if you have had a bad experience in the past (such as facing discrimination because of a hidden condition such as a mental health problem) or if you prefer to remain private, you may prefer not to disclose but to find out discreetly whether your requirements will be met. The decision on disclosure is yours. Some accommodation providers may be inclined to make assumptions about prospective disabled guests. It may be annoying to be asked irrelevant questions but this can be preferable to not being asked anything and certainly better than a disinclination to answer your specific questions.

- **Point out the facilities you are looking for at your destination** - it may be useful to have in mind those features that are absolutely essential and those that are desirable. Facilities can include the physical accessibility of the premises and the surroundings, the availability of equipment or the provision of any services.

Planning & booking a holiday in Britain

■ **Seek adjustments when making a booking** - for instance, if you need to discuss the booking by textphone or email rather than telephone or if you need to contact accommodation directly rather than only a central reservations service. If this is not agreed, remind the provider of their duties under the Disability Discrimination Act.

■ **Make arrangements for transport to and from your holiday accommodation** - if you are likely to require any form of assistance, make sure that the transport provider knows well in advance.

■ **Ensure you have adequate insurance cover** - check whether your own requirements will be covered by any policy offered by holiday providers (see page 14).

Before you go

■ **Double check that all your arrangements are satisfactory.**

■ **Make a checklist of extra equipment you may need to take with you.**

■ **Check that you have a valid passport** if you are going abroad.

■ **Take a more than sufficient supply of all medicines you may need** - it is also advisable to take a written prescription in case of emergency and, if you are having to go through customs or border controls, a note explaining what they are.

■ **Consider the security of your home** - remember to cancel regular deliveries.

If things go wrong

■ **Try to sort things out on the spot** – often problems can be solved if they are brought to the attention of the provider as soon as they occur.

■ **If you experience discrimination or reluctance to make adjustments for your needs** - you do have legal rights under the Disability Discrimination Act, which requires service providers not to discriminate and to make adjustments that are reasonable. Reminding a holiday provider of this can prompt them to be more flexible. If you have faced or experience discrimination contact the for Equality and Human Rights Commission.

■ **Non-disability complaints** - if general standards in the accommodation are not what might be expected there may be several routes to make a complaint, for example to the headquarters of the accommodation group or to the tourism body or The AA that have carried out a quality assessment. Your local trading standards office should be able to give advice.

If things go right

■ **Tell the provider** – when people provide a good service tell them and their bosses.

■ **Tell others** – RADAR welcomes comments about accommodation that readers have found good, just as much as places that have been found to be unsatisfactory and uses the information to improve this guide from year to year.

Planning & booking a holiday in Britain

This book is mainly concerned with holidays in Britain. However, many disabled people take holidays overseas. In some cases, the choice of destination may be affected by climate or dietary factors or by the availability of particular services. Voluntary organisations concerned with specific impairments can often give information on these and many are listed under Voluntary Organisations (see page 18).

Most mainstream holiday brochures give little or no information on what is offered for disabled people, or only refer to the subject in off-putting terms in the small print. Good travel agents may be able to find out more information from the tour operators and efficiently pass on your needs to all concerned.

However, It may be better to deal direct with a tour operator. Indeed even if you book through a travel agent it is probably advisable to contact the tour operator and the transport provider to reinforce your specific needs. Some tour operators specialise in some way, for example in a particular locality or type of activity. Their staff will often have personal contact with the accommodation and transport providers on the ground. There are also a few organisations that actually own the accommodation for which they make bookings.

While RADAR believes that disabled people should be able to enjoy mainstream holiday opportunities and that individuals should have the maximum choice in holiday options, it may also be worth considering those companies that specialise in catering for disabled customers. The fact that they will have knowledge, and often personal experience, of disability and will have directly inspected the accessibility of the accommodation and resorts that they offer may provide the necessary confidence to make a booking. For information on these organisations see page 28.

National Key Scheme for Toilets for Disabled People – although the NKS is used widely throughout the UK, many people make little use of public toilets in their home areas and only become aware of it when travelling, especially as rail companies and some motorway service providers are among the organisations using the scheme for their toilets for disabled people.

The principle of the NKS is that if local authorities and other organisations decide to lock toilets for disabled people to prevent misuse they should use a standard lock. Local authorities taking part should have arrangements for disabled people in their areas to obtain a NKS key that can be used throughout the country. Disabled people who have difficulty getting a key can obtain one from RADAR (price £3.50) by calling 0870 770 7930 or through www.radar.org.uk.

RADAR also maintains a list of the toilets fitted with the NKS, of which there are currently almost 8000. This is published annually in the National Key Scheme Guide.

Insurance

It is essential to have adequate insurance for travel. Although travel insurance is generally associated with overseas journeys, it is also available and should be considered for leisure and business travel in the UK as well. Even if loss of possessions in this country is covered by household insurance, there may still be the risk of financial loss if the trip has to be cancelled.

In many countries the cost of medical treatment in the event of illness or accident has to be met in full and can be frighteningly high. Even in areas with which Britain has reciprocal health care agreements, part of the cost of treatment often has to be paid and in extreme cases there may be repatriation costs. Insurance may also be required to cover the cost of property that is damaged or lost while away from home, to recoup money if a holiday has to be cancelled or cut short or to provide some compensation for delays.

While any blanket refusal to provide insurance cover, or charge unjustifiable higher rates, for disabled people is unlawful there can still be difficulties or higher costs for some people. It is worth checking whether a standard policy offered by a travel company meets an individual's situation, including that of any equipment that has to be taken. Some voluntary organisations can assist their members, or people with the condition with which they are concerned, to obtain appropriate cover which would otherwise be difficult.

Some companies with insurance packages designed specifically for disabled people are:

AllClear Travel Insurance

6th Floor, Regents House, Hubert Road, Brentwood CM14 4JE.

☎ 0871 2088 579. W www.allcleartravel.co.uk

Chartwell Insurance

Chartwell House, 229-294 Hale Lane, Edgware HA8 8NP.

☎ 0845 260 7051. @ info@chartwellinsurance.co.uk W www.chartwellinsurance.co.uk

En Route Insurance

Grove Mills, Cranbrook Road, Hawkhurst, Kent TN18 4AS.

☎ 0800 783 7245. W www.enrouteinsurance.co.uk

Fogg Travel Insurance Services Ltd

Crow Hill Drive, Mansfield NG19 7AE.

☎ 01623 631331. @ sales@fogginsure.co.uk W www.fogginsure.co.uk

Free Spirit

P J Hayman & Company Ltd, Stansted House, Rowlands Castle, Hampshire PO9 6DX.

☎ 0845 230 5000. @ freespirit@pjhayman.com W www.free-spirit.com

Travelbility

J & M Insurance Services, Peregrine House, Bakers Lane, Epping CM16 5DQ.

☎ 0845 338 1638 or 01992 566919. W www.jmi.co.uk

The Tourism For All National Accessible Accommodation Standard

The principle behind the National Accessible Scheme is that tourist accommodation is inspected against agreed access criteria; the inspections being carried out either by the national/regional tourist boards or Holiday Care. The scheme was first introduced in 1993. A new set of criteria was introduced in 2002 in England where it has superseded the original scheme, which however remains in use in Scotland, Wales and Northern Ireland.

In England the scheme comprises four categories of standards of access for mobility impairment and also standards for two levels each for people with hearing and visual impairment. These are indicated as follows:

Typically suitable for a person with sufficient mobility to climb a short flight of steps but would benefit from points of fixtures and fittings to aid balance.

Typically suitable for a person with restricted walking ability and for those that may need to use a wheelchair some of the time.

Typically suitable for a person who depends on the use of a wheelchair and transfers unaided to and from a wheelchair in a seated position.

Typically suitable for a person who depends on a wheelchair and who requires personal/mechanical assistance (a carer or a hoist) to aid transfer.

Minimum requirements to meet the National Accessible Standards for guests with hearing impairment, from mild hearing loss to profoundly deaf.

Recommended additional requirements to meet best practise.

Minimum entry requirements to meet the National Accessible Standards for visually impaired guests.

Recommended additional requirements to meet best practise.

Full details of the criteria can be found on **www.qualityintourism.com**

Elsewhere there are three categories of access, depicted by the following symbols with their brief descriptions:

 Category 1 - Accessible to a wheelchair user travelling independently.

 Category 2 - Accessible to a wheelchair user travelling with assistance

 Category 3 - Accessible to someone with limited mobility but able to walk a few paces and up to a maximum of 3 steps.

Within this guide we have used the symbols where appropriate in the accommodation entries.

Tourism for All

☎ **0845 124 9971.**

@ **info@tourismforall.org.uk**

W **www.tourismforall.org.uk**

Tourism for All, previously Holiday Care, is a registered charity that is the UK's central source of holiday and travel information and support for disabled and older people and carers. It provides information on accessible accommodation, visitor attractions and transport, both in the UK and at selected overseas destinations. It also identifies sources of funding for disabled people on low incomes. A reservations service for inspected accessible accommodation is also offered. In addition Tourism for All works with all sectors of the tourism industry to improve accessibility and carry out inspections under the National Accessible Scheme.

In addition the following voluntary organisations are involved in various ways in holiday provision for disabled people. For those with their own accommodation, numbers in brackets indicate the regional sections of this guide in which further information may be found. Other organisations with a more localised remit are listed in the regional sections.

Action Against Allergy

PO Box 278, Twickenham, TW1 4QQ.

☎ **020 8892 4949**

W **www.actionagainstallergy.co.uk**

Action Against Allergy publish a large number of information leaflets for people with allergies including '***Holiday Accommodation – a useful list of places to stay for allergic people'***, price £2.

Action for Blind People

14-16 Verney Road, London SE16 3DZ.

☎ **020 7635 4906/7.**

@ **info@actionforblindpeople.org**

W **www.actionforblindpeople.org**

Operate 4 holiday hotels for blind and partially sighted people, see entries for Russell Hotel, Bognor Regis (3), Lauriston Hostel, Weston-super-Mare (4), Cliffden Hotel, Teignmouth (5) and Windermere Manor, Windermere (10). Self catering units are also available at Teignmouth and Windermere. Brochures are available in large print, Braille and cassette.

Arthritis Care

18 Stephenson Way, London NW1 2HD.

☎ **020 7380 6500.**

W **www.arthritiscare.org.uk**

Arthritis Care campaigns and provides a range of services and information for people with arthritis and their families including on holiday options. Although Arthritis Care has decided to withdraw from direct provision of holiday accommodation bookings are still being taken for its hotels in Blackpool, Largs, Nairn and Poole.

Asthma UK

Summit House, 70 Wilson Street, London EC2A 2DB.

☎ **020 7786 4900.**

Advice Line: 08457 010203.

W **www.asthma.org.uk**

Asthma UK runs Kick Asthma adventure holidays for children and young people with asthma and related conditions. Fun and adventure activities are combined with educational sessions on managing asthma. Holidays are held at a variety of locations in the UK and are divided into 6-11 and 12-17 age groups. For more information call the Kick Asthma Information Team on ☎ 0845 603 8143.

Voluntary organisations

BREAK

Davison House, 1 Montague Road, Sheringham NR26 8WN.
☎ **01263 822161.**
@ **office@break-charity.org**
W **www.break-charity.org**

Offers holidays and respite care for disabled children and adults at centres in Norfolk, see under Sheringham (6). BREAK also has holiday chalets at Westward Ho!, Devon (5).

British Kidney Patient Association

Bordon, Hants GU35 9JZ.
☎ **01420 472021/2.**
W **www.britishkidney-pa.co.uk**

BKPA are able to offer financial assistance to kidney patients for holidays and any requests should be made on their behalf by their renal social worker. Group holidays are arranged for young kidney patients at three activity centres and arrangements can be made for adults at some Mediterranean resorts. For information contact the Holiday Secretary.

British Limbless Ex-Service Men's Association

Frankland Moore House, 185/187 High Road, Chadwell Heath RM6 6NA.
☎ **020 8590 1124.**
@ **headquarters@blesma.org**
W **www.blesma.org**

Holiday accommodation is available at BLESMA residential and nursing homes in Blackpool and Crieff, Perthshire for limbless ex-service men and their wives and to widows of former members. Convalescent and holiday accommodation may also be available to other ex-service men.

British Lung Foundation

73-75 Goswell Road, London EC1V 7ER.
☎ **0845 850 5020.** @ **enquiries@blf-uk.org**
W **www.lunguk.org**

Among a range of free information sheets and booklets on lung diseases and related issues is Going on Holiday with a Lung Condition. Some information on services in other countries can also be given.

British Polio Fellowship

Unit A, Eagle Office Centre, The Runway, Ruislip HA4 6SE.
☎ **0800 0180586.**
W **www.britishpolio.org.uk**

BPF have a self-catering bungalow equipped for wheelchair users at Burnham-on-Sea (4). Holiday information and grants are available to their members.

Calvert Trust

W **www.calvert-trust.org.uk**

The Calvert Trust has three outdoor activity centres equipped for disabled people in the Lake District, Northumbria and Exmoor (see page 499). At each there is also accessible self-catering for families and similar sized groups. See under Barnstaple (5), Keswick (10) and Kielder (11)

Contact a Family

209-211 City Road, London EC1V 1JN.
☎ **0808 808 3555.**
Textphone: 0808 808 3556.
@ **info@cafamily.org.uk**
W **www.cafamily.org.uk**

Among a range of publications offering information to families with disabled children is a free factsheet on holidays.

Cystic Fibrosis Trust

11 London Road, Bromley BR1 1BY.

☎ **0845 859 1000.**

www.cftrust.org.uk

Can give information to people with cystic fibrosis and their families on holidays, travel and travel insurance.

Diabetes UK

10 Parkway, London NW1 7AA.

☎ **020 7424 1000.**

info@diabetes.org.uk

www.diabetes.org.uk

Offers advice to people with diabetes on travel planning and has a Travel Guide booklet (price £2). Also available are guides on around 60 countries. Activity holidays are arranged at a number of locations during the summer for children and young people with diabetes. A Catalogue and information are available from Careline at the above address or ☎ 0845 120 2960 Textphone: 020 7424 1031 (9am-5pm weekdays).

DIAL UK

St Catherines, Tickhill Road, Doncaster DN4 8QN.

☎**/Textphone: 01302 310123.**

dial-uk@hotmail.co.uk

www.dialuk.org.uk

The national organisation of the DIAL network of around 130 local disability advice centres run by and for disabled people. Independent advice on all aspects of disability, mainly by phone but also in person. Local DIAL groups are listed in the regional sections of this guide.

Disability Snowsport UK

Cairngorm Mountain, via Aviemore PH22 1RB.

☎ **01479 861272.**

admin@disabilitysnowsport.org.uk

www.disabilitysnowsport.org.uk

Disability Snowsport (The Uphill Ski Club) offers ski instruction by fully qualified instructors for disabled people at a purpose built adaptive ski school at Cairngorm. Similar services are based at the ski slopes around the country. In addition, activity weeks are held in Europe and USA.

Disabled Christians Fellowship/Through the Roof

PO Box 353, Epsom KT18 5WS.

☎ **01372 749955.**

www.throughtheroof.org

Organises holidays for disabled people of all ages both in the UK and overseas. Personal help may be available as required.

Disabled Holiday Information

PO Box 185, Oswestry, Shropshire SY10 1AF.

info@disabledholidayinfo.org.uk

www.disabledholidayinfo.org.uk

Organisation providing information on the accessibility of places to visit and some places to stay largely based on the direct experience of a wheelchair user. In addition to regularly expanded website, they have printed information on facilities in and around Shropshire, see page 228.

Voluntary organisations

Disabled Ramblers
c/o Little Croft, Guildford Road,
Shamley Green,
GU5 0RT.
☎ **01483 893159.**
@ **helby@disabledramblers.org**
W **www.disabledramblers.co.uk**

This is an organisation of disabled people promoting improved access in the country-side. They have an annual programme of one and two day supported rambles in a variety of settings mainly for users of mobility vehicles including wheelchairs, scooters and buggies. Advice on accommodation can be given to participants if required.

Disaway Trust
55 Tolworth Park Road,
Surbiton, Surrey KT6 7RJ.
☎ **020 8390 2576.**
W **www.disaway.co.uk**

Organises group holidays abroad and in Britain for physically disabled people aged 16-80. Helpers are available on a one-to-one basis and partners of disabled people are welcome.

Livability Holidays
PO Box 36, Cowbridge CF71 7GB.
☎ **0845 6584478.**
@ **holidays@johngrooms.org.uk**
W **www.groomsholidays.org.uk**
Livability Holidays offers a range of holiday accommodation including three hotels and a variety of self-catering units around England and Wales, including the former Farrell Holiday Properties. See under Bognor Regis, Brackle-sham Bay, Felpham and Selsey (2); New Milton and Poole (3); Minehead, South Cerney and Weymouth (4); Torquay (5); Clacton and Wroxham (6); Ambleside (10); Llandudno (13a) and Minehead (13c).

3H Fund
147A Camden Rd, Tunbridge Wells TN1 2RA
☎ **01892 547474.** @ **info@3hfund.org.uk**
W **www.3hfund.org.uk**

Provide subsidised group holidays for physically disabled people, from 13 years upwards, who would otherwise be unable to take a break. Holidays are inclusive of accommodation and transport. Experienced volunteers and nursing staff provide help. The programme, including weeks in Britain and abroad, is planned to give variety.

Hearing Concern
95 Gray's Inn Road, London WC1X 8TX.
☎ **020 7440 9871.**
Textphone: 020 7440 9873.
W **www.hearingconcern.org.uk**

A number of holidays and short breaks in Britain and abroad are organised each year for people who would like to share their time with others who understand hearing difficulties. A lipspeaker usually accompanies each group, but BSL support is not provided. Contact Philip Barron, 4 Anselm Close, Croydon CR0 5LY. ☎ 020 8680 2229. @ philbarron@waitrose.com

Holidays for Disabled People
Holidaymaker Liaison Team, PO Box 164,
Totton, Southampton SO40 9WZ.
@ **disholspw@aol.com**
W **www.holidaysfordisabled.com**

Organises an annual group holiday for people with physical disabilities at a holiday centre in the UK. Assistance provided by volunteers as required with medical and nursing cover. Participants can take their own companions.

Holidays with Help

4 Pebblecombe, Adelaide Road,
Surbiton, Surrey KT6 4LL.
☎ 020 8390 9752.
@ holidays.with.help@lineone.net
W www.holidayswithhelp.org.uk

Organisation running respite care breaks for disabled people at holiday centres in England. Activities and outings are arranged. Applications accepted from groups, families and individuals. Experienced helpers and medical and nursing personnel are available. Apply to Rosemary McIntyre at the above address.

Incontact

SATRA Innovation Park,
Rockingham Road, Kettering NN16 9JH.
☎ 0870 770 3246. @ info@incontact.org
W www.incontact.org

Incontact is the leading UK advocacy charity which campaigns for people living with bladder & bowel control problems. Dedicated to raising awareness and improving the understanding of continence issues, they provide user-friendly booklets and fact sheets, offer an on-line support forum, a specialist nurse and counsellor helpline and a magazine three times a year. Call confidentially on 01536 533255, email info@incontact.org or visit www.incontact.org. Registered charity number 1085095.

MENCAP

Advice & Information Service, 4 Swan Courtyard, Coventry Road, Birmingham B26 1BU.
☎ 0121 707 7877. @ help@mencap.org.uk
W www.askmencap.info

Local Gateway Clubs offer a range of leisure activities for people with learning disabilities. Mencap also administers the AdCare Holiday Fund which gives grants to enable people with learning disabilities to go on holiday.

Multiple Sclerosis Society

MS National Centre, 372 Edgware Road,
London NW2 6ND.
☎ Helpline: 020 8438 0700.
@ info@mssociety.org.uk
W www.mssociety.org.uk

The Society publishes information on holidays suitable for people with multiple sclerosis including an online respite directory and owns several respite care homes and hotels. See under Horley (2), Leamington Spa (7), York (9) and North Berwick (13a).

The National Autistic Society

393 City Road, London EC1V 1NG.
☎ 020 7833 2299. @ nas@nas.org.uk
W www.autism.org.uk

Issues Holiday Help: A Guide giving information on places that may be appropriate for children and adults with autism and Asperger syndrome.

National Blind Children's Society

Bradbury House, Market Street,
Highbridge, Somerset TA9 3BW.
☎ 01278 764764. @ enquiries@nbcs.org.uk
W www.nbcs.org.uk

Among their services NBCS provide and organise activity holidays for children with a visual impairment, family weekends and have a specially adapted mobile home at Burnham-on-Sea.

National Deaf Children's Society

15 Dufferin Street, London EC1Y 8UR.
☎/Textphone: 0121 234 9820.
@ events@ndcs.org.uk
W www.ndcs.org.uk

Among the services and events organised for deaf children and their families, NDCS arrange a series of residential and day adventure and activity events at centres around the country. Volunteer signers and lip speakers provide communication support.

National Federation of Shopmobilty

PO Box 6641, Christchurch, BH23 9DQ.
☎ 08456 442446.
@ info@shopmobility.org
W www.shopmobilityuk.org

Shopmobility schemes, listed in the regional sections of this Guide, provide wheelchairs and scooters for use in around 300 shopping and other areas areas throughout UK. A Directory giving details of the services offered by each scheme is published each year by NFS UK and an online version is on the website.

National Kidney Federation

The Point, Coach Road, Shireoaks, Worksop S81 8BY.
☎ 01909 544999 (Helpline).
W www.kidney.org.uk

The Holiday Pages on the NKF website give general advice for kidney patients travelling away from home and contact details for dialysis units in the UK that are particularly geared up for people on holiday.

National Society for Epilepsy

Chalfont Centre for Epilepsy, Chalfont St Peter, Bucks SL9 0RJ.
☎ 01494 601300.
W www.epilepsynse.org.uk

Provides respite and residential care and medical services including assessment for people living with epilepsy. Contact Epilepsy Helpline 01494 601400, 10am-4pm weekdays.

Papillon Holidays

1 Exeter Drive, Ashton-under-Lyne OL6 8BZ.
☎ 0774 959 8423.
W www.papillonholidays.co.uk

Papillon Holidays offers a range of holidays with support in Britain particularly for people with learning and physical disabilities. The programme, which runs through the year, includes a variety of activity and themed breaks as well as less structured seaside holidays.

Parkinson's Disease Society of the UK

215 Vauxhall Bridge Road, London SW1V 1EJ.
☎ 020 7931 8080 or 0808 800 0303 (☎Helpline).
Textphone: 020 7963 9380.
W www.parkinsons.org.uk

Advice and information on Parkinson's Disease and travel is available through the Helpline. The PDS publishes an information sheet on International Travel & Parkinson's.

Phab England

Summit House, 50 Wandle Road, Croydon CR0 1DF.
☎ 020 8667 9443.
@ info@phab.org.uk W www.phab.org.uk

The Phab Kids Integrated Living Experience offer one week breaks at Activity Centres for young people with and without disibilities aged 9-18. Details on these and information on the network of Phab clubs throughout the country are available from the above address.

P.I.N.N.T

PO Box 3126, Christchurch BH23 2XS.
☎ 01202 481625. W www.pinnt.co.uk

A self-help organisation for people requiring intravenous, naso-gastric and other artificial nutrition therapy. They produce Holiday Guidelines giving information on planning a holiday, transporting and obtaining equipment and supplies and other matters.

Rethink

28 Castle Street, Kingston-Upon-Thames KT1 1SS
☎ 0845 456 0455. @ info@rethink.org
W www.rethink.org

Rethink provides services and advice to people affected by severe mental illness including information on holidays and respite care and it has a respite centre, 'Foresters', on the edge of the New Forest.

Voluntary organisations

Riding for the Disabled Association

Norfolk House, 1A Tournament Court,
Edgehill Drive,
Warwickshire CV34 6LG.

☎ **0845 658 1082.**

@ **info@rda.org.uk**

W **www.rda.org.uk**

The RDA has local riding and carriage driving groups for disabled people throughout the country. The Association organises Group, County, Regional and National holidays for its members. Contact the above address for details on joining a RDA Group.

Royal British Legion

48 Pall Mall, London SW1Y 5JY.

☎ **0845 772 5725**

W **www.britishlegion.org.uk**

The Legion has 4 Poppy Break Centres for serving and ex-Service people, their dependants and carers recovering from an illness or bereavement. The Centres are in Bridlington, Portrush, Southport and Weston-super-Mare for people who do not need personal or nursing care. Personal and nursing care is not provided.

Royal National Institute of the Blind

105 Judd Street, London WC1H 9NE.

☎ **0845 766 9999.**

W **www.rnib.org.uk**

RNIB's Leisure Service provide holiday and leisure information for people with sight loss and run vacation schemes for blind and partially sighted children. They also work with the leisure industry to improve access to leisure. A Hotel Guide Book is available, see page 47.

RYA Sailability

RYA House, Ensign Way, Hamble,
Southampton SO31 4YA.

☎ **0845 345 0403.**

Textphone: 023 8060 4248

@ **sailability@rya.org.uk**

W **www.rya.org.uk/sailability**

RYA Sailability is an initiative with the aim of promoting and co-ordinating participation by disabled people in the sailing community. It provides information to the public on where they can sail and supports sailing centres and clubs in improving opportunities open to people with disabilities.

Scope

Scope Response, PO Box 833,
Milton Keynes MK12 5NY.

☎ **0808 800 3333.**

@ **response@scope.org.uk**

W **www.scope.org.uk**

Scope is a national disability organisation with a focus on people with cerebral palsy. For more information contact the Scope Response, 9am-7pm weekdays and 10am-2pm Saturdays.

Scout Holiday Homes Trust

Gilwell Park, Bury Road, Chingford,
London E4 7QW.

☎ **020 8433 7290.**

@ **lynda.peters@scout.org.uk**

W **www.scoutbase.org.uk/hq/holhomes**

Offers low cost self-catering holidays in 6-berth chalets and caravans at a number of holiday parks. Any family with a disabled member welcomed - not only those in Scouting. The season is generally from Easter-October and bookings are taken from the previous October. See entries in this Guide under New Milton and Poole(3); Burnham-on-Sea (4); Exmouth, Paignton and St Austell (5); Clacton and Great Yarmouth (6); Skipsea (9); Berwick (11), Prestatyn (13a) and Kidwelly (13c).

Scripture Union Holidays

207-209 Queensway, Bletchley,
Milton Keynes MK2 2EB.
☎ **01908 856177.**
@ **holidays@scriptureunion.org.uk**
W **www.scriptureunion.org.uk**

Organises holidays for young people. One each year is for physically disabled and able-bodied youngsters aged 15-19 and another for 13-19 year-olds with learning difficulties. Applications via the Holidays Administrator.

Sense (The National Deafblind & Rubella Association)

101 Pentonville Road, London N1 9LG.
☎ **0845 127 0060**
Textphone: 0845 127 0062.
@ **holiday@sense.org.uk**
W **www.sense.org.uk**

Sense organises over 25 holidays each year for 120 deafblind children and adults. Each holiday has one or more paid leaders supported by a team of volunteers to ensure that each holiday is centred on individual needs and choices of holidaymakers. Sense holidays enable participants to have fun in a supportive environment, gain new experience and meet new people.

For further information contact the Holidays Co-ordinator.

Spinal Injuries Association

SIA House, 2 Trueman Place, Oldbrook,
Milton Keynes MK6 2HH.
☎ **0845 678 6633.**
@ **sia@spinal.co.uk**
W **www.spinal.co.uk**

The SIA's website includes information on holiday opportunities taken from information provided by SIA members and articles and advertisements placed in the Association's magazine. An Advice Line is available on 0800 980 0501

Vitalise

Shaproad Industrial Estate, Shap Road,
Kendal, Cumbria, LA9 6NZ
☎ **0845 345 1970.**
@ **bookings@vitalise.org.uk**
W **www.vitalise.org.uk**

Vitalise (formerly Winged Fellowship Trust) provides breaks for disabled people and carers in 5 accessible centres, see under Southampton (3), Bodmin (5), Chigwell (6), Nottingham (8) and Southport (10). Each centre provides a programme of short breaks with personal support and four of the five centres provide 24-hour care on-call. Over 500 activities are offered throughout the year with 35 special interest weeks, including special Alzheimer's Society Weeks and rooms sponsored by the MS Society. Vitalise also runs holidays for visually impaired people, accompanied by sighted guides and offers independent holidays, without care support, at selected accessible hotels in germany and Spain.Two accessible self-catering lodges are available at Vitalise Churchtown in Cornwall. Holidays for disabled groups can be arranged.

Specialist commercial organisations

The following companies and organisations offer holidays or other tourist services specifically geared to meet the needs of disabled people.

Access at Last Ltd

18 Hazel Grove, Tarleton, Preston PR4 6DQ.
☎ **01772 814555.**
W **www.accessatlast.com**

Travel company, formed by a wheelchair user, that can book accessible hotels, adapted vehicles, equipment and holiday packages. The website has details of inspected hotels, all of which have at least one room with a wheel-in shower, on which users can post their comments.

Access Travel Ltd

6 The Hillock, Astley, Lancashire M29 7GW.
☎ **01942 888844.**
@ **office@access-travel.co.uk**
W **www.access-travel.co.uk**

This long-established company offers a programme of holiday packages designed for disabled people in destinations around the Mediterranean, the Canaries and Florida. Sailing around the Greek Islands and holiday homes in France are also offered. A variety of self-catering and hotel accommodation options are available. ATOL protected.

Accessible Travel & Leisure

Avionics House, Naas Lane, Quedgeley, Gloucester GL2 4SN.
☎ **01452 729739.**
@ **info@accessibletravel.co.uk**
W **www.accessibletravel.co.uk**

Specialist travel service offering a wide range of holidays and related services for disabled people including Mediterranean holidays, cruises and tours in South Africa and Egypt. Accessible villas, apartments and hotels are offered together with accessible transfers or car hire, local representatives and insurance.

ATS Travel Ltd

1 Tank Lane, Purfleet, Essex RM16 1TA.
☎ **01708 863198.**
@ **aatstravel@aol.com**
W **www.assistedholidays.com**

Tour operator arranging holidays for disabled people and their families in Britain and abroad. Accessible accommodation is used and transport, trips and holiday insurance can be arranged. A variety of hotel, self-catering, and touring holidays are offered throughout the country.

Can Be Done Ltd

11 Woodcock Hill, Harrow HA3 0XP.
☎ **020 8907 2400.**
@ **holidays@canbedone.co.uk**
W **www.canbedone.co.uk**

Tour Operator founded by a wheelchair user, offering holidays for people with access or mobility problems. Their brochure includes a wide range of destinations in Europe (including Britain and Ireland), Asia, Australia, Africa and America but tailor made holidays can be arranged anywhere.

Chalfont Line

Chalfont House, 4 Providence Road, West Drayton UB7 8HJ.
☎ **01895 459540.**
@ **info@chalfont-line.co.uk**
W **www.chalfont-line.co.uk**

Chalfont Line, a long-established adapted coach hire company, has a programme of leisurely paced holidays for wheelchair users and others with impaired mobility mainly to destinations in Britain and Europe. Their own wheelchair accessible coaches are used for these. A door-to-door service and personal assistance can be provided at extra cost. Assistance with planning can also be given to groups hiring coaches for their own programmes.

Diana's Supported Holidays

18 Parish Close, St Peters, Broadstairs, Kent CT10 2UJ

☎ **0844 800 9373.**

@ **enquiries@dsh.org.uk**

W **www.dsh.org.uk**

A range of holidays are offered with support for people with learning disabilities at seaside resorts and countryside areas in Britain and a number destinations abroad. Groups are of at least six with a qualified leader and support staff, up to one-to-one support if required although a lower ratio is normally provided. In addition to the programmed holidays, other destinations can be arranged for groups.

Enable Holidays Ltd

The Green, Kings Norton, Birmingham B38 8SD.

☎ **0871 222 4939.**

W **www.enableholidays.com**

Company offering overseas package holidays at selected resorts in the Mediterranean, Canaries and Florida at hotels chosen as being accessible. Powered wheelchairs and other equipment can be pre-booked and adapted vehicles arranged for transfers and outings in many locations. All properties personally checked for accessibility.

Have Horse Will Travel

Ash Wells, Pilgrims Way, Postling, Hythe CT21 4EY.

☎ **01303 862996.** W **www.hhwtravel.co.uk**

Company providing a range of equestrian holidays including two each year to a dude ranch in Arizona designed and equipped for disabled guests.

Katalan Travels

☎ **01494 580816.**

@ **katalan.travels@ntlworld.com**

W **www.holidayswithaccess.com**

A travel company offering a specialist holiday consultancy and booking service for disabled people, whether travelling individually, in families or larger groups. All aspects of any type of holiday in Britain or worldwide can be covered including transport, transfers, accommodation, insurance, equipment hire and care services. An initial £25 consultancy is charged that is deducted from any subsequent booking fee.

Mosaic Community Care Ltd

Unit 1 Chiswick Court, Chiswick Grove, Preston New Road, Blackpool FY3 9TW.

☎ **01253 764500**

W **claire@mosaiccommunitycare.co.uk**

Mosaic Community Care specialises in the provision of supported luxury holidays and respite breaks for disabled people who require support and care with daily living tasks. Their programme includes cruises and destinations in Florida and UK.

Redpoint Holidays

PO Box 634, Wolverhampton WV6 0FT.

☎ **0845 6801214.** W **www.redpoint.co.uk**

A mainstream winter sports company that also offers adaptive ski programmes for disabled people wanting a skiing holiday with their family or friends. They also offer a 'Buddy Course' for companions.

Traveleyes

PO Box 511, Leeds LS5 3JT.

☎ **0870 922 0221.** @ **info@traveleyes.co.uk**

W **www.traveleyes.co.uk**

Travel company organising small group holidays for visually impaired and sighted people, with the latter acting as guides in exchange for a discounted price. Destinations in 2009 will include Peru, New Zealand, Sorrento, Sicily, Grand Canaria and Turkey. Groups are kept to around 16 and the air holidays are ATOL protected.

Specialist commercial organisations

William Forrester

1 Belvedere Close,
off Manor Road, Guildford GU2 9NP.
☎ **01483 575401.**

A wheelchair user who is a registered Blue Badge tour guide. He can help plan an itinerary in London or throughout the country, give lectures and assist visiting study groups. A telephone advice service is offered for wheelchair users visiting this country. For further information see page 00.

Wings on Wheels

8 Cornfields, Church Lane,
Tydd St Giles, Wisbech PE13 5LX.
☎ **01945 871111.**
@ **wingsonwheels@btconnect.com**
W **www.wingsonwheels.co.uk**

Offer a programme of small escorted group holidays for disabled and non-disabled people throughout the year to overseas destinations and also tailored holidays for individuals and organisations in Britain, Europe and Worldwide.

www.matchinghouses.com

A recently established website for disabled people who wish to house-swap for their holidays based on the principle that if an exchange can be arranged between people with similar access needs they should both be able to travel with greater confidence within this country or further afield. They have over 850 members worldwide.

Accommodation groups

The hotel groups and other organisations listed below are not specialist providers of accommodation for disabled people but have some properties which may be suitable and include an indication of this in their directories and brochures.

Best Western Hotels GB

Consort House, Amy Johnson Way, Clifton Moor, York YO30 4GP.

☎ **0845 773 7373 (Reservations).**

W www.bestwestern.co.uk

A consortium of independently owned hotels both in England, Scotland, Wales and the Channel Islands. Some member hotels have been inspected for accessibility and infor-mation on these can be found by on the Accessible Information section of their web-site. A number of Best Western Hotels are included in the regional sections of this guide.

Campanile Hotels

Europa House, Church Street, Old Isleworth TW7 6DA.

☎ **020 8326 1500.**

W www.campanile.com

A chain of purpose built hotels by main roads and in city centres. Parking is adjacent to the bedrooms and to the building housing reception, bar, restaurant and meeting room. All have rooms designed for disabled guests and most are included in this guide.

The Camping and Caravanning Club

Greenfields House, Westwood Way, Coventry CV4 8JH.

☎**/Textphone: 0845 130 7633.**

W www.campingandcaravanningclub.co.uk

Operates sites throughout Great Britain, most of which are open to non-members. About 70 have unisex toilet and shower facilities designed for disabled people. This together with information on their sites and membership can be obtained from the above address.

The Caravan Club

East Grinstead House, East Grinstead RH19 1UA.

☎ **01342 326944.**

W www.caravanclub.co.uk

The Caravan Club has about 200 sites throughout UK. Over 140 have unisex toilet/shower rooms designed for wheelchair users and a further 24 have handrails in amenity blocks. 70 sites have been assessed under the National Accessible Scheme and received the M1 grading; The Caravan Club is the first organisation of its kind to participate in this scheme. Full details are given in their annual brochure, and on their website.

Choice Hotels Europe

Premier House, 112 Station Road, Edgware HA8 7BJ.

☎ **0800 444444.**

W www.choicehotelseurope.com

A hotel group including Sleep Inn, Comfort, Quality and Clarion Hotels. Their directory indicates those with facilities for disabled guests. A number of these are included in the regional sections of this guide.

The Circle

20 Church Road, Horspath, Oxford OX33 1RU.

☎ **0845 345 1965.**

@ info@circlehotels.co.uk

W www.circlehotels.co.uk

A consortium of individual family run hotels, located throughout the British Isles, with a central reservations office. The Circle Hotel Directory indicates those whose managers say have access to bedrooms for disabled guests. A number are included and indicated in the regional sections of this guide.

Accommodation groups

Days Inn

☎ **0800 0280400.**

W **www.daysinn.com**

Accommodation, mainly at Welcome Break Service Areas on motorways and main routes, that have rooms for disabled guests. Listed under Lodge Accommodation in the regional sections of this guide.

Etap Hotels

W **www.etaphotel.com**

Limited service hotels in cities listed under Lodge Accommodation in the regional sections of this guide. Each has rooms with shower rooms designed for disabled guests. No restaurants but continental breakfast available. Part of the international Accor Group.

Forest Holidays

Bath Yard, Moira, Derbyshire DE12 6BD.

☎ **0845 130 8224 (campsites),**
0845 130 8223 (cabins).

@ **contact@forestholidays.co.uk**

W **www.forestholidays.co.uk**

The Forestry Commission has 20 caravan and camping sites, most of which have WCs and shower for wheelchair users, and also 3 self-catering log cabin sites, in Cornwall, north Yorkshire and The Trossachs that each have 6 person cabins designed for disabled people.

Formule 1 Hotels

W **www.hotelformule1.com**

Budget hotels listed under Lodge Accommodation in the regional sections of this guide. Each has two rooms for disabled guests with a double and bunk beds. One shared shower room has a roll-in shower, handrails and space for side transfer to the WC. Continental breakfast served. When reception is not open an electronic machine will sell rooms by credit card; an entry code is provided for pre-paid bookings. Reservations may be made through the website or by contacting the hotel.

Haven Holidays, Reservations

1 Park Lane, Hemel Hempstead HP2 4TU.

☎ **0870 242 2222 (Customer Care).**

W **www.havenholidays.com**

Haven UK operate 34 holiday parks in Great Britain, mainly on the coast. Their brochure, available from travel agents or by calling the above telephone number, indicates that most of these have some units designed for use by disabled people. These are included in the regional sections of this guide. For detailed information contact a Special Needs Advisor on ☎ 0870 381 1111. Haven also have some parks with accessible units in France.

Helpful Holidays

Mill Street, Chagford, Devon TQ13 8AW.

☎ **01647 433593.**

@ **help@helpfulholidays.com**

W **www.helpfulholidays.com**

Offers over 650 self-catering properties in Cornwall, Devon, Dorset and Somerset, all of which are regularly inspected. Several have been designed for wheelchair users. These are indicated in their brochure, and can be searched for on the website, as are others that may be suitable for people with mobility difficulties.

Hilton Hotels

Maple Court, Watford WD24 4QQ.

☎ **0870 551 5151**

W **www.hilton.co.uk**

International hotel group with hotels in cities, at airports and in other locations throughout the country. Although mainly used for business travel during the week special offers for leisure guests are available at weekends. There are entries for a number of Hilton hotels in the regional sections of this guide.

InterContinental Hotel Group

☎ 0800 405060.

🅆 www.ichotelsgroup.com

An international hotel group comprising the limited service ***Express by Holiday Inn*** brand, middle range ***Holiday Inn*** hotels, high class ***Crowne Plaza*** hotels and luxury ***InterContinental*** hotels. They have a programme of improving their accessibility and services for disabled guests. Most of their hotels in UK are included in the regional sections of this guide. Information on weekend breaks and other special offers is available by phoning Central Reservations and on their website.

Ibis Hotels

255 Hammersmith Road, London W6 8SJ.

☎ 020 8283 4500 (Reservations).

🅆 www.ibishotel.com

A group of 2 star hotels, part of the international Accor group, which have rooms designed for disabled guests. Most of the 46 Ibis Hotels are included in the regional sections of this guide.

Innkeeper's Lodge

☎ 0870 243 0500 (Reservations).

🅆 www.innkeeperslodge.com

A chain of lodge hotels attached to Mitchells & Butlers pubs and restaurants. The more recent properties have rooms for disabled guests and are indicated in their directory. Some are included in the regional sections of this guide.

National Trust

Holiday Cottage Booking Office, PO Box 536, Melksham SN12 8SX.

☎ 0844 800 2072 (brochures).

@ cottages.nationaltrust.org.uk

🅆 www.nationaltrustcottages.co.uk

The National Trust has holiday cottages with adaptations for disabled people in a number of parts of England, Wales and Northern Ireland, some of which are included in the regional sections of this guide. Further information on these and on other cottages with ground floor accommodation that may be suitable for people with restricted mobility can be obtained from the above address and website.

Novotel Hotels

255 Hammersmith Road,
London W6 8SJ.

☎ 020 8283 4500 (Reservations).

🅆 www.novotel.com

A group of three star hotels, part of the international Accor group, all with rooms designed for disabled guests. At present there around 30 Novotel Hotels in Britain, with more planned, and most of these are included in the regional sections of this guide.

Parkdean Holidays

2nd Floor, 1 Gosforth Park Way,
Gosforth Business Park,
Newcastle upon Tyne NE12 8ET.

☎ 0870 220 4646.

🅆 www.parkdeanholidays.co.uk

Parkdean operate 24 holiday parks in South West England, East Anglia, Wales and Scotland. Most have some units that have been adapted for disabled guests and a number of these are included in the regional sections of this guide.

Premier Cottages

☎ 0114 275 1477.

🅆 www.premiercottages.co.uk

An annual brochure of independently owned and managed holiday cottages in many parts of Great Britain. Bookings are made direct with the owners who can answer enquiries. Those that have been assessed under the National Accessible Scheme are shown. A number of these are included and indicated in the regional sections of this guide.

Accommodation groups

Premier Travel Inn

Oakley House, Oakley Road, Leagrave, Luton, LU2 9HG.

☎ **0870 242 8000.**

W www.premiertravelinn.com

A group of over 470 lodge hotels around Great Britain mainly adjoining restaurants or pubs where meals are available, although some have integral restaurants. Almost all have rooms designed for disabled guests and the number of these is indicated in their directory. Bookings can be made online, or by telephone to the central reservations number or to the individual hotels which are listed under Lodge Accommodation in the regional sections of this guide.

Recommended Cottage Holidays

Eastgate House, Eastgate, Pickering YO18 7DW.

☎ **01751 475547.**

W www.recommended-cottages.co.uk

Company offering self-catering holiday cottages in many parts of Great Britain. Their brochure and website indicate those that have adaptations for wheelchair users and also those with some ground floor accommodation.

Travelodge

Reservations Centre.

☎ **08700 850 950.**

W www.travelodge.co.uk

Travelodges are located beside main roads and in city centres in over 300 locations. All but 3, in Central London, have rooms designed for disabled guests and also those for people with limited mobility. These can be specified when booking. A directory is available. Travelodges are listed under Lodge Accommodation in the regional sections of this guide.

Venuemasters

The Workstation, Paternoster Row, Sheffield S1 2BX.

☎ **0114 249 3090.**

@ info@venuemasters.co.uk

W www.venuemasters.co.uk

Offers holiday accommodation at Universities and Colleges throughout Britain during vacations on self-catering, bed & breakfast and fully serviced terms. Some of the venues with facilities for disabled guests appear in the regional sections of this guide.

Youth Hostels Association (England & Wales)

Trevelyan House, Dimple Road, Matlock DE4 3YH.

☎ **0870 770 8868. W www.yha.org.uk**

Scottish Youth Hostels Association

7 Glebe Crescent, Stirling FK8 2JA.

☎ **0870 155 3255. W www.syha.org.uk**

Hostelling International Northern Ireland

22-32 Donegal Road, Belfast BT12 5JN.

☎ **028 9032 4733. W www.hini.org.uk**

Irish Youth Hostel Association (An Oige)

61 Mountjoy Street, Dublin 7.

☎ **+353 (0)1 830 4555.**

W www.irelandyha.org

Youth Hostels offer inexpensive accommodation with meals or self-catering. A small but growing number of hostels have some adaptations for disabled people and some of these are included in the regional sections of this guide. Other hostels vary considerably in the extent of their accessibility. Especially for groups it is recommended that an advance visit is made before booking. Some hostels can be block-booked by groups or offer special activity programmes. For information on membership, hostels and other matters contact the associations at the above addresses.

GET AHEAD - plan your journey

The most important part of any journey takes place before you set off. The Highways Agency is reponsible for England's motorways and major 'A' roads and Lucy Fitzhenry from the Agency explains some of the different tools available to readers of Holidays in Britain and Ireland to plan their journeys - helping you get to your destination on time, with the minimum of fuss.

Plan ahead

We all want easy, free-flowing journeys. However, with increasing amounts of traffic on our roads, it is not simply just about the time spent in your car travelling, it is also about the time you invest in planning your journey. We have an important role to play in helping you do this by providing you with an increasing number of different ways you can access the most up-to-date traffic information about our motorways and major 'A' roads. A useful tool is the Highways Agency's Think Ahead Move Ahead journey planning guide. A hard copy, including a free map book is available through the Highways Agency Information Line, 08457 50 40 30. The advice is also on our website, www.highways.gov.uk . We have a range of information services to help you and your family plan your journeys and avoid the queues.

Before you go

Check your route using .....

• TRANSPORT DIRECT
Britain' free online journey planner which gives you information on travel by either road or public transport. www.transportdirect.info

Check the traffic conditions using ...

• TRAFFIC ENGLAND
Our website and automated telephone service gives you real-time traffic information www.trafficengland.co.uk and 08700 660115.

• HIGHWAYS AGENCY INFORMATION LINE
Professional advisors provide you with information relating to the Highways Agency business 24/7 365 days a year on 08457 50 40 30. You can also contact us via RNID typetalk.

• TRAFFIC RADIO
Whenever you're planning a journey, Traffic Radio can help you, live traffic updates 24 hours a day. Available on DAB Digital Radio and the internet.

And remember ....

• Plan your journey to allow for a 15 minute break every two hours
• Make sure your vehicle is roadworthy and always carry a spare tyre in good condition
• Take emergency items for very hot or very cold weather
• Check you have enough fuel before you set off
• Don't start a long trip if you are already tired.

Further information

The following websites contain valuable journey planning tools for other parts of the UK:

Transport for London: www.tfl.gov.uk
Scotland: www.trafficscotland.org
Wales: www.traffic-wales.com
Northern Ireland: www.trafficwatchni.com

Transport

TRANSPORT CONTENTS

TRANSPORT INFORMATION

Local transport guides for disabled people are available in a number of areas and some of these are listed in the regional sections of this publication.

General information on journeys by public transport throughout UK can be obtained from **Traveline** ☎ 0870 608 2 608. W www.traveline.org.uk

MOTORING

The following give information on motoring matters and provide other services for members:

Disabled Motorists Federation

c/o 145 Knoulberry Road, Blackfell, Washington, Tyne & Wear NE37 1JN.

W www.freewebs.com/dmfed

The Mobilise Organisation

Ashwellthorpe, Norwich NR16 1EX.

☎ 01508 489449.

W www.mobolise.info

Formed by a merger between the Disabled Drivers' Association and the Disabled Drivers' Motor Club, Mobilise has almost a century of successful campaigning history behind us. We campaign for and support disabled drivers, passengers, scooter and wheelchair users, families and carers. We provide information & advice on various subjects including the Blue Badge scheme, disabled parking bays, access issues, public transport, adapted vehicles and mobility aids.

Automobile Association

The AA has a freephone travel information and advice helpline specifically for disabled motorists. A discount off full AA membership is offered to Blue Badge holders. The AA Helpline is ☎ 0800 262050. Textphone: 0800 3282810. SMS text: 07900 444999. W www.theaa.com

Forum of Mobility Centres

☎ 0800 559 3636.

W www.mobility-centres.org.uk

The 17 Mobility Centres around the country provide advice and information to disabled people on driving, car adaptations for both drivers and passengers and factors to consider when buying a car.

Motorhome Information Service

Maxwelton House, Boltro Road,
Haywards Heath RH16 1BJ.

☎ **01444 458889.**

@ **info@motorhomeinfo.co.uk**

W **www.motorhomeinfo.co.uk**

Information for disabled people can be supplied on motorhomes, or campervans, including the addresses of dealers who have experience of carrying out adaptations.

National Caravan Council

Catherine House, Victoria Road,
Aldershot GU11 1SS.

☎ **01252 318251.**

W **www.thecaravan.net**

The NCC is the representative trade body for the UK caravan industry. Its website lists sites throughout Great Britain and Ireland for both touring and with static caravans to hire and this can be searched for those with 'disabled access'. It has published Guidance for Welcoming Disabled Visitors for its member parks

VEHICLE HIRE

Atlas Vehicle Conversions

3 Aysgarth, Road, Waterlooville, Hampshire PO7 7UG.

☎ **023 9226 5600.**

W **www.avcltd.co.uk**

In addition to selling adapted cars, Atlas has a number of wheelchair accessible vehicles for hire including the Renault Kangoo, which can carry one passenger in a wheelchair and a minibus with removable seats that can carry up to two. Daily, weekly and monthly terms are available with special rates for weekends. Drivers must be over 25.

Autobility

Tower Garage, Main Road,
Abernethy, Perth PH2 9JN.

☎ **0800 298 9290.**

W **www.autobility.co.uk**

Autobility have wheelchair accessible vehicles for hire on weekend, weekly and monthly rates. From their base in central Scotland they can arrange delivery throughout Britain or to airports and railway stations for an additional charge.

Brotherwood Automobility

Lambert House, Pillar Box Lane, Beer Hackett, Sherborne, Dorset DT9 6QP.

☎ **01935 872605.**

@ **sales@brotherwood.com**

W **www.brotherwood.com**

Brotherwood have long experience of converting cars for wheelchair users and have a range of cars available for long or short term hire from their premises in north Dorset.

Caldew Coaches

6 Caldew Drive, Dalston, Carlisle,
Cumbria CA5 7NS.

☎ **01228 711690.**

@ **caldewcoachesltd@aol.com**

W **www.caldewcoaches.co.uk**

Company with a range of accessible coaches for hire. These are available for holidays and day trips for groups of 8 and above. Caldew won the Accessibility Award in the 2004 Bus Industry Awards.

Flanagans Coach Travel

Unit 1a, Stretton Distribution Centre, Grappenhall, Warrington, WA4 4QT.

☎ 01925 266115.

@ admin@flanagancoaches.co.uk

W www.flanaganscoaches.co.uk

This company has coaches equipped with lifts that can carry passengers in wheelchairs that are available for hire by groups for day and longer trips. Holidays can be arranged in UK, Ireland and Holland for groups.

Jumbulance Trust

Delaport Coach House, Lamer Lane, Wheathampstead, St Albans AL4 8RQ.

☎ 01582 831444.

W www.jumbulance.org.uk

The Trust has a fleet of Jumbulances which can carry groups including severely disabled adults and children. These are available for hire for holidays and day trips in Britain and abroad.

Motorvation Hull & East Riding

31a Northfield Close, West End, South Cave, Brough HU15 2EW.

☎ 01430 422809.

@tenn@tenn.karoo.co.uk

Have 3 vehicles adapted to carry a passenger in a wheelchair and 3 others. Mainly used in east Yorkshire. Available with a voluntary driver on a daily basis. A donation towards running costs based on mileage used is requested. Contact Mike Tennison.

Nirvana Motorhomes

Court Farm, Pilgrims Road, Upper Halling, Rochester, Kent ME2 1HR.

☎ 0800 328 1475.

@ info@nirvanarv.com

W www.nirvanarv.com

Nirvana can hire out a motor home that is purpose designed to be accessible for a wheelchair user and companions. It is equipped with a lift at the wide entrance, lower level kitchen fitments and a shower room with sliding walls to increase the size. Clamps are available to enable a passenger in a wheelchair to sit alongside the driver or both front seats can swivel to aid transfer. This can be used both in Britain and continental Europe. Similar models are available for sale.

Pyehire

Ovangle Road, Morcambe LA3 3PF.

☎ 01524 598641.

@ pye.hire@pye-motors.co.uk

W www.pyemotors.co.uk

Pyehire have a range of self-drive accessible vehicles that can carry between 1 and 4 passengers in wheelchairs and 2-8 other people. These are available on daily or weekly hire. Contact Steve or Mary.

Thorntrees Garage

Wigan Road, Leyland, Lancashire PR25 5SB.

☎ 01772 622688.

W www.thorntreesgarage.co.uk

Cars and vans that can carry passengers in wheelchairs are available for hire at daily, weekly and monthly rates. Thorntrees Garage is near the M6, M61 and M65 or customers can be picked up from Preston mainline rail station. Secure parking available.

Wheelchair Accessible Vehicles

Unit I4, Morton Park, Darlington DL1 4PJ.

☎ **01325 389900.**

@ **martdisdemon@hotmail.com**

W **www.wheelchairaccessiblevehicles.co.uk**

This company has for hire a range of self drive adapted vans that can carry wheelchair users. Delivery or collection from Darlington Station can be arranged at additional cost.

Wheelchair Travel

1 Johnston Green, Guildford GU2 9XS.

☎ **01483 233640.**

@ **info@wheelchair-travel.co.uk**

W **www.wheelchairtravel.co.uk**

A self-drive rental company with wheelchair accessible cars and minibuses available for any period of domestic and continental use by both UK and non-UK licences holders. Minibuses have lifts, wheelchair securing points and seatbelts. Fiat Doblo cars can carry one wheelchair only, driver and 2 passengers. Cars with hand controls also available. Vehicles can be delivered to home, hotel or airport. Also offered is a wheelchair taxi service, using luxury adapted minibuses.

Vehicle Hire

RAIL TRAVEL

Despite continuing improvements, the railway system still has problem areas and many disabled passengers will need help at some points of their journey. Anyone who may need assistance is asked to give as much advance notice as possible. Requests for information and assistance should be made to the train operating company with which you will be travelling or starting your journey on the following numbers:

Arriva Trains Wales
☎ 0845 300 3005; Text: 0870 410 0355

C2C
☎ 01702 357640; Text: 0845 7125 988

Chiltern Railways
☎ 0845 600 5165; Text: 0845 078051

CrossCountry
☎ 0844 811 0125; Text: 0844 811 0126

East Midlands Trains
☎ 0845 712 5678; Text: 0845 707 8051

First Capital Connect
☎ 0800 058 2844; Text: 0800 975 1052

First Great Western ☎ 0800 197 1329
Textphone: 0800 294 9209

First ScotRail
☎ 0800 912 2901; Text: 0800 912 2899

TransPennine
☎ 0800 197 2149; Text: 0800 107 2061

Gatwick Express ☎ 0845 850 1530

Heathrow Express ☎ 0845 600 1515

Hull Trains
☎ 0845 071 0222; Text: 0845 678 6967

Island Line
☎ 0800 528 2100; Text: 0800 692 0792

London Midland
☎ 0845 601 4867; Text: 0845 712 5988

Merseyrail ☎ 0870 055 2681
Textphone: 0151 702 2071

National Express East Anglia
☎ 0800 028 2878; Text: 0845 606 7245

National Express East Coast
☎ 0845 722 5444; Text: 0845 720 2067

Northern Rail
☎ 0845 600 8008; Text: 0845 604 5608

National Express East Anglia
☎ 0800 028 2878; Text: 0845 606 7245

Southeastern
☎ 0800 783 4524; Text: 0800 783 4548

South West Trains
☎ 0800 528 2100; Text: 0800 692 0792

Southern
☎ 0800 138 1016; Text: 08451 272 940

Virgin Trains
☎ 0845 744 3366; Text: 0845 744 3367

In planning a journey by rail it may be worth noting that there are a number of through services between major population centres and popular holiday areas. Using these may avoid the need to change trains or enable changes to be made at "easier" stations. Information can be obtained from the **National Train Enquiry Bureau** ☎ 08457 484950 Textphone: 0845 6050600. W www.nationalrail.co.uk

Rail Travel for Disabled Passengers is a leaflet available from major stations and rail enquiry offices. It gives general advice about services on trains and at stations for disabled people and an application form for the Disabled Person's Railcard.

Transport

AIR TRAVEL

A number of airlines operate internal flights within the British Isles and these may provide the most convenient means of travel for some destinations.

A travel agent will be able to give further information. It is particularly important that the airline is given advance notice of any relevant information and special requirements of a disabled passenger at the time of booking, whether this is done directly or through a travel agent. It is advisable to re-check that these requirements have been noted a day or so before the flight and, on the day, to check in early.

Access to Air Travel: Guidance for disabled and less mobile passengers, which was issued by the Disabled Persons' Transport Advisory Committee in 2003 to compliment a Code of Practice on Access to Air Travel issued by the Department of Transport to the air transport industry in UK. It is available from DPTAC Secretariat, Great Minster House, 76 Marsham Street, London SW1P 4DR. ☎ 020 7944 8011. Textphone: 020 7944 3277. W www.dptac.gov.uk

Advice is also available from the official consumer body for air transport - **Air Transport Users' Council**, Room K705, CAA House, 45-59 Kingsway, London WC2B 6TE. ☎ 020 7240 6061. W ww.caa.co.uk/auc

Some airports produce information leaflets on their accessibility and services for disabled passengers and others refer to the subject in general information leaflets. These are usually available from the customer services or public relations department of the airport.

Under European regulations that came into effect in July 2007, it is unlawful for an airline or travel company to refuse to let a disabled person with a booking board an aircraft, although they do have to maintain a regard for safety.

SEA TRAVEL

Information on ferry operators between the British mainland and the Isle of Wight, the Scottish islands, the Channel Islands, Isle of Man and Ireland is given in the appropriate regional sections of this guide. If any assistance may be required the ferry company should be notified in advance. Often price concessions on car ferries are available to disabled people, frequently to those who are members of one of the organisations for disabled motorists, see page 00

There & Back is a RADAR guide giving information for disabled people on non-local transport by road, rail, sea and air and the links between them. The 2008/9 edition is available from RADAR price £7.25 including postage.

Equipment hire & other services

This section includes bodies that operate nationally or at least over a large part of the country. Some organisations that hire wheelchairs and other equipment to people living in or visiting their area are included in the regional sections of this guide. A full list may be obtained from the **British Healthcare Trades Association**, Suite 4.06 New Loom House, Back Church Lane, London E1 1LU. ☎ 020 7702 2141.
@ bhta@bhta.com W www.bhta.com

British Red Cross

44 Moorfields. London EC2Y 9AL.
☎ 0870 170 7000.
W www.redcross.org.uk

Most Branches of British Red Cross can help people with disabilities in some or all of the following ways - referring people to other holiday facilities; providing voluntary assistance to disabled holiday-makers; providing short-term loan of equipment such as wheelchairs. Enquiries should be made to the area office, addresses in local telephone directories or on the website.

Direct Mobility Hire Ltd

Warren House, 201A Bury Street, Edmonton, London, N9 9JE.
☎ 0800 0929322.
@ info@directmobility.co.uk
W www.directmobility.co.uk

Hire and sell a wide range of mobility, bath, toilet and bed equipment. Pressure relief and incontinence products also available. Next day delivery in area around London.

St John Ambulance

National Headquarters, 27 St Johns Lane, London EC1M 4BU.
☎ 0870 010 4950.
W www.sja.org.uk

For road ambulance services, escorts, nursing and other care services in England, Wales and Northern Ireland apply to the County Headquarters listed in the telephone directory or on the website.

Theraposture Ltd

Kingdom Avenue, Northacre Industry Park, Westbury BA13 4WE.
☎ 0800 834654.
@ info@theraposture.co.uk
W www.theraposture.co.uk

This company offers a sale and rental scheme for adjustable beds for short-term use, 2 weeks minimum.

Useful publications & websites

RADAR PUBLICATIONS

RADAR publishes a wide range of publications for disabled people. The following may be particularly relevant to those travelling but a full list including prices and other details is available from RADAR, 12 City Forum, 250 City Road, London EC1V 8AF.
☎ 020 7250 3222. Text: 020 7250 4119. W radar@radar.org.uk

Get Mobile: a guide to buying a scooter or power chair (2007)

Get Motoring: a guide to buying a car (2007)

Leisure Time: Days Out (2005)

National Key Scheme Guide (2008)

There & Back: a Guide for Disabled Travellers (2008/9)

Up to date information on RADAR publications is given on RADAR's website - **www.radar.org.uk**

VISIT BRITAIN PUBLICATIONS

The official "Enjoy England" guides each list a particular type of holiday accommodation throughout England. The appropriate National Accessible Scheme symbol indicates those establishments meeting the relevant criteria. The following are available in bookshops and many tourist information centres. They can also be ordered on www.visitengland.com:

Enjoy England: Hotels, £10.99

Enjoy England: Bed & Breakfast Guest Accommodation, £11.99

Enjoy England: Self-Catering Holiday Homes, £11.99

Britain's Camping & Caravan Parks, £8.99

Much information on all aspects of tourism in Britain is given on the Visit Britain website. This includes some information on accessibility for disabled people of both attractions and accommodation that has been inspected under the National Accessible Scheme. The site also provides a link to many other relevant websites including those of the national and regional tourist boards. It also includes contact information for local tourist information centres. It can be reached on **www.visitbritain.com**.

PUBLICATIONS & WEBSITES FROM OTHER SOURCES

AA's Guide for the Disabled Traveller - two-yearly publication giving information on facilities for disabled people at motorway service areas, toll bridges and tunnels. An overseas section gives information on the Channel Tunnel, car ferries, French motorways and some hotels in Europe. The guide is free to AA members.

www.caravanable.co.uk - this website has been created by the mother of a wheelchair user. It lists caravan sites in the UK which have an adapted toilet, shower and basin with level or ramped access that are suitable for a disabled person.

Useful publications & websites

www.careinthecountryside.net - a website established by CaRE (Care and Rural Enterprise) a network of rural and farm-based bed & breakfast and self-catering providers offering specialist holiday accommodation for disabled and older people and their families and carers. A directory of members is included on their website. Contact CaRE, Harper-Adams University College, Edgmond, Newport, Shropshire TF10 8NB. ☎ 01952 815330. @ enquiries@careinthecountryside.net

---

www.deaftravel.co.uk - this website has been launched for Deaf people travelling independently abroad. As well as advice, information and local contacts it includes travel stories both in written and signed video clip forms.

---

www.directenquiries.com - This website gives information from a database on the accessibility of a wide range of business premises around the country. It can be searched geographically, by type of business and by the nature of the access required.

Disability Now - monthly magazine for disabled people containing regular features on holidays in Britain and abroad written by disabled people and also holiday advertisements. DN is available on subscription, in print or free on tape, £28 per year for individuals and organisations. For sample copy contact Disability Now Subscriptions ☎ 0845 120 7001. @ dnsubs@servicehelpline.co.uk

---

www.disabledgo.info - the DisabledGo website gives access details on premises including shops, leisure facilities, catering establishments, etc in an increasing number of towns and cities. Those available currently are listed in the appropriate regional sections of this guide.

---

www.disabledholidaydirectory.co.uk - website giving detailed information on accessible holiday accommodation in the UK, Ireland and worldwide. The site also gives a useful list of questions that disabled people may wish to ask accommodation owners.

English Heritage: Access Guide - annual booklet giving information on accessibility and facilities for disabled people at around 100 historic buildings and sites owned by English Heritage. The booklet, and information on alternative formats, is available from English Heritage Customer Services Department, PO Box 569, Swindon SN2 2YP ☎ 0870 333 1181. Textphone: 0800 0150516. It is available on W www.english-heritage.org.uk/accessguide

---

Farm Stay - the official guide of Farm Stay UK lists holiday accommodation of all kinds on farms throughout the UK. Some information on accessiblity is included. It can be obtained from Farm Stay (UK) Ltd, National Agricultural Centre, Stoneleigh Park, Warwickshire CV8 2LG. ☎ 024 7669 6909. @ info@farmstayuk.co.uk W www.farmstayuk.co.uk

---

www.glutenfreeholidays.com - an independent website giving information on accommodation and travel services in Britain and abroad suitable for coeliacs and others needing a gluten-free diet. The site was set up in 2003 and is expanding although it includes a limited range of places at present.

Good Beer Guide - annual publication containing information on 4500 pubs throughout the UK recommended by members of the Campaign for Real Ale. Those that are said to have easy access for wheelchair users to bars and toilets are indicated. Available, price £14.99 (2008), from bookshops or from CAMRA, 230 Hatfield Road, St Albans AL1 4LW. ☎ 01727 867201. W www.camra.org.uk/books

Useful publications & websites

The National Trust Access Guide - an annual book giving information on the accessibility and services for disabled visitors at National Trust properties throughout England, Wales and Northern Ireland. Individual copies are free from National Trust Membership Department, PO Box 39, Warrington WA5 7WD. Tel: 0870 458 4000. Textphone 0870 240 3207. For a taped version, brailled sections or information on bulk orders contact Jane Satchwell, Access for All Office, The National Trust, Heelis, Kemble Drive, Swindon SN2 2NA. Tel: 01793 817634. The Guide is also available on W www.nationaltrust.org.uk

---

RNIB Hotel Guide – gives information on over 100 hotels and guesthouses that have been recommended by blind and partially sighted people. Available in print, Braille, audio or on disk price £8.49 from RNIB Customer Services, PO Box 173 Peterborough PE2 6WS. ☎ 0845 702 3153.

RSPB Disabled Access to Reserves - the Royal Society for the Protection of Birds welcomes disabled visitors to many of its nature reserves. Information on accessibility is given on their website and information on over 30 sites is included in this free leaflet, available from RSPB, The Lodge, Sandy SG19 2DL. ☎ 01767 680551.
@ enquiries@rspb.org.uk W www.rspb.org.uk

Time to Learn - directory published by City & Guilds of learning holidays, residential courses, day schools and overseas study tours. It indicates centres with facilities for people with a disability, some of which are included under Special Interest Centres/Courses in the Activity Holidays section of this Guide. Specific details both in relation to the premises and the course should be checked before booking. The directory is published twice a year and can be obtained, price £7.95 plus £2.50 p&p (2007), from Publication Sales, Educate Ltd, 91-93 Southwark Street, London SE1 0HX. ☎ 020 7294 2850. It is also available viewed online – W www.timetolearn.org.uk

---

The Yellow Book - the National Gardens Scheme's annual Guide to around 3500 gardens, most of which are not normally open to the public. Many are indicated in the Guide and on the website as being accessible to wheelchair users. Available from bookshops or by post, price £7.99, (2007) from The National Gardens Scheme, Hatchlands Park, East Clandon, Surrey GU4 7RT. @ ngs@ngs.org.uk
W www.ngs.org.uk.

Explanation of symbols

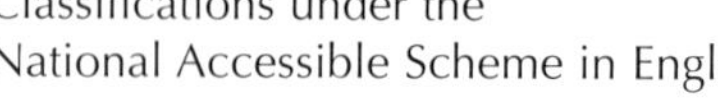

Classifications under the National Accessible Scheme in England

Classification under the National Accessible Scheme elsewhere, see page 14.

The ● symbol gives an indication of the suitability for disabled people of accommodation listed in this guide. It gives an idea of access, and in the final three categories, of levels of assistance and support available. It is NOT a guide to the quality of accommodation, service or food. Ii is, however, advisable to check direct with owners/managers that your own requirements can be met before making reservations at the accomodation.

● Welcomes disabled guests and their companions but facilities are not considered suitable for full-time wheelchair users. Disabled guests will usually need to be accompanied. Specific access details must be checked before booking.

●● Welcomes disabled guests, including wheelchair users, and their companions. Disabled guests will need to be accompanied if they cannot manage independently. The premises will have design features or adaptations for disabled guests, which will be mentioned in the text, but specific access details and other details must be checked before booking.

●●● Welcomes disabled guests, including wheelchair users and their companions. Some assistance and/or equipment is available beyond that which might be expected from the type of accommodation. Guests who cannot manage independently or with the help of their companion should make absolutely sure that this will be sufficient for their needs and specific access details should also be checked.

●●●● Welcomes disabled guests. Some personal help and nursing support is available and guests will not need to be accompanied. A range of equipment and adaptations will be available. Probably registered with the social services department.

●●●●● Welcomes disabled guests and provides full day and night nursing cover and extensive personal help. Accommodation will be purpose-built or adapted for severely disabled people and a range of equipment and services will be available. Probably registered as a nursing home.

D Special diets available with advance notice. Not all establishments can cater for every diet.
E People with epilepsy, who may need to be accompanied, accepted.
I Incontinent people accepted. Please check in advance whether they need to be accompanied and whether precautionary materials should be supplied.
F Feather-free bedding available. Advance notice may be required.
G Assistance dogs accepted.
H Hoist available. Please check on location and suitability.
Unisex WC Public WC designed for wheelchair users.
⭯ Turning space for wheelchairs

Rates

BB - Bed & breakfast DBB - Dinner, bed & breakfast FB - Full Board

Accommodation Facilities

NOTE - these relate to general facilities in the accommodation and may not be accessible or suitable for disabled guests. So if any particular feature is important, its suitability should be checked before booking

- Parking close to entrance.
- Non-smoking bedrooms available or more extensive smoking restrictions.
- Pets accepted, advance notice may be required.
- Room service at most times.
- Telephone available (self-catering only).
- Laundry facilities (self-catering only).
- Swimming pool.
- Gym or fitness equipment.
- Special facilities for young children.
- Golf on premises or arranged nearby.
- Fishing on premises or arranged nearby.
- Tennis.
- Riding on premises or arranged nearby.
- Birdwatching in the area.
- Facilities for touring caravans.
- Facilities for tents.
- Groups accepted.
- Information on access in the area available.

Gradings & classification in England

Where relevant the general holiday accommodation grading and classification symbols are given in the regional sections of this guide. These are determined by annual inspections for the appropriate regional tourist board.

CLASSIFICATIONS

Accommodation can be classed as a hotel, a guest house, a farm, an inn, a hostel or as other accommodation.

Grades

Within those categories properties are graded for quality by one to 5 stars, using inspection criteria that are aligned with those of the AA and RAC, as follows:

★ - Fair and acceptable
★★ - Good
★★★ - Very good
★★★★ - Excellent
★★★★★ - Exceptional

Self-catering Accommodation

A grading system using one to 5 stars is in operation for self-catering properties.

Holiday caravan, chalet and camping parks

A grading system using one to 5 stars is in operation.

More detailed information on all tourist board grading and classification schemes can be obtained at any tourist information centre or regional tourist board.

Map of Great Britain & tourist areas

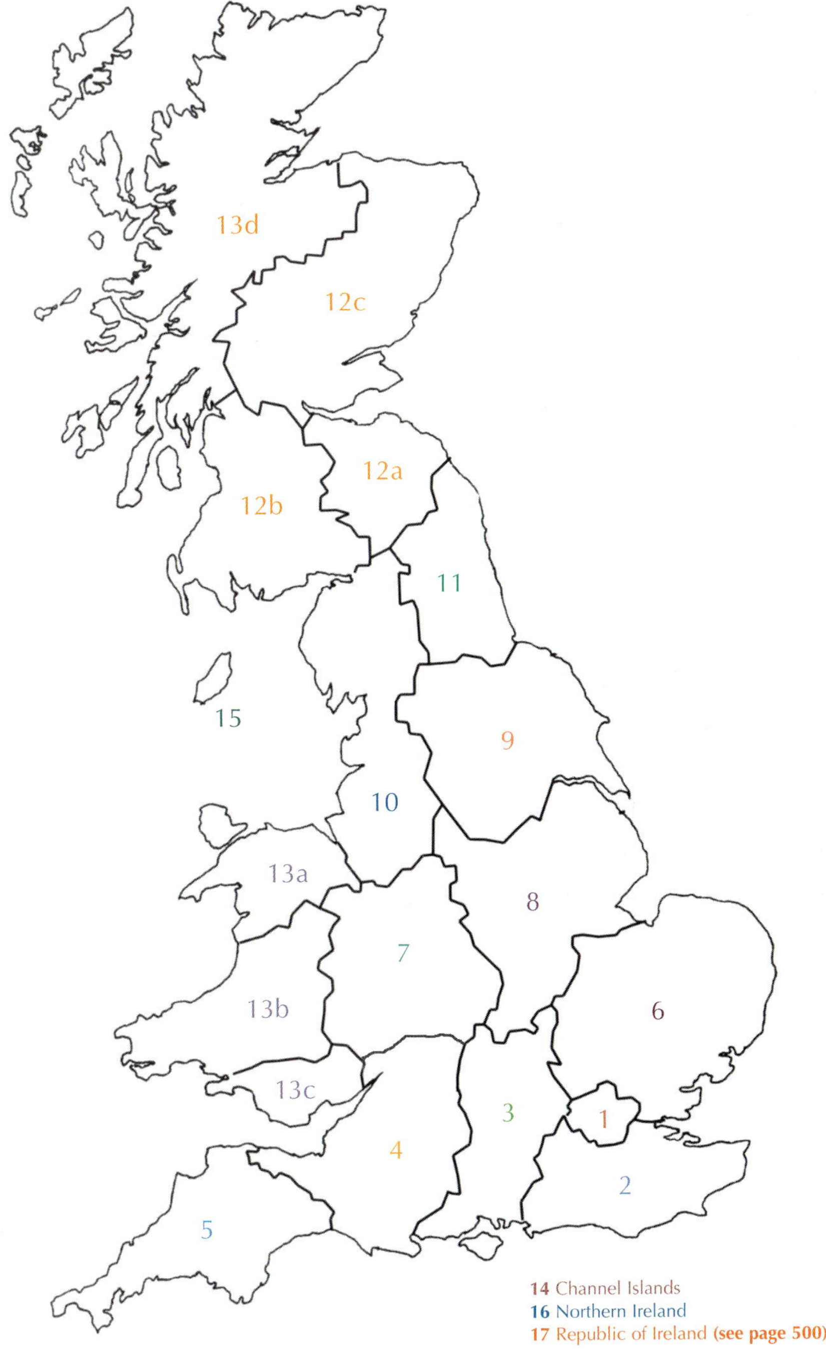

Harrods

London is one of the world's most important tourist destinations as well as hosting more British visitors than any other city or area, whether their trip is for pleasure or business, for a particular event or general sightseeing.

Many of London's major sights are well-known - Buckingham Palace, Trafalgar Square, Marble Arch, Piccadilly Circus, Westminster Abbey, St Paul's Cathedral, Tower Bridge and the Tower of London.

London is the home of many internationally important museums and art collections including the British Museum in Bloomsbury and the National Gallery and the National Portrait Gallery off Trafalgar Square. The national British art collection is in Tate Britain near Westminster. The Victoria & Albert, the Natural History and the Science Museums are clustered in South Kensington. Other accessible attractions include the London Transport Museum in Covent Garden, the Imperial War Museum in Kennington and Somerset House between the river and Strand.

Photo: © Sharadon Dublin - Britainonview.com

1 London

A string of attractions now exist along the riverfront. The most dramatic are the London Eye opposite Westminster and Tate Modern at Bankside with its international collection of 20th century art. Nearby Southwark Cathedral has a recently opened visitor centre as does The Globe, a reconstructed Elizabethan theatre. Families may visit the London Aquarium in the old County Hall while adults can explore the history and taste of wine at Vinopolis near London Bridge.

There is much to see outside the centre of London. The accessible Docklands Light Railway serves the centre of Greenwich with its many historic buildings. An access leaflet covering the National Maritime Museum, the Queen's House and the Royal Observatory is available. Greenwich and the Thames Barrier can be visited by river. English Heritage premises include the home of Charles Darwin at Down House in the extreme south east of Greater London and Eltham Palace with its restored 1930s interior.

Central London has more open spaces, large and small, than many comparable cities and these are home to attractions such as the Serpentine Gallery in Hyde Park and London Zoo in Regents Park. In the outer areas there are large open areas at Hampstead Heath to the north, Epping Forest in the east and Richmond Park in west London. Also to the west the London Wetlands Centre is at Barnes across the river from Hammersmith and Kew Gardens is a designated World Heritage Site.

Shopping opportunities include famous retail streets, stores and markets in both central London and major suburban centres. For live entertainment, London offers an enormous variety of theatre and concerts, many in venues with recently improved access. Visitors to London may well encounter an event, be it pageantry like the Changing of the Guards or a State Visit, celebrations such as the Lord Mayor's Show or the Chinese New Year, a colourful demonstration or a major exhibition or sports fixture.

USEFUL ADDRESSES

Visit London

6th Floor, 2 More London Riverside,
London SE1 2RR.
☎ 020 7234 5800.
W www.visitlondon.com

The organisation representing the tourist industry in London. Some information for disabled people is included on their website.

Transport for London

☎ 020 7222 1234 (Information).
Text: 020 7918 3015. W www.tfl.gov.uk

Historically the public transport networks in London were not designed for wheelchair users and other people with mobility problems. Although considerable barriers still exist, a range of developments have made it easier for disabled people to use at least parts of London's public transport system.

London Buses – All bus routes regulated by Transport for London use buses with low, level floors with improved circulation space, space for a wheelchair user and entrance ramps. Along some routes work has been carried out to adjust the kerbs at bus stops. However, the extent to which buses are easily accessible to wheelchair users is limited by the inability to draw up close to the pavement at bus stops not least because of bad parking by other vehicles.

London Underground - On the Underground all the stations on the Jubilee Line Extension from Westminster to Stratford have lifts between street and platform levels with only a small gap between platform and train. There are a number of other stations with step-free access to platforms either at the outer parts of the network or where there has been substantial work carried out. Transport for London has a long-term programme to create a network of 100 accessible Underground stations and carry out other improvements. A map showing which stations are accessible for wheelchair users is available.

Docklands Light Railway runs from near Tower Hill and Bank to Stratford, Beckton, the Isle of Dogs, Greenwich, Lewisham and London City Airport with an extension under construction to Woolwich. There are lifts or ramps to all station platforms and passengers in wheelchairs can be carried. For further information ☎ 020 363 9700.

Tramlink, a network running through Croydon to Beckenham and Wimbledon in South London, has been designed to be accessible for disabled passengers. For further information ☎ 020 8760 5729.

journeyplanner.tfl.gov.uk is Transport for London's internet travel planner. It can be searched for routes using accessible vehicles and stepfree stations and interchanges.

Blue badge holders can apply for 100% discount from the **Congestion Charge** in central London for an initial registration fee of £10. Therefore for disabled visitors to London it would be worth registering for the discount if they are going to be using a car in central London for more than 2 weekdays. The Registration Pack can be obtained by calling 0845 900 1234, Text: 020 7649 9123. Vehicles exempt from Vehicle Excise Duty are automatically exempt from the charge. For further information see W www.cclondon.com

Taxis – all licensed public hire taxis (Black Cabs) in London have space for a passenger in a manual wheelchair and carry or are equipped with a ramp.

London

DIAL

DIAL offers a free, impartial and confidential service of information and advice by telephone to disabled people, their relatives and professionals. The following groups are members of DIAL UK and may be able to help disabled residents and visitors in their areas:

Disability Action Barnet

☎ **020 8446 6935**
W www.dab.org.uk

Bexley Assn. of Disabled People

☎ **01322 350988**

Mind in Croydon

☎ **020 8763 2037**
W www.mindincroydon.org.uk

Greenwich Assn of Disabled People

☎ **020 8305 2221.**
Textphone 020 8858 9307

Choice in Hackney

☎ **020 7613 3206.**
Textphone: 020 7613 3208

DIAL Havering

☎ **01708 730226.**
Textphone: 01708 751844

Disability Network Hounslow

☎ **020 8758 2048.**
Textphone: 020 8758 2065
W www.disabilitynetworkhounslow.org
@ christina@disabilitynetworkhounslow.org

Kingston CIL

☎ **020 8540 9603**

Lambeth DAS

☎ **020 7738 5656.**
Textphone: 020 7978 8765

Richmond A&ID

☎ **020 8831 6070.**
Textphone: 020 8831 6078

DAN Tower Hamlets

☎ **020 8980 2200**

DIAL Waltham Forest

☎ **020 8539 8884.**
Textphone: 020 8539 8077

Wandsworth DAS

☎ **020 8333 6949**

Bromley Association of People with Disabilities

Lewis House, 30 Beckenham Road, Beckenham BR3 4LS.
☎ **020 8663 3345.**
@ respite@bath-disability.org
W www.bath-disability.org

Organises a range of respite holidays for disabled people living in Bromley Borough.

The Original Tour

Jews Row, Wandsworth, London SW18 1TB.
☎ **020 8877 1722.**
@ info@theoriginaltour.com
W www.theoriginaltour.com

This company is the largest provider of bus tours around central London with recorded and live commentaries in English or recorded other languages and the ability to get on and off at places of interest. Their most recent vehicles, introduced in 2005, have a ramp at the entrance and spaces on the lower deck for wheelchair users.

OSL

153-157 Kingston Road, Wimbledon, London SW19 1LJ.
☎ **020 8543 9737**
@ j.murphy@olympic-cars.co.uk
W www.olympic-cars.co.uk

OSL has a variety of vehicles for hire including wheelchair accessible vans and minibuses and drivers with wide experience of disability. These are available for outings and airport/station transfers.

William Forrester

1 Belvedere Close, off Manor Road, Guildford GU2 9NP.
☎ 01483 575401.

A wheelchair user who is a registered Blue Badge tour guide. He can help plan an itinerary in London or throughout the country, give lectures and assist visiting study groups. Specialist tours of the British Museum, St Paul's Cathedral, and Westminster Abbey are offered and also tailor-made tours of London in accessible taxis and buses. Lectures are available on a large number of English country houses.

USEFUL PUBLICATIONS

Access to London – 4th edition published in 2003. Prepared by Pauline Hephaistos Survey Projects teams of disabled and able-bodied people. Gives information on getting around the London area, accommodation, attractions, entertainment, sports venues, shopping, places to eat and pubs. Available from: Access Project, 39 Bradley Gardens, London W13 8HE. W www.accessinlondon.org

Access London Theatre – quarterly brochure listing audio described, sign-interpreted and captioned performances in London theatres. The Access Guide to London's Theatres, published 2004, gives details on access and facilities at 58 theatres including those in the West End. These are available, in print, tape, Braille or large print from the Society of London Theatre, 32 Rose Street, London WC2E 9ET. ☎ 020 7557 6700. @ enquiries@solttma.co.uk or can be downloaded together with listings of assisted performances from W www.officiallondontheatre.co.uk/access

Access for Disabled People in the City of London - a booklet, regularly revised, listing parking bays for blue badge holders, accessible toilets and places of interest in The City, the historic core of London, and information on Congestion Charging. Also available in alternative formats, it can be obtained from the Access Office, City of London, PO Box 270, Guildhall, London EC2P 2EJ. ☎ 020 7332 1995, Typetalk available. @ access@cityoflondon.gov.uk. It is also available on www.cityoflondon.gov.uk

www.disabledgo.org - this website includes detailed information on the accessibility of many premises in Brent, City of London, Croydon, Enfield, Harrow, Islington, Kensington and Chelsea, Kingston-on-Thames, Lewisham, Richmond, Southwark, Tower Hamlets and Wandsworth and also Tourist London covering the West End.

EQUIPMENT HIRE

All Handling (Movability) Ltd

492 Kingston Road, Raynes Park, London SW20 8DX.

☎ **020 8542 2217.**

@ **info@movability.com**

W **www.movability.com**

Hires manual and powered wheelchairs and scooters at weekly rates. Also supplier of new and second hand equipment, including installation of new stairlifts. Free catalogue also available on request.

B.A.T.H. Shopmobility

30 Beckenham Road, Beckenham BR3 4LS.

☎ **020 8663 3345.**

@ **Shopmobility@bath-disability.org**

A hire service of wheelchairs and scooters is available for both members and visitors to the Bromley area.

City Mobility

267 Southwark Park Road, London SE16 3TP.

☎ 020 7394 0591.

W www.citymobility.co.uk

Manual and electric wheelchairs and scooters are available to rent on daily, weekly or monthly rates.

Direct Mobility Hire Ltd

Warren House, 201A Bury Street, Edmonton N9 9JE.

☎ **0800 0929322.**

@ **info@directmobility.co.uk**

W **www.directmobility.co.uk**

Hire and sell a wide range of mobility, bath, toilet and bed equipment. Pressure relief and incontinence products also available. Next day delivery in London and surrounding areas.

Harrow Shopmobility

37 St George's Centre, St Ann's Road, Harrow HA1 1HS.

☎ **020 8427 1200.**

@ **harrowshopmo@tiscali.co.uk**

Wheelchairs can be borrowed by visitors to Harrow and residents for use on holiday. ID required and donations requested. A service is also available in the Wealdstone part of the area.

Havering Shopmobility

1 The Brewery, Waterloo Road, Romford RM1 1AU.

☎ **01708 765764.**

@ **haveringshopmo@onetel.com**

In addition to the usual services, Havering Shopmobility can provide manual and electric wheelchairs and scooters, including models that can be carried in a car, on longer hire at daily rates. This service is available both to residents and visitors.

Opt4Mobility

9/11 The Causeway, Teddington TW11 0HA.

☎ **020 8943 8890.**

@ **info@opt4mobility.com**

W **www.opt4mobility.com**

As well as selling a wide range of mobility and daily living equipment this company also offers a hire service for transit and manual wheelchairs.

Sutton Shopmobility

Level 3, St Nicholas Shopping Centre, Sutton SM1 1AY.

☎ **020 8770 0691.**

W **www.suttonshopmobility.org.uk**

Manual wheelchairs are available to residents and visitors to the area at daily, overnight, weekend and weekly rates. Photo and address ID are required.

Shopmobility schemes exist to provide wheelchairs and/or scooters for use in shopping centres in the following areas. For information on availability, etc. telephone in advance.

Barking ☎ 020 8594 1687

Beckenham ☎ 020 8663 3345

Bexleyheath ☎ 020 8301 5237

Brent Cross ☎ 020 8457 4070

Bromley ☎ 020 8313 0031

Camden ☎ 020 7482 5503

Croydon ☎ 020 8688 7336

Harrow ☎ 020 8427 1200

Hounslow ☎ 020 8570 3343

Ilford ☎ 020 8478 6864

Kingston ☎ 020 8547 1255

Lewisham ☎ 020 8297 2735

Romford, Brewery ☎ 01708 722570

Romford, The Liberty ☎ 01708 765764

Sutton ☎ 020 8770 0691

Uxbridge ☎ 01895 271510

Walthamstow ☎ 020 8520 3366

Wandsworth ☎ 020 8875 9585

Wealdstone ☎ 020 8881 5402

Wood Green ☎ 020 8881 5402

LONDON

For ease of reference accommodation entries for London are divided into five sections as follows:

Entries for self-catering accommodation in London, where they exist, have been included with other accommodation entries. As elsewhere in this Guide, lodge accommodation is listed at the end of each section.

CENTRAL LONDON

Brown's Hotel

Albemarle Street, London W1S 4BP.

☎ **020 7493 6020.**

@ **reservations.browns@roccofortecollection.com**

●● D/E/I/F/G ★★★★★

Luxury hotel off Piccadilly that was recently refurbished. Street or valet parking. Main entrance 1 step, ramp available. Main public rooms ground floor. Unisex WC. Lift to other floors. Two double bedrooms designed for disabled guests. Bathroom ⟲, roll-in shower, space by bath and WC. Other bedrooms level. Waterproof sheet, induction loops and Teletext TV available. Carers and nannies can be arranged.

Rates: from £310 per night (2007).

City Inn Westminster

30 John Islip Street, London SW1P 4DD.

☎ **020 7630 1000.**

@ **westminster.res@cityinn.com**

●● D/E/F/G

Modern hotel near Westminster and Tate Britain. Reserved parking bays. Automatic doors. Public rooms level. Unisex WC. Lifts to upper floors. 23 bedrooms designed for disabled guests. Shower rooms with roll-in shower and seat, handrails, space by WC. Other bedrooms level.

Rates: on application.

Copthorne Tara

Scarsdale Place, London W8 5SR.
☎ **020 7937 7211.**
@ **sales.tara@milleniumhotels.co.uk**
●●● D/E/I/G/H ★★★★

Hotel off Kensington High Street. Entrance level, automatic doors. Low reception desk. Public rooms level or ramped. Unisex WCs. Lifts 47" to all floors. 10 specially adapted bedrooms with bathrooms for disabled guests, two with hoists and Clos-o-Mat WCs, some roll-in showers. Some other equipment available. Other bedrooms level.

Rates: special rates for adapted rooms on application to Tourism for All ☎ 0845 124 9973.

Crowne Plaza London – The City

19 New Bridge Street, London EC4V 6DB.
☎ **0870 400 9190.**
@ **loncy.info@ihg.com**
 D/E/I/F/G

Hotel near Blackfriars Bridge. No parking. Entrance level. Lobby level. Restaurants 1st floor, ramp to one. Bar and unisex WC lower floor. Lifts 110cm, inside 130x160cm. 10 bedrooms designed for disabled guests, 80cm, lowered fittings, can connect to neighbouring rooms. Bathrooms 90cm, ↺, handrails, space by bath and WC. Bath and raised WC seats, waterproof sheets, sound amplifiers, vibrating alarms and large print information available. Other bedrooms level.

Rates: on application.

Express by Holiday Inn London City

275 Old Street, London EC1V 9LN.
☎ **020 7300 4300.**
@ **reservations@expressbyholidayinn-london.co.uk**
 F/G

Limited service hotel on north edge of the City. Parking for disabled motorists can be arranged in advance. Entrance level. Public rooms level, open plan. Unisex WC. Lift to all floors. Six bedrooms designed for disabled guests. Shower rooms ↺, roll-in shower, handrail by basin and WC, space for side transfer to WC. Other bedrooms level.

Rates: from £79 per room (2007).

Grange City Hotel

8-14 Coopers Row, London EC3N 2BD.
☎ **020 7863 3700.**
@ **city@grangehotels.com**
 D/E/I/F/G 

Luxury hotel near Tower Hill. 2 reserved parking bays. Automatic doors. Low reception desk. Public rooms ground floor. Unisex WCs ground and 1st floors. 14 family rooms designed for disabled guests 90cm. Bathrooms 77cm sliding door, ↺, handrail by bath, space by bath and WC. Other bedrooms level.

Rates: on application.

Grange Holborn Hotel

50-60 Southampton Row, London WC1B 4AR.
☎ **020 7242 1800.**
@ **holborn@grangehotels.com**
● D/E/I/F/G 

Luxury hotel in Bloomsbury area. Parking in street. Side entrance level; ramp available. Restaurant and bar level. Unisex WC. Lift 90cm, inside 148x130cm. 4 rooms adapted for disabled guests on 2nd-6th floors, 90cm, ↺. Bathrooms with handrails and shower, no ↺ or space by WC. Other bedrooms level.

Rates: on application.

Hilton London Metropole

225 Edgware Road, London W2 1JU.
☎ **020 7402 4141.**
www.hilton.co.uk/londonmet
●● D/E/F/G

Large hotel near Paddington Station. Reserved parking spaces by ramp. Entrances level, automatic revolving doors. Low reception desk. Most public rooms ground and mezzanine floors, level or ramp. Unisex WCs. Lifts to all floors. 25 bedrooms adapted for disabled guests with roll-in shower rooms. Other bedrooms level. Bathlift, adapted cutlery, wheelchair and induction loop available. Hoist and adapted changing room in Leisure Club.

Rates: on application.

Holiday Inn London Bloomsbury

Coram Street, London WC1N 1HT.
☎ **0870 400 9222.**
bloomsbury@ihg.com
●● D/E/I/F/G/H 

Hotel near British Museum. Private underground car park; 2 blue badge bays on street. Entrance level, automatic doors. Low reception desk. Public rooms ground floor. Unisex WCs, ground and 1st floors. Lift 90cm, inside 148x143cm. 8 bedrooms designed for disabled guests 85cm, ⟲; one has fitted hoist. Bathrooms 85cm, ⟲, handrails, space for side transfer to bath and WC. Other bedrooms level. Portable hoist, waterproof sheet, vibrating pager, induction loop available. Large print information

Rates: on application.

Holiday Inn London Kensington Forum

97 Cromwell Road, London SW7 4DN.
☎ **0870 400 9100.**
hikensingtonforum@ihg.com
●● D/E/I/G/H 

Recently refurbished large hotel in South Kensington. 2 reserved parking bays. Entrance ramp or one step, automatic and revolving doors. Lounge off reception level, part 1 step or ramp. Restaurants on ground and 1st floors, level or ramped, large print menus. Bar level from within hotel. Unisex WC on 1st floor. Lifts 110cm, inside 113x193cm. Eight bedrooms designed for disabled guests. Bathrooms 89cm, ⟲, handrails, space by bath and WC. Hoist in one room. Other bedrooms level. Waterproof sheets, vibrating pager and pillow alarms, evac chair and portable induction loops available.

Rates: on application.

Holiday Inn London Kings Cross/Bloomsbury

1 Kings Cross Road, London WC1X 9HX.
☎ **020 7833 3900.**
sales@holidayinnlondon.com
●● D/E/I/G 

Large hotel. Limited parking on site. Entrance ramp or 6 steps. Reception and bar open plan. Ramp or 6 steps to lounge and restaurant. Unisex WC on lower ground floor. Three large lifts. Four bedrooms designed for disabled guests with doors to adjoining rooms. Bathroom 32", ⟲, handrails, space for side transfer to bath and WC. Other bedrooms level.

Rates: on application.

London

Holiday Inn London Regents Park

Carburton Street, London W1W 5EE.
☎ **0870 400 9111.**
www.londonregentspark.holiday-inn.co.uk

 D/E/I/F/G 

Hotel between Oxford Street and Regents Park. Underground NCP car park, reserved bay by lift. Entrance ramp or 2 steps, automatic door. Low reception desk. Public rooms 1st floor, open plan. Unisex WC. Lifts to all floors, largest 105cm, inside 200x120cm. Six double bedroom designed for disabled guests 84cm, alarm call, door to adjoining room. Bathroom 84cm, ⟲, handrails, space for side transfer to bath and WC. Other bedrooms level. Large print menus, induction loops, alarm pagers.

Rates: on application.

Holiday Inn Mayfair

3 Berkeley Street, London W1J 8NE.
☎ **0870 400 9110.**
himayfair-reservations@ihg.com

 D/E/I/F/G 

Hotel north of Piccadilly. Reserved bays in surface car park can be booked through concierge, also valet underground parking. Step to entrance, porter available, improvements planned. Induction loop at reception and low check-in desk. Public rooms ground floor, level. Unisex WC 1st floor. Lift 87cm, inside 153x108cm. Four 2-person bedrooms designed for disabled guests on 1st floor, 2 have alarm cords and 2 have flashing alarms. Bathrooms 84cm ⟲, handrails, transfer bench at bath, space by bath and WC. Waterproof sheets, flashing door bells and portable induction loops available.

Rates: on application.

Hyatt Regency London - The Churchill

30 Portman Square, London W1H 7BH.
☎ **020 7486 5800.**
www.london.churchill.hyatt.com

●● D/E/F/G ★★★★★

Luxury hotel north of Oxford Street. Reserved parking bays by ramp to side entrance. Main entrance level. Low reception desk with induction loop. Main public rooms level, except part of lounge. Unisex WC. Lifts 106cm, inside 164x120cm. Two double bedrooms adapted for disabled guests ⟲, low door spyholes, alarm call by bed. Bathroom ⟲, handrails, space for side transfer to bath and WC. Other bedrooms level. Wheelchair available.

Rates: on application.

Ibis Hotel Euston St Pancras

3 Carrington Street, London NW1 2LW.
☎ **020 7388 7777. H0921@accor.com**

●● D/E/I/G

Hotel near Euston Station. A parking space may be available with advance notice. Entrance level. Public rooms level, open plan. Unisex WC. Lift 50", inside 50"x50". Eight bedrooms designed for disabled guests. Bathrooms 32", ⟲, handrails, space by bath and WC. Other bedrooms level.

Rates: from £76 - £135 per room (2008).

Ibis Hotel London City

5 Commercial Street, London E1 6BF.
☎ **0870 429 5095. H5011@accor.com**

●● D/E/I/G

Hotel by Aldgate Underground Station. Entrance level. Public rooms open plan. Lifts to upper floors. 19 bedrooms with bathrooms designed for disabled guests. Other 329 bedrooms level.

Rates: from £69 - £109 per room (2008).

London Bridge Hotel

8/18 London Bridge St, London SE1 9SG.
☎ 020 7855 2200.
W www.londonbridgehotel.com
●● D ★★★★

Hotel by London Bridge Station. Car park 5 minutes away. Entrance one 3" step. Automatic door. Lounge ground floor. Restaurant and unisex WC lower ground floor. Lift to all floors. Six bedrooms designed for disabled guests. Bathrooms ↺, handrails, space for side transfer to bath and WC. Other bedrooms level.

Rates: on application.

London Marriott Marble Arch

134 George Street, London W1H 5DN.
☎ 020 7723 1277.
W www.marriott.co.uk/lonma
●● D/G ★★★★

High class hotel north of Oxford Street. Entrance level. Lounge and restaurant level. Bar 3 steps or lift. Unisex WC. Two bedrooms designed for wheelchair users. Roll-in shower rooms with handrails. Two bedrooms equipped for guests with hearing impairment and two for those with partial sight. Other bedrooms level.

Ⓟ

Rates: on application.

Mercure London City Bankside

71-79 Southwark Street, London SE1 0JA.
☎ 020 7902 0800. @ H2814@accor.com
●● D/F/G ★★★★

Hotel by Tate Modern Gallery. Small car park for residents. Wheelchair lift at Southwark Street entrance, automatic doors. Public rooms ground floor. Unisex WC. Lift to other floors. Five ground floor bedrooms designed for disabled guests. Bathrooms ↺, handrails, space by WC. Alarm systems available. Other bedrooms level.

Ⓟ

Rates: from £150 per room (2007).

Novotel London City South

53-61 Southwark Bridge Road, London SE1 9HH.
☎ 0870 850 4540.
@ H3269-re@accor.com
●● D/E/F/G ★★★★

Modern hotel near Tate Modern and London Bridge. Entrances level. Low reception desk. Main public rooms ground floor. Unisex WCs on ground and 1st floors. Lifts 90cm, inside 130x135cm, visual, audible announcements. 10 bedrooms designed for disabled guests with low level fittings. Shower rooms 80cm, ↺, roll-in shower, handrails and space by WC. Other bedrooms level.

Rates: from £89-£300 double per night (2008).

Novotel London Euston

100-110 Euston Road, London NW1 2AJ.
☎ 020 7666 9000.
@ H5309@accor.com
●● D/E/F/G

Hotel near Euston and St Pancras stations. No car park but with advance notice a space can be made available for disabled guests or valet parking in private car parks arranged. Entrance 6 steps with wheelchair lift. Automatic revolving door with reduced speed button. Restaurant and bar ground floor open plan. Unisex WC. Wheelchair lift to basement lounge. Lift to upper floors 100cm, inside 150x150cm. 13 rooms for disabled guests with interconnecting door to neighbouring room. Bathrooms 200cm, roll-in shower with seat, handrails, space for side transfer to bath and WC. Other bedrooms level.

Rates: from £79-£195 per night (2007).

Novotel London Tower Bridge

10 Pepys Street, London EC3N 2NR.

☎ **0870 850 4530.** @ **H3107@accor.com**

●● D/E/I/F/G ★★★

Modern hotel near Tower of London. Entrance level. Public rooms level, open plan. Unisex WC. Lifts to upper floors. 12 bedrooms designed for disabled guests, single and double. 6 have bathroom with low level bath and 6 have roll-in shower and seat; all with handrails, space by WC. Other bedrooms level.

Rates: from £79-£250 per room (2007).

Novotel London Waterloo

113 Lambeth Road, London SE1 7LS.

☎ **020 7793 1010.** @ **H1785@accor.com**

 D/E/F/G ★★★

Modern hotel near Waterloo and Westminster. Reserved bays in underground car park. Entrance ramp, automatic doors. Main public rooms level, open plan. Unisex WC. Lifts 35", inside 63"x55", Braille buttons. Ten bedrooms designed for disabled guests, Bathrooms ⟲, handrails, space for side transfer to WC. 6 have baths and 4 roll-in showers. Interconnecting rooms available.

  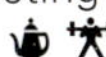

Rates: from £150 per room weekdays and from £89 at weekends.

Ramada Hyde Park

150 Bayswater Road, London W2 4RT.

☎ **020 7229 1212.**

@ **sales.hydepark@ramadajarvis.co.uk**

●● D/E/I/F/G 

Hotel overlooking Kensington Gardens. A reserved parking space by lift to reception. Entrance ramp or 2 steps, automatic door. Public rooms, ground floor, level. Unisex WC mezzanine. Lift 70cm, inside 180x100cm. 5 twin/double ground floor bedrooms adapted for disabled guests. Shower rooms ⟲, roll in shower. Other bedrooms level.

Rates: on application.

Royal National Hotel

Bedford Way, London WC1H 0DG.

☎ **020 7637 2488.**

W **www.imperialhotels.co.uk**

●● D/E/I/F/G

Large hotel in Bloomsbury. Underground car park. Level entrance, double doors. Public rooms ground floor. Unisex WC. 15 lifts to upper floors. Ten twin bedrooms adapted for disabled guests, 85cm, ⟲. Bathrooms ⟲, handrails, space by WC. 1620 other bedrooms level.

Rates: from £68 per person sharing (2007).

St Pancras International Youth Hostel

79-81 Euston Road, London NW1 2QE.

☎ **020 7388 9998.**

@ **stpancras@yha.org.uk**

●● D/E/F ★★★★

Modern hostel near British Library. Entrance level. Ramp to lift, 30", to all floors. Public rooms level. Unisex WC ground floor. 39 bedrooms, twin, double and family. Shower rooms 30", shower trays, seat available, no adaptations. For more information on Youth Hostels see page 34.

Rates: from £25 adult overnight (2007).

Tavistock Hotel

Tavistock Square, London WC1H 9EW.

☎ **020 7636 8383.**

W **www.imperialhotels.co.uk**

●● D/E/I/F

Hotel in Bloomsbury. Underground car park nearby. Small step at entrance. Double door. Public rooms ground floor. Unisex WC. 4 lifts to upper floors. Nine rooms adapted for disabled guests. Bathrooms 88cm sliding door, ⟲, grabrails. Other bedrooms level.

Rates: from £62 per person sharing (2007).

1a London

Thistle Charing Cross
Strand, London WC2N 5HX.
☎ **0870 333 9105**
@ **CharingCross@Thistle.co.uk**
●● D/E/G

Hotel by railway station. Very limited parking. Entrance level or ramp. Public rooms level. Lift 36". Two bedrooms adapted for disabled guests. Bathrooms ↺, handrails. Other bedrooms level. Wheelchair available.

Rates: on application.

Thistle City Barbican Hotel
120 Central Street, London EC1V 8DS.
☎ **0870 333 9101**
@ **CityBarbican@Thistle.co.uk**
 D/E/I/F/G 

Hotel in Clerkenwell, north of the City. One reserved parking space or meters. Entrance ramp or 4 steps. Public rooms ground floor, open plan. Unisex WC. Lift 44", inside 81"x86". Double bedroom adapted for disabled guests. Bathroom 32½", ↺, space for side transfer to bath and WC. Other bedrooms level.

Rates: on application.

Thistle Marble Arch
Bryanston Street, London W1A 4UR.
☎ **0870 333 9116.**
@ **Marble.Arch@Thistle.co.uk**
 D/E/I/G 

High class hotel near Marble Arch. APCOA car park adjoining. Level entrance. Lift or 4 steps to reception. Public rooms 1st fl. Unisex WC. Lift 38½", inside 61"x33". 10 double bedrooms adapted for disabled guests 39", ↺. Shower rooms ↺, roll-in shower, handrails, space for side transfer to WC. Other bedrooms level. Wheelchair available.

Rates: on application.

Victoria Park Plaza
239 Vauxhall Bridge Road,
☎ **020 7769 9999.**
W **www.victoriaparkplaza.com**
 D/E/I/F/G 

High class hotel near Victoria Station and Westminster. Parking space for disabled guests can be provided. Entrance level, swing and revolving doors. Public rooms ground floor. Adapted WC cubicles. Lifts 120cm, inside 150x150cm, braille controls. 26 bedrooms designed for disabled guests. Bathrooms 100cm, ↺, roll-in shower with seat, space by bath and WC. Wheelchair available.

Rates: on application.

Waldorf Hilton
Aldwych, London WC2B 4DD.
☎ **020 7836 2400.**
W **www.hilton.co.uk/waldorf**
●● D/E/I/F/G

High class hotel in Strand/Covent Garden area. Entrance 2 steps, ramp available. 8 steps with stairlift to reception. 7 steps with stairlift to restaurant. Bar external entrance level. Other main public rooms level. Unisex WCs on ground and lower ground levels. Lifts from reception to most bedroom floors. Six bedrooms adapted for disabled guests 90cm, ↺, low hanging rails and spy holes, vibrating and visual alarms, can connect to neighbouring rooms. Bathrooms ↺, handrails; 5 with roll-in showers, 1 low bath with transfer platform. Nine other rooms accessible but with fewer adaptations. Braille information. Portable induction loop, adapted cutlery and wheelchair available.

Rates: on application.

LODGE ACCOMMODATION

There are Premier Travel Inn (see page 38) and Travelodge (see page 38) properties in the following localities:

City Road - Travelodge .... ☎ 0871 984 6333
County Hall - Premier Travel Inn .... ☎ 0870 238 3300
Euston - Premier Travel Inn .... ☎ 0870 238 3301
Kensington - Premier Travel Inn .... ☎ 0870 238 3304
Kings Cross - Premier Travel Inn .... ☎ 0870 990 6414
Travelodge .... ☎ 0871 984 6256
Kings Cross Royal Scot - Travelodge .... ☎ 0870 191 1773
Liverpool Street - Travelodge .... ☎ 0871 984 6190
Marylebone - Travelodge .... ☎ 0871 984 6311
Southwark - Premier Travel Inn .... ☎ 0870 990 6402
Travelodge .... ☎ 0871 984 6352

OUTER LONDON - EAST

The Clarendon Hotel

Montpelier Row, Blackheath,
London SE3 0RW.
☎ **020 8318 4321.**
www.clarendonhotel.com
●● D/E/F/G ★★★

Hotel in Georgian terrace overlooking Blackheath. Parking bay can be reserved. Ramp to level entrance 84cm. Restaurant, lounge and bar ground floor; lounge and bar on lower ground floor with WCs. Lift from Reception 80cm, inside 90x81cm. Two ground floor bedrooms ↺. Bathrooms with some adaptations.

Ⓟ

Rates: from £80 single, £100 double BB (2007).

Crowne Plaza London Docklands

Western Gateway, Royal Victoria Dock,
London E16 1AL.
☎ **0870 990 9692.**
crowneplazadocklands.co.uk
●● D/E/I/F/H ★★★★

Hotel by ExCel exhibition centre in Docklands. Reserved parking bays. Main entrance level, automatic doors; ramp at rear entrance. Low reception desk. Main public rooms ground floor, open plan. Lifts to other floors. Unisex WC 1st floor. 11 bedrooms designed for disabled guests. Shower rooms 2m, ↺, roll-in shower with seat, handrails, alarm. Other bedrooms level. Vibrating pillow alarm and waterproof sheets available.

Ⓟ

Rates: on application.

Custom House Hotel

272-283 Victoria Dock Road,
London E16 3BY.
☎ **020 7474 0011.**
www.customhouse-hotel.co.uk
●● D/I/F/G ★★★

Hotel near Custom House Station and ExCel. Reserved parking bays. Entrance level. Wheelchair lift or steps to reception. Lounge ground floor. Restaurant 1st floor. Unisex WCs. Lift 30" to all floors. 14 bedrooms designed for disabled guests. Shower rooms ↺, roll-in shower with seat. Other bedrooms level. Waterproof sheets can be provided with advance notice.

Ⓟ

Rates: from £80 per night (2007).

Express by Holiday Inn London Chingford

5 Walthamstow Avenue, Chingford,
London E4 8ST.
☎ **0870 444 2789.**
managerchingford@express-holidayinn.co.uk
●● D/E/I/F/G ★★★

Limited service hotel off North Circular Road between Chingford and Walthamstow. Reserved parking bays. Slight slope to entrance, level, automatic door. Low reception desk. Public rooms open plan. Unisex WC. Lift 36", inside 54"x42". 5 bedrooms designed for disabled people on 1st floor. Shower rooms 32", ↺, roll-in shower with seat, handrails, space by WC. Other bedrooms level. Waterproof sheets, vibrating and flashing alarms available. Teletext TV. Air conditioning in every room.

Ⓟ

Rates: From £49 per night.

Express by Holiday Inn London Limehouse

469-475 The Highway, London E1W 3HN.

☎ **020 7791 3850.**

@ **info@exhi-limehouse.co.uk**

●● I/F

Limited service hotel in Docklands near Limehouse DLR Station. Reserved parking bays. Entrance level, automatic door. Public rooms on 1st floor. Unisex WC. 2 lifts. 6 bedrooms designed for disabled guests. Shower rooms ⟲, roll-in shower with seat, space by WC. Other bedrooms level.

Rates: on application.

Express by Holiday Inn London Stratford

196 High Street, London E15 2NE.

☎ **020 8536 8000.**

W **www.express-holidayinn.com**

 G 

Hotel in the centre of Stratford. Reserved parking bays. Entrance from car park level, automatic doors; main entrance also level. Low reception desk. Public rooms open plan. Unisex WC. 6 double bedrooms designed for disabled guests 79cm, vibrating and strobe alarms. Shower room 80cm, ⟲, roll-in shower with seat, handrails, space by WC.

Rates: from £75 per night BB (2007).

Holiday Inn London Bexley

Black Prince Interchange, Southwold Road, Bexley DA5 1ND.

☎ **0870 400 9006.**

@ **bexley@ihg.com**

●● D/E/G 

Hotel east of Bexley on A2. Reserved parking bays. Ramp or 2 steps to entrance, automatic doors. Public rooms ground floor, level. Large print menu. Unisex WC. Lift to all floors. 2 ground floor bedrooms adapted for disabled guests. Bathrooms 75cm, handrail.

Rates: on application.

Ibis London Barking

Highbridge Road, Barking IG11 7BA.

☎ **020 8477 4100.**

@ **H2042@accor.com**

●● D/E/G 

Hotel off A406. Entrance level. Public rooms open plan. Lifts to upper floors. Four bedrooms with bathrooms designed for disabled guests. Other 82 bedrooms level.

Ⓟ 🚭 🐕

Rates: from £56-£66 per room (2008).

Ibis London Docklands

1 Baffin Way, London E14 9PE.

☎ **020 7517 1100.**

@ **H2177@accor.com**

●● D/E/G

Hotel near A13 and Blackwall DLR Station. Entrance level. Public rooms open plan. Lifts to upper floors. Five bedrooms with bathrooms designed for disabled guests. Other 82 bedrooms level.

Ⓟ 🚭 🐕

Rates: from £69-£89 per room (2008).

Ibis London ExCel

9 Western Gateway, Royal Victoria Dock, London E16 1AB.
☎ **020 7055 2300.**
@ **H3655@accor.com**
●● D/E/G
Hotel by exhibition centre. Entrance level. Public rooms open plan. Lifts to upper floors. 15 bedrooms with bathrooms designed for disabled guests. Other bedrooms level.
Ⓟ 🚭 🐕
Rates: from £55-£69 per room (2008).

Ibis London Greenwich

30 Stockwell Street, London SE10 9JN.
☎ **020 8305 1177.**
@ **H0975@accor.com**
●● E/G
Hotel in centre of Greenwich. Entrance ramp. Public rooms level, open plan. Lifts 30", inside 50"x48". Two ground floor bedrooms with bathrooms designed for disabled guests. Other bedrooms level.
🚭 🐕
Rates: from £70-£90 per room (2008).

Ibis London Stratford

1A Romford Road, London E15 4LJ.
☎ **020 8536 3700.**
@ **H3099@accor.com**
●● D/E/G
Hotel near Stratford Station. Entrance level. Public rooms open plan. Lifts to upper floors. Six bedrooms with bathrooms designed for disabled guests. Other bedrooms level. Public car park nearby.
🚭 🐕
Rates: from £62-£75 per room (2008).

The Mitre Hotel

291 Greenwich High Road, London SE10 8NA.
☎ **020 8293 0037.**
W **www.mitregreenwich.com**
●● D/G
Traditional pub/hotel in centre of Greenwich. Entrance level. Bar ground floor. Unisex WC basement. Lift 31", inside 60"x33". 1 twin and 1 double bedroom 30", ⟲. Bathrooms ⟲, no handrails. Other bedrooms level.
Ⓟ 🚭
Rates: from £69 single, £89 double BB (2007).

Novotel London ExCeL

Western Gateway, Royal Victoria Dock, London E16 1AA.
☎ **0870 850 4560.** @ **h3656@accor.com**
●● D/E/F/G ★★★★
Modern hotel on waterside by exhibition centre. Reserved parking bays. Entrance and public rooms level. Unisex WC. Lifts to upper floors. 13 bedrooms with bathrooms designed for disabled guests. Other bedrooms level.
Ⓟ 🚭 🐕 ☕ 🏋
Rates: from £75-£275 per room (2007).

YHA London Riverside

Island Yard, Salter Road, London SE16 1PP.
☎ **0870 770 6010.**
@ **thameside@yha.org.uk**
●● D/E/I/F/G ★★
Hostel on south bank of Thames. Entrance level, swing and double doors. Dining room and lounge/bar level. Unisex WC, limited ⟲. Lift 67", inside 66"x54". Six 4-bed rooms designed for disabled people. En suite shower rooms with sliding door, ⟲, roll-in shower with seat, space for side transfer to WC. Other bedrooms level. For more information on Youth Hostels, see page 34.
Ⓟ 🚭 🐴 🚌 ⓘ
Rates: from £24 adult per night BB (2007).

LODGE ACCOMMODATION

There are Etap (see page 34) Formule 1 (see page 34), Premier Travel Inn (see page 38) and Travelodge (see page 38) properties in the following areas in this section.

Barking	Etap	☎ 020 8507 8500
	Formule 1	☎ 020 8507 0789
	Premier Travel Inn	☎ 0870 990 6318
Beckton	Premier Travel Inn	☎ 0870 197 7029
Chadwell Heath	Premier Travel Inn	☎ 0870 990 6450
City Airport	Etap	☎ 0207 474 91 06
	Travelodge	☎ 0871 984 6333
Docklands	Premier Travel Inn	☎ 0870 238 3322
	Travelodge	☎ 0871 984 6192
Gants Hill	Travelodge	☎ 0871 984 6193
Ilford	Premier Travel Inn	☎ 0870 197 7140
	Travelodge	☎ 0871 984 6194
Rainham	Premier Travel Inn	☎ 0870 197 7217
Romford	Premier Travel Inn	☎ 0870 197 7220
	Travelodge	☎ 0871 984 6255
Tower Bridge	Premier Travel Inn	☎ 0870 238 3303

OUTER LONDON - NORTH

Hendon Hall Hotel

Ashley Lane, Hendon, London NW4 1HF.

☎ **0870 3339109.**

🅆 **www.hendonhall.com**

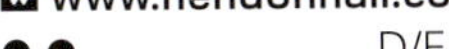 D/F/G ★★★★

Country house hotel in North London suburb. 2 reserved parking bays. Entrance level. Public rooms ground floor. Unisex WC. Lift 85cm, inside 105x172cm. Twin bedroom on 3rd floor adapted for disabled guests. Shower room 82cm, roll-in shower, handrails, space by WC.

Rates: on application.

Hilton London Islington

53 Upper Street, London N1 0UY.

☎ **020 7354 7700.**

🅆 **www.hilton.co.uk/islington**

●● D/E/I/F/G

Hotel beside Business Design Centre. Drop off point at entrance. Ramp to entrance. Public rooms open plan. Unisex WC. Lift. 10 bedrooms designed for disabled guests with doors to neighbouring rooms. Bathrooms, handrails, space for side transfer to bath and WC. Flashing and vibrating alarms. Remote control door openers. Other bedrooms level.

Rates: on application.

Holiday Inn London Brent Cross

Tilling Road, Brent Cross, London NW2 1LP.

☎ **0870 400 9112.**

@ **bregc.reservations@ihg.com**

Hotel at south end of M1 off A5, A4 and A406 junction. Reserved parking bays. Entrance level, automatic revolving door and side entrance. Public rooms level, open plan. Unisex WC. Lift 80cm, inside 107x138cm. Four bedrooms designed for disabled guest, door to adjoining room. Bathrooms sliding door, handrails, space for side transfer to bath and WC. Bath seat available. Other bedrooms level.

Rates: on application.

Holiday Inn London Camden Lock

30 Jamestown Road, London NW1 7BY.

☎ **020 7485 4343.**

🅆 **www.holidayinncamden.co.uk**

●● D/E/I/F/G 

Hotel near Camden Town and Regents Park. Entrance level, automatic doors. Lounge and Bar ground floor, open plan. Restaurant and unisex WC mezzanine. Lift 89cm, inside 107x139cm. 4 double bedrooms designed for disabled guests. Shower rooms, roll-in shower, handrails, space by WC. Other bedrooms level. Induction loops and large print menus.

Rates: on application.

Jurys Inn Islington

60 Pentonville Road, London N1 9LA.
☎ **020 7282 5500.**
●● D/E/I/F/G
3 star hotel between Kings Cross and Islington. Limited parking at rear. Ramp or 5 steps to entrance, automatic door. Low reception desk. Public rooms ground floor level. Unisex WC. Lift 31½", inside 51½"x54½", Braille buttons. 8 double and 3 twin bedrooms designed for disabled guests. Bathrooms 35", ⟲, handrails, space for side transfer to bath and WC. Waterproof sheets with advance notice. Other bedrooms level.
Ⓟ 🚭
Rates: on application.

LODGE ACCOMMODATION

There are Premier Travel Inn (see page 38) and Travelodge (see page 38) properties in the following area in this section:

Edgware - Premier Travel Inn .... ☎ **0870 990 6522**
Enfield - Premier Travel Inn .... ☎ **0870 238 3306**
Hampstead - Premier Travel Inn .... ☎ **0870 850 6328**
Harrow - Premier Travel Inn .... ☎ **0870 197 7146**
Wembley - Premier Travel Inn .... ☎ **0870 990 6484**
Travelodge .... ☎ **0871 984 6466**

OUTER LONDON - SOUTH

Duke's Head Hotel

6 Manor Road, Wallington SM6 0AA.
☎ **020 8401 7410.**
www.dukesheadsurrey.co.uk
●● D/E/I/F/G 

Hotel and pub in suburban town. Parking space can be reserved with advance notice. Slope to front entrance, double doors. Public rooms level. Unisex WC. Bedroom designed for disabled guests 56cm. Bathroom 82cm sliding door ⟲, handrails, space for side transfer to bath and WC. Other ground floor rooms level. A Youngs Hotel.

Rates: £79 per night on weekdays, £75 per night at weekends.

Express by Holiday Inn Wandsworth

Smugglers Way, London SW18 1EG.
☎ **0870 720 1298.**
Wandsworth@morethanhotels.com
●● E/F/G

Limited service hotel near Wandsworth town centre. Reserved parking bays. Entrance level, automatic door. Low reception desk. Public rooms open plan. Unisex WC. Lift to all floors. 8 bedrooms designed for disabled guests. Shower room with roll-in shower, seat and space by WC. Other bedrooms level.

Rates: from £79 per room BB (2007).

Express by Holiday Inn Wimbledon South

200 High Street, Colliers Wood, London SW19 2BH.
☎ **020 8545 7300.**
www.exhiwimbledon.co.uk
●● E/I/F/G

Limited service hotel by Colliers Wood tube station, between Wimbledon and Mitcham. Reserved parking bays at entrance and in underground car park. Entrance level, automatic door. Low reception desk. Public rooms open plan. Unisex WC. Lift 36", inside 36"x72", Braille buttons. Five bedrooms designed for disabled guests. Shower rooms 33", ⟲, roll-in shower with seat, handrails, space by WC. Waterproof sheets, vibrating alarms available. Other bedrooms level.

Rates: from £70-£85 per room BB (2007).

Greyhound Hotel

2 High Street, Carshalton SM5 3PE.
☎ **020 8647 1511.**
www.greyhoundhotel.net
 D/G 

Hotel and inn in suburban town. 5 steps with stairlift to Reception. Public rooms level. Unisex WC. Ramp or 6 steps to bedroom block. Bedroom designed for disabled guests 80cm, ⟲. Bathroom 83cm, ⟲, handrails, space by WC. Other ground floor bedrooms level. A Youngs Hotel.

Rates: from £65-£115 per person BB (2007).

Holiday Inn London Sutton

Gibson Road, Sutton SM1 2RF.
☎ **0870 400 9113.**
sales-sutton@ihg.com
●● E/I/F/G

Town centre hotel. Reserved parking bays. Entrance ramp or 5 steps, automatic door. Main public rooms level. Unisex WC. Lift 31", inside 54"x71". Two double/twin bedrooms designed for disabled guests. Bathrooms 36", ⟲, low bath space for side transfer to bath and WC. Other bedrooms level. Induction loop in public areas.

Rates: on application.

Jurys Inn Croydon

Wellesley Road, Croydon CR0 9XY.
☎ **020 8448 6000.**
@ **jurysinncroydon@jurysdoyle.com**
●● D/E/I/F/G ★★★

Hotel in centre of Croydon. 3 reserved parking bays, otherwise meters on street. Ramp with handrails or 3 steps to entrance. Low reception desk. Public rooms open plan. Unisex WCs on ground and 2nd floors. Lift 150cm, inside 150x200cm. 12 bedrooms designed for disabled guests. Bathrooms 100cm, ⟲, handrails, 2 with roll-in showers, 10 with baths. Other bedrooms level. Teletext TV. Wheelchair available.

Ⓟ

Rates: on application.

Rose & Crown Hotel

55 High Street, Wimbledon, London SW19 5BA.
☎ **020 8947 4713.**
W **roseandcrownwimbledon.co.uk**
●● D/E/I/G ★★★

Inn with rooms in Wimbledon Village. Public rooms level. Unisex WC. One bedroom designed for disabled guests 35", ⟲, door to adjoining room. Bathroom 33", ⟲, handrails, space for side transfer to bath and WC. A Youngs Hotel.

Ⓟ

Rates: from £95-£140 per room BB (2007).

The Windmill on the Common

Clapham Common Southside, London SW4 9DE.
☎ **020 8673 4578.**
W **www.windmillclapham.co.uk**
●● D/E/I/G ★★★

Hotel attached to inn. Reserved parking bay. Ramp from car park to side entrance, 31½". Main bar entrance level. Public rooms level. Unisex WC. One bedroom designed for disabled guests 35", ⟲, door to adjoining room. Bathroom 33", ⟲, handrails, space for side transfer to bath and WC. A Youngs Hotel.

Ⓟ

Rates: from £85-£115 per night BB (2007).

LODGE ACCOMMODATION

There are Premier Travel Inn (see page 38) and Travelodge (see page 38) properties in the following areas in this region.

Battersea - Travelodge .... ☎ 0871 984 6189
Chessington - Premier Travel Inn .... ☎ 0871 977 057
Croydon - Travelodge .... ☎ 0871 984 6318
Croydon West - Premier Travel Inn .... ☎ 0870 990 6554
Morden - Travelodge .... ☎ 0871 848484

OUTER LONDON - WEST

Bridge Hotel

Western Avenue, Greenford UB6 8ST.
☎ **020 8566 6246.**
www.thebridgehotel.com
●● D/E/F/G ★★★

Hotel and pub at A40/A4127 junction. Reserved parking bays. Entrance level. Public rooms level. Unisex WC. Lift 85cm, inside 107x124cm. 2 ground floor bedrooms, twin and double, designed for disabled guests. Bathrooms 77cm sliding door, ⟲, handrails, space for side transfer to WC. Other bedrooms level. A Youngs Hotel.

Ⓟ 🚭

Rates: from £55-£85 per room BB (2007).

Coach & Horses Hotel

8 Kew Green, Kew TW9 3BH.
☎ **020 8940 1208.**
www.coachandhorseskew.co.uk
●● D/F

Hotel in 17th century coaching inn by Kew Gardens. Public rooms level. Unisex WC. Bedroom designed for disabled guests 80cm, ⟲. Bathroom 83cm, ⟲, handrails, space by WC. Other ground floor bedrooms level.

Ⓟ 🚭

Rates: from £90-£120 per room BB (2007).

Wyndham Grand Hotel

Chelsea Harbour, London SW10 0XG.
☎ **020 7823 3000.**
lonch-salesadm@Hilton.com
●● D/G

Luxury suite hotel. Reserved bays in basement car park. Entrance level, swing and revolving doors. Public rooms level. Unisex WCs. Lifts 48", inside 60"x60". Two suites designed for disabled guests. Bathrooms ⟲, roll-in shower, handrails, space for side transfer to bath and WC alarm. Other rooms level.

Ⓟ 🚭

Rates: on application.

Crowne Plaza London Heathrow

Stockley Road, West Drayton UB7 9NA.
☎ **0870 400 9140.**
reservations.cplhr@ihg.com
●● D/E/I/G/H

High class hotel near Heathrow airport. Reserved parking bays. Entrance level, automatic sliding doors. Public rooms level. Unisex WCs. Low level payphone. Eight ground floor bedrooms and bathrooms designed for disabled guests. Hoist available. Other bedrooms level.

Ⓟ 🚭

Rates: on application.

Express by Holiday Inn London Earl's Court

295 North End Road, London W14 9NS.
☎ 020 7384 5151.
@ info@exhiearlscourt.co.uk
●● E/I/F/G

Limited service hotel near Earls Court Exhibition Centre. Reserved parking spaces. Entrance level, automatic door. Low reception desk. Public rooms open plan. Unisex WC. Lift 90cm, inside 110x110cm. 5 double/twin bedrooms designed for disabled guests with lowered controls and clothes rail. Shower rooms 95cm, ⟲, roll-in shower, handrails, space by WC. Other bedrooms level. Vibrating alarm and portable induction loop. Teletext TV.

Ⓟ

Rates: on application.

Express by Holiday Inn London Hammersmith

124 King Street, London W6 0QU.
☎ 020 8746 5100.
W www.hiexpresshammersmith.co.uk
●● D/E/F/G

Limited service hotel in central Hammersmith. Reserved parking bays. Ramp with handrail or 4 steps to entrance, automatic door. Public rooms open plan. Unisex WC. Lift 90cm, inside 110cmx212cm, raised button marking, voice announcements. Seven double bedrooms designed for disabled guests, 3 connect with neighbouring rooms. Vibrating and strobe alarms. Shower rooms 90cm, roll-in shower, handrails, space by WC. Other bedrooms level.

Ⓟ

Rates: on application.

Hilton London Heathrow Airport

Terminal 4, Heathrow Airport, Hounslow TW6 3AF.
☎ 020 8759 7755.
W www.hilton.co.uk/heathrow
●● D/E/I/G

Airport hotel with walkway to Terminal 4. Valet parking. Entrance automatic doors. Public areas level. Lifts to all floors. Four bedrooms designed for disabled guests with door to adjoining room. Shower rooms ⟲, roll-in shower with seat, handrails, space for side transfer to WC. Other bedrooms level, four with wide doors.

Ⓟ

Rates: on application.

Crowne Plaza London Ealing

Western Avenue, Hanger Lane, London W5 1HG.
☎ 0870 400 9114.
●● D/E/I/F/G

Hotel at junction of A40 and North Circular Road. Reserved parking bays. Public rooms level, Large print menus. Unisex WC. Lift, 80cm, to all floors. 6 ground floor bedrooms adapted for disabled guests. Bathrooms 100cm, ⟲, space by bath and WC. Other bedrooms level.

Ⓟ

Rates: on application.

Holiday Inn London Heathrow

Bath Road/Sipson Way, West Drayton UB7 0DP.

☎ **020 8990 0000.**

www.london-heathrow.holiday-inn.com

●● D/E/I/F/G

Hotel near airport and M4 junction 4a. Reserved parking bays in underground car park with lift to hotel. Entrance level, automatic door. Low reception desk. Main public rooms ground floor open plan. Unisex WC. Lifts to all floors, Braille buttons.17 bedrooms designed for disabled guests. Shower rooms ↺, roll-in shower with seat, handrails, space by WC, alarm cord. Other bedrooms level. Wheelchair available.

Rates: on application.

Holiday Inn London Heathrow Ariel

118 Bath Road, Hayes UB3 5AJ.

☎ **020 8757 7008.**

www.holiday-inn.com/hiheathrow

●● D/E/I/F/G

Hotel near airport. Reserved parking bays by entrance. Entrance level, automatic door. Low reception desk. Public rooms level, open plan. Unisex WC. Lift 38", inside 64"x60". Four bedrooms adapted for disabled guests. Bathrooms, 34", ↺, handrails by WC, space by bath and WC. Visual and vibrating alarms. Large print information. Other bedrooms level.

Rates: on application.

Holiday Inn London Heathrow M4 J4

Sipson Road, West Drayton UB7 0JU.

☎ **0870 400 8595.**

reservations-heathrowm4@ihg.com

●● D/E/I/F/G

Hotel near airport. Reserved parking bays. Entrance level, automatic doors. Low reception desk. Public rooms ground floor, level. Unisex WC and adapted cubicles in toilets off bar. Lifts 106cm, inside 135x200cm. 9 bedrooms designed for disabled guests. Bathrooms 90cm, ↺, handrails, space by bath transfer platform and WC. Other bedrooms level. Vibrating alarms, waterproof sheets, induction loops and large print menus and information available.

Rates: on application.

Ibis London Earls Court

47 Lillie Road, London SW6 1UD.

☎ **020 7610 0880.**

H5623-re@accor.com

●● D/E/G

Hotel near Earls Court Exhibition Centre. Entrance ramp. Public rooms level, open plan. Unisex WC. Lift 30", inside 50"x48". Ten bedrooms with bathrooms designed for disabled guests. Other 500 bedrooms level.

Rates: from £72-£99 per room (2008).

Ibis London Heathrow

112-114 Bath Road, Hayes UB3 5AL.

☎ **020 8759 4888.** **H0794@accor.com**

●● D/E/G

Hotel near airport. Parking for resident guests only. Entrance ramp. Public rooms level, open plan. Lift 30", inside 50"x48". Seven double/twin bedrooms with bathrooms designed for disabled guests. Other 344 bedrooms level.

Rates: from £49-£87 per room (2008).

Novotel London Heathrow

M4 Junction 4,Cherry Lane,
West Drayton UB7 9HB.
☎ 0870 850 4570. @ H1551@accor.com
●● D/E/I/F/G ★★★

Hotel near airport and M4 junction 4. Reserved parking bays. Entrance level, automatic doors. Public rooms open plan, level or ramp. Unisex WC. Five ground floor bedrooms designed for disabled guests with door to adjoining room. Bathrooms 30", ⟲, handrails, space for side transfer to bath and WC. Other bedrooms level.

Rates: from £69-£145 per night (2007).

Novotel London West

1 Shortlands, London W6 8DR.
☎ 020 8741 2120. @ H0737@accor.com
●● D/E/I/F/G ★★★

Hotel in central Hammersmith. Reserved parking bays. Public rooms 1st floor open plan. Adapted WC cubicles. Lift to all floors. Eight bedrooms designed for disabled guests. Five have roll-in shower rooms and the others have bathrooms ⟲, handrail by bath, space for side transfer to bath and WC. Other bedrooms level.

Rates: from £69-£215 per room (2007).

Popes Grotto Hotel

Cross Deep, Twickenham TW1 4RB.
☎ 020 8892 3050.
W www.popesgrotto.co.uk
●● D/G

Hotel and bar facing river. Entrance level. Public rooms level. Unisex WC. Bedroom designed for disabled guests 80cm, ⟲. Bathroom 83cm, ⟲, handrails, space by WC. Other ground floor bedrooms level. A Youngs hotel.

Rates: from £75 -120 per room BB (2007).

Ramada Ealing

Ealing Common, London W5 3HN.
☎ 020 8896 8400.
W sales.londonwest@ramadajarvis.co.uk
●● D/E/F/G

Hotel in town centre. Reserved parking bays. Ramp to entrance, automatic doors. Induction loop at reception. Public rooms open plan, level except par of bar. Unisex WC. Lift 80cm, inside 130x107cm, audible announcements. 4 double bedrooms designed for disabled guests, restricted ⟲. Shower rooms 80cm, roll-in shower with seat, handrails, space by WC, alarm. Other bedrooms level. Teletext TV.

Rates: from £140 per night (2007).

Renaissance London Heathrow Hotel

Bath Road, Hounslow TW6 2AQ.
☎ 020 8897 6363.
W www.renaissancelondonheathrow.co.uk
●● D/E/I/F/G ★★★★

Hotel on A4 beside airport. Reserved parking bays. Ramp to entrances, automatic doors. Public rooms ground floor, ramp or 2 steps to bar. Unisex WC 1st floor, adapted cubicles ground floor. Lifts to upper floors and separate wheelchair lift to ground floor bedrooms. 6 double bedrooms adapted for disabled guests 90cm. Shower rooms 90cm, ⟲, roll-in shower with seat, handrails, space by WC. Flashing alarm, Braille room number and induction loop. Other bedrooms level. Wheelchair available.

Rates: from £82-£170 per night (2007/8).

LODGE ACCOMMODATION

There are Premier Travel Inn (see page 38) and Travelodge (see page 38) properties in the following areas in this section.

Brentford - Premier Travel Inn .... ☎ 0870 990 6304
Feltham - Travelodge .... ☎ 0871 984 6319
Greenford - Premier Travel Inn .... ☎ 087197 7119
Hammersmith - Premier Travel Inn .... ☎ 0870 850 6310
Hayes - Premier Travel Inn .... ☎ 0870 197 7132
Heathrow, Bath Road - Premier Travel Inn .... ☎ 0870 607 5075
Heathrow, M4/J4 - Premier Travel Inn .... ☎ 0870 990 6612
Heathrow, terminals 4&5 - Travelodge .... ☎ 0871 984 6353
Heston - Travelodge .... ☎ 0871 91 1537/1762
Kew Bridge - Travelodge .... ☎ 0871 984 6040
Kingston - Travelodge .... ☎ 0871 984 6241
Park Royal - Travelodge .... ☎ 0871 984 6195
Putney Bridge - Premier Travel Inn Metro .... ☎ 0871 238 3302
Tolworth - Travelodge .... ☎ 0871 984 6210
Twickenham - Premier Travel Inn Metro .... ☎ 0871 990 6416

2 South East England

Broadstairs- Kent

Although sometimes overshadowed by London, the counties of Kent, Surrey and East and West Sussex have their own special features and many attractions for holiday makers and day visitors.

Resorts large and small are found around the coast. Brighton with its distinctive Royal Pavilion and a thriving arts and entertainment scene can claim to be Britain's first seaside resort. Eastbourne has a long level seafront but is close to the South Downs and the cliffs of Beachy Head. Other resorts include Margate, Hastings, Worthing, Littlehampton and Bognor Regis.

Historically, the area has always been important. The Romans landed here and among the many reminders of their civilisation is Fishbourne Palace near Chichester. At the famous historic site of the Battle of Hastings, at Battle north of Hastings, English Heritage have opened a new visitor centre, although access difficulties remain for the battlefield itself. Since 1066, the military emphasis has been on repelling invasions. Examples of this include Dover Castle, the Military Aviation Museum at the Battle of Britain airfield at Tangmere in West Sussex and a cluster of attractions in north Kent including the Chatham Historic Dockyard. Also at Chatham, Dickens World is a family attraction bringing to life the work of the region's leading literary figure.

Photo: Britainonview/Thanet District Council © Rod Edwards

At Canterbury, disabled people can get to most parts of the great cathedral. There are also historic cathedrals in Chichester and Rochester and a more modern one at Guildford. Historic secular buildings include the beautiful Leeds Castle near Maidstone, the imposing 17th century Petworth House in West Sussex owned by the National Trust and the modernist De La Ware Pavilion at Bexhill.

Arundel

Before the Industrial Revolution the forested Weald was a major centre for iron manufacture. A variety of old industrial and transport buildings are on display at the Amberley Museum north of Arundel. The several heritage railways in the area include the Bluebell Railway, which has a coach for wheelchair users. More modern industries are represented at Mercedes-Benz World and the Brooklands Museum of motor racing and aviation at Weybridge and at The Body Shop Tour in Littlehampton.

Animal attractions in the area include the WWT Wetlands Centre at Arundel, Wildwood north of Canterbury, Birdworld near Farnham and the South of England Rare Breeds Centre near Ashford, which is run by people with learning disabilities. Noted gardens include Painshill Landscape Garden near Cobham. Other outdoor attractions include the award-wining Seven Sisters Country Park in East Sussex and Capstone Farm Country Park near Gillingham. Thorpe Park in north west Surrey is a destination for family outings. There is also the possibility of a shopping trip to Bluewater near Dartford or a day trip to France by ferry or through the Channel Tunnel.

Photo: Britain on View / South East Tourism © Simon Kreitem

Ivy House Country Hotel

with spacious accommodation is known as Oulton Broad's hidden Oasis. Enjoy a tranquil setting with a lovely country garden and lily ponds frequented by kingfishers. Delicious cuisine – from bread to ice-cream made by our chefs. Special breaks available throughout the year. Dogs welcome.

Contact details: Ivy House Country Hotel, Ivy Lane, Oulton Broad, Lowestoft, Suffolk NR33 8HY
Tel: (0) 1502 501 353 Fax: (0) 1502 501 539
Email: radar@ivyhousecountryhotel.co.uk

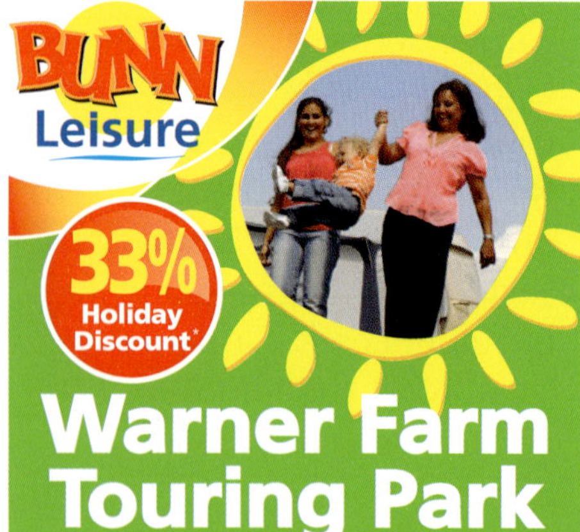

Warner Farm offers great value holidays with modern facilities, disabled access, FREE daytime activities and evening entertainment. Choose from Standard, Electric and Service Pitches here in sunny Selsey, West Sussex.

Call today 01243 604499
or visit warnerfarm.co.uk
quoting: RADAR09

*Pay for 2 nights and we'll give a 3rd night FREE based on the cheapest night booked. Offer only available on certain dates. Visit web site for details and conditions

CHICHESTER DISTRICT COUNCIL

For details of tourist attractions throughout the District or any other information please visit our website at:

www.chichester.gov.uk

or email: **helpline@chichester.gov.uk**

or telephone: **01243 785166**

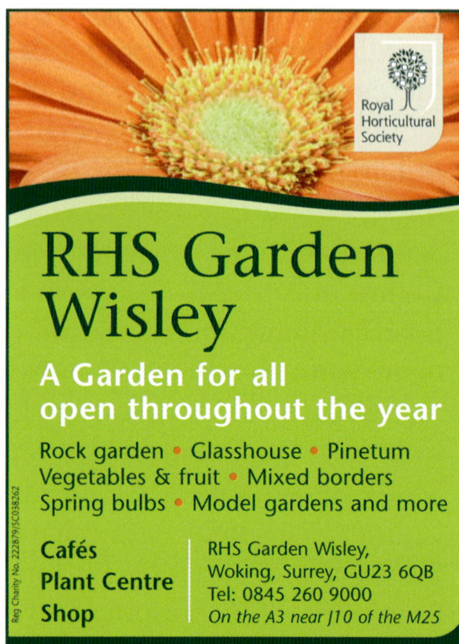

USEFUL ADDRESSES

Tourism South East
40 Chamberlayne Road, Eastleigh
Hampshire SO50 5JH.
☎ **023 8062 5505.**
W **www.visitsoutheastengland.com**

Issues a number of publications on accommodation and attractions in the region.

East Sussex Disability Association
1 Faraday Close, Eastbourne BN22 9BH.
☎ **01323 514500.** @ **info@esda.org.uk**
W **www.esda.org.uk**

Provides a wide variety of services including advice on direct payments, equipment, welfare rights and an information service.

Kent Association for Disabled People
The Chequers Centre Management Suite, Pads Hill, Maidstone ME15 6AT.
☎ **01622 756444.**

Organises 3 one-week holidays for disabled people at hotels on the south coast. Some care is provided by voluntary helpers but no medical or night care.

Voluntary Association for Surrey Disabled
10 Havenbury Estate, Station Road, Dorking RH4 1ES.
☎ **01306 741500/741600.**
@ **info@vasd.org.uk** W **www.vasd.org.uk**

Two adapted vehicles and manual wheelchairs can be hired by individuals and organisations in Surrey. Self-catering properties are available in Bognor and Bracklesham Bay, see pages 102 and 103.

West Sussex Association for Disabled People
9a South Pallant, Chichester PO19 1SU.
☎ **01243 774088.** @ **info@wsad.org.uk**
W **www.wsad.org.uk**

General advice is given on holiday opportunities.

DIAL
DIAL offers a free, impartial and confidential service of information and advice by telephone to disabled people, their relatives and professionals. The following groups are members of DIAL UK and may be able to help disabled residents and visitors in their areas:

Brighton & Hove DAC
☎**/Textphone: 01273 203016**

DIAL Kent
☎ **01227 771155; Textphone: 01227 771645**

DIS Kent (Folkestone)
☎**/Textphone: 01303 226464**

DIAL N W Kent
☎**/Textphone: 01474 537666**

DIS Sussex ☎ **01273 585575**

South East England

USEFUL PUBLICATIONS & WEBSITES

Access to Places in and around Eastbourne is a booklet, published annually, giving information on accessible places in and around Eastbourne and includes a wheelchair route map. The wheelchair route map can be downloaded from the website. It is available free of charge from Eastbourne Tourist Information Centre, Cornfield Road, Eastbourne. East Sussex BN21 4QA. ☎ 0871 663 0031 (premium rate). Text: 01323 45111.
W www.visiteastbourne.com

Walks for All in Kent & Medway gives detailed information on 16 country routes in the area that can be used by disabled people. These can be downloaded free via W www.kent.gov.uk/explorekent

Maidstone: a Disabled Person's Guide to the Town Centre - a map showing the location of dropped kerbs, reserved parking bays and toilets for disabled people. Available from Maidstone Visitor Information Centre, Town Hall, High Street, Maidstone ME14 1TF. ☎ 01622 602169. @ tourism@maidstone.gov.uk

---

Accessible Worthing - an access guide is available from Worthing Tourist Information Centre, Chapel Road, Worthing, West Sussex BN11 1HL.
☎ 01903 221066.
W www.visitworthing.co.uk

---

www.disabledgo.org - this website includes detailed information on the accessibility of many premises in Arun, Canterbury, Chichester, Crawley and Woking.

EQUIPMENT HIRE

Brighton & Hove Shopmobility

Grenville Street, Brighton BN1 2RF.

☎ **01273 323239.**

@ **Shopmobility@bhfederation.org.uk**

In addition to the daily Shopmobility service in the area, which can be used by visitors, manual wheelchairs are available for hire at £25 per week.

Canterbury & Herne Bay Shopmobility

14 Gravel Walk, Canterbury CT1 2TF.

☎ **01227 459889.**

@ **canterbury@cshopmobility.freeserve.co.uk**

Long-term hire, up to 4 weeks, of wheelchairs and electric scooters is available both for residents and visitors to the Canterbury area. Advance booking is required.

Southern Mobility Centres

Mobility House, Cavendish Avenue, Eastbourne BN22 8EN.

☎ **01323 645067.**

W **www.southernmobility.com**

Manual wheelchairs and a range of hoists are available to hire at weekly and monthly rates.

Weald Mobility Care Centre

149 Tideswell Road, Eastbourne.

☎ **01323 721223.** W **www.wealdmobility.co.uk**

Scooters and manual wheelchairs are available for hire for 2 days and over. Free local delivery and collection.

The Wheelchair Shop

Queen Elizabeth's Foundation Resource Centre, Brent Way, Dartford DA2 6DA.

☎ **01322 394100/108. Text: 01322 290728.**

@ **info@qefresourcecentre.org.uk**

Manual and powered wheelchairs and scooters are available for hire on a daily or longer term basis. A repair service and collection and delivery are also available.

Shopmobility schemes exist to provide wheelchairs and/or scooters for use in shopping centres in the following towns. For information on availability, etc. telephone in advance.

Ashford ☎ 01233 650063

Bluewater ☎ 01322 427427

Bognor Regis ☎ 01243 830077

Brighton ☎ 01273 323239

Broadstairs ☎ 04843 871444

Canterbury ☎ 01227 459889

Chatham ☎ 01634 830555

Chichester ☎ 07932 802778

Crawley ☎ 01293 522852

Eastbourne ☎ 01323 439585

Folkestone ☎ 01303 226500

Guildford ☎ 01483 453993

Hastings ☎ 01424 447847

Herne Bay ☎ 01227 372487

Horsham ☎ 01403 249015

Leatherhead ☎ 01372 362400

Littlehampton ☎ 01903 733004

Maidstone ☎ 01622 678777

Redhill ☎ 01737 772718

Staines ☎ 01784 459416

Tunbridge Wells ☎ 01892 544355

Woking ☎ 01483 776612

Worthing ☎ 01903 820980

ACCOMMODATION WITH MEALS

AMBERLEY, West Sussex

Woodybanks

Rackham Road, Amberley BN18 9NR.

☎ **01798 831295.**

www.woodybanks.co.uk.

peaceful@woodybank.co.uk

● D/E/I/F ★★★★

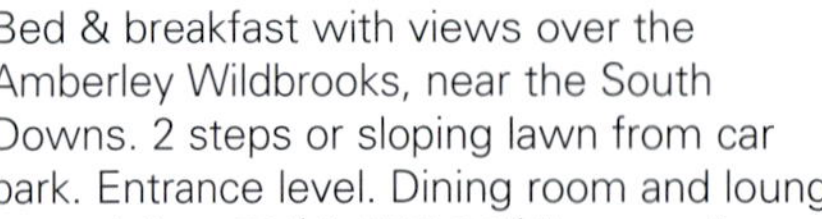

Bed & breakfast with views over the Amberley Wildbrooks, near the South Downs. 2 steps or sloping lawn from car park. Entrance level. Dining room and lounge ground floor 28½". WC 28½", space for wheelchair and helper, no handrails. Stairlift to 1st floor. Twin and double bedrooms. Also double room. Waterproof sheet can be supplied. Shower room with fixed seat and handrail. Shower tray cubicle. Private guest lounge. Downstairs toilet. Wheelchair available. Pub/restaurant next door.

Rates: from £28.50 per person BB (2007).

ARUNDEL, West Sussex

Mill Lane House

Slindon, Arundel BN18 0RP.

☎ **01243 814440.**

www.mill-lane-house.co.uk

●● D/F/G

Bed & breakfast house in National Trust village west of Arundel. Entrance 2x2 steps. Dining room and hall/lounge level. In annexe a family bedroom designed for disabled guests, ⭯. Bathroom with roll-in shower and space by WC. Breakfast can be served in bedroom.

Rates: from £40 per person sharing BB (2007).

ASHFORD, Kent

Ashford International Hotel

Simone Weil Avenue, Ashford TN24 8UX.

☎ **01233 219988.** **www.qhotels.co.uk**

●● D/E/I/G ★★★★

Hotel on edge of town. Entrance level, automatic doors. Public rooms level. Unisex WC. Lift 36". Three double bedrooms designed for disabled guests. Bathrooms 33", roll-in shower, handrails, adjustable height basin, space for side transfer to WC.

Rates: on application.

Holiday Inn Ashford Central

Canterbury Road, Ashford TN24 8QQ.

☎ **0870 400 9001.**

reservations-ashford@ihg.com

●● D/E/I/F/G ★★★

Hotel on edge of town. Reserved parking bays. Entrance level. Public rooms ground floor, slope to restaurant. Large print menu. Unisex WC. Bedrooms with bathrooms des-igned for disabled guests. Ramp to garden.

Rates: on application.

Holiday Inn Ashford North

Maidstone Road, Ashford TN26 1AR.

☎ **01233 713333.**

enquiries@HIashford.com

●● D/E/F/G ★★★

Hotel on A20 west of Ashford. Reserved parking bays. Entrance level. Public rooms open plan. Unisex WC. Lift to all floors. Two double bedrooms designed for disabled guests with door to adjoining rooms. Bathrooms ⭯, space for side transfer to bath and WC. Other bedrooms level.

Rates: on application.

BOGNOR REGIS, West Sussex

Russell Hotel

King's Parade, Bognor Regis PO21 2QP.

01243 869377.

russell.hotel@actionforblindpeople.org.uk

●●● D/G

Hotel near seafront and park designed for blind and partially sighted people and their companions. 41 bedrooms with own bath-rooms, some designed for wheelchair users. Full facilities for guide dogs. Volunteers can be arranged for some assistance. Outings and activities organised. Owned by Action for Blind People, see page 19.

Rates: from £36-£48 per night DBB (2007).

BRIGHTON & HOVE, East Sussex

Jurys Inn Brighton

101 Stroudley Road, Brighton BN1 4DJ.

01273 862121. **www.jurysinns.com**

●● D/E/I/F/G 

Hotel near railway station. Station car park opposite. Entrance level, automatic door. Low reception desk. Public rooms ground floor, level. Unisex WC and adapted cubicle in ladies. Lift 90cm, inside 157x139cm. 12 double bedrooms designed for disabled guests, automatic door opener. Two interconnect to adjoining room. Shower rooms 90cm, roll-in shower with seat, handrail, space by WC, lowered basin. Pillow alarms available.

Rates: from £69-£129 room only (2008).

Quality Hotel Brighton

West Street, Brighton BN1 2RQ.

01273 220033.

www.qualityhotelbrighton.co.uk

●● D/E/G 

Hotel by Conference Centre. Entrance level, automatic door. Public rooms open plan, level except ramp to bar. Unisex WCs. Lifts 31", inside 55"x64". Two bedrooms designed for disabled guests. Bathrooms with roll-in shower. Other bedrooms level.

Rates: on application.

RNIB Wavertree House

Somerhill Road, Hove BN3 1RN.

01273 262200.

wavertree@rnib.org.uk

●●●● G

Purpose-built residential accommodation for older visually impaired people offering holiday and short-term breaks, subject to availability. Accessible by wheelchair users. 24 hour care and assistance if required. Activities and outings arranged.

Rates: on application.

BROADSTAIRS, Kent

The Fayreness Hotel

Marine Drive, Kingsgate, Broadstairs CT10 3LG.

01843 868641.

www.fayreness.co.uk

reservations-ashford@ihg.com

●● D/E/I/G 

Clifftop hotel with sea views between Broadstairs and Cliftonville. Reserved parking bay. Level entrance. Public rooms ground floor. Braille menus. Unisex WC. One bedroom adapted for disabled guests. Bathroom 32", handrails, space by bath and WC. 4 other ground floor bedrooms.

Rates: from £57 - £158 (2007)

South East England

CANTERBURY, Kent

Express by Holiday Inn Canterbury

Upper Harbledown, Canterbury CT2 9HX.
☎ **01227 865000.**
canterbury@exbhi.co.uk
●● D/E/I/F/G

Limited service hotel on A2, 4 miles from city. Reserved parking bays. Entrance ramp or 3 steps. Automatic door. Low reception desk. Public rooms open plan. Unisex WC. 5 double bedrooms designed for disabled guests connect with neighbouring rooms. Shower rooms 36", roll-in shower with seat, handrails, space by WC. Other ground floor rooms level.

Rates: on application.

CHATHAM, Kent

Holiday Inn Rochester-Chatham

Maidstone Road, Chatham ME5 9SF.
☎ **0870 400 9069.**
reservations-rochester@ihg.com
●● D/E/I/F/G

Hotel south of Chatham near M2 junction 3. Reserved parking bays with ramp to level entrance. Main entrance automatic doors and internal steps. Public rooms level, open plan. Unisex WC. Lift 31", inside 42"x54". Two bedrooms, twin and double, designed for disabled people with low level fittings. Bathrooms 33", handrails, shower tray, space by bath and WC. Fixed and portable induction loops, audible and flashing alarms, vibrating pager, waterproof sheets available. Other bedrooms level.

Rates: on application.

CHERTSEY, Surrey

The Crown Hotel

7 London Street, Chertsey KT16 8AP.
☎ **01932 564657.**
www.crownchertsey.co.uk
●● D/E/I/F/G

Town pub and hotel. Entrance by car park level, double doors. Public rooms level. Unisex WC. Double bedroom designed for disabled guests. Bathroom, handrails, bathseat, space for side transfer to bath and WC. Other ground floor bedrooms level. A Youngs Hotel.

Rates: from £75-£120 per room BB (2007).

CHICHESTER, West Sussex

Crouchers Country Hotel & Restaurant

Birdham Road, Apuldram,
Chichester PO20 7EH.
☎ **01243 784995.**
www.croucherscountryhotel.com
●● D/E/F/G ★★★

Hotel near Chichester Harbour. Ramp to entrance 35". Public rooms level. Unisex WC. Twin bedroom with patio and double bedroom designed for disabled guests. Bathrooms 31", handrails, space for side transfer to bath and WC. Other ground floor bedrooms level including double with space for wheelchair.

Rates: from £95-£115 double BB (2007).

University College Chichester

Bishop Otter Campus, College Lane, Chichester PO19 4PE.

☎ 01243 816070.

@ conference@ucc.ac.uk

●● D/F/G

Student accommodation. Reception level. Restaurant 4 steps or ramp. Bar 10 steps or ramp. Unisex WC. Eight single bedrooms designed for disabled people. Own shower rooms 82cm, turning space, roll-in shower, no handrails. Other level bedrooms available. Available September-May.

Rates: from £27.50-£35.50 per night BB (2007).

CRAWLEY, West Sussex

Ibis Hotel Gatwick Airport

London Road, County Oak, Crawley RH11 0PF.

☎ 01293 590300.

@ H0794@accor.com

●● D/E/G

Hotel between Crawley and Airport. Entrance level. Public rooms open plan. Unisex WC. Lift to upper floors. Ten bedrooms with bathrooms designed for disabled guests. Other 130 bedrooms level. Shuttle bus to Airport.

Rates: from £52-£65 per room (2008).

Ramada Plaza Gatwick

Tinsley Lane South, Three Bridges, Crawley RH10 8XH.

☎ 01293 561186.

@ sales.plazagatwick@ramadajarvis.co.uk

●● D/E/I/F/G ★★★★

Modern hotel. Reserved parking bays. Entrance level. Public rooms open plan. Unisex WC. Lift 35", inside 47"x55". Four twin bedrooms designed for disabled guests. Bathrooms turning space, handrails, space for side transfer to bath and WC. Other bedrooms level.

Rates: from £99 single weekdays (2007).

DARTFORD, Kent

Campanile Dartford

1 Clipper Boulevard West, Crossways Business Park, Dartford DA2 6QN.

☎ 01322 278925.

@ dartford@campanile.com

●●

Hotel at south end of Dartford River Crossing. Reserved parking bays. Public rooms level. Unisex WC. 6 twin bedrooms designed for disabled guests. Bathroom turning space, handrails, space for side transfer. Other ground floor bedrooms level. See page 31.

Ⓟ

Rates: on application.

Thistle Brands Hatch - Dartford

Brands Hatch, Dartford DA3 8PE.

☎ 0870 333 9128.

@ reservations.brandshatch@thistle.co.uk

●● D/E/F/G ★★★★

Modern hotel south of Dartford. Reserved parking bays. Ramp to entrance. Public rooms level. Unisex WC. Four bedrooms, double and twin, with adaptations for disabled guests. Bathrooms 90cm sliding door, handrails, turning space and space for side transfer to WC in one of the rooms.

Rates: on application.

Accommodation with meals

South East England

DORKING, Surrey

The Felbury Centre

Holmbury St Mary, Dorking RH5 6NL.

☎/Text: 01306 730929.

www.felburycentre.org.uk

●●● D/E/I

Centre for groups and training owned by the Lifetrain Trust. Fully accessible for wheelchair users. Accommodation for up to 45 in twin and triple bedrooms. En suite bathrooms equipped for disabled guests.

Ⓟ

Rates: on application.

DYMCHURCH, Kent

Dolly Plum Cottage Guest House

Burmarsh Road, Burmarsh,
Dymchurch TN29 0JT.

☎ 01303 874558.

● E/F/G

Country guest house between Hythe and Dymchurch on Romney Marsh. Ramp to entrance. Dining room ground floor. One level ground floor bedroom. Shower room with shower tray, handrails, no space for side transfer to WC. Level garden.

Rates: from £30 per person sharing BB (2007).

EAST PRESTON, West Sussex

Bradbury Hotel

Station Road, East Preston BN16 3AL.

☎ 01903 770339.

www.royalblindsociety.org.uk

●●● D/G

Small hotel for visually impaired people and their companions owned by Royal Blind Society near West Sussex coast. Accommodation for up to 23 guests. Talking lift to upper floors. Designed and equipped with features for blind and partially sighted people including library of cassettes and audio described videos. Outings and entertainment arranged. Support available but not personal care.

Ⓟ

Rates: on application.

EASTBOURNE, East Sussex

Best Western York House Hotel

14-22 Royal Parade,
Eastbourne BN22 7AP.

☎ 01323 412918.

www.bw-yorkhouse.co.uk

●● D/E/F/G ★★★

Hotel on seafront. Street parking. Entrance ramp or 7 steps, revolving door that can be folded. Restaurant, lounge and bar ground floor level. Unisex WC. Also basement bar/dance floor. Lifts, largest 80cm, inside 135x110cm. One bedroom on ground floor adapted for disabled guests, 82cm, ⟲. Bathroom 80cm, restricted ⟲. Other bedrooms level. Teletext TVs.

Rates: from £57 per person BB (2007).

Cavendish Hotel

Grand Parade, Eastbourne BN21 4DH.

☎ 01323 410222.

www.cavendishhotel.co.uk

●● D/E/I/F/G

Seafront hotel. Ramp with handrail or 4 steps from car park and then lift to all floors; 8 steps at main entrance. Public rooms ground floor, level. Unisex WCs in basement and ground floor. Lift 90cm, inside 100x170cm. 7 bedrooms adapted for disabled guests, 92cm, ⟲. Shower rooms 92cm, ⟲, roll-in shower with seat, handrails, space by WC. Other bedrooms level. Waterproof sheets available. Teletext TV.

Ⓟ

Rates: on application.

Hydro Hotel

Mount Road, Eastbourne BN20 7HZ.
☎ **01323 720643.** **www.hydrohotel.com**
●● D/E/I/F/G
Hotel near seafront out of town centre. Reserved parking bays. Entrance from car park level; front entrance 3 steps. Steps to reception desk. Public rooms ground floor. Lift 30", inside 39"x42". Unisex WC. One bedroom designed for disabled guests. Shower room 38", ⟲, roll-in shower with seat, handrails, space by WC. Other bedrooms level. Waterproof sheet, raised WC seat and wheelchair available. Large print hotel directory and induction loop.

Rates: from £45-£80 per person BB (2007).

Langham Hotel

Royal Parade, Eastbourne BN22 7AH.
☎ **01323 731451.**
www.langhamhotel.co.uk
●● D/E/F/G ★★★
Privately owned seafront hotel. Reserved parking bays. Ramp to entrance 59". Public rooms ground floor level. Unisex WC. Lift 30", inside 53"x38". 85 bedrooms with bath-rooms, most level from lift, no adaptations.
Rates: on application.

EGHAM, Surrey

Runnymede Hotel & Spa

Windsor Road, Egham TW20 0AG
☎ **01784 436171.**
www.runnymedehotel.com
●● D/E/F/G ★★★★
High class hotel by Thames. Reserved parking bays. Ramp to side entrance; main entrance 3 steps. Public rooms level. Unisex WC. Lift 80cm, inside 110x110cm. Two bedrooms designed for disabled people on 1st floor. Bathrooms 84cm ⟲, roll-in shower with seat, handrails, space by WC and bath. Waterproof sheet and mobile ramps available. Other bedrooms level.

Rates: on application.

GATWICK AIRPORT, West Sussex (see also Crawley and Horley)

Copthorne London Gatwick

Copthorne RH10 3PG
☎ **0870 890 0212.**
sales.gatwick@milleniumhotels.co.uk
●● D/F/G ★★★★
Country house hotel 6 miles east of Airport. Reserved parking bays. Entrance ramp or 1 step. Public rooms level. Unisex WC. Lift 76cm, inside 86x118cm. Twin bedroom adapted for disabled guests. Bathroom ⟲, handrails, space for side transfer to bath and WC. Some other level bedrooms.
Rates: on application.

Hilton London Gatwick Airport

South Terminal, Gatwick Airport, RH6 0LL.
☎ **01293 518080.**
www.hilton.co.uk/gatwick
●● D/E/I/F/G ★★★★
Hotel at airport with walkway to South Terminal. Entrance level, 67". Public rooms level. Unisex WC. Six bedrooms adapted for disabled guests. Bathrooms 31", ⟲, low bath, handrails. Other bedrooms level.
Rates: on application.

Sofitel London Gatwick

North Terminal, Gatwick Airport RH6 0PH.
☎ **01293 567070.**
●● D/G ★★★★
Hotel with walkway from North Terminal. Multi-storey and surface parking. Public rooms level. Unisex WC. Two bedrooms with bathrooms designed for disabled guests. Other bedrooms level.
Rates: on application.

South East England

GILLINGHAM, Kent

Medway Youth Hostel

377 Capstone Road, Gillingham ME7 3JE.
☎ 0870 7705964. @ medway@yha.org.uk
● D/E/I/F/G

Hostel at Country Park. Reserved parking bays. Ramp from car park to entrance. Public rooms level. Unisex WCs on Ground and 1st floors. Chairlift on stairs. Twin and family bedrooms level. Shower room with shower tray, no ⟲. For further information on Youth Hostels see page 34.

Rates: from £14 adult per night (2007).

GUILDFORD, Surrey

Holiday Inn Guildford

Egerton Road, Guildford GU2 7XZ.
☎ 0870 400 9036.
●● D/E/I/F/G

Hotel off A3, 1½ miles from town centre. Reserved parking bays. Entrance level. Public rooms open plan. Unisex WC. Four bedrooms designed for disabled guests 36", ⟲. Bathroom ⟲, handrail by WC, space for side transfer to bath. Other bedrooms level. Complementary room for carer.

Rates: from £119 per room weekdays, £55 weekends (2008).

HASTINGS, East Sussex

Grand Hotel

Grand Parade, St Leonards, Hastings TN38 0DD.
☎ 01424 428510.
W www.grandhotelhastings.co.uk
●● D/E/F/G ★

Seafront hotel. Designated parking for disabled people in front of hotel. Entrance ramp. Lounge and bar level. Restaurant lower floor, meals can be served in lounge/bar. Double and family bedrooms ground floor, ⟲. Bathrooms ⟲. Bathseat available. Other bedrooms upstairs. Star hotel rating.

Rates: from £24-£50 per night (2007).

HORLEY, Surrey

Brambles MS Respite Care Centre

Suffolk Close, Massetts Road, Horley RH6 7DU.
☎ 01293 771644. W www.brambles.org.uk
●●●●● D/I/H

Purpose-built centre for respite care for people with multiple sclerosis. 28 single bedrooms with hoists and WCs, of which 24 have shower cubicle and air conditioning. Bathrooms and WCs with range of fittings and equipment. Other facilities include physiotherapy, aromatherapy, hydrotherapy beauty salon and bar. Outings and entertainment arranged. Full care provided. Designated smoking room.

Rates: on application.

Holiday Inn Gatwick

Povey Cross Road, Horley RH6 0BA.
☎ 0870 400 9030.
@ reservationsgatwick@ihg.com
●● D/E/F/G

Hotel near airport. Reserved parking bays. Entrance level, automatic door. Low reception desk. Public rooms level. Unisex WC. Lifts to upper floors. 4 ground floor bedrooms adapted for disabled guests. Bathrooms 90cm, ⟲, handrail by bath, space by bath and WC. Other bedrooms level. Induction loops in most public areas.

Rates: from £165 per night (2007).

Masslink House

70 Massetts Road, Horley RH6 7ED.

☎ 01293 785798.

W www.masslinkguesthouse.co.uk

●●● D/E/F

Guesthouse near Gatwick Airport. Longterm parking available. Entrance ramp, 33". Dining room level 29". Twin bedroom level, 29½". Shower room, handrails, shower seat, space for side transfer to WC. Some assistance offered.

Ⓟ

Rates: from £29 single, £46 double BB (2007).

Renaissance London Gatwick Hotel

Povey Cross Road, Horley RH6 0BE.

☎ 01293 820169.

W www.renaissancelondongatwick.co.uk

●● D/E/I/F/G ★★★★

Hotel near airport. Reserved parking bays. Entrance level, automatic doors. Public rooms level. Unisex WC and adapted cubicles in other toilets. Lift 36", inside 50"x70". Four bedrooms adapted for disabled guests. Bathroom ⟲ roll-in shower with seat, handrail by bath, space by WC. Other bedrooms level.

Ⓟ

Rates: from £79 room only weekends (2007/8).

HYTHE, Kent

Maccassil Guest House

50 Marine Parade, Hythe CT21 6AW.

☎ 01303 261867.

@ info@maccassil.co.uk

● E/F

Guesthouse on the seafront. Entrance step, ramp available. Dining room level, limited ⟲. Three ground floor bedrooms with own bathrooms. No adaptations.

Ⓟ

Rates: from £30 single, £45 double BB (2007).

LINGFIELD, Surrey

Claridge House Centre for Healing

Dormans Road, Lingfield, Surrey RH7 6QH.

☎ 01342 832150.

W www.claridgehouse.quaker.eu.org

●● D/E/I/F/G

For information on this Quaker-run centre which can take bookings for individual stays, see page 503. Purpose built annex for wheelchairs.

MAIDSTONE, Kent

Hilton Maidstone

Bearstead Road, Maidstone ME14 5AA.

☎ 01622 734322.

W www.hilton.co.uk/maidstone

●● D/E/F/G

Hotel in country between M20 junction 7 and Maidstone. Reserved parking bays. Entrance level, automatic door. Public rooms ground floor, level except ramp or 4 steps to bar. Unisex WC. 4 twin/double bedrooms designed for disabled guests 80cm. Bathrooms 71cm, ⟲, handrails and space by bath and WC, low bath and basin. Other ground floor rooms level. Bath lift and seat and raised WC seat available. Used by Guide Dogs for the Blind.

Ⓟ

Rates: on application.

Marriott Tudor Park Hotel & Country Club

Ashford Road, Bearsted, Maidstone ME14 4NQ.

☎ 0870 400 7226.

W www.marriott.co.uk/TDMGS

●● D/E/F/G ★★★★

Country hotel east of Maistone. Reserved parking bays. Entrance level. Main public rooms 1st floor. Unisex WC ground floor. Lift 79cm, inside 89x132cm. 3 doubled bedrooms designed for disabled guests 77cm. Bathrooms 77cm, restricted ⟲, low bath, handrails, space by WC. Other bedrooms level. Wheelchair available.

Ⓟ

Rates: on application.

RYE, East Sussex

Woodlands

Whitebread Lane, Beckley, Rye TN31 6UA.

☎ **01797 260486.**

www.woodlandsrye.co.uk

 D/E/I/F/G

Farmhouse guesthouse north of Rye. Ramp with handrails to entrance from patio. Dining room and conservatory level. Twin ground floor bedsitting room designed for disabled guests with adjustamatic beds. Shower room 80cm, ⟲, roll-in shower with seat, handrails, space by WC. Fridge and microwave in bedroom. Some equipment available. Second bedroom upstairs. Some assistance and extended hospitality offered. Owner has nursing experience.

Rates: from £35 per person BB (2007).

SELSEY, West Sussex

St Andrews Lodge

Chichester Road, Selsey PO20 0LX.

☎ **01243 606899.**

www.standrewslodge.co.uk

●● D/F/G

Family run hotel 7 miles south of Chichester. Reserved parking bay. Entrance level. Public rooms level. One bedroom in annexe designed for disabled guests, with double and single beds. Shower room 36" sliding door, roll-in shower, handrails, space for side transfer to WC. Teletext TV. Other ground floor bedrooms available.

Rates: from £30-£50 per person BB (2007).

SEVENOAKS, Kent

Holiday Inn Maidstone-Sevenoaks

London Road, Wrotham Heath, Sevenoaks TN15 7RS.

☎ **0870 400 9054.**

reservationsmaidstone@ihg.com

●● D/E/I/F/G

Hotel in country between Sevenoaks and West Malling near M26 junction 2. Reserved parking bays. Ramp with handrails or 2 steps to entrance. Public rooms ground floor, level. Unisex WC. 2 bedrooms, family and double, designed for disabled guests. Bathrooms ⟲, handrails, space by bath and WC. Other ground floor rooms level. Waterproof sheets, vibrating alarms, induction loop and telephone amplifier available.

Rates: on application.

SITTINGBOURNE, Kent

Palace Farm Hostel

Down Court Road, Doddington, Sittingbourne ME9 0AU.

☎ **01795 886200.**

www.palacefarm.com

●● D/E/F/G ★★★

Bed & breakfast single storey hostel in country between Sittingbourne and Ashford. Parking bays can be reserved. Entrance level. Lounge/dining room and self-catering kitchen with standard worktops. Family bedroom designed for disabled guests with roll-in shower, handrails, space by WC. Step to other bedrooms.

Rates: from £18-£20 per adult, £14-£16 for children BB (2007).

TUNBRIDGE WELLS, Kent

Ramada Tunbridge Wells

8 Tonbridge Road, Pembury,
Tunbridge Wells TN2 4QL.
☎ 01892 823567.
@ sales.tunwells@ramadajarvis.co.uk
●● D/G ★★★

Hotel east of town off A21. Reserved parking bays. Entrance ramp or 1 step. Main public rooms ground floor. Unisex WC. Two twin bedrooms designed for disabled guests. Bathroom ⟲, handrails, telephone, space for side transfer to bath and WC. Other ground floor bedrooms level.

Rates: on application.

The Spa Hotel

Mount Ephraim, Tunbridge Wells TN4 8XJ.
☎ 01892 520331.
W www.spahotel.co.uk
●● D/I/F/G ★★★★

Hotel in own grounds near town centre. Reserved parking bays. Step at main entrance; side entrance level. Restaurant ramp or 3 steps. Lounge and bar level. Unisex WC. Ramp to lift. Two twin bedrooms adapted for disabled guests. Bathrooms ⟲, handrails, space for side transfer. Waterproof sheet available. Other bedrooms level.

Rates: from £150 double BB (2007).

WOKING, Surrey

Holiday Inn Woking

Victoria Way, Woking GU21 8EW.
☎ 01483 221000.
@ sales@wokingholiday-inn.com
●● D/E/I/F/G

Hotel in town centre. Reserved parking bays by entrance and in underground car park. Entrance level, automatic doors. Public rooms open plan, ramp or 3 steps to restaurant. Unisex WC. Lift 90cm, inside 89x130cm. 8 double bedrooms designed for disabled guests. Shower rooms 80cm, ⟲, roll-in shower with seat, handrails, space by WC. Other bedrooms level.

Rates: on application.

WORTHING, West Sussex

Best Western Berkeley Hotel

Marine Parade, Worthing BN11 3QD.
☎ 01903 820000.
W www.bw-berkeleyhotel.co.uk
●● D/E/F/G

Hotel on seafront. Reserved parking bay. Lift to entrance from car park. Low reception desk. Public rooms. Unisex WC. Lift to all floors. One twin room adapted for disabled guests on first floor ⟲, 42". Bathroom sliding door, ⟲, handrails and space by toilet and bath. Other bedrooms level.

Rates: £86 single, £130 double BB (2007).

Chatsworth Hotel

Steyne, Worthing BN11 3DU.
☎ 01903 236103.
W www.chatsworthworthing.co.uk
●● D/E/F/G ★★★

Hotel near beach and town centre. Street parking. Entrance 5 steps or ramp, automatic doors. Public rooms ground floor, level. Unisex WC. Lifts 75cm, inside 130x140cm, one with Braille and voice announcements. Three 2 person rooms adapted for wheelchair users. Bathrooms 78cm, ⟲, handrails, one with roll-in shower. Other bedrooms level.

Rates: on application.

South East England

LODGE ACCOMMODATION

There are Premier Travel Inn (see page 38) and Travelodge (see page 38) properties in the following areas in this region.

Arundel - Premier Travel Inn ☎ 0870 197 7016
Ashford - Premier Travel Inn ☎ 0870 197 7305
Travelodge ☎ 0870 191 1504
Ashford, North - Premier Travel Inn ☎ 0870 197 7018
Bagshot - Premier Travel Inn ☎ 0870 197 7021
Billingshurst - Travelodge ☎ 0870 191 1513
Bognor Regis - Premier Travel Inn ☎ 0870 990 6434
Brighton - Premier Travel Inn ☎ 0870 9906340
Travelodge ☎ 0870 191 1517
Camberley - Premier Travel Inn ☎ 0870 197 7047
Travelodge ☎ 0870 191 1815
Canterbury, West - Travelodge ☎ 0870 191 1523
Caterham - Travelodge ☎ 0870 191 1817
Chichester - Premier Travel Inn ☎ 0870 990 6578
Cobham - Premier Travel Inn ☎ 0870 990 6358
Crawley - Premier Travel Inn ☎ 0870 197 7067
Crawley South - Premier Travel Inn ☎ 0870 990 6390
Dartford - Travelodge ☎ 0870 191 1525
Dorking - Travelodge ☎ 0870 191 1526
Dover - Premier Travel Inn ☎ 0870 990 6517
Dover, East - Premier Travel Inn ☎ 0870 197 7075
Dover, West - Premier Travel Inn ☎ 0870 197 7076
East Grinstead - Premier Travel Inn ☎ 0870 197 7088
Eastbourne - Premier Travel Inn ☎ 0870 197 7089
Travelodge ☎ 0870 085 0950
Eastbourne North - Premier Travel Inn ☎ 0870 850 0959
Epsom - Premier Travel Inn ☎ 0870 197 7096
Epsom North - Premier Travel Inn ☎ 0870 990 6466
Folkestone - Premier Travel Inn ☎ 0870 197 7103
Fontwell - Travelodge ☎ 0870 191 1514
Gatwick - Premier Travel Inn ☎ 0870 238 3305
Travelodge ☎ 0870 191 1531
Gatwick South - Premier Travel Inn ☎ 0870 990 6354

Gillingham - Premier Travel Inn ☎ 0870 197 7105
Gravesend - Premier Travel Inn ☎ 0870 197 7118
Gravesend South - Premier Travel Inn ☎ 0870 990 6352
Guildford - Premier Travel Inn Metro ☎ 0870 197 7122
Travelodge ☎ 0870 191 1795
Hailsham - Travelodge ☎ 0870 191 1535
Hastings - Premier Travel Inn ☎ 0870 197 7128
Travelodge ☎ 0870 191 1810
Hickstead - Travelodge ☎ 0870 191 1538
Hollingbourne - Premier Travel Inn ☎ 0870 197 7169
Horsham - Premier Travel Inn ☎ 0870 197 7136
Leatherhead - Travelodge ☎ 0870 191 1748
Littlehampton - Travelodge ☎ 01903 725469
Maidstone, Allington - Premier Travel Inn ☎ 0870 197 7168
Maidstone, Leybourne - Premier Travel Inn ☎ 0870 197 7170
Maidstone, Sandling - Premier Travel Inn ☎ 0870 197 7308
Margate - Premier Travel Inn ☎ 0870 197 7182
Travelodge ☎ 0870 085 0950
Medway M2- Travelodge ☎ 0870 191 1697
Newhaven - Premier Travel Inn ☎ 0870 197 7192
Redhill - Premier Travel Inn ☎ 0870 197 7218
Sevenoaks - Premier Travel Inn ☎ 0870 197 7227
Sittingbourne - Premier Travel Inn ☎ 0870 197 7229
Staines - Travelodge ☎ 0870 191 1746
Sunbury- Travelodge ☎ 08709 085 0950
Tonbridge - Premier Travel Inn ☎ 0870 990 6552
Tonbridge North - Premier Travel Inn ☎ 0870 850 6344
Wateringbury - Premier Travel Inn ☎ 0870 990 6346
Westerham - Premier Travel Inn ☎ 0870 197 7265
Whitstable - Premier Travel Inn ☎ 0870 197 7269
Travelodge ☎ 0870 191 1522
Woking - Premier Travel Inn ☎ 0870 197 7276

SELF-CATERING ACCOMMODATION

ASHFORD, Kent

Gill Farm

Gill Lane, Mersham, Ashford TN25 7HZ.
W **www.gillfarm.co.uk**
@ jan@gillfarm.co.uk
●● F/G ★★★★

Converted barn for up to 4 people south of Ashford. Ramps on approach. Entrance threshold, portable ramp available. Lounge/kitchen open plan. Double and twin bedrooms 29½", ⟲. Bathroom 29½", ⟲, space for side transfer to bath and shower but not WC. Breakfast can be provided. Free internet connection also provided.

Apply: Mrs Jan Bowman ☎ 01233 720345.
Rates: from £220-£400 per week (2007).

BATTLE, East Sussex

Crowhurst Park

Telham, Battle TN33 0SL.
☎ **01424 773344.**
W **www.crowhurstpark.co.uk**
●● I/F/G ★★★★★

Holiday park in grounds of country house. Two chalets designed for disabled people. Ramp or 3 steps to entrance, 57" double doors. Lounge/kitchen open plan, controls useable from wheelchair. Twin bedroom with bathroom 28" sliding door, ⟲, handrails, bath seat, space for side transfer to bath and WC. Also double bedroom and bathroom. Clubhouse with bar, restaurant and ballroom. Adapted changing room in Leisure Club.

Rates: from £295-£690 per week (2006).

BOGNOR REGIS, West Sussex

Farrell House

27 Nelson Road, Bognor Regis.
●● I/G/H

Chalet-bungalow adapted and equipped for disabled people sleeping up to 8. Ground floor lounge, kitchen, bathroom, twin and single bedrooms. Two double bedrooms and bathroom upstairs. Electric hoists and shower chair. Ramp to garden.

Ⓟ

Apply: Grooms Holidays ☎ 08455 584478
@ selfcatering@johngrooms.org.uk
Rates: on application.

Invicta Warren

Elmer Sands, Middleton, Nr. Bognor Regis.
●●● E/I/F/G/H

Bungalow designed for wheelchair users, sleeping up to 10 people including 5 wheelchair users. Entrance level. Kitchen useable from wheelchair. Four twin bedrooms and sofabed in lounge. Hoist in 1 bedroom and bathroom. Shower room with seat. Shower chair and commode available.

Ⓟ

Apply: Voluntary Association for Surrey Disabled, 10 Havenbury Estate, Station Road, Dorking RH4 1ES. ☎ 01306 741500.
W www.vasd.org.uk
Rates: from £325-£465 per week (2007).

BRACKLESHAM BAY, West Sussex

Tamarisk

Farm Road, Bracklesham Bay.

●● I/G/H

Bungalow near beach adapted and equipped for disabled people. 3 bedrooms, lounge/dining room, kitchen, roll-in and second shower rooms. Mobile and electric hoists and other equipment available.

Apply: Grooms Holidays ☎ 08455 584478
@ selfcatering@johngrooms.org.uk
Rates: on application.

VASD Holiday Chalet

Sussex Beach Holiday Village, Earnley, Bracklesham Bay.

●● G/H

Chalet sleeping 3 designed for wheelchair user on holiday park by beach. Sofa bed in lounge. Double bedroom ↺, hoist and also single bedroom. Roll in shower room. Shop and pub on site.

Apply: Voluntary Association for Surrey Disabled, 10 Havenbury Estate, Station Road, Dorking RH4 1ES. ☎ 01306 741500.
W www.vasd.org.uk
Rates: from £150-£200 per week (2007).

BRIGHTON & HOVE, East Sussex

Varley Halls of Residence

Coldean Lane, Brighton.

●● G ★★★

Student accommodation north of town centre. Reserved parking bays. Entrance ramp. Ground floor living room and kitchen, controls useable from wheelchair. Shower room ↺, roll-in shower, handrail and space for side transfer to WC. Two flats have 3 ground floor bedrooms and 3 downstairs; the others have 3 on the ground floor and 3 downstairs. Battery recharging space. Available July-September.

Apply: Conferences & Events, University of Brighton, Lewes Road, Brighton BN2 4AT.
☎ 01273 643167/8.
@ conferences@brighton.ac.uk
Rates: from £498 per flat per week (2007).

CHICHESTER, West Sussex

Canute Cottages

Cobnor Farm, Chidham,
Nr. Chichester PO18 8TE.
☎ 01243 572123.
W www.canutecottages.co.uk

●● E/I/F/G 

Two, of 4 cottages by Chichester Harbour, designed for disabled people. Each sleeps up to 7. Entrance ramp, 81cm. Lounge with sofabed ↺. Kitchen/dining room open plan, controls useable from wheelchair. Double and twin bedrooms ↺. One cottage has roll-in shower room with raised seat, handrails and space for side transfer to WC. The other has a bathroom ↺ with handrails by bath and WC. Leisure barn. Accessible waterfront path nearby.

Apply: Diana Beale
Rates: from £285-£630 per week (2008).

DIAL POST, West Sussex
Honeybridge Park

Honeybridge Lane, Dial Post, Nr. Horsham RH13 8NX.

☎ **01403 710923.**

www.honeybridgepark.co.uk

●● G ★★★★

Park for touring caravans and camping off A24 in country south of Horsham with 145 pitches, half with hard standing. Site mainly level. Road surfaces mainly tar and brick paths. Unisex toilet block with NKS lock, 2 roll-in showers/WCs with ⟲, handrails, space by WC. Ramp to shop and games room. Ramp to reception and shop. Launderette and washing up area level. Holiday lodges for sale.

Rates: on application.

DORKING, Surrey
Bulmer Farm

Holmbury St Mary, Dorking RH5 6LG

☎ **01306 731871.**

www.bulmerfarm.co.uk

●● I/F/G ★★★★

Self-catering units in barn. "Badgerholt" has entrance ramp. Lounge/kitchen open plan. Twin bedroom. Bath and shower room ⟲, shower stool in tray, handrails. Other unit ground floor but with entrance steps. Bed & breakfast in farmhouse, not accessible to wheelchair users.

Rates: from £260-£360 (2007).

FARNHAM, Surrey
High Wray

73 Lodge Hill Road, Farnham GU10 3RB.

●● I/F/G ★★

"Rose" is a purpose-built flat for disabled people a mile from town. It has twin bed-sitting room, kitchen and roll-in shower/WC. All doors 36". Controls useable from wheelchair. Bedblocks, waterproof sheet and bath aid available. Accessible garden. Bed & breakfast may be available for short periods.

Apply: Mrs Alexine Crawford ☎ 01252 715589. crawford@highwray73.co.uk

Rates: from £220-£265 per week (2007).

FELPHAM, West Sussex
Beach Lodge

Strandway, Felpham, Nr Bognor Regis.

●●● I/G/H

Detached house facing the sea, east of Bognor. Adapted for wheelchair users with a lift and roll-in shower. Sleeps up to 9 people. Electric and mobile hoists available.

Apply: Grooms Holidays ☎ 08455 584478 selfcatering@johngrooms.org.uk

Rates: on application.

HASTINGS, East Sussex

Combe Haven Holiday Park

Harley Shute Road, St Leonards-on-Sea, Hastings TN38 8BZ.

☎ **01424 427891.**

●● I/G ★★★★

Haven holiday park between Hastings and Bexhill with range of facilities and entertainment. Caravans for 5 people adapted for disabled guests. Entrance ramp. Lounge/kitchen open plan. Two bedrooms, sliding door 75cm, ↺ in double. Shower room 75cm, handrails, restricted ↺, no space beside WC. Open Late March-October.

Ⓟ

Apply: Haven Holiday Reservations ☎ 0870 2422222.

Rates: on application.

HERNE BAY, Kent

Strode Park Foundation

Strode Park House, Herne CT6 7NE.

☎ **01227 373292.**

W www.strodepark.org.uk

●●● I/F/G/H

Two holiday bungalows, each for 4 people, designed for severely disabled people and their companions. Entrance level 85cm. Lounge/kitchen open plan, worktops and controls useable from wheelchair. Two bedrooms, one with variable height bed. Shower room 101cm, roll-in shower with seat, handrails, space by WC. Hoist tracking between bedroom and shower room. Level patio doors from lounge and one bedroom.

Ⓟ

Rates: from £175-£625 (2007).

MARDEN, Kent

Tanner Farm Touring Caravan & Camping Park

Goudhurst Rd, Marden, Tonbridge TN12 9ND.

☎ **01622 832399.**

W www.tannerfarmpark.co.uk

●● G ★★★★★

15 acre site for up to 100 touring caravans and tents. Toilet blocks include unisex roll-in shower room with seat, handrails, space for side transfer to WC. Office and shop level. Open all year.

Ⓟ

Rates: on application.

RYE, East Sussex

The Blacksmith's Cottage

Great Knelle Farm, Beckley, Rye TN31 6UB.

W www.greatknellefarmcottage.com

●● F ★★★★

One cottage, of three, designed for disabled people on working farm. Entrance level 91cm. Open plan lounge/kitchen, worktops 90cm. Twin bedroom ↺, also double sofa bed. Shower room ↺, roll-in shower with seat, space and handrails by WC. Electric wheelchair and buggy available. Shop on site.

Ⓟ

Apply: Jenny Farrant. ☎ 01797 260250.

Rates: £325-£475 per week (2007).

WINCHELSEA, East Sussex

Winchelsea Sands Holiday Park

Pett Level Road, Winchelsea Beach, Rye TN36 4NB.

☎ **01797 226442.**

●● I/F/G ★★★★★

Holiday park between Hastings and Rye with range of facilities. Caravan for 5 people adapted for disabled guests. Entrance ramp. Lounge/kitchen open plan. Two bedrooms, sliding door 75cm, ↺ in double. Shower room 75cm, handrails, restricted ↺. Open Easter-October.

Ⓟ

Rates: on application.

WOOLBEDING, West Sussex

Eastshaw Farm House

Eastshaw Lane, Woolbeding.

●● F/G

18th century farmhouse for up to 11 people. Lounge and open plan kitchen/ dining room. Twin bedroom level. Roll-in shower room. 5 bedrooms, bathroom and shower room upstairs.

Apply: National Trust Holiday Booking Office ☎ 0870 4584422. See page 33.

Rates: from £601-£1874 per week (2007).

Self catering accomodation

This is a large and varied region stretching from Buckinghamshire and Oxfordshire, through Berkshire and Hampshire to eastern Dorset and the Isle of Wight. It includes much of the Chiltern and Cotswold hills and the Thames Valley as well as the New Forest and stretches of attractive coastline.

There are many opportunities for seaside holidays. The largest resort is Bournemouth where there is entertainment and attractions for both young and old. Other resorts include Poole and Southsea, while Ryde, Sandown and Shanklin are on the Isle of Wight.

At Portsmouth, many attractions in the Historic Dockyard depict the military and naval heritage of the city including the Royal Naval Museum, the Mary Rose display and HMS Victory. An access trail has been laid out around the site and a panoramic view can be obtained from the Spinnaker Tower. The D-Day Museum and Overlord Embroidery are elsewhere in the city. There are other military museums in Aldershot, Winchester and elsewhere in the region.

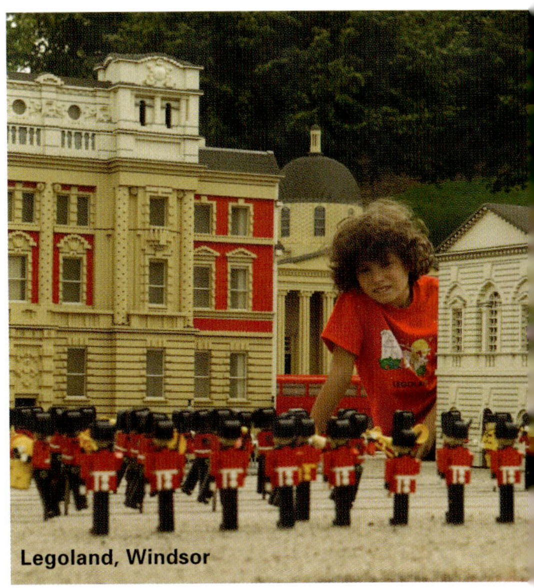
Legoland, Windsor

Photo: britainonview © Martin Brnet

There is also a full range of urban amenities in Reading and Southampton where part of the harbour has been redeveloped as Ocean City with waterfront restaurants, bars and shops. In Oxford, guided walks are open to disabled people around the historic university buildings. Other historic towns in the region include the cathedral city of Winchester, the Royal Borough of Windsor dominated by the castle, the old port of Poole and market towns such as Banbury and Aylesbury. Riverside towns along the Thames

Bridge of sighs, Oxford

include Marlow, Maidenhead and Henley, home of the River & Rowing Museum.

Two areas have their own specific characteristics - the New Forest, England's newest National Park, and the Isle of Wight. A good starting point to learn more about the natural and human history of the former is the New Forest Museum and Visitor Centre at Lyndhurst. The Isle of Wight has been a tourist destination since the middle of the 19th century when Queen Victoria made her home at Osborne House near Cowes. This is now run by English Heritage and is partly accessible to disabled visitors. The many other attractions on the island include the Isle of Wight Steam Railway, Needles Park overlooking Alum Bay, Isle of Wight Pearl and just watching the boats in the Solent.

Historic houses that can be visited elsewhere in the region include the National Trust's Basildon Park near Reading and Blenheim Palace at Woodstock in Oxfordshire. Beaulieu Abbey in the New Forest houses a large collection of veteran and classic cars. Outdoor attractions include the restored Greenham Common near Newbury, Marwell Zoo and Old Winchester Hill National Nature Reserve both in Hampshire and the Cotswold Wild Life Park at Burford. Most children, and many adults, will enjoy Legoland outside Windsor.

USEFUL ADDRESSES

Tourism South East

40 Chamberlayne Road, Eastleigh
Hampshire SO50 5JH.
☎ 023 8062 5505.
W www.visitsoutheastengland.com

Issues a number of publications on accommodation and attractions in the region.

Berkshire Disability Information Network

Brakenhale School, Rectory Lane,
Bracknell RG12 7BA.
☎ 01344 301572/426500.
Textphone: 01344 427757.
@ ask@bdin.org.uk
W www.bdin.org.uk

Provides information on a wide range of subjects, including holidays, to callers. Information Centres throughout Berkshire.

British Red Cross Berkshire Branch

Community Services, 90 Eastern Avenue,
Reading RG1 5FS.
☎ 0118 929 0500.

Can give some information on holidays to disabled and elderly people and may be able to provide transport for groups and individuals.

Dorset Association for the Disabled

Unit 18a Enterprise Park, Piddlehinton,
Dorchester DT2 7UA.
☎ 01305 849122.
@ dad.hq@tesco.net

Provides holidays for Association members and can respond to enquiries.

Green Island Holiday Trust,

c/o Peter Viney, 3 Gleneagles Avenue,
Parkstone, Poole BH14 9LJ.
☎ 01202 740470. @ pviney@aol.com

Organises holidays for disabled people with volunteer helpers at Holton Lee on the shore of Poole Harbour. Activities include birdwatching, painting, boat trips and barbecues. Priority given to people living in Dorset and Hampshire. For information on Holton Lee see page 134.

DIAL

DIAL offers a free, impartial and confidential service of information and advice by telephone to disabled people, their relatives and professionals. The following members of DIAL UK may be able to help disabled residents and visitors in their areas:

DIAL Isle of Wight
☎ 01983 522823. Textphone: 01983 525424

Milton Keynes CIL
☎ 01908 231344. Textphone: 01908 231505

New Forest DIS
☎ 01425 628750. Textphone: 01425 610062

Dialability Oxford
☎ 01865 763600. Textphone: 01865 203636

Sorrell DIAL, Portsmouth
☎ 023 9282 4853

Disability Wessex, Bournemouth
☎ 01202 589999

Hovertravel Ltd

Quay Road, Ryde, Isle of Wight PO33 2HB.
☎ 01983 811000. W www.hovertravel.co.uk

Operate a fast crossing for foot passengers by hovercraft between Southsea (Portsmouth) and Ryde on the Isle of Wight. There is a lift and space for 2 manual wheelchairs on each craft. Wheelchairs are available at each terminal and there are toilets for disabled people at Southsea and Ryde. A major new transport interchange is under construction at Ryde which should open in early 2008.

Red Funnel Ferries

12 Bugle Street, Southampton SO14 2JY.
☎ **0870 444 8898.**
@ **post@redfunnel.co.uk**
W **www.redfunnel.co.uk**

Operate car ferries and hi-speed passenger services between Southampton and Cowes on the Isle of Wight. Ferries have lifts and there are toilets for disabled passengers on board and at terminals.

Wightlink Isle of Wight Ferries

PO Box 59, Portsmouth PO1 2XB.
☎ **0870 582 7744.**
W **www.wightlink.co.uk**

Operate car ferries on the Portsmouth-Fishbourne and Lymington-Yarmouth routes and FastCat catamaran services for foot passengers only between Portsmouth and Ryde. The vessels on the Portsmouth-Fishbourne service are equipped with lifts and toilets for disabled passengers. Wheelchairs are available at all terminals. A Wightlink Disabled Persons Card is available giving discounted fares. For assistance ☎ 023 9281 2011.

USEFUL PUBLICATIONS & WEBSITES

Bournemouth: Accessibility Guide - regularly up-dated guide giving information on accommodation, attractions, places to eat & drink and entertainment. Available free of charge from Bournemouth Tourism, Westover Road, Bournemouth BH1 2BU. ☎ 0845 0511 700. Text: 01202 454800. @ accessibility@bournemouth.gov.uk
W www.bournemouth.co.uk

Accessible Portsmouth – A Guide for Visitors with Disabilities – Access guide produced by the City Council working with disabled people. The guide is available in print, audio, Braille and large print formats from ECCS, Portsmouth City Council, Civic Offices, Guildhall Square, Portsmouth PO1 2AD. ☎ 023 9283 4109.
@ tourism@portsmouthcc.gov.uk
W www.visitportsmouth.co.uk

Reading Access Guide – Published Summer 2002. It is also available and regularly updated on the web. For information contact the Access Officer, Civic Centre, Reading RG1 7TD.
☎ 0118 939 0581.
@ access.officer@reading-council.org.uk
W www.reading.gov.uk

www.visitthames.co.uk - this website, managed by the Environment Agency, gives information on activities, attractions and places to stay along the Thames from its source in the Cotswolds to Teddington. Some contacts for disabled people are included.

Winchester: Visitor Trail by Wheelchair – A leaflet for visitors to the city prepared by Winchester Shopmobility and Winchester City Council. Available from the Tourist Information Centre, Guildhall, High Street, Winchester SO23 9GH. ☎ 01962 840500.
@ tourism@winchester.gov.uk
W www. visitwinchester.co.uk

www.disabledgo.org - this website includes detailed information on the accessibility of many premises in Aylesbury.

EQUIPMENT HIRE

All Handling (Movability) Ltd

492 Kingston Road, London, SW20 8DX.

☎ **01252 319130.**

@ **info@movability.com**

W **www.movability.com**

Hires and sells manual and powered wheelchairs and scooters at weekly rates.

Andover Shopmobility

Bus Station, West Street, Andover SP10 1QP.

☎ **01264 352000.**

@ **andovershopmo@waitrose.com**

Members, whether residents or visitors to the area, can hire equipment for £12 a week. If a vehicle is to be taken abroad, proof of insurance is required.

Aylesbury Shopmobility

Civic Centre Car Park, Exchange Street, Aylesbury HP20 1DG.

☎ **01296 336725.**

@ **Shopmobility@aylesburyvaledc.gov.uk**

Manual wheelchairs and travel scooters can be hired to visitors to the area and to residents for holidays elsewhere. A copy of the insurance cover is required if the vehicle is to be taken overseas.

Eastleigh Shopmobility

Unit 2 Swan Centre, Wells Place, Eastleigh SO50 9SG.

☎ **023 8090 2402.**

@ **eastleighshopmo@btconnect.com**

In addition to the regular Shopmobility service, manual wheelchairs are available for longer hire by residents and visitors to the area who would have to register with the scheme. A deposit of £25 and proof of identity is required for extended loans. Proof of insurance is required if a wheelchair is to be taken abroad. Hire charges must be paid in advance.

British Red Cross

Isle of Wight Branch, Red Cross House, Hunnycross Way, Newport PO30 5ZD.

☎ **01983 522718.**

Can lend wheelchairs, walking and bathing equipment for holidaymakers. Advance booking required.

Buckingham Engineering Company

Old Leighton Farm, Mursley Road, Stewkley, Leighton Buzzard LU7 0ES.

☎ **01296 720800.**

Company hiring a range of manual, lightweight and powered wheelchairs and scooters for hire on weekly or monthly terms. A repair service is also offered.

Dunbar Dean Electric Transport Ltd

31 St Catherine's Road, Southbourne, Bournemouth BH6 4AE.

☎ **01202 426135**

Electric and manual wheelchairs and scooters are available for hire. Delivery can be arranged.

Island Mobility

32 Dodnor Lane, Newport, Isle of Wight PO30 5XA.

☎ **01983 530000.**

W **www.island-mobility.co.uk**

Manual wheelchairs, walkers and mobile hoists for hire on daily or weekly terms. Powered scooters available for experienced users on a weekly basis. A range of other equipment is stocked. Collection and delivery service offered throughout the Isle of Wight.

Poole Shopmobility

Level B, Multi Storey Car Park, Kingland Crescent, Poole BH15 1TA.
☎ **01202 661770.**
@ **ross@pooleshopmobility.org.uk**

In addition to regular Shopmobility services, wheelchairs, power chairs and scooters are available to both residents and visitors to their area for up to a month. There is a charge of £20 per week for manual wheelchairs and £50 per week for others and a £40 deposit.

Southampton City Shopmobility

7 Castle Way, Southampton SO14 2BX.
☎**/Textphone: 023 8063 1263.**
@ **city.shopmobility@southamptonvs.org.uk**

As well as usual Shopmobility Services, Southampton Shopmobility can provide manual wheelchairs for extended hire to both residents and visitors. Two forms of identification are required to register.

Shopmobility Winchester

Upper Parking, The Brooks Shopping Centre, Winchester SO23 8QY.
☎ **01962 842626.**
@ **winchestershopmobility@waca.org.uk**

Winchester Shopmobility can hire both wheelchairs and scooters to members and casual users on overnight, weekly and monthly rates. It also has, for local members a lightweight scooter that can be folded to fit in a car boot.

Shopmobility schemes exist to provide wheelchairs and/or scooters for use in shopping centres in the following towns. For information on availability, etc. telephone in advance.

Andover ☎ **01264 352000**
Aylesbury ☎ **01296 336725**
Banbury ☎ **01295 252722**
Basingstoke ☎ **01256 476066**
Bicester ☎ **01869 320132**
Boscombe ☎ **01202 399700**
Bournemouth ☎ **01202 598295**
Bracknell ☎ **01344 861316**
Eastleigh ☎ **023 8090 2402**
Fareham ☎ **01329 282929**
Gosport ☎ **023 9250 2692**
Havant ☎ **023 9245 5444**
High Wycombe ☎ **01494 472277**
Maidenhead ☎ **01628 543038**
Textphone: 01628 796056
Marlow ☎ **01623 405218**
Newbury ☎ **01635 523854**
Oxford ☎ **01865 248737**
Petersfield ☎ **01730 710474**
Poole ☎ **01202 661770**
Portsmouth ☎ **023 9281 6973**
Reading ☎ **0118 965 9008**
Slough ☎ **01753 691133**
Southampton ☎ **023 8063 1263**
Southampton, West Quay
☎ **023 8063 6100**
Winchester ☎ **01962 842626**
Windsor ☎ **01753 622330**
Wokingham ☎ **0118 977 0332**

In addition Poole Shopmobility operates a mobile scheme visiting a number of towns and other venues in the area.

ACCOMMODATION WITH MEALS

ABINGDON, Oxfordshire

Abbey Guest House

136 Oxford Road, Abingdon OX14 2AG.

☎ **01235 537020.**

www.abbeyguest.com

●● D/E/F/G ★★★★

Guesthouse to north of town centre. Slight slope to entrance, level 76cm. Lounge/breakfast room. Twin bedroom designed for disabled guests. Shower room 84cm, roll-in shower with seat, handrails, space by WC. Other bedrooms upstairs. Teletext TV.

Rates: £45-£78 per night BB (2007).

Kingfisher Barn

Rye Farm, Abingdon OX14 3NN.

☎ **01235 537538.**

www.kingfisherbarn.com

●● E/I/G/H

Bed & breakfast in barn conversion close to town centre. Reserved parking bays. Reception level. 10 ground floor rooms with own entrances. Two designed for disabled guests with roll-in shower rooms. Breakfast delivered to rooms. Mobile hoist with slings, commode, shower chair and waterproof sheet available. Self-catering also available, see page 131.

Rates: from £57 per night (2007).

ALDERSHOT, Hampshire

Potters International Hotel

1 Fleet Road, Aldershot GU11 2ET.

☎ **01252 344000.**

www.pottersinthotel.com

●● D/F/G ★★★

Hotel 1 mile from town off A325. Reserved parking bays. Side entrance level; 4 steps at front entrance. Low reception desk. Public rooms level. Unisex WC. Lift 31", inside 43½"x55", Braille controls. 100 bedrooms, all level with own bathrooms, no adaptations.

Rates: on application

ANDOVER, Hampshire

Esseborne Manor Hotel

Hurstbourne Tarrant,
Nr. Andover SP11 0ER.

☎ **01264 736444.**

www.esseborne-manor.co.uk

●● D/E/F/G ★★★

Country house hotel north of Andover. Reserved parking bay. Entrance level. Low reception desk. Public rooms ground floor, min. door width 77cm. Unisex WC. One ground floor bedroom. Bathroom 90cm, space by bath and WC. Other rooms upstairs.

Rates: on application.

Be Amazed...

The Look Out Discovery Centre

A Great Family Day Out, Whatever the Weather!

Hands on Science and Nature Exhibition - Over 70 Exhibits

The Look Out Discovery Centre
Nine Mile Ride, Bracknell
Berkshire, RG12 7QW
Tel: 01344 354400
www.bracknell-forest.gov.uk/be

Open Daily
10am - 5pm

Be LEISURE

Havant & Hayling Island

If you are mobility impaired then Havant & Hayling Island is a wonderful place to visit, especially if you want to be beside the sea.

- Beach boardwalks for mobility impaired
- Specially designed picnic tables
- Radar key toilets
- Special parking areas
- Specially adapted beach huts for hire
- Variety of accommodation with range of access
- Topography suitable for wheelchairs

For a full colour brochure contact:
Hayling Island Visitor Centre,
Sea Front, Hayling Island PO11 0AG
Tel/Fax: 023 9246 7111
e-mail: tourism@havant.gov.uk
www.visithavant.co.uk

COTSWOLD Wildlife Park and Gardens

OPEN DAILY FROM 10AM

The premier choice for gardeners and their children in 160 acres of landscaped parkland.

INFORMATION HOTLINE:
01993 825728

BURFORD • OXON OX18 4JP (MID-WAY BETWEEN OXFORD & CHELTENHAM)

www.cotswoldwildlifepark.co.uk

AYLESBURY, Buckinghamshire

Holiday Inn Aylesbury

Aston Clinton Road, Aylesbury HP22 5AA.
☎ 01296 734017.
@ aylesbury@ihg.com
●● D/E/I/F/G

Hotel in country east of Aylesbury. 7 reserved parking bays. Entrance level, automatic doors. Low reception desk. Main public rooms open plan, level. Unisex WC. Two bedrooms, twin and double, designed for disabled guests. Bathrooms ⟲, space by bath and WC. Other ground floor bedrooms level. Portable induction loops available. Health Club accessible.

Rates: on application.

Holiday Inn Garden Court Aylesbury

Buckingham Road, Watermead, Aylesbury HP19 0FY.
☎ 01296 398839.
@ aylesbury@holidayinns.co.uk
●● E/I/G

Hotel on A413, west of town centre. Reserved parking bays. Entrance level. Restaurant and bar level. Unisex WC. Two bedrooms designed for disabled guests 31", ⟲. Bathroom 36", ⟲, handrails, space for side transfer to WC. Waterproof sheet available. Other ground floor bedrooms level.

Rates: on application.

Olympic Lodge

Guttmann Road, Stoke Mandeville, Aylesbury HP21 9PP.
☎ 01296 484848.
W www.stokemandevillestadium.co.uk
●●● D/E/I/G/H

Accomodation in Stoke Mandeville Stadium complex owned by British Wheelchair Sports Foundation on outskirts of Aylesbury. 25 reserved parking bays. All public areas and the 50 bedrooms and bathrooms designed for wheelchair users. Equipment available includes hoist, raised WC seats, bed raisers. Meals and bar in Stadium. Also dormitory accommodation for up to 300 people. Sports and conference facilities can be made available for groups.

Rates: on application.

BASINGSTOKE, Hampshire

Audleys Wood Hotel

Alton Road, Basingstoke RG25 2JT.
☎ 01256 817555.
W www.handpicked.com
●● D/E/I/G

Country house hotel. Reserved parking bays. Ramp to side entrance; main entrance 3 steps. Public rooms level. Unisex WC. Double bedroom adapted for disabled guests 74cm. Door to adjoining twin room. Bathroom 77cm sliding door, ⟲, handrails, space for side transfer to bath and WC. Other ground floor bedrooms level.

Rates: from £55 per person weekends (2007).

Hilton Basingstoke

Old Common Road, Black Dam, Basingstoke RG21 3PR.
☎ **01256 460460.**
www.hilton.co.uk/basingstoke
●● D/E/F/G

Hotel near town centre. Reserved parking bays. Entrance level, automatic doors. Public rooms level, open plan. Unisex WC. Two twin bedrooms adapted for disabled guests. Bathrooms with sliding door, ⟲, handrails, space for side transfer. Other bedrooms level.

Rates: on application.

Holiday Inn Basingstoke

Grove Road, Basingstoke RG21 3EE.
☎ **0870 400 9004.**
reservations-basingstoke@ihg.com
●● D/E/I/F/G

Hotel south of town centre. Reserved parking bays at side and front. Ramp or steps to entrance, automatic doors. Low reception desk. Public rooms, ground floor, open plan. Unisex WC. Four double rooms designed for disabled guests. Bathrooms 32", ⟲, handrails, space by bath and WC. Other ground floor bedrooms level.

Rates: on application.

BOURNEMOUTH, Dorset

Belvedere Hotel

Bath Road, Bournemouth BH1 2EU.
☎ **01202 293336.**
www.belvedere-hotel.co.uk
●● D/E/F/G ★★★

Hotel in town centre. Reserved parking bay. Ramp at entrance, automatic door. Public rooms level. Unisex WC. Lift 78cm, inside 90x35cm. One twin/double bedroom adapted for disabled guests. Shower room 70cm, ⟲, roll-in shower with seat, handrails. Some other bedrooms level. Steps to pool.

Rates: from £33-£90 per person BB (2007).

Best Western East Anglia Hotel

6 Poole Road, Bournemouth BH2 5QX.
☎ **01202 765163.**
www.eastangliahotel.com
●● D/F/G

Reserved parking bays. Entrance level. Public rooms level. WCs adapted. Small lift. Two ground floor bedrooms 33", ⟲. Bathroom 33", handrails, space by WC. Other level bedrooms available.

Rates: from £63 per person BB (2007).

Cumberland Hotel

East Overcliffe Drive, Bournemouth BH1 3AF.
☎ **01202 290722.**
www.cumberlandbournemouth.co.uk
●● D/E/I/F/G ★★★

Hotel near to east of town centre. 3 reserved parking bays. Entrance level, 155cm. Public rooms ground floor, level. Adapted cubicle in ladies toilet, unisex toilet planned. Lift 70cm, inside 97x88cm. 10 bedrooms more suitable for disabled guests, 78cm, ⟲. Bathrooms 78cm, ⟲, handrail by bath, space by WC. Other bedrooms level. Wheelchairs available. Regular disabled guests.

Rates: on application.

Heathlands Hotel

Grove Road, East Cliff, Bournemouth BH1 3AY.
☎ **01202 553336.**
www.heathlandshotel.com
●● D/E/G ★★★

Reserved parking bay. Front entrance step, portable ramp available, automatic door. Rear entrance level. Public rooms level. WCs not adapted. Lift 45", inside 54"x54". Twin bedroom with bathroom adapted for disabled guests. Other level bedrooms available.

Rates: on application.

Lawnswood Hotel

22A Studland Road, Alum Chine,
Bournemouth BH4 8JA.
☎ **01202 761170.**

● D/F

Guesthouse west of town centre. Reserved parking bays. Entrance level. Public rooms level. Twin bedroom level, 32". Shower room 27", no ⟲, 1⟲" step to shower with seat, grabrails by shower and WC. Raised WC seat available. Also double room on ground floor. Teletext TV. Scooter recharging point.

Ⓟ ⊘

Rates: from £25 per person BB (2007).

Quality Hotel Bournemouth

47 Gervis Road, East Cliff,
Bournemouth BH1 3DD.
☎ **01202 316316.**
www.qualityhotelbournemouth.com

●● D/E/F/G ★★★

Hotel near town centre. Reserved parking bay. Entrance level, double doors. Public rooms level. Lift to 1st and 2nd floors. Unisex WC. One double or twin bedroom designed for wheelchair users with own level entrance. Shower room 84cm, roll-in shower with seat, handrails, space for side transfer to WC. 53 other bedrooms.

Ⓟ ⊘

Rates: from £32-£55 per person BB (2007).

BRACKNELL, Berkshire

Coppid Beech Hotel

John Nike Way, Bracknell RG12 8TF.
☎ **01344 303333.**
www.coppidbeech.com

●● D/E/I/F/G ★★★★

Hotel on edge of town. Reserved parking bays. Entrance ramp or 10 steps, automatic door. Low reception desk. Public rooms level, except step in part of night club. Unisex WC. Lifts 35½", inside 41"x 62". Two bedrooms designed for disabled guests. Bathrooms 35", ⟲, handrails, space for side transfer to bath and WC. Waterproof sheet available. Other bedrooms level.

Ⓟ ⊘

Rates: on application.

Grange Bracknell

Charles Square, Bracknell RG12 1DF.
☎ **01344 474000.**
Bracknell@grangehotels.com

●● D/E/I/F/G ★★★★

Hotel in town centre. 3 reserved parking bays. Entrance level, automatic doors. Public rooms ground floor. Unisex WCs. Lift 90cm, inside 175x160cm. 9 bedrooms, double/twin, designed for disabled guest 90cm Bathrooms 80cm, no ⟲, handrail by bath, space by bath and WC. Other bedrooms level. Portable induction loop.

Ⓟ ⊘

Rates: on application.

BROCKENHURST, Hampshire

The Watersplash Hotel

The Rise, Brockenhurst SO42 7ZP.
☎ **01590 622344.**
www.watersplash.co.uk

●● D/E/F/G ★★

Country hotel in New Forest village. Reserved parking bays. Entrance level, double doors. Public rooms level. Two twin bedrooms on ground floor, ⟲ with bathrooms.

Ⓟ ⊘

Rates: on application.

EASTLEIGH, Hampshire

Holiday Inn Southampton-Eastleigh

197 Leigh Road, Eastleigh SO50 9PG.
☎ **0870 400 9075.**

●● D/E/F/G

Hotel on edge of town near M3 Junction 13. 4 reserved parking bays. Ramp to entrance, automatic door. Low reception desk. Public rooms level, open plan, large print menus. Unisex WC. Lift 82cm, inside 115x132cm. Two ground floor bedrooms adapted for disabled guests. Bathrooms ⟲, handrails, space by bath and WC. Other bedrooms level. Vibrating and flashing alarms, sound amplifier and large print information available.

Ⓟ ⊘

Rates: on application.

FAREHAM, Hampshire

Holiday Inn Fareham-Solent

Cartwright Drive, Titchfield, Fareham PO15 5RJ.

☎ **0870 400 9028.**

@ **fareham@ihg.com**

●● D/E/I/F/G

Hotel 2 miles west of town centre near M27 Junction 9. Reserved parking bays. Entrance level, automatic doors. Low reception desk. Public rooms level, open plan. Unisex WC. Two bedrooms designed for disabled guests. Bathrooms ⟲, handrails, space by WC. Other ground floor bedrooms level. Portable induction loop, large print menus available. Ramp to garden.

Ⓟ

Rates: on application.

FARINGDON, Oxfordshire

Sudbury House Hotel

56 London Street, Faringdon SN7 8AA.

Tel: 01367 241272.

W **www.sudburyhouse.co.uk**

●● D/E/F/G ★★★

Modern hotel in country between Oxford and Swindon. Entrance and public rooms level. Ground floor twin bedroom adapted for disabled guests 32". Bathroom with shower 35", handrails by bath, no space by WC. 48 other level rooms. A Best Western Hotel. AA Rosett restaurant.

Ⓟ

Rates: £95 single, £105 double BB (2007).

FARNBOROUGH, Hampshire

Holiday Inn Farnborough

Lynchford Road, Farnborough GU14 6AZ.

☎ **0870 400 9029.**

@ **farnborough@ichotelsgroup.com**

●● D/E/I/F/G

Hotel between Farnborough and Aldershot near Aerospace Centre. Ramp or 3 steps to entrance. Public rooms level. Unisex WC. Two bedrooms adapted for disabled guests ⟲. Bathrooms ⟲, handrails, space by bath and WC, Other ground floor bedrooms level. Teletext TV and induction loop.

Ⓟ

Rates: on application.

HIGH WYCOMBE, Buckinghamshire

Holiday Inn High Wycombe

Crest Way, High Wycombe HP11 1TL.

☎ **0870 400 9042.**

@ **highwycombe@ichotelsgroup.com**

●● D/E/I/F/G

Hotel in town. Reserved parking bays. Slope to entrance, automatic doors. Public rooms ground floor, level and mainly open plan. Unisex WC. Two rooms designed for disabled guests, 88cm. Bathroom 85cm, ⟲, handrails, space by bath and WC. Other ground floor rooms level. Induction loops, vibrating alarms and large print information and menus available.

Ⓟ

Rates: on application.

ISLE OF WIGHT

Country Garden Hotel

Church Hill, Totland Bay PO39 0ET.

☎ **01983 754521.**

W **www.thecountrygardenhotel.co.uk**

●● D/E/G

Small hotel in gardens. Side entrance ramp; 2 steps at main entrance. Public rooms level. WCs level, not adapted. Ground floor bedroom 28", limited ⟲. Shower room ⟲, roll-in shower, handrails, space for side transfer to WC. Other ground floor rooms.

Ⓟ

Rates: on application.

Koala Cottage Retreat
Church Hollow, Godshill PO38 3DR.
☎ **01983 842031.**
🆆 **www.koalacottage.co.uk**

●● ★★★★
Guesthouse in village. Reserved parking bay. Level entrance. Dining room and conservatory level. Three ground floor double bedrooms ⟲. Bathrooms ⟲, space by bath and WC, 2 with roll-in shower.
Ⓟ 🚭
Rates: on application for 3 & 4 night breaks.

Marlborough Hotel
16 Queens Road, Shanklin PO37 6AN.
☎ **01983 862588.**
@ **eugenio.pascoal@btopenworld.com**

●● D ★★
Hotel in own grounds near town centre. Ramp or 6 steps to entrance. Public rooms ground floor level. One twin bedroom adapted for disabled guests. Shower room ⟲, roll-in shower, handrails, space by WC. Other ground floor bedrooms level. Stairlift to 1st floor. Regular disabled guests.
Ⓟ 🚭 ☕ 🚌
Rates: from £50-£80 per room BB (2007).

LEE-ON-SOLENT, Hampshire
West Wind Guest House
197 Portsmouth Road, Lee-on-Solent, Gosport PO13 9AA.
☎ **023 9255 2550.**
🆆 **www.west-wind.co.uk**
● D/E/F
Guesthouse close to beach. Reserved parking bay. Entrance 29", one step. Dining room level. Double bedroom ground floor 29", Shower room 25" sliding door, handrails by WC and in shower cubicle. Shower stool available.
Ⓟ 🚭
Rates: from £45-£60 per person BB (2007).

MAIDENHEAD, Berkshire
Holiday Inn Maidenhead/Windsor

Manor Lane, Maidenhead SL6 2RA.
☎ **0870 400 9053.**
@ **maidenhead-reservations@ihg.com**
●● D/E/I/F/G ★★★★
Hotel a mile south of central Maidenhead. Reserved parking spaces by main and side entrances. Ramp to side entrance. Public rooms level, open plan. Braille and large print menus. Adapted cubicles in toilets. Lift to upper floors. Five double bedrooms designed for disabled guests which can connect with neighbouring room. Bathrooms ⟲, handrails, some with roll-in showers. Other bedrooms level. Wheelchair, vibrating pager and induction loops available.
Ⓟ 🚭 ☕ 🏊 🏋 🚌
Rates: on application.

MARLOW, Buckinghamshire
Crowne Plaza Marlow

Fieldhouse Lane, Marlow SL7 1GJ.
☎ **0870 444 8940.**
🆆 **www.crowneplazamarlow.co.uk**
●● D/E/I/F/G ★★★★
Luxury hotel by lake to east of town in Thames Valley. Reserved parking bays. Entrance level, swing and revolving doors. Low reception desk. Public rooms ground floor, mainly open plan. Unisex WC 1st floor. Lift 35½", inside 63"x55". 8 double bedrooms designed for disabled guests on ground floor, low controls and clothes rail. Shower rooms ⟲, roll-in shower with seat, space and handrails by WC. Other bedrooms level. Vibrating alarm and waterproof sheet available.
Ⓟ 🚭 ☕ 🏊 🏋 ⚑
Rates: on application.

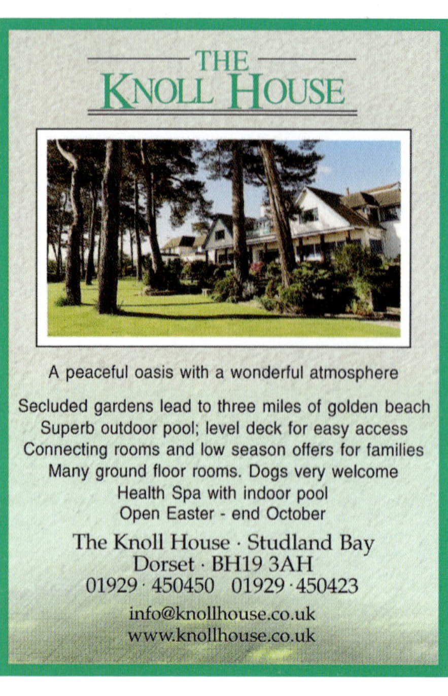
THE
KNOLL HOUSE
A peaceful oasis with a wonderful atmosphere
Secluded gardens lead to three miles of golden beach
Superb outdoor pool; level deck for easy access
Connecting rooms and low season offers for families
Many ground floor rooms. Dogs very welcome
Health Spa with indoor pool
Open Easter - end October
The Knoll House · Studland Bay
Dorset · BH19 3AH
01929 · 450450 01929 · 450423
info@knollhouse.co.uk
www.knollhouse.co.uk

Looking for a great day out for the whole family?
Try the Hawk Conservancy Trust, Andover.
• Large disabled parking area
• Fully accessible and flat tarmac paths around grounds
• 22 acres of beautiful grounds, with seats for rest breaks
• Over 100 birds on display and 3 exciting flying displays daily
• Reserved disabled viewing areas in our arenas and hides
• Hands on experience sessions
• Manual and powered scooters available
See how learning about nature can be fun!
Call 01264 773850 or visit
www.hawkconservancy.org

...more to see than you ever imagined
Art gallery, Museum, Gardens, Café and Stunning Views
ADMISSION FREE
RENAISSANCE SOUTH WEST museums for changing lives
Bournemouth
Russell-Cotes
Art Gallery & Museum
East Cliff, Bournemouth BH1 3AA
Telephone: 01202 451858 Minicom: 01202 451820
www.russell-cotes-bournemouth.gov.uk
Open: tuesday-Sunday 10am-5pm
Bournemouth's best kept secret - and it is just 2 minutes from Bournemouth Pier

WICKED ROMAN STUFF
at Brading Roman Villa
There's something for all the family at Brading Roman Villa.
Brading Roman Villa. Morton Old Road. Brading. Isle of Wight. PO36 0PH
01983 406223 www.bradingromanvilla.org.uk
Open Daily: 9.30am - 5pm
Reg Charity No: 1044506

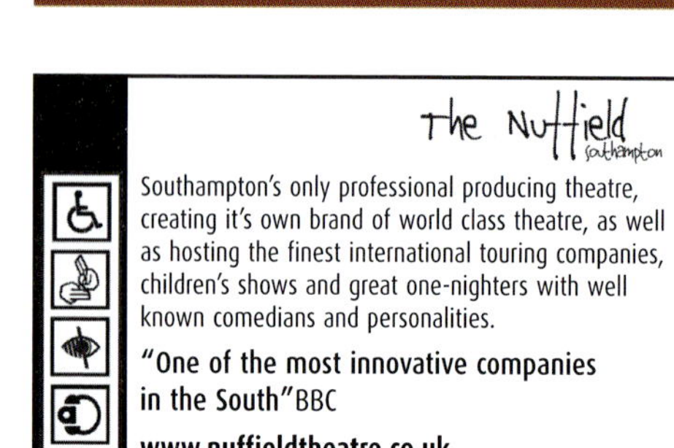
The Nuffield
southampton
Southampton's only professional producing theatre, creating it's own brand of world class theatre, as well as hosting the finest international touring companies, children's shows and great one-nighters with well known comedians and personalities.
"One of the most innovative companies in the South" BBC
www.nuffieldtheatre.co.uk
023 8067 1771
Love live theatre

MILTON KEYNES, Buckinghamshire

Campanile Milton Keynes

40 Penn Road, Fenny Stratford,
Milton Keynes MK2 2AU.
☎ **01908 649819.**
@ **mk@campanile-hotels.com**

Hotel at A5/B4140 junction south of town centre. Reserved parking bays. Public rooms level. Unisex WC. 2 twin bedrooms designed for disabled guests with bathroom, handrails, space for side transfer. Other ground floor bedrooms level. See page 31.

Rates: on application.

Express by Holiday Inn Milton Keynes

Eastlake Park, Tongwell Street, Fox Milne,
Milton Keynes MK15 0YA.
☎ **01908 681000.**
@ **miltonkeynes@expressbyholidayinn.co.uk**
 E/I/F/G

Limited service hotel in suburbs near M1 junction 14. Reserved parking bays. Entrance level. Low reception desk. Public rooms level, open plan. Unisex WC. Lift 89cm, inside 110x140cm, braille buttons. Six double bedrooms designed for disabled guests. Shower rooms, roll-in shower, space by WC. Other bedrooms level.

Rates: on application.

Hilton Milton Keynes

Timbold Drive, Kents Hill Park,
Milton Keynes MK7 6HL.
☎ **01908 694433.**
W **www.hilton.co.uk/miltonkeynes**
●● D/E/I/F/G

Hotel between town centre and M1. Reserved parking bays. Entrance level, automatic doors. Public rooms open plan. Unisex WC. Lift 30", inside 41"x53". Three bedrooms designed for disabled guests with doors to neighbouring room. Bathrooms 33", sliding doors, handrail, space by WC and bath. Waterproof sheet, raised WC seat and bed raisers available. Vibrating alarms. Other bedrooms level.

Rates: on application.

Holiday Inn Milton Keynes

500 Saxon Gate West,
Milton Keynes MK9 2HQ.
☎ **0870 4009057.**
@ **reservations-miltonkeynes@ihg.com**
●● D/E/F/G ★★★★

Town centre hotel. Reserved parking bays. Entrance level, automatic doors. Public rooms level, open plan. Unisex WC. Lifts 59" to all floors. Four bedrooms designed for disabled guests. Bathrooms, space for side transfer to bath and WC. Other bedrooms level.

Rates: on application.

Jurys Inn Milton Keynes

Midsummer Boulevard, Milton Keynes
MK9 2HP.
☎ **01908 843700.**
@ **jurysinnmiltonkeynes@jurysinns.com**
●● D/E/I/F/G

Hotel in town centre. Street parking. Entrance level, automatic door. Low reception desk with induction loop. Public rooms open plan. Unisex WC. Lift to all floors. 14 bedrooms for 1 or 2 people designed for disabled guests, low cloths rail and spyhole, 4 have automatic doors. Shower rooms 90cm, roll-in shower with seat, handrails, space by WC. Other bedrooms level. Vibrating pillow available.

Rates: from £51-£119 room only (2008).

Novotel Milton Keynes

Saxon Street, Heelands,
Milton Keynes MK13 7RA.
☎ 01908 322212. @ H3272@accor.com

●● D/E/I/G ★★★

Hotel north of town centre. Reserved parking bays. Entrance level, automatic doors. Main public rooms open plan. Unisex WCs. Lift to all floors. 7 ground floor rooms designed for disabled guests. Bathrooms ⟲, roll-in shower, space by WC. Other bedrooms level.

Rates: on application.

NEW MILTON, Hampshire

St Ursula

30 Hobart Road, New Milton BH25 6EG.
☎ 01425 613515.

●● D/E/F/G

Guesthouse in town near coast and New Forest. Entrance ramp, 33". Dining room and lounge level, min. door width 30". Ground floor suite with twin bedroom, sitting room and kitchenette and shower room ⟲, roll-in shower with seat and handrails. Other bedrooms upstairs.

Rates: from £60 per night for suite (2007).

NEWBURY, Berkshire

Ramada Elcot Park Hotel

Elcot, Nr Newbury RG20 8NJ.
☎ 01488 658100.
@ sales.elcotpark@ramadajarvis.co.uk

●● D/G

Country house hotel. Reserved parking bays. Entrance level. Public rooms level. Adapted WC cubicles. Two ground floor bedrooms designed for disabled guests. Bathrooms ⟲, handrails, space for side transfer to bath and WC.

Rates: on application.

OXFORD, Oxfordshire

Holiday Inn Oxford

Peartree Roundabout, Woodstock Road, Oxford OX2 8JD.
☎ 0870 400 9086.
@ oxford-reservations@ihg.com

●● D/E/I/F/G

Modern hotel on northern edge of city. Reserved parking bays. Entrance level, automatic doors. Public rooms level. Unisex WC. Lift 35", inside 61.5"x55.5". 7 bedrooms designed for disabled guests with interconnecting rooms if required. Bathrooms 36" sliding door, ⟲, handrails, space by bath and WC. Room for carers, subject to availability. Other bedrooms level. Vibrating alarms, waterproof sheets, portable induction loops and Braille information available. Pool level, stairs to gym.

Rates: on application.

Oxford Spires Four Pillars Hotel

Abingdon Road, Oxford OX1 4PS.
☎ 01865 324324.
@ spires@four-pillars.co.uk

●● D/E/F/G ★★★★

Hotel near city centre. Reserved parking bays. Entrance level, automatic door. Restaurant, lounge and bar ground floor. Drawing Room 1st floor. Unisex WCs in public areas and Leisure Club. Lift 80cm, inside 110x140cm. Five twin bedrooms designed for disabled guests. Bathrooms 82cm, ⟲, handrails, space by WC and bath. Other bedrooms level.

Rates: on application.

POOLE, Dorset

Orton Rigg Hotel

53 Cliff Drive, Canford Cliffs,
Poole BH13 7JF.
☎ **01202 707946.**
@ **www.ortonrigghotel.co.uk**
●● D/E/I/F/G

Hotel adapted for disabled guests in secluded setting. Reserved parking bays. Entrance level. Public Rooms level. Unisex WC. Lift 31", inside 49"x36". Most bedrooms with bathrooms adapted for wheelchair users, 33", ⟲. Some have roll-in showers with seat. Some equipment available. Entertainment and outings arranged.

Ⓟ

Rates: on application.

PORTSMOUTH, Hampshire

Express by Holiday Inn Portsmouth

The Plaza, Gunwharf Quays,
Portsmouth PO1 3FD.
☎ **023 9289 4240.**
W **www.exhiportsmouth.com**
●● E/I/F/G

Limited service hotel in city centre waterfront development. Underground car park with attendant. Ramp or 2 steps to entrance, automatic doors. Low reception desk. Lift to all floors. Public rooms 1st floor open plan. Unisex WC. 7 bedrooms designed for disabled guests, interconnect with neighbouring room. Shower room ⟲, roll-in shower, handrails, space by WC. Other bedrooms level. Waterproof sheets, induction loop, vibrating alarms and Teletext TV available.

Ⓟ

Rates: £120 per room BB (2007).

Hilton Portsmouth

Eastern Road, Farlington,
Portsmouth PO6 1UN.
Tel: 023 9221 9111.
@ **gm-portsmouth@Hilton.com**
●● D/E/I/F/G

Hotel on outskirts of city. Reserved parking bays. Entrance level, automatic doors. Public rooms level, open plan. Unisex WC. Bedroom designed for disabled guests. Bathroom 80cm, ⟲, handrails, space by bath and WC. Other ground floor bedrooms level.

Ⓟ

Rates: on application.

Holiday Portsmouth

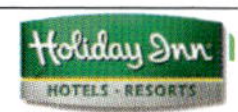

Pembroke Road, Portsmouth PO1 2TA.
☎ **0870 400 9065.**
@ **reservations-portsmouth@ihg.com**
●● D/E/I/F/G

Hotel in city centre and near Southsea seafront. Reserved spaces in small hotel car park and street parking. Ramp to entrance, automatic door. Public rooms ground floor. Unisex WC. Ramp to lift 31", inside 56"x40". 4 bedrooms designed for disabled guests, ground floor with ramp on approach. Bathrooms ⟲, handrails, space by WC. Wheelchair, vibrating alarms and menu and information in large print available.

Ⓟ

Rates: on application.

Ibis Hotel Portsmouth

Winston Churchill Avenue,
Portsmouth PO1 2LX.
☎ **023 9264 0000.** @ **H1461@accor.com**
●● D/E/I/F/G

City centre hotel. Entrance level 36". Public rooms level, open plan. Unisex WC. Lifts. Four twin and double bedrooms designed for disabled guests. Shower room ⟲, roll-in shower, handrails space for side transfer to WC. Other 140 bedrooms level.

Ⓟ

Rates: from £55-£65 per room (2008).

Portsmouth Marriott Hotel

Southampton Road, Portsmouth PO6 4SH.

☎ **0870 400 7285.**

www.marriotthotels.com/pmeha

●● D/G ★★★★

Hotel north of Portsmouth with 174 bedrooms. Entrance level, 35". Public rooms level. Unisex WC. Lift, inside 65"x54". Four bedrooms and bathrooms adapted for disabled guests. Other rooms level.

Rates: on application.

Queens Hotel

Clarence Parade, Southsea, Portsmouth PO5 3LJ.

☎ **023 9282 2466.**

www.queenshotelportsmouth.com

●● D/E/I/F/G ★★★

Edwardian hotel overlooking Southsea seafront. 2 reserved parking bays. Side entrance level, 10 steps at main entrance. Lift, inside 48"x84", from side entrance to reception and other floors. Public rooms level. Unisex WC. Two double bedrooms with bathrooms adapted for disabled guests.

Rates: on application.

Premier Travel Inn Portsmouh

Binnacle Way, Kingsway North, Portsmouth PO6 4FB.

☎ **0870 423 6456**

www.premierinn.com

●● D/E/F/G

Hotel in north Portsmouth near M27 junction 12. Reserved parking bays. Entrance level, automatic doors. Low reception desk. Restaurant, lounge and bar ground floor level. Unisex WC. Lift 80cm, inside 108x213cm. 5 double rooms designed for disabled guests, vibrating alarm, large button phone. Shower room ⟲, roll-in shower with seat, handrails, space by WC. Other bedrooms level. Induction loop.

Rates: from £67 double room only (2007).

READING, Berkshire

Holiday Inn Reading South

500 Basingstoke Road, Reading RG2 0SL.

☎ **0870 400 9067.**

reservations-reading@ihg.com

●● D/E/I/F/G

Hotel 3 miles south of town centre near M4 junction 11. Reserved parking bays. Entrance level, automatic door. Public rooms ground floor open plan. Unisex WC. 4 bedrooms adapted for disabled guests. Bathrooms ⟲, handrails, space by bath and WC, seat by bath. Induction loops, vibrating alarm, sound amplifier available. Other ground floor bedrooms level.

Rates: from £60-£180 per room (2007).

Holiday Inn Reading West

Bath Road, Padworth, Reading RG7 5HT.

☎ **00870 400 9670.**

reservations@reading.kewgreen.co.uk

●● D/E/I/F/G ★★★

Hotel off A4 west of Reading. Reserved parking bays. Entrance level, double doors. Public rooms open plan. Unisex WC. Two double/twin bedrooms designed for disabled guests. Bathrooms have sliding door, ⟲, handrails, space for side transfer. Other ground floor bedrooms level.

Rates: on application.

Ibis Hotel Reading

25a Friar Street, Reading RG1 1DP.

☎ **0118 953 3500** **H5431@accor.com**

●● D/E/I/G

Hotel in city centre. Entrance level, automatic doors. Low reception desk. Public rooms open plan. Unisex WC. Lifts to upper floors. Nine Bedrooms designed for disabled guests. Shower rooms ⟲ roll-in shower with seat, space by WC. Other bedrooms level.

Rates: from £52-£72 per room (2008).

Novotel Reading Centre

25b Friar Street, Reading RG1 1DP.
☎ 0118 952 2600. @ h5432@accor.com
●● D/E/I/F/G ★★★★

Modern hotel in city centre. Reserved parking bay. Entrance level, swing and revolving doors. Low reception desk. Public rooms open plan. Unisex WC. Lifts 90cm, inside 130x100cm. 10 bedrooms for two people designed for disabled guests. Bathrooms 83cm, ⟲, some with roll-in showers. Other bedrooms level. Vibrating pillow alarm and portable induction loop available.

Rates: from £65-£160 per room (2007).

Millennium Madejski Hotel

Junction 11 M4, Reading RG2 0FL.
☎ 0118 925 3500.
@ reservations.reading@millennium hotels.co.uk
●● D/E/I/F/G ★★★★

High class hotel in suburbs by sports stadium. Reserved parking bays. Entrance level, revolving and swing door. Low reception desk. Public rooms level. Unisex WC and adapted cubicles. Lifts 33", inside 42"x84". Seven twin bedrooms and four suites designed for disabled guests. Bathrooms 36", ⟲, handrails, space by bath and WC. Other rooms level. Waterproof sheets, wheelchairs and portable induction loop available.

Rates: on application.

SLOUGH, Berkshire

Copthorne Hotel Slough-Windsor

400 Cippenham Lane, Slough SL1 2YE.
☎ 01753 516222.
@ sales.slough@mill-cop.com
●● D/E/F/G ★★★★

Modern hotel. Reserved parking bays. Entrance level, revolving and swing doors. Public rooms open plan. Unisex WC. Lift 43", inside 60"x60". Double bedroom designed for disabled guests. Shower room 34", roll-in shower, handrails, space for side transfer to WC. Waterproof sheet available. 9 other bedrooms with wheelchair access and all level.

Rates: on application.

SOUTHAMPTON, Hampshire

Chilworth Manor Hotel

Chilworth, Southampton SO16 7PT.
☎ 023 8076 7333.
W www.chilworth-manor.co.uk
●● D/E/F/G 

Hotel and Conference Centre in own grounds north of Southampton. Reserved parking bays. Entrance level. Low reception desk. Public rooms ground floor. Unisex WC. Lift 80cm, inside 110x140cm. Single and double bedrooms on ground floor designed for disabled guests 78cm, ⟲. Bathrooms 82cm, ⟲, handrails, space by WC. Other bedrooms level. Induction loop and Teletext TV available.

Rates: From £55-£95 single BB (2007).

Express by Holiday Inn Southampton M27 J7

Botley Road, West End, Southampton SO30 3XA.
☎ 023 8060 6060.
@ reservations@expressbyholidayinn.uk.net
●● E/I/G

Limited service hotel east of city by motorway and Hampshire Cricket Ground. Reserved parking bays. Level entrance, automatic doors. Low reception desk. Public rooms open plan. Unisex WC. Lift 100cm, inside 110x135cm. Six double/twin bedrooms designed for disabled guests. Shower rooms ⟲, roll-in shower with seat, handrails, space by WC. Other bedrooms level, some interconnecting. Vibrating alarm and induction loop available.

Rates: from £65 per room BB (2007).

Express by Holiday Inn Southampton West

Adanac Park, Redbridge Lane, Nursling, Southampton SO16 0YP.

☎ **0870 720 1252.**

@ **southampton@morethanhotels.com**

●● D/E/I/F/G

Limited service hotel off M271, 5 miles from city centre. Reserved parking bays. Entrance level, automatic door. Low reception desk with induction loop. Public rooms open plan. Unisex WC. Lift to upper floors. 6 double bedrooms designed for disabled guests. Shower room ⟲, roll-in shower with seat, handrails, space by WC. Adjoining bedrooms available for carers.

Rates: from £49-£135 per room BB (2007).

Hilton Southampton

Bracken Place, Chilworth, Southampton SO16 3RB.

☎ **023 8070 2700.**

W **www.hilton.co.uk/southampton**

●● D/E/F/G

Hotel north of city near M3 and M27. Reserved parking bays. Entrance level, automatic doors. Public rooms level. Unisex WC. Lift 31", inside 42"x53". Two twin bedrooms designed for disabled guests 30½", flashing alarm. Bathroom 32", ⟲, handrails and space for side transfer by WC. Other bedrooms level. Vibrating alarm available.

Rates: on application.

Holiday Inn Southampton

Herbert Walker Avenue, Southampton SO15 1HJ.

☎ **0870 400 9073.**

@ **reservations-southampton@ihg.com**

●● D/E/I/F/G

Hotel on waterfront in city centre. Reserved parking bays. Slope to level entrance, automatic doors. Public rooms ground floor. Unisex WC and adapted cubicles. Lift 82cm, inside 115x132cm. 4 bedrooms adapted for disabled guests. Bathrooms ⟲, handrails, space by WC, low basin. Vibrating and flashing alarms. Other bedrooms level. Induction loops and sound amplifiers. Large print information.

Rates: on application.

Ibis Hotel Southampton

West Quay Road, Western Esplanade, Southampton SO15 1RA.

☎ **023 8063 4463.** @ **H1039@accor.com**

●● D/E/I/F/G

Hotel near city centre and station. Entrance level. Public rooms open plan. Unisex WC. Lift to all floors. Two bedrooms designed for disabled guests, left or right access to bed. Bathrooms ⟲, handrails, space for side transfer to bath and WC. Other bedrooms level. Walk-in shower.

Rates: from £58-£64 per room (2008).

Jurys Inn Southampton

1 Charlotte Place, Southampton SO14 0TB.
☎ **023 8037 1111.**
@ **jurysinnsouthampton@jurysinns.com**
●● D/E/I/F/G ★★★

City centre hotel. Lift from NCP car park under hotel. Entrance ramp, automatic door. Low reception desk. Public rooms open plan. Unisex WC. Lift 35.5", inside 43"x48". 2 bedrooms designed for disabled guests. Showers rooms ↺, roll-in shower with seat, space by WC. Other bedrooms level. Deaf alerter available.

Rates: from £69-£145 per room (2008).

Novotel Southampton

1 West Quay Road,
Southampton SO15 1RA.
☎ **023 8033 0550.** @ **H1073@accor.com**
●● D/F/G ★★★

City centre hotel. Reserved parking bays. Entrance level, automatic doors. Public rooms level. Unisex WC. Lift to all floors. Four bedrooms designed for disabled guests. Bathrooms ↺, handrails, space for side transfer to bath and WC. Other bedrooms level.

Rates: on application.

Vitalise Netley Waterside House

Abbey Hill, Netley Abbey, Southampton SO31 5FA.
☎ **023 8045 3686.**
●●●●● D/E/I

Centre by Southampton Water purpose-built for breaks by people with physical disabilities and carers. Single and twin bedrooms and also also two suites in a seperate wing. Activities, outings and entertainment arranged. 24-hour care on-call and personal support provided.

Apply: Vitalise ☎ 0845 345 1970 (see page 27).
Rates: on application.

UFFINGTON, Oxfordshire

The Craven

Fernham Road, Uffington SN7 7RD.
☎ **01367 820449.**
W **www.thecraven.co.uk**
● D

Thatched farmhouse with garden on edge of village in south west Oxfordshire. Entrance 36", threshold. Dining room level 36". Lounge 30", step. One ground floor bedroom with shower room 28", ↺.

Rates: from £40 per person BB (2007).

WINCHESTER, Hampshire

The Winchester Hotel

Worthy Lane, Winchester SO23 7AB.
☎ **01962 709988.**
W **www.pedersenhotels.com/winchester**
●● D/E/F/G

Hotel near city centre. Entrance level. Public rooms level. Unisex WC. Twin bedroom designed for disabled guests. Bathroom 80cm, ↺, space for side transfer to bath, no handrails. Other ground floor bedrooms level.

Rates: on application.

WITNEY, Oxfordshire

The Bird In Hand Inn

Whiteoak Green, Hailey, Witney OX29 9XP.
☎ **01993 868321.**
W **www.birdinhandinn.co.uk**
●● D/E/I/F/G

Hotel on edge of Cotswold village north of Witney. Reserved parking bays. Entrance ramp or 2 steps, min door width 82cm. Low reception desk. Large print check-in forms. Public rooms open plan, ramp to restaurant. Unisex WC. Two twin bedrooms designed for disabled guests in courtyard 81cm with small lip. Bathrooms 82cm, ↺, handrails, space by bath and WC. Small step to other ground floor rooms. Teletext TV. Courtyard garden and outdoor dining area level.

Rates: from £70-£120 per night BB (2007).

Crofters

29 Oxford Hill, Witney OX28 3JU.
☎ **01993 778165.**
@ **crofters.ghouse@virgin.net**
● D/F

Guest house in market town. Doorstep at entrance. Dining room and lounge level. 2 ground floor bedrooms, twin and double. Shower rooms with grabrails by WC and shower.

Ⓟ 🚭

Apply: Mr & Mrs Crofts
Rates: from £45 single, £55 double BB (2007).

Witney Four Pillars Hotel

Ducklington Lane, Witney OX28 4TJ.
☎ **01993 779777.**
@ **witney@four-pillars.co.uk**
●● D/G ★★★

Hotel on A40. Reserved parking bays. Entrance level. Public rooms level. Unisex WC. Double/twin bedroom designed for disabled guests. Bathroom 33", ↺, handrails, space for side transfer to WC. 18 other level bedrooms.

Ⓟ 🚭

Rates: on application.

LODGE ACCOMMODATION

There are Days Inn (see page 34), Premier Travel Inn (see page 38) and Travelodge (see page 38) properties in the following areas in this region.

Abingdon - Premier Travel Inn ☎ 0870 197 7014
Aldershot - Premier Travel Inn ☎ 0870 197 7015
Alton - Travelodge ☎ 0870 191 1502
Andover - Travelodge ☎ 0870 850 6304
Travelodge ☎ 0870 191 1507
Aylesbury - Premier Travel Inn ☎ 0870 197 7019
Banbury - Premier Travel Inn ☎ 0870 990 6512
Basingstoke - Premier Travel Inn ☎ 0870 197 7028
Travelodge ☎ 0870 191 1509
Basingstoke South - Premier Travel Inn ☎ 0870 990 6476
Bicester - Travelodge ☎ 0870 191 1512
Bournemouth - Travelodge ☎ 01202 295 708
Bracknell - Premier Travel Inn ☎ 0870 197 7036
Travelodge ☎ 0870 191 1515
Buckingham - Travelodge ☎ 0870 191 1587
Burford - Travelodge ☎ 0870 191 1518
Christchurch, East - Premier Travel Inn ☎ 0870 197 7062
Christchurch, West - Premier Travel Inn ☎ 0870 197 7063
Didcot - Premier Travel Inn ☎ 0870 197 7073
Eastleigh - Premier Travel Inn ☎ 0870 197 7090
Travelodge ☎ 0870 191 1712
Emsworth - Travelodge ☎ 0870 191 1524
Fareham - Premier Travel Inn ☎ 0870 197 7100
Farnborough - Premier Travel Inn ☎ 0870 197 7101
Ferndown - Premier Travel Inn ☎ 0870 197 7102
Fleet - Days Inn ☎ 01252 815587
Havant - Premier Travel Inn ☎ 0870 197 7130
High Wycombe - Premier Travel Inn ☎ 0870 197 7135
Liphook - Travelodge ☎ 0870 191 1544
Lyndhurst - Travelodge ☎ 0870 191 1699
Membury - Days Inn ☎ 01488 872 336
Milton Keynes - Premier Travel Inn ☎ 0870 197 7184
Travelodge ☎ 0870 191 1698
Milton Keynes Central SW - Premier Travel Inn ☎ 0870 990 6396
Milton Keynes East - Premier Travel Inn ☎ 0870 197 7185
Milton Keynes, Old Stratford - Travelodge ☎ 0870 191 1501
Milton Keynes South - Premier Travel Inn ☎ 0870 990 6558
Newbury - Premier Travel Inn ☎ 0870 990 6556
Newbury, Chieveley - Travelodge ☎ 0870 191 1702
Newbury, South - Travelodge ☎ 0870 191 1703
Newport, IOW - Premier Travel Inn ☎ 0870 197 7144
Travelodge ☎ 0870 085 0950
Newport Pagnell - Days Inn ☎ 01908 610878
Oxford - Days Inn ☎ 01865 877 000
Premier Travel Inn ☎ 0870 197 7204
Travelodge ☎ 0870 191 1705

South of England

Petersfield	Premier Travel Inn	0870 850 6306
Poole	Premier Travel Inn	0870 197 7210
Poole North	Premier Travel Inn	0870 990 6332
Portsmouth	Premier Travel Inn	0870 197 7213
	Travelodge	0870 191 1707
Portsmouth, Southsea	Premier Travel Inn	0870 197 7236
Reading	Travelodge	0870 191 1710
Reading, M4	Travelodge (2)	0870 191 1768/9
Reading, South	Premier Travel Inn	0870 990 6454
	Travelodge	0870 191 1708
Ringwood	Travelodge	0870 191 1736
Slough	Premier Travel Inn	0870 990 6500
	Travelodge	0870 191 1754
Southampton	Premier Travel Inn	0870 238 3308
	Travelodge	0870 191 1711
Southampton Airport	Premier Travel Inn	0870 990 6436
Southampton North	Premier Travel Inn	0870 197 7233
Southampton, Rownhams	Premier Travel Inn	0870 197 7234
Southampton, West	Premier Travel Inn	0870 990 6350
Thame	Travelodge	0870 191 1714
Wheatley	Travelodge	0870 191 1706
Winchester	Premier Travel Inn	0870 197 7272
	Travelodge	0870 191 171 1766
Windsor	Travelodge	0870 085 0950

Lodge accommodation

SELF-CATERING ACCOMMODATION

ABINGDON, Oxfordshire

Kingfisher Barn Holiday Cottages

Rye Farm, Culham, Abingdon OX14 3NN.

☎/Fax 01235 537538.

www.kingfisherbarn.com

●●● E/I/F/G/H ★★★-★★★★

A mixture of cottages available for wheelchair users, sleeping from 4 people to 10 people per cottage. Ground floor rooms have ceiling tracking for the use of a mobile hoist. Hoist facility in bedrooms and bathrooms. Wheel in shower rooms are in some cottages. We provide hoists, slings, cot-sides, showerchairs and commades free of charge upon booking. Situated in the countryside and close to Abingdon Town Centre we are a great base for explaining Oxfordshire. Indoor pool available, and b&b rooms. Call for your free brochure

Rates: from £486-£1,367 per week (2008).

CHRISTCHURCH, Dorset

Number 31

c/o 40 Walcott Avenue, Dorset BH23 2NG.

www.31aha.co.uk

●●● I/F/G/H

Bungalow originally adapted for wheelchair using owner, a mile from centre of coastal town. Level entrance 90cm. Lounge 90cm with double sofabed. Kitchen 75cm, with controls, sink and cooker useable from wheelchair. Twin bedroom with ceiling hoist and a bed raiser, also second twin bedroom. Shower room 75cm, roll-in shower with seat, handrails, space by Clos-o-Mat WC and under basin, ceiling hoist. Shower chair available. Level patio. Teletext TV.

Apply: Liz Cox ☎ 01202 481597.

info@31aha.co.uk

Rates: from £300-£500 per week (2008).

EXTON, Hampshire

Beacon Hill Farm Cottages

The Farm Office, Manor Farm, Warnford Road, Exton, Southampton SO32 3NW.

☎ 01730 829724.

www.beaconhillcottages.co.uk

●● F/G ★★★★

One cottage, of 4, designed for disabled people in the Meon Valley near Bishops Waltham. Lip on kerb from parking area then entrance level, double doors. Lounge /kitchen open plan. Twin and double bedrooms, furniture can be moved for. Shower room, roll-in shower with seat. Handrail but no space for side transfer by WC.

Rates: from £300-£480 per week (2006).

FORDINGBRIDGE, Hampshire

Sandy Balls Holiday Centre

Godshill, Fordingbridge SP6 2JZ.

☎ 01425 653042.

www.sandy-balls.co.uk

●● F/G ★★★★★

120 acre woodland holiday centre by New Forest. Four chalets for up to 6 people designed for disabled guests. Ramp to level patio door. Lounge/kitchen open plan, controls useable from wheelchair. Twin and double bedrooms; one unit also has bunkroom. Bathroom 73cm sliding door, handrails, space for side transfer to bath and WC. Roll-in shower in one unit. Raised WC seat available Teletext TV. Site facilities level. Access statement available.

Rates: on application.

ISLE OF WIGHT

Atherfield Green Farm Holiday Cottages

Chale, nr. Ventnor

●● F/G ★★★★

4 cottages designed for disabled people near the south west coast of the island. One accommodates 2 people, one up to 5 and the others have room for 8. The two smaller can be linked. Entrances level. Minimum internal door width 84cm. One twin/double bedroom in each ⟲. Shower room with roll-in shower and seat, handrails, space by WC.

Ⓟ

Apply: Alistair Jupe, The Laurels, High Street, Newchurch, Isle of Wight PO36 0NJ. ☎ 01983 867613.
W www.btinternet.com/~alistair.jupe/
Rates: £270-£990 per week (2007).

Borthwood Cottages

Borthwood, Sandown, IOW

●● I/F/G ★★★

Three cottages in country 2 miles from Sandown for up to 6 people. All with ramp to double door entrance. 'Rose Cottage' has open plan living room/kitchen, controls usable from wheelchair. The others have a separate lounge and kitchen. All have ground floor double bedroom and roll-in shower room with handrails, shower seat and space by WC. Also a separate WC and bedrooms upstairs. Wheeled shower chair available.

Ⓟ

Apply: Anne Finch, Sandlin, Borthwood Lane, Borthwood, Sandown PO36 0HH. ☎ 01988 403967.
Rates: from £250-£690 per week (2007).

Brambles Chine Bungalow

194 Brambles Chine, Monks Lane, Freshwater, IOW.

●● I/F

Chalet owned by Isle of Wight ASBAH on holiday park at west of Island. Slope to entrance 30". Lounge/kitchen open plan. Controls useable from wheelchair, adjustable height sink. Two twin bedrooms, ⟲ in one, and double sofabed in lounge. Shower room, 29" sliding door, ⟲, roll-in shower with seat, handrails, space by WC. Mattress cover available. Shop and clubhouse on site. Available end-February to end-October.

Ⓟ

Apply: Mrs S Griffiths, Chalet Secretary, Isle of Wight ASBAH, 3 Western Road, Shanklin, PO37 7NF. ☎ 01983 863658.
W www.iwasbah.co.uk
Rates: on application.

Laramie

Howard Road, Shanklin

●● I/F/G ★★★

Bungalow for up to 5 people near cliff top walk and town centre. Entrance level, 36". Internal doors 33". Lounge and kitchen /diner ⟲. Two bedrooms, one with grabrails and underbed space for hoist. Shower room, sliding door, ⟲, small step to shower with seat, handrails, space by WC. Also separate WC. Raised WC seat, waterproof sheet and some other equipment available. Adjustable bed can be supplied. Ramp to garden. Owners live in adjoining house.

Ⓟ

Apply: Sally Ranson, Saddlers, Howard Road, Shanklin PO37 6HD.
☎ 01983 862905. @ sally.ranson@tiscali.co.uk
Rates: from £250 per week (2006).

Lower Hyde Holiday Park

Shanklin PO37 7LL.

☎ **01983 866131.**

●● I/F/G ★★★★★

Park Resorts holiday centre on edge of Shanklin with range of facilities and entertainment. Caravans for 5 people adapted for disabled guests. Entrance ramp. Lounge/kitchen open plan. Two bedrooms, sliding door 75cm, ⟲ in double. Shower room 75cm, handrails, restricted ⟲. Open Easter-October.

Apply: Park Resorts Reservations ☎ 08701 299299. W www.park-resorts.com

Rates: on application.

Old Club House

The Duver, St Helens, Isle of Wight

●● F/G

National Trust cottage near beach for up to 5 people. Entrance ramp, 35". Min. internal door width 33". Lounge, kitchen and bedrooms all level, no adaptations. Bathroom 36", ⟲, handrails, transfer bath seat.

Apply: National Trust Holiday Booking Office ☎ 0870 4584422. See page 35.

Rates: from £282-£802 per week (2007).

Thorness Bay Holiday Park

Thorness, Nr Cowes PO27 7LL.

☎ **01983 523109.**

●● I/F/G ★★★

Park Resorts holiday centre in wooded countryside with range of facilities and entertainment. Caravans for 5 people adapted for disabled guests. Entrance ramp. Lounge/kitchen open plan. Two bedrooms, sliding door 75cm, ⟲ in double. Shower room 75cm, handrails, restricted ⟲. Open Easter-October.

Apply: Park Resorts Reservations ☎ 08701 299299. W www.park-resorts.com

Rates: on application.

LYMINGTON, Hampshire

Bench Cottage & Little Bench

Pennington, Nr. Lymington

●●● I/F/G/H

Two cottages designed for wheelchair users in grounds of owner's home near New Forest. Both have level entrance 90cm. Open plan lounge/kitchen with split level worktops. Shower room with roll-in shower and seat, handrails and space by WC. "Bench Cottage" has two bedrooms and "Little Bench" has one double or twin. Electric foot and riser beds and chair. In addition a self-contained annexe, "Grandma's Retreat" has level entrance, open plan lounge/bedroom with double/twin beds, a small kitchen and a roll-in shower room. Portable hoist and other equipment available.

Apply: Mrs Mary Lewis, Our Bench, Lodge Road, Pennington, Lymington SO41 8HH. ☎ 01590 673141. W www.ourbench.co.uk

Rates: from £270-£750 per week (2007).

MAIDENHEAD, Berkshire

Hurley Riverside Park

The Park Office, Hurley, nr. Maidenhead SL6 5NE.

☎ **01628 824493/823501.**

W **www.hurleyriversidepark.co.uk**

●● G ★★★★

Park for touring caravans and camping by the Thames between Maidenhead and Henley. Level site with pitches for 138 caravans and 62 tents. Smooth gravel roads and paths. Unisex toilet, fitted with NKS lock, for disabled people near entrance with roll-in shower with seat, handrails, space by WC. Reception, shop and launderette level or ramped. Step to washing-up area. Induction loop in reception. Open March-October.

Rates: on application.

Self catering accommodation

NEW MILTON, Hampshire

Hoburne Naish Holiday Village

Christchurch Road, New Milton BH25 7RE

Large clifftop site with chalets and static caravans, including those listed below. Site facilities including restaurant and club house level or ramped. Open March-October. The following units are owned by voluntary organisations.

Scout Holiday Homes Trust Caravans

●● E/I/F/G

2 adapted units for up to 5 people and child. Entrance ramp, 40″. Open plan lounge/kitchen. Worktops 36″. Two bedrooms, in double. Shower room 30″ sliding door, handrails, space for side transfer to WC and shower seat. Available April-October.

Apply: Scout Holiday Homes Trust ☎ 020 8433 7290. See page 26.

Rates: from £185-£495 per week (2007).

Smugglers View Chalets

●● I/G

Two chalets adapted for wheelchair users with entrance ramp, hoists, specially designed shower/WC. Each sleeps 4 people in two bedrooms, double and twin.

Apply: Grooms Holidays ☎ 08455 58448

@ selfcatering@johngrooms.org.uk

Rates: on application.

POOLE, Dorset

Holton Lee

East Holton, Poole BH16 6JN.

☎ 01202 631063. W www.holtonlee.co.uk

●●● E/I/F/G/H

Purpose built centre for disabled people and carers in countryside overlooking Poole Harbour. Accommodation for up to 8 each in Gateway and Woodland Cottages and 9 in The Barn. Powered wheelchairs available. Catered as well as self-catering options available. For further information see page 503.

Rates: on application.

Grooms Chalet

Rockley Park, Hamworthy Poole BH15 4LZ

●● E/I/H

Chalet on holiday park overlooking Poole Harbour adapted for disabled holiday-makers. Sleeps up to 6 in two bedrooms and on sofa bed in lounge. Roll-in shower with shower chair and mobile hoist. Open April-October.

Apply: Grooms Holidays ☎ 01446 771311.

@ selfcatering@johngrooms.org.uk

Rates: on application.

Scout Holiday Homes Trust Caravan

Rockley Park, Hamworthy Poole BH15 4LZ

●● E/I/F/G

Adapted unit for up to 6 people on holiday park overlooking Poole Harbour. Entrance ramp, 32″. Open plan lounge/kitchen. Worktops 36″. Two bedrooms, in double. Shower room 30″, handrails, space for side transfer to WC and shower seat. Available April-October.

Apply: Scout Holiday Homes Trust ☎ 020 8433 7290. See page 26.

Rates: from £190-£490 per week (2007).

WIMBORNE, Dorset

Grange Farm Holiday Cottages

Grange, Wimborne BH21 4HX.

www.grangeholidaycottages.co.uk

●● I/F/G ★★★★

Three single storey cottages in east Dorset designed for disabled guests. Slope to level entrance. All doors 85cm. Open plan lounge/kitchen, controls useable from wheelchair. Double and twin bedrooms in 2 units, twin in the other all ⟲. Shower rooms ⟲, roll-in shower with seat, handrails, space by WC. Shower chair, waterproof sheet, wheelchair and some other mobility equipment available. Teletext TV, visual and vibrating fire alarms, large button telephone. A larger unit for up to 10 people is also available. Information on care agencies and meal service can be provided in advance.

Ⓟ

Apply: Jane Craigmyle ☎ 01202 884426.
@ craigmyle@btinternet.com
Rates: £278-£885 per week (2007).

WITNEY, Oxfordshire

Swallows Nest

Springhill Farm, Cogges, Witney OX29 6UL.

●● F/G ★★★★

Ground floor cottage on farm in Windrush valley. Entrance level, double door. Lounge/kitchen open plan, worktops 900mm. Two double/twin bedrooms. One has ⟲ for wheelchair users; the other with low allergy features. Shower rooms 80cm, roll-in shower, handrails, space by WC and under basin. Shower chair, raised WC seat, toilet frame and some other equipment available. Teletext TV.

Ⓟ

Apply: Mr & Mrs Strainge ☎ 01993 704919. @ jan@strainge.fsnet.co.uk
Rates: from £300-£450 per week (2007).

4 West Country

This region comprises Somerset, Wiltshire, Gloucestershire, much of Dorset and the area around Bristol. It includes the rolling chalk uplands of the Salisbury Plain in the east, part of the Exmoor National Park in the west, the Mendip Hills, the Forest of Dean, much of the Cotswolds, the Somerset Levels and two distinctive coastlines.

Many of the most important signs of Britain's pre-history can be found in the area. Stonehenge in Wiltshire is world famous. Perhaps of equal significance are the stone rings of Avebury and there are several examples of ancient figures cut into chalk hillsides, such as the Cerne Abbas Giant in Dorset. Much of the Dorset and East Devon "Jurassic coast" has been declared a World Heritage Site because the many fossils found in the area were vital in the development of knowledge of early life on Earth.

Montacute House - Somerset

The region's leading city is Bristol. As well as a history that equals any other major town, there are a range of modern museums, theatrical and music performances, shops and a thriving nightlife. The docks in the heart of the city now contain many attractions including SS Great Britain, the 2006 Museum of the Year, and @ Bristol with its interactive displays of science and wildlife.

The city of Bath has attracted visitors since the Romans bathed in its thermal springs, a practice that today's visitors can copy. Its status as a World Heritage Site comes from its later tourist development at the end of the 18th century when it was the smartest

Bibury - Gloucestershire

resort in the country. The hilly nature of the town means there are restrictions for some disabled people, but a number of attractions are accessible, including the Assembly Rooms and the medieval Abbey, and the massed Georgian architecture can be appreciated.

Other towns to visit include Salisbury with its famed cathedral and Close. Wells boasts a magnificent cathedral and the oldest continuously populated street in Europe. Gloucester Cathedral appears in the Harry Potter films and the city's docks now house a waterways museum and other attractions. Also in Gloucestershire, Cheltenham developed as a Georgian spa town. Dorchester, the historic county town of Dorset, was Thomas Hardy's Casterbridge. In part of the old railway works at Swindon, Steam depicts the history of the Great Western Railway and its workers.

On the Bristol Channel coast the largest resort is Weston-super-Mare with a long, level seafront and a wide range of entertainment. Other resorts on this coast include Minehead on the edge of Exmoor and Burnham-on-Sea. The Dorset coast includes Weymouth on a sheltered bay behind Portland Bill and picturesque Lyme Regis.

Other attractions in the area with facilities for disabled visitors include the Tank Museum at Bovington in Dorset and Longleat House and Safari Park in Wiltshire. The West Somerset Railway has coaches adapted to carry wheelchair users between Minehead and the outskirts of Taunton.

Photos: Montacute © Britainonview.com. Bibury ©Britainonview.com-Tony Pleavin

USEFUL ADDRESSES

South West Tourism

Woodwater Park, Exeter EX2 5WT.

☎ 0870 442 0880.

@ post@swtourism.co.uk

W www.visitsouthwest.co.uk

General tourist information is given on their website. More specific information for disabled people is given on W www.accessiblesouthwest.co.uk

Dorset Association for the Disabled

Unit 18a, Enterprise Park, Piddlehinton, Dorchester DT2 7UA.

☎ 01305 849122.

@ dad.hq@tesco.net

Provides holidays for Association members and can respond to enquiries.

DIAL

DIAL offers a free, impartial and confidential service of information and advice by telephone to disabled people, their relatives and professionals. The following members of DIAL UK may be able to help disabled residents and visitors in their areas:

DIAS Bristol ☎/Textphone: 0117 983 2828

Nailsea Disability Initiative ☎ 01275 812183

NORDIS Gillingham ☎ 01747 821010

Dial Weston-Super-Mare ☎/Textphone: 01934 419426

Disability Wessex ☎ 01202 589999

Wiltshire & Bath ILC ☎ 01380 871007; Textphone: 01380 871747

USEFUL PUBLICATIONS & WEBSITES

www.accessiblesouthwest.co.uk – a website giving information on accessible accommodation and attractions in the region that also includes sections on equipment hire, services and public toilets for disabled people.

---

www.visitforestofdean.co.uk – contains "Facilities and Information for those with disabilities visiting the Forest of Dean", with information regularly updated by Forest of Dean Council's Tourism & Marketing Services.

---

www.visitkennet.co.uk – contains a "Disabled Guide" for visitors to central Wiltshire including Avebury, Devizes, Marlborough and Pewsey. This includes information on accommodation, places to visit and a range of other services.

---

www.salisbury.gov.uk – information for disabled people visiting Salisbury can be found in the Living section of the website.

---

www.visitsomerset.co.uk – the website of Somerset Tourism includes information for disabled visitors to the county including accommodation that has been inspected for accessibility, attractions that are said to have facilities for disabled visitors, a countywide list of unisex public toilets and organisations that can provide further information. General advice on the area is also available from The Somerset Visitor Centre ☎ 01934 750833.
@ somersetvisitorcentre@somerset.gov.uk

South Somerset: a Guide for People with Disabilities – published 2003 by the South Somerset District Council. A booklet giving information for disabled people on attractions, accommodation, car parking, public toilets and organisations. Available from information centres in the area or from Tourism Unit South Somerset District Council, Brympton Way, Yeovil BA20 2HT. ☎ 01935 462462.
@ tourism@southsomerset.gov.uk

West Dorset for Visitors with Special Needs – free booklet published by West Dorset District Council. It gives information on visiting the towns of Dorchester, Bridport, Sherborne, Beaminster and Lyme Regis. Available from Tourist Information Centres in the area or from West Dorset District Council, Community Enabling Division, Stratton House, High West Street, Dorchester DT1 1UZ.
@ tourism@westdorset-dc.gov.uk.
W www.westdorset.com

EQUIPMENT HIRE

Wareham & District Development Trust

LifeWheels Mobility Centre, St Johns Hill, Wareham BH20 4NB.

☎ 01929 552623. @ info@wddt.org.uk

Wareham Shopmobility scheme can provide wheelchairs and scooters to visitors to the Purbeck area on daily and weekly rates, which if required can be delivered to holiday accommodation. The associated Mobility Centre sells equipment and accessories.

Weston Mobility Centre

215 Milton Road,
Weston-super-Mare BS22 8EG.

☎ 01934 642071.

W www.westonmobilitycentre.co.uk

In addition to hiring wheelchairs, this company can supply a wide range of other disability equipment including spare parts.

Shopmobility schemes exist to provide wheelchairs and/or scooters for use in shopping centres of the following towns. For information on availability, etc. telephone in advance.

Bath ☎ **01225 481744**
Bridgwater ☎ **01278 434254**
Bristol ☎ **0117 922 6342**
Cheltenham ☎ **01242 255333**
Gloucester ☎ **01452 302871**
Salisbury ☎ **01722 328068**
Swindon ☎ **01793 512621**
Taunton ☎ **01823 327900**
Wareham ☎ **01929 552623**
Warminster ☎ **01985 217438**
Yate ☎ **01454 228519**

ACCOMMODATION WITH MEALS

BATH, Somerset

Carfax Hotel

13-15 Great Pulteney Street,
Bath BA2 4BS.
☎ **01225 462089.**
www.carfaxhotel.co.uk
●● D/E/F/G

Townhouse hotel in city centre. Main entrance 2 steps. Car park at rear. Ramp at entrance from car park and lift to reception and public rooms. Unisex WC. Double bedroom designed for disabled guests. Shower room ⟲, handrails. Other ground floor bedrooms level.

Rates: from £71 single, £99 double BB (2007).

Express by Holiday Inn Bath

Brougham Hayes, Lower Bristol Road,
Bath BA2 3QU.
☎ **0870 444 2792.**
www.expressbath.co.uk
●● E/I/F/G

Limited service hotel a mile west of city centre. Reserved parking bays. Entrance level, automatic door. Low reception desk. Public rooms open plan, level. Unisex WC. 7 rooms for 2 people designed for disabled guests 76cm. Shower rooms 77cm, ⟲, roll-in shower with seat, handrails, space by WC. Other bedrooms level. Mattress protectors, vibrating pillows and Teletext TV available.

Rates: from £85 per room BB (2007).

BRIDGWATER, Somerset

Blackmore Farm

Blackmore Lane, Cannington,
Bridgwater TA5 2NE.
☎ **01278 653442.** **www.dyerfarm.co.uk**
●● D/E/F/G

Farmhouse bed & breakfast, 3 miles from Bridgwater. Entrance level 32". Breakfast room 1 step, ramp available. Lounge level. Three ground floor bedrooms in converted barn. Entrance level 95cm. Shower room 100cm sliding door, roll-in shower, handrails, space for side transfer to WC. Bed blocks, raised WC seat, wheeled shower chair available. Six other rooms available. Breakfast can be served in bedroom. Self catering also available.

Rates: from £37.50-£45 per person BB (2007).

BRIDPORT, Dorset

Britmead House

West Bay Road, Bridport DT6 4EG.
☎ **01308 422941.**
www.britmeadhouse.co.uk
● F/G ★★★★

Guesthouse south of Bridport, 10 minutes from West Bay. Reserved parking bays. Slope to entrance, 1 step, ramp available. Public rooms level. 2 ground floor bedrooms 28", ⟲. Bathroom 23", no ⟲ or adaptations. Accessible garden.

Rates: from £30 per person BB (2007).

BRISTOL

The Bowl Inn

16 Church Road, Lower Almondsbury, Bristol BS32 4DT.

☎ **01454 612757.** **www.thebowlinn.co.uk**

●● D/E/F/G ★★

Country inn 8 miles from Bristol. Reserved parking bay. Main entrance 1 step; level entrance available. Public rooms level. Unisex WC, no handrails. One ground floor bedroom 36". Shower room ⟲, seat for shower tray, handrails, space by WC. Other bedrooms upstairs.

Ⓟ

Rates: from £51.50 per person BB (2007).

City Inn Bristol

Temple Way, Bristol BS1 6BF.

☎ **0117 925 1001.**

Bristol.reservations@cityinn.com

●● D/E/F/G

City centre hotel. Reserved parking bays. Level entrance, automatic and revolving doors. Low reception desk. Public rooms level. Unisex WC. Lift to all floors. Two double bedrooms designed for disabled guests. Shower rooms with roll-in shower and seat, handrails, space by WC. Other bedrooms level.

Ⓟ

Rates: from £70 per room (2007).

Express by Holiday Inn Bristol City Centre

Temple Gate, Bristol BS1 6PL.

☎ **0870 720 2293.**

Bristol@morethanhotels.com

●● E/I/F/G

Limited service hotel near Temple Meads Station. Reserved parking bay. Entrance level, automatic door. Low reception desk. Public rooms open plan. Unisex WC. Lift 97cm, inside 145x110cm. Double bedroom designed for disabled guests. Shower room ⟲, roll-in shower, handrails, space by WC. Other bedrooms level.

Ⓟ

Rates: on application.

Express by Holiday Inn Bristol North

New Road, Bristol Parkway Business Park, Bristol BS34 8SJ.

☎ **0870 443 0036.**

managerbristolnorth@expressholidayinn.co.uk

●● E/I/F/G

Limited service hotel north of city off A4174, near M32/M4 and M5. Reserved parking spaces. Entrance level, automatic door. Public rooms open plan. Unisex WC. Lift 90cm, inside 100x140cms. 7 bedrooms, twins and doubles, designed for disabled guests. Shower rooms 77cm, ⟲, roll-in shower with seat, handrails and space by WC. Other bedrooms level. Teletext TV on request. Pub/restaurant opposite.

Ⓟ

Rates: from £39-£109 per room BB (2007).

Holiday Inn Bristol Filton

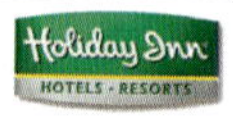

Filton Road, Hambrook, Bristol BS16 1QX.

☎ **0870 400 9014.**

Bristol@ihg.com

●● D/E/I/G

Hotel north of city near M32 junction 1. Reserved parking bays. Ramp to entrance, automatic doors. Public rooms level, open plan. Unisex WC. Lift 77cm, inside 100x140cm. 4 bedrooms adapted for disabled guests. Bathrooms 91cm, ⟲, handrails, space by bath and WC. Induction loop and Teletext TV. Wheelchair available.

Ⓟ

Rates: from £45-£180 per room (2007).

Ibis Bristol Centre

Explore Lane, Bristol BS1 5TY.

☎ **0117 989 7200.** @ **H5547@accor.com**

●● D/E/I/G ★★

Waterfront hotel in city centre. Car park across road. Entrance level, automatic doors. Low reception desk. Public rooms open plan. Unisex WC. Lifts to upper floors. 10 bedrooms designed for disabled guests. Shower rooms ↻ roll-in shower with seat, space by WC. Other bedrooms level.

Rates: from £57-£65 per room (2008)

Mercure Holland House Hotel & Spa

Redcliffe Hill, Bristol BS1 6SQ.

☎ **0117 968 9900.** @ **H6698@accor.com**

●● D/E/I/F/G

City centre hotel. Reserved parking bays. Entrance 7 steps with lift fitted, automatic doors. Reception level. 5 steps or lift to main public rooms. Unisex WC. 7 bedrooms designed for disabled guests, each with 2 double beds. Bathrooms 100cm, no ↻, space by bath and WC, handrails by WC, shower cubicles in some. Other bedrooms level.

Rates: on application.

Novotel Bristol Centre

Victoria Street, Bristol BS1 6HY.

☎ **0117 925 5040.** @ **H5622@accor.com**

●● D/E/F/G ★★★★

City centre hotel. Reserved parking bays. Ramp to entrance, automatic doors. Public rooms level, open plan. Unisex WC. Lift 36", inside 59"x55", braille buttons. Six bedrooms designed for disabled guests. Bathroom ↻, handrails, space by bath and WC. Bathseat available. Other bedrooms level. Vibrating alarm and telephone induction loop available.

Rates: from £55-£134 per room (2006).

Ramada Plaza Bristol

Redcliffe Way, Bristol BS1 6NJ.

☎ **0117 926 0041.**

W **sales.plazabristol@ramadajarvis.co.uk**

●● D/F/G

Hotel near city centre and rail station. Reserved parking bays. Entrance ramp or 5 steps, automatic door. Lounge and bar level. Chair lift on 5 steps to restaurant. Unisex WC. Three bedrooms designed for disabled guests. Shower rooms ↻, roll-in shower with seat, handrails. Other bedrooms level.

Rates: from £70 per night (2007).

BURNHAM-ON-SEA, Somerset

RNIB Kathleen Chambers House

97 Berrow Rd, Burnham-on-Sea TA8 2PG.

☎ **01278 782142.**

●●●● D/G

Registered residential home for blind, partially sighted and deaf/blind older people. Building and garden accessible for wheelchair users. Facilities include library, activities room and hairdressing. Short term bookings available.

Rates: on application.

Yew Tree House

Hurn Lane, Berrow, Nr. Brean, Burnham-on-Sea TA8 2QT.

☎ **01278 751382.**

W **www.yewtree-house.co.uk**

● D/E/F/G

Rural guesthouse near beach and 4 miles from Burnham. Reserved parking bay. Level entrance. Dining room and lounge level. Two ground floor bedrooms with bathrooms in stables annexe.

Rates: from £27.50 per person BB (2007).

CHELTENHAM, Gloucestershire

Bridge House Bed & Breakfast

88 Lansdown Road, Cheltenham GL51 6QR.
☎ **01242 583559.**
www.bridgehouse88.co.uk
●● D/E/F/G ★★★★

Bed & breakfast house near railway station. Ramp to guest entrance 90cm; step at front door. Breakfast room level. One ground floor bedroom, single or double, 90cm, ⟲. Shower room 100cm sliding door, roll-in shower with seat, handrails, space by WC. One other ground floor bedroom.

Ⓟ ⊗

Rates: from £40 single, £55 double BB (2007).

Cheltenham Chase Hotel

Shurdington Road, Brockworth, Gloucester GL3 4PB.
☎ **01452 519988.**
●● D/E/F/G

Modern hotel between Cheltenham & Gloucester. Reserved parking bays 50 yards. Entrance level, automatic doors. Public rooms level, open plan. Unisex WC. Lift 31", inside 36"x60". Two twin/double bedrooms designed for disabled guests 27". Bathroom sliding door, ⟲, handrails, space for side transfer to bath and WC. Bath seat available. Other bedrooms level. Text phone and portable induction loop.

Ⓟ ⊗

Rates: from £120 per night (2007).

CHIPPING CAMPDEN, Gloucestershire

Three Ways House

Mickleton, Nr. Chipping Campden GL55 6SB.
☎ **01386 438429.** **www.puddingclub.com**
● D/E/F/G ★★★

Hotel with noted restaurant in Cotswold village. Side entrance ramp 30"; main entrance 6 steps. Public rooms level, min. door width 30". Fully adapted unisex WC. Lift. 14 ground floor bedrooms, Bathrooms⟲, no adaptations.

Ⓟ ⊗

Rates: from £65 per person sharing BB (2007)

COMBE FLOREY, Somerset

Redlands

Treble's Holford, Combe Florey, Taunton TA4 3HA.
☎ **01823 433159.**
www.escapetothecountry.co.uk
●● D/E/F/G

Country bed & breakfast 8 miles from Taunton. Reserved parking space. Entrance 75cm with ramped 5cm sill. Lounge and dining room level. Courtyard Room has separate level entrance and twin/double bed and also a small cooking/eating area. Own shower room 78cm, roll-in shower, handrails, space by shower and WC. Also upstairs bedroom in main house and self-catering cottages available. Owned by a wheelchair user.

Ⓟ ⊗ ⓘ

Rates: from £26-£40 per person BB (2007).

FOREST OF DEAN, Gloucestershire

Dryslade Farm

English Bicknor, Coleford GL16 7PA.
☎ **01594 860259.**
www.drysladefarm.co.uk
●● D/E/I/F/G

Farmhouse bed & breakfast 3 miles from Coleford. Reserved parking bay. Entrance level, 30". Conservatory/breakfast room and lounge level. Ground floor double bedroom 33". Shower room 30" sliding door, shower tray, space by WC. 2 other bedrooms upstairs. Teletext TV. Regular disabled guests.

Rates: from £30-£45 per person BB (2007).

The Fountain Inn

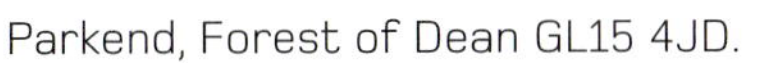

Parkend, Forest of Dean GL15 4JD.
☎ **01594 562189.**
thefountaininn@aol.com
●● D/E/F/G ★★★

Village inn. Entrance ramp or 2 steps. Lounge and 1 bar level. Restaurant 2 steps. Unisex WC. Twin bedroom designed for disabled guests with own level entrance 36". Shower room ⟲, shower tray, seat available, handrails, space for side transfer to WC. One other ground floor bedroom. Hostel accommodation in adjoining building.

Ⓟ

Rates: from £62 twin BB (2007).

The Speech House Hotel

Coleford GL16 7EL
☎ **01594 822607.**
www.thespeechhouse.co.uk

 D/E/I/F/G 

Country hotel. Reserved parking bays. Rear entrance level; step at front entrance. Public rooms ground floor. Lounge and bar level. Restaurant 1 step. Twin bedroom in annexe designed for disabled guests. Shower room ⟲, roll-in shower, space for side transfer to WC. Other level bedrooms available.

Rates: on application

Tudor Farmhouse Hotel & Restaurant

High Street, Clearwell,
Nr. Coleford GL16 8JS.
☎ **01594 833046.**
www.tudorfarmhousehotel.co.uk
●● D/E/I/F/G ★★★

Hotel in village. Reserved parking bay with paved path to level entrance. Public rooms ground floor, level. Unisex WC. 4 ground floor level bedrooms ⟲. Bathrooms 100cm, ⟲, space by bath and WC, no handrails. Other ground floor bedrooms level. Induction loop available.

Rates: from £45-£60 per person BB (2007).

Wyndham Arms Hotel

Clearwell, Nr. Coleford GL16 8JT.
☎ **01594 833666.**
www.thewyndhamhotel.co.uk
●● D/E/I/F/G ★★★

Village inn and hotel. Reserved parking bays. Side entrance level. Bar level. Ramp to restaurant. WCs not adapted. Lounge upstairs. Six ground floor bedrooms in annexe. Bathrooms ⟲, space for side transfer, no handrails. Waterproof sheets available.

Rates: from £80-£100 per room BB (2007).

GLOUCESTER, Gloucestershire

Brookthorpe Lodge

Stroud Road, Brookthorpe,
Gloucester GL4 0UQ.
☎ **01452 812645.**
www.brookthorpelodge.demon.co.uk
●● D/F/G

Guesthouse in country south of Gloucester. Reserved parking bay. Entrance level. Lounge and dining room level. One ground floor bedroom 28". Shower room ⟲, handrails, space by WC. Other bedrooms upstairs. Teletext TV.

Rates: from £60 double BB (2007).

Express by Holiday Inn Gloucester South

Telford Way, Nr. Quedgeley, Gloucester GL2 4SA.
☎ **0870 720 0953.**
@ **gloucester@morethanhotels.com**
●● E/F/G

Limited service hotel off A38 a mile from M5 junction 12. Reserved parking bays. Entrance level, automatic doors. Low reception desk. Public rooms open plan, level. 4 bedrooms designed for disabled guests. Shower room ⟲, roll-in shower with seat, handrails, space by WC. Other ground floor rooms level.

Rates: from £69 per night BB (2007)

Holiday Inn Gloucester-Cheltenham

Crest Way, Barnwood, Gloucester GL4 3RX.
☎ **0870 400 9034.**
@ **reservations-gloucester@ihg.com**
●● D/E/F/G

Hotel 2 miles from Gloucester and 7 from Cheltenham. Reserved parking bays. Entrance level, automatic doors. Public rooms level, open plan. Unisex WC. Double bedroom adapted for disabled guests 36", ⟲. Bathroom ⟲, handrails, space for side transfer to bath and WC. Emergency call to neighbouring room if required. Other ground floor rooms level. Mobile induction loops available. Menus available in large print and Braile.

Rates: on application.

LONGHOPE, Gloucestershire

The Farmer's Boy Inn

Ross Road, Longhope GL17 0LP.
☎ **01452 831300.**
W **www.thefarmersboyinn.co.uk**
●● D/E/F/G

Inn with rooms between Gloucester and Ross-on-Wye. Entrances level. Public rooms level. Unisex WC. Five bedrooms in ground floor annexe with shower rooms ⟲, shower tray, no handrails. Teletext TV.

Rates: £45-£55 per room BB (2007).

MINEHEAD, Somerset

The Promenade

Esplanade, Minehead TA24 5QS.
☎ **01643 702572.**
@ **promenade@livability.org.uk**
●●● D/E/I/G/H

Hotel owned by Livability specially adapted for disabled guests. 11 bedrooms with 8 fully accessible. Some equipment available, including fixed and manual hoists. Guests needing personal help should be accompanied or make arrangements through local agency.

Rates: on application

PORTLAND, Dorset

Portland Lodge

Easton Lane, Portland DT5 1BW.
☎ **01305 820265.**
W **www.portlandlodge.com**
●● D/F/G

Motel accommodation. Reserved parking bays. Entrance level, 92cm. Low reception desk. Breakfast room level. Unisex WC. Seven double bedrooms designed for disabled guests 90cm. Shower rooms ⟲, handrails, space by WC; two have shower trays, the other 5 have a roll-in shower with seat. A shared bathroom nearby with hand-rails, seat and bathboard. 4 other level bed-rooms. Large print information.

Rates: from £60 per room (2007).

SALISBURY, Wiltshire

Clovelly Hotel

17/19 Mill Road, Salisbury SP2 7RT.
☎ **01722 322055.**
www.clovellyhotel.co.uk
●● D/E/G

Guesthouse near city centre. Entrance level. Dining room level. Ground floor bedroom ⟲, door to car park. Shower room ⟲, roll-in shower, space for side transfer to WC. Two other ground floor bedrooms.

Ⓟ 🚭
Rates: from £40-£70 per person BB (2007).

Cricket Field House Hotel

Wilton Road, Salisbury SP2 9NS.
☎ **01722 322595.**
www.cricketfieldhouse.co.uk
●● D/F/G

Guesthouse south west of city centre. Ramp to entrance. Dining room and lounge level. Double bedroom designed for disabled people in annexe. Roll-in shower room with seat, space for side transfer and handrail by WC. Four ground floor bedrooms level.

Ⓟ 🚭
Rates: from £60-£85 double BB (2006).

Grasmere House

Harnham Road, Salisbury SP2 8JN.
☎ **01722 338388.**
www.grasmerehotel.com
●● D/G ★★★

Country house hotel by river south of city centre. Reserved parking bays. Entrance level. Low reception desk. Public rooms level, min. door width 30". Unisex WC. Five bedrooms designed for disabled guests, one has roll-in shower room Two others adapted for disabled guests ⟲, handrails, space for side transfer to bath and WC. Raised WC seat available. Other ground floor bedrooms level. Access to riverside garden.

Ⓟ 🚭
Rates: on application.

Websters

11 Hartington Rd, Salisbury SP2 7LG.
☎ **01722 339779.**
www.websters-bed-breakfast.com
●● D/E/F/G

Bed & breakfast house in city. Reserved parking bay. Entrance level, ramp in hall. Dining room and lounge level. Twin/double bedroom designed for disabled guests. Shower room 33" sliding door, roll-in shower, handrails, space for side transfer to WC. Raised WC seat, shower chair and waterproof sheet available. Other bedrooms upstairs. No small children.

Ⓟ 🚭 ⓘ
Rates: from £50-£58 per room BB (2007).

SHAFTESBURY, Dorset

Coppleridge Inn

Motcombe, Shaftesbury SP7 9HW.
☎ **01747 851980.**
www.coppleridge.com
● D/E/I/F/G ★★★

Country inn north of Shaftesbury. Entrance level. Public rooms level. WCs not adapted. 10 double bedrooms in annexe level. Shower rooms ⟲, no handrails. Waterproof sheets available. Other bedrooms 1 step.

Ⓟ 🚭
Rates: from £40-£45 per person BB (2007).

STUDLAND, Dorset

The Knoll House

Studland BH19 3AH.
☎ **01929 450450.**
www.knollhouse.co.uk
●● D/F/G

Family country hotel. Entrance 33", ramp. Public rooms ground floor. Unisex WC. 15 bedrooms with external doors and bathrooms with narrow doors. Level deck to pool. Open April-October. Regular disabled guests.

Ⓟ
Rates: on application.

SWINDON, Wiltshire

Best Western Premier Blunsdon House Hotel

Blunsdon, nr. Swindon SN26 7AS.
☎ **01793 721701.**
www.blunsdonhouse.co.uk
●● D/E/I/F/G ★★★★

High class hotel with leisure facilities in 30 acres of grounds between Swindon and Cirencester. Entrance level, revolving and swing doors. One restaurant and bar level; 6 steps and lift to 2nd restaurant and bar. Unisex WC. Lift 31", inside 42"x57". Ground floor bedroom adapted for disabled guests 31", ↺. Bathroom 30", ↺, space beside WC. Also 2 bedrooms for disabled guests in executive wing. Other bedrooms level.

Rates: on application.

Express by Holiday Inn Swindon Town Centre

Bridge Street, Swindon SN1 1BT.
☎ **0870 444 3758.**
info@exhiswindon.co.uk
 G

Limited service hotel in town centre. Reserved parking bays with level approach to rear lobby. Main entrance level, automatic door. Lift to reception and open plan public areas. Unisex WC. 8 family bedrooms designed for disabled guests. Shower rooms ↺, roll-in shower with seat, handrails, space by WC. Other rooms level.

Rates: from £60-£80 per room BB (2007).

Express by Holiday Inn Swindon West

Frankland Road, Blagrove, Swindon SN5 8UD.
☎ **01793 818800.**
www.hiexpressswindon.co.uk
●● E/I/F/G

Modern hotel on edge of town. Reserved parking bays. Slight slope to entrance. Low reception desk. Public rooms open plan. Unisex WC. Lift 90cm, textured buttons. Six double bedrooms designed for disabled guests. Vibrating and strobe alarms. Shower rooms 92cm, roll-in shower with seat, handrails, space by WC. Other bedrooms level. Wheelchair available. Staff receive disability awareness training.

Rates: on application.

Hilton Swindon

Lydiard Fields, Great Western Way, Swindon SN5 8UZ.
☎ **01793 881777.**
www.hilton.co.uk/swindon
●● D/E/I/F/G

Business hotel by M4 junction 16. Reserved parking bays. Entrance level, revolving door with slow turn control and swing door. Low reception desk. Main public rooms level, open plan. Unisex WC. Lift 44", inside 46"x81". Ground floor bedrooms designed for disabled guests. Bathrooms 31", ↺, handrails, space by bath and WC. Two rooms with strobe and vibrating alarms. Other bedrooms level.

Rates: on application.

Holiday Inn Swindon

Marlborough Road, Swindon SN3 6AQ.

☎ **0870 400 9079.**

@ **swindon@ihg.com**

●● D/E/F/G

Hotel east of town centre near M4 junction 15. Reserved parking spaces. Level entrance, automatic door. Main public rooms open plan, ground floor. Unisex WC. Two ground floor bedrooms adapted for disabled guests. Bathrooms 90cm, ⟲, handrails, space by bath and WC. Induction loop, vibrating alarms and large print menu available.

Rates: on application.

The Campanile Hotel Swindon

Delta Business Park, Swindon SN5 7XG.

☎ **01793 514777.**

@ **swindon@campanile.com**

●● D/E/G ★★

Hotel west of town centre. Reserved parking bays. Public rooms level or ramped. Two ground floor bedrooms designed for disabled guests. Bathrooms ⟲, handrails, space for side transfer to bath and WC. Other bedrooms level.

Rates: from £40-£59 per room (2007).

TAUNTON, Somerset

Express by Holiday Inn Taunton

Blackbrook Business Park, Blackbrook Park Avenue, Taunton TA1 2PX.

☎ **01823 624000.**

@ **taunton@expressholidayinn.co.uk**

●● E/F/G

Limited service hotel east of town centre near M5 junction 25. Reserved parking bays. Entrance level automatic door. Low reception desk. Open plan public rooms. Unisex WC. Lift 90cm, inside 100x140cm. 6 bedrooms designed for disabled guests. Shower room ⟲, roll-in shower with seat, handrails, space by WC. Other bedrooms level. Vibrating alarms and Teletext TV available. Induction loop also available.

Rates: from £72 per room BB (2007).

Holiday Inn Taunton M5 J25

Deane Gate Avenue, Taunton TA1 2UA.

☎ **0870 4009080.**

W **www.isg.com/taunton**

●● D/E/I/F/G ★★★

Hotel near M5 junction 25. Reserved parking bays. Entrance level. Induction loop at reception. Public rooms level. Unisex WC. Lift. Two double bedrooms adapted for disabled guests, one with door to adjoining room. Bathroom ⟲, space for side transfer to bath and WC. Other bedrooms level. Portable induction loop, vibrating and visual alarms, telephone amplifier.

Rates: on application.

TEMPLECOMBE, Somerset

The Half Moon Inn

Horsington, Templecombe BA8 0EF.
☎ **01963 370140.** 🅆 **www.horsington.co.uk**
●● D/E/I/F/G

Village inn between Wincanton and Templecombe. Reserved parking bays. Level entrance 76cm; steps at main entrance. Bar and restaurant level. Unisex WC. Bedrooms in separate buildings. 3 double/twin bedrooms designed for disabled guests. Shower rooms 90cm, ⟲, roll-in shower with seat, handrails, space by WC. Induction loop, vibrating and strobe fire alarm, vibrating alarm clock, Teletext TV, large print information and menus available. 7 Other bedrooms.

Rates: from £40-£80 per room BB (2007).

TOLLER PORCORUM, Dorset

The Kingcombe Centre

Toller Porcorum, Dorchester DT2 0EQ.
☎ **01300 320684.**
🅆 **www.kingcombecentre.org.uk**
●● D/E/I/F/G

For information on this rural Study Centre, which is also available for groups see page 504.

WELLS, Somerset

Double-Gate Farm

Double-Gate Farm, Godney, Wells BA5 1RX.
☎ **01458 832217.**
🅆 **www.doublegatefarm.com**
●● D/E/F/G

Converted barn near Somerset Levels. Slope with handrail to entrance, 36". Dining room and lounge ground floor 33". Twin bedroom designed for disabled guests. Shower room, 33", wheel-in shower, handrails, low level and standard height basins, space for side transfer to WC. Other bedrooms upstairs. Tactile alarm. Large print and Braille menu and brochure. Games room accessible. Also available as self-catering. New for 2009 4 fully accessible triple bedrooms, please contact for information.

Ⓟ 🚭 🦆 🚌 ⓘ

Rates: from £30-£32 per person sharing BB (2007).

Manor Farm

Dulcote, Wells BA5 3PZ.
☎ **01749 672125.**
🅆 **www.wells-accommodation.co.uk**
●● D/F/G

Bed & breakfast in village, one mile from Wells. Entrance level. Lounge and dining room ground floor, min. door width 34". Ground floor suite with double or twin bedroom, bathroom with shower, ⟲, handrails, space for side transfer to WC, adjoining private sitting room with additional single bed. French windows to patio and walled garden. Other bedrooms upstairs.

Ⓟ 🚭 🦆

Rates: from £95 BB garden suite (2007).

WESTON-SUPER-MARE, Somerset

The Lauriston Hotel

6-12 Knightsbridge Road, Weston-super-Mare BS23 2AN.
☎ **01934 620758.** @ **lauriston.hotel@actionforblindpeople.org.uk**
●●● D/G

Hotel in own grounds near seafront for blind and partially sighted people and their companions. Accessible throughout. All 38 bedrooms have bathrooms with handrails. Full facilities for guide dogs. Entertainment and outings arranged. Volunteers can provide some assistance. Owned by Action for Blind People, see page 19.

Ⓟ 🚭 🚌

Rates: from £38-£47 per night DBB (2007).

WEST QUANTOXHEAD, Somerset

Stilegate

Staple Close, West Quantoxhead, Taunton TA4 4DN.

☎ **01984 639119.**

W www.stilegate.co.uk

 D/E/F/G 

Bed & breakfast in village between coast and Quantock hills. Reserved parking bay. Ramp to entrance. Dining room and lounge level. Ground floor double bedroom, 77cm, ↺, own outside door. Shower room ↺, roll-in shower, handrails, space by WC, shower chair, alarm cord. Two other bedrooms upstairs. Teletext TV. Refrigerator. Ramp to level garden.

Rates: from £55-£80 per room BB (2007).

WEYMOUTH, Dorset

Hotel Central

15 Maiden Street, Weymouth DT4 8BB.

☎ **01305 760700.**

W www.kingshotels.co.uk

●● D/G 

Town centre hotel. Step from rear car park. Front entrance level. Dining room ground floor. Lounge and bar 1st floor. Unisex WC. Lift 32", inside 44"x45". Three ground floor bedrooms adapted for disabled guests. Showers, handrails, space for side transfer to bath and WC, adjustable height basin. Other bedrooms level. Closed December-February.

Ⓟ

Rates: on application.

Oaklands Edwardian Guesthouse

1 Glendinning Avenue, Weymouth DT4 7QF.

☎ **01305 767081.**

W www.oaklands-guesthouse.co.uk

●● D/F

Guesthouse in residential area of resort. Reserved parking bay. 3" step at entrance, ramp available, low doorbell. Dining room and lounge ground floor level, min. door width 75cm. Twin/double bedroom on ground floor adapted for disabled guests. Shower room 90cm, ↺ roll-in shower, handrails, space by WC. Other bedrooms upstairs.

Ⓟ ⓘ

Rates: £28-£41 per person BB (2007).

WOTTON-UNDER-EDGE, South Gloucestershire

Tortworth Court Four Pillars Hotel

Tortworth, Wotton-under-Edge GL12 8HH.

☎ **01454 263000.**

@ tortworth@four-pillars.co.uk

●● D/E/I/F/G

Country hotel between Bristol and Stroud. Reserved parking bays. Entrance step, ramp available. One restaurant and bar ground floor. Orangery restaurant in separate building. 1st floor lounge level. Unisex WCs on ground and 1st floors. Lift 90cm, inside 110x210cm. Six bedrooms, double, twin and single, designed for disabled guests 83cm, ↺. Bathrooms 71cm sliding door, ↺, space by bath and WC. Other bedrooms level. Grounds mainly level. Wheelchair available.

Rates: on application.

4 West Country

LODGE ACCOMMODATION

There are Days Inn (see page 34), Premier Travel Inn (see page 38) and Travelodge (see page 38) properties in the following areas in this region.

Alveston - Premier Travel Inn ☎ 0870 990 6496
Amesbury - Travelodge ☎ 0870 191 1717
Bath - Travelodge ☎ 0870 191 1718
Beckington - Travelodge ☎ 0870 191 1719
Bridgwater - Premier Travel Inn ☎ 0870 197 7284
Travelodge ☎ 0870 191 1743
Bristol - Premier Travel Inn ☎ 0870 990 6424
Travelodge ☎ 0870 191 1722
Bristol Airport - Premier Travel Inn ☎ 0870 990 6302
Bristol, East - Premier Travel Inn ☎ 0870 197 7042
Bristol, South - Premier Travel Inn ☎ 0870 197 7043
Bristol, Haymarket - Premier Travel Inn ☎ 0870 238 3307
Cheltenham - Premier Travel Inn ☎ 0870 197 7056
Travelodge ☎ 0870 191 1701
Cheltenham West - Premier Travel Inn ☎ 9879 197 7055
Chippenham - Premier Travel Inn ☎ 0870 197 7061
Cirencester - Travelodge ☎ 0870 191 1732
Cribbs Causeway - Premier Travel Inn ☎ 0870 990 6570
Travelodge ☎ 0870 191 1721
Filton - Premier Travel Inn ☎ 0870 990 6456
Frome - Premier Travel Inn ☎ 0870 850 6322
Glastonbury - Travelodge ☎ 0870 085 0950
Gloucester Business Park - Premier Travel Inn ☎ 0870 850 0347
Gloucester, East - Premier Travel Inn ☎ 0870 990 6322
Gloucester, Longford - Premier Travel Inn ☎ 0870 197 7115
Gloucester, North - Premier Travel Inn ☎ 0870 990 6560
Gloucester, Witcombe - Premier Travel Inn ☎ 0870 197 7116
Gordano - Days Inn ☎ 01275 373709
Ilminster - Travelodge ☎ 0870 191 1728
Leigh Delamere - Travelodge (2) ☎ 0870 191 1765/1726
Michaelwood - Days Inn ☎ 01454 261513
Portishead - Premier Travel Inn ☎ 0870 197 7212
Salisbury - Premier Travel Inn ☎ 0870 197 7225
Sedgemoor - Days Inn ☎ 01934 750831
Severn View - Travelodge ☎ 0870 191 1552

Stonehouse - Travelodge ☎ 0870 191 1554
Strensham - Premier Travel Inn ☎ 0870 197 7252
Stroud - Premier Travel Inn ☎ 0870 990 6378
Swindon - Premier Travel Inn ☎ 0870 197 7310
Travelodge ☎ 0870 085 0950
Swindon, North - Premier Travel Inn ☎ 0870 990 6356
Swindon, West - Premier Travel Inn ☎ 0870 197 7247
Taunton - Premier Travel Inn ☎ 0870 197 7293
Travelodge ☎ 0870 191 1556
Taunton Deane - Premier Travel Inn ☎ 0870 197 7250
Taunton, East - Premier Travel Inn ☎ 0870 197 7249
Taunton, Ruishton - Premier Travel Inn ☎ 0870 990 6534
Tewkesbury - Premier Travel Inn ☎ 0870 850 1845
Warminster - Travelodge ☎ 0870 191 1558
Weston-Super-Mare - Premier Travel Inn ☎ 0870 197 7266
Weymouth - Premier Travel Inn ☎ 0870 197 7267
Yeovil - Travelodge ☎ 0870 191 1559

SELF-CATERING ACCOMMODATION

ARNE, Dorset
The Farmhouse

Middlebere Farm, Arne, Purbeck.

●●

Cottage for up to 7 people near Arne Bird Sanctuary. Entrance level 42". Lounge, dining room and kitchen level. Sofabed in lounge. Shower room 31", ⟲, handrails, roll-in shower with seat, handrails, space by WC. 4 bedrooms and bathroom upstairs.

Ⓟ

Apply: National Trust Holiday Cottages ☎ 0870 4584422. See page 35.

Rates: from £526-£1231 per week (2007).

BATH, Somerset
Newton Mill Camping Park

Newton Road, Bath BA2 9JF.

☎ **01225 333909.**

www.campinginbath.co.uk

●● G ★★★★

Site for touring caravans and camping 2 miles west of city centre. Site mainly level with 2 sloped areas. Pitches for 85 caravans and 105 tents with 110 electric hook-ups. Most paths are tarmac with rolled gravel to restaurant/bar. Unisex toilet for disabled people with roll-in shower, seat and handrails. Site facilities level or ramped except washing-up area.

Ⓟ

Rates: on application.

BEAMINSTER, Dorset
Stable Cottage

Meerhay Manor, Beaminster DT8 3SB.

www.meerhay.co.uk

●● F/G ★★★★

Barn conversion a mile from Beaminster in grounds of thatched Manor House. Entrance level, 83cm. Lounge with sofabed. Kitchen 77cm sliding door, no ⟲. Twin bedroom 81cm sliding door ⟲. Bathroom 83cm sliding door, roll-in shower, handrails, space for side transfer to bath and WC.

Ⓟ

Apply: Mrs Diana Clarke ☎ 01308 862305.

Rates: from £175-£400 per week (2007).

BLANDFORD FORUM, Dorset
The Ellwood Centre

Wooland, Blandford Forum DT11 0ES.

☎ **01258 818196.**

www.theellwoodcentre.co.uk

●● I/F/G ★★★★

Three single storey cottages designed for disabled people in country between Blandford and Shaftesbury. Entrances level, 76cm. Open plan lounge/kitchen, controls useable from wheelchair, space under sink and hob. Each has 2 bedrooms; one sleeps 3, the second 4 and the other 4 and two cots. Shower rooms ⟲, roll-in shower, handrails, space by WC, shower chair, direct access from bedroom in two cottages. Hoists and other equipment can be hired. Teletext TV and loop in living room. Recreation room. Treatment room. Pool with hoist.

Ⓟ

Rates: from £550-£980 per week (2007).

Houghton Lodge

Winterbourne Houghton,
Blandford DT11 0PE.

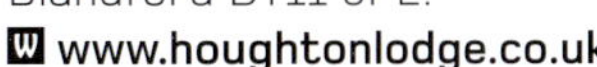

F/G

Cottage, sleeping up to 8, designed for disabled people in country west of Blandford. Ramp with handrail to entrance. Open plan lounge/kitchen. Worktop 85cm, controls useable from wheelchair. Ground floor double/twin bedroom. Shower room, roll-in shower with seat, handrails, space by WC and under basin. Also bedroom and bathroom upstairs and double sofabed in lounge. Equipment can be hired and carers service provided. Pool with hoist available. Teletext TV and induction loop. Meals can be provided with advance orders. Premier Cottages member.

Apply: Lucy Flander ☎ 01258 882170.
Rates: from £1650-£2495 per week (2007).

BLUE ANCHOR, Somerset

Primrose Hill Holidays

Wood Lane, Blue Anchor TA24 6LA.
www.primrosehillholidays.co.uk
●● G

Four bungalows overlooking Blue Anchor Bay near Exmoor. Entrances level 31" or 28". Lounge open plan. Kitchen 36", worktops 25"-36"; variable height sink in one unit. Two or 3 bedrooms 31". Shower rooms 31", roll-in shower, handrails, space for side transfer to WC. Shower chair and raised WC seat available.

Apply: Jo Halliday ☎ 01643 821200.
Rates: from £240-£540 per week (2008).

BRIDPORT, Dorset

Binghams Farm

Melplash, Bridport DT6 3TT
●● F/G ★★★

Holiday flat designed for disabled people on small touring park north of Bridport. Ramp to entrance 43". Lounge/ kitchen open plan, controls useable from wheelchair. Two bedrooms level, double and single. Shower room 35", shower with seat. 2nd flat upstairs. Adults only.

Apply: Mr & Mrs Herbert. ☎ 01308 488234.
www.binghamsfarmbarns.co.uk
Rates: from £215-£475 per week (2007).

Shepherds Cottage

Rudge Farm, Chilcombe, Bridport DT6 4NF.
●● F/G ★★★★

Converted barn on farm east of Bridport, 2 miles from coast. Paved approach. Entrance level. Lounge/kitchen open plan; controls not useable from wheelchair. Twin bedrooms and also double bedroom. Bathroom, handrails, space for side transfer to bath and WC. Raised WC seat available. 5 other cottages have ground floor accommodation.

Apply: Mike Hamer. ☎ 01308 482630.
www.rudgefarm.co.uk
Rates: from £360-£670 per week (2006).

BRUTON, Somerset

Discove Farm

Dropping Lane, Bruton BA10 0NQ.
●●● F/G

"Owl Barn" designed for disabled guests. Level entrance. Min. door width 80cm. Lounge with single sofa bed. Kitchen, worktops 90cm. Ground floor double/twin bedroom and roll-in shower room/WC with handrails. Twin bedroom upstairs. Sundeck, and utility room. Some portable equipment available.

Apply: Tony Eldridge ☎ 01749 812284.
www.discove-farm.co.uk
Rates: from £285-£540 per week (2007).

Self-catering accomodation

BURNHAM-ON-SEA, Somerset

BPF Bungalow

Burnham-on-Sea

●● E/I/H

Purpose-built bungalow on seafront for up to 6 people in double and two twin bedrooms. Hoist in double bedroom. Adapted kitchen and bathroom. Suitable for wheelchair users.

Ⓟ

Apply: British Polio Fellowship, Eagle Office Centre, The Runway, Ruislip HA4 6SE.
☎ 01903 529057. @ info@britishpolio.org.uk
W www.britishpolio.org.uk
Rates: on application.

Scout Holiday Homes Trust Caravan

Burnham-on-Sea Holiday Village, Burnham-on-Sea TA8 1LA.

●● E/I/F/G

Adapted units for up to 6 people on holiday park near town centre. Entrance ramp, 30". Open plan lounge/kitchen. Worktops 36". Two bedrooms, in double. Shower room 30" sliding door, handrails, shower seat, space for side transfer to WC. Available April-October.

Ⓟ

Apply: Scout Holiday Homes Trust
☎ 020 8433 7290. See page 25.
Rates: from £170-£545 per week (2006).

CASTLE CARY, Somerset

The Birds Nest

Orchard Farm, Cockhill, Castle Cary BA7 7NY.
W **www.orchard-farm.co.uk**

●● I/F/G

Cottage for up to 4 people. Ramp to level entrance. Open plan lounge/kitchen, controls may be useable from wheelchair. Two double bedrooms, a single bed can be provided for . Bathroom 36", , handrails, space for side transfer to bath and WC. A neighbouring unit with ground floor accommodation is also available.

Ⓟ ⓘ

Apply: Helen Boyer ☎ 01963 350418.
@ boyer@orchard-farm.co.uk
Rates: from £175-£320 per week (2007).

CHARD, Somerset

Tamarack Lodge

Fyfett Farm, Otterford, nr. Chard TA20 3QP.
W **www.tamaracklodge.co.uk**

●● F ★★★★

Log cabin designed for use by disabled people on farm in Blackdown Hills. Paved approach to level patio door 35". Lounge/kitchen open plan. Worktops and controls useable from wheelchair. Double and twin bedrooms ground floor, 35", automatic height beds. Shower room 36", , roll-in shower with seat, handrails, space by WC. 3rd bedroom for 2 people upstairs. Decked seating area. Teletext TV.

Ⓟ

Apply: Matthew Sparks. ☎ 01823 601270.
Rates: from £195 - £705 per week (2007).

CHARMOUTH, Dorset

The Poplars

Wood Farm Caravan Park, Axminster Road, Charmouth DT6 6BT.
☎ **01297 560697.**
W **www.woodfarm.co.uk**

●● F/G ★★★

One apartment for 4 people and a baby on caravan park at edge of Charmouth. Entrance ramp, 84cm. Lounge/kitchen open plan. Double and twin bedrooms . Bathroom 90cm, , roll-in shower with seat, handrails, space for side transfer to bath and WC. Shop and meals on site. Facilities for disabled people in toilet block for tourers. Open Easter-October.

Ⓟ

Rates: from £250-£600 per week (2007).

CORFE CASTLE, Dorset

Isolation Hospital

Soldiers Lane, Corfe Castle, Nr. Wareham

●● G

Cottage a mile from village. Entrance level, 30". Lounge ⟲. Kitchen 36", controls useable from wheelchair. Two ground floor twin bedrooms 30", ⟲. Shower room ⟲, roll-in shower with seat, handrails, space for side transfer to WC. Double sleeping balcony upstairs. Uneven path to main road. Two other single storey cottages available.

Ⓟ

Apply: National Trust Holiday Booking Office ☎ 0870 4584422. See page 35.
Rates: from £312-£1055 per week (2007).

Scoles Manor Barns

Kingston, Corfe Castle BH20 5LG.

☎ 01929 480312. W www.scoles.co.uk

● G ★★★★

Three converted barns. "Dairy" has ground floor lounge, kitchen and 4 double bedrooms with en suite WCs. Shower room ⟲ and 2 bathrooms, no adaptations.

Ⓟ

Rates: from £375-£1100 per week (2007).

DEVIZES, Wiltshire

Stable End

Easterton, Devizes

●● G ★★★

Cottage for 2 people on edge of village near Salisbury Plain. Entrance 48", small step, ramp available. Min. door width 32". Lounge/kitchen open plan, worktop 28". Twin bedroom ⟲. Shower room ⟲, roll-in shower, space for side transfer to WC. No young children.

Ⓟ

Apply: Mrs Blagborough, Canfield Yard, White Street, Easterton, Devizes SN10 4NZ. ☎ 01380 812426.
@ anne@ablagbrough.fsnet.co.uk
Rates: from £150-£260 per week (2006).

EXFORD, Somerset

Westermill Farm

Exford, Minehead TA24 7NJ.

W www.westermill.com

●● F/G ★★★★

Group of Scandinavian-style cottages on Exmoor farm. "Bracken" sleeps up to 8. Small ramp at entrance. Lounge open plan. Kitchen sliding door. Twin bedroom level with en suite roll-in shower room with seat, handrails and space for side transfer to WC. 3 bedrooms and bathroom upstairs. "Molinia" has similar accommodation except two bedrooms on 1st floor and single bed downstairs.

Ⓟ

Apply: Jackie Edwards ☎ 01643 831238.
@ info@westermill.com
Rates: from £280-£520 per week (2007).

HIGH LITTLETON, Somerset

Greyfield Farm Cottages

Greyfield Road, High Littleton BS39 6YQ.

W www.greyfieldfarm.com

●● E/F/G ★★★★★

Three, of 5, cottages adapted for disabled people in Mendips, 8 miles south of Bath. Entrance level or ramp, 31". Internal doors 30". Lounge and kitchen ⟲, no adaptations. Two bedrooms, sleeping 3 or 4 people. Bathroom ⟲, handrails, space for side transfer.

Ⓟ

Apply: Mrs June Merry ☎ 01761 471132.
Rates: from £211-£450 per week (2007).

Self-catering accomodation

LANGPORT, Somerset

Bowdens Crest Caravan & Camping Park

Bowdens, Langport TA10 0DD.
☎ **01458 250553.**
www.bowdenscrest.co.uk
●● F/G ★★★

Site overlooking Somerset Levels with a total of 30 static caravans and 30 touring pitches. One static caravan for up to 5 designed for disabled people. Ramp with handrail to double door entrance. Sliding internal doors to single and double bedrooms. Bathroom ⟲, handrail and space by WC. Unisex WC and roll-in shower for tourers. Site facilities include shop, games room, restaurant and bar.

Rates: from £175-£395 per week (2007).

LONG BREDY, Dorset

The Stables

Whatcombe House, Long Bredy DT2 9HN.
●● F/G

Stable conversion in country between Dorchester and Bridport. Ramp with handrail to entrance. All doors 32". Open plan lounge/kitchen, controls useable from wheelchair. Double and single bedrooms, ⟲ in single and also child's bed. Bathroom ⟲, handrails, roll-in shower with seat, space by WC.

Apply: Dream Cottages, 5 Hope Square, Weymouth DT4 8TR. ☎ 01305 789000.
www.dream-cottages.co.uk
Rates: from £217-£468 per week (2007).

LYMPSHAM, Somerset

Hope Farm Cottages

Brean Road, Lympsham, Weston-super-Mare BS24 0HA.
www.hopefarmcottages.co.uk
● F/G ★★★★

Courtyard of 4 single-story cottages on farm 5 miles from Weston-super-Mare and Burnham. Entrances 1 step, portable ramp available. Lounge/kitchen open plan. Double and twin bedrooms, ⟲ in some. En suite bathrooms, ⟲ in one cottage, no handrails. Wheelchair and some portable equipment available. Free broadband connection also available.

Apply: John & Liz Stirk ☎ 01934 750506.
@ stirkhopefarm@aol.com
Rates: from £229-£618 per week (2007).

MINEHEAD, Somerset

Woodcombe Lodges

Bratton, Minehead TA24 8SQ.
●● F ★★★★

Eight holiday cottages and lodges on the edge of Exmoor, 1½ miles from Minehead. "Holly Lodge" sleeps up to 12. Entrance and all rooms level. Roll-in shower room and two bathrooms. "Cherry Tree Lodge", designed for disabled guests. 2 steps on approach can be avoided. Level entrance by French doors. Lounge/kitchen open plan, controls useable from wheelchair. Double and twin bedrooms. Bathroom ⟲, handrails, space by bath and WC. Teletext TV. Guide dogs taken in some other units.

Apply: Mrs Hanson ☎ 01643 702789.
www.woodcombelodge.co.uk
Rates: from £195-£1295 per week (2006).

SALISBURY, Wiltshire

The Old Stables

Bridge Farm, Britford, Salisbury SP5 4DY.
☎ **01722-349002.**
www.old-stables.co.uk

●● F/G 

Three self-catering units attached to farmhouse bed & breakfast ½ mile from Salisbury. Entrance level 45". Lounge/ kitchen open plan, controls useable from wheelchair. Double/twin bedroom sliding door. En suite shower room 36" sliding door, ⟲, shower tray with seat, handrails, space by WC. Double and single bedrooms upstairs. Accessible farm shop on site. Free broadband connection included.

Rates: from £195-£645 per week (2006).

SHAFTESBURY, Dorset

Hartgrove Farm

Hartgrove, Shaftesbury SP7 0JY.

●●● I/G/H 

Four cottages on farm south of Shaftesbury with 2 designed for wheelchair users. Both have entrances level or ramped. Ground floor lounge, kitchen, twin bedroom, roll-in shower room and WC designed for wheelchair users. Second twin bedroom 1st floor. One cottage has kitchen fittings useable from a wheelchair. A third cottage has ground floor accommodation. Waterproof sheets, mobile hoist, raised WC seat and bathseat available. Paved gardens. Accessible games barn. Support services can be arranged.

Apply: Mrs S Smart. ☎ 01747 811830.
www.hartgrovefarm.co.uk
Rates: on application.

SOUTH CERNEY, Gloucestershire

Lakeside Chalets

Cotswold Water Park, Broadway Lane, South Cerney

2 lakeside chalets, each sleeping 4 people in double and twin bedrooms. Adaptations include ramped entrance, and specially designed WC/shower room. Shower chair available. Clubroom, entertainment and restaurant on site. Open March-November.

Apply: Hoburne Cotswolds
☎ 01285 860216
hoburne.cotswold@hoburne.com
Rates: on application.

SPARKFORD, Somerset

Long Hazel Park

High Street, Sparkford, Yeovil BA22 7JH.
☎ **01963 440002.**
longhazelpark@hotmail.com

 G 

A holiday pine lodge designed for disabled people on adult only level site. Entrance ramp. Kitchen controls useable from wheelchair. 2 bedrooms. Shower room ⟲ with seat and handrails. Also 75 touring pitches, 40 with hard standing and 50 with electric hook-ups. Tarmac and rolled gravel roads. Toilets include unisex unit for disabled people with WC, roll-in shower ⟲ with seat and basin, handrails. Ramp to reception and launderette. Pub/restaurant and shop nearby.

Rates: on application

Self-catering accomodation

STAWLEY, Somerset

Stawley Wood Farm

Stawley, Wellington TA21 0HP.
www.stawleywood.co.uk
●● F/G ★★★★

Three courtyard cottages with 1, 2 and 3 bedrooms in country west of Wellington near Blackdown Hills. Ramp to upper level entrance. Lounge/kitchen open plan ⟲. Sofa bed in lounge. Bedrooms downstairs with entrance from courtyard. The two bedroom unit, "Cider Cottage" has a ramped entrance, a shower room designed for wheelchair users, a stairlift and a separate bathroom.

Apply: James & Julia Luard.
☎ 01823 672300. jandjluard@tiscali.co.uk
Rates: from £275-£725 per week (2006).

TEMPLECOMBE, Somerset

Lois Country Cottages

Lois Farm, Horsington,
Templecombe BA8 0EW.
www.loisfarm.com
● G ★★★★

Two barn conversions in Blackmore Vale for 4 and 6 people. Entrance level 80cm. Lounge and kitchen/dining room 70cm ⟲. Double bedroom ground floor. Shower room ⟲, shower tray, space by WC. Other bedrooms upstairs.

Apply: Paul & Penny Constant
☎ 01963 370496. www.loisfarm.com
Rates: from £299-£536 per week (2007).

TEWKESBURY, Gloucestershire

Croft Farm Water Park

Bredons Hardwick, Tewkesbury GL20 7EE.
☎ 01684 772321.
www.croftfarmleisure.co.uk
●● G ★★★

Privately owned site for touring caravans and camping beside lake between Tewkesbury and Bredon. The site is mainly level with 40 hard standing pitches and 60 with electric hook-ups. Tarmac and stone paths. Toilet unit for disabled people with roll-in shower and handrails. Office, bar/restaurant and other facilities level or ramped. Water sports available. Closed December-February.

Rates: on application.

WATCHET, Somerset

Doniford Bay Holiday Park

Watchet TA23 0TJ.
☎ 01984 632423.
●● I/F/G

Haven holiday park on Somerset coast with range of facilities and entertainment. Caravans for 5 people adapted for disabled guests. Entrance ramp. Lounge/kitchen open plan. Two bedrooms, sliding door 75cm, ⟲ in double. Shower room 75cm, handrails, restricted ⟲, no space by WC, no space by WC. Open April-October.

Apply: Haven Holiday Reservations
☎ 0870 2422222.
Rates: on application.

Roseville

Brendon Road, Watchet TA23

● F/G ★★★★

Bungalow with garden for 6-7 people. Front entrance 1 step, 33". Patio door from paved area. Lounge and kitchen, no adaptations. Three bedrooms ↺, one with en suite bathroom. 2nd bathroom ↺, handrail by bath. Owners live next door.

Ⓟ

Apply: Country Holidays (ref 10619)
☎ 0870 192 1617.
Rates: on application.

WELLS, Somerset

St Mary's Lodge

Croscombe, Nr. Wells.
🆆 **www.st-marys-lodge.co.uk**

●● I/F/G ★★★★

House for up to 7 people in village 2 miles from Wells. Ramp to entrance by parking area; 1 step at front entrance. Internal doors 80cm. Lounge/diner and kitchen/breakfast room ↺, lowered worktop and kitchen controls useable from wheelchair. Ground floor double bedroom ↺. Shower room ↺, roll-in shower with seat, handrails, space by WC. Other bedrooms and bathrooms upstairs. Accessible patio.

Ⓟ

Apply: Jane Hughes, St Mary Mead, Long Street, Croscombe, Wells BA5 3QL. ☎ 01749 342157.
@ hirtemp@hotmail.co.uk
Rates: from £500-£725 per week (2007).

WEST BAY, Dorset

West Bay Holiday Park

West Bay, Bridport DT6 4HB.

●● I/F/G ★★★★

Holiday Park on west Dorset coast with range of facilities. Caravans for 5 people adapted for disabled guests. Entrance ramp. Lounge/kitchen open plan. Two bedrooms, sliding door 75cm, ↺ in double. Shower room 75cm, handrails, restricted ↺. Open March-November.

Ⓟ

Apply: Parkdean Holidays ☎ 0871 641 2066.
🆆 www.parkdeanengland.co.uk
Rates: Holiday homes from £199 per week. Short breaks (3 or 4 nights) from £120

WEST BEXINGTON, Dorset

Tamarisk Farm Holiday Cottages

Tamarisk Farm, West Bexington, Chesil Beach.
🆆 **www.tamariskfarm.co.uk**

●● F/G ★★★★

"Mimosa" cottage designed for disabled people by organic farm 13 miles west of Weymouth on coast. Entrance level 80cm. Internal doors 77cm. Lounge and conservatory with double sofabed. Kitchen with adjustable height sink & hobs, controls useable from wheelchair. Double and twin bedrooms. Bathroom and roll-in shower room both ↺, handrails and space for side transfer to WCs. Some equipment available. Chlorine water filter. Large dial telephone. Level patio. "Granary Lodge" bungalow in the village sleeps up to 7. Ramp to entrance. Very large ounge/dining room, conservatory and kitchen, controls not useable from wheelchair. Double, twin and bunk bedrooms. Bathroom ↺, roll-in shower, handrails, space by bath and WC. Raised WC seat and toilet frame available. 4 other cottages available without disabled facilities

Ⓟ

Apply: Josephine Pearse, Tamarisk Farm, West Bexington, Dorchester DT2 9DF.
☎ 01308 897784.
Rates: from £360-£980 per week (2007).

WEYMOUTH, Dorset

Anchor House

3 Holland Road, Weymouth

●● E/I/H

Victorian house owned by Livability Holidays, adapted for wheelchair users. Ramp to entrance. Lift to 1st floor. Accommodation for up to 10 people in 6 bedrooms of which 3 are accessible. Roll-in shower. Shower chair and mobile hoist available.

Apply: Livability Holidays. ☎ 01446 771311. @ selfcatering@livability.org.uk

Rates: on application.

Chesil Beach Holiday Park

Portland Road, Weymouth DT4 9AG.

☎ 01305 773233.

W www.chesilholidays.co.uk

●● I/F/G ★★★★

Holiday Park 3 miles west of Weymouth with range of facilities. Caravans for 6 people adapted for disabled guests. Entrance ramp. Lounge/kitchen open plan. Two bedrooms, sliding door 75cm, ↻ in double. Shower room 75cm, handrails, restricted ↻. Open Easter-October.

Rates: on application.

Littlesea Holiday Park

Lynch Lane, Weymouth DT4 9DT.

☎ 01305 774414.

●● F/G

Haven holiday park west of Weymouth by Chesil Beach with range of facilities and entertainment. Caravans for 5 people adapted for disabled guests. Entrance ramp. Lounge/kitchen open plan. Two bedrooms, sliding door 75cm, ↻ in double. Shower room 75cm, handrails, restricted ↻ no space by WC. Open Mid March-October. For information on units owned by voluntary organisation on this site, see below.

Apply: Haven Holiday Reservations ☎ 0870 2422222.

Rates: on application.

Wimborne & Ferndown Lions Club Caravans

Littlesea Holiday Park, Nr. Weymouth

6 berth caravan designed for disabled people sited on Haven holiday park by Chesil Beach. Entrance ramp. Kitchen. Double and twin bedrooms, ↻. Shower /WC with handrails and wheelchair access.

Apply: Frank Fortey, 23 Egdon Drive, Wimborne BH21 1TY. ☎ 01202 886022. W www.lions.org.uk/wimborne-ferndown/

Rates: on application.

Seaview Holiday Park

Preston, Weymouth DT3 6DZ.

☎ 01305 833037

●● F/G

Haven holiday park east of Weymouth with wide range of facilities and entertainment. Caravans for 5 people adapted for disabled guests. Entrance ramp. Lounge/kitchen open plan. Two bedrooms, sliding door 75cm, ↻ in double. Shower room 75cm, handrails, restricted ↻, no space beside WC. Open Mid March-October.

Apply: Haven Holiday Reservations ☎ 0870 2422222.

Rates: on application.

Waterside Holiday Park

Bowleaze Cove, Weymouth DT3 6PP.

☎ 01305 833103.

W www.watersideholidays.co.uk

●● F/G 

Holiday Park on coast 1½ miles east of Weymouth with caravans designed for disabled guests. Ramp to entrance, double doors. 2 bedrooms, no ↻, and sofabed in lounge. Handrails by bath and shower, no ↻ or space by WC. Level site with entertainment. Closed November-March.

Rates: on application.

Weymouth Bay Holiday Park

Preston, Weymouth DT3 6BQ.
☎ **01305 832271.**

●● I/F/G ★★★

Haven holiday park 2 miles east of Weymouth with wide range of facilities and entertainment. Caravans for 5 people adapted for disabled guests. Entrance ramp. Lounge/kitchen open plan. Two bedrooms, sliding door 75cm, ⟲ in double. Shower room 75cm, handrails, restricted ⟲, no space by WC. Open Mid March-October.

Ⓟ

Apply: Haven Holiday Reservations ☎ 0870 2422222.
Rates: on application.

WHITMINSTER, Gloucestershire

Walk Close

Whitminster House, Whitminster, Nr. Stroud.

●● I/F/G ★★★

Cottage in village between Stroud and the Severn. Entrance ramp. Living room with door to terrace. Dining room/kitchen ⟲, cooker controls useable from wheelchair. Double and single bedrooms ⟲. Shower room/WC ⟲, roll-in shower with seat, handrails. Can be booked with adjoining cottages available.

Ⓟ

Apply: Mrs Teesdale, Whitminster House, Whitminster GL2 7PN. ☎ 01452 740204.
W www.whitminsterhousecottages.co.uk
Rates: from £225-£375 per week (2006).

WINSFORD, Somerset

Halse Farm Caravan & Tent Park

Winsford, Exmoor TA24 7JL.
☎ **01643 851259.** W **www.halsefarm.co.uk**

●● G ★★★

Small site for up to 22 touring caravans and tents on working Exmoor stock farm. 21 pitches with electric hook-ups. Site mainly level. Toilet/ shower designed for disabled people. Laundry room level. Open mid-March to October.

Ⓟ

Rates: on application.

Self-catering accomodation

Babara Hepworth Museum - St Ives

Photo: Henrietta Creedy

The two counties of England's south west peninsula have for long been a major holiday destination and offer a wide range of attractions for visitors.

Nowhere is far from the sea and there are a series of resorts around the coast. The Torbay towns of Torquay and Paignton are known as the English Riviera because of their mild climate and high-class entertainment. Much of the coast is hilly, although east Devon resorts such as Exmouth and Sidmouth are fairly level as is Penzance in the far west. At other resorts such as Ilfracombe, St Ives, Newquay or Falmouth a car may be needed away from the seafront itself.

Much of the coastal scenery is dramatic. Among the places where this can be experienced are at the cliff-top National Trust car park at Wheel Coates near St Agnes, with its view over the north Cornwall cliffs and old tin mines, and Land's End. Marine life can be experienced at the National Seal Sanctuary near Helston and the National Marine Aquarium at Plymouth.

Inland, the country can also be wild, particularly in the National Parks of Dartmoor and Exmoor and areas such as Bodmin Moor in Cornwall. However, there are plenty of opportunities to experience

Dartmouth Castle, Devon

the countryside and its activities at attractions such as Mount Edgcumbe Country Park overlooking Plymouth Sound, or the Crealy Farm Adventure Park in east Devon. At the Eden Project, outside St Austell, a dramatic global garden has been developed in a disused china clay pit. Longer established planting can be enjoyed at the Royal Horticultural Society's Rosemoor Garden at Torrington.

Historic buildings in the area include Okehampton Castle in Devon owned by English Heritage, Buckfast Abbey and a number of National Trust properties such as Saltram House and Killerton House & Garden both near Exeter.

In the region's largest city, the Plymouth Dome, on the Hoe, uses multi-media displays to show the civic and maritime history of the area. Exeter, county town of Devon, still has many old buildings especially in the area around the cathedral. Truro is the location of the Royal Cornwall Museum. Other attractive towns include Barnstaple and Bideford in north Devon.

For family outings there is Dobwells Family Adventure Park near Liskeard or a trip on the Seaton Tramway in east Devon, both having facilities for disabled visitors. Finally, this is a region with distinctive food, be it genuine Cornish pasties, fresh caught fish or the widely available cream teas.

Photo: britainonview.com

USEFUL ADDRESSES

South West Tourism

Woodwater Park, Exeter EX2 5WT.
☎ **0870 442 0880.**
@ **post@swtourism.co.uk**
W **www.visitsouthwest.co.uk**

General tourist information is given on their website. More specific information for disabled people is given on
@ www.accessiblesouthwest.co.uk

Cornwall Disabled Association

1 Riverside House, Heron Way, Newham, Truro TR1 2XN.
☎/Fax 01872 273518.
@ **info@cornwalldisabled.co.uk**
W **www.cornwalldisabled.co.uk**

Provides holidays, in conjunction with the social services, for disabled residents of Cornwall and has adapted caravans at Par and Rejerrah that are also available to people from outside the county (see pages 186 and 187).

The Association also has 20 and 48 seat accessible coaches for group hire and runs monthly outings.

Richard Willson Accessible Transport

49 Carne View Road, Probus, Truro TR2 4HZ.
☎ **01726 883460.**

A well-established transport provider offering ambulance and accessible minibus services for wheelchair users, with or without their companions. Escorts and care attendants can be supplied. Journeys to and from the region are undertaken and guided tours can be arranged. Information on a range of disability matters can be given.

DIAL

DIAL offers a free, impartial and confidential service of information and advice by telephone to disabled people, their relatives and professionals. The following member of DIAL UK may be able to help disabled residents and visitors in its area.

DIAC Plymouth ☎ 01752 201065; Textphone: 01752 201766

USEFUL PUBLICATIONS & WEBSITES

www.accessiblesouthwest.co.uk – a website giving information on accessible accommodation and attractions in the region that also includes sections on equipment hire, services and public toilets for disabled people.

Easy-Going Dartmoor – a pack giving information on walks, driving routes and viewpoints suitable for disabled people price £3 + p&p.

Access Guide to Dartmoor Town and Villages – providing access information on businesses in the main settlements. Both booklets are available from Dartmoor National Park Authority, The High Moorland Visitor Centre, Old Duchy Hotel, Princetown, Yelverton PL20 6QF. ☎ 01822 890414 or at W www.dartmoor-npa.gov.uk

The English Riviera: Access for All – regularly updated leaflet for Torquay, Paignton and Brixham. Available free at Tourist Information Centres in each town or from English Riviera Tourist Board, The Tourist Centre, Vaughan Parade, Torquay TQ2 5JG. ☎ 01803 296296.
@ tourist.board@torbay.gov.uk or on their website W www.theenglishriviera.co.uk

www.disabledgo.org – this website includes detailed information on the accessibility of many premises in Torbay.

EQUIPMENT HIRE

Braunton Mobility

3 Cross Tree Centre, Braunton, Devon EX33 1AA.
☎ 01271 814577.

Manual wheelchairs and scooters are available for hire as well as a wide range of equipment for sale.

Exeter Community Transport Association

8- 10 Paris street, Exeter EX1 1GA.
☎ 01392 494001. @ exetercta@aol.com

In association with Exeter Shopmobility there is a long term loan service for both residents and visitors for use anywhere. They have manual wheelchairs at £2.50 a day and two portable scooters at £5 per day.

HSC Mobility

Units 1c/1d Guildford Road Industrial Estate, Hayle, Cornwall TR27 4QZ.
☎ 01736 755927.
W www.hsc-mobility.co.uk

Wheelchairs, scooters, hoists, adjustable beds and other equipment are available for hire.

Mid Devon Shopmobility

Phoenix Lane MSCP, Tiverton EX16 6NB.
☎ 01884 242099.

Manual wheelchairs are available for holiday loan both to residents and visitors to the area.

Newton Abbot Shopmobility

Multi-Storey Car Park, Sherborne Road, Newton Abbot, TQ12 2QY.
☎ 01626 335775.

Manual wheelchairs are available for use in the UK for up to 3 months and in Europe for 2 weeks. A refundable deposit is required and a small daily charge is made.

North Devon Shopmobility

Albert Lane, Barnstable EX32 8RL.
☎ 01271 328866.
@ gonorthdevon@hotmail.co.uk

In addition to a regular Shopmobility service in Barnstaple and a mobile service visiting other towns in the area and events in the region, manual wheelchairs can be hired by people who register with the scheme for holidays and short breaks.

Pluss

22 Marsh Green Road, Exeter EX2 8PQ.
☎ 01392 438329. W www.pluss.org.uk

Pluss have manual and electric wheelchairs, scooters and some other equipment are available for hire. They also have centres at:

Riverside Road, Pottington Business Park, Barnstaple EX31 1QB.
☎ 01271 347934.

Clittaford Road, Southway, Plymouth PL6 6DF.
☎ 01752 306630.

Waddeton Close, Brixham Road, Paignton TQ4 7RZ.
☎ 01803 696568.

Tremorvah Industries

Unit 8, Threemilestone Industrial Estate, Truro, Cornwall TR4 9LD.
☎ 01872 324340.
Textphone: 01872 324364.
W www.tremorvah.co.uk

Tremorvah Industries can hire manual and powered wheelchairs, scooters, commodes, hoists and a range of other equipment. Deliveries can be made throughout Cornwall.

Devon & Cornwall

Shopmobility schemes exist to provide wheelchairs and/or scooters for use in shopping centres of the following towns. For information on availability, etc., call in advance.

Barnstaple ☎ **01271 328866**
Brixham ☎ **01803 585304**
Exeter ☎ **01392 494001**
Falmouth ☎ **01326 313553**
Honiton ☎ **01404 46529**
Newton Abbot ☎ **01626 335775**
Paignton ☎ **01803 521771**
Penzance ☎ **01736 351792**
Plymouth ☎ **01752 600633**
Teignmouth ☎ **01626 777775**
Tiverton ☎ **01884 242099**
Torquay ☎ **01803 380982**

North Devon Shopmobility operates Leisure Mobility across north Devon and Somerset and can be contacted at the Barnstable number above.

ACCOMMODATION WITH MEALS

BARNSTAPLE, Devon

Bracken House

Bratton Fleming, Barnstaple EX31 4TG.
☎ **01598 710320.**
www.brackenhousehotel.co.uk

 D/F/G 

Country hotel on edge of Exmoor. Entrance 3 steps, portable ramp available. Public rooms level, min. door width 33". Twin bedroom ground floor, ⟲. Bathroom 31" ⟲, handrails, bath lift, space by bath and WC. No children under 12.

Rates: from £62-£77 per person DBB (2007).

BODMIN, Cornwall

Vitalise Churchtown

Lanlivery, Bodmin, Cornwall PL30 5BT.
☎ **01208 872148.**

●●●●● D/E/I/G/H

For information on Churchtown, which provides regular holidays with outings throughout the year, in addition to activity breaks during the summer months see page 501.

Apply: Vitalise (See page 27)
Rates: on application.

BOSCASTLE, Cornwall

The Old Coach House

Tintagel Road, Boscastle PL35 0AS.
☎ **01840 250398.**
www.old-coach.co.uk

●● D/G 

Guesthouse in village. Ramp to side entrance from parking area; main entrance 1 step. Ramp to lounge. Dining room level or 3 steps from lounge. Double and twin ground floor bedrooms, 33", limited ⟲. Shower room 33", ⟲, roll-in shower, space for side transfer to WC.

Ⓟ

Rates: from £25-£28 per person sharing BB (2007).

BUDLEIGH SALTERTON, Devon

Hansard House Hotel

3 Northview Road,
Budleigh Salterton EX9 6BY.
☎ **01395 442773.**
www.hansardhousehotel.co.uk
●● D/E/I/F/G ★★★★

Hotel near town centre. Ramp or 3 steps to entrance, double door. Low reception desk. Public rooms ground floor. Adapted WC cubicles. Ramp to lift manual door 75cm, inside 85x90cm. Ground floor bedroom designed for disabled guests 81cm, ⟲. Shower room 81cm, ⟲, roll-in shower with seat, space by WC. Other bedrooms level. Raised WC seat and wheelchair available. Teletext TVs.

Rates: £36-£46 per person BB (2008).

COLYTON, Devon

Smallicombe Farm

Northleigh, Colyton EX24 6BU.
☎ **01404 831310.**
www.smallicombe.com
●● D/E/I/F

Farmhouse in East Devon. Ramp to level entrance 31". Dining room level. Twin bedroom with own lounge ground floor. Bathroom 31", ⟲, handrails, space for side transfer to bath and WC. Some equipment available. Self-catering also available, see page 178.

Rates: from £30-£35 per person BB (2008).

CRANTOCK, Cornwall

Crantock Bay Hotel

West Pentire, Crantock TR8 5SE.
☎ **01637 830229.**
www.crantockbayhotel.co.uk
●● D/E/IF/G ★★★

Hotel overlooking north Cornwall coast west of Newquay. Entrance level 32". Public rooms ground floor, min. door width 44". Twin bedroom ground floor designed for disabled guests. Shower room 31", ⟲, roll-in shower with seat, handrails, space by WC. Other ground floor bedrooms level. Closed December and January

Rates: from £59-£99 per person DBB (2007).

DAWLISH, Devon

Langstone Cliff Hotel

Mount Pleasant Road, Dawlish EX7 0NA.
☎ **01626 868000.**
www.langstone-hotel.co.uk
● D/F/G

Resort hotel. Entrance level, double doors. Main public rooms level. Unisex WC. Lift 27". 66 bedrooms with bathrooms; 10 on ground floor, ⟲ in some. Paths to beach. Cabaret weekends.

Rates: from £50-£75 per person BB (2007).

FALMOUTH, Cornwall

Falmouth Beach Resort Hotel

Gyllyngvase Beach, Seafront,
Falmouth TR11 4NA.
☎ **01326 310500.**
www.falmouthbeachhotel.co.uk
●● D/E/F/G ★★★

Hotel in level grounds. Reserved parking bays with lift to hotel. Slope to entrance. Main public rooms ground floor. Unisex WC and adapted cubicles. Lifts to most floors, max. 80cm, inside 93x138cm. One ground floor bedroom adapted for disabled guests with roll-in shower room 79cm, ⟲, handrails. Other level bedrooms available. Bath seat and waterproof sheets available. Teletext TV. Lift to pool with hoist. A Best Western Hotel.

Rates: on application.

Penmorvah Manor Hotel

Budock Water, Falmouth TR11 5ED.
☎ **01326 250277.**
www.penmorvah.co.uk
● D/E/F/G 

Privately owned country hotel in wooded garden. Ramp to entrance, 40". Restaurant ramp, 29". Lounge and bar level 38". 10 ground floor bedrooms level with bathrooms, no adaptations.

Rates: from £50 per person BB (2007).

NEWQUAY, Cornwall

Chynoweth Lodge Hotel

1 Eliot Gardens, Newquay TR7 2QE.
☎ **01637 876684.**
www.chynowethlodge.co.uk
● D/E/F/G 

Small guesthouse. Reserved parking bays. Ramp or 2 steps with handrail to entrance. Lounge and dining room level. Double and two family rooms ground floor with bathrooms ⟲, space by bath and WC. Regular disabled guests.

Rates: from £25-£33 BB per night (2007).

PLYMOUTH, Devon

Copthorne Hotel Plymouth

Armada Way, Plymouth PL1 1AR.
☎ **01752 224161.**
sales@milleniumhotels.co.uk
●● D/E/F/G 

City centre hotel. Reserved parking bays in underground car park, no lift to ground level. Ramp to entrance, 67". Public rooms ground floor, open plan. Unisex WC. Lift to reception and 135 bedrooms. One bedroom adapted for disabled guests. Bathroom ⟲, handrails, space for side transfer to bath and WC

Rates: on application.

Holiday Inn Plymouth

Armada Way, Plymouth PL1 2HJ.
☎ **01752 639988.**
@ **hiplymouth@qmh-hotels.com**
●● D/E/I/F/G ★★★★

Hotel near city centre. Reserved parking bays. Ramp with handrails to entrance, automatic door. Low reception desk. Bar/lounge ground floor. Restaurant and unisex WC on penthouse level. Lifts 115cm, inside 210x142cm. 2 bedrooms for disabled guests on ground floor, vibrating and flashing alarms. Bathroom 86cm, ⟲, hand rail by WC, space by bath and WC. Bath seat available. Other bedrooms level. Induction loop, large print menus and wheelchair available.

Rates: from £69-£89 per night (2007).

Ibis Hotel Plymouth

Marsh Mills, Longbridge Road, Plymouth PL6 8LD.
☎ **01752 601087.** @ **H2093@accor.com**
●● D/E/G ★★

Hotel off A38 on approach to city. Entrance level. Public rooms open plan. 2 rooms with bathrooms designed for disabled guests. Other bedrooms level.

Rates: from £52-£56 per room (2008).

Novotel Plymouth

Marsh Mills, Plymouth PL6 8NH.
☎ **01752 221422.** @ **H0508@accor.com**
●● D/E/I/F/G

Hotel on edge of city. Entrance ramp, automatic doors. Public rooms ground floor, open plan. Unisex WC. Lifts 30". Two bedrooms with bathrooms designed for disabled guests ⟲. Other bedrooms level.

Rates: on application.

TEIGNMOUTH, Devon

Cliffden

Dawlish Road, Teignmouth TQ14 8TE.
☎ **01626 770052.** @ **cliffden.hotel@actionforblindpeople.org.uk**
●● D/G

Hotel in large grounds near seafront and town centre for visually impaired people and their companions. Public rooms level. 48 bedrooms with bathrooms. Full facilities for guide dogs. Outings and activities organised. Volunteers can be arranged for some assistance. A self-catering unit for 6 is also available. Owned by Action for Blind People (see page 19).

Rates: from £45-£52 per night DBB (2007).

TORQUAY, Devon

Brunel Manor

Teignmouth Road, Torquay TQ1 4SF.
☎ **01803 329333.**
W **www.brunelmanor.com**
●● D/E/F/G

Holiday and conference centre owned by Christian Trust, in large grounds at edge of town. 3 reserved parking bays. 2 steps or ramp to entrance. Low reception desk. Public rooms level, min. door width 101cm. Unisex WC and adapted cubicles. Lift, inside 136x140cm. 8 bedrooms adapted for disabled guests. 3 have roll-in shower rooms with shower seat, handrails and space by WC. Wheelchair available. Special interest breaks arranged.

Rates: on application.

TRURO, Cornwall
Tregoninny Farm
Tresillian, Truro TR2 4AR.
☎ 01872 520145.
W www.tregoninny.com
●● D/E/F/G/H

Farm bed and breakfast in secluded setting 3 miles from Truro. Breakfast room and conservatory/lounge on ground floor, small step, portable ramp available. Unisex WC. Bedrooms created from farm buildings. Double and 4 twin/double designed for disabled guests with own entrances level, 85cm. Some can interconnect. Bath/shower rooms, ⟲, handrails, space by WC, 4 have roll-in shower rooms. Shower chairs, mobile hoist, raised WC seat, bath board and some other equipment available. Accessible paths planned for surrounding woodland.

Rates: from £50 per room per night BB (2007).

WOODBURY, Devon
Woodbury Park Hotel, Golf & Country Club
Woodbury Castle, Woodbury, Exeter EX5 1JJ.
☎01395 233382.
W www.woodburypark.co.uk
●● D/E/I/F/G ★★★★

Country hotel with leisure facilities in East Devon. Reserved parking bays. Entrance level, automatic door. Public rooms ground floor. Unisex WC. Lift 30½", inside 52"x54". Four bedrooms with double and single beds designed for disabled guests. Shower rooms 34", ⟲, seat in shower tray, handrails, space by WC and under basin. Other bedrooms level.

Rates: on application.

WOOLACOMBE, Devon

Sunnymeade Country Hotel
Dean Cross, West Down, nr. Woolacombe EX34 8NT.
☎ 01271 863668.
W www.sunnymeade.co.uk
●● D/E/F/G ★★★

Hotel in country near North Devon coast. Reserved parking bays. Ramp to entrance, 33" automatic door. Low reception desk. Lounge and bar open plan. Restaurant 30". Two ground floor bedrooms 32", variable height bed. Shower room 32" sliding door ⟲, roll-in shower with seat, handrails, space by WC. Two other ground floor bedrooms and 8 upstairs. Teletext TV, vibrating alarms available and BSL can be used.

Rates: from £60 double per night (2007).

YEALMPTON, Devon

Kitley House Hotel
Kitley Estate, Yealmpton, Nr Plymouth PL8 2NW.
☎ 01752 881555.
W www.kitleyhousehotel.com
●● D/E/F/G ★★★

Country house hotel east of Plymouth. Reserved parking bays. 3 steps or ramp to entrance. Public rooms ground floor level. Unisex WC. One ground floor bedroom adapted for disabled guests 86cm door, ⟲. Bathroom 86cm, ⟲, handrails, space by bath and WC. Other bedrooms upstairs. Grounds accessible.

Rates: from £75 per room BB (2007).

LODGE ACCOMMODATION

There are Premier Travel Inn (see page 38) and Travelodge (see page 38) properties in the following areas in this region.

Barnstaple - Premier Travel Inn ..... ☎ 0870 197 7025
Travelodge ..... ☎ 0870 191 1845
Bodmin - Premier Travel Inn ..... ☎ 0870 197 7107
Exeter - Premier Travel Inn ..... ☎ 0870 197 7097
Travelodge ..... ☎ 0870 191 1727
Hayle - Premier Travel Inn ..... ☎ 0870 197 7133
Travelodge ..... ☎ 0870 191 1804
Newquay - Premier Travel Inn ..... ☎ 0870 197 7194
Okehampton, East - Travelodge ..... ☎ 0870 191 1547
Okehampton, West - Travelodge ..... ☎ 0870 191 1548
Plymouth - Premier Travel Inn ..... ☎ 0870 990 6458
Travelodge ..... ☎ 0870 191 1752
Plymouth Coxside - Premier Travel Inn ..... ☎ 0870 197 7207
Plymouth, East - Premier Travel Inn ..... ☎ 0870 197 7208
St Austell - Travelodge ..... ☎ 0870 191 1660
Saltash - Travelodge ..... ☎ 0870 191 1551
Tiverton - Travelodge ..... ☎ 0870 191 1557
Truro - Premier Travel Inn ..... ☎ 0870 197 7255

Lodge & self-catering accomodation

SELF-CATERING ACCOMMODATION

ASHBURTON, Devon

Robin & Wren Cottages

Poundsgate, Nr. Ashburton.

www.newcott-farm.co.uk

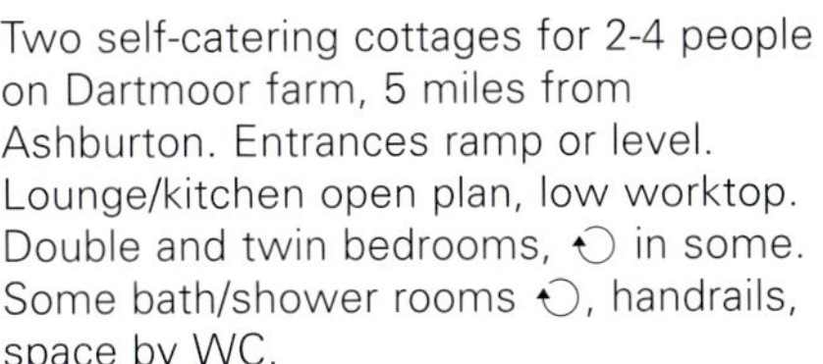

●● F/G ★★★★

Two self-catering cottages for 2-4 people on Dartmoor farm, 5 miles from Ashburton. Entrances ramp or level. Lounge/kitchen open plan, low worktop. Double and twin bedrooms, ⟲ in some. Some bath/shower rooms ⟲, handrails, space by WC.

Apply: Mrs Margaret Phipps, New Cott Farm, Poundsgate, Newton Abbot Q13 7PD. ☎ 01364 631421.

Rates: on application.

Wooder Manor Holiday Homes

Widecombe-in-the Moor, Newton Abbot TQ13 7TR.

www.woodermanor.com

●● I/F/G ★★★-★★★★★

Two units, each for 4 people, near Dartmoor village 6 miles from Ashburton. Each entrance 81cm, ramp to one. Open plan kitchen/living area. "Lower Hameldown" has one level bedroom with sliding door to shower room ⟲, roll-in shower, space by WC. Second double room with bathroom up 2 steps. "Lower Chinkwell" has two level bedrooms. Bathroom with sliding door, ⟲, space by WC. Raised WC seat, monkey pole and waterproof sheets available. 5 other units on site including house for 12 with a ground floor bedroom and bathroom.

Apply: Mrs Angela Bell. ☎ 01364 621391.

Rates: from £220 per week (2006).

BAMPTON, Devon

The Barn

Huntsham, Nr. Tiverton EX16 7NQ.

www.huntshambarn.co.uk

●● E/F/G

Cottage for up to 5 people in hamlet close to Exmoor. Ramp between courtyard and entrance. Double doors. Lounge/kitchen open plan. Twin bedroom level. Step to other two double bedrooms. Bathroom ⟲, handrails, space for side transfer to WC, transfer chair for bath/shower. Also 2nd WC. Equipment can be hired locally. Bed & breakfast and special interest breaks also available.

Apply: Carol Salter ☎ 01398 361519.

Rates: from £200-£500 per week (2007).

BARNSTAPLE, Devon

Calvert Trust Exmoor

Wistlandpound, Kentisbury, Barnstaple EX31 4SJ.

☎/Text: 01598 763221.

exmoor@calvert-trust.org.uk

●● I/F/G/H

Four self-catering units attached to Activity Centre for disabled people with their families and friends, sleeping 4-7. Two designed for full wheelchair access and a third has a ground floor bedroom with stairlift giving access to upstairs bedrooms. Entrances level. Open plan lounge/kitchen with adjustable height sink. 5, 4 or 1 bedrooms level. Bathrooms with roll-in shower or bath with hoist, handrails, space for side transfer to WC. Waterproof sheet available. Activities at the Centre are available and evening meals can be booked, see page 499.

Rates: from £620-£1195 per week (2007).

BEAWORTHY, Devon

Anglers Utopia

The Gables, Winsford, Halwill Junction, Beaworthy EX21 5XT.
☎ **01409 221559.**
W www.anglers-paradise.co.uk

 F/G 

Group of villas with associated fishing lakes. "Anglers Utopia", designed for disabled people, one sleeps up to 7. Entrance ramp. Open plan lounge/kitchen, controls useable from wheelchair. Ground floor bedroom and shower room ⟲, roll-in shower, handrails, space for side transfer to WC. 3 bedrooms upstairs. Also two other villas with accommodation for up to 3 disabled people. Accessible paths to most lakes.

Rates: on application.

Blagdon Farm Country Holidays

Ashwater, Beaworthy EX21 5DF.
☎ **01409 211509.**
W www.blagdon-farm.co.uk

 I/F/G/H 

Eight cottages on centre designed to be useable by disabled people. In country 1½ miles from village in West Devon. All with level entrance, open plan lounge/kitchen. Controls useable from wheelchair, low worktops in one cottage. 6 cottages have two bedrooms, the others have one, all 37cm. Shower rooms 37cm, ⟲, roll-in shower with seat, handrails, space by WC. Shower chairs, hoists, powered wheelchair and a range of other equipment available. Bar and meal service on site. Hoist for swimming pool. Level paths round nature reserve. Regional Tourism for All Winner 2004.

Rates: from £275-£855 per week (2006).

BIDEFORD, Devon

West Hele

Buckland Brewer, Bideford EX39 5LX.
W www.westhele.co.uk

●● I/F/G ★★★-★★★★

Cottages designed for disabled people on farm south of Bideford. "Orchard Barn" sleeps up to 6. Entrance ramp or 3 steps, 80cm to lounge. Kitchen 80cm. "Garden Wing" sleeps up to 4. Entrance 90cm, level. Lounge/kitchen 88cm. Both have a level twin bedroom and shower room 78cm, roll-in shower, handrails, space by WC. Other bedrooms upstairs. Shower chairs and some other equipment available. Alarm system. Large garden.

Apply: Lorna Hicks ☎ 01237 451044.
Rates: from £230-£825 per week (2007).

BIGBURY-ON-SEA, Devon

Challaborough Bay Holiday Park

Challaborough Beach, Bigbury-on-Sea TQ7 4HU.

●● I/F/G ★★★★

Holiday Park on South Devon coast with range of facilities. Two caravans for 5 people adapted for disabled guests. Entrance ramp. Lounge/kitchen open plan. Two bedrooms, sliding door 75cm, ⟲ in double. Shower room 75cm, handrails, restricted ⟲. Open March-November.

Apply: Parkdean Holidays
☎ 0871 641 2066
W www.parkdeanengland.co.uk
Rates: Holiday homes from £189 per week. Short breaks from (3 or 4 nights) from £114

BODMIN, Cornwall

Churchtown Lodges

Churchtown, Lanlivery, Bodmin PL30 5BT.

●● I/F/G/H

Two Vitalise chalets designed for disabled people at Adventure Centre. Open plan lounge/kitchen. Each sleeps up to 6 people. One bedroom has ceiling hoist and en-suite roll-in shower room. For further information on Churchtown, see page 501.

Apply: Vitalise Bookings Office
☎ 0845 345 1970.
Rates: on application.

East Rose Farm

St Breward, Bodmin Moor PL30 4NL.
☎ **01208 850674.**
www.eastrose.co.uk

●● F/G

Cottages on farm on edge of Bodmin Moor with 2 designed for disabled people. Each has level entrance, minimum internal door width 90cm, ↺ in kitchen. "Shippen" has a double bedroom ↺ and roll-in shower room with seat, handrails and space by WC. "Mowhay" has a twin bedroom with roll-in shower room designed for wheelchair users and also a double bedroom and bathroom.

Rates: from £165-£875 per week (2007).

Penrose Burden Cottages

St Breward, Nr. Bodmin PL30 4LZ.
www.penroseburden.co.uk

●● E/I/G

9 cottages for 2 or 6 people. Two cottages designed for disabled people with 3 bedrooms ↺, each with own roll-in shower rooms. Entrances level, 33". Ground floors level, doorways 33". 5 cottages have roll-in showers as well as baths. Some portable equipment available. Meals available. Many years experience of catering for wheelchair users.

Apply: Mrs Hall ☎ 01208 850277.
Rates: on application.

BROADCLYST, Devon

Paynes Farm

Broadclyst, Exeter EX5 3BJ.
☎ **01392 466720.**
www.paynes-farm.co.uk

●● I/F/G ★★★★

'Hue's Piece' barn conversion for up to 4 people designed for disabled guests on farm north east of Exeter. Entrance level 75cm. Open plan lounge/kitchen. Controls useable from wheelchair with space under worktop and sink. Double and 2 single bedrooms, ↺ in double and one single. Shower room 75cm, roll-in shower, space by WC, handrails, shower chair, toilet frame and raised WC seat. Meals provided by arrangement.

Apply: Anna Hamlyn
Rates: from £230-£735 per week (2007).

BUDE, Cornwall

Sharlands Farm

Marhamchurch, Nr. Bude EX23 0HP.
www.sharlandsfarm.co.uk

●● I/F/G ★★★★

Single storey barn conversion on farm in North Cornwall half mile from village and 2 miles from Bude. Entrance level, 81cm. Lounge 82 cm. Kitchen 82cm ↺. Double and twin bedrooms. Waterproof sheet available. Bathroom, ↺, handrails, space for side transfer to WC. A similar sized adjoining cottage and a detached 2 person cottage are also available. Meals available.

Apply: Mr K H Miller. ☎ 01288 361322.
Rates: from £202-£492 per week (2008).

COLYTON, Devon

Smallicombe Farm

Northleigh, Colyton EX24 6BU.
☎ **01404 831310.**
www.smallicombe.com

 E/I/F 

Two units, of four in converted barns, designed for disabled people. Entrance level 31". Open plan lounge/kitchen, worktops 30" and 35", controls useable from wheelchair. Double and twin bedrooms, ⟲ in double. Roll-in shower room with seat and shower chair. Bathroom ⟲, handrails, space for side transfer to bath and WC. Some equipment available or can be hired locally. Video available. For information on farmhouse accommodation see page 169.

Rates: from £175-£595 per week (2008).

CRANTOCK BAY, Cornwall

Crantock Beach Holiday Park

Nr. Newquay TR7 5RH.

 I/F/G 

Holiday park overlooking Crantock Beach. One 5-person caravan adapted for disabled guests. Entrance ramp. Lounge/kitchen open plan. Two bedrooms, ⟲ in double. Shower room 75cm, handrails, restricted ⟲. Open March-October.

Apply: Parkdean Holidays ☎ 0871 641 2099.
www.parkdeanengland.co.uk
Rates: Holiday homes from £169 per week. Short breaks (3 or 4 nights) from £102

CREDITON, Devon

Creedy Manor

Long Barn, Crediton EX17 4AB.
www.creedymanor.com

  I/F/G 

One apartment, of 4, designed for disabled people on farm a mile from Crediton. Slope to level entrance, 42". Lounge 31" with sofa bed. Kitchen 32", cooker controls useable from wheelchair. Two bedrooms. Bathroom 34", ⟲, roll-in shower, handrails, space for side transfer to WC. Other units have ground floor accommodation.

Apply: Mr & Mrs Turner ☎ 01363 772684.
Rates: from £297-£427 per week (2007).

CROYDE BAY, Devon

Ruda Holiday Park

Croyde Bay EX33 1NY.

●● I/F/G 

Holiday park by Blue Flag beach in North Devon. 5-person caravans adapted for disabled guests. Entrance ramp. Lounge /kitchen open plan. Two bedrooms, ⟲ in double. Shower room 75cm, handrails, restricted ⟲. Also adapted 3 bedroom lodge. Open March-November.

Apply: Parkdean Holidays
☎ 0871 641 2066.
www.parkdeanengland.co.uk
Rates: Holiday homes from £189 per week. Short breaks (3 or 4 nights) from £114.

EXMOUTH, Devon

Devon Cliffs Holiday Park

Sandy Bay, Exmouth EX8 5BT.
☎ 01395 226226.

●● I/F/G 

Haven holiday park overlooking Sandy Bay with wide range of facilities and entertainment. Caravans for 5 people adapted for disabled guests. Entrance ramp. Lounge/kitchen open plan. Two bedrooms, sliding door 75cm, ↺ in double. Shower room 75cm, handrails, restricted ↺, no space by WC. Doctor's surgery on site. Open Mid March-October.

For information on separately owned units see below.

Apply: Haven Holiday Reservations
☎ 0870 2422222.
Rates: on application.

Scout Holiday Homes Trust Caravans

●● E/I/F/G

Two adjacent adapted units each for up to 6 people. Entrance ramp, 30". Open plan lounge/kitchen, worktops 36". Two bedrooms, ↺ in double. Shower room/WC 30" sliding door, handrails, space for side transfer to WC and shower seat. Available April-October.
Apply: Scout Holiday Home Trust
☎ 020 8433 7290. See page 25.
Rates: from £195-£495 per week (2007).

Exmouth Seafront Flats

6 Alston Terrace, Exmouth EX8 1BH.
W www.exmouthseafrontflats.co.uk

●●● E/I/F/G

Ground floor flat by seafront near town centre. Street parking. Ramp to entrance. Lounge and kitchen level, controls not useable from wheelchair. Electric recliner chair. Twin bedroom level with electric adjustable bed. En suite shower room, ↺, roll-in shower with seat, handrails, space by WC. Three additional bedrooms and 2 bathrooms.

Apply: Judith Olisa ☎ 01395 275367.
Rates: from £450-£1000 per week (2007).

FOWEY, Cornwall

Penmarlam Caravan & Camping Park

Bodinnick by Fowey, Fowey PL23 1LZ.
☎ 01726 870088.
W www.penmarlanpark.co.uk

●● G ★★★★

Site overlooking the Fowey Estuary for touring caravans and camping. The site with 65 pitches with electric hook-ups, and 6 fully serviced, comprises two level areas with gentle slopes. Tarmac or concrete roads around Reception, amenity blocks and lower field. Unisex toilet designed for disabled people with roll-in shower, handrails and space by WC. Ramp to reception and shop. BSL can be used in reception and shop and there is an induction loop in reception. The surrounding areas are hilly. Boat landing stage available. Open Easter-October.

Ⓟ

Rates: from £2-£18 per pitch. (2007).

GUNNISLAKE, Cornwall

Todsworthy Farm Holidays

Todsworthy Farm, Albaston, Gunnislake PL18 9AW.
☎ **01822 834744.**
www.todsworthyfarmholidays.co.uk
●● I/F/G/H ★★★★

Two barn conversion cottages on farm in Tamar Valley. Entrances level 100cm. Lounge/kitchen open plan. Kitchen controls useable from wheelchair. Ground floor double/twin bedroom with hoist and roll-in shower room, ⟲, handrails, shower seat. Two other bedrooms and bathrooms upstairs. Teletext TV. Owned by wheelchair user.

Rates: £300-£750 per week (2007).

HAYLE, Cornwall

Riviere Sands Holiday Park

Riviere Towans, Hayle TR27 5AF.
☎ **01736 752132.**
●● I/F/G

Haven holiday park on cliffs overlooking St Ives Bay with range of facilities and entertainment. Caravans for 5 people adapted for disabled guests. Entrance ramp. Lounge/kitchen open plan. Two bedrooms, sliding door 75cm, ⟲ in double. Shower room 75cm, handrails, restricted ⟲, no space beside WC. Open April-October.

Ⓟ

Apply: Haven Holiday Reservations
☎ 0870 2422222.
Rates: on application.

Sea Haven

Riviere Towans, Hayle.
●● F/G

Privately owned bungalow overlooking St Ives Bay for up to 6 people. Ramp to entrance 36". Lounge/kitchen open plan, controls useable from wheelchair. Two double bedrooms ⟲ and bunkroom. Shower room 32" sliding door, roll-in shower with seat, handrails, space for side transfer to WC. Shop nearby and café in summer. Available Easter-October and Christmas.

Apply: Toms Self-Catering Holidays, 3A Riviere Towans, Hayle TR27 5AF.
☎ 01736 753010.
@ john@tomsholidays.co.uk
Rates: from £174-£756 per week (2007).

HELSTON, Cornwall

Chyvarloe Base Camp

Chyvarloe, Gunwalloe, Helston.
●● I/G

National Trust accommodation for groups of up to 12. Living areas level, no adaptations in kitchen. Two 6 bed dormitories, one on 1st floor and two bedrooms on ground floor. Shower room/WC adapted for wheelchair users and two other bathrooms. Not available July and August.

Apply: Property Manager, National Trust, The Stables, Penrose, Helston TR13 0RD.
☎ 01326 561407.
Rates: on application.

Elm Cottage

Cadgwith, Ruan Minor, nr. Helston.
●● G

Single storey National Trust cottage on Lizard Peninsula. Lounge, kitchen and two twin bedrooms. Bathroom with some adaptations for disabled guests.

Apply: National Trust Holiday Booking Office ☎ 0870 4584422. See page 33.
Rates: from £285-£871 per week (2006).

Lower Pentire Barn

Degibna, Helston

●● G

Single storey cottage on National Trust's Penrose Estate. Open plan lounge/kitchen. Twin bedroom. Bathroom with some adaptations for disabled guests.

Ⓟ

Apply: National Trust Holiday Booking Office ☎ 0870 4584422. See page 33.
Rates: from £269-£723 per week (2007).

The Stables

Penrose, Helston

● G

Ramp to entrance. Open plan lounge/kitchen. 3 bedrooms, double, twin and single. Bathroom with separate shower.

Ⓟ

Apply: National Trust Holiday Booking Office ☎ 0870 4584422. See page 33.
Rates: from £506-£1161 per week (2007).

HOLCOMBE ROGUS, Devon

Old Lime Kiln Cottages

Holcombe Rogus, nr. Wellingon.

●● I/G ★★★★

'Hopper Cottage' is one of 5 cottages between Tiverton and Wellington. Ramp with handrail to entrance. Doors 93cm. Lounge/kitchen open plan, controls useable from wheelchair. Two 2-person bedrooms. Shower room ⟲, handrails, roll-in shower, space by WC. Teletext TV.

Ⓟ

Apply: Sue Gallagher, Whipcott Heights, Holcombe Rogus, Wellington TA21 0NA. ☎ 01823 672339.
W www.oldlimekiln.co.uk
Rates: from £241-£615 per week (2007).

ILFRACOMBE, Devon

Hidden Valley Park

West Down, Ilfracombe EX34 8NU.
☎ **01271 813837.**
W **www.hiddenvalleypark.com**

●● G ★★★★

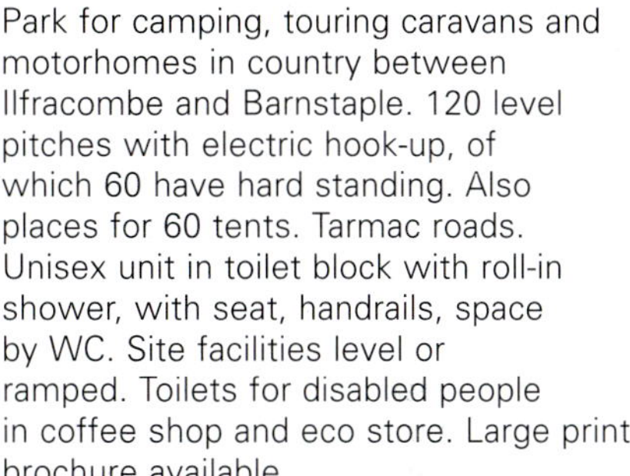

Park for camping, touring caravans and motorhomes in country between Ilfracombe and Barnstaple. 120 level pitches with electric hook-up, of which 60 have hard standing. Also places for 60 tents. Tarmac roads. Unisex unit in toilet block with roll-in shower, with seat, handrails, space by WC. Site facilities level or ramped. Toilets for disabled people in coffee shop and eco store. Large print brochure available.

Ⓟ

Rates: on application.

Watermouth Lodges

Watermouth, nr. Ilfracombe EX34 9SJ.
☎ **01271 865361.**
W **www.watermouth.co.uk**

●● I/F/G

Group of 35 lodges overlooking North Devon coast. 4 units, for 8 and 6 people, designed for disabled guests. Ramp to entrance 36", also French doors. Internal doors 36". Lounge/kitchen open plan. 3 and 2 bedrooms and sofabed in lounge. Bathroom ⟲, one has handrails and roll-in shower. Raised WC seat and wheelchair available. Shop, restaurant and bar on site with level entrances. Some other lodges have a single entrance step and a portable ramp is available. Closed January and February.

Ⓟ

Rates: from £450-£900 per week (2007).

ISLES OF SCILLY

Altamira Flat

St Marys, Isles of Scilly.

● F/G

Ground floor flat for up to 6 people near Porth Loo beach on west coast. Entrance 1 step, then a step down to hallway. Lounge/dining room level. Kitchen ½" step, no ⟲. Twin and double bedrooms 33", ⟲ in double. Bunkroom 26½". Bathroom 30", no adaptations. 3 steps to part of garden. Three other units with ground floor accommodation available.

Ⓟ

Apply: Island Properties, Porthmellon, St Mary's, Isles of Scilly TR21 0JY.
Rates: from £453-£753 per week (2007).

IVYBRIDGE, Devon

Hannah's Holiday Lets

Dame Hannah Rogers School, Ivybridge PL21 9HQ.
☎ 01752 898100.
@ jane@dhrs.co.uk

●●● E/I/F/H

Five bungalows designed for wheelchair users. Each sleeps up to 6 people in 4 or 6 bedrooms and has lounge, utility room and kitchen with adjustable height sink. The number of bath and shower rooms varies between units but all have fittings for disabled people. All bungalows have ceiling hoists installed in bathrooms and bedrooms. Extensive grounds. Available Easter and Summer holidays.

Rates: from £567-£963 per week (2007).

Venn Farm

Ugborough, Ivybridge PL21 0PE.

●● I/G ★★★★

Three cottages on farm 3 miles from Ivybridge. All have entrance ramp. Open plan lounge/kitchen. "The Granary" sleeps up to 8 and has two bedrooms and a shower room designed for disabled people on the ground floor with additional accommodation upstairs. This can be booked with "The Hams" which sleeps up to 4 in two level bedrooms and also has a roll-in shower room. "The Byre" has one twin bedroom with an en-suite shower room. Shower chair available. Access to courtyard and ponds.

Ⓟ

Apply: Mrs Pat Stephens. ☎ 01364 73240.
Rates: on application.

KENNACK SANDS, Cornwall

Sea Acres Holiday Park

Kennack Sands TR12 7LT.

●● I/F/G ★★★★

Holiday park on Lizard Penninsula. One 5- person caravan adapted for disabled guests. Entrance ramp. Lounge/kitchen open plan. Two bedrooms, sliding door 75cm, ⟲ in double. Shower room 75cm, handrails, restricted ⟲. Open April-November.

Ⓟ

Apply: Parkdean Holidays
☎ 0871 641 2066
W www.parkdeanengland.co.uk
Rates: Holiday homes from £159 per week. Short breaks (3 or 4 nights) from £96

KINGSBRIDGE, Devon

Beeson Farm Holidays

Beeson, Kingsbridge TQ7 2HW.
☎ 01548 581270.
www.beesonhols.co.uk
info@beesonhols.co.uk
●● F/G ★★★★

Farm near coast with 5 holiday cottages. "Linhay" is single storey and sleeps 4 people. Entrance step, portable ramp available. Lounge/kitchen open plan, controls useable from wheelchair. 5cm sill to sundeck. Twin bedroom with shower room 75cm, roll-in shower with seat, handrails, space by WC and under basin. Also double bedroom and bathroom. "Dairy Cottage" sleeps up to 6. Entrance level 82cm. Lounge/kitchen open plan, worktops 95cm. Double bedroom ground floor 86cm. En suite shower room 75cm folding door, roll-in shower with seat, handrails, space for side transfer to WC. Double and twin bedrooms with bath and shower rooms upstairs. Teletext TV and induction loop in "Linhay" lounge. No animals in "Linhay". M2 accredited 2008.

Rates: from £395-£875 per week (2007).

Parkland Caravan & Camping Site

Sorley Green, Kingsbridge TQ7 4AF.
☎ 01548 852723.
www.parklandsite.co.uk
●● G

Level touring site in country a mile from Kingsbridge. Pitches for 30 caravans and 20 tents; 20 with hardstanding and 50 with electric hook-ups. Tarmac drive and concrete pathways. Toilet designed for disabled people, handrails, roll-in shower, space by WC. Site facilities level or ramped. Large print brochure available.

Rates: on application.

Post Office Apartments

Beesands, Nr. Kingsbridge.
● F
★★★★

2 apartments in fishing village with ground floor accommodation. 'The Old Bakery' has ramp available for rear entrance 31". Open plan lounge/kitchen. Two bedrooms sleep up to 6 people. Shower room, no handrails. Separate WC. 'The Old Post Office' has 2 small steps at entrance. Open plan lounge/kitchen. 2 bedrooms with 1 step. Shower room 27". Teletext TV in each. Steps to garden.

Apply: Paul Gilbey, The Old Coach House, Stokenham, Kingsbridge TQ7 2ST.
☎ 01548 580175. paulmgilbey@aol.com
Rates: from £240-£540 per week (2007).

LADOCK, Cornwall

Treworgans Farm Holidays

Treworgans Farm, Ladock, Truro TR2 4QD.
☎ 01726 883240.
www.treworgansfarm.co.uk
●● I/F/G

Two barn conversions designed for disabled guests in mid Cornwall between Truro and St Austell. Each has ramp at entrance. Lounge/kitchen open plan, controls useable from wheelchair and adjustable hob. Twin/double bedroom. En suite shower room 83cm, roll-in shower with seat, handrails, space by WC. One has a second bedroom and a bathroom on the ground floor; the second has two bedrooms and bathrooms upstairs. Shower chair, raised WC seat and bathboard available. Teletext TV and induction loop. Also four section electric profiling bed with cot size. Electric hoist.

Rates: from £315-£875 per week (2007).

LOOE, Cornwall

Bocaddon Holiday Cottages

Bocaddon Farm, Lanreath, Looe PL13 2PG.
☎ **01503 220192.** @ **bocaddon@aol.com**

●● F/G/H ★★★-★★★★

3 cottages in converted barns on farm between Looe and Lostwithiel. Entrances level. Doors 33". Lounge/kitchen open plan. Two units have 2 twin/double ground floor bedrooms, the 3rd has a ground floor double and twin room upstairs. Bed raisers available. Bathroom level, roll-in shower with seat, handrails, space by bath and WC. Hoist available.

Rates: from £180-£560 per week (2007).

Trelawne Manor Holiday Park

Pelynt, Looe PL13 2NA.
☎ **01503 272151.**

●● I/F/G ★★★★

Holiday Park 3 miles from Looe with range of facilities and entertainment. Three caravans for 5 people adapted for disabled guests. Entrance ramp. Lounge/kitchen open plan. Two bedrooms, sliding door 75cm, ↺ in double. Shower room 75cm, handrails, restricted ↺. Open Easter-October.

Rates: on application.

Tudor Holiday Lodges

Morval, Looe PL13 1PR.
☎ **01579 320344.** W **www.tudorlodges.co.uk**

●● I/F/G

6 new lodges, for up to 6 people, designed to be used by disabled guests. Ramp to balcony, French doors level. Open plan lounge/kitchen, controls usable from wheelchair. 3 bedrooms, 2 with door to balcony. Electric single beds available. Shower room 33" sliding door, handrails, roll-in shower with seat, space by WC. Shower chair available. Scooter for hire. 2 units animal-free. Restaurant and bar adjoining.

Rates: from £150-£755 (2007).

LOSTWITHIEL, Cornwall

Hartswheal Farm

St Winnow, Lostwithiel PL22 0RB.

●● I/F/G/H

Cottages designed for disabled people on a farm a mile from Lostwithiel. "Hartswheal Barn" sleeps up to 6. Entrance level, 37". Lounge/kitchen open plan. 3 bedrooms, double and twin, 32" sliding doors, ↺. Shower room 32" sliding door, ↺, roll-in shower with seat, handrails, space for side transfer to WC, adjustable basin. "Hartswell Stables" is for 4 people. Open plan lounge/kitchen, adjustable table and worktop, controls useable from wheelchair. Double and twin bedrooms with own bath/shower rooms. One with electric adjustable bed and ceiling tracking to bath and WC. Adjustable basins. Shower chair and raised WC seat available. Teletext TV. Electric scooter for use round farm and also wheelchair available.

Apply: Wendy Jordan ☎ 01208 873419.
W www.connexions.co.uk/hartswheal
Rates: from £350-£700 per week (2007).

Manelly Fleming Farm

St Veep, Lostwithiel PL22 0NS.
☎ **01208 872564.**
W www.alittlebitofheaven.co.uk
●● I/F/G/H

Two apartments designed for disabled people in barn conversion on family farm 4 miles south of Lostwithiel. Entrance level; external lift to upper flat. Lounge/kitchen open plan, adjustable height kitchen fittings. Twin/double bedroom with adjustable beds and sofa bed in lounge. Shower room, ↻, roll-in shower with seat, space by WC, handrails, adjustable basin. Hoist in bedroom and shower room Powered wheelchair can be supplied.

Rates: from £400 per week (2007).

MAWNAN SMITH, Cornwall

Bosloe

Durgan, Mawnan Smith, Nr. Falmouth
●● G

National Trust country house overlooking the Helford River, with 3 self-catering apartments. The west wing, "Chatham", has lounge, kitchen and twin bedroom with own bathroom on ground floor and 3 bedrooms and bathroom upstairs. Some adaptations for disabled guests.

Apply: National Trust Holiday Booking Office ☎ 0870 4584422. See page 33.
Rates: from £601-£1875 per week (2007).

NEWQUAY, Cornwall

Holywell Bay Holiday Park

Holywell, Newquay TR8 5PR.
●● I/F/G ★★★★

Holiday Park on coast west of Newquay with a range of facilities. Caravans for 5 people adapted for disabled guests. Entrance ramp. Lounge/kitchen open plan. Two bedrooms, sliding door 75cm, ↻ in double. Shower room 75cm, handrails, restricted turning space. Open March-November.

Apply: Parkdean Holidays
☎ 0871 641 2066.
W www.parkdeanengland.co.uk
Rates: Holiday homes from £169 per week. Short breaks (3 or 4 nights) from £102

Mawgan Porth Holiday Park

Mawgan Porth, Newquay TR8 4BD.
☎ **01637 860322.**
W www.mawganporth.co.uk
●● F/G ★★★★★

Holiday park on coast north of Newquay. One 6-person bungalow designed for disabled guests. Level entrance through patio door. Open plan lounge/kitchen 96cm. Double and twin bedrooms, ↻ in twin with a bed removed. Bathroom ↻, handrails, space by WC. Raised WC seat and bathboard available. Also en-suite shower room from double bedroom. Shop and other site facilities level.

Rates: from £295-£840 per week (2007).

Newquay Holiday Park

Newquay TR8 4HS.

●● I/F/G ★★★★

Holiday Park in countryside 2 miles from Newquay with a range of facilities. Two caravans for 5 people adapted for disabled guests. Entrance ramp. Lounge/kitchen open plan. Two bedrooms, sliding door 75cm, ⟲ in double. Shower room 75cm, handrails, restricted turning space. Open March-November.

Apply: Parkdean Holidays ☎ 0871 641 2066.
W www.parkdeanengland.co.uk
Rates: Holiday homes from £169 per week. Short breaks (3 or 4 nights) from £102.

White Acres Holiday Park

White Cross, Newquay TR8 4LW.

●● I/F/G ★★★★★

Holiday park with extensive facilities. 6-person caravans adapted for disabled guests. Entrance ramp. Lounge/kitchen open plan. Two bedrooms, sliding door 75cm, ⟲ in double. Shower room 75cm, handrails, restricted ⟲. Open March-November.

Apply: Parkdean Holidays ☎ 0871 641 2066.
W www.parkdeanengland.co.uk
Rates: Holiday homes from £199 per week. Short breaks (3 or 4 nights) from £120

OKEHAMPTON, Devon

Acorn Cottage

Beer Farm, Okehampton EX20 1SG.
W **www.beerfarm.co.uk.**

●● F/G ★★★★

Cottage designed for disabled guests on farm on edge of Dartmoor. Entrance level, 80cm. Bed-sitting room with double bed 84cm. Kitchen 84cm, ⟲, controls useable from wheelchair. Shower room, ⟲ , roll-in shower with seat, handrails, space by WC. Twin bedroom and small lounge on 1st floor. Can interconnect with adjoining 3 bedroom cottage. Teletext TV.

Apply: Bob & Sue Annear ☎ 01837 840265.
Rates: £195-£480 per week (2007).

PAIGNTON, Devon

Scout Holiday Homes Trust Caravan

Hoburne Torbay, Grange Road, Goodrington, Paignton TQ4 7JP.

●● E/I/F/G

Adapted units each for up to 5 adults and small child on site with views over Torbay. Entrance ramp, 40". Open plan lounge/kitchen, worktops 36". Two bedrooms, ⟲ in double. Shower room/WC 30" sliding door, handrails, space for side transfer to WC and shower seat. Available April-October.

Apply: Scout Holiday Home Trust ☎ 020 8433 7290. See page 26.
Rates: from £165-£520 per week (2007).

PAR, Cornwall

CDA Caravan

Par Beach Sands Holiday Park, Par Beach.

●● I/F/G

Purpose-built caravan for 5/6 people on level coastal holiday park near Eden Project. Ramp with handrails to entrance 42". Kitchen controls useable from wheelchair. Two bedrooms with 32" sliding doors. Bathroom 32", ⟲, handrails, space for side transfer to WC.

Apply: Cornwall Disabled Association. ☎ 01872 273518. See page 166.
Rates: from £175 per week (2007).

PENZANCE, Cornwall

Nanceglos House

Madron, Penzance.

●● G

National Trust cottage for up to 9 in woodlands. Ground floor lounge, kitchen, twin bedroom and shower room. Other bedrooms upstairs.

Apply: National Trust Holiday Booking Office ☎ 0870 4584422. See page 33.
Rates: from £576-£1830 per week (2007).

PERRANPORTH, Cornwall
Perran Sands Holiday Park

Perranporth TR6 0AQ. ☎ **01872 573551.**

●● I/F/G ★★★

Haven holiday park on north Cornwall coast with wide range of facilities and entertainment. Caravans for 5 people adapted for disabled guests. Entrance ramp. Lounge/kitchen open plan. Two bedrooms, sliding door 75cm, ⟲ in double. Shower room 75cm, handrails, restricted ⟲, no space by WC. Open April-October.

Ⓟ

Apply: Haven Holiday Reservations ☎ 0870 2422222.
Rates: on application.

PORT ISAAC
Carnweather

Doyden House, Port Quinn, Port Isaac.

●● G

Ground floor apartment with sea views in National Trust property. Some adaptations for disabled people. Lounge, kitchen/diner and double and twin bedrooms. Bathroom with separate WC. Three other apartments on site, one ground floor.

Ⓟ

Apply: National Trust Holiday Booking Office ☎ 0870 4584422. See page 33.
Rates: from £298-£928 per week (2007).

PORTSCATHO, Cornwall
Major's Quarter & Captain's Quarter

St Anthony Head, Portscatho, Nr. Truro.

●● F/G

Two adapted cottages overlooking Falmouth Bay. One sleeps 4 in two twin bedrooms, the other has one twin bedroom. Each has level entrance. Min. door width 30". Bathrooms ⟲, handrails, space for side transfer to WC.

Ⓟ

Apply: National Trust Holiday Booking Office ☎ 0870 4584422. See page 33.
Rates: from £239-£871 per week (2006).

REDRUTH, Cornwall
Tehidy Holiday Park

Harris Mill, Illogan, Redruth TR16 4JQ.
☎ **01209 216489.** **W** **www.tehidy.co.uk**

●● F/G ★★★★

Two bungalows designed for disabled guests on small holiday park between Redruth and Portreath. Entrances 90cm, level except threshold. Lounge/kitchen open plan; no ⟲ in kitchen. Twin and double bedrooms. Shower room 90cm, roll-in shower with seat, handrails. Shower chair and raised WC seat available. DigitalTV. Other bungalows and caravans available. Steep slopes elsewhere on site. David Berllamy conservation award.

Ⓟ

Rates: from £250-£580 per week (2007).

REJERRAH, Cornwall
CDA Caravan

Monkey Tree Holiday Park, Scotland Road, Rejerrah TR8 5QR.

●● I/F/G

Purpose-built caravan for 5/6 people on site in central Cornwall a few miles from north coast. Ramp with handrails to entrance 42". Kitchen controls useable from wheelchair. Two bedrooms with 32" sliding doors. Bathroom 32", ⟲, handrails, space for side transfer to WC, accessible shower. Entertainment on site in summer.

Ⓟ

Apply: Cornwall Disabled Association. ☎ 01872 273518. See page 166.
Rates: from £175 per week (2007).

ST AGNES, Cornwall

Trenerry Farm

Mingoose, Mount Hawke, Truro TR4 8BX.
☎ 01872 553755.
www.babatrenerry.co.uk
●● I/F/G

Three lodges for on farm between Truro and the North Cornwall coast, designed for disabled guests. Back door by parking area level, ramp to patio door. Lounge/kitchen open plan, most controls useable from wheelchair. Lodge 1 has double and twin bedrooms and folding bed in lounge. The others have a double bedroom. En-suite shower rooms, roll-in shower with seat, handrails, space by WC. Wheelchair and some other equipment available. Teletext TV. Large balcony and garden.

Rates: from £160-£780 per week (2007/8).

ST AUSTELL, Cornwall

Bosinver Cottages

Bosinver Farm, St Austell PL26 7DT.
☎ 01726 72128. www.bosinver.co.uk
●● I/G ★★★-★★★★

A group of cottages in secluded grounds. "Olearia" has a ramp to entrance 31". All rooms have turning space, min. door width 30". Lounge/kitchen open plan. Double bedroom with bathroom with handrails and bathseat. Two other bedrooms and second bathroom. "Buddleia" has open plan lounge/kitchen and conservatory. Double bedroom with roll-in shower room designed for disabled guests. Also twin room with bathroom. Other units may be suitable for ambulant disabled people.

Rates: from £375-£1000 per week (2007).

Scout Holiday Homes Trust Caravans

Pentewan Sands Holiday Park, St Austell PL26 6BT.
●● E/I/F/G

Two adjacent adapted units each for up to 6 people on coastal site. Entrance ramp, 30". Open plan lounge/kitchen, worktops 36". Two bedrooms, in double. Shower room/WC 30" sliding door, handrails, space for side transfer to WC and shower seat. Available April-October.

Apply: Scout Holiday Home Trust
☎ 020 8433 7290. See page 26.
Rates: from £135-£495 per week (2007).

SALTASH, Cornwall

Notter Mill Country Park

Notter Bridge, Saltash PL12 4RW.
☎ 01752 843694.
www.nottermill.co.uk
●● F/G

Small rural holiday centre. Three bungalows for up to 7 people designed for disabled guests. Ramp to entrance 75cm. Lounge/kitchen open plan, . Double bedroom 90cm, also room with bunks and single bed. Shower room , roll-in shower with seat, space for side transfer to WC. Shower chair and WC frame available. 22 other bungalows, some pet-free. Pub serving meals nearby.

Rates: from £269-£661 per week (2007).

TORQUAY, Devon

Park House

1 Park Road, St Marychurch, Babbacombe, Torquay.

●● E/I/H

Ground floor flat. Double bedroom and two sofabeds in lounge. Fully adapted for wheelchair users. Roll-in shower. Electric hoist and shower chair available.

Apply: Grooms Holidays ☎ 08456 584478 @ selfcatering@johngrooms.org.uk
Rates: on application.

Torquay Holiday Park

Kinkerwell Road, Torquay TQ2 8JU.

●● F/G ★★★★

Holiday park on outskirts of Torquay with wide range of facilities and entertainment. Caravans for 5 people with adaptations for disabled guests. Entrance ramp. Lounge /kitchen open plan. Two bedrooms, ↺ in double. Shower room 75cm, handrails, restricted ↺, no space by WC. Open late March-October.

Apply: Parkdean Holidays ☎ 0870 990 4138. W www.parkdeanholidays.co.uk
Rates: on application.

TRURO, Cornwall

The Engine House

Trelissick, Feock, Truro.

●● F/G

Adapted cottage for up to 3 in National Trust Garden south of Truro. Entrance ramp, 74cm. Lounge 78cm, ↺. Kitchen 71cm, controls useable from wheelchair, no ↺. Double bedroom. Bathroom 70cm, roll-in shower with seat, space for side transfer to bath and WC. Restaurant on site and a batricar is available for use in the grounds.

Apply: National Trust Holiday Booking Office ☎ 0870 4584422. See page 33.
Rates: from £285-£815 per week (2007).

UMBERLEIGH, Devon

Country Ways

Little Knowle Farm, High Bickington, Umberleigh EX37 9BJ.
☎ **01769 560503.** W **www.country-ways.net**

●● F/G ★★★★

6 cottages on farm in North Devon. "The Stables" designed for disabled guests. Entrance level. Lounge/kitchen open plan, controls useable from wheelchair. Single and double bedrooms level and also hayloft bed. Waterproof sheet and bedblocks available. Shower room 90cm, ↺, roll-in shower with seat, handrails.

Rates: from £350-£780 per week (2006).

VERYAN, Cornwall

Dairy Cottage

Gwendra, Veryan, Truro

●● F/G

One of a group of National Trust cottages overlooking Gerrans Bay. Single storey with open plan lounge/kitchen, twin bedroom and bathroom.

Apply: National Trust Holiday Booking Office ☎ 0870 4584422. See page 33.
Rates: from £269-£723 per week (2007).

WADEBRIDGE, Cornwall

St Minver Holiday Park

St Minver, Rock, Wadebridge PL27 6RR.

●● I/F/G ★★★★

Holiday Park between Wadebridge and north Cornwall coast with range of facilities. Two caravans for 5 people adapted for disabled guests. Entrance ramp. Lounge/kitchen open plan. Two bedrooms, sliding door 75cm, ↺ in double. Shower room 75cm, handrails, restricted ↺. Open March-October.

Apply: Parkdean Holidays ☎ 0871 641 2066. W www.parkdeanengland.co.uk
Rates: Holiday homes from £169 per week Short breaks (3 or 4 nights) from £102

WARBSTOW, Cornwall
Trenannick Cottages

Trenannick Farmhouse, Warbstow, nr. Launceston PL15 8RP.

☎ **01566 781443.**

www.trenannickcottages.co.uk

●● I/F/G ★★★

"Roundhouse Cottage", one of 5, between Camelford and Bude originally converted for disabled family member. Entrance level 35½". Internal doors 32". Kitchen worktops 32". Twin bedroom ↺ and double sofabed in lounge. Waterproof sheets available. Shower room ↺, roll-in shower with shower stool, handrails, space for side transfer to WC. Separate WC. 2 other cottages with ground floor accommodation.

Rates: from £145-£430 per week (2007).

WEMBURY, Devon
Traine Farm

Wembury, Nr. Plymouth PL9 0EW.

☎ **01752 862264**

www.traine-holiday-cottages.co.uk

●● E/I/F/G ★★★★

2 cottages designed for disabled guests on farm in coastal village 7 miles south of Plymouth. Entrance level, 90cm minimum. Open plan lounge/kitchen with controls useable from wheelchair. Double bedroom ground floor; one cottage also has 4 single beds in upstairs gallery. Shower room 85cm, roll-in shower with seat, handrails, space for side transfer to WC. One unit also has a bath. Ramp to garden.

Rates: from £180-£650 per week (2007).

WESTWARD HO!, Devon
BREAK Chalets

Golden Bay Holiday Village, Westward Ho!, Nr. Bideford.

●●

2 chalets on holiday park overlooking Bideford Bay. One, sleeping up to 6 is purpose-built for disabled people. The second sleeps up to 4. Open March-December.

Apply: BREAK, 1 Montague Road, Sheringham NR26 8WN. ☎ 01263 822161. office@break-charity.org (see page 20)

Rates: on application.

WOOLACOMBE, Devon
Lions Bungalow

Golden Coast Holiday Village, Woolacombe.

●● E/I/H/G

Purpose-built bungalow for wheelchair users and their families. Lounge, kitchen/dining room and 2 twin bedrooms. Adjustable bed. Wheel in shower and non-slip flooring in bathroom. Portable hoist, commode and shower chair available. Club house on site. Open Easter-October.

Apply: Mr Taylor, Ilfracombe & District Lions Club, Danesbury, King Street, Combe Martin EX34 0AD. ☎ 01271 883677.

Rates: from £100-£245 per week (2007).

6 East of England

Norfolk

The East of England region includes Bedfordshire, Cambridgeshire, Essex, Hertfordshire, Norfolk and Suffolk. It stretches from the fringes of London and the Thames Estuary to the Wash and encompasses historic towns, varied countryside and a long coastline.

A string of coastal resorts, most with level promenades, cater for every taste of seaside holiday. Great Yarmouth, Clacton and Southend have a long tradition of proving a range of lively entertainment for their visitors, whether staying in the area or on day trips. Quieter resorts include Hunstanton and Sheringham on the north Norfolk coast, Lowestoft and the old port of Southwold in Suffolk and Frinton in Essex. Harwich and Felixstowe are still important commercial ports as well as resorts.

The region is rich in historic houses and other buildings, including Colchester Castle in England's oldest town, Tilbury Fort, run by English Heritage where Elizabeth I rallied her troops before the Spanish Armada, Melford Hall in Suffolk and Hatfield House in Hertfordshire. Ancient cathedrals and churches can be visited in Ely, Norwich, Peterborough, Bury St Edmund's and St Alban's.

In Cambridge, visitors can join the regular walking tours to see the colleges and other historic buildings. Norwich, which was once the second largest town in the England, contains the largest collection of medieval buildings and street patterns in the country. Other notable towns in the area include Bedford, Huntingdon, Kings Lynn, Saffron Walden, Sudbury and Woodbridge. The countryside between Ipswich and Colchester was immortalised by John Constable.

The Norfolk Broads just inland from the coast on the Norfolk/Suffolk border is now the equivalent of a National Park and offers many opportunities for boating, bird watching and enjoying the unique scenery. Other sites of interest to country lovers include the Wildfowl & Wetlands Trust site at Welney near Peterborough, the National Trust's Wicken Fen near Ely and Needham Lake in Suffolk. Country parks with facilities for disabled visitors include Sandringham in west Norfolk and Aldenham at Elstree, Hertfordshire.

More formal gardens in the area include the Swiss Garden at Biggleswade in central Bedfordshire, the extensive Gardens of the Rose at St Albans and the University Botanic Garden at Cambridge. Near King's Lynn, Norfolk Lavender is a commercial lavender farm holding the national collection of the plant. Other outdoor attractions include the Museum of East Anglian Life at Stowmarket, Woburn Park in Bedfordshire and the Raptor Foundation near Huntingdon. The North Norfolk Railway, running between Sheringham and Holt has a restored coach equipped for wheelchair users. For an up-to-the-minute shopping experience the region has the Lakeside Shopping Centre at Thurrock.

St John's College, Cambridge

Photo: britainonview.com © Ingrid Rasmussen

East of England

USEFUL ADDRESSES

East of England Tourist Board

Dettingen House, Dettingen Way, Bury St Edmunds IP33 3TU.
☎ **0870 225 4800.**
visiteastofengland.com

Disability Essex

Rochford Adult Community College, Rocheway, Rochford, Essex, SS4 1DQ.
☎ **0844 4412 1771**
info@essexdpa.org
www.disabilityessex.org

Disability Essex (EDPA) can provide holiday information to disabled people in Essex as well as general information on disability.

Awayadays

Stone Cottage, Front Road, Wood Dalling, Norwich NR11 6RN.
☎ **01263 587005.**
awayadays@clara.co.uk
www.awayadays.com

Operates day and package tours in Norfolk and evening tours of Norwich in a 15-seat coach equipped with a lift that can carry up to 4 passengers in wheelchairs. Accessible refreshment and toilet stops can be included. Pick-ups at railway stations can be arranged, as can tailor-made tours including the booking of accommodation. Contact David McMaster.

Norfolk Country Cottages

Carlton House, Market Place, Reepham NR10 4JJ.
☎ **01603 871872.**
info@norfolkcottages.co.uk
www.norfolkcottages.co.uk

A leading provider of self-catering holiday accommodation in Norfolk. Their brochure indicates properties that have features for or may be suitable for disabled people. One of these is included in this guide.

DIAL

DIAL offers a free, impartial and confidential service of information and advice by telephone to disabled people, their relatives and professionals. The following DIAL UK members may be able to help disabled residents and visitors in their areas:

DIAL Basildon ☎ **0845 450 3001/2**
Optua Bury St Edmunds ☎ **01284 748800**
Directions Plus, Cambridge
☎ **01223 569600**
Textphone: 01223 569601
DRC Dunstable ☎ **01582 470900;**
Textphone: 01582 470959
DAS East Suffolk ☎ **01394 387070**
Essex DPA ☎ **0844 4412 1771;**
Textphone: 01245 253400
DIAL Great Yarmouth ☎
DIS Huntingdonshire ☎ **01480 830833**
Ipswich DAB ☎ **01473 217313**
DIAL Lowestoft ☎ **01502 511333;**
Norfolk Coalition ☎ **01603 666951**
DIAL Peterborough ☎ **01733 265551**
DIAL Southend ☎ **0800 731 6372;**
Textphone: 01702 356031
Optua Stowmarket ☎ **01449 672781;**
Textphone: 01449 775999
West Norfolk DIS ☎ **01553 774599;**
Textphone: 01553 774766

USEFUL PUBLICATIONS & WEBSITES

Access to Bedford – a range of leaflets giving information on accommodation, places to eat, transport, etc. Produced by the Borough Council in association with Bedford Access Group. Available free from Bedford Tourist Information Centre, Town Hall, St Paul's Square, Bedford MK40 1SJ. ☎ 01234 215226 or on www.bedford.gov.uk

---

Accessible South Lincolnshire & West Norfolk by John Killick – a book published by the Disabled Motorists Federation in 2005 giving information on the accessibility of places to visit and eat in the Fens. Available price £3.50 from Mr J E Killick, 145 Knoulberry Road, Blackfell, Washington, Tyne & Wear NE37 1JN.

---

www.disabledgo.info - this website includes detailed information on the accessibility of many premises in Norwich, St Albans and Watford.

East of England

EQUIPMENT HIRE

Buckingham Engineering Company

Old Leighton Farm, Mursley Road, Stewkley, Leighton Buzzard LU7 0ES.

☎ **01296 720800.**

Company hiring a range of manual, lightweight and powered wheelchairs and scooters for hire on monthly and weekly terms from their centre in Milton Keynes. A repair service is also offered.

The Disability Resource Centre

Poynters House, Poynters Road, Dunstable LU5 4TP.

☎ **01582 470900.**

@ **equipment@drcbeds.org.uk**

W **www.drcbeds.org.uk**

The DRC for Bedfordshire and Luton has manual wheelchairs to hire on a short-term basis. They also have a number of small items of equipment for sale and can advise on local suppliers.

Hatfield Shopmobility

Rear of Bill Salmon Centre, 88 Town Centre, Hatfield AL10 0JW.

☎ **01707 262731.**

@ **shopmobility@welhat.gov.uk**

A long-term loan service is provided for residents of Welwyn Hatfield for up to 3 months. People living in the area who have disabled relatives staying with them can borrow wheelchairs

The HAND Partnership

38A Bull Close, Norwich NR3 1SX.

☎ **01603 415999.**

W **countywidemobility.org**

Wheelchairs and scooters are available to hire for people living or on holiday in Norfolk. They also carry out scooter repairs.

Hertfordshire Action on Disability

The Woodside Centre, The Commons, Welwyn Garden City AL7 4DD.

☎ **01707 384260 (equipment hire) or 375159 (transport).**

@ **info@hadnet.org.uk**

W **www.hadnet.org.uk**

Operate a wheelchair hire scheme and an accessible transport service.

Luton Shopmobility

Level 3, Market Car Park, Arndale Centre, Luton LU1 2LJ.

☎ **01582 738936.**

@ **lutonshopmobility@tiscali.co.uk**

Manual wheelchairs are available for holiday loan for £10 for up to 10 days and a subsequent daily fee if required.

Maple Mobility DGT Services

Unit 7, Buckingham Court, Dairy Road, Dukes Park Industrial Estate, Chelmsford CM2 6XW.

☎ **01245 451514.**

W **www.maplemobility.co.uk**

Manual and powered wheelchairs and scooters are available at weekly rates. Delivery and collection in the Chelmsford area.

Peterborough Shopmobility

Level 11, Queensgate Car Park, Peterborough PE1 1NT.

☎ **01733 313133.**

Manual wheelchairs are available for holiday loan for £1 a night. ID including address and a contactable telephone number are required.

Rainbow Services

Lattonbush Business Centre, Unit 2, Southern Way, Harlow, Essex, CM18 7BH.

☎ 01279 308151.

@ jean@rainbowservices.org.uk

This community organisation has manual wheelchairs to hire for a moderate fee to residents and people visiting Harlow.

South East Mobility

59 Jesmond Road, Grays, Essex RM16 2QS.

☎ 0845 644 2892.

W www.southeastmobility.co.uk

Company supplying a wide range of equipment for disabled people has available for hire scooters, wheelchairs and some other equipment including a commode and bath lift.

Watford Shopmobility

Church Car Park, Exchange Road, Watford W18 0BU.

☎ 01923 211020.

@ shopmobilitywatford@btinternet.com

As well as regular shopmobility services, Watford Shopmobility can supply manual wheelchairs for longer periods on advance payment of £2 a day. Details on insurance cover are required if taking it abroad.

Shopmobility schemes exist to provide wheelchairs and/or scooters for use in shopping centres in the following towns. For information on availability, etc. telephone in advance.

Basildon ☎ **01268 533644**

Bedford ☎ **01234 348000**

Bury St Edmunds ☎ **01284 757175**

Cambridge ☎ **01223 457452**

Cambridge, Grafton Centre

☎ **01223 461858**

Chelmsford ☎ **01245 250467**

Chelmsford, The Meadows

☎ **01245 357097**

Clacton-on-Sea ☎ **01255 435566**

Colchester ☎ **01206 505256**

Ely ☎ **01353 666655**

Harlow ☎ **01279 419196**

Hatfield ☎ **01707 262731**

Haverhill ☎ **01440 858051**

Hemel Hempstead ☎ **01442 259259**

Hitchin ☎ **01462 423399**

Ipswich ☎ **01473 222225**

Kings Lynn ☎ **01553 770310**

Lakeside ☎ **01708 869933**

Lowestoft ☎ **01502 588857**

Luton ☎ **01582 738936**

Norwich ☎ **01603 753350**

Peterborough ☎ **01733 313133**

St Albans ☎ **01727 819339**

Stevenage ☎ **01438 350300**

Stowmarket ☎ **01449 616234**

Watford ☎ **01923 211020**

Hatfield Shopmobility also operates in Welwyn Garden City and The Galleria Hatfield, St Albans Shopmobility has a satellite scheme at Harpenden and Kings Lynn Shopmobility also operates in Swaffham and Downham Market.

ACCOMMODATION WITH MEALS

BASILDON, Essex

Campanile Basildon

Southend Arterial Road, Pipps Hill, Basildon SS14 3AE.

☎ **01268 530810.**

@ **basildon@campanile.com**

 ★★

Hotel off Inner Ring Road. Reserved parking bays. Public rooms level. Unisex WC. 4 twin bedroom designed for disabled guests. Bathroom ⟲, handrails, space for side transfer. Other ground floor bedrooms level. See page 31.

Rates: on application.

Holiday Inn Basildon

Waterfront Walk, Basildon SS14 3DG.

☎ **0870 400 9003.**

@ **reservations-basildon@ihg.com**

 D/E/I/F/G 

Hotel at leisure complex north of town centre. Reserved parking bays. Level entrance, automatic door. Lounge, bar and unisex WC ground floor. Restaurant 1st floor, Braille menu meals can be served in lounge. Lift 80cm. Two ground floor bedrooms designed for disabled guests, low level controls. Bathrooms ⟲, bath transfer seat, space by WC and bath. Other bedrooms level.

Rates: from £75-£130 per room (2007).

BEDFORD, Bedfordshire

Express by Holiday Inn Bedford

Elstow Interchange A6/A421, Wilstead Road, Bedford MK42 9BS.

☎ **0870 112 1807.**

@ **bedford@expressholidayinn.co.uk**

●● F/G

Limited service hotel south of town centre. Reserved parking bays. Entrance level. Low reception desk. Open plan public rooms. Unisex WC. Lift 90cm, inside 140x1235cm. Five bedrooms designed for disabled guests. Shower rooms 92cm, ⟲, roll-in shower with seat, handrails, space by WC. Other bedrooms level. Induction loop and Teletext TV.

Rates: on application.

Mill House Hotel & Restaurant

Mill Road, Sharnbrook, Bedford MK44 1NP.

☎ **01234 781678.**

W **www.millhouse-riverside.co.uk**

●● D/E/I/F/G

Country restaurant with rooms north of Bedford. Reserved parking bay. Entrance level. Public rooms ground floor, level, lounge/bar open plan, restaurant 140cm. Unisex WC. Twin bedroom, ground floor, 87cm, ⟲. Bathroom 90cm, ⟲, handrails, space by bath and WC. Other bedrooms upstairs.

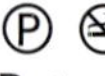

Rates: on application.

BOREHAMWOOD, Hertfordshire

Holiday Inn London – Elstree M25 J23

Barnet Bypass, Borehamwood WD6 5PU.
☎ **020 8214 9988.**
@ **hielstree@qmh-hotels.com**
●● D/E/I/F/G

Hotel near M25 junction 23. Reserved parking bays. Entrance level, automatic doors. Public rooms level. Unisex WC. Lift to all floors. Two bedrooms designed for disabled guests. Bathrooms 94cm, ⟲, space for side transfer to bath and WC. Waterproof sheets available. Other bedrooms level.

Rates: on application.

Ibis London Elstree Borehamwood

Elstree Way, Borehamwood WD6 1JY.
☎ **0871 663 0632.** @ **H6186@accor.com**
●● D/E/I/F/G ★★

Hotel in town centre, near A1. Designated parking bays. Rear entrance level. Low reception desk. Public rooms open plan. Adapted cubicles in WCs. Lifts 92cm, inside 112x138cm. Six bedrooms designed for disabled guests. Wheel-in shower rooms ⟲, handrails, space by WC. Other bedrooms level. Portable induction loop available.

Rates: from £49-£69 per night.

BRAINTREE, Essex

Express by Holiday Inn Braintree

Galley's Corner, Cressing Road, Braintree CM7 8DJ.
☎ **01376 551141.**
●● E/F/G

Limited service hotel off A120 south of town. Reserved parking bays. Entrance level. Public areas level. Restaurant across car park. Two double bedrooms designed for disabled guests. Shower room ⟲, roll-in shower, space for side transfer to WC. Other ground floor bedrooms level.

Rates: on application.

BRENTWOOD, Essex

Holiday Inn Brentwood

Brook Street, Brentwood CM14 5NF.
☎ **0870 400 9012.**
@ **brentwoodm25@ihg.com**
●● D/E/I/F/G ★★★

Hotel off M25 J28 west of town. 6 reserved parking bays. Ramp to main entrance, automatic doors. Main public rooms level. Unisex WC. Lift 30", inside 41"x56". Two ground floor bedrooms designed for disabled guests, low level controls and wardrobe rail. Bathrooms 30", ⟲, handrails, transfer platform to bath, space by bath and WC. Other bedrooms level.

Rates: on application.

BROXBOURNE, Hertfordshire

Cheshunt Marriott Hotel

Halfhide Lane, Turnford,
Broxbourne EN10 6NG.
☎ **01992 451245.**
www.cheshuntmarriott.co.uk
●● D/E/I/F/G 

Hotel off A10, north of M25. Reserved parking bays. Entrance level, automatic doors. Public rooms ground floor, open plan. Unisex WC. Large lift to all floors. 8 double bedrooms designed for disabled guests, 4 with connecting rooms. Bathrooms have low bath with handrails, space by WC, no ⟲. Other bedrooms level. Braille menus. Courtyard garden.

Rates: £89-£139 per room (2007).

CAMBRIDGE, Cambridgeshire

Crowne Plaza Cambridge

Downing Street, Cambridge CB2 3DT.
☎ **0870 400 9180.**
www.crowneplaza.com/cambridgeuk
●● D/E/I/G

Modern city centre hotel. Entrance level. Lift to public rooms, 1st floor, open plan. Unisex WC. Lift from 1st floor 43", inside 66"x66". Two double bedrooms designed for disabled guests. Bathrooms 36", ⟲, handrails, space for side transfer to bath and WC. Other bedrooms level.

Rates: on application.

Holiday Inn Cambridge

Lakeview, Bridge Road,
Impington, Cambridge CB24 9PH.
☎ **0870 400 9015.**
cambridge@ihg.com
●● D/E/I/F/G

Hotel in suburb to the north of Cambridge off A16 J32. Reserved parking bays. Ramp to entrance, automatic door. Low reception desk. Public rooms level, mainly open plan. Unisex WC. 4 double bedrooms adapted for disabled guests, restricted ⟲. Bathrooms have 36" sliding door, ⟲, handrails, space by bath and WC. Other ground floor rooms level. Large print information and menus.

Rates: from £60-£185 per night (2007).

CHELMSFORD, Essex

Atlantic Hotel

New Street, Chelmsford CM1 1PP.
☎ **01245 268168.**
www.atlantichotel.co.uk
●● D/E/F/G

Modern town centre hotel. Reserved parking bays. Slope to level entrance, double doors. Public rooms level, open plan. Unisex WC. 3 family rooms designed for disabled guests. Bathroom 80cm, ⟲, handrails, space by WC and bath. Other ground floor rooms level.

Rates: from £120 per room weekdays (2007).

CHIGWELL, Essex

Vitalise Jubilee Lodge

Grange Farm, High Road, Chigwell IG7 6DP.
☎ **020 8501 2331.**
●●●●● D/E/I/H

Centre on the edge of Epping Forest for breaks by people with physical disabilities and carers. Accommodates 36 guests in twin and single bedrooms with bathrooms. Activities, outings and entertainment arranged. 24-hour care on-call and personal support provided.

Ⓟ

Apply: Vitalise ☎ 0845 345 1970 (see page 27).
Rates: on application.

COLCHESTER, Essex

Best Western Rose & Crown Hotel

East Street, Colchester CO1 2TZ.
☎ **01206 866677.**
www.rose-and-crown.com
● D/E/F/G ★★★

Historic town centre hotel. Parking spaces can be reserved. Slope to level entrance. Public rooms ground floor, open plan. Unisex WC. Double bedroom designed for disabled guests. Bathroom, space for side transfer to bath and WC. Two level ground floor bedrooms with shower rooms, no adaptations.

Ⓟ

Rates: from £99-£118 BB (2007).

Holiday Inn Colchester

Abbotts Lane, Eight Ash Green, Colchester CO6 3QL.
☎ **0870 400 9020.**
@ **colchester@ihg.com**
●● D/E/I/F/G

Hotel on edge of town. Reserved parking bays, ½" kerb. Entrance level, double doors. Lounge and bar level, open plan. Restaurant 3 steps or chair lift. Unisex WC, approach doors 74cm. 3 double/twin bed-rooms designed for disabled guests 74cm. Door to adjoining room. Bathrooms 76cm sliding door, handrails, alarm, space for side transfer to bath and WC. Other ground floor bedrooms level. Wheelchair available.

Ⓟ

Rates: on application.

Marks Tey Hotel

London Road, Marks Tey, Colchester CO6 1DU.
☎ **01206 210001.**
www.markstheyhotel.co.uk
●● D/E/I/G

Hotel west of Colchester. Reserved parking bays. Entrance level. Public rooms level, open plan. Unisex WC. Two twin bedrooms adapted for disabled guests with roll-in shower rooms. Other ground floor bedrooms level.

Ⓟ

Rates: on application.

Old Courthouse Inn

Harwich Road, Great Bromley, Colchester CO7 7JG.

☎ **01206 250322.**

www.theoldcourthouseinn.co.uk

●● D/G ★★★★

Inn in village east of Colchester. Ramp to entrance. Public rooms level. Unisex WC. In annexe 5 bedrooms with bathrooms designed for disabled guests.

Rates: from £55-£70 per person BB (2007).

CROSTWICK, Norfolk

The Old Rectory Hotel

North Walsham Road, Crostwick, Norwich NR12 7BG.

☎ **01603 738513.**

www.oldrectorycrostwick.com

●● D/F/G

Country hotel north of Norwich. Reserved parking bays. Entrance level, double doors. Public rooms level, mainly open plan. Adapted WCs. One bedroom adapted for disabled guests level, 80cm. Bathroom 80 cm, restricted ⟲, handrails, space for side transfer to bath and WC. Bath seat available. Other ground floor bedrooms level.

Rates: from £32.75-£50 per person BB (2007).

ELY, Cambridgeshire

The Nyton Hotel

7 Barton Road, Ely CB7 4HZ.

☎ **01353 662459.**

www.thenytonhotel.co.uk

● ★★★

Family run hotel. Entrance 2 steps, 45". Public rooms level with 1/2" threshold to restaurant and sun lounge. 2 steps to garden. Two ground floor bedrooms. WC and shower room, no ⟲. Commode available.

Rates: from £37.50-£60 per person BB (2007).

GREAT YARMOUTH, Norfolk

Burlington Palm Hotel

North Drive, Great Yarmouth NR30 1EG.

☎ **01493 844568.**

www.burlington-hotel.co.uk

●● D/E/F/G ★★★

Family run adjoining hotels on seafront. Parking bays can be reserved. Entrance ramp or 3 steps. Public rooms level. Unisex WC. Lift 36", inside 36"x42". Five bedrooms may be suitable for disabled guests, 3 twins and 2 family/doubles. Bathrooms 42" sliding door. Other bedrooms level. Closed January.

Rates: from £329 DBB per night (2007).

HATFIELD, Hertfordshire

Ramada Hatfield

St Albans Road West, Hatfield AL10 9RH.

☎ **01707 265411.**

sales.hatfield@ramadajarvis.co.uk

●● D/E/I/F/G

Hotel near town centre. Reserved parking bays. Ramp or 3 steps to entrance revolving and swing doors. Public rooms level. Unisex WC. Twin bedroom adapted for disabled guests 77cm. Shower room 76cm, ⟲, roll-in shower with seat, handrails, space by WC. Waterproof sheet can be provided. Other ground floor rooms level.

Rates: from £45-£149 per night (2007).

HEMEL HEMPSTEAD, Hertfordshire

Express by Holiday Inn Hemel Hempstead

Stationers Place, Apsley, Hemel Hempstead HP3 9RH.

☎ **0870 458 5485.**

@ hemel@expressholidayinn.co.uk

●● E/F/G ★★★

Limited service hotel south of town centre near M25 junction 20. Reserved parking bays. Entrance level. Low reception desk. Open plan public rooms. Unisex WC. Lift 35", inside 53"x87". 6 bedrooms designed for disabled people, doubles and twin. Shower rooms ⟲, roll-in shower with seat, handrails, space by WC. Other bedrooms level.

Ⓟ

Rates: on application.

Holiday Inn Hemel Hempstead

Breakspear Way,
Hemel Hempstead HP2 4UA.

☎ **0870 400 9041.**

@ hemelhempsteadm1@ihg.com

●● D/E/I/F/G ★★★

Hotel at edge of town near M1 junction 8. Reserved parking bays. Entrance level, automatic door. Wheelchair lift or 3 steps to restaurant. Other public rooms level, except part of bar. Unisex WCs on ground and lower ground floors. Lifts 100cm, inside 153x120cm. Two ground floor bedrooms adapted for disabled guests, low controls and clothes rail. Bathrooms 92cm, ⟲, low bath, handrails, space by WC. Other bedrooms level. Vibrating alarm, portable and fixed induction loops and sound system available.

Ⓟ

Rates: on application.

HUNSTANTON, Norfolk

Claremont Guest House

35 Greevegate, Hunstanton PE36 6AF.

☎ **01485 533171.**

@ claremontg@tiscali.co.uk

●● D/E/F/G ★★★★

Bed & breakfast in town centre. Ramp or 2 steps at entrance. Public rooms level. A twin bedroom adapted for disabled guests. Shower room 30", roll-in shower with seat, handrails.

Ⓟ

Rates: £30 per person BB (2007).

HUNTINGDON, Cambridgeshire

The George Hotel & Restaurant

High Street, Buckden PE19 5XA.

☎ **01480 812300.**

@ www.thegeorgebuckden.com

●● D/E/G ★★★

Hotel in village south of Huntingdon. Foyer entrance level. Public rooms level, open plan. Unisex WC. Lift 91cm, inside 99x149cm, manual door. Bedroom adapted for disabled guests. Bathroom 78cm, ⟲, space and handrail by bath but not WC. Other bedrooms level.

Rates: from £80-£130 per night BB (2007)

Huntingdon Marriott

Kingfisher Way, Hinchingbrooke Business Park, Huntingdon PE29 6FL.

☎ **01480 446000.**

●● D/E/I/F/G ★★★★

Modern hotel by A14 and Huntingdon race-course. Reserved parking bays. Entrance level, automatic door. Low reception desk. Public rooms level, open plan. Unisex WC. Lift inside 54"x60". Eight bedrooms designed for disabled guests. Bathrooms 36", ⟲, handrails, space for side transfer to bath and WC. Other bedrooms level. Bedblocks, chair & table raisers, magnifying pads and vibrating pillow alarms available.

Ⓟ

Rates: on application.

IPSWICH, Suffolk

Express by Holiday Inn Ipswich

Old Hadleigh Road, Sproughton, Ipswich IP8 3AR.

☎ **01473 222279.**

@ **ebhi-ipswich@btconnect.com**

●● E/I/G ★★★★

Limited service hotel on eastern edge of town off A14. Reserved parking bays. Ramp to entrance, double doors. Low reception desk. Public rooms open plan. Unisex WC, no space for side transfer. 3 double bedrooms designed for disabled people. Shower rooms ↻, roll-in shower with seat, space by WC. Other ground floor bedrooms level. Teletext TVs and vibrating alarms available. Meals available in adjoining Beagle Inn.

Rates: from £47-£65 per room BB (2007).

Holiday Inn Ipswich

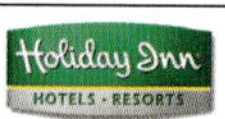

London Road, Ipswich IP2 0UA.

☎ **0870 400 9045.**

@ **reservations-ipswich@ihg.com**

●● D/E/I/F/G ★★★★

Hotel on outskirts of town. Reserved parking bays. Entrance level, automatic doors. Stairlift to restaurant, lounge and bar level. Unisex WC planned. Stair lift to 1st floor. Three double bedrooms designed for disabled guests, one on ground floor. Bathroom 88cm, ↻, handrail, space by bath and WC. Induction loop, telephone and TV amplifiers, vibrating alarm and waterproof sheet available.

Rates: on application.

Holiday Inn Ipswich Orwell

The Havens, Ransomes Europark, Ipswich IP3 9SJ.

☎ **01473 272244.**

@ **reservations@ipswich.kewgreen.co.uk**

●● D/G ★★★

Hotel east of town centre. Reserved parking bays. Entrance level. Low reception desk. Public rooms ground floor level. Unisex WC. Lift to all floors. Two twin bedrooms with bathrooms designed for disabled guests. Other rooms level.

Ⓟ 🚭

Rates: on application.

Lattice Lodge

499 Woodbridge Road, Ipswich IP4 4EP.

☎ **01473 712474.**

W **www.latticelodge.co.uk**

@ **info@latticelodge.co.uk**

●● D/F/G

Guest house on outskirts of town. Entrance ramp or 1 step. Dining room, lounge and conservatory level. Dooway not suitable for wheelchairs. Ground floor twin bedroom 31", ↻. Shower room 31", roll-in shower and seat, handrails, space by WC. One other bedroom on ground floor. Regular disabled guests.

Ⓟ 🚭

Rates: from £48 single, £68 twin BB (2007).

Novotel Ipswich Centre

Greyfriars, Ipswich IP1 1UP.

☎ **01473 232400.** @ **H0995@accor.com**

●● D/E/G ★★★

Town centre hotel. Entrance level, automatic doors. Public rooms level. Unisex WC. Lift to all floors. Three bedrooms designed for disabled guests with doors to adjoining rooms. Bathroom ↻, handrails, space for side transfer to bath and WC. Other bedrooms level.

Rates: on application.

LATCHINGDON, Essex

Crouch Valley Lodge

Burnham Road, Latchingdon CM3 6EX.

☎ **01621 740770.**

W www.crouchvalley.com

●● D/E/F/G ★★★

Lodge with licensed restaurant & cafe between Burnham-on-Crouch and Maldon. Ground floor level reception and restaurant. Two chalets designed for disabled guests, level 33". Shower rooms 39", ⟲, roll-in shower, handrails, space for side transfer to WC. Other units level.

Rates: from £50 double per room (2007).

LUTON, Bedfordshire

Express by Holiday Inn London Luton Airport

2 Percival Way, Luton LU2 9GB.

☎ **0870 444 8920.**

W www.hiexpressluton.co.uk

●● D/E/I/G

Hotel by airport. Reserved parking bays. Entrance level, double doors each 90cm. Low reception desk. Public rooms open plan. Unisex WC. Lift 90cm, inside 150x125cm, braille buttons, voice announcements. Four double and a family room designed for disabled guests 83cm, low level controls. Shower room 83cm, turning space, roll-in shower with seat, handrails, space by WC. Vibrating and strobe alarms. Other bedrooms level.

Rates: from £65 per room BB (2007).

Ibis Luton Airport

Spittlesea Road, Luton LU2 9NZ.

☎ **01582 424488.** @ **H1040@accor.com**

●● G

Hotel by airport. Entrance level. Public rooms level, open plan. Unisex WC. 8 bedrooms designed for disabled guests. Bathroom ⟲, handrails. Other 94 bedrooms level.

Rates: from £58-£75 per room (2008).

NEWMARKET, Suffolk

Best Western Heath Court Hotel

Moulton Road, Newmarket CB8 8DY.

☎ **01638 667171.**

W www.heathcourthotel.com

@ reservations@heathcourthotel.com

● D/E/F/G 

Town centre hotel. Parking space can be reserved. Entrance level. Public rooms level. WCs not adapted. Lift 33", inside 44"x52". Small step to all bedrooms 28", ⟲. Bathrooms 28", ⟲ in some.

Ⓟ

Rates: on application.

NORWICH, Norfolk

Beeches Hotel & Victorian Garden

2-6 Earlham Road, Norwich NR2 3DB.

☎ **01603 621167.** **W www.beeches.co.uk**

●● D/F/G

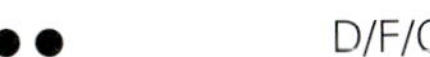

Hotel with large garden near city centre. Reserved parking bays. Entrance from car park level, 31"; main entrance 1 step. Public rooms level, min. door width 30". WCs 2 steps. Double bedroom designed for disabled guests 31". Bathroom 31", ⟲, handrails, space for side transfer to bath and WC. Other ground floor bedrooms level. Access to garden from drive.

Ⓟ

Rates: on application.

Holiday Inn Norwich

Ipswich Road, Norwich NR4 6EP.

☎ **0870 400 9060.**

@ **reservations-norwich@ihg.com**

●● D/F/G

Hotel 2 miles south of city centre. Reserved parking bays. Entrance level, automatic doors, ramps at other entrances. Main public rooms level, open plan. Unisex WC. 3 bedrooms adapted for disabled guests; neighbouring rooms for carers if required. Bathrooms 88cm, ⟲, handrails, space by bath and WC. Induction loops and sound amplifiers, vibrating alarms, Teletext TV. Other ground floor bedrooms level. Leisure club not accessible.

Rates: on application.

University of East Anglia

UEA Conferences, Norwich NR4 7TJ.

☎ **01603 593297.**

@ **guestsuite@uea.ac.uk**

●● D/G

Campus 3 miles from city centre. One bedroom with shower room adapted for disabled people, with adjacent carers room, available all year in the guest suite. Other student accommodation available during vacations with some rooms adapted for disabled people. Check specific details on booking.

Rates: from £49 singleper night BB (2007).

OULTON BROAD, Suffolk

Ivy House Country Hotel

Ivy Lane, Oulton Broad NR33 8HY.

☎ **01502 501353.**

W **www.ivyhousecountryhotel.co.uk**

●● D/E/F/G ★★★

Country hotel by Broad. Entrance level. Restaurant and lounge level. Unisex WC. Two bedrooms, double and twin, designed for disabled guests. Shower rooms 35", roll-in shower, handrails, space for side transfer to WC. Raised WC seat available. Two other level bedrooms.

Rates: from £125 double BB (2007).

PETERBOROUGH, Cambridgeshire

Express by Holiday Inn Peterborough

East of England Way, Alwalton, Peterborough PE2 6HE.

☎ **0870 720 1197.**

@ **peterborough@morethanhotels.com**

●● E/F/G

Hotel west of city centre. Reserved parking bays. Entrance level. Public rooms open plan. Unisex WC. Four bedrooms designed for disabled guests. Shower rooms ⟲, roll-in shower with seat, space for side transfer to bath and WC. Other ground floor bedrooms level.

Rates: from £39.

POTTERS BAR, Hertfordshire

Holiday Inn South Mimms

Swanland Road, South Mimms,
Potters Bar EN6 3NH.

0870 400 9072. @ southmimms@ihg.com

●● D/E/I/F/G

Hotel at M25/A1(M) junction north of London. Reserved parking bays. Entrance level, automatic door. Public rooms open plan. Unisex WCs. 4 two-person bedrooms designed for disabled guests. Bathroom 36", ⟲, handrails, bathseat, space by bath and WC. Other ground floor bedrooms level. Wheelchair, waterproof sheet, vibrating alarm, Teletext TV, large print information available.

Rates: on application.

ROLLESBY, Norfolk

Horse & Groom Hotel

Main Road, Rollesby, Great Yarmouth
NR29 5ER.

01493 740624.

@ sales@horseandgroomrollesby.co.uk

●● D/E/F/G ★★

Hotel six miles from Great Yarmouth, near Norfolk Broads. Reserved parking bays. Ramp to restaurant, bar and reception. Accommodation entrance level. Twin bedroom designed for wheelchair users 30", ⟲. Bathroom 32", handrails, space for side transfer to bath and WC. 2 other rooms may be suitable for disabled guests.

Rates: from £55 per room (2007).

SAFFRON WALDEN, Essex

Rockells Farm

Duddenhoe End,
Nr. Saffron Walden CB11 4UY.

01763 838053. W www.rockellsfarm.co.uk

● E/G

Farmhouse on Cambridgeshire/Essex border. Rear Entrance 1 step, 30". Dining room 3 steps. Lounge level. One ground floor family bedroom ⟲. Shower room 30", ⟲, space by WC. Self-catering cottages also available, see page 222.

Rates: from £25 per person BB (2007).

SANDRINGHAM, Norfolk

Park House

Sandringham, King's Lynn PE35 6EH.

01485 543000.

W www.parkhousehotel.org.uk

@ parkinfo@lcdisability.org

●●●● D/E/I/G/H

Country house hotel for disabled people and their companions run by the Leonard Cheshire Disability. Entrance level, 40". Public rooms level, min. door width 32". Games room and leisure area. Two lifts. 16 bedrooms 30", ⟲. Bathrooms ⟲, handrails. Bathroom with Arjo bath. Equipment for incontinent guests. In house 24-hour care team available. Activities and outings arranged.

Rates: on application.

SWAFFHAM, Norfolk

Corfield House

Sporle, Nr. Swaffham PE32 2EA.

☎ **01760 723636.**

www.corfieldhouse.co.uk

●● D/F/G ★★★★

Country guesthouse 3 miles from Swaffham. Conservatory entrance level, 28"; main entrance 3 steps. Dining room and lounge level. One ground floor twin bedroom 28". Bathroom 28", ⟲, space for side transfer to WC, no handrails.

Rates: from £28 BB per night (2007).

THURROCK, Essex

Ibis Thurrock

Weston Avenue, West Thurrock, Grays RM20 3JQ.

☎ **01708 686000.** @ **H2176@accor.com**

●● E/G

Suburban hotel near M25 and Lakeside Shopping Centre. 4 reserved parking bays. Entrance level, double doors each 85cm. Low reception desk. Public rooms ground floor, open plan. Unisex WC. Lift 80cm, inside 140x135cm. 5 bedrooms designed for disabled guests. Shower room 90cm, roll-in shower, handrails, space by WC. Light and vibrating alarm. Other bedrooms level.

Ⓟ

Rates: from £47-£59 per room (2008).

WALTHAM ABBEY, Essex

Waltham Abbey Marriott Hotel

Old Shire Lane, Waltham Abbey EN9 3LX.

☎ **01992 717170.**

www.marriott.com/lonwa

●● D/E/I/F/G 

Hotel near M25, junction 26. Reserved parking bays. Slope to level entrance, automatic door. Low reception and concierge desks. Public rooms ground floor. Unisex WC. Four family bedrooms designed for disabled guests. Bathrooms ⟲, handrails, space for side transfer to bath and WC. Waterproof sheet available. Other ground floor bedrooms level.

Ⓟ

Rates: on application.

WALTON-ON-THE-NAZE, Essex

Bufo Villae

31 Beatrice Road, Walton-on-the-Naze CO14 8HJ.

☎ **01255 672644.** **www.bufovillae.co.uk**

●● D/E/I/F/G 

Guesthouse facing sea. Ramp to entrance 75cm. Dining room level, 72cm. Twin bedroom level 70cm, ⟲. Shower room with roll-in shower, shower chair, handrails by WC, no space for side transfer. 2 other bedrooms upstairs. Waterproof sheet, transfer board and walking frame available.

Ⓟ ⓘ

Rates: from £25 per person BB (2007).

Radisson SAS Hotel London Stansted Airport

Waltham Close,
Stansted Airport CM24 1PP.
☎ **01279 661012.**
www.stansted.radissonsas.com
●● D/E.I/F/G

High class hotel at airport with walkway to terminal and station. Reserved parking bays. Entrance level, automatic doors. Main public rooms ground floor, open plan. Unisex WC. Lifts to all floors. 20 double rooms designed for disabled guests with roll-in shower room, no seat. Other bedrooms level. Wheelchair and waterproof sheet available.

Rates: from £125 per night (2007).

STEVENAGE, Hertfordshire

Express By Holiday Inn Stevenage

Danestrete, Stevenage SG1 1XB.
☎ **01438 344300.**
stenenage@morethanhotels.com
●● E/F/G

Limited service hotel in town centre. Reserved parking spaces. Ramp to entrance, automatic door. Low reception desk. Public rooms open plan. Unisex WC. Lift to all floors. 5 bedrooms designed for disabled guests. Shower rooms ⟲, roll-in shower with seat, handrails, space by WC. Vibrating alarms. Other bedrooms level.

Rates: from £49-£85 per room BB (2007).

Ibis Stevenage

Danestrete, Stevenage SG1 1EJ.
☎ **01438 779955.** **H2794@accor.com**
●● G

Hotel in town centre. Entrance level. Swing and revolving doors. Public rooms level, open plan. Unisex WC. One bedroom designed for disabled guests. Bathroom ⟲, handrails. Other bedrooms level.

Rates: from £37-£47 per room (2008).

Novotel Stevenage

Knebworth Park, Stevenage SG1 2AX.
☎ **01438 346100.** **H0992@accor.com**
●● D/E/I/F/G ★★★

Modern hotel. Reserved parking bays. Entrance level, automatic doors. Public rooms level, open plan. Low level payphone. Adapted cubicles in WCs. Two ground floor bedrooms designed for disabled guests. Bathrooms ⟲, handrails, space for side transfer to bath and WC. Other bedrooms level.

Rates: from £42-£95 per room (2007).

STILTON, Cambridgeshire

The Bell Inn

7 High Street, Stilton,
Peterborough PE7 3RA.
☎ **01733 241066.**
www.thebellstilton.co.uk
●● D/E/F/G ★★★

Historic coaching inn in village south of Peterborough. Reserved parking bays with level entrance to most areas; one step at front entrance to reception and bar, ramp available. Bar/bistro and lounge ground floor. Adapted WC cubicles. Bedroom in Courtyard designed for disabled guests, level, ⟲. Shower room ⟲, roll-in shower, handrails. Shower chair available. Other ground floor rooms level.

Rates: from £72.50-£129.50 per night BB (2007).

SHERINGHAM, Norfolk

Rainbow Holiday Centre Sheringham

●●●●● D/E/I/G/H

9 bed centre offering holidays, short breaks and respite care for children and adults with disabilities including those with high level needs and challenging behaviour. Lift and other adaptations and facilities for disabled people. 24 hour care. Indoor pool, soft play and sensory room. Entertainment and outings arranged. Group and emergency placements taken.

Apply: BREAK ☎ 01263 822161 (see page 19)

Rates: on application.

Sheringham Youth Hostel

1 Cremers Drift,
Sheringham NR26 8HX.

☎ **0870 7706024.**

@ **sheringham@yha.org.uk**

●● D/E/I/G ★★

Hostel in town centre. Entrance 35", level with ramp from gravel drive. Public rooms level. WCs not adapted. Three 4-bedded rooms with en suite WCs 35", ⟲, handrails space for side transfer. Ground floor bathroom ⟲, handrails, bath seat. Other ground floor bedrooms available. Induction loop in classrooms. Portable induction loop and Braille information pack available. For more information on Youth Hostels see page 34.

Rates: from £17.50 adult BB (2007).

SHOTLEY, Suffolk

Hill House Farm

Wades Lane, Shotley, nr. Ipswich IP9 1EW.

☎ **01473 787318.**

@ **hazel@wrinchfarmstay.co.uk**

●● D/F/G ★★★★

Farmhouse bed & breakfast near River Orwell estuary. Brick path from parking. Entrance level 78cm. Lounge and dining room level, min. door width 85cm. Two ground floor bedrooms in annexe, 80cm, ⟲. Shower rooms no ⟲ or space by WC, seat can be provided for shower tray. No small children.

Rates: from £30-£45 per person BB (2007).

SNETTISHAM, Norfolk

The Rose & Crown

Old Church Road, Snettisham PE31 7LX.

☎ **01485 541382.**

W **www.roseandcrownsnettisham.co.uk**

●● D/E/I/F/G ★★

Old inn in village between King's Lynn and Hunstanton. Reserved parking bays. Ramp to Garden Room entrance 30"; main entrance from street level. Lounge and restaurant level, 2 steps to bar. Unisex WC. Two ground floor bedrooms designed for disabled guests. Shower rooms 30", ⟲, roll-in shower, space by WC. A Circle hotel.

Rates: from £45-£70 per night BB (2007).

STANSTED, Essex

Express by Holiday Inn London Stansted Airport

Thremhall Avenue, Stansted CM24 1PY.

☎ **01279 680015.**

@ **admin.stansted@kewgreen.co.uk**

●● D/E/I/F/G

Limited service hotel at airport. 13 reserved parking bays. Ramp to entrance, automatic door. Low reception desk. Open plan public areas. Unisex WC. Lift to upper floors. 12 bedrooms designed for disabled guests with roll-in shower rooms. Other bedrooms level. Accessible shuttle bus to Terminal.

Rates: on application.

POTTERS BAR, Hertfordshire

Holiday Inn South Mimms

Swanland Road, South Mimms, Potters Bar EN6 3NH.

☎ **0870 400 9072.** @ **southmimms@ihg.com**

●● D/E/I/F/G

Hotel at M25/A1(M) junction north of London. Reserved parking bays. Entrance level, automatic door. Public rooms open plan. Unisex WCs. 4 two-person bedrooms designed for disabled guests. Bathroom 36", ↺, handrails, bathseat, space by bath and WC. Other ground floor bedrooms level. Wheelchair, waterproof sheet, vibrating alarm, Teletext TV, large print information available.

Ⓟ

Rates: on application.

ROLLESBY, Norfolk

Horse & Groom Hotel

Main Road, Rollesby, Great Yarmouth NR29 5ER.

☎ **01493 740624.**

@ **sales@horseandgroomrollesby.co.uk**

●● D/E/F/G ★★

Hotel six miles from Great Yarmouth, near Norfolk Broads. Reserved parking bays. Ramp to restaurant, bar and reception. Accommodation entrance level. Twin bedroom designed for wheelchair users 30", ↺. Bathroom 32", handrails, space for side transfer to bath and WC. 2 other rooms may be suitable for disabled guests.

Rates: from £55 per room (2007).

SAFFRON WALDEN, Essex

Rockells Farm

Duddenhoe End, Nr. Saffron Walden CB11 4UY.

☎ **01763 838053.** W **www.rockellsfarm.co.uk**

● E/G

Farmhouse on Cambridgeshire/Essex border. Rear Entrance 1 step, 30". Dining room 3 steps. Lounge level. One ground floor family bedroom ↺. Shower room 30", ↺, space by WC. Self-catering cottages also available, see page 222.

Rates: from £25 per person BB (2007).

SANDRINGHAM, Norfolk

Park House

Sandringham, King's Lynn PE35 6EH.

☎ **01485 543000.**

W **www.parkhousehotel.org.uk**

@ **parkinfo@lcdisability.org**

●●●● D/E/I/G/H

Country house hotel for disabled people and their companions run by the Leonard Cheshire Disability. Entrance level, 40". Public rooms level, min. door width 32". Games room and leisure area. Two lifts. 16 bedrooms 30", ↺. Bathrooms ↺, handrails. Bathroom with Arjo bath. Equipment for incontinent guests. In house 24-hour care team available. Activities and outings arranged.

Rates: on application.

WENDLING, Norfolk

Greenbanks Country Hotel & Restaurant

Wendling NR19 2AB.

Tel: 01362 687742.

www.greenbankshotel.co.uk

 D/E/I/F/G 

Small country hotel between Dereham and Swaffham. Reserved parking bays. Entrances level 76cm and 100cm. Restaurant and bar level. Unisex WC with adjustable height seat. Five ground floor suites ⟲. Three have level shower rooms 100cm sliding door, ⟲, roll in showers with seat, no handrails, space by WC. One with level shower room and threshold to shower. 4 rooms upstairs. Raised toilet seat and commode available. Hydrotherapy pool with hoist.

Rates: from £66 per person BB (2007).

WEST RUNTON, Norfolk

Links Country Park Hotel

West Runton, Cromer NR27 9QH.

☎ 01263 838383.

www.links-hotel.co.uk

 D/E/F/G 

Country hotel near north Norfolk coast. Level entrance to Reception; main entrance 3 steps. Public rooms level. Unisex WC. Lift 72cm, inside 88x114cm. Two family bedrooms ground floor 102cm. Bathrooms ⟲, handrails, space for side transfer to bath and WC. Other bedrooms level.

Rates: from £65-£80 per night BB (2007).

WISBECH, Cambridgeshire

Crown Lodge Hotel

Downham Road, Outwell,
Nr. Wisbech PE14 8SE.

☎ 01945 773391.

www.thecrownlodgehotel.co.uk

●● D/E/I/F/G ★★★★

Hotel in village between Wisbech and Downham Market. Reserved parking bays. Level entrance, automatic doors. Public rooms level. Unisex WC. Two double and one twin bedrooms designed for disabled guests. Bathrooms ⟲, handrails, space for side transfer to bath and WC. Other bedrooms level.

Rates: from £40-£60 per person BB (2007).

WOODBRIDGE, Suffolk

Grove House Hotel

39 Grove Road, Woodbridge IP12 4LG.

☎ 01394 382202.

www.thegrovehousehotel.co.uk

●● D/E/I/F/G ★★★

Small hotel on edge of town. Slope to level entrance, 36". Low reception desk. Bar and dining room level. 1 step down to lounge. Double/twin bedroom designed for disabled guests. Shower room 36" sliding door, ⟲, roll-in shower with seat, handrails, space for side transfer to WC. Other ground floor bedrooms level.

Rates: £65 twin/double per night BB (2007).

East of England

LODGE ACCOMMODATION

There are Days Inn (see page 34), Formule 1 (see page 34), Premier Travel Inn (see page 38) and Travelodge (see page 38) properties in the following areas in this region.

Baldock - Travelodge ☎ 0870 191 1505
Basildon - Premier Travel Inn ☎ 0870 197 7026
Basildon, Festival Park - Premier Travel Inn ☎ 0870 990 6598
Basildon, South - Premier Travel Inn ☎ 0870 197 7027
Bedford - Premier Travel Inn ☎ 9870 197 7030
Travelodge ☎ 01234 270793
Bedford, East - Travelodge ☎ 0870 191 1510
Bedford, South West - Travelodge ☎ 0870 191 1511
Bishops Stortford - Days Inn ☎ 01279 656477
Borehamwood - Premier Travel Inn ☎ 0870 990 6616
Braintree - Premier Travel Inn ☎ 0870 197 703
Brentwood - Travelodge ☎ 0870 191 1516
Cambridge - Travelodge ☎ 0870 191 1601
Cambridge, South - Travelodge ☎ 0870 191 1519
Cambridge, West - Travelodge ☎ 0870 191 1521
Chelmsford - Premier Travel Inn ☎ 0870 238 3310
Chelmsford, Boreham - Premier Travel Inn ☎ 0870 990 6394
Cheshunt - Travelodge ☎ 0870 085 0950
Premier Travel Inn ☎ 0870 197 7064
Colchester - Premier Travel Inn ☎ 0870 197 7065
Travelodge ☎ 0870 191 1529
Dunstable - Premier Travel Inn ☎ 0870 197 7083
Travelodge ☎ 0870 191 1527
Dunstable, South - Premier Travel Inn ☎ 0870 197 7082
Eaton Socon - Premier Travel Inn ☎ 0870 990 6314
Ely - Travelodge ☎ 0870 191 1528
Great Dunmow - Travelodge ☎ 0870 191 1913
Great Yarmouth - Travelodge ☎ 0870 191 1532
Harlow - Premier Travel Inn ☎ 0870 197 7125
Travelodge ☎ 0870 191 1789
Harwich - Premier Travel Inn ☎ 0870 850 0904
Hatfield - Premier Travel Inn ☎ 0870 197 7129
Travelodge ☎ 0870 191 1816
Haverhill - Days Inn ☎ 0870 423 088
Hemel Hempstead - Premier Travel Inn ☎ 0870 990 6622
Travelodge ☎ 0870 191 1536

Hemel Hempstead West - Premier Travel Inn ☎ 0870 238 3309
Huntingdon - Premier Travel Inn ☎ 0870 197 7139
Travelodge ☎ 0870 191 1539
Ipswich, Capel - Travelodge ☎ 0870 191 1542
Ipswich, North - Premier Travel Inn ☎ 0870 238 3311
Ipswich, South - Premier Travel Inn ☎ 0870 197 7143
Kings Langley - Premier Travel Inn ☎ 0870 990 6372
King's Lynn - Premier Travel Inn ☎ 0870 197 7149
Lolworth - Travelodge ☎ 0870 191 1546
Lowestoft - Travelodge ☎ 0870 085 0950
Luton - Premier Travel Inn ☎ 0870 197 7166
Luton Airport - Premier Travel Inn ☎ 0870 197 7166
Mildenhall - Travelodge ☎ 0870 191 1506
Needham Market - Travelodge ☎ 0870 191 1541
North Weald - Travelodge ☎ 0870 191 1533
Norwich - Premier Travel Inn ☎ 0870 990 6632
Travelodge ☎ 0870 191 1797
Norwich Airport - Premier Travel Inn ☎ 0870 197 7291
Norwich, Cringleford - Travelodge ☎ 0870 191 1704
Norwich Nelson - Premier Travel Inn ☎ 0870 850 6346
Norwich Showground - Premier Travel Inn ☎ 0870 197 7197
Norwich, South East - Premier Travel Inn ☎ 0870 197 7198
Peterborough - Premier Travel Inn ☎ 0870 197 7205
Travelodge ☎ 0870 191 1803
Peterborough A1(M) J16 - Premier Travel Inn ☎ 0870 850 6330
Peterborough, Alwalton - Travelodge ☎ 0870 191 1503
Peterborough, Eye Green - Travelodge ☎ 0870 191 1597
Peterborough, Hampton - Premier Travel Inn ☎ 0870 197 7206
Radlett - Premier Travel Inn ☎ 08760 197 7040
St Neots - Premier Travel Inn ☎ 0870 197 7238
South Mimms - Days Inn ☎ 01707 665440
Premier Travel Inn ☎ 0870 850 6326
Southend - Premier Travel Inn ☎ 0870 197 7235
Travelodge ☎ 01702 612694
Southend, Thorpe Bay - Premier Travel Inn ☎ 0870 990 6370
Stevenage - Premier Travel Inn ☎ 0870 990 6628
Stevenage North - Premier Travel Inn ☎ 0870 197 7240
Stowmarket - Travelodge ☎ 0870 191 1543
Thurrock - Formule 1 ☎ 01708 891302
Travelodge ☎ 0870 191 1715
Thurrock, East - Premier Travel Inn ☎ 0870 197 7253
Thurrock, West - Premier Travel Inn ☎ 0870 990 6490

Toddington - Travelodge ☎ 01525 876753
Tring - Premier Travel Inn ☎ 0870 197 7254
Waltham Abbey - Premier Travel Inn ☎ 0870 990 6568
Watford - Premier Travel Inn ☎ 0870 990 6620
Travelodge ☎ 0870 197 1820
Watford, Croxley Green - Premier Travel Inn ☎ 0870 850 0328
Watford, North - Premier Travel Inn ☎ 0870 197 7261
Welwyn Garden City - Premier Travel Inn ☎ 0870 197 7263

SELF-CATERING ACCOMMODATION

BELTON, Norfolk

Wild Duck Holiday Park

Howard's Common, Belton,
Great Yarmouth NR31 9NE.
☎ **01493 780268.**

●● I/F/G ★★★

Haven holiday park in woodland, inland from Great Yarmouth with range of facilities and entertainment. Caravans for 5 people adapted for disabled guests. Entrance ramp. Lounge/kitchen open plan. Two bedrooms, sliding door 75cm, ⟲ in double. Shower room 75cm, handrails, restricted ⟲, no space by WC. Open mid-March-October.

Ⓟ

Apply: Haven Holiday Reservations ☎ 0870 2422222.
Rates: on application.

BROXBOURNE, Hertfordshire

Old Mill Meadows

Mill Lane, Broxbourne

●● E/G

"Mill View" chalet designed for disabled people and sleeps up to 5. Entrance ramp, 32". Interior doors 32". Low kitchen worktops. Double and bunk bedrooms and sofa bed. Adapted WC and bathroom with seat. Specify chalet for disabled visitors when booking. Accessible boat trips available.

Ⓟ

Apply: The Manager, Lee Valley Boat Centre, Old Nazeing Road, Broxbourne EN10 6LX. ☎ 01992 462085.
Rates: from £190-£295 per week (2007).

BURGH CASTLE, Norfolk

Breydon Water Holiday Park

Burgh Castle, Great Yarmouth NR31 9QB.
☎ **01493 780357.**

●● F/G

Park Resorts Holiday park by Broads. Two static caravans designed for disabled people. Ramp to entrance, double doors. Open plan lounge/kitchen. Double bedroom 73cm, ⟲ and twin bedroom. Bathroom 84cm sliding door, seat for bath/shower, no ⟲. Ramp to clubroom and amusements. Unisex WC in general toilet area. Closed November-February.

Ⓟ

Apply: Park Resorts ☎ 0870 1299 299.
W www.park-resorts.com
Rates: on application.

Cherry Tree Holiday Park

Mill Road, Burgh Castle,
Great Yarmouth NR31 9QR.

●● F/I/G ★★★★

Holiday park on edge of Norfolk Broads with range of facilities and entertainment. Caravans for 5 people with adaptations for disabled guests. Entrance ramp. Lounge /kitchen open plan. Two bedrooms, ⟲ in double. Shower room, 75cm, handrails, restricted ⟲, no space by WC. Open late March-November.

Ⓟ

Apply: Parkdean Holidays ☎ 0871 641 2066
W www.parkdeanengland.co.uk
Rates: Holiday homes from £179 per week. Short breaks (3 or 4 nights) from £108

CAISTER, Norfolk
Caister Holiday Park
Caister-on-Sea,
Great Yarmouth NR30 5NQ.
☎ 01493 728931.

●● I/F/G ★★★★

Haven holiday park 3 miles north of Great Yarmouth with wide range of facilities and entertainment. Caravans for 5 people adapted for disabled guests. Entrance ramp. Lounge/kitchen open plan. Two bedrooms, sliding door 75cm, ⟲ in double. Shower room 75cm, handrails, restricted ⟲, no space by WC. Open Easter-October.

Ⓟ

Apply: Haven Holiday Reservations
☎ 0870 2422222.
Rates: on application.

CHEDGRAVE, Norfolk
Barn Own Holidays
Bryons Green, Big Back Lane,
Chedgrave NR14 6BH.
www.barnowlholidays.co.uk

●● G ★★★

Three cottages each for up to 6 people. Level entrances. All doors 33". Lounge with wall-bed. Kitchen controls not useable from wheelchair. Bathroom level, ⟲, handrails, roll-in shower, space by WC. Twin and double bedrooms upstairs.

Ⓟ

Apply: Rosemary Beattie.
☎ 01508 528786.
Rates: from £240-£660 per week (2007).

CLACTON-ON-SEA, Essex
Groomshill
8 Holland Road, Clacton-on-Sea

●● E/I/H

Holiday bungalow specially adapted for disabled people near town centre and sea-front. Three twin bedrooms and sofa bed. Roll-in shower. Hoist and shower chair available.

Ⓟ

Apply: Grooms Holidays
☎ 08456 584478.
@ selfcatering@johngrooms.org.uk
Rates: on application.

Scout Holiday Homes Trust Caravan
The Orchards Holiday Village, St Osyth,
Clacton-on-Sea CO16 8LJ.

●● E/F/F/G

Adapted unit for 5 adults and a small child. Ramp to entrance 30". Open plan lounge/kitchen, worktops 36". Two bedrooms, ⟲ in double. Shower room/WC 30" sliding door, handrails, space for side transfer to WC and shower seat. Veranda. Activities and entertainment on site. Available April-October.

Ⓟ

Apply: Scout Holiday Homes Trust
☎ 020 8433 7290. See page 25.
Rates: from £165-£410 per week (2007).

CLIPPESBY, Norfolk
Clippesby Hall
Clippesby, Nr. Great Yarmouth NR29 3BL.
☎ 01493 367800.
www.clippesby.com

● E/I/G ★★★★

Award winning park in Norfolk Broads. Pine lodges with ramped entrance to wide deck. Check requirements on booking. Pub, shop and cafe level or ramped. Adapted WC and shower cubicles for tourers and campers.

Ⓟ

Rates: from £375-£799 per week (2007).

Self-catering accomodation

CROMER, Norfolk

Woodhill Park

Cromer Road, East Runton,
Cromer NR27 9PX

☎ **01263 512242.**

www.woodhill-park.com

● G ★★★★

Coastal site for touring caravans and camping. Amenity block includes WC and shower designed for disabled people.

Rates: on application.

DEREHAM, Norfolk

Moor Farm Stable Cottages

Foxley, Dereham NR20 4QN.

www.moorfarmstablecottages.co.uk

●● I/F/G ★★-★★★

Two stable cottages in village between Dereham, Fakenham and Norwich. Both are level, min. door width 32". Kitchen worktops and controls may be useable from wheelchair. Single and double bedrooms. Shower room, handrails, space by WC, shower chair.

Apply: Mr & Mrs Davis ☎ 01362 688523.
Rates: on application.

DISS, Norfolk

Ivy House Farm Cottages

Wortham, Diss IP22 1RD.

☎ **01379 898395.**

www.ivyhousefarmcottages.co.uk

●● F/G ★★★★

Self-catering cottages on Norfolk/Suffolk border 3 miles from Diss. "Owl Cottage" is a purpose built chalet bungalow for disabled guests. Ramp to entrance 33". Lounge/kitchen open plan. Double bedroom ground floor with roll-in shower room, handrails, space by WC. Shower chair and bedblocks available. 2 bedrooms and bathroom upstairs. Three other cottages in "The Stables" have one step to ground floor accommodation. Premier Cottages member.

Rates: £560-£1110 per week (2007).

DUNWICH, Suffolk

Coastguard Apartments

Dunwich Heath, Nr. Saxmundham.

●● E/I/F/G

Ground floor flat adapted for disabled people near Minsmere Nature Reserve. Approach slope. Entrance level 33". Lounge/kitchen open plan, no adaptations. Twin bedroom and sofa-bed in lounge. Shower room 35", roll-in shower with seat, handrails, space for side transfer to WC, raised WC seat. Two other units available.

Apply: National Trust Holiday Booking Office ☎ 0870 4584422. See page 35.
Rates: from £243-£610 per week (2007).

EAST HARLING, Norfolk

Berwick Cottage

East Harling.

www.thelinberwicktrust.org.uk

●●● I/G/H ★★★★

Purpose-built cottage in village between Thetford and Diss for up to 6 people including 2 who are disabled. Min. door width 90cm. Lounge and kitchen level. Twin bedroom ground floor, adjustable height beds. Ceiling hoist to bathroom with adjustable height bath and basin, roll-in shower with seat, handrails and Clos-o-Mat WC. Induction loop, vibrating alarm clock, angled cutlery and other equipment available. Two bedrooms and bathroom upstairs. Accessible garden.

Apply: The Lin Berwick Trust, Eastgate House, Upper East Street, Sudbury CO10 1UB. ☎ 01787 372343.
@ info@thelinberwicktrust.org.uk
Rates: from £355-£745 per week (2009).

FAKENHAM, Norfolk
Cranmer Cottages
Home Farm, Cranmer, Fakenham NR21 9HY.
Tel: 01328 823135
www.homefarmcranmer.co.uk
●● F/G 

Two cottages in group of converted buildings north of Fakenham near Burnham Market, 7 miles from coast. Parking across road. Portable ramp available for small entrance step. Lounge/kitchen open plan. Each has two bedrooms with at least one accessible to a wheelchair user. Roll-in shower rooms with, handrails and space by WC. Raised WC seats and stool available. Shallow steps to pool. Premier Cottages member. Please request copy of access statement at time of booking.

Rates: from £350-£750 per week (2007).

FELIXSTOWE, Suffolk
Felixstowe Beach Holiday Village
Walton Avenue, Felixstowe IP11 2HA.
☎ 01394 283393.
●● I/F/G 

Holiday centre 2 miles from Felixstowe with range of facilities. Caravans for 5 people adapted for disabled guests. Entrance ramp. Lounge/kitchen open plan. Two bedrooms, sliding door 75cm, ↺ in double. Shower room 75cm, handrails, restricted ↺. Open Easter-October.

Rates: from £90-£360 per week (2007).

GISSING, Norfolk
Norfolk Cottages

Malthouse Farm, Malthouse Lane, Gissing IP22 5UT.
☎ 01379 651177.
www.norfolkcottages.net
●● I/F/G ★★★★

Three cottages, of 4, designed for disabled people in south Norfolk countryside. All have level or ramped entrance, min. 80cm. Open plan lounge/kitchen with controls useable from wheelchair. "Primrose" and "Bluebell" are single storey with a twin bedroom and a bathroom with sliding door, roll-in shower, handrails, space by bath and WC. These can be booked and linked together. "Rose" and "Honeysuckle" Cottage have one and two ground floor bedrooms and a roll-in shower room and additional bedrooms and bathroom upstairs.Leisure facilities with hoist in pool. Raised flower beds. Shower chair and some other equipment available.

Rates: from £387-£1224 per week (2007).

GREAT YARMOUTH, Norfolk
Seashore Holiday Park
North Denes, Great Yarmouth NR30 4HG.
☎ 01493 851131.
●● I/F/G ★★★

Haven holiday park at end of Great Yarmouth promenade with wide range of facilities and entertainment. Caravans for 5 people adapted for disabled guests. Entrance ramp. Lounge/kitchen open plan. Two bedrooms, sliding door 75cm, ↺ in double. Shower room 75cm, handrails, restricted ↺, no space beside WC. Open Mid March-October. For information on unit owned by voluntary organisation see below.

Apply: Haven Holiday Reservations
☎ 0870 2422222.
Rates: on application.

Scout Holiday Homes Trust Caravan
●● E/I/F/G

Adapted unit for up to 6 people. Entrance ramp 31½". Open plan lounge/kitchen. Worktops 36". Two bedrooms, ↺ in double. Shower room 30", handrails, space for side transfer to WC and shower seat. Veranda. Available April-October.
Apply: Scout Holiday Homes Trust.
☎ 020 8433 7290. See page 26.
Rates: from £170-£475 per week (2007).

HALSTEAD, Essex

Rareview Holidays

Shardlowes Farm, Gosfield,
Halstead CO9 1PZ.
☎ **01787 474696.**
www.rareviewholidays.com

●● D/E/I/F/G 

Converted farm buildings in country between Braintree and Halstead. One unit designed for disabled guests. Entrance ramp. Lounge/kitchen open plan. Family bedroom 83cm. Shower room ⭯, roll-in shower with seat, handrails, space by WC. Wheelchair, bed rails, raised WC seat and some other equipment available. Breakfast can be served to unit.

Rates: on application.

HEACHAM, Norfolk

Heacham Beach Holiday Park

South Beach Road, Heacham,
King's Lynn PE31 7BD.
☎ **01485 570270.**

 I/F/G

Park Resorts holiday park between Dersingham and Hunstanton with range of facilities and entertainment. Caravans for 5 people adapted for disabled guests. Entrance ramp. Lounge/kitchen open plan. Two bedrooms, sliding door 75cm, ⭯ in double. Shower room 75cm, handrails, restricted ⭯. Open Easter-October.

Apply: Park Resorts Reservations
☎ 08701 299299. www.park.resorts.com
Rates: on application.

HERTFORD, Hertfordshire

Petasfield Cottages

Mangrove Lane, Hertford SG13 8QQ.
☎ **01992 504201.**
www.petasfieldcottages.co.uk

●● F/G/H 

Four ground floor cottages on rural riding centre south of Hertford. All have level or ramped entrance. Doors 30". Lounge with double sofabed, kitchen/dining room, twin/double bedroom and roll-in shower room with handrails, space by WC and under basin, all ⭯. One has adjustable height sink and hob in kitchen. Shower chair, bed blocks, raised WC seat, wheelchair and walking frame available. Hoist installed in one unit. Other equipment can be hired locally. Large print information. Teletext TV. Carriage driving can be arranged.

Rates: from £300-£450 per week (2007).

HORNING, Norfolk

Eagle Cottage

Ferry Road, Horning.

●● F 

House fronting onto River Bure, sleeping up to 9 people. Ramp to patio door and a two bedroom annexe designed for disabled guests with a roll-in shower room. One of the 3 bedrooms in the main cottage is on the ground floor. Wheelchair available. Leisure centre and inn nearby. A day cruiser that can carry wheelchair users can be hired.

Apply: King Line Cottages, Ferry Road, Horning, Norwich NR12 8SP.
☎ 01692 630297.
www.norfolk-broads.co.uk
Rates: from £882-£1735 per week (2007).

Hall Farm Cottages

Hall Farm, Horning, Norwich NR12 8NJ.

☎ **01692 630385.** 🅆 **www.hallfarm.com**

●● I/F/G ★★★★

Eight cottages in Norfolk Broads. Entrance 33" level or 48" french window from terrace. Lounge/kitchen open plan. Double/twin bedroom level ⟲. En suite shower room ⟲, roll-in shower with seat, handrails, space for side transfer to WC. Raised WC seat and some other equipment available. 2 or 3 bedrooms and bathroom upstairs. Teletext TV.

Rates: from £225-£692 per week (2007).

King Line Cottages

Ferry Road, Horning, Norwich NR12 8PS.

☎ **01692 630297.**

🅆 **www.norfolk-broads.co.uk**

●● F ★★★

Horning Lodges are a group of chalets by River Bure. Four designed for disabled people, sleeping 4 and 6. Ramp with handrails to entrances, double doors. Internal doors 33". Lounges and kitchens ⟲. Bath or shower rooms have roll-in showers, handrail and space for side transfer in two units. A further unit, "Lady Lodge", has ground floor accommodation and a shower room designed for wheelchair users. Raised WC seat and wheelchairs available. Leisure centre and inn nearby. A day cruiser that can carry wheelchair users can be hired.

Rates: from £280-£923 per week (2007).

HORSEY, Norfolk

Horsey Barns

The Street, Horsey.

●● F/G

One cottage, of three, in National Trust barn conversion near Norfolk Broads. Entrance level from paved path. Open plan lounge/kitchen. Double and single bedroom. Shower room/WC. All level.

Apply: National Trust Holiday Booking Office ☎ 0870 4584422. See page 33.

Rates: from £281-£772 per week (2007).

HOVETON, Norfolk

Broomhill

Station Road, Hoveton, Nr. Wroxham.

●● E/I/H

Two self-contained flats by Wroxham Broad, owned by Grooms Holidays, designed for wheelchair users. One on ground floor, the other has lift access to 1st floor. Each has double, twin and bunk bedrooms and sofabed and a roll-in shower. Shower chair and hoist available. Flats can be booked separately or together.

Apply: Grooms Holidays

☎ 08456 584478.

@ selfcatering@johngrooms.org.uk

Rates: on application.

IPSWICH, Suffolk
Damerons Farm Holidays

Damerons Farm, Main Road, Henley, Ipswich IP6 0RU.
☎ **01473 832454.**
www.dameronsfarmholidays.co.uk

  I/F/G 

"The Old Dairy" cottage designed for disabled people on farm in country north of Ipswich. Entrance level entrance. Open plan lounge/kitchen, controls useable from wheelchair with adjustable hob and sink. Twin bedroom and sofabed in lounge. Shower room ⟲, roll-in shower with seat, handrails, space by WC, raised WC seat available. Teletext TV and portable induction loop available. 4 other cottages, one with all ground floor accommodation but an entrance step.

Rates: from £255-£365 per week (2007).

LOWESTOFT, Suffolk
Four Winds Retreat

Holly Grange Road, Kessingland Beach, Nr. Lowestoft NR33 7RR.

  I/F/G ★★★★

Purpose built, spacious single storey annexe to owners' house on edge of coastal village. Entrances level, min. 90cm. Open plan lounge/kitchen, controls useable from wheelchair. Double and twin bedrooms. Shower room 84cm, ⟲, roll-in shower with seat, handrails, space by WC and under basin. Raised WC seat, wheelchair and alarm system available. List of care agencies can be supplied.

Apply: Mr & Mrs Garner.
☎ 01502 740044.
info@four-winds-retreat.co.uk
Rates: from £340-£420 per week (2007).

Kessingland Beach Holiday Park

Nr. Lowestoft NR33 7RN.
☎ **01502 740636.**

●●  I/F/G 

Park Resorts holiday park on coast south of Lowestoft with range of facilities and entertainment. Caravans for 5 people adapted for disabled guests. Entrance ramp. Lounge/kitchen open plan. Two bedrooms, sliding door 75cm, ⟲ in double. Shower room 75cm, handrails, restricted ⟲. Open Easter-October.

Apply: Park Resorts Reservations
☎ 08701 299299.
www.park-resorts.com
Rates: on application.

MERSEA ISLAND, Essex
Waldegraves, Holiday Park

Mersea Island, Colchester CO5 8SE.
☎ **01206 382898.**
www.waldegraves.co.uk.

●● I/F/G 

Small rural holiday park on coast with a caravan adapted for disabled people. Ramp with handrails to entrance. Sliding door 72cm to open plan lounge/kitchen. Double and single bedrooms. Shower room 70cm sliding door, ⟲, roll in shower with seat, handrails. Restaurant and shop level. Closed December-February.

Rates: from £220-£450 per week (2007).

NAYLAND, Suffolk

Gladwins Farm

Harper's Hill, Nayland,
Nr. Colchester CO6 4NU.
☎ **01206 262261.**
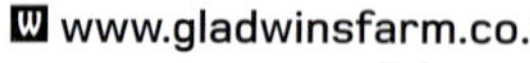
www.gladwinsfarm.co.uk

●● F/G ★★★★★

Two cottages, for 6 and 8 people, designed for disabled guests in south Suffolk. Ramps to level entrances. Doors 90cm. Lounge and kitchen ⭯, controls useable from wheelchair. Twin bedrooms on ground floor. Bathroom with handrails. Other bedrooms upstairs.

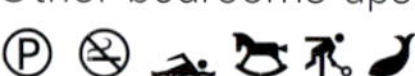

Rates: from £755-£1975 per week (2007).

NORWICH, Norfolk

Spixworth Hall Cottages

Grange Farm, Buxton Road, Spixworth, Norwich NR10 3PR.
☎ **01603 898190.**
www.hallcottages.co.uk
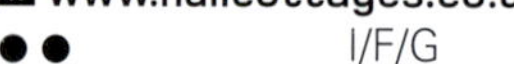
●● I/F/G ★★★★

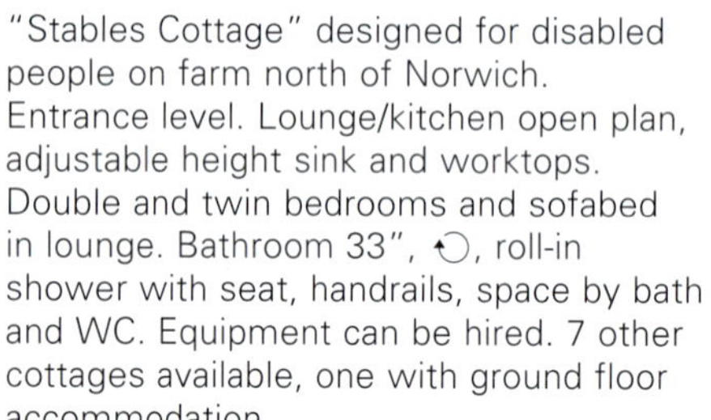

"Stables Cottage" designed for disabled people on farm north of Norwich. Entrance level. Lounge/kitchen open plan, adjustable height sink and worktops. Double and twin bedrooms and sofabed in lounge. Bathroom 33", ⭯, roll-in shower with seat, handrails, space by bath and WC. Equipment can be hired. 7 other cottages available, one with ground floor accommodation.

Rates: from £245-£470 per week (2007).

OTLEY, Suffolk

Blacksmiths Cottage

Hall Farm, Otley, Nr. Ipswich.

●● I/F/G

Cottage for 3 adults on farm north of Ipswich. Entrance level 90cm. Lounge/kitchen open plan. Double bedroom ⭯. Shower room ⭯, roll-in shower, shower chair, handrails, space for side transfer to WC. Single bedroom upstairs. Owner a nurse.

Apply: Mrs T Holmes, Tithe Barn, Hall Lane, Otley, Ipswich IP6 9PA.
☎ 01473 890766.
@ tessa.holmes@virgin.net
Rates: £190-£370 per week (2007).

SAFFRON WALDEN, Essex

Fishermans Lodge

Rockells Farm, Duddenhoe End, nr. Saffron Walden CB11 4UY.
●● F/G

2 lodges overlooking fishing lake on farm south of Cambridge. Ramp to entrance. All doors 82 cm. Living room/kitchen open plan. Double and twin bedrooms. One unit has roll-in shower room, the other a bathroom: each ⭯, space by WC. Bed & breakfast in farmhouse, see page 207.

Apply: Mrs Westerhuis ☎ 01763 838053.
Rates: from £250-£500 per week (2007).

ST IVES, Cambridgeshire

The Raptor Foundation

The Heath, St Ives Road, Woodhurst, Cambridgeshire PE28 3BT.

☎ **01487 741140.**

www.raptorfoundation.org.uk

●● I/F

5 ground floor units for up to 5 couples at Bird of Prey centre near St Ives and east of Huntingdon. One designed for disabled guests. Ramp on approach to level entrance. Twin/double bedroom and double sofa bed. Shower room with roll-in shower and seat. Space by WC and under basin. Teletext TV. Restaurant and other public areas of centre accessible.

Rates: from £40 per night (2007).

SANDY, Bedfordshire

Highfield Farm

Highfield Farm, Tempsford Road, Sandy SG19 2AQ.

www.highfield-farm.co.uk

●● G ★★★★

2 cottages designed for disabled guests on farm north of Sandy. Ramp to entrance, 90cm. Double door to open plan lounge/kitchen, some low worktops, controls useable from wheelchair. Double bedroom designed for disabled guests with shower room 90 cm, ↻, roll-in shower with adjustable seat, handrails, space by WC and under basin. Teletext TV. 'Acorn' has 3 other bedrooms and bathrooms and 'Ash' has one. Additional units and also bed and breakfast available in the farmhouse with ground floor bedrooms.

Apply: Margaret Codd ☎ 01767 682332.
Rates: from £450-£900 per week (2007).

SAXMUNDHAM, Suffolk

Rose Farm Barns

Middleton, Nr. Saxmundham.

● ★★★★

Cottages near coast. "Stable Cottage", entrance 2 steps, has ground floor accommodation for 2 people, wide doors and a roll-in shower room.

Apply: Sandra Dean, Rose Farm Barns, Mill Street, Middleton, Saxmundham IP17 3NG. ☎ 01728 648456.
Rates: from £250-£420 per week (2007).

SCRATBY, Norfolk

California Cliffs Holiday Park

Rottenstone Lane, Scratby, Great Yarmouth NR29 3QU.

☎ **01493 730584.**

●● I/F/G ★★★

Park Resorts holiday park 5 miles north of Great Yarmouth with range of facilities and entertainment. Caravans for 5 people adapted for disabled guests. Entrance ramp. Lounge/kitchen open plan. Two bedrooms, sliding door 75cm, ↻ in double. Shower room 75cm, handrails, restricted ↻. Open Easter-October.

Apply: Park Resorts Reservations ☎ 08701 299299. www.park-resorts.com
Rates: on application.

SIZEWELL, Suffolk

Wardens

Ness House, Sizewell IP16 4UB.

☎ **01728 830007.**

wardeneil@explorer.co.uk

●●

Camp site in 4-acre site on coast for supervised parties of up to 30. Recreation hall with 2 unisex WCs, shower and kitchen with adaptations for disabled people. Residential bunk bed accommodation for 12 people with 2 showers designed for disabled people and 4 WCs. A self-catering one bedroom flat with a double and a single adjustable bed is also available. Owned by a registered charity.

Rates: on application.

SNETTISHAM, Norfolk

Orangery Lodge

Snettisham, nr. Hunstanton.

●● F/G

Single storey accommodation in style of a Georgian Orangery in grounds of country house 5 miles from Hunstanton. Level entrance. Double and bunk bed-rooms. Shower room with roll-in shower. Patio garden.

Apply: Norfolk Country Cottages.

☎ 01603 871872 (see page 194).

Rates: on application.

WELLS-NEXT-THE-SEA, Norfolk

YHA Wells-next-the Sea

Church Plain,

Wells-next-the-Sea NR23 1EQ.

☎ **0870 770 6084.**

wellsnorfolk@yha.org.uk

●● E/F/G ★★★★

Self-catering hostel in coastal town. Reserved parking bay. Entrance level, double doors. Public rooms ground floor. Members' kitchen with low level hob and controls useable from wheelchair. Unisex WC. Ground floor bedroom designed for disabled guests. Own roll-in shower room, handrails, shower seat. Braille signs. Open Easter-mid November. For further information on Youth Hostels, see page 34.

Rates: from £20 per night (2007).

The Heart of England region comprises Herefordshire, Shropshire, Staffordshire, Warwickshire, West Midlands and Worcestershire. It is an area that combines a major urban centre, a rich historic and industrial heritage and some of England's most typical and unspoilt countryside.

The rivers Severn and Wye flow through Shropshire, Worcestershire and Herefordshire on the Welsh border. Fruit blossom attracts visitors to the Vale of Evesham in the spring. To the north, Staffordshire shares the Peak District with its neighbouring counties.

Birmingham, the country's second largest city, provides the full range of urban attractions and has more miles of canals than Venice. Recent developments in the city centre include a concert hall and the National Indoor Sports Centre and a rebuilt shopping area around the Bullring. There is also a wide range of museums, shops, parks, sporting venues and other activities. Outside the city centre the National Exhibition Centre and Arena hosts a full programme of concerts, exhibitions and other events.

Spirit of Enterprise and forward sculpture, Birmingham

Ironbridge in Shropshire, the birthplace of the Industrial Revolution, is a World Heritage Site supporting a cluster of museums that are largely accessible. The Black Country Museum at Dudley is a large open-air site depicting life and industry in the area. The pottery industry can be explored at visitor centres and factory shops in Stoke-on-Trent and Worcester.

Photo: britainonview.com

Heart of England

Shrewsbury, Shropshire

The canal docks have been refurbished in Gloucester and, in Birmingham, a late 19th century jewellery factory has been recreated as the Jewellery Quarter Discovery Centre. The development of the motor industry can be experienced at the Heritage Motor Centre near Warwick and the Museum of British Road Transport in Coventry. For other tastes there are museums devoted to beer in Burton-on-Trent and cider in Hereford, Cadbury World in Birmingham and Vegetable Kingdom at the Ryton Organic Gardens near Coventry.

The literary and artistic heritage of the area is considerable. Pride of place must go to Stratford-upon-Avon, birthplace of William Shakespeare, where the Shakespeare centre is accessible. The hills of Shropshire and Worcestershire were immortalised by A E Houseman. Other notables include Dr Johnson from Lichfield, George Elliot from Nuneaton and Edward Elgar from Worcester.

At Britain's first major theme park, Alton Towers in Staffordshire, the grounds and many of the attractions are accessible and help can be provided in getting onto rides. Dedicated holiday shoppers can visit the Merryhill Centre near Dudley.

Photo: www.britainonview.com

USEFUL ADDRESSES

DIAL

DIAL offers a free, impartial and confidential service of information and advice by telephone to disabled people, their relatives and professionals. The following DIAL UK members may be able to help disabled residents and visitors in their areas:

Liseux Trust Birmingham
☎ 0121 382 6660;
Textphone: 0121 350 8182

ABLE Herefordshire ☎ 01432 277770

DIAL North Worcestershire
☎ 0800 970 7202; Textphone: 01562 68248

DIAL Nuneaton & Bedworth
☎ 024 7634 9954

CARES Sandwell
☎/Textphone: 0121 558 7003

A4U
☎ 0845 602 5561

DIAL Solihull
☎/Textphone: 0121 770 0333

DIAL South Worcestershire
☎ 01905 27790; Textphone: 01905 22191

Disability Solutions, Stoke
☎ 01782 683100; Textphone: 01782 683804

Walsall DIAL ☎ 01922 635588

CDP Warwickshire & Coventry
☎/Textphone: 01926 889349

USEFUL PUBLICATIONS & WEBSITES

Getting Around Acess Guide – a guide to accessible public transport in the West Midlands PTA area. It also lists public toilets for disabled people in the area and other useful information. A new edition is published each April and includes information on the accessible Midland Metro light rail service between Birmingham and Wolverhampton. Available in standard or large print, Braille or on tape or CD from CENTRO Customer Relations, 16 Summer Lane, Birmingham B19 3SD. ☎ 0121 214 7214.
@ customerrelations@centro.org.uk
W www.centro.org.uk

Access in Ludlow, prepared by the South Shropshire Access Group, is available from the Ludlow Tourist Information Centre ☎ 01584 875053. It can also be downloaded from W www.ludlow.org.uk

Wheelchair User's Guide to Accessible Tourist Attractions and Accomodation for Shropshire (re-published late 2006).
Wheelchair User's Guide to Accessible Countryside Sites & Trails in Shropshire & the Borderlands (2007/8) and **Wheelchair User's Guide to Accessible Activities in & around Shropshire** (new edition for 2008/9) - all researched by a wheelchair user. Send an A5 addressed envelope with a first class stamp for each title to Disabled Holiday Information, PO Box 185, Oswestry SY10 1AF. They can be downloaded with other information from W www.disabledholidayinfo.org.uk

www.stratford-upon-avon.co.uk - quite detailed information on access at tourist attractions and other facilities is given on this site.

www.disabledgo.info - this website includes detailed information on the accessibility of many premises in Burton-on-Trent, Solihull, Stoke-on-trent and Wolverhampton.

EQUIPMENT HIRE

Birmingham Shopmobility

Snow Hill Railway Station, 7 Colmore Row, Birmingham B3 2BJ.

☎/Textphone: 0121 236 8980.

@ shopmobs@freeuk.com

Manual wheelchairs are available for weekly hire by both visitors and locals. Proof of ID and address are required. Contact above for booking and other details. There is also a Shopmobility scheme based in the Bullring in Birmingham.

Burton-upon-Trent Shopmobility

Unit 35a Octagon Shopping Centre, Park Street, Burton-upon-Trent DE14 3TN.

☎ 01283 210770.

@ administrator@burtonshopmobility.freeserve.co.uk

In addition to a regular Shopmobility service, the Shopmobility Extended Loan Scheme (Sh.els) can hire smaller scooters, electric and manual wheelchairs and some other items of equipment. This is available to East Staffordshire residents and people visiting the area. People have to register with proof of ID.

DIAL

DIAL Nuneaton & Bedworth, New Ramsden Centre, School Walk, Attleborough, Nuneaton CV11 4PJ.

☎ 024 7634 9954.

In addition to their information service they run a short-term wheelchair loan service, with a small refundable deposit, for periods of up to 6 weeks. There is a 15 stone weight limit.

Evesham Riverside Shopmobility

Top Level Multi-Storey Car Park, Bridge Street, Evesham WR11 4RY.

☎ 01386 49230.

@ shopmobilityeva@aol.com

In addition to a regular Shopmobility service, people on holiday in the Evesham area can hire manual wheelchairs on a weekly basis. Both manual wheelchairs and lightweight folding scooters are available for local residents to take on holiday whether in Britain or abroad.

Leamington Spa Shopmobility

Level 4, Royal Priors Car Park, Park Street, Leamington Spa CV32 4XT.

☎ 01926 470450.

@ info@leamingtonshopmobility.org.uk

Long term hire of mobility equipment is available to members and disabled people visiting the area can join at no cost although should produce two pieces of address identification.

Shrewsbury Shopmobility

Raven Meadows MSCP, Shrewsbury SY1 1PL.

☎ 01743 236900.

@ shopmobshrews@freeuk.com

A Home Loan Service is available to visitors to the area and residents for holiday use. Manual wheelchairs and scooters that can be carried in the boot of a car are available.

Stratford Shopmobility

Level 2, Bridgefoot Car Park, Stratford upon Avon CV37 6YY.

☎ 01789 414534.

@ shop.mobility@stratford-dc.gov.uk

Manual wheelchairs and powered scooters can be hired to residents for holidays and to visitors. In addition scooters and power chairs can be delivered to hotels with suitable access in the town.

Walsall Shopmobility

☎ **01922 613959.**

@ **wallsallshopmobility@btopenworld.com**

Manual and powered wheelchairs and scooters can be hired by visitors to the area and Walsall residents for holiday use in Britain and Europe. A membership form can be sent by post or fax.

Wolverhampton Shopmobility

12 Cleveland Street,
Wolverhampton WV1 3HH.

☎ **01902 556021.**

@ **Shopmobility.wmbc@dial.pipex.com**

Manual wheelchairs are available for up to 3 weeks on holiday loan to residents and disabled people visiting the area. Proof of identity is required and also details of holiday or household insurance.

Worcester Shopmobility

54 Friary Walk, Crowngate Centre,
Worcester WR1 3LE.

☎ **01905 610523.**

@ **shopmoworcs@aol.com**

As well as a regular Shopmobility service, they can hire travel scooters to members and manual wheelchairs to both members and visitors on a daily rate for to use in the UK.

Shopmobility schemes exist to provide wheelchairs and/or scooters for use in shopping centres in the following towns. For information on availability etc telephone in advance.

Birmingham
☎/Textphone: 0121 236 8980

Birmingham Bullring ☎ 0121 616 2942

Bromsgrove ☎ 01527 837736

Burton-on-Trent ☎ 01283 515191

Coventry ☎ 024 7683 2020

Evesham ☎ 01386 49230

Hereford ☎ 01432 342166

Leamington Spa ☎ 01926 470450

Ledbury ☎ 01531 636001

Leominster ☎ 01568 616755

Lichfield ☎ 01543 308999

Nuneaton ☎ 024 7632 5908

Oswestry ☎ 01691 656882

Redditch ☎ 01527 63271

Shrewsbury ☎ 01743 236900

Solihull ☎ 0121 704 0380

Stafford ☎ 01785 619456

Stoke-on-Trent ☎ 01782 233333;
Textphone: 01782 236919

Stratford-on-Avon ☎ 01789 414534

Sutton Coldfield ☎ 0121 355 1112

Tamworth ☎ 01827 709392

Telford ☎ 01952 238005

Walsall ☎ 01922 613959

West Bromwich ☎ 0121 553 1943

Wolverhampton ☎ 01902 556021

Worcester ☎ 01905 610523

Heart of England

ACCOMMODATION WITH MEALS

ABBERLEY, Worcestershire

The Manor Arms Inn

Netherton Lane, Abberley WR6 6BN.
☎ 01299 896507.
www.themanorarms.co.uk
● D/E/F/G

Inn in village between Tenbury Wells and Worcester. Reserved parking bay. Level entrance from car park. Restaurant and lounge bar level. Unisex WC, no space for side transfer. Single and two twin bedrooms on ground floor. Bathrooms not suitable for wheelchair users. Terrace level, steps to lawn.

Rates: from £55-£70 per room BB (2007).

BIRMINGHAM, West Midlands

Campanile Birmingham

Chester Street, Aston,
Birmingham B6 4BE.
☎ 0121 359 3330.
@ birmingham@campanile.com

Hotel off ring road near city centre. Reserved parking bays. Public rooms level. Unisex WC. 5 twin bedrooms designed for disabled guests. Bathroom, handrails, space for side transfer. Other ground floor bedrooms level. See page 31.

Rates: on application.

City Inn Birmingham

Brunswick Square, Brindleyplace,
Birmingham B1 2HW.
☎ 0121 643 1003.
@ birmingham.reservations@cityinn.com
●● D/E/F/G

City centre hotel. Reserved parking bays. Level entrance, automatic and revolving doors. Low reception desk. Public rooms level. Unisex WC. Lift to all floors. 14 double bedrooms designed for disabled guests. Shower rooms with roll-in shower and seat, handrails, space by WC. Other bedrooms level.

Rates: on application.

Copthorne Hotel Birmingham

Paradise Circus, Birmingham B3 3HJ.
☎ 0121 200 2727.
@ reservations.birmingham@mill-cop.com
●● D/G/P ★★★★

City centre hotel. Limited parking. Entrance level, automatic doors. Public rooms level or ramp. Unisex WC. Lift 43″, inside 59″x76″. One bedroom designed for disabled guests 27″, handrails, space for side transfer to WC. Other bedrooms level.

Rates: on application.

Crowne Plaza Birmingham

Central Square, Birmingham B1 1HH.
☎ 0870 400 9150
●● D/E/G ★★★★

High class city centre hotel. Entrance level, revolving and swing doors. Public rooms level. Large lifts. Six bedrooms with adaptations for disabled guests. Other bedrooms level with large bathrooms.

Rates: on application.

Express by Holiday Inn Birmingham City Centre

65 Lionel Street, Birmingham B3 1JE.
☎ **0845 112 6151.**
@ **ebhi.bhamcc@mbplc.com**
●● E/F/G

Limited service hotel in city centre. Reserved parking spaces. Ramp or 10 steps to entrance, automatic door. Low reception desk. Open plan public rooms. Unisex WC. Lift to upper floors. 8 double bedrooms designed for disabled guests. Shower room 93cm, ⟲, roll-in shower with seat, handrails, space by WC. Other bedrooms level. Vibrating alarm.

Rates: from £62-£95 per room BB (2007).

Holiday Inn Birmingham City Centre

Smallbrook Queensway, Birmingham B5 4EW.
☎ **0870 400 9008.**
@ **reservations- birminghamcity@ihg.com**
●● D/E/I/F/G ★★★

Hotel in city centre. Reserved bays in adjoining car park. Entrance level, automatic and swing doors. Public rooms and unisex WC level from lifts 160cm, inside 184x120cm. 2 bedrooms adapted for disabled guests, connect to neighbouring rooms if required. Bathroom ⟲, handrails, space by bath and WC. Other bedrooms level. Teletext TV and vibrating alarms.

Rates: on application.

Holiday Inn Birmingham M6 Junction 7

Chapel Lane, Great Barr, Birmingham B43 7BG.
☎ **0870 400 9009.**
@ **birminghamgreatbarr@ihg.com**
●● D/E/I/F

Hotel by M6 north west of Birmingham. Reserved parking bays. Entrance level, automatic doors. Public rooms ground floor, open plan. Unisex WC. Four twin/double bedrooms designed for disabled guests. Bathrooms have ⟲ and space by WC and bath. Other ground floor bedrooms level.

Rates: on application.

Ibis Birmingham Bordesley Circus

1 Bordesley Park Road, Birmingham B10 0PD.
☎ **0121 506 2600.** @ **H2178@accor.com**
●● D/E/G

Hotel east of city centre off A45. Entrance level. Public rooms open plan. Unisex WC. Lift to upper floors. 6 bedrooms with bathrooms designed for disabled guests. Other bedrooms level.

Rates: from £59 per room (2008).

Ibis Birmingham City Centre

Arcadian Centre, Ladywell Walk, Birmingham B5 4ST.
☎ **0121 622 6010.** @ **H1459@accor.com**
●● D/E/G

City centre hotel. Entrance level, automatic doors. Public rooms on Ground floor open plan. Unisex WC. Lift 30", inside 42"x55". Four double bedrooms designed for disabled guests 37", ⟲. Shower rooms 37", ⟲, roll-in shower and seat, handrails, space for side transfer to WC. Other 155 bedrooms level.

Rates: from 60 per room (2008).

Ibis Birmingham Holloway Circus

55 Irving Street, Birmingham B1 1DH.
☎ 0121 622 4925. @ H2092@accor.com
●● D/E/G
Hotel south of city centre off A38. Entrance level. Public rooms open plan. Unisex WC. Lift to upper floors. Two bedrooms with bathrooms designed for disabled guests. Other bedrooms level.
Rates: from £52 per room (2008).

Jurys Inn Birmingham

245 Broad Street, Birmingham B1 2HQ.
☎ 0121 626 0626.
@ jurysinnbirmingham@jurysdoyle.com
●● D/E/I/F/G ★★★
City centre hotel. 2 reserved parking bays by rear entrance. Ramp or 4 steps at main entrance. Steps to reception desk; guest services area level. Public areas on upper ground floor level, open plan. Adapted cubicles in WCs. Lift 110cm, inside 190x120cm. 22 bedrooms designed for disabled guests 103cm, ⟲, interconnect with adjoining room. Bathrooms 93cm, ⟲, handrails, space by WC. Other bedrooms level.
Rates: from £69 per room (2007).

Novotel Birmingham Centre

70 Broad Street, Birmingham B1 2HT.
☎ 0121 643 2000. @ H1077@accor.com
●● D/E/I/G ★★★
Modern city centre hotel. Underground car park. Entrance level, automatic doors. Induction loop at reception and bar. Public rooms level, open plan. Unisex WC. Lift to all floors. Four bedrooms designed for disabled guests with bathroom ⟲. Other bedrooms level. Portable induction loop and vibrating pillow available.
Rates: on application.

Radisson SAS Hotel Birmingham

12 Holloway Circus, Queensway, Birmingham B1 1BT.
☎ 0121 654 6000.
@ info.birmingham@radissonsas.com
●● D/E/F/G
High class hotel in city centre. Entrance level, automatic door. Low reception desk. Public rooms ground and 1st floors. Low service counter in bars. Unisex WCs. Lifts 108cm, inside 157x151cxm. 11 double bedrooms designed for disabled guests, 80cm, low clothes rail. Ramp to shower room ⟲, roll-in shower with seat, handrails, space by WC. Other rooms level, some interconnect. Large print menus. Vibrating alarms.
Rates: on application.

BIRMINGHAM AIRPORT & NEC, West Midlands

Crowne Plaza Birmingham NEC

CROWNE PLAZA HOTELS & RESORTS

Pendigo Way, National Exhibition Centre, Birmingham B40 1PS.
☎ 0870 400 9160.
W www.necsales@ihg.com
●● D/E/I/F/G ★★★★
High class hotel by NEC and close to Birmingham Airport. 8 designated parking bays. Entrance level. Lounge and bar open plan on ground floor. Restaurant lower ground floor. Unisex WCs on ground and lower ground floors. Lifts 110cm, inside 136x130cm, Brailled buttons. 12 double bedrooms designed for disabled guests. Bathrooms 90cm, turning space, handrails, space by bath and WC. Bath seats available. Other bedrooms level. Interconnecting rooms available.
Rates: from £69 per night (2007).

Express by Holiday Inn Birmingham NEC

Bickenhill Parkway B40 1QA.

☎ **0870 720 2297.**

@ **Birmingham@morethanhotels.com**

●● E/I/F/G

Limited service hotel between NEC and M42 J6. Reserved parking bays. Entrance level, automatic door. Low reception desk. Public rooms open plan. Unisex WC. Lift to upper floors. 10 bedrooms designed for disabled people. Shower rooms 32½", ⟲, roll-in shower with seat, handrails, space by WC. Other bedrooms level. Restaurant adjoining.

Rates: on application.

Hilton Birmingham Metropole National Exhibition Centre

Birmingham B40 1PP.

☎ **0121 780 4242.**

W **www.hilton.co.uk/birminghammet**

●● D/E/I/F/G

Large, high class large hotel and conference centre. Reserved parking bays. Entrance level, automatic revolving door. Public rooms open plan, level except ramp to bar. Unisex WCs. Lifts 105cm, inside 160x160cm. 20 double bedrooms adapted for disabled guests, remote control door, connection to adjoining room. Shower room 70cm, ⟲, roll in shower, handrails, space for side transfer to WC. Other bedrooms level. Waterproof sheet, shower chair and wheelchairs available.

Rates: on application.

Novotel Birmingham Airport

Birmingham International Airport, Birmingham B26 3QL.

☎ **0121 782 4111.** @ **H1158@accor.com**

●● D/G ★★★

Hotel close to Airport Terminal. Parking at surrounding airport car parks. Entrance level. Public rooms level, open plan. Unisex WC. Lift to all floors. Six bedrooms designed for disabled guests. Bathrooms ⟲, handrails, space for side transfer to bath and WC. 4 other accessible bedrooms and all level.

Rates: from £75 per night single (2007).

BISHOPS CASTLE, Shropshire

Boars Head Hotel

Church Street, Bishops Castle SY9 5AE.

☎ **01588 638521.**

W **www.boarsheadhotel.co.uk**

● D/E/G

Inn in small country town. Rear entrance level. Public rooms ground floor, 1 step in bar. Unisex WC. Two twin bedrooms in annexe, 1 step. Bathrooms level, no adaptations.

Rates: from £30-£40 per person BB (2007).

BRANDON, Warwickshire

Mercure Brandon Hall Hotel

Main Street, Brandon, Coventry CV8 3FW.

☎ **024 7654 6000.** @ **H6625@accor.com**

● D/E/I/F/G

Country house hotel east of Coventry. Reserved parking bays. Ramp at Restaurant entrance; small step at front door and then 3 steps to Reception. Three steps internal steps to restaurant. Four steps to Bar, Lounge and toilets. Lift 31", inside 43"x57". Four bedrooms, 2 on ground floor, 2 in annexe, designed for disabled guests. Bathrooms 33", level.

Rates: from £55 per person BB (2008).

BROMSGROVE, Worcestershire

Hilton Bromsgrove Hotel

Birmingham Road, Bromsgrove B61 0JB.
☎ **0121 447 7888.**
www.hilton.co.uk/bromsgrove
●● D/F/G ★★★★

Modern hotel. Main entrance level from car park. Public rooms level except ramp to bar. Unisex WC. Three bedrooms adapted for disabled guests with flashing alarms. Bathrooms ⟲, handrails, space under basin and by bath and WC.

Rates: on application.

BURTON-ON-TRENT, Staffordshire

Express by Holiday Inn Burton-Upon-Trent

2nd Avenue, Centrum 100, Burton-on-Trent DE14 2WF.
☎ **01283 504300.**
@ **info@exhiburton.co.uk**
●● E/I/F/G

Limited service hotel between town centre and A38. 7 reserved parking spaces. Entrance level, double doors. Public rooms ground floor level. Unisex WC. Lift 36", inside 42"x60". Five double bedrooms designed for disabled guests. Shower room ⟲, roll-in shower with seat, handrails, space for side transfer to WC. Other bedrooms level. Vibrating and light alarms available. Evening meals can be delivered.

Rates: from £55 per room weekends BB (2007).

CASTLE BROMWICH, West Midlands

Express by Holiday Inn Castle Bromwich

1200 Chester Road, Castle Bromwich, Birmingham B35 7AJ.
☎ **0121 747 6633.** @ **castlebromwich@holidayinnexpress.co.uk**
●● D/E/I/F/G

Limited service hotel 5 miles east of central Birmingham near M6 Junction 5. Reserved parking bays. Slope to level entrance. Low reception desk. Public rooms open plan. Unisex WC. Lift to upper floors. 3 bedrooms designed for disabled guests one with roll-in shower room. Other bedrooms level. Induction loop and large print information sheet.

Rates: on application.

CHELMARSH, Shropshire

The Bulls Head Inn

Chelmarsh, Bridgnorth WV16 6BA.
☎ **01746 861469.** **www.virtual-shropshire.co.uk/bulls-head-inn**
●● D/E/F/G

Country inn south of Bridgnorth overlooking Severn Valley. Small step at entrance 30". Bar level. Step down to restaurant. Toilets level. One twin and 2 double bedrooms with ramped entrance 36", ⟲. Shower rooms 36", roll-in shower, handrails, chair in shower. Other bedrooms upstairs. Self catering accommodation also available, see page 246.

Rates: from £55-£60 twin BB (2006).

CLEOBURY MORTIMER, Worcestershire

Pioneer Centre & Forest Lodge Conference Centre

Cleobury Mortimer,
Kidderminster DY14 8JG.
☎ 01299 271217.
@ pioneer@actioncentres.co.uk
●● D/E/I/F/G

Activity and conference centre for groups. Reserved parking bays. Entrance level, double doors. Public rooms ground floor, level or ramp. Unisex WC. Ten bedrooms, twin and family, designed for disabled guests. En suite shower room 90cm, ⟲, roll-in shower with seat, handrails, space for side transfer to WC. Waterproof sheets and shower chairs available. Other bedrooms level.

Rates: on application.

COVENTRY, West Midlands

Campanile Coventry North

4 Wigston Road, Walsgrave,
Coventry CV2 2SD.
☎ 024 7662 2311.
@ coventry@campanile.com
●●

Hotel between M6 junction 2 and city centre. Reserved parking bays. Public rooms level. Unisex WC. 2 twin bedroom designed for disabled guests. Bathroom ⟲, handrails, space for side transfer. Other ground floor bedrooms level. See page 31.

Ⓟ

Rates: on application.

Hilton Coventry

Paradise Way, Walsgrave Triangle,
Coventry CV2 2ST.
☎ 024 7660 3000.
●● D/E/F/G ★★★★

Hotel off M6 junction 2. Reserved parking bays. Entrance level, automatic doors. Restaurant and lounge open plan. Bar ramp or 2 steps. Café and leisure complex level. Unisex WC. Lift 120cm, inside 140x140cm. 4 double/twin bedrooms designed for disabled guests with roll-in shower rooms ⟲, handrails. Other bedrooms level. Vibrating alarm and induction loop available.

Rates: on application.

Holiday Inn Coventry M6 J2

Hinckley Road, Walsgrave,
Coventry CV2 2HP.
☎ 0870 400 9021. @ reservations-coventrym6@ichotelsgroup.com
●● D/E/I/F/G ★★★

Hotel on eastern edge of city, near M6. Reserved parking bays. Entrance level, automatic doors. Public rooms open plan, level except ramp to part of bar. Unisex WC. Lift 32", inside 36"x48". Bedrooms designed for disabled guests with low-level fittings. Bathrooms 36", ⟲, handrails, low bath with transfer seat, space by WC and bath. Waterproof sheet, induction loops, large print information and vibrating pillow alarms available. Other bedrooms level.

Rates: on application.

Ibis Coventry Centre

Mile Lane, Coventry CV1 2LN.
☎ 024 7625 0500. @ H2793@accor.com
●● D/E/G

Hotel off St John's Ringway near city centre. Entrance level. Public rooms open plan. Lift to upper floors. Five rooms with bathrooms designed for disabled guests. Other rooms level.

Rates: from £49-£58 per room (2008).

Novotel Coventry

Wilsons Ln, Longford, Coventry CV6 6HL.
☎ 024 7636 5000. @ H0506@accor.com

●● D ★★★

Hotel on edge of city near M6 junction 3. Entrance 59", double doors. Lounge level. Ramp or 4 steps to restaurant and bar. Two ground floor bedrooms with bathrooms adapted for disabled guests. Other bedrooms level.

Rates: on application.

CRAVEN ARMS, Shropshire

Tugford Farm Holiday Cottages

Tugford, Craven Arms SY7 9HS.
☎ 01584 841259. W www.tugford.com
@ tugfordfarm@yahoo.co.uk

●● E/I/F/G

Bed & breakfast on farm in South Shropshire between Craven Arms and Ludlow. Entrance level. Breakfast room ground floor. Twin bedroom designed for disabled guests, adjustable bed and roll-in shower room with handrails, shower chair and space by WC. 1 other bedroom and self-catering cottages also available. Livery stables on site.

Rates: from £25-£45 per person BB (2007).

DROITWICH, Worcestershire

Express by Holiday Inn Droitwich

Worcester Road, Wychbold, Droitwich WR9 7PA.
☎ 0870 442 5658.
W hiexpressdroitwich.co.uk

●● E/I/F/G ★★

Limited service hotel near M5 junction 5 north of Droitwich. 6 reserved parking bays. Entrance level, automatic door. Low reception desk. Ramp to open plan public rooms. Unisex WC. Lift 90cm, inside 110x140cm. 6 bedrooms designed for disabled guests. Shower rooms ⟲, handrails, roll-in shower with seat, space by WC. Other bedrooms level. Teletext TV and vibrating pillows available.

Rates: on application.

DUDLEY, West Midlands

The Copthorne Hotel Merry Hill Dudley

The Waterfront, Level Street, Brierley Hill, Dudley DY5 1UR.
☎ 01384 482882.

●● D/E/G ★★★★

Modern hotel by marina and shopping centre. Reserved parking bays. Entrance level, large revolving door. Public rooms level. Unisex WC. Lifts 31", inside 34"x82", Braille buttons. Double bedroom designed for disabled guests. Bathroom 31", ⟲, handrails, space for side transfer to bath and WC. Other bedrooms level.

Rates: on application.

HEREFORD, Herefordshire

Castle House

Castle Street, Hereford HR1 2NW.
☎ 01432 356321. W www.castlehse.co.uk

●● D/E/I/F/G

High class hotel in town centre. 15 reserved parking spaces in car park 50 yards from entrance; valet parking available. Entrances ramped. Public rooms ground floor. Unisex WC. Lift 42", inside 42"x250". Ground floor suite designed for disabled guests. Electric bed. Roll-in shower room. Bathroom 40", ⟲, space for side transfer to WC. Other bedrooms level. AA Accessible Hotel of the Year 2003/4.

Rates: from £220 per night for suite (2007).

ILAM, Staffordshire

YHA Ilam Hall

Ilam, Nr. Ashbourne DE6 2AZ.

☎ 0870 770 5876. @ ilam@yha.org.uk

●● D/E/F/G 

Youth hostel in mansion in southern Peak District. Reserved parking bays. Side entrance level; step at main entrance. Dining room and lounge level. Step to common room. Unisex WC. Two family rooms with 4 and 6 beds in separate wing with shared shower room designed for disabled people. Other accommodation upstairs in main house. For more information on Youth Hostels see page 34.

Rates: from £17 adult per night (2007).

KIDDERMINSTER, Worcestershire

Brockencote Hall

Chaddesley Corbett,
Nr. Kidderminster DY10 4PY.

☎ 01562 777876.

W www.brockencotehall.com

●● D/F/G 

Privately owned country house hotel between Kidderminster and Bromsgrove. Reserved parking bay. Entrance 1 step, portable ramp available. Public rooms level. Unisex WC. One bedroom designed for disabled guests, ⟲, adjustable height clothes rail. Bathroom ⟲, handrails, seat in shower cubicle, space by WC and bath and under basin. Teletext TV. Other ground floor bedrooms level.

Rates: from £95 single BB per night (2007).

LEAMINGTON SPA, Warwickshire

Helen Ley House

Bericote Road, Blackdown,
Leamington Spa CV32 6QP.

☎ 01926 313550. W www.helenley.org.uk

●●●●● D/I/G/H

Purpose built respite care home for people with multiple sclerosis between Leamington and Kenilworth. 24 single bedrooms. Staffed by nurses and experienced care attendants, the home is registered for nursing and care. Outings and activities organised.

Rates: on application.

LEEK, Staffordshire

Croft Meadows Farm

Horton, Leek ST13 8QE.

☎ 01782 513039.

●● D/E/F

Country cottage. Slope to level entrance. Dining room and lounge level. One double bedroom ground floor. Shower room level, roll-in shower, handrails, space for side transfer to WC. 4 other bedrooms upstairs.

Rates: from £20 per person BB (2007).

LICHFIELD, Staffordshire

Express by Holiday Inn Lichfield

Wall Island, Shenstone, Lichfield WS14 0QP.

☎ 0870 720 1078.

@ Lichfield@morethanhotels.com

●● E/F/G

Limited service hotel off A5 near M6 (Toll) J15. Reserved parking bays. Entrance level, automatic doors. Low reception desk. Public rooms open plan. Unisex WC. Lift 31", inside 422x57". 6 ground floor bedrooms designed for disabled guests that can link with neighbouring rooms. Shower rooms ⟲, roll-in shower with seat, handrails, space by WC. Other bedrooms level. Teletext TV.

Rates: from £72.50 per room (2007).

LUDLOW, Shropshire

The Clive Bar & Restaurant with Rooms

Bromfield, Ludlow SY8 2JR.

☎ 01584 856565. 🅆 www.theclive.co.uk

●● D/E/F/G ★★★★

Restaurant and bar with rooms two miles from Ludlow. Reserved parking bays. Ramp to entrance. Restaurant and bar level, 1 step to lounge. Unisex WC. One bedroom in annexe designed for disabled guests, ramp at entrance, ⟲. Shower room 90cm, roll-in shower, handrails, space by WC. 11 ground floor rooms.

Rates: from £60-£110 per night (2007).

PATTINGHAM, Shropshire

Patshull Park Hotel, Golf & Country Club

Pattingham, Shropshire WV6 7HR.

☎ 01902 700100.

🅆 www.patshull-park.co.uk

●● D/E/I/F/G

Country hotel with golf course between Bridgnorth and Wolverhampton. Reserved parking bays. Side entrance level; 8 steps at front entrance. Public rooms ground floor level. Unisex WC. 2 bedrooms with bathrooms ⟲, no adaptations. Other ground floor bedrooms level. Waterproof sheet and wheelchair available. Large print and audio brochures.

Rates: from £99 single, £119 twin BB (2007).

REDDITCH, Worcestershire

Campanile Redditch

Far Moor Lane, Winyates Green, Redditch B98 0SD.

☎ 01527 510710.

@ redditch@campanile-hotels.com

●● ★

Hotel off Inner Ring Road. Reserved parking bays. Public rooms level. Unisex WC. Twin bedroom designed for disabled guests. Bathroom ⟲, handrails, space for side transfer. Other ground floor bedrooms level. See page 31.

Rates: on application.

ROSS-ON-WYE, Herefordshire

Merton House Hotel

Edde Cross Street, Ross-on-Wye HR9 7BZ.

☎ 01989 563252.

@ merton.house@clara.co.uk

●●● D/G/H

Hotel in own grounds specially adapted for disabled and elderly guests. Accommodates up to 36 people in 17 double and 2 single rooms. Roll-in showers, bath hoists, toilet frames, bed blocks, wheelchairs and other equipment available. Outings and entertainment arranged. Personal care, but not nursing, may be arranged.

Rates: on application.

Portland House

Whitchurch, Ross-on-Wye HR9 6DB.

☎ 01600 890757.

🅆 www.portlandguesthouse.co.uk

●● D/E/I/F/G ★★★★

Guesthouse in village on River Wye between Ross and Monmouth. Reserved parking space. Entrance level 84cm. Dining room and lounge level. One bedroom with double and single beds designed for disabled guests 77cm, ⟲. Bathroom 78cm sliding door, roll-in shower with seat, handrails, space by bath and WC. Other bedrooms upstairs. Teletext TVs. Evening meals may be provided with advance notice. Ramp to garden terrace. Closed January.

Rates: from £35 per person BB (2007).

SOLIHULL, West Midlands

Ramada Solihull-Birmingham

The Square, Solihull B91 3RF.

☎ **0121 711 2121.**

@ **sales.solihull@ramadajarvis.co.uk**

●● D/E/G

Town centre hotel. Entrance level. Restaurant level. Ramp to bar, Small step to lounge. Unisex WC. Lift 31", inside 42"x55". 4 ground floor bedrooms with bathrooms designed for disabled guests. Other bedrooms level.

Rates: on application.

STAFFORD, Staffordshire

Express by Holiday Inn Stafford

Acton Court, Acton Gate, Stafford ST18 9AR.

☎ **0870 720 2295.**

@ **stafford@morethanhotels.co.uk**

●● E/I/F/G

Limited service hotel off M6 junction 13 south of Stafford. Reserved parking bays. Level entrance, automatic door. Low reception desk. Public rooms open plan. Unisex WC. Lift 36". Rooms designed for disabled guests with shower rooms ⟲, roll-in shower, space by WC. Other bedrooms level. Wheelchair and vibrating alarms available. Restaurants adjacent.

Rates: from £69 per room BB (2007).

STOKE-ON-TRENT, Staffordshire

Best Western Stoke-on-Trent Moat House

Etruria Hall, Festival Way, Etruria, Stoke-on-Trent ST1 5BQ.

☎ **0870 225 4601.**

@ **www.bw-stokeontrentmoathouse.qmh-hotels.com**

 D/E/I/F/G/H 

High class hotel near city centre. Reserved parking bays. Entrance level, automatic doors. Public rooms level. Unisex WC. Lift to all floors except 1st. Double and twin bedrooms designed for disabled guests. Bathrooms ⟲, handrails, space for side transfer to bath and WC. Most other bedrooms level. Bath hoist and seat and wheelchair available. Braille signs and directory.

Rates: on application.

Holiday Inn Stoke-on-Trent

Clayton Road, Newcastle-under-Lyme ST5 4DL.

☎ **0870 400 9077.**

@ **stoke@ihg.com**

● D/E/I/F/G

Hotel in own grounds near M6 junction 15, south of Stoke. Reserved parking bays. Small step at entrance, automatic doors. Public rooms level. Adapted cubicles in toilets. Two bedrooms on lower floor with some adaptations 70cm, ⟲. Bathroom 74cm, ⟲, space by bath and WC. Vibrating alarm, induction loop and large print menus.

Rates: on application.

STRATFORD-UPON-AVON, Warwickshire

Best Western Grosvenor Hotel

Warwick Road, Stratford-upon-Avon CV37 6YT.

☎ **01789 269213.**

W **www.bwgh.co.uk**

●● D/E/I/F/G ★★★

Town centre hotel. Reserved parking bays. Rear entrance level; step and handrail at main entrance. Public rooms level, min. door width 30½". Unisex WC. 2 twin bedrooms adapted for disabled guests, ground floor, lowered switches. Bathrooms ⟲, grabrails, space by WC. One twin/double room with alarm cord and vibrating alarm.

Rates: on application.

Legacy Falcon Hotel
2 Chapel Street,
Stratford-upon-Avon CV37 6HA.
☎ **0870 832 9905**
@ **res-falcon@legacy-hotels.co.uk**
●● D/E/I/F/G ★★★

Hotel in town centre. Reserved parking bays. Entrance from car park ramp; main entrance 1 step. Public rooms ground floor open plan. WCs not adapted. Lift. Double bedroom and bathroom adapted for disabled guests. Other bedrooms level.

Rates: on application.

Stratford Manor Hotel
Warwick Road,
Stratford-upon-Avon CV37 0PY.
☎ **01789 731173.**
@ **stratfordmanor@marstonhotels.co.uk**
●● D/E/I/F/G ★★★★

Hotel in own grounds 3 miles from town centre. Reserved parking bays. Ramp, or 8 steps, to entrance, automatic door. Public rooms ground floor, mainly open plan. Unisex WC in Leisure Centre; other toilets level. Lift to all floors. 5 bedrooms, twin and double, designed for disabled guests of which 3 are level from car park. Bathrooms 93cm, ⟲, space by bath and WC. Other bedrooms level.

Rates: on application.

SUTTON COLDFIELD, West Midlands

Innkeepers Lodge Sutton Coldfield
Chester Road North, Streetly,
Sutton Coldfield B73 6SP.
☎ **0121 353 7785.**
●● D/E/I/F/G

Lodge accommodation on A452 by Toby Carvery near Sutton Coldfield. Reserved parking bays. Entrances level. Low reception desk. Restaurant and bar level. Unisex WC. Four bedrooms designed for disabled guests with roll-in shower rooms. Other ground floor bedrooms level.

Rates: from ££49.95 per room BB (2007).

TELFORD, Shropshire

Holiday Inn Telford/Ironbridge

St Quentin Gate, Telford TF3 4EH.
☎ **01952 527000.**
@ **holidayinntelford@thl.uk.com**
●● D/E/I/F/G

Hotel near town centre. Reserved parking bays. Entrance level, automatic door. Low reception desk with induction loop. Public rooms level, mainly open plan. Unisex WC. Lift 80cm, inside 110x135cm. Four ground floor bedrooms designed for disabled guests. Bathrooms 90cm, ⟲, handrails, space for side transfer to bath and WC. Bathseat, raised WC seat and waterproof sheets available. Other bedrooms level. Librating alarms, portable induction loop. Wheelchair access to pool.

Rates: on application.

YHA Ironbridge

John Rose Building, High Street, Coalport, Telford TF8 7HT.

☎ 0870 770 5882.

@ ironbridge@yha.org.uk

●● D/E/I/F/G ★★★

Hostel in converted building. Parking by museum 300m. Entrance level, induction loop at reception. Public rooms ground floor. External entrance with stairlift to restaurant. Unisex WC. Three family bunkrooms and 1 single bedroom level. Roll-in shower room, shower chair. For more information on Youth Hostels see page 34.

Rates: from £15.50 adult per night (2008).

WOLVERHAMPTON, West Midlands

Holiday Inn Wolverhampton

Dunstall Park, Wolverhampton WV6 0PE.

☎ 0870 220 0102.

@ enquiries@dunstallpark.com

●● D/E/I/F

Hotel north of town centre at racecourse. Reserved parking bays. Entrance level, double doors. Public rooms ground floor, open plan. Unisex WC. Lift 80cm, inside 116x130cm. Bedrooms designed for disabled guests 80cm. Bathrooms 90cm, handrails, space for side transfer to bath and WC. Waterproof sheet available. Other bedrooms level. Some staff trained in sign language.

Rates: on application.

Novotel Wolverhampton

Union Street, Wolverhampton WV1 3JN.

☎ 01902 871100.

@ H1188@accor.com

●● D/E/I/G ★★★

Hotel near town centre. Reserved parking bays. Entrance level, automatic doors. Public rooms ground floor, open plan. Unisex WC. Lift 31", inside 31"x41". Three bedrooms designed for disabled guests. Bathrooms 35", handrails, space for side transfer to bath and WC. Other bedrooms level.

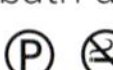

Rates: on application.

WORCESTER, Worcestershire

Fownes Hotel

City Walls Road, Worcester WR1 2AP.

☎ 01905 613151.

@ Reservations@Fowneshotel.co.uk

●● D/G ★★★

Hotel in city centre. Reserved parking bay. Entrance level. Public rooms ground floor. Unisex WC. Lift to parts of upper floors. One bedroom with some adaptations for disabled guests. Bathroom 36", level. Some other bedrooms level.

Rates: from £70-£98.50 per person BB (2008).

Pigeon Racing

The sport for all the family
- The sport for all abilities

For more information

The Royal Pigeon Association, The Reddings,
Near Cheltenham, Glos GL516RN
Telephone: 01452 713529
Web: www.rpra.org Email: gm@rpra.org

GEDDINGTON ROAD CORBY,
NN18 8ET ENGLAND
Hotel Front Desk: 44-1536-401020
Hotel Fax: 44-1536-400767

The perfect place from which to discover Northamptonshire, the Holiday Inn Corby-Kettering boasts accessible public areas including reception, lounge, bar and restaurant as well as fully air-conditioned spacious accessible bedrooms. Relax and enjoy our health club which provides a pool hoist to access our 15 metre swimming pool before enjoying a treatment in our beauty rooms.

Country Parks with Facilities for Disabled People

Cannock Chase Country Park
Visitor Centre with RADAR keyed toilets and accessible café. Self-guided trail for the visually impaired and is wheelchair friendly (taped commentary available f.o.c.), 3 electric scooters for use on marked routes f.o.c.

Highgate Country Park, Enville
Wheelchair route around woodland heath.

Apedale Country Park, Chesterton
Wheelchair route to viewpoint.

RADAR keyed toilets and wheelchair accessible visitor centre at:
Consall Nature Park, Wetley Rocks.
Deep Hayes Country Park, Cheddleton.
Greenway Bank Country Park, Knypersley.
Oakamoor Picnic area, Cheadle.

Contact 01785 277264

www.staffordshire.gov.uk Staffordshire County Council

Wayfinder Talking Signs

in Birmingham City Centre

For more information on Wayfinder, please visit **www.birmingham.gov.uk/wayfinder** or phone Birmingham City Centre Partnership on

0121 616 2894

Birmingham Museums

Many of Birmingham's finest museums are fully accessible for people with disabilities.

At Birmingham Museum and Art Gallery, visitors will be able to enjoy the world's largest collection of Pre-Raphaelite art, as well as contemporary works, silver, ceramics and archaeology.

There is also access for people with disabilities at the Museum of the Jewellery Quarter (Tel: 0121 554 3598) and Soho House (Tel: 0121 554 9122, only open Easter to October).

For enquiries and information on current exhibitions, Tel: 0121 303 2834
www.bmag.org.uk

Birmingham City Council

LODGE ACCOMMODATION

There are Days Inn (see page 34) Etap (see page 34) Formule 1 (see page 34), Premier Travel Inn (see page 38) and Travelodge (see page 38) properties in the following areas in this region.

Alcester - Travelodge ☎ 0870 191 1607
Balsall Common - Premier Travel Inn ☎ 0870 197 7022
Bedworth - Travelodge ☎ 0870 191 1562
Birmingham - Etap ☎ 0121 622 7575
Premier Travel Inn ☎ 0870 990 6404
Travelodge ☎ 0870 191 1564
Birmingham, Canal Side - Premier Travel Inn ☎ 0870 197 7031
Birmingham, East - Premier Travel Inn ☎ 0870 238 3312
Birmingham Five Ways - Travelodge ☎ 0870 191 1825
Birmingham Frankley - Travelodge ☎ 0870 191 1567
Birmingham, Fort Dunlop - Travelodge ☎ 0870 191 1812
Birmingham, Maypole - Travelodge ☎ 0870 191 1804
Birmingham, South - Formule 1 ☎ 0121 773 9583
Premier Travel Inn ☎ 0870 990 6538
Birmingham, Yardley - Travelodge ☎ 0870 191 1565
Birmingham Airport/NEC - Premier Travel Inn ☎ 0870 990 6326
Brierley Hill - Travelodge ☎ 0870 191 1563
Bromsgrove - Premier Travel Inn ☎ 0870 197 7044
Bromsgrove South - Premier Travel Inn ☎ 0870 990 6408
Burton A38 - Travelodge (2) ☎ 0870 191 1568/9
Cannock - Premier Travel Inn ☎ 0870 197 7048
Cannock M6 Toll - Premier Travel Inn ☎ 0870 197 7070
Coventry - Formule 1 ☎ 024 7623 4560
Premier Travel Inn ☎ 0870 197 7066
Coventry, East - Premier Travel Inn ☎ 0870 990 6472
Droitwich - Travelodge ☎ 0870 191 1574
Dudley - Premier Travel Inn ☎ 0870 197 7303
Evesham - Premier Travel Inn ☎ 0870 198 7288
Hagley - Premier Travel Inn ☎ 0870 197 7123
Hereford - Premier Travel Inn ☎ 0870 197 7134
Travelodge ☎ 0870 191 1843
Hilton Park - Travelodge ☎ 0870 191 1566

7 Heart of England

Kidderminster - Travelodge ☎ 0870 191 1579
Leamington Spa - Travelodge ☎ 0870 191 1738
Lichfield - Premier Travel Inn ☎ 0870 990 6438
Ludlow - Travelodge ☎ 0870 191 1586
Newcastle-under-Lyme - Premier Travel Inn ☎ 0870 197 7191
Nuneaton - Days Inn ☎ 024 7635 7370
Premier Travel Inn ☎ 0870 197 7201
Travelodge ☎ 0870 191 1594
Oldbury - Premier Travel Inn ☎ 0870 197 7202
Travelodge ☎ 0870 191 1595
Oswestry - Travelodge ☎ 0870 191 1596
Redditch - Premier Travel Inn ☎ 0870 990 6392
Travelodge ☎ 0870 085 0950
Ross-on-Wye - Premier Travel Inn ☎ 0870 197 7221
Rugby - Premier Travel Inn ☎ 0870 197 7223
Travelodge ☎ 0870 191 1599
Rugeley - Travelodge ☎ 0870 191 1602
Shrewsbury North - Travelodge ☎ 0870 191 1620
Shrewsbury South - Travelodge ☎ 0870 191 1603
Solihull, Hockley Heath - Premier Travel Inn ☎ 0870 197 7230
Solihull, North - Premier Travel Inn ☎ 0870 197 7231
Solihull, Shirley - Premier Travel Inn ☎ 0870197 7232
Stafford - Premier Travel Inn ☎ 0870 990 6478
Stafford North - Premier Travel Inn ☎ 0870 859 0689
Stafford Services M6 - Premier Travel Inn ☎ 0870 197 7239
Travelodge ☎ 0870 191 1605
Stoke - Travelodge ☎ 0870 191 1606
Stratford-on-Avon - Days Inn ☎ 01926 651681
Sutton Coldfield - Premier Travel Inn ☎ 0870 990 6320
Travelodge ☎ 0870 191 1608
Tamworth - Premier Travel Inn ☎ 0870 197 7248
Travelodge ☎ 0870 191 1609
Telford - Days Inn ☎ 01952 238400
Premier Travel Inn ☎ 0870 197 7251
Travelodge ☎ 0870 191 1610
Uttoxeter - Premier Travel Inn ☎ 0870 197 7256
Travelodge ☎ 0870 191 1614

Walsall - Premier Travel Inn ☎ 0870 197 7258
Travelodge ☎ 0970 191 1823
Warwick South - Days Inn ☎ 01926 650168
West Bromwich - Premier Travel Inn ☎ 0870 197 7264
West Bromwich, Central - Premier Travel Inn ☎ 0870 950 6340
Wolverhampton - Premier Travel Inn ☎ 0870 197 7277
Worcester - Premier Travel Inn ☎ 0870 197 7278
Travelodge ☎ 01905 22592

SELF-CATERING ACCOMMODATION

ABBERLEY, Worcestershire

Old Yates Cottages

Old Yates Farm, Abberley WR6 6AT.

www.oldyatescottages.co.uk

F/G ★★★

Ground floor cottage designed for disabled people. Entrance level. Min. door width 82cm. Cooker controls useable from wheelchair. Twin bedroom, restricted ⟲. Bathroom ⟲, handrails. Can be let with adjoining cottage with upstairs bedroom.

Apply: Mr & Mrs Goodman ☎ 01299 896500.
Rates: from £175-£295 per week (2008).

ALTON, Staffordshire

Jay's Barn

Bradley, Nr. Alton Towers.

 I/F/G 

Chalet designed for disabled guests in countryside, 2 miles from Alton Towers. Accessible parking. Entrance level. Lounge/kitchen open plan level. Ground floor twin bedroom. Shower room with roll-in shower and seat ⟲, handrails, lever taps, non-slip floor, low-level mirror. Specially designed garden for visually impaired people.

Apply: Mrs Christine Babb, Rest Cottage, Bradley, Alton, Stoke-on-Trent ST10 4DF ☎ 01889 507444. www.jaysbarn.co.uk
Rates: £300-£400 per week (2007).

The Star Caravan & Camping Park

Cotton, Nr. Alton Towers, Stoke-on-Trent ST10 3DW.

☎ 01538 702219.

www.starcaravanpark.co.uk

●● G ★★★★

Family owned park for touring caravans, tents and motorhomes 1½ miles north of Alton Towers. 120 pitches in total including 16 with hard standing and 40 with electric hook-up. Roadways tarmac but some quite steep. Unisex unit for disabled people in toilet block - NKS lock, small ramp, roll-in shower with seat, handrails, space by WC. Ramp to reception with low counter and induction loop. Accessible laundry/washing-up building. 9 static caravans for hire including one designed for disabled people. Open late March to October.

Rates: on application.

BISHOPS CASTLE, Shropshire
The Byre
Minsterley, nr. Bishops Castle.

●● I/F/G

Converted level barn for 2 people on small working farm in south Shropshire between Ludlow and Shrewsbury. Entrance level, 32". Open plan lounge/kitchen and bedroom area with stow away double bed. Single bed can be provided. Kitchen controls useable from wheelchair. Shower room 33" sliding door, ⟲, roll-in shower, handrails, space by WC, tilting mirror. Shower chair, waterproof sheets and raised WC seat available. Garden and patio. Farmyard level.

Apply: Yvonne & John Hart, Crosfields, Gravels Bank, Minsterley SY5 0HG.
☎ 01743 891412. @ yj.hart@virgin.net
Rates: from £200-£280 per week (2008).

BRIDGNORTH, Shropshire
Stanmore Hall Touring Park
Stourbridge Road, Bridgnorth WV15 6DT.
☎ 01746 761761.
@ stanmore@morris-leisure.co.uk

● G ★★★★★

Parkland site on edge of town with pitches for 130 touring caravans and tents. Mainly level grass site with tarmac paths. Ramp to toilet block which has unisex WC designed for wheelchair users. Office and shop level.

Rates: on application.

CHELMARSH, Shropshire
Stable Mews
Chelmarsh, Nr. Bridgnorth.
W www.virtual-shropshire.co.uk/bulls-head-inn

●● F/G ★★★

Ground floor apartment adjoining country inn in Severn Valley. Ramp at entrance, 30". Internal doors 36". ⟲ in lounge and kitchen. Double bedroom and sofa bed in lounge. Shower room ⟲, roll-in shower with seat, handrails, space by WC. Two other units have ground floor accommodation. Meals and bed & breakfast available in Inn, see page 234.

Apply: Mr & Mrs Baxter, Bulls Head Inn, Chelmarsh, Bridgnorth WV16 6BA.
☎ 01746 861469.
Rates: from £245-£380 per week per cottage, £45-£65 per BB (2008).

CHURCH STRETTON, Shropshire
Brook House Farm
Wall-under-Heywood,
Church Stretton SY6 7DS.
W www.churchstretton.co.uk

●● F ★★★★

Cottage in grounds of farmhouse 3 miles from Church Stretton. Entrance level, 36". Internal doors 33". Kitchen controls useable from wheelchair. Two double bedrooms ⟲. Shower room ⟲, roll-in shower, handrails, space by WC.

Apply: Leslie & Joan Egerton ☎ 01694 771308
Rates: on application

CRAVEN ARMS, Shropshire

Swallows Nest

Strefford Hall, Strefford,
Craven Arms SY7 8DE.
www.streffordhall.co.uk

●● F/G ★★★★

Ground floor flat on farm in south Shropshire. Entrance level 39". Lounge open plan with sofabed. Kitchen 30", ⟲, cooker controls useable from wheelchair. Double bedroom 31", ⟲. Shower room 30" sliding door, roll-in shower with seat, handrails, space for side transfer to WC. Upstairs flat and farmhouse bed & breakfast also available.

Apply: Mrs Caroline Morgan
☎ 01588 672383.
Rates: £180-£275 per week (2006).

HEREFORD, Herefordshire

Grafton Villa

Grafton, Hereford HR2 8ED.
☎ **01432 268689.**
www.graftonvilla.co.uk

●● I/F/G ★★★★

Cottages designed for disabled people on farm 2 miles south of Hereford. "Anvil Cottage" sleeps 4. Entrance ramp, 32". Lounge and kitchen/dining room level. Cooker useable from wheelchair. Double and twin bedrooms. Shower room 32", ⟲, handrails and space for side transfer to WC. Also separate bathroom, handrail by WC. "Apple Bough" sleeps up to 6. Ramp with handrail to entrance 32". Open plan lounge/kitchen, cooker controls useable from wheelchair. Ground floor bedroom with roll-in shower room, ⟲, shower seat, handrails, space by WC. 2 other bedrooms and shower room upstairs. Raised WC seat available. Inn serving meals nearby.

Rates: from £230-£600 per week (2007).

The Granary

Little Dewchurch, Nr. Hereford.

●● I/F/G ★★★★

Converted barn on organic farm 6 miles from Hereford overlooking Wye Valley. Two 10cm steps on approach. Lounge 81cm. Dining room/kitchen 100cm, cooker controls useable from wheelchair. Ground floor twin bedroom 81cm, ⟲. En suite shower room ⟲, roll-in shower with seat, handrails, space by WC. 2 double bedrooms on 1st floor. Level terrace and lawn. Long lets also available.

Apply: Karen Tibbetts, Henclose Farm, Little Dewchurch, Hereford HR2 6PP.
☎ 01432 840826.
Rates: from £240-£500 per week (2006).

ILAM, Staffordshire

The Cottage by the Pond

Beechenhill Fm, Ilam, Ashbourne DE6 2BD.

●● I/F/G ★★★★

Cottage on organic farm in south Peak District. Entrance level, 36". All accommodation, except one bedroom, level. Lounge 31" sliding door. Kitchen worktops 30", with space below, and 35". Two level bedrooms, twin and twin/double ⟲ and 3rd bedroom upstairs. Bathroom sliding door, ⟲, roll-in shower with shower chair, handrails, space for side transfer to WC. Waterproof sheet, bath board and seat available and hoist may be hired. Second ground floor cottage on site. Ready meals and puddings available.

Apply: Sue & Terry Prince
☎ 01335 310274. www.beechenhill.co.uk
Rates: from £230-£680 (2007).

Self-catering accommodation

KNIGHTCOTE, Warwickshire

Knightcote Farm Cottages

The Bake House, Knightcote, Southam CV47 2EF.

 www.farmcottages.com

●● I/F/G ★★★★★

Cottages on farm between Stratford and Warwick. 'Home Cottage' bungalow for 6 people. Entrance level 93cm. Lounge/kitchen open plan. Adjustable height worktop, hob and sink. Three bedrooms, double and twin, ⟲, one with en suite roll-in shower room. Bathroom ⟲, roll-in shower with seat, hand-rails, space for side transfer to bath and WC. 'Chestnut Cottage' has ground floor accom-modation for up to 4 people in two bedrooms. Two bathrooms, one with a roll-in shower. 'Oak House' sleeps up to 10. Lounge/kitchen open plan. Ground floor twin bedroom ⟲ with roll-in shower room, handrails, space by WC. Other accom-modation upstairs. Raised WC seat and some other equipment available. Teletext TV. Meals can be provided. Two other cottages available. Premier Cottages member.

Apply: Fiona Walker ☎ 01295 770637.
Rates: from £391-£1534 per week (2007).

LEOMINSTER, Herefordshire

YHA Leominster

The Old Priory, Leominster HR6 8EQ.
☎ **0780 770 5916.**
 Leominster@yha.org.uk

●● E/F/G ★★★★

Self-catering hostel in town centre. Parking nearby. Level entrance, double doors each 34". Lounge, dining room and self-catering kitchen level. Kitchen has low worktop and accessible microwave and kettle. Bedroom designed for disabled people with double and single beds. En suite shower room 40", ⟲, roll-in shower with seat, space by WC. Other bedrooms upstairs. Closed November to March. For further information on Youth Hostels see page 34.

Rates: £15 adult per night (2007).

LUDLOW, Shropshire

Sutton Court Farm Holiday Cottages

Little Sutton, Stanton Lacy, Ludlow SY8 2AJ.
☎ **01584 861305.**
 www.suttoncourtfarm.co.uk

●● F/G ★★★★

"Holly Cottage" is a ground floor cottage for 2 people 5 miles from Ludlow. Ramp or 1 step on approach. Entrance level. Min. door width 31". Lounge/kitchen open plan. Twin bedroom ⟲. Bathroom ⟲, handrails, space for side transfer to bath and WC, bath seat. Own courtyard garden. Five other cottages on site. Some meals can be provided.

Rates: from £220-£360 per week (2008).

MALVERN, Worcestershire

Hidelow House Cottages

Acton Green, Acton Beauchamp, Nr. Malvern WR6 5AH.

☎ **01886 884547.** **www.hidelow.co.uk**

●●● I/F/G/H ★★★★-★★★★★

"Hidelow Lodge" is a single storey rural cottage for 5 people between Malvern and Bromyard. Entrance ramp or 2 steps. Lounge 78cm. Kitchen 82cm, cooker but not taps useable from wheelchair. Twin bedroom with en suite shower room, roll-in shower, shower chair, handrails, space for side transfer to WC. Also a double bedroom with additional single bed and bathroom. "St Katherine's" is a two-person cottage designed for disabled people. Level approach to large entrance porch, door level 90cm. Open plan lounge/kitchen, controls useable from wheelchair, split-level worktops. Twin/ double bedroom, bed blocks and low hanging rail available. Shower room 82cm, turning space, roll-in shower, handrails, wheeled shower chair, space by WC. 4 other cottages and shop with local produce on site. Home-made freezer meals can be supplied. Electric hoist and bed can be hired. Some personal assistance can be provided. Heart of England Tourism for All Award Winner 2005.

Rates: £345-£685 per week (2007).

Whitewells Farm Cottages

Ridgeway Cross, Malvern WR13 5JR.

☎ **01886 880607.**

www.whitewellsfarm.co.uk

●● G ★★★★

"Cider Press Cottage" is a ground floor cottage for 2 people. Paved paths. Entrance level 34". Lounge/kitchen open plan. Worktops 33". One bedroom. Bathroom 34", handrails, space beside bath and WC. Raised toilet seat available. 6 other cottages available.

Rates: from £280-£395 per week (2007).

NEWPORT, Shropshire

The Owl House

Hawthorn House, Church Lane, Moreton, Nr. Newport TF10 9DQ.

www.owlhouseshropshire.co.uk

●● I/F/G

Cottage for up to 4 people in country south east of Newport. Gravel drive, paved approach to cottage. Entrance 1 step. Internal doors 86cm. Lounge. Kitchen controls useable from wheelchair, no. Twin bedroom and roll-in shower room with handrails and space by WC. Double bedroom and WC upstairs. Teletext TV available. Level gardens.

Apply: Fiona Asson ☎ 01952 691305 or 07929 350895.

Rates: from £340-£600 per week (2007).

OSWESTRY, Shropshire

The Engine House

Quarry Lane, Nantmawr, Oswestry SY10 9HJ.

www.nantmawrquarry.co.uk

●● G

Accommodation for groups of up to 20 on Welsh border south of Oswestry. Ramp to entrance. Internal doors 29". Large lounge and kitchen, no adaptations. Ground floor bedroom with bunks, 10 lower level. Ground floor shower room, roll-in shower, handrail and space by WC. 10 bunk beds and bathroom upstairs. Activities and catering can be arranged.

Apply: Caroline Williams ☎ 01691 659358.

Rates: on application.

ROSS-ON-WYE, Herefordshire

Wye Lea Country Manor

Wye Lea, Bridstow,
Ross-on-Wye HR9 6PZ.
☎ 01989 562880. W www.wyelea.co.uk

●● F/G

"Wye Lea Lodge", designed for disabled guests, is one of a 15 cottages on riverside country estate just north of Ross-on-Wye. Ramp with handrails to rear door. Doors 84cm. Lounge/dining room and kitchen ⟲. Kitchen controls not useable from wheelchair. Twin bedroom with own shower room, handrails, roll-in shower with seat, space by WC. Also double bedroom with bathroom. Teletext TV. Powered scooter available for hire. Restaurant on site. Leisure facilities. Short breaks available.

Ⓟ

Rates: from £675-£1040 per week (2007).

SHREWSBURY, Shropshire

Newton Meadows

Wem Rd, Harmer Hill, Shrewsbury SY4 3DZ.

●● F/G ★★★★

Three cottages in country 6 miles north of Shrewsbury. Entrances level. Lounge/kitchen open plan, controls useable from wheelchair. One cottage sleeps 4 people in two bedrooms, one on ground floor; the others sleep up to 7 in 4 bedrooms, two on ground floor. All have a shower room 39" sliding door, ⟲, roll-in shower with seat, handrails, space for side transfer to WC.

Ⓟ ⓘ

Apply: Mr & Mrs Simcox.
☎ 01939 290346.
W www.newtonmeadows.co.uk
Rates: from £240-£615 per week (2008).

Oxon Hall Touring Park

Welshpool Road, Shrewsbury SY3 5FB.
☎ 01743 340868.
@ oxon@morris-leisure.co.uk

●● G ★★★★★

Landscaped level site by park & ride facility on edge of town. Pitches for 130 touring caravans and tents. Tarmac paths. Ramp to toilet block that has unisex WC designed for wheelchair users. Office and shop level.

Ⓟ

Rates: on application.

TELFORD, Shropshire

Church Farm

Rowton, Nr, Wellington, Telford TF6 6QY.

●● I/F/G ★★★

Three barn conversions for 2-8 people. "The Old Shippon" sleeps up to 8. Small step at entrance. Min. door width 33". Lounge, Open plan kitchen/dining room, taps and sink not useable from wheelchair. Twin bedroom ground floor. Shower room level, ⟲, roll-in shower with seat, handrails, space for side transfer to WC. Other bedrooms and toilets upstairs. Two cottages for 5 people each with a double ground floor bedroom also available. Breakfast can be served in farmhouse.

Ⓟ ⓘ

Apply: Mr & Mrs Evans. ☎ 01952 770381.
W www.virtual-shropshire.co.uk/churchfarm
Rates: from £200-£600 per week (2008).

WHITCHURCH, Shropshire
Combermere Abbey Cottages

Whitchurch SY13 4AJ.
☎ **01948 662876.**
W www.combermereabbey.co.uk
●● F/G ★★★★★

A courtyard of 7 cottages on estate on Shropshire/Cheshire border. One, "Stapleton", designed for disabled guests. Entrance level. Lounge/kitchen open plan. Twin bedroom with en-suite shower room sliding door, ↺, roll-in shower with seat, handrails, space by WC. Double bedroom and bathroom upstairs. Some other cottages have ground floor bedrooms.

Rates: from £525-£721 per week (2007).

WORCESTER, Worcestershire
Roseland Bungalow Annexe

Roseland, Clifton, Severn Stoke, Worcester WR8 9JF.
W www.roselandworcs.demon.co.uk
● I/F/G ★★★★

Self-contained annexe to owners house in country 5 miles south of Worcester. Conservatory entrance has 3 shallow steps, portable ramp available. Lounge 28", ↺. Sliding door from conservatory to kitchen/dining room ↺, controls not useable from wheelchair. Double and single bedrooms, space under double bed. Also double sofa bed. Bathroom 28", limited ↺, curtained shower, grabrails by bath and shower, space by WC. Teletext TV. Garden mainly level. Floor plan and other details available. Bed & breakfast in main house.

Apply: Guy & Mary Laurent
☎ 01905 371463.
Rates: from £185-£325 per week (2007).

8 East Midlands

Photo: Britainonview - visit Peaks and Derbyshire © Daniel Bosworth

This region, ranging from the wide, flat Fens to the mountainous Peak District, comprises the counties of Derbyshire, Leicestershire, Lincolnshire, Northamptonshire, Nottinghamshire and Rutland.

Around the Lincolnshire coast, resorts such as Cleethorpes, Skegness and Mablethorpe provide the opportunity for seaside holidays with a level seafront and much traditional entertainment. Inland there is a choice between staying in historic towns or more rural localities.

Many important historic events and myths focus on the area. You can learn more of Hereward the Wake in the Fens around Crowland or Robin Hood in Nottingham and Sherwood Forest. The Wars of the Roses ended at Bosworth in Leicestershire, where there is a Visitor Centre and Country Park, and the Civil War began at Nottingham Castle, now an art gallery and museum.

The two largest cities in the region are Leicester and Nottingham. Both provide opportunities to enjoy music, theatre and sporting events and have a variety of attractions depicting the history and industries of the area. Other important towns include Derby, Northampton and Lincoln, with its magnificent cathedral towering over the surrounding countryside at the top of a steep hill.

Many smaller towns are also worth visiting. At Boston the church tower dominates the surrounding fenland. In nearby Spalding the Springfields Gardens are renowned, as befits a town that is the centre of Britain's major flower growing area. Another town proud of its parks is Buxton where the museum has an exhibition on the surrounding Peak District. The twisted spire on the parish church of Chesterfield is another of the noted landmarks of the region.

Pavillion Gardens, Buxton

Most of the Peak District National Park is in Derbyshire. Other countryside attractions include accessible trails in Grafton Park and Boughton Park near Kettering, the Saltfleetby National Nature Reserve on the Lincolnshire Coast and the National Trust's Clumber Park in north Nottinghamshire. There are opportunities for water sports, birdwatching, fishing and many other activities at Rutland Water. Life on an Edwardian estate can be experienced at Elvaston Country Park near Derby.

The region is the home of a number of transport attractions including the Crich Tramways Village in Derbyshire, the Great Central Railway in Leicestershire and the National Space Science Centre at Leicester. Those with literary interests can compare the background of D H Lawrence at the Durban House Heritage Centre at Eastwood near Nottingham with that of Lord Byron at Newstead Abbey only a few miles away. For family outings, help is offered to disabled visitors at the American Adventures theme park near Ilkeston.

Photo: www.britainonview

USEFUL ADDRESSES

Mosaic: shaping disability services

2 Richard III Street, Leicester LE3 5QT.
☎ 0116 251 5565.
@ aspire@mosaic1898.co.uk
W www.mosaic1898.co.uk

Voluntary organisation providing a range of services to disabled people, their families and carers. They have two accessible self-catering bungalows at Overstrand, North Norfolk. Priority is given to people living in, or having a connection with Leicester, Leicestershire and Rutland. In the off-season consideration can be given to people from outside the area.

Disability Lincs Ltd

Ancaster Day Centre, Boundary Street, Lincoln LN5 8NJ.
☎ 01522 870602.
W www.disabilitylincs.org.uk
Enquiries to the Administrative Officer.

DIAL

DIAL offers a free, impartial and confidential service of information and advice by telephone to disabled people, their relatives and professionals. The following groups may be able to help disabled residents and visitors in their areas:

Brigg Carers' Support Centre
☎ 01652 650585

Disability Direct, Derby
☎ 01332 299449: 01332 368585

Leicester CIL ☎ 0116 222 5005

DIAL Mansfield ☎ 01623 625891

DIAL Northants Corby ☎ 01536 204742

DIAL Northants Daventry
☎ 01327 701646

Translinc

Jarvis House, 157 Sadler Road, Lincoln LN6 3RS.
☎ 01522 503400. W www.translinc.co.uk

Translinc run a range of transport services in and around Lincolnshire and have vehicles equipped to carry wheelchair users in their fleet. They have a programme of coach excursions and holidays from their bases in Lincoln and Boston.

Useful addresses

USEFUL PUBLICATIONS

Access for All - guides giving information for disabled visitors to the Peak District including car parks, public transport, easy-going trails, public toilets and other matters. Available in print and other formats from Peak District National Park, Aldern House, Baslow Road, Bakewell DE45 1AE. ☎ 01629 816200. @ customer.service@peakdistrict.gov.uk. The information is also available on W www.peakdistrict.org

Accessible South Lincolnshire & West Norfolk by John Killick – a book published by the Disabled Motorists Federation in 2005 giving information on the accessibility of places to visit and eat in the Fens. Available price £3.50 from Mr J E Killick, 145 Knoulberry Road, Blackfell, Washington, Tyne & Wear NE37 1JN.

www.disabledgo.info - this website includes detailed information on the accessibility of many premises in Newark and North East Lincolnshire.

EQUIPMENT HIRE

Boston Community Transport

The Len Medlock Centre,
St Georges Road, Boston PE21 8TY.
☎ 01205 315936.
@ transport@bostoncvs.org.uk

As part of a Shopmobility Scheme, scooters and both powered and manual wheelchairs are available for hire for both residents for use elsewhere and people visiting the area. Users have to be members of the scheme for insurance purposes. Vehicles can be delivered, at an additional charge, to addresses within 10 miles of Boston.

Daventry Shopmobility

New Street, Daventry NN11 4BT.
☎ 01327 312555.

Manual wheelchairs can be hired for up to 3 months by residents for use on holiday and also people visiting the Daventry area.

Scooter Serv

Moat Lane, Towcester,
Northamptonshire NN12 6AD.
☎ 0845 612 1912. W www.scooterserv.com

This company can hire manual and powered wheelchairs and scooters for use on the UK mainland.

Shopmobility schemes exist to provide wheelchairs and/or scooters for use in shopping centres in the following towns. For information on availability, etc. telephone in advance.

Alfreton **☎ 01773 835199**
Arnold **☎ 0115 966 1331**
Beeston **☎ 0115 917 3788**
Chesterfield **☎ 01246 559331**
Daventry **☎ 01327 312555**
Derby **☎ 01332 200320**
Glossop **☎ 01457 861632**
Hinckley **☎ 01455 633920**
Ilkeston **☎ 0115 932 4956**
Lincoln **☎ 01522 514477**
Long Eaton **☎ 0115 946 5392**
Loughborough **☎ 01509 634706**
Mansfield **☎ 01623 655222**
Market Harborough **☎ 01858 410864**
Melton Mowbray **☎ 01664 480677**
Northampton **☎ 01604 233714**
Nottingham **☎ 0115 915 3888**
Retford **☎ 01777 705432**
Swadlincote **☎ 01283 210770**
Wellingborough **☎ 01933 228844**
West Bridgford **☎ 0115 981 5451**
Worksop **☎ 01909 479070**

ACCOMMODATION WITH MEALS

ANNESLEY, Nottinghamshire

Dakota Nottingham

Lakeview Drive, Sherwood Business Park, Annesley, Nottingham NG15 0DA.

☎ 0870 442 2727.

W www.dakotanottingham.co.uk

●● D/I/F/G

Hotel off M1 J27 north of Nottingham. Reserved parking bays. Entrance level, automatic doors. Public rooms level, open plan. Unisex WC. Lifts to upper floors. 5 double bedrooms designed for disabled guests ⟲. Shower rooms ⟲, roll-in shower with seat, handrails, space by WC, low basin. Other bedrooms level. Teletext TV.

Ⓟ ⊗

Rates: from £86 per room (2007).

ASHBY-DE-LA-ZOUCH, Leicestershire

Forest Court Accommodation

Annwell Place,
Ashby-de-la-Zouch LE65 2TA.

☎ 01530 411711.

W www.forestcourt.co.uk

● G

Motel in National Forest. 6 ground floor bedrooms level 77cm, restricted ⟲. No adaptations in shower rooms. Evening meals available. Also 2 self-catering bungalows with level or ramped entrances.

Ⓟ ⊗

Rates: from £40-£50 per room (2007).

BARLBOROUGH, Derbyshire

Ibis Sheffield South

3 Tallys End, Chesterfield Road, Barlborough, Sheffield S43 4TX.

☎ 01246 813222. @ H3157@accor.com

●● G

Hotel between Chesterfield and Sheffield, off M1 junction 30. Entrance level. Public rooms open plan. Lifts to upper floors. One bedroom with bathroom designed for disabled guests. Other bedrooms level.

Ⓟ ⊗

Rates: from £42-£49 per room (2008).

BOSTON, Lincolnshire

Special Needs Activity Centre Lincolnshire

14 Croppers Way, Freiston,
Boston PE22 0QT.

☎ 01205 761373. W www.snac.org.uk

●●● D/E/I/F/G

For information on this Centre for self-catering groups at which meals can be supplied by prior arrangement see page 273.

BUXTON, Derbyshire

Gradbach Mill Youth Hostel

Gradbach, Quarnford, Buxton SK17 0SU.

☎ 0870 770 4834.

@ gradbach@yha.org.uk

● D/E/I/F/G

Youth hostel in Peak District 7 miles from Buxton. Entrance step, 40". Dining room ground floor 29". Lounge upstairs. Five ground floor dormitories 31", ⟲. One with adapted shower room/WC. Waterproof sheets provided. Closed November-March. Advanced booking required. For more information on Youth Hostels see page 34.

Ⓟ ⊗

Rates: from £14 adult per night (2007).

CASTLE DONINGTON, Leicestershire

Donington Park Farmhouse Hotel

Melbourne Road, Isley Walton, Castle Donington DE74 2RN.

☎ **01332 862409.**

www.parkfarmhouse.co.uk

●● D/G ★★★★

Small country hotel in old farmhouse. Reserved parking bays. Entrance level then 1 step. Lounge/bar level. Dining room 1 step. Twin/double bedroom designed for disabled guests level. Shower room ⟲, roll-in shower, space for side transfer to WC. A Circle hotel.

Rates: from £75 single, £110 double BB (2007).

Express by Holiday Inn East Midlands Airport

Pegasus Business Park, Castle Donington DE74 2TQ.

☎ **01509 678000.**

@ **ema@expressholidayinn.co.uk**

●● D/E/F/G

Modern hotel near airport. Reserved parking bays. Slight slope to entrance. Low reception desk. Public rooms open plan. Unisex WC. Lift to all floors. Five double rooms designed for disabled guests. En suite roll-in shower room with shower seat, handrails, space by WC. Other bedrooms level.

Rates: on application.

Hilton East Midlands Airport Junction 24

Castle Donington DE74 2YW.

☎ **01509 674000.**

www.hilton.co.uk/eastmidlands

●● D/E/I/F/G ★★★★

Hotel near motorway and airport. Reserved parking bays. Entrance level, automatic doors. Public rooms ground floor open plan. Braille menus. Unisex WC. Lift 34", inside 53"x58". Two twin bedrooms designed for disabled guests ⟲. Bathrooms 31", ⟲, handrails, space for side transfer to WC. Waterproof sheet and vibrating pillow alarm available. Other bedrooms level.

Rates: on application.

CHESTERFIELD, Derbyshire

Ibis Chesterfield

Lordsmill Street, Chesterfield S41 7RW.

☎ **0124 622 1333.**

@ **H3160@accor.com**

●● D/E/G

Hotel on edge of town. Entrance level. Public rooms open plan. Unisex WC. Two bedrooms with bathrooms designed for disabled guests. Other bedrooms level.

Rates: from £50-£54 per room (2008).

CLEETHORPES, N E Lincolnshire

The Comat Hotel

26 Yarra Road, Cleethorpes DN35 8LS.

☎ **01472 694791.**

www.comat-hotel.co.uk.

● D/G 

Seaside guest house. Street parking. Step at entrance, ramp available. Reception/lounge/bar open plan. Dining room level 27". Two ground floor bedrooms 30", ⟲. Bath or shower room ⟲, no adaptations. Other bedrooms upstairs.

Rates: from £50 per person BB (2007).

COALVILLE, Leicestershire

Hermitage Park Hotel

Whitwick Road, Coalville LE67 3FA.

☎ **01530 814814.**

www.hermitageparkhotel.co.uk

●● D/E/I/F/G ★★★

Modern hotel off A511. Reserved parking bay. Entrance level. Low reception desk. Public rooms level, open plan. Unisex WC. Double bedroom designed for disabled guests. Bathroom 30", no ↻, handrails, space by bath and WC. Other ground floor bedrooms level.

Rates: from £65- £77.50 double BB (2006).

CORBY, Northamptonshire

Holiday Inn Corby-Kettering

Geddington Road, Corby NN18 8ET.

☎ **01536 401020.**

reservations@hicorby.com

●● D/E/F/G

Hotel on edge of town on A43. Reserved parking bays. Entrance level, automatic door. Public rooms level. Unisex WC. Lift to all floors. Two twin bedrooms designed for disabled guests. Shower rooms ↻. Other bedrooms level.

Rates: on application.

CRICK, Northamptonshire

Holiday Inn Rugby/Northampton

Crick NN6 7XR.

☎ **0870 400 9059.**

rugbyhi@ihg.com

● D/E/I/F/G ★★★

Hotel near M1 Junction 18. Reserved parking bays. Slope and ramp or 10 steps to entrance, automatic door. Public rooms level, open plan. Unisex WC. Lift 95cm, inside 102x137cm. Bedrooms and bathrooms level, no adaptations at present. Induction loop, large print information and teletext TV available.

Rates: on application.

Ibis Rugby East

Parklands, DIRFT East, Crick NN6 7EX.

☎ **01788 824331.** **H3588@accor.com**

●● D/E/F/G

Hotel between Daventry and Rugby near M1 junction 18. Entrance level. Public rooms open plan. Lifts to upper floors. Two bedrooms with bathroom designed for disabled guests. Other bedrooms level.

Rates: from £45-£57 per room (2008).

DERBY, Derbyshire

Days Hotel Derby

Derbyshire County Cricket Ground, Nottingham Road, Derby DE21 6DA.

☎ **01332 363600.**

www.dayshotelderby.com

●● D/E/I/F/G ★★★

Hotel off A52 approach to town. Reserved parking bays. Slope to level entrance, automatic doors. Low reception desk. Public rooms open plan. Unisex WC. Lift 80cm, inside 110x220cm. 2 bedrooms with bathrooms designed for disabled guests 93cm, ↻. Adjoining leisure centre level.

Rates: from £57-£95 per night (2008).

Express by Holiday Inn Derby

Wheelwright Way, Pride Park,
Derby DE24 8HX.

☎ 01332 388000.

@ derby@expressholidayinn.co.uk

●● E/I/G

Limited service hotel near city centre and football stadium. Reserved parking bays. Level entrance, automatic door. Low reception desk. Public rooms open plan, level. Unisex WC. Lift 35″. 8 double bedrooms designed for disabled guests. Shower rooms 31.5″, ↺, roll-in shower with seat, handrails, space by WC. Other bedrooms level. Teletext TVs. Restaurant adjacent.

Rates: from £65.95-£109 per room BB (2007).

Innkeepers Lodge Derby

Nottingham Road, Chaddesden,
Derby DE21 6LZ.

☎ 0845 112 6047.

●● D/E/I/F/G

Limited service hotel by Toby Carvery on A6005. Reserved parking bays. Entrances level. Restaurant and bar level. Unisex WC. Two bedrooms designed for disabled guests with roll-in shower rooms. Other ground floor rooms level. Teletext TV.

Rates: £53-£59.95 per room BB (2007).

EDWINSTOWE, Nottinghamshire

Sherwood Forest Youth Hostel

Forest Corner, Edwinstowe,
Mansfield NG21 9RH.

☎ 0870 770 6026. @ sherwood@yha.org.uk

●● D/E/I/F/G ★★★★

Youth hostel on edge of Sherwood Forest Country Park. Reserved parking bays. Entrance level, double doors. Low reception desk. Dining room and one lounge level. Main lounge upstairs. Unisex WC. Two bedrooms designed for disabled guests. En suite or adjoining shower room ↺, roll-in shower with seat, handrails. 9 other ground floor rooms. For more information on Youth Hostels see page 34.

Rates: from £15.50 adult per night (2007).

GAINSBOROUGH, Lincolnshire

Black Swan Guest House

21 High Street, Marton,
Gainsborough DN21 5AH.

☎ 01427 718878.

W www.guesthouse-hotel-gainsborough.co.uk

●● D/E/G

Country guesthouse near Gainsborough. Entrance level. 2 steps or ramp to dining room. 5 double and 3 family bedrooms. One bedroom is adapted for disabled guests. Bathroom ↺, roll-in shower and seat. One other level bedroom. Breakfast served in bedroom if required. 2 ground floor self-catering apartments are also available.

Rates: from £34-£45 per person BB (2005).

GRANTHAM, Lincolnshire

Best Western Kings Hotel

130 North Parade, Grantham NG31 8AU.

☎ 01476 590800.

@ kings@bestwestern.co.uk

● D/E/I/F/G

Hotel on edge of town. Entrance level, double doors. Lounge open plan. Restaurant level 60″. Bar ramp 30″. Unisex WC. Three ground floor bedrooms 27″, ↺. Shower rooms no ↺.

Rates: from £79-£115 double BB (2007).

Grantham Marriott Hotel

Swingbridge Road, Grantham NG31 7XT.

☎ **01476 593000.**

●● D/E/I/G ★★★★

Hotel A1/A607 junction. Reserved parking bays. Entrance level, automatic door. Public rooms level. Unisex WC. Two twin bedrooms designed for disabled guests. Bathrooms 32", ⟲, handrails, space for side transfer to bath and WC. Other ground floor bedrooms level.

Rates: on application.

GRIMSBY, N E Lincolnshire

The Beeches Hotel & Brasserie

42 Waltham Road, Scartho,
Grimsby DN33 2LX.

☎ **01472 278830.**

www.thebeecheshotel.com

●● D/E/I/F/G ★★★

Hotel in village south of Grimsby. Entrance level, double doors. Table by reception desk. Public rooms ground floor, mainly open plan. Unisex WC. Lift to upper floor. One twin bedroom adapted for disabled guests. Bathroom with space by bath and WC. Also 4 level double bedrooms on ground floor.

Rates: from £60 weekend BB (2008).

HARTINGTON, Derbyshire

YHA Hartington Hall

Hall Bank, Hartington, Buxton SK17 0AT.

☎ **01298 84223.**

Hartington@yha.org.uk

●● D/E/I/F/G ★★★★

Hostel in 17th century mansion on edge of Peak District village. Reserved parking bays. Slope to level front entrance. Low reception desk. Public rooms ground floor, level or ramped, including restaurant, bar and self-catering kitchen. Unisex WC. One family bedroom designed for disabled people with bathroom 38", ⟲, handrails, bathseat. Other ground floor bedrooms available. Induction loop. For further information, see page 34.

Rates: from £16-£24.50 adult per night (2008).

HINCKLEY, Leicestershire

Paramount Hinckley Island Hotel

A5 Watling Street, Hinckley LE10 3JA.

☎ **01455 631122.**

hinevents@paramount-hotels.co.uk

●● D/E/I/F/G ★★★★

Large hotel near M69/A5 junction. Reserved parking bays. Entrance level, automatic doors. Public rooms level. Unisex WC. Lift 48", inside 60"x60". Eight ground floor bedrooms adapted for disabled guests. Bathrooms 30", ⟲, handrails by WC. Other bedrooms level.

Rates: on application.

HUMBERSTON, N E Lincolnshire

The Tertia Trust Residential Centre

South Sea Lane, Humberston,
Grimsby DN36 4JX.

☎ 01472 812378 or 07881 887602

●●

Residential centre close to Cleethorpes & Pleasure Island designed for groups of young people including those with disabilities. Accommodation in single storey dormitories or tents with separate accommodation for group leaders. 6 acre site with facilities for activities. Full board or self-catering options available.

Ⓟ

Rates: on application.

LAXTON, Northamptonshire

Spanhoe Lodge

Laxton, nr. Corby NN17 3AT.

☎ 01780 450328.

www.spanhoelodge.co.uk

● ● D/E/F/G

Guesthouse in Rockingham Forest between Corby and Stamford. Reserved parking bay. Entrance 1 step or portable ramp. Low reception desk. Public rooms level, sill from lounge to conservatory. Unisex WC. 2 double bedrooms with interconnecting door, ramp to french doors. Bathrooms 75cm, ⟲, no handrails. Extension with restaurant and 2 additional bedrooms for disabled people.

Ⓟ

Rates: from £80-£100 per room BB (2007).

LEICESTER, Leicestershire

Campanile Leicester

St Matthews Way, Bedford Street North,
Leicester LE1 3JE.

☎ 0114 261 6601.

leicester@campanile-hotels.com

●● ★

Hotel near city centre off Inner Ring Road. Reserved parking bays. Public rooms level. Unisex WC. 4 bedrooms designed for disabled guests. Bathroom ⟲, handrails, space for side transfer. Other ground floor bedrooms level. See page 31.

Ⓟ

Rates: on application.

Hilton Leicester

Junction 21 Approach, Leicester LE19 1WQ.

☎ 0116 263 0066.

www.hilton.co.uk/leicester

●● D/E/I/F/G ★★★★

Modern hotel near M1/M69 junction. Reserved parking bays. Entrance level, automatic door. Public rooms, open plan, ramp or 3 steps to bar. Unisex WC. Lift to 1st floor. Six ground floor double bedrooms designed for disabled guests with remote control door opener, intercom, vibrating pillow alarm, door to adjoining room in 4 rooms. Bathroom ⟲, handrails, space for side transfer to bath and WC. Bath seat and some other equipment available. Other ground floor bedrooms level. Adapted changing room in Health Club and hoist to pool. Teletext TVs and induction loop at reception.

Ⓟ

Rates: on application.

Holiday Inn Leicester

129 St Nicholas Circle, Leicester LE1 5LX.
☎ **0870 400 9048**
@ **leicestercity.reservations@ihg.com**
●● D/G ★★★★
City centre hotel. Reserved parking bays. Entrance ramp, automatic doors. Reception and restaurant level. WCs adapted. Lifts to all floors. Two bedrooms designed for disabled guests. Bathroom ⟲, handrails. Other bedrooms level.
Ⓟ ⊗
Rates: on application.

Ibis Leicester

St George's Way, Constitution Hill, Leicester LE1 1PL.
☎ **0116 248 7200.** @ **H3061@accor.com**
●● D/E/G
Hotel near city centre. Entrance level. Publicrooms open plan. Unisex WC. Lift from ent-rance to all floors. 5 bedrooms with bathrooms designed for disabled guests. Other bedrooms level.
Ⓟ ⊗
Rates: from £53-£58 per night (2008).

LINCOLN, Lincolnshire

The Bentley Hotel & Leisure Club

Newark Rd, South Hykeham, Lincoln LN6 9NH.
☎ **01522 878000.**
W **www.thebentleyhotel.uk.com**
●● D/E/F/G ★★★
Hotel on western approach to city. Reserved parking bays. Entrance level, automatic door. Public rooms ground floor level. Unisex WC. Lift 81cm, inside 100x140cm. Three twin bedrooms designed for disabled guests. Shower rooms 90cm, ⟲, roll-in shower with seat, handrails, space by WC. Other bedrooms level. A Best Western hotel.
Ⓟ ⊗
Rates: from £88-£102 double BB (2008).

Damon's Motel

997 Doddington Road, Lincoln LN6 3SE.
☎ **01522 887733.** W **www.damons.co.uk**
●● E/F/G
Motel on south west edge of city. Slope to entrance. Restaurant and bar with separate entrance level. Unisex WC. Three bedrooms, twins and double, designed for disabled guests. Bathrooms ⟲, handrails space for side transfer. Other bedrooms level.
Ⓟ ⊗
Rates: from £59 room only (2007).

Ibis Lincoln

A46 off Whisby Road, South Hykeham, Lincoln LN6 3 QZ.
☎ **01522 698333.** @ **H3161@accor.com**
●● D/E/G
Hotel south of city off A46. Entrance level. Public rooms open plan. Lifts to upper floors. One bedroom with bathroom designed for disabled guests. Other bedrooms level.
Ⓟ ⊗
Rates: from £49 per room (2008).

Newport Guest House

26-28 Newport, Lincoln LN1 3DF.
☎ **01522 528590.**
W **www.newportguesthouse.co.uk.**
●● D/E/F/G
City centre guesthouse. Reserved parking bay. Rear entrance level 73cm; 2 steps at front entrance. Dining room and lounge ground floor. Twin bedroom ground floor 77cm, restricted ⟲. Shower room 88cm, roll-in shower with seat, handrails, space by WC. One other ground floor bedroom. Regular disabled guests.
Ⓟ ⊗
Rates: from £37-£55 per room BB (2008).

LONG EATON, Derbyshire

Novotel Nottingham/Derby

Bostocks Lane, Long Eaton, Nottingham NG10 4EP.

☎ 0115 946 5111. @ H0507@accor.com

●● D/E/F/G ★★★

Hotel off M1 junction 25. Reserved parking bays. Step on approach to entrance 66". Public rooms level. Adapted cubicles in WCs, no ⟲. Lift 66"x66". Eight bedrooms designed for disabled guests 30", ⟲. Bathroom 48" sliding door, ⟲, handrail, space for side transfer to bath and WC. Other bedrooms level.

Ⓟ

Rates: from £50-£95 per room (2007).

Ramada Nottingham Hotel

Bostocks Lane, Long Eaton, Nottingham NG10 4EP.

☎ 0115 946 0000.

@ sales.nottingham@ramadajarvis.co.uk

●● D/E/I/F/G ★★★

Hotel near M1. Reserved parking bays. Entrance level, heavy swing door. Public rooms level. Unisex WC. Stair lift to 1st floor. 4 ground floor bedrooms adapted for disabled guests. Bathrooms ⟲. Other ground floor bedrooms level. Teletext TVs.

Ⓟ

Rates: on application.

LOUGHBOROUGH, Leicestershire

Ramada Loughborough Hotel

High Street, Loughborough LE11 2QL.

☎ 01509 233222.

W www.ramadaloughboroughhotel.com

●● D/E/F/G ★★★

Hotel in town centre. Reserved parking bays. Ramp or 3 steps to car park entrance. Public rooms, ground floor, open plan. Unisex WC on lower floor. Lift to all floors. 2 bedrooms for two people designed for disabled guests. Shower rooms ⟲, roll-in shower. Other bedrooms level.

Ⓟ

Rates: on application.

LOUTH, Lincolnshire

The Beaumont Hotel

Victoria Road, Louth LN11 0BX.

☎ 01507 605005.

W www.thebeaumonthotel.co.uk

● D/G ★★★

Hotel on edge of town. Reserved parking bays. Entrance level. Public rooms level, min. door width 75cm. Unisex WC. Lift 90cm, inside 100x200cm. Twin and double bedrooms level, 85 cm, ⟲. Bathrooms no ⟲ or handrails.

Ⓟ

Rates: from £85 double BB (2008).

MOUNTSORREL, Leicestershire

Mountsorrel Hotel

217 Loughborough Road,
Mountsorrel LE12 7AR.
☎ **01509 412627.**
www.mountsorrelhotel.co.uk
●● D/E/F/G

Privately owned hotel in village between Leicester and Loughborough. Side entrance level; 3 steps at front entrance. Low reception desk. Public rooms ground floor. Double bedroom designed for disabled guests. Bathroom 36", ⟲, roll-in shower with seat, handrails, space by bath and WC. Other ground floor bedrooms level.

Rates: on application.

NORTH KILWORTH, Leicestershire

Kilworth House Hotel

Lutterworth Road,
North Kilworth LE17 6JE.
☎ **01858 880058.**
www.kilworthhouse.co.uk
●● D/E/G ★★★★

Country hotel between Lutterworth and Market Harborough, 4 miles from M1 junction 20. Reserved parking bays. Slight ramp to entrance. Public rooms level. Unisex WC. Lift to upper floors. Two ground floor bedrooms designed for disabled guests. Bathrooms ⟲, roll-in shower with seat, space by bath and WC. Other bedrooms level. Teletext TV. Wheelchair available.

Rates: from £150-£165 per night BB (2007).

NORTHAMPTON, Northamptonshire

Express by Holiday Inn Northampton

Grange Park, Northampton NN4 5FB.
☎ **01604 432800.** **northampton@expressbyholidayinn.net**
●● E/I/F/G

Limited service hotel off M1 junction 15 south of Northampton. Reserved parking bays. Entrance level, automatic doors. Low reception desk. Open plan public rooms. Unisex WC. Lift to upper floors. 7 double bedrooms designed for disabled guests. Shower room 32", ⟲, roll-in shower with seat, handrails, space by WC, vibrating and visual alarms. Other bedrooms level. Wheelchair and portable induction loop available. Teletext TV. Meals in nearby Harvester restaurant.

Rates: on application.

Hilton Northampton Hotel

100 Watering Lane, Collingtree,
Northampton NN4 0XW.
☎ **01604 700666.**
www.hilton.co.uk/northampton
●● D/E/I/F/G

Hotel near M1 junction 15. Reserved parking bays. Entrance level, automatic doors. Public rooms level open plan. Unisex WC. Two double bedrooms designed for disabled guests 40", door intercom, flashing light and vibrating pillow alarms. Bathroom 28", ⟲, handrails, space for side transfer to bath and WC. Interconnecting rooms available. Other level bedrooms.

Rates: on application.

Holiday Inn Northampton West M1 J16

High Street, Flore,
Nr. Northampton NN7 4LP.

☎ 01327 349022.

●● D/E/I/G 

Hotel near M1 between Northampton and Daventry. Entrance level. Public rooms level. Unisex WC. Two bedrooms designed for disabled guests 31". Bathrooms, no space for side transfer to WC.

Rates: on application.

Ibis Northampton

Sol Central, Marefare,
Northampton NN1 1SR.

☎ 01604 608900. @ H3657@accor.com

●● G

Hotel in town centre. Entrance level. Public rooms level, open plan. Unisex WC. 2 lifts to all floors. Eight bedrooms with bathrooms designed for disabled guests. Other 143 bedrooms level.

Rates: from £50-£57 per room (2008).

King's Park Conference Centre

King's Park Road, Moulton Park,
Northampton NN7 1NG.

☎ 01604 493111.

@ kingsparkcentre@actioncentres.co.uk

●● D/E/F/G

Conference centre on edge of town. Reserved parking bays. Slope to level entrance. Low reception desk. Public rooms ground floor level. Unisex WC. Five twin bedrooms designed for disabled guests 100cm. Shower rooms 85cm, roll-in shower with seat, handrails, space for side transfer to WC. 89 other bedrooms, half on ground floor. Induction loop in conference room and restaurant.

Rates: on application.

NOTTINGHAM, Nottinghamshire

Express by Holiday Inn Nottingham

Chapel Bar, Maid Marion Way,
Nottingham NG1 6JS.

☎ 0870 417 6000.

W www.exhinottingham.com

●● E/I/F/G

Limited service hotel in city centre. Car park across road. Entrance level. Low reception desk. Public rooms open plan. Unisex WC. Lift to upper floors. Six bedrooms designed for disabled guests. Shower rooms, roll in shower with seat, handrails and space by WC. Waterproof sheet, vibrating alarm and induction loop available. Other bedrooms level.

Rates: on application.

Holiday Inn Nottingham

Castle Marina Park, Nottingham NG7 1GX.

☎ 0115 993 5000.

@ holidayinn.nottingham@zoom.co.uk

●● D/F/G

Business hotel near city centre. Reserved parking bays. Entrance ramp, automatic doors. Public rooms open plan, level. Unisex WC. Lift to all floors. Three ground floor double bedrooms designed for disabled guests. Bathroom with handrails and space by bath and WC. Other 125 bedrooms level.

Rates: on application.

Ibis Nottingham Centre

16 Fletchergate, Nottingham NG1 2FS.
☎ **0115 985 3600.** @ **H6160@accor.com**
●● D/E/G

Hotel in Lace Market area of city centre. Entrance level. Public rooms open plan. Lifts to upper floors. Seven bedrooms with bathroom designed for disabled guests. Other bedrooms level.

Rates: on application.

Nottingham Gateway Hotel

Nuthall Road, Nottingham NG8 6AZ.
☎ **0115 979 4949.**
W **www.nottinghamgatewayhotel.co.uk**
●● D/E/I/F/G ★★★

Hotel in suburb near M1 J26. Reserved parking bays. Entrance level. Public rooms level. Unisex WC. Two lifts 76cm, inside 220x156cm. 6 bedrooms designed for disabled guests. Bathrooms 78cm, ⟲, handrails, space for side transfer to bath and WC. Other bedrooms level. Regular disabled guests.

Rates: on application.

Village Hotel & Leisure Club

Brailsford Way, Chilwell,
Nottingham NG9 6DL.
☎ **0115 946 4422.**
@ **reservations.vn@village-hotels.com**
●● D/E/F/G

Modern hotel outside city near M1 junction 25. Reserved parking bays. Entrance ramp or 7 steps, automatic door. Restaurant and bar level. Lounge 2 steps. Unisex WC. Lift 90cm, inside 135x140cm. One twin and 4 double bedrooms designed for disabled guests. Bathrooms 86cm, ⟲, handrails, space for side transfer to bath and WC.

Rates: on application.

Vitalise Skylarks

Adbolton Road, West Bridgford,
Nottingham NG2 5AS.
☎ **0115 982 0962.**
●●●●● D/E/I/H

Centre in country park by National Water Sports Centre . Purpose-built for breaks by people with physical disabilities and carers. 26 single and and 5 twin ensuite bedrooms. Activities, outings, entertainment and special breaks offered. Own nature reserve. 24-hour care on-call and personal support provided.

Apply: Vitalise ☎ 0845 345 1970.
See page 27.
Rates: on application.

OSGATHORPE, Leicestershire

Royal Oak House

20 Main Street, Osgathorpe,
Loughborough LE12 9TA.
☎ **01530 222443.**
● D/E/I/F/G

Guesthouse in village between Ashby-de-la-Zouch and Shepshed. Accommodation in chalet bedrooms with own parking. Entrance 1 step. Shower room ⟲, step into shower, handrail by WC. Breakfast served in bedroom.

Rates: from £25-£35 BB (2008).

SANDIACRE, Nottinghamshire

Holiday Inn Derby/Nottingham

Bostocks Lane, Sandiacre, Nottingham NG10 5NJ.

☎ **0870 400 9062.**

@ **reservations-nottingham@ihg.com**

●● D/E/I/F/G

Hotel between Derby and Nottingham off M1 junction 25. Reserved parking bays. Ramp or 5 steps to entrance. Public rooms open plan. Unisex WC. 5 steps or ramp to bedroom corridor. 2 double bedrooms adapted for disabled guests. Bathroom ⟲, handrail by bath, space by bath and WC. Other ground floor bedrooms level. Waterproof sheets, vibrating alarm, induction loops available.

Rates: from £52 per person BB (2008).

SKEGNESS, Lincolnshire

Chatsworth Hotel

16 North Parade, Skegness PE25 2UB.

☎ **01754 764177.**

W **www.chatsworthskegness.co.uk**

●● D/E/I/F/G

Seafront hotel. Entrance ramp. Public rooms level. WC level, 33". Stairlifts to upper floors. Bedroom with bathroom designed for disabled guests ⟲, handrails, adjustable height basin, raised WC seat, space for side transfer to low bath. Other bedrooms level.

Rates: on application.

Crown Hotel

Drummond Road, Skegness PE25 3AB.

☎ **01754 610760.** W **www.crownhotel.biz**

●● D/E/F/G ★★★

Hotel on coast to south of town. Level entrance. Public rooms ground floor, ramp at one entrance to bar. Lift 80cm, inside 89x122cm. Bedroom with double and single beds 76cm, ⟲. Bathroom 72cm, ⟲, handrails and space by bath and WC. Other bedrooms level. Level access to pool.

Rates: from £40-£50 per person BB (2008).

Mayfair Hotel

10 Saxby Avenue, Skegness PE25 3JZ.

☎ **01754 764687.**

W **www.mayfair-skegness.co.uk**

●● D/E/I/F/G

Family owned licensed hotel. Entrance 60", threshold. Public rooms level. Unisex WC. Three ground floor bedrooms ⟲ with bathrooms. One has 30" door, roll-in shower with seat, handrails. Shared shower room/WC 30", roll-in shower, seat, handrails. Stairlift to upper floor. Some equipment available.

Ⓟ ⊗

Rates: on application.

North Parade Hotel

20 North Parade, Skegness PE25 2UB.

☎ **01754 762309.**

W **www.north-parade-hotel.co.uk**

● D/E/I/F/G

Family-run hotel on seafront. Ramp with handrails to entrance, 34". Restaurant and lounge ground floor, level. Stair lift to bar/games room. Unisex WC, no space for side transfer. Lift to upper floors 28", inside 28"X37". Bedrooms level with bathrooms, no ⟲ or adaptations.

Ⓟ ⊗

Rates: from £25 per person BB (2007).

Accommodation with meals

SOUTH NORMANTON, Derbyshire

Renaissance Derby/ Nottingham Hotel

Carter Lane East,
South Normanton DE55 2EH.
☎ **01773 812000.** **W** **www.renaissancederbynottingham.co.uk**

D/E/F/G ★★★★

Hotel off M1 junction 28. Reserved parking bays. Dropped kerb to entrance, automatic door. Low reception desk. Public rooms level with wheelchair lift to Leisure Club. Adapted WC cubicles. Four bedrooms, double and twin, adapted for disabled guests. Bathrooms , handrails. Other ground floor bedrooms level.

Rates: on application.

SUTTON-ON-SEA, Lincolnshire

The Bacchus Hotel

17 High Street, Sutton-on-Sea,
Mablethorpe LN12 2EX.
☎ **01507 441204.**
W **www.bacchushotel.co.uk**

●● D/E/I/F/G ★★★★

Hotel/Inn in seaside town. Reserved parking bays. Small ramp to entrance. Public rooms ground floor. Unisex WC. Stair lift to 1st floor. Six bedrooms with bathrooms; all level, limited . 14 other bedrooms with bathrooms. Regular disabled guests.

Rates: from £76 twin BB (2008).

WELLINGBOROUGH, Northamptonshire

Euro-Hotel

90-92 Midland Road,
Wellingborough NN8 1NB.
☎ **01933 228761.**

●● D/E/G

Privately owned hotel near town centre and station. Entrance ramp, 53". Lounge and bar ground floor level. Dining room on lower floor with separate entrance at rear; breakfast can be served in bedrooms. Unisex WC. Three ground floor bedrooms with bathrooms 39", turning space, space for side transfer.

Ⓟ

Rates: from £35-£45 BB (2008).

Ibis Wellingborough

Enstone Court,
Wellingborough NN8 2DR.
☎ **01933 228333.** **@** **H3164@accor.com**

●●

Hotel off A45 south of town centre. Reserved parking bays. Entrance level. Low reception desk. Public rooms open plan. Unisex WC. Lift 90cm. Two bedrooms designed for disabled guests. Shower room 82cm, turning space, roll-in shower, handrails, space for side transfer to WC. Other 77 bedrooms level. Visual alarm.

Ⓟ 🚭 🐕

Rates: from £46-£56 per room (2008).

WOODHALL SPA, Lincolnshire

Kirkstead Old Mill Cottage

Tattershall Road, Woodhall Spa LN10 6UQ.
☎ 01526 353637.
W www.woodhallspa.com
●●● D/E/F/G

Bed & breakfast in riverside cottage on farm track a mile from road. Slope from parking area to level entrance, 91cm, main entrance 2 steps. Breakfast room and lounge level. Ground floor double bedroom designed for disabled guests with touch sensitive lights and fridge. Shower room 91cm, ⟲, roll-in shower with stool and trolley, handrails, adjustable basin, space by WC. Ionizer and filter ceiling fans. Teletext TV, personal hearing loop and vibrating alarm. Some other equipment available. Other bedrooms upstairs. Raised flower beds and fishpond in garden.

Rates: from £30-£40 per person BB (2008).

Petwood House Hotel

Woodhall Spa LN10 6QF.
☎ 01526 352411. W www.petwood.co.uk
●● D/E/F/G ★★★

Country house hotel. Reserved parking bays. Entrance ramp. Restaurant and bar level; 2 steps to lounge. Unisex WC. Lift to all floors. A double bedroom adapted for disabled guests. Shower room 29", roll-in shower with seat, space for side transfer. Raised WC seat available. Other bedrooms level.

Rates: from £99 single, £145 double BB (2008).

LODGE ACCOMMODATION

There are Days Inn (see page 34), Premier Travel Inn (see page 38) and Travelodge (see page 38) properties in the following areas in this region.

Alfreton - Travelodge ..... ☎ 0870 191 1619
Ashby de la Zouch - Premier Travel Inn ..... ☎ 0870 197 7281
Blyth - Travelodge ..... ☎ 0870 191 1623
Boston - Premier Travel Inn ..... ☎ 0870 197 7035
Castle Donington - Days Inn ..... ☎ 01332 798666
Travelodge ..... ☎ 0870 191 1573
Chesterfield - Premier Travel Inn ..... ☎ 0870 197 7060
Travelodge ..... ☎ 0870 191 1629
Colsterworth - Travelodge ..... ☎ 0870 191 1575
Daventry - Premier Travel Inn ..... ☎ 0870 990 6364
Derby - Travelodge ..... ☎ 0870 191 1572
Derby, East - Premier Travel Inn ..... ☎ 0870 238 3313
Derby, North West - Premier Travel Inn ..... ☎ 0870 990 6606

East Midlands

Derby South - Premier Travel Inn ☎ 0870 990 6306
Derby, West - Premier Travel Inn ☎ 0870 197 7072
Grantham - Premier Travel Inn ☎ 0870 850 0329
Grantham, New Fox - Travelodge ☎ 0870 191 1576
Grantham, North - Travelodge ☎ 01476 577500
Grimsby - Premier Travel Inn ☎ 0870 197 7121
Kettering - Premier Travel Inn ☎ 0870 197 7147
Travelodge ☎ 0870 191 1581
Leicester - Premier Travel Inn ☎ 0870 990 6398
Travelodge ☎ 0870 191 1755
Leicester, Braunstone - Premier Travel Inn ☎ 0870 197 7154
Leicester, Braunstone S - Premier Travel Inn ☎ 0870 850 6332
Leicester Forest East - Days Inn ☎ 0116 239 0534
PremierTravel Inn ☎ 0870 197 7155
Leicester, Markfield - Travelodge ☎ 0870 191 1583
Leicester, North - Travelodge ☎ 0870 191 1584
Leicester, North West - Premier Travel Inn ☎ 0870 990 6520
Lincoln - Premier Travel Inn ☎ 0870 197 7156
Travelodge ☎ 0870 191 1585
Long Sutton - Travelodge ☎ 0870 191 1582
Lutterworth - Travelodge ☎ 0870 191 1681
Mansfield - Premier Travel Inn ☎ 0870 197 7180
Travelodge ☎ 0879 191 1640
Mansfield, Tibshelf - Premier Travel Inn ☎ 0870 197 7181
Market Harborough - Premier Travel Inn ☎ 0870 850 6300
Newark - Premier Travel Inn ☎ 0870 197 7186
Travelodge ☎ 0870 191 1588
Northampton - Premier Travel Inn ☎ 0870 990 6510
Travelodge ☎ 0870 191 1589
Northampton, East - Premier Travel Inn ☎ 0870 197 7196
Northampton, South - Premier Travel Inn ☎ 0870 990 6426
Northampton. West - Premier Travel Inn ☎ 0870 197 7195
Nottingham - Premier Travel Inn ☎ 0870 238 3314
Travelodge ☎ 0870 191 1780
Nottingham, Castle Marina - Premier Travel Inn ☎ 0870 187 7199

Nottingham, London Rd - Premier Travel Inn ☎ 0870 990 6574
Nottingham, North - Premier Travel Inn ☎ 0870 990 6328
Nottingham, Riverside - Travelodge ☎ 0870 191 1592
Nottingham, Trowell - Travelodge ☎ 0870 191 1593
Nottingham, South - Premier Travel Inn ☎ 0870 990 6422
Nottingham, West - Premier Travel Inn ☎ 0870 197 7200
Oadby - Premier Travel Inn ☎ 0870 990 6452
Retford - Travelodge ☎ 0870 191 1598
Rushton - Travelodge ☎ 0870 191 1615
Scunthorpe - Premier Travel Inn ☎ 0870 197 7226
Travelodge ☎ 0870 191 1786
Silverstone - Premier Travel Inn ☎ 0870 990 6382
Travelodge ☎ 0870 191 1612
Sleaford - Travelodge ☎ 0870 191 1604
Thrapston - Travelodge ☎ 0870 191 1611
Uppingham - Travelodge ☎ 0870 191 1613
Watford Gap - Premier Travel Inn ☎ 0870 197 7301
Wellingborough - Premier Travel Inn ☎ 0870 197 7262
Worksop - Travelodge ☎ 0870 191 1684

SELF-CATERING ACCOMMODATION

APPLEBY MAGNA, Leicestershire
Upper Rectory Farm Cottages

Snarestone Road, Appleby Magna, Nr. Swadlincote.
W **www.upperrectoryfarmcottages.co.uk**
●● F/G

9 cottages in country in north west Leicestershire and the National Forest. Six have ground floor accommodation sleeping 2-8 people. All entrances 33", 1 step, portable ramp available. Lounge/kitchen open plan, cooker controls useable from wheelchair. ⟲ in some bedrooms. Standard en-suite bathrooms. A separate roll-in shower room with handrails, low basin, lever controls and space by WC is available for people staying in all cottages. Teletext TV. Assistance dogs in one cottage only. Access statement available.

Apply: Mrs Jean Corbett, Cottage Farm, Norton-juxta-Twycross, Atherstone CV9 3QH. ☎ 01827 880448.
Rates: on application.

ASHBOURNE, Derbyshire
Ancestral Barn

Church Farm, Stanshope, nr. Ashbourne
● F/G ★★★★

Converted barn on organic Peak District Farm near Dovedale. Entrance level, small step from hallway to lounge. Kitchen 31", no ⟲. Level bedroom with double canopy bed. Shower room 31", roll-in shower with seat and handrails, raised WC seat available. Double and twin bedrooms with bath/shower rooms upstairs. Teletext TV. A second cottage also available.

Apply: Sue & Steve Fowler, Church Farm, Stanshope, Ashbourne DE6 2AD.
☎ 01335 310243.
W www.dovedalecottages.co.uk
Rates: from £345-£876 per week (2008).

ASHOVER, Derbyshire
Holestone Moor Barns

Holestone Moor Farm, Holestone Moor, Ashover S45 0JS.
☎ **01246 591263.**
W **www.hmbarns.co.uk**
●● I/F/G

Two cottages on farm between Chesterfield and Matlock. "The Barn", sleeping up to 12, designed for disabled people. Ramp from courtyard. Entrance 130cm. Lounge, dining room and kitchen on ground floor. Kitchen controls useable from wheelchair. Twin bedroom level ⟲. Shower room ⟲, roll-in shower, handrails, space by WC. Shower chair and raised WC seat available. Four bedrooms with bathrooms upstairs. One step to "The Stables", a second cottage with ground floor accommodation for up to 4 people.

Rates: £226-£1929 per week (2008).

BAKEWELL, Derbyshire
Bolehill Farm

Moneyash Road, Bakewell DE45 1QW.
☎ **01629 812359.**
W **www.bolehillfarm.co.uk**
●● G ★★★★

"Derwent Cottage", adapted for disabled people. Entrance ramp, 42". Lounge/kitchen open plan. Worktops 36". Three bedrooms, min. door width 32". Bathroom 37", ⟲, handrails, space for side transfer to bath and WC. Three other ground floor cottages available.

Rates: from £280-£610 per week (2007).

BARLOW, Derbyshire

Heron Lodge

Oxton Rakes Hall Farm, Barlow S18 7SE.

●● F/G ★★★★

Lodge 2 miles from village on edge of Peak District. Ramp to veranda then entrance level, 33". Open plan lounge/kitchen. Open plan sleeping area with double bed level and two single beds upstairs. Bathroom level 32", space by bath and WC, no handrails.

Apply: Mrs Lynne Phillips

☎ 0114 289 1592.

W http://heronlodge.hypermart.net

Rates: on application.

BOSTON, Lincolnshire

Special Needs Accommodation Centre

14 Croppers Way, Freiston, Boston PE22 0QT.

☎ **01205 761373.**

W **www.snac.org.uk**

●●● D/E/I/F/G

Centre for groups of disabled people and carers east of Boston. Entrance 1 step. Living room and kitchen level. Two twin bedrooms level. Shower rooms have ⟲, roll-in shower, space for side transfer to WC. Four twin bedrooms with bath/shower rooms upstairs. Neighbouring house has recreation room, dining room and sleeping accommodation for a further 10 guests. Selected help available. Some games and activities at the Centre and advice on those in the surrounding area. Space for mini-golf, football and cycling; tandem and cycles provided. Self catering or meals on site by prior arrangement.

Rates: on application.

BRASSINGTON, Derbyshire

Hoe Grange Holidays

Brassington, Matlock DE4 4HP.

☎ **01629 540262.**

W **www.hoegrangeholidays.co.uk**

●● F/G ★★★★

Log cabins on dairy farm in southern Peak District. "Hipley", sleeps 4, has ramp to entrance, 34". Internal doors. Open plan lounge/kitchen, controls useable from wheelchair. Twin bedroom ⟲ with roll-in shower room handrails, low basin, space by WC. Also double bedroom with bath. Shower chair, bath board, raised WC seat and waterproof sheet available. Vibrating alarm clock. Hoist can be hired. Level veranda. 2nd cabin available.

Rates: on application.

BURGH-LE-MARSH, Lincolnshire

Chestnuts Farm & Country Cottages

Wainfleet Road, Burgh-le-Marsh PE24 5AH.

☎ **01754 810904.**

W **www.thechestnutsfarm.co.uk**

●● E/G

Holiday cottages on farm with private fishing waters between Skegness and Spilsby. "Farm Cottages" include adapted units. Entrance ramp, 33". Lounge and kitchen 33", ⟲. Two bedrooms and bathroom/WC ⟲. Three "Country Cottages", away from the main farm, have ground floor accommodation.

Apply: Mrs Mackinder

Rates: on application.

BUXTON, Derbyshire

Cressbrook Hall

Cressbrook, Nr. Buxton SK17 8SY.
☎ **01298 871289.**
www.cressbrookhall.co.uk
●● F ★★★

Cottages in grounds of 19th Century mansion between Buxton and Bakewell. "High Spy", "Top Spot", "Carriage Cottage", "Rubicon Retreat" and "Hidesaway" are said to be suitable for wheelchair users. Check specific access details before booking. Meals service available.

Apply: Mrs Hull-Bailey
Rates: on application.

CHESTERFIELD, Derbyshire

Ashgate Holiday Bungalow

Ashgreen, Ashgate Road, Ashgate, Chesterfield S42 7JE.
●●● I/F/G/H

Holiday bungalow owned by Mencap on outskirts of Chesterfield. Purpose-built for people with learning/physical disabilities and their companions. Entrance level. Two lounges, one with sofabed. Kitchen ⟲, controls and worktop useable from wheelchair. Single bedroom with adjustable height bed and ceiling hoist to en suite bathroom with roll-in shower. Waterproof sheets and mobile hoist available. Also two twin bedrooms, bathroom and 2 WCs.

Ⓟ

Apply: Julie Harbottle, Mencap, 96 Douglas Road, Long Eaton, Nottingham NG10 4BD. ☎ 0115 983 5731.
julie.harbottle@mencap.org.uk
Rates: on application.

High Hazel

Hardwick Hall, Doe Lea, Chesterfield.
●● F/G

One of 2 cottages in the Hardwick Hall Estate accommodates up to 11 people. Ground floor has kitchen, dining room, lounge with sofa bed and bathroom designed for disabled guests. 6 bedrooms, bathroom and WC on upper floors.

Ⓟ

Apply: National Trust Holiday Booking Office ☎ 0870 4584422. See page 33.
Rates: from £576-£1830 per week (2007).

DONINGTON, Lincolnshire

The Barn

110 Quadring Road, Donington, Spalding PE11 4SJ.
● I/F/G ★★★

Converted barn beside waterfowl garden, 6 miles from Spalding. Ramp to entrance. Open plan lounge/kitchen. Two bedrooms upstairs. Ground floor bathroom ⟲, handrail by bath, shower with seat, space by bath and WC. Owner is a nurse.

Ⓟ

Apply: Mrs Margaret Smith
☎ 01775 821242.
Rates: £200-£250 per week (2007).

HOGSTHORPE, Lincolnshire

Helsey House Cottages

Helsey, Hogsthorpe, nr. Skegness PE24 5PE.
☎ **01754 872927.**
www.helseycottagrs.co.uk
●● I/F/G

Two single storey cottages in country near coast. Entrances level 113 cm. Lounge/kitchen open plan, worktops 90cm. Twin and double bedrooms, furniture can be moved for ⟲. Bathrooms level, one also has a roll-in shower, space and handrail by WC. Shower chair available. Families with children with special needs welcome.

Rates: from £280-£400 per week (2008).

KIRK IRETON, Derbyshire

Grange Cottages

Tinkerley Lane, Kirk Ireton, Nr. Ashbourne.

●● F/G ★★★★

A single storey cottage between Ashbourne and Matlock. "Doveholes" has open plan lounge/kitchen, cooker controls useable from wheelchair. Double and twin bedrooms, plus sofa-bed in lounge. 3 steps at entrance and no specific adaptations. Wheelchair, raised WC seat and bath seat.

Apply: Malcolm Race, Grange Holidays, Tinkerley Lane, Kirk Ireton, Ashbourne DE6 3LF. ☎ 01335 370880.

www.malcolmrace.co.uk

Rates: from £230-£450 per week (2008).

MABLETHORPE, Lincolnshire

Golden Sands Holiday Park

Quebec Road, Mablethorpe LN12 1QJ.

☎ **01507 477871.**

●● I/F/G 

Haven holiday park near Mablethorpe with wide range of facilities and entertainment. Caravans for 5 people adapted for disabled guests. Entrance ramp. Lounge/kitchen open plan. Two bedrooms, sliding door 75cm, in double. Shower room 75cm, handrails, restricted, no space by WC. Open Late March-October.

Apply: Haven Holiday Reservations ☎ 0870 2422222.

Rates: on application.

MATLOCK, Derbyshire

Darwin Forest Country Park

Two Dales, Matlock DE4 5LN.

☎ **01629 732428.**

www.pinelodgeholidays.co.uk

●● G 

Three lodges designed for disabled people. Two sleep 4 people and one sleeps 6. Approach ramp. Entrance level 54" double doors. Lounge/kitchen open plan, controls useable from wheelchair. in twin bedroom. Bathroom 36" sliding door, , handrails, space for side transfer to bath and WC. Meals available on site. Shop level.

Rates: from £280-£980 per week (2008).

MELTON MOWBRAY, Leicestershire

Amberley Gardens Holiday Annexe

4 Church Lane, Asfordby-by-the-Wreake, Melton Mowbray LE14 3RU.

☎ **01664 812314.**

www.amberleygardens.net

 G 

Annexe to a riverside bungalow in village 3 miles from Melton. One step at entrance. Lounge and kitchen/diner, restricted. Double bedroom. Bathroom/WC no adaptations. Access to large garden. Full accessibility details on request.

Rates: from £175-£225 per week (2007).

MILFORD, Derbyshire

The Ebenezer Chapel

Derwent River Bridge, Milford.

W www.derbyshire-holidays.com

●● I/F/G

Converted former chapel in riverside village accommodating up to 22 people. Ramp or 1 step on approach. Entrance, 4" sill. Ground floor split level with two short flights of steps fitted with stairlifts. Three bedrooms on lower floor 38", ⟲. Bathroom 38", ⟲, handrails, space for side transfer to bath and WC. Lounge, dining room, kitchen and sauna. 2nd lounge and 4 bedrooms on 2nd floor. Ramp to garden. Pub/restaurant next door.

Apply: Derbyshire Holidays, The Cedars, Field Lane, Belper DE56 1DD.
☎ 01332 840 564
@ annwayne@derbyshire-holidays.com
Rates: from £855-£1595 per week (2008).

SKEGNESS, Lincolnshire

37 Langton Court

Burgh Road, Skegness

●● E/I/F

Bungalow adapted for wheelchair users. Entrance ramp. Open plan lounge/kitchen. Shower room/WC ⟲, roll-in shower, handrails. Shower chair and raised WC seat available. Sleeping up to four people in two bedrooms. Central heating.

Apply: Mrs Trudy Bennett, D.A.S.H. Holiday Homes, 6 Windsor Drive, Spalding PE11 2RP. ☎ 01775 768433.
Rates: from £185-£225 per week (2006).

Sunkist Caravan Park

Sea Road, Anderby Creek, Skegness PE24 5XW.

☎ **01754 872374.**

W **www.sunkistcaravanpark.co.uk**

●● I/F/G

Holiday park close to beach north of Skegness. One caravan for up to 6 designed for disabled guests. Entrance ramp or 3 steps, 84cm. Lounge/kitchen open plan, controls useable from wheelchair. Two bedrooms, ⟲ in one. Shower room 84cm sliding door, roll-in shower with seat, handrails, space by WC and under basin. Available mid March-October.

Rates: from £220-£400 per week (2008).

Newry Abbey, Ripon

The broad acres of England's largest county form this region stretching from the Tees to the Humber and the top of the Pennines to the North Sea. Within its borders are attractions for all types of holiday or short break.

Scarborough with its two bays, castle and surrounding hills is Britain's oldest and Yorkshire's largest seaside resort. Other centres for traditional seaside holidays include Bridlington and Filey with long, level seafronts and many attractions for families.

Many rural areas in Yorkshire are familiar through television programmes. The North York Moors provided the setting for "Heartbeat", the area around Northallerton is still known as Herriot Country and "The Last of the Summer Wine" is filmed in the Pennine valleys west of Halifax. Throughout the area there are opportunities to enjoy the countryside. In addition to two National Parks, covering the Yorkshire Dales and the North York Moors, there are many country parks run by local authorities and other organisations.

For many visitors the star attraction of Yorkshire is York itself, with its pedestrianised centre of medieval streets leading to York

Photo: www.britainonview.com/Joanna Henderson

Minster. The Association of York Guides can arrange a tour of the city using a route planned for disabled visitors. Other attractions of the city include Jorvic, showing life in the town at the time of the Vikings, and the award-wining National Railway Museum.

Historic buildings and stately homes that can be visited in the area include Fountains Abbey & Studley Royal, near Ripon, which is in the care of the National Trust, Brodsworth Hall near Doncaster that is run by English Heritage, Castle Howard east of York and Temple Newsam outside Leeds.

A number of important museums can be found in the region. The enormous Magna Science Adventure Centre at Rotherham is a Millennium projects. In Leeds there are the Medical Museum and the Royal Armouries. The National Museum of Photography, Film & Television is in central Bradford and the National Coal Mining Museum is near Wakefield. Children have their own museum, the award-winning Eureka, in Halifax. The Eden Camp Modern History Museum near Malton has a variety of World War II exhibits.

The major urban centres of Leeds and Sheffield offer an array of entertainment and sport of all types. Visitors are attracted to the Meadowhall Shopping Centre from all over the region. Other towns, large and small, have their own attractions. The oceans can be explored at The Deep in Hull. There are Cathedrals at Ripon and Doncaster, the home of the Brontes at Haworth, historic abbey ruins overlooking Whitby, magnificent gardens in Harrogate and many more attractions.

The Shambles, York

Photo: www.britainonview.com

USEFUL ADDRESSES

Yorkshire Tourist Board

312 Tadcaster Road, York YO24 1GS.
☎ 01904 707961.
@ info@ytb.org.uk.
W www.yorkshire.com

The Regional Tourist Board issues a number of publications on the area including **Make Yorkshire Yours** and the **Yorkshire Accommodation Guide**, which includes and indication of places that may cater for disabled people.

DIAL

DIAL offers a free, impartial and confidential service of information and advice by telephone to disabled people, their relatives and professionals. The following DIAL UK members may be able to help disabled residents and visitors in their areas:

DIAL Barnsley ☎ 01226 240273

Disability Advice Bradford
☎ 01274 594173;
Textphone: 01274 530951

Calderdale DART ☎ 01422 346040

DIAL Doncaster ☎ 01302 327800;
Textphone: 01302 768297

Choices & Rights, Hull ☎ 01482 878778;
Textphone: 01482 370986

DIAL Leeds ☎ 0113 214 3630;
Textphone: 0113 214 3627

Rotherham DIS
☎ 01709 373658

Scarborough DAG
☎/Text: 01723 379397

DIAL Selby
☎ 01757 210495

DIAL Wakefield ☎ 01977 723933/4;
Textphone: 01977 724081

DIAC York ☎ 01904 638467

USEFUL PUBLICATIONS & WEBSITES

Easy Going North York Moors – prepared by the National Park Authority in 2002 this guide gives information for disabled people on easy-going paths, view points, attractions, accommodation, toilets and transport in the North York Moors National Park. It can be ordered from Sutton Bank National Park Centre, Sutton Bank, Thirsk YO7 2EH. ☎ 01845 597426. Price £4.50 + £1.25 p&p. It is also available on the Access For All pages of www.visitthemoors.co.uk

www.disabledgo.info - this website includes detailed information on the accessibility of many premises in Bradford, Hull, Kirklees, Leeds, Wakefield and York.

EQUIPMENT HIRE

Bayliss Mobility Ltd

Enterprise Complex, Walmgate,
York YO1 9TT.
☎ **01904 611516.**
www.livingindependent.co.uk

This company has wheelchairs for hire as well as selling a wide range of mobility and other equipment.

Skipton & Craven Action for Disability

46/48 Newmarket Street,
Skipton BD23 2DB.
☎ **01756 701005.** **info@scad.org.uk**
www.scad.org.uk

SCAD operate a hire service for manual wheelchairs, an accessible minibus service and has a specially adapted canal boat for day trips. Advance booking necessary.

Whitby & District Disablement Action Group

Church House Centre, Flowergate,
Whitby YO21 3BA.
☎ **01947 821001.**
whitbydag@btconnect.com
www.whitbydag.org.uk

Offer a wheelchair hire scheme and have manual wheelchairs, scooters, a powered wheelchair and a chair with a power pack. Deposits and hire charges payable in advance. All-terrain wheelchairs are available to hire for use on Whitby beach. Arrangements can be made for people arriving at weekends or on bank holidays.

Shopmobility schemes provide wheelchairs and/or scooters for use in shopping centres in the following towns. For information on availability, etc. telephone in advance.

Barnsley ☎ **01226 786006**

Bradford ☎ **01274 434076**

Dewsbury ☎ **01924 325075**

Doncaster ☎ **01302 760742**

Goole ☎ **01405 837113**

Halifax ☎ **01422 344040**

Harrogate ☎ **01423 556778**

Huddersfield ☎ **01484 416668**

Huddersfield, Kingsgate ☎ **01484 559006**

Hull ☎ **01482 225686**

Leeds ☎**/Textphone: 0113 246 0125**

Leeds, White Rose ☎ **0113 277 3636**

Meadowhall ☎ **0845 600 6800**

Otley ☎ **01943 466335**

Scarborough ☎ **01732 369910**

Sheffield ☎ **0114 281 2278**

Wakefield ☎ **01924 787788**

York ☎ **01904 679222**

Bradford Shopmobility has satellite schemes in Shipley and Keighley.

ACCOMMODATION WITH MEALS

BEDALE, North Yorkshire

The Lodge at Leeming Bar

The Great North Road, Leeming Bar, Bedale DL8 1DT.

☎ **01677 422122.**

www.leemingbar.com

●● D/E/F/G

Hotel in country by A1/A684 junction. Reserved parking bays. Level entrance, double doors. Public rooms ground floor. Unisex WC. One bedroom designed for disabled guests on ground floor. Bathroom 150cm, ↺, handrails. Other ground floor bedrooms level.

Rates: from £80 double BB (2008).

BEVERLEY, East Yorkshire

Rudstone Walk

South Cave, Brough, Nr. Beverley HU15 2AH.

☎ **01430 422230.**

www.rudstone-walk.co.uk

●● D/E/F/G ★★★★

Rural accommodation west of Hull. Reserved parking bays. Entrance 1 step. Restaurant and lounge 1 step. Bar level. Function room level. WCs not adapted. Single and double/ twin bedrooms designed for disabled people in annexe, 1 step. One has a bathroom and the other a roll-in shower with space for side transfer to WC. Self-catering also available, see page 298.

Rates: from £49 single per night BB (2007).

BINGLEY, West Yorkshire

Ramada Bradford Leeds

Bradford Road, Bingley BD16 1TU.

☎ **01274 567123.**

sales.bradford@ramadajarvis.co.uk

●● D/E/I/F/G ★★★

Country house hotel. 11 reserved parking bays. Ramped entrance through Conference Centre; 2 steps at main entrance. Public rooms level. Adapted WC. Lift to all floors. Two double bedrooms adapted for disabled guests ↺. Bathroom ↺, space for side transfer to bath and WC. Other bedrooms level.

Rates: on application.

BRADFORD, West Yorkshire

Novotel Bradford

6 Roydsdale Way, Bradford BD4 6SA.

☎ **01274 683683.** **H0510@accor.com**

●● D/E/I/G ★★★

Hotel on edge of city. Reserved parking bays. Low kerb to entrance 66", automatic door. Public rooms level, open plan. Adapted cubicles in WCs. Lift 30" to all floors. Two bedrooms designed for disabled guests. Bathrooms 33", ↺, handrails. Other bedrooms level.

Rates: on application.

BRIGHOUSE, West Yorkshire

Holiday Inn Leeds/Brighouse

Clifton Village, Brighouse HD6 4HW.

☎ **0870 400 9013.**

@ **reservations-brighouse@ihg.com**

●● D/E/I/F/G

Hotel between Huddersfield and Bradford near M62 junction 25. Reserved parking bays. Slope to level entrance, swing and automatic doors. Low reception desk. Public rooms level, open plan. Unisex WC. 2 bedrooms, double and twin adapted for disabled guests, low controls and clothes rail. Bathrooms ↺, handrails space by bath and WC. Vibrating and visual alarms. Other ground floor bedrooms level. Waterproof sheet, induction loop and Braille menus available. Accessible changing room in Leisure club.

Rates: on application.

CASTLEFORD, West Yorkshire

Tulip Inn Leeds/Castleford

Colorado Way, Castleford WF10 4TA.

☎ **0870 4326458.**

W **www.tulipinnleedscastleford.co.uk**

●● D/E/I/G ★★★

Hotel off M62 junction 32, by leisure and retail centres. Reserved parking bays. Entrance level, automatic door. Low reception desk. Public rooms open plan. Unisex WC. Lift 100cm, inside 150x200cm. 6 bedrooms designed for disabled guests on ground floor. Shower rooms ↺, handrails, roll-in shower with seat, space by WC. Vibrating and strobe alarms and induction loop. Other bedrooms level.

Rates: from £55 per room (2008).

CLAPHAM, North Yorkshire

New Inn Hotel

Clapham, nr. Settle, LA2 8HH.

☎ **01524 251203.**

W **www.newinn-clapham.co.uk**

●● D/E/F/G

Inn and hotel in Yorkshire Dales village. Reserved parking space. Entrances level. Low reception desk. Restaurant and bars ground floor. Adapted WC cubicles. Ground floor twin/double bedroom adapted for disabled guests. Shower room 90cm, ↺, roll-in shower with seat, handrails. Mobile shower chair available. A second ground floor bedroom also available Accessible picnic table and nature trail.

Rates: from £65 per person BB (2007).

DONCASTER, South Yorkshire

Campanile Doncaster

Doncaster Leisure Park, Bawtry Road, Doncaster DN4 7PD.

☎ **01302 370770.**

@ **doncaster@campanile-hotels.com**

●●

Hotel near racecourse. Reserved parking bays. Public rooms level. Unisex WC. 2 twin bedrooms designed for disabled guests. Bathroom ↺, handrails, space for side transfer. Other ground floor bedrooms level. See page 31.

Rates: on application.

Holiday Inn Doncaster A1(M) J36

High Road, Warmsworth,
Doncaster DN4 9UX.

☎ **0870 442 8761.**

@ **hidoncaster@qmh-hotels.com**

●● D/E/I/G

Hotel near A1(M) junction 36. Entrance level, double doors. Public rooms level. Unisex WC. Three twin bedrooms designed for disabled guests 32", ⟲. Alarm call. Shower room ⟲, roll-in shower, handrails, space for side transfer to WC. Waterproof sheets available. Other bedrooms upstairs.

Rates: on application.

DRIFFIELD, East Yorkshire

Best Western Bell in Driffield

46 Market Place, Driffield YO25 6AN.

☎ **01377 256661.**

W **www.bw-bellhotel.co.uk**

●● D/E/I/F/G ★★★

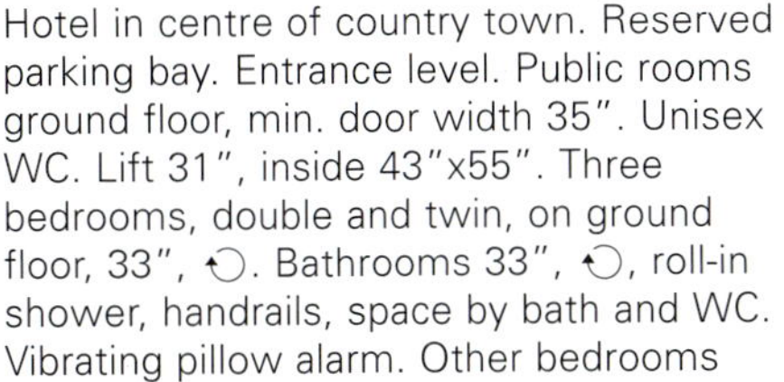

Hotel in centre of country town. Reserved parking bay. Entrance level. Public rooms ground floor, min. door width 35". Unisex WC. Lift 31", inside 43"x55". Three bedrooms, double and twin, on ground floor, 33", ⟲. Bathrooms 33", ⟲, roll-in shower, handrails, space by bath and WC. Vibrating pillow alarm. Other bedrooms level. No children.

Rates: from £78 single, £98 double BB (2008).

GOATHLAND, North Yorkshire

The Beacon Country House

Goathland, Whitby YO22 5AN.

☎ **01947 896409.**

W **www.thebeaconguesthouse.co.uk**

@ **abcherdman@hotmail.co.uk**

 D/E/I/F/G 

Guesthouse in North York Moors village. Ramp to entrance. Dining room and lounge level, ramp to conservatory. Ground floor bedroom designed for disabled guests. Shower room ⟲, roll-in shower with seat, handrails, space by WC. One other ground floor bedroom.

Rates: from £40 per person BB (2008).

GRASSINGTON, North Yorkshire

Threshfield Court Care Centre

Station Road, Threshfield,
Skipton BD23 5ET.

☎ **01756 752200.**

W **www.barchester.com/threshfield**

●●●●● D/E/I/F/G/H

Nursing home for elderly people in former country hotel. Entrance level. Public rooms ground floor. Lifts to upper floors. 55 single and 3 twin bedrooms with own WC and basin. 6 rooms designed for wheelchair users. Bathrooms and roll-in shower rooms with handrails. Equipment available and qualified nursing and care staff. Short stay bookings taken. There is also a specialist dementia unit that offers holiday/respite stays

Rates: on application

HARROGATE, North Yorkshire

Cedar Court Hotel Harrogate

Park Parade, Harrogate HG1 5AH.
☎ 01423 858585.
@ sales@cedarcourtharrogate.co.uk
●● D/F/G ★★★★

Traditional hotel in town centre. Reserved parking bays. Entrance level, automatic door. Public rooms ground floor. Unisex WC. Lift to upper floors. Ground floor bedrooms ↺ with bathrooms. Other bedrooms level. A Best Western Hotel.

Rates: on application.

Holiday Inn Harrogate

Kings Road, Harrogate HG1 1XX.
☎ 01423 849988.
@ reservations.harrogate@qmh.hotels.com
●● D/E/I/G ★★★★

High class town centre hotel. Reserved parking bays. Entrance level, automatic door. Low reception desk. Lounge and Bar ground floor, open plan. Restaurant 1st floor. Unisex WCs on ground and first floors. Lifts 80cm, inside 133x135cm. Two bedrooms adapted for disabled guests with bathrooms 78cm, ↺, handrails, space by WC. Raised WC seat available. Other bedrooms level. Portable induction loop. Braille hotel directory.

Rates: on application.

Rudding Park

Follifoot, Harrogate HG3 1JH.
☎ 01423 871350. W www.ruddingpark.com
●● D/E/I/F/G
★★★★

Country house hotel with large grounds south of Harrogate. Reserved parking bay. Entrance level, automatic door. Main public rooms ground floor, level. 2 unisex WCs. Lift 75cm, inside 140x110cm. Two ground floor bedrooms adapted for disabled guests. Bathroom 80cm sliding door ↺, space by bath and WC; toilet rails, bath seat and other equipment can be provided. Amplified telephone and vibrating alarm clock available. Other bedrooms level. Golf course, holiday park and camping / caravanning site in grounds.

Rates: on application.

HEDON, East Yorkshire

Little Weghill Farm

Weghill Road, Preston, nr. Hull HU12 8SX.
☎ 01482 897650.
W www.littleweghillfarm.co.uk
●● D/E/F/G ★★★★

Farmhouse bed and breakfast in country 6 miles east of Hull. Threshold at back door, ramp available if required. Dining room and lounge level 74cm. In converted barn annexe one double bedroom is designed for disabled guests, ramp with handrail to 83cm entrance. Shower room ↺, roll-in shower with seat, handrails, space by WC. Two other ground floor rooms. Raised WC seat. Large print menus. Teletext TV.

Rates: £32-£34 per person BB (2008).

HELMSLEY, North Yorkshire

Pheasant Hotel

Harome, Helmsley YO62 5JG
☎ **01439 771241.**
www.thepheasanthotel.com
●● D/F/G ★★★

Country hotel. Entrance Level 60". Public rooms level. One ground floor bedroom with bathroom 30", ⟲. Closed mid-December to mid-March

Rates: from £65 BB, £85 DBB (2008).

HESSLE, East Yorkshire

Redcliffe House Luxury B&B

Redcliff Road, Hessle HU13 0HA.
01482 648655
www.redcliffehouse.co.uk
●● D/E/I/F/G ★★★★

Guesthouse in large garden near Humber Bridge. Entrance step, portable ramp available. Dining room level, 28". One double ground floor bedroom with ramped approach. Shower room 32", roll-in shower with seat, space by WC. Other bedrooms upstairs.

Rates: from £50-£65 per person (2008).

HULL, East Yorkshire

Campanile Hotel

Beverley Road, Freetown Way,
Hull HU2 9AN.
☎ **01482 325530.**
hull@campanile-hotels.com

●●

Hotel in city centre. Reserved parking bays. Public rooms level. Unisex WC. 2 twin bedrooms designed for disabled guests. Bathroom ⟲, handrails, space for side transfer. Other ground floor bedrooms level. See page 31.

Rates: on application.

Holiday Inn Hull Marina

Castle Street, Hull HU1 2BX.
☎ **0870 400 9043.**
reservations-hull@ihg.com
●● E/I/F/G

City centre hotel by marina. Reserved parking spaces. Level entrance, automatic doors. Low reception desk available. Main public rooms open plan and level. Unisex WC. Lift 79cm, inside 107x138cm. 2 bedrooms adapted for disabled guests. Bathroom 90cm, ⟲, handrails, space by bath and WC. Other bedrooms level. Teletext TV, induction loops and large print information available.

  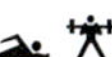

Rates: on application.

Ibis Hull

Ferensway, Hull HU1 2NL.
☎ **01482 387500.**
H3479@accor.com
●● G

Hotel in city centre. Entrance level. Public rooms level, open plan. Unisex WC. Six bedrooms with adaptations for disabled guests. Bathrooms ⟲, handrails. Other 100 bedrooms level.

Rates: from £45-£49 per room (2008).

Ramada Hull

Grange Park Lane, Willerby,
Hull HU10 6EA.
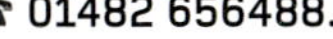
☎ **01482 656488.**
sales.hull@ramadajarvis.co.uk
●● D/E/G ★★★

Hotel in own grounds west of Hull. Entrance level. Public rooms level. Unisex WC. 3 bedrooms designed for disabled guests. Bathrooms ⟲, handrails, space for side transfer to bath and WC.

Rates: on application.

INGLETON, North Yorkshire

Riverside Lodge

24 Main Street, Ingleton,
via Carnforth LA6 3HJ.
☎ **015242 41359.**
www.riversideingleton.co.uk
●● D/E/F/G ★★★★

Guesthouse in Pennine village. Entrance level, double doors. Dining room and lounge level. Two ground floor twin/double bedrooms, no ⟲. Shower rooms, no ⟲, handrails, space for side transfer to WC, shower seat available. 2 external steps to sauna and games room. Evening meals available.

Rates: from £30 per person BB (2008).

KEIGHLEY, West Yorkshire

Currer Laithe Farm

Long Lee, Keighley BD21 4SL.
☎ **01535 604387.**
www.currerlaith.co.uk
●● D/E/I/G

Farm guesthouse. Ramp to entrance 33". Public rooms level 33". Two level en-suite bedrooms 33". Shower room 1 step, 30", shower seat, handrails, space for side transfer to WC. Own transport essential. Self-catering also available, see page 302.

Rates: from £18.50 BB, £23 DBB on request (2007).

KIRKBYMOORSIDE, N. Yorkshire

The Cornmill

Kirby Mills, Kirkbymoorside, York YO62 6NP.
☎ **01751 432000.**
www.kirbymills.demon.co.uk
●● D/E/F ★★★★

Licensed guesthouse by River Dove on edge of National Park. Entrance level. Dining Room and Lounge level. One twin/double bedroom designed for disabled guests 78cm, ⟲. Bathroom 76cm, ⟲, wheel-in shower, handrails, restricted space for side transfer to WC. One other ground floor bedroom and 3 upstairs. Evening meals can be pre-arranged.

Rates: from £37.50-£52.50 per person BB (2008).

George and Dragon Hotel

17 Market Place, Kirkbymoorside YO62 6AA.
☎ **01751 433334.**
www.georgeanddragon.net
● D/E/F/G

Old coaching inn in market town. Slope to entrance 70cm. Step to restaurant and lounge, ramp available. Bar level. Handrails in WC level cubicles. Bedrooms in neighbouring buildings, some ground floor with bathrooms ⟲, no specific adaptations.

Rates: from £45-£60 per person BB (2007).

LEEDS, West Yorkshire

Corn Mill Lodge Hotel

Pudsey Road, Bramley, Leeds LS13 4JA.
☎ **0113 257 9059.**
●● D/E/F/G ★★★

Hotel in city outskirts. Reserved parking bays. Entrance level. Public rooms level, open plan. Unisex WC. Lift 80cm, inside 110x150cm. 3 twin bedrooms on ground floor designed for disabled guests. Bathrooms ⟲, space by bath and WC. Other bedrooms level.

Rates: from £52.95 per room (2008).

Crowne Plaza Leeds

Wellington Street, Leeds LS1 4DL.
☎ **0870 400 9170.**
www.leeds.crowneplaza.com
●● D/E/I/F/G ★★★★

High class city centre hotel. Reserved parking bays. Entrance level. Restaurant ground floor. Lounge and bar 1st floor. Unisex WC on 1st floor, adapted cubicles in ground floor toilets. Lift 80cm, inside 130x138cm. Two bedrooms designed for disabled guests 93cm, ⟲. Bathrooms 90cm, ⟲, handrails, space for side transfer to bath and WC. Other rooms level. Adapted changing rooms in Health Club.

Rates: on application.

Express by Holiday Inn Leeds City Centre

Cavendish Street, Leeds LS3 1LY.
☎ **0113 242 6200.**
@ **res.leeds@expressholidayinn.co.uk**
●● E/I/F/G

Limited service hotel near city centre. Reserved parking bays. Entrance level, double doors. Low reception desk. Public rooms open plan. Unisex WC. Lift 31.5", inside 43"x55". Bedroom designed for disabled guests. Shower room 32", ⟲, roll-in shower with seat, handrails, space by WC. Portable induction loop and vibrating alarm available. Mattress protectors. Other bedrooms level including 5 with ⟲ but no adaptations.

Rates: £49-£99 per room BB (2007).

Hilton Leeds City

Neville Street, Leeds LS1 4BX.
☎ **0113 244 2000.**
www.hilton.co.uk/leedscity
●● D/E/I/F/G ★★★★

City centre hotel. Reserved parking bays. Entrance level 92cm. Induction loop at reception. Main public rooms 3rd floor level. Unisex WC with 64cm sliding door. Lift 117cm, inside 200x200cm, Braille buttons, audio announcements. Four bedrooms adapted for disabled guests. Bathrooms 82cm, ⟲, handrails, 2 have roll-in shower with seat. Other bedrooms level. Vibrating and strobe alarms and Evac chair available. Accessible changing room and hoist to swimming pool.

Rates: on application.

NYMR

Ibis Leeds Centre

Marlborough Street, Leeds LS1 4PB.
☎ 0113 220 4100. @ H3652@accor.com
●● G
Hotel near city centre. Car park across road. Entrance level. Public rooms level, open plan. Unisex WC. Lifts to all floors. 8 bedrooms designed for disabled guests. Bathrooms ⟲, handrails. Other 160 bedrooms level.
Rates: £50 per night (2008).

Innkeepers Lodge Leeds East

Aberford Road, Oulton, Leeds LS26 8EJ.
☎ 0845 112 6039.
●● E/I/F/G
Limited service hotel between Leeds and Wakefield. Reserved parking spaces. Entrance level. Low reception desk. Four bedrooms designed for disabled guests. Shower room ⟲, handrails, space for side transfer to WC. Other ground floor rooms level. Meals in adjoining Toby Carvery.
Ⓟ
Rates: from £49.95-£55 per room BB (2007).

Novotel Leeds Centre

4 Whitehall Quay, Whitehall Road LS1 4HR.
☎ 0113 242 6446. @ H370@accor.com
●● D/E/F/G
Modern hotel in city centre. Entrance level, 83cm. Low reception desk. Main public rooms, ground floor, open plan. Unisex WC. Lift 85cm, inside 100x120cm, Braille keypad. Ten double bedrooms designed for disabled guests. Vibrating pillow and audible and visual alarms. Shower rooms 100cm sliding door, ⟲, roll-in shower, handrails and space by WC. Other bedrooms level.
Ⓟ
Rates: from £50-£119 per night (2007).

Leeds Marriott Hotel

Trevelyan Square, Boar Lane, Leeds LS1 6ET.
☎ 0113 236 6366.
W www.leedsmarriott.co.uk
●● D/E/F/G
City centre hotel. NCP car park nearby. Entrance level, revolving and swing doors. Restaurant and bar ground floor. Unisex WC. Lift to 1st floor and service lift to other bedroom floors. 6 double rooms adapted for disabled guests, 1st floor. Shower rooms 92cm, ⟲, roll-in shower with seat, handrails, space by WC. Vibrating pillow alarms available.
Rates: from £84 BB (2008).

Ramada Leeds North

Mill Green View, Ring Road, Leeds LS14 5QF.
☎ 0113 273 2323.
@ sales.leedsnorth@ramadajarvis.co.uk
●● D/E/I/F/G ★★★
Hotel in residential area northwest of city centre. Reserved parking bays. Ramp or 1 step to entrance, automatic door. Public rooms open plan. Unisex WC. Lift 31", inside 47"x84". 3 bedrooms designed for disabled guests, low clothes rail and spyhole, restricted ⟲. Shower rooms 34", shower tray with seat, handrails, no space by WC. Other bedrooms level.
Ⓟ
Rates: on application.

Weetwood Hall

Otley Road, Leeds LS16 5PS.

☎ **0113 230 6000.**

www.weetwood.co.uk

●● D/E/I/F/G 

Business hotel 4 miles from city centre. Entrance level. Public rooms ground floor. Unisex WC. Lift 30", inside 55"x62". Two ground floor bedrooms designed for disabled guests with bathrooms 32", ⭮, handrails, space for side transfer to bath and WC. Other bedrooms level.

Rates: from £45 per person weekends (2008).

RIPLEY, North Yorkshire

Boar's Head Hotel

Ripley Castle Estate, Ripley, Harrogate HG3 3AY.

☎ **01423 771888.**

www.boarsheadripley.co.uk

●● D/F/G 

Historic country inn and hotel. Reserved parking bays. Entrance from car park level; front entrance 2 steps. Public rooms level. Unisex WC. One ground floor double/twin bedroom designed for disabled guests. Bathroom 110cm sliding door, ⭮, handrails, space for side transfer to WC. Some other bedrooms level.

Rates: from £105 single, £125 double per room BB (2007).

RIPON, North Yorkshire

Best Western Ripon Spa Hotel

Park Street, Ripon HG4 2BU.

☎ **01765 602172.** **www.riponspa.com**

●● D/E/F/G ★★★

Hotel in own grounds near town centre. 2 reserved parking bays. Ramp or 1 step to entrance. Public rooms ground floor level. Unisex WC. Lift 120cm, inside 160x220cm. 1 double bedroom on ground floor adapted for disabled guests. Bathroom 120cm, handrails, no ⭮ or space by WC. Other bedrooms level. Gardens mainly accessible.

Ⓟ

Rates: on application.

ROTHERHAM, South Yorkshire

Hellaby Hall

Old Hellaby Lane, Hellaby, Rotherham S66 8SN.

☎ **01709 702701.**

www.hellabyhallhotel.co.uk

●● D/E/I/F/G 

Country house hotel near M18 junction 1. Car park 100m, valet parking available. Entrance ramp or 3 steps. Reception, bar and lounge ground floor. Restaurant and bar 2nd floor. Lift 120cm, inside 140x140cm. Unisex WCs. Two twin bedrooms designed for disabled guests. Bathroom ⭮, handrails, space for side transfer to bath and WC. Waterproof sheets available. Other 88 bedrooms level.

Ⓟ

Rates: on application

Holiday Inn Rotherham -Sheffield M1 J33

West Bawtry Road, Rotherham S60 4NA.
☎ **01709 830630.**

 D/E/F/G 

Modern hotel in suburbs near M1 junction 33. Reserved parking bays. Ramp to entrance, automatic doors. Public rooms level. Unisex WCs. Lift to all floors. Double and twin bedrooms designed for disabled guests. Bathrooms ⟲, handrails, space for side transfer to WC. Waterproof sheet can be provided. Other bedrooms level.

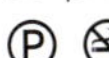  

Rates: from £52-£129 double BB (2007).

Ibis Rotherham East

Moorhead Way, Bramley,
Rotherham S66 1YY.
☎ **01709 730333.** @ **H3163@accor.com**

 D/E/G

Hotel off M18 and M1 junction 32. Entrance level. Public rooms open plan. Lift to upper floors. Five bedrooms with bathrooms designed for disabled guests. Other bedrooms level.

Rates: from £44-£54 per room (2008).

SCARBOROUGH, North Yorkshire

The Moorings

3 Burniston Road, Scarborough YO12 6PG.
☎ **01723 373786.**
W **www.scarboroughmoorings.co.uk**

 D/E/F/G 

Guesthouse in North Bay area. Level entrance to annexe. Twin bedroom with shower room level, handrails, roll-in shower. Shower stool and raised WC seat available. Level access to dining room. Regular disabled guests.

Rates: from £35 per person BB (2008).

Hotel St Nicholas

St Nicholas Cliff, Scarborough YO11 2EU.
☎ **01723 364101.**
@ **res.stnicolas@crerarmgmt.com**

●● G ★★★

Traditional hotel. Parking space can be arranged. Entrance ramp and 1 step. Split level reception desk. Wheelchair lift to bar. Restaurant split level, 3 steps at one entrance. Lift to all floors, braille buttons. Two bedrooms adapted for disabled guests. Shower room with seat and handrails. Some other bedrooms level.

Rates: on application.

SHEFFIELD, South Yorkshire

Ibis Sheffield City

Shude Hill, Sheffield S1 2AR.
☎ **0114 241 9600.** @ **H2891@accor.com**

●● E/I/F/G

City centre hotel. Car park nearby. Entrance level and low reception desk. Public rooms open plan. Unisex WC. Lift to all floors. 6 bedrooms adapted for disabled guests, one on each floor. Shower room with roll-in shower and seat designed for wheelchair user. Other bedrooms level

Rates: from £55 per room (2008).

Novotel Sheffield

Arundel Gate, Sheffield S1 2PR.
☎ **0114 278 1781.**
@ **H1348-re@accor.com**

●● D/E/G 

Modern city centre hotel. Reserved parking bays by lower level entrance with lift to reception. Main entrance level, automatic doors, low reception desk. Public rooms open plan, level except part of bar. Low level payphones. Unisex WC. Lift to all floors. Four bedrooms designed for disabled guests ⟲. Bathrooms ⟲, handrails, space for side transfer to bath and WC. Other bedrooms level.

Rates: on application.

Sheffield Park Hotel

Chesterfield Road South,
Sheffield S8 8BW.
☎ **0114 282 9988.**
www.sheffieldparkhorel.co.uk
●● D/E/G

Hotel south of city. Entrance level, automatic doors. Public rooms level. Unisex WC and adapted cubicles in ground floor toilets. Two bedrooms designed for disabled guests. Bathrooms 36" sliding door, handrails, space for side transfer to bath and WC. Other bedrooms level.

Rates: on application

SCISSETT, West Yorkshire

Bagden Hall Hotel

Wakefield Road, Scissett,
Huddersfield HD8 9LE.
☎ **01484 865330.**
info.bagdenhall@classiclodges.co.uk
●● D/E/G 

Country house hotel between Huddersfield and Barnsley. Orchard entrance level, automatic doors; main entrance 6 steps. Ramp for step in reception and restaurant. Lounge and bar level. Unisex WC. Ramp to double bedroom adapted for disabled guests. Bathroom ⟲, space by bath and WC. Other ground floor rooms available.

Rates: from £90-£155 per room BB (2007).

SHIPLEY, West Yorkshire

Ibis Bradford Shipley

Quayside, Saltsmill Rd, Shipley BD18 3ST.
☎ **01274 589333.**
H3158@accorhotels.com
●● D/E/G

Hotel by Leeds-Liverpool Canal near town centre. Entrance level. Public rooms open plan. Lifts to upper floors. Two bedrooms with bathroom designed for disabled guests. Other bedrooms level.

Rates: from £45-£53 per room (2008).

SKIPTON, North Yorkshire

Craven Heifer Inn

Grassington Road, Skipton BD23 3LA.
☎ **01756 792521.**
www.cravenheifer.co.uk
●● D/G ★★★

Country inn. Reserved parking bay. Entrance level 32". Public rooms level. Unisex WC. One bedroom designed for disabled guests 32", ⟲. Shower room 32", shower tray with seat and handrail, no space for side transfer to WC. 13 other ground floor bedrooms.

Rates: from £49.95 double BB (2007).

THORNE, South Yorkshire

The Belmont Hotel

Horsefair Green, Thorne,
Doncaster DN8 5EE.
☎ **01405 812320.**
www.belmonthotel.info
●● D/G

Hotel in market town east of Doncaster near M18 and Robin Hood Airport. Ramp for entrance sill. Public rooms ground floor. WCs level, no adaptations. One double bedroom with adaptations for disabled guests. Bathroom ⟲, space by bath and WC, no handrails. 4 other level bedrooms.

Rates: from £60 double per night BB (2007).

WAKEFIELD, West Yorkshire

Campanile Wakefield

Monckton Road, Wakefield WF2 7AL.
☎ **01924 201054.**
wakefield@campanile-hotels.com
●●

Hotel near M1 junction 39. Reserved parking bays. Public rooms level. Unisex WC. 2 twin bedrooms designed for disabled guests with bathroom ⟲, handrails and space for side transfer. Other ground floor rooms level. See page 31.

Rates: on application.

Cedar Court Hotel

Denby Dale Road, Calder Grove, Wakefield WF4 3QZ.

☎ 01924 276310.

@ sales@cedarcourthotels.co.uk

●● D/E/I/G ★★★★

Hotel near M1 junction 39. Entrance level. Public rooms level. Unisex WC. Two lifts and large goods lift. Two ground floor bedrooms designed for disabled guests. Bathrooms 36", ⟲, handrail by bath, space for side transfer to WC. Other bedrooms level.

Rates: from £100 per room (2008).

Express by Holiday Inn Wakefield

Denby Dale Road, Wakefield WF4 3BB.

☎ 0845 112 6153.

@ ebhi_wakefield@btconnect.com

●● E/I/F/G

Limited service hotel near M1 junction 39, south of Wakefield. Reserved parking bays. Entrance level, automatic doors. Public areas open plan. Unisex WC. Lift 80cm, inside 100x140cm. 4 bedrooms designed for disabled guests. Shower rooms 92cm, ⟲, roll-in shower with seat, handrails, space by WC. Other bedrooms level. Vibrating alarm. Restaurant/pub adjoining with level entrance.

Rates: from £50 per room BB (2007).

Holiday Inn Leeds - Wakefield M1 J40

Queens Drive, Ossett, Wakefield WF5 9BE.

☎ 0870 400 9082.

@ reservations-wakefield@ihg.com

●● D/E/I/F/G ★★★

Hotel off M1 between Wakefield and Dewsbury. Reserved parking bays. Slope to level entrance, automatic door. Wheelchair lift or 3 steps to ground floor public rooms. Unisex WC. Lift 76cm, inside 102x129cm, level from rear entrance, lift or 3 steps from reception. Two double bedrooms designed for disabled people on ground floor. Bathrooms 89cm, ⟲, handrails, space by bath and WC. Other bedrooms level. Mattress protectors, sound amplifiers, vibrating pagers, induction loops at reception and bar, large print menus and information sheets.

Rates: on application.

WHITBY, North Yorkshire

The Olde Ford

1 Briggswath, Whitby YO21 1RU.

☎ 01947 810704.

W www.theoldeford.com

●● D/E/F/G ★★★★

Guesthouse on edge of North York Moors, 3 miles from Whitby. Entrance level, 32". Dining room level. Twin bedroom level 31". Shower room ⟲, shower tray, seat available, handrails, space for side transfer to WC. 2 other bedrooms upstairs.

Rates: from £60 per cupple BB (2007).

YORK, North Yorkshire

Best Western Monkbar Hotel

St Maurice's Road, York YO31 7JA.
☎ **01904 638086.** **www.monkbar.co.uk**
●● D/E/F/G ★★★

Hotel in centre of city. Reserved parking bays. Entrance level. Low reception desk. Public rooms level. Unisex WCs. Lift to upper floor. Two ground floor rooms with own entrance designed for disabled guests ⟲. Bathroom ⟲, roll-in shower with seat, handrails, space by WC and bath.

Rates: from £85-£150 per room BB (2007).

Fifth Milestone Cottage

Hull Road, Dunnington, York YO19 5LR.
☎ **01904 489361.**
www.milestonecottage.co.uk
●● D/E/I/F/G

Bed & Breakfast in country about 2 miles east of York. Ramp to entrance 31". Lounge and breakfast room level. Three ouble/family bedrooms rooms in ground floor annexe designed for disabled guests. Entrance ramp, 36". Shower rooms 36", ⟲, roll-in shower with seat, handrails, space by WC. Varied height fittings and some equipment available. Accessible garden.

Rates: on application.

The Groves Hotel

St Peter's Grove, York YO30 6AQ.
☎ **01904 559777.**
www.ecsyork.co.uk
●● D/E/I/F/G ★★

Hotel near city centre. Designated parking bays. Ramp to rear entrance; front entrance 1 step. Low reception desk. Public rooms level. 2 bedrooms designed for disabled guests ⟲. Shower rooms with roll-in shower and seat, handrails, space by WC. Other ground floor bedrooms level. Teletext TVs, taped hotel information.

Rates: from £40 per person BB (2008).

Hilton York

1 Tower Street, York YO1 9WD.
☎ **01904 648111.**
www.hilton.co.uk/york
●● D/E/I/F/G ★★★★

Hotel in city centre. One parking space may be made available. Ramp or 4 steps to entrance, automatic door. Low reception desk. Main public rooms open plan. Adapted WC cubicles. Lift 75cm, inside 110x136cm. Three bedrooms for 2 people adapted for disabled guests. Bathrooms 89cm space by bath and WC.

Rates: on application.

Holiday Inn York

Tadcaster Road, York YO24 1QF.
☎ **0870 400 9085.**
reservationsyork@ihg.com
●● D/E/I/F/G

Hotel south of city centre near racecourse. Reserved parking bays. Entrance level, automatic doors. Public rooms level, open plan. Unisex WC. Lift 30", inside 52"x34".Two ground floor bedrooms adapted for disabled guests. Bathrooms 30", ⟲, handrails, space by bath and WC. Other bedrooms level. Induction loops, alarms and amplifier available.

Rates: on application.

Ibis York Centre

77 The Mount, York YO24 1BN.
☎ **01904 658301.** **H6390@accor.com**
●● D/E/G

Hotel near city centre. Entrance level. Public rooms open plan. Lifts to upper floors. Three bedrooms with bathroom designed for disabled guests. Other bedrooms level.

Rates: from £67per room (2008).

Novotel York Centre

Fishergate, York YO10 4FD.
☎ 01904 611660.
@ H0949@accor.com
●● D/E/I/F/G ★★★

City centre hotel. Reserved parking bays. Level entrance, automatic doors. Public rooms level. Unisex WC. Two lifts. Four bedrooms designed for disabled guests with door to neighbouring room. Bathrooms, handrails, space for side transfer to WC. Other bedrooms level.

Rates: from £59-£209 per room (2007).

Woodlands Respite Care Centre

120 Thief Lane, Hull Road, York YO10 3HU.
☎ 01904 430600.
@ enquiries@woodlands.org.uk
●●●●● D/E/I/G/H

Centre purpose-built to meet the needs of people with multiple sclerosis. Located in own grounds to the east of the city. All bedrooms are single with en suite facilities. Fully equipped for respite care with 24 hour nursing, physiotherapy and hydro-therapy. Outings and activities arranged.

Rates: from £749 per week FB (2007).

YHA York

Water End, Clifton, York YO30 6LP.
☎ 0870 770 6102.
@ york@yha.org.uk
●● D/E/I/F/G ★★★

Youth hostel a mile from city centre. Entrance ramp, double doors. Restaurant and one lounge level. Step to self-catering kitchen and laundry; TV lounge upstairs. WC level with adaptations. Annexe with entrance level from car park, key from reception. two ground floor bedrooms with adaptations and shared roll-in shower room designed for wheelchair users. Portable induction loop. Braille signage. For more information on Youth Hostels see page 34.

Rates: from £13.95-£24.50 adult BB (2008).

York Marriott Hotel

Tadcaster Road, York YO24 1QQ.
☎ 01904 701000.
@ york@marriotthotels.co.uk
●● D/E/F/G ★★★★

Hotel south of city centre by racecourse. Reserved parking bays. Entrance level, automatic door. Public rooms level. Unisex WC. Lifts to upper floors. Two ground floor bedrooms, double and twin, with bathrooms designed for disabled guests. Other bedrooms level. Adapted changing room and shower in leisure club.

Rates: on application.

LODGE ACCOMMODATION

There are Days Inn (see page 34), Etap (see page 34) Formule 1 (see page 34), Premier Travel Inn (see page 38) and Travelodge (see page 38) properties in the following areas in this Region.

Barnsley - Premier Travel Inn	☎ 0870 197 7024
Travelodge	☎ 0870 191 1621
Barnsley, Tankersley - Premier Travel Inn	☎ 0870 197 7228
Bradford - Travelodge	☎ 0870 191 1624
Brighouse - Premier Travel Inn	☎ 0870 990 6360
Castleford - Premier Travel Inn	☎ 0870 990 6592
Cleckheaton - Premier Travel Inn	☎ 0870 990 6360
Doncaster - Premier Travel Inn	☎ 0870 197 7074
Travelodge	☎ 0870 191 1631
Doncaster M18/M180 - Travelodge	☎ 0870 191 1632
Ferrybridge - Days Inn	☎ 01977 621129
Travelodge	☎ 0870 191 1669
Goole - Premier Travel Inn	☎ 0870 197 7177
Halifax - Premier Travel Inn	☎ 0870 990 6308
Travelodge	☎ 0870 191 1644
Harrogate - Premier Travel Inn	☎ 0870 197 7126
Travelodge	☎ 0870 191 1737
Hartshead Moor - Days Inn	☎ 01274 851706
Huddersfield - Premier Travel Inn	☎ 0870 990 6488
Hull, North - Premier Travel Inn	☎ 0870 197 7137
Hull, West - Premier Travel Inn	☎ 0870 197 7138
Travelodge	☎ 0870 191 1647
Keighley - Premier Travel Inn	☎ 0870 197 7038
Knottingley - Premier Travel Inn	☎ 0870 197 7209
Leeds - Premier Travel Inn	☎ 0870 197 7150
Travelodge	☎ 0870 191 1655
Leeds, Drighlington - Premier Travel Inn	☎ 0870 197 7152
Leeds, East - Premier Travel Inn	☎ 0870 197 7151
Travelodge	☎ 0870 191 1734
Leeds, West - Premier Travel Inn	☎ 0870 990 6448
Leeds/Bradford Airport - Premier Travel Inn	☎ 0870 197 7153
Travelodge	☎ 0870 191 1775
Mirfield - Travelodge	☎ 0870 191 1646

Rotherham - Premier Travel Inn ☎ 0870 197 7222
Scotch Corner - Travelodge ☎ 0870 191 1672
Sheffield - Premier Travel Inn ☎ 0870 238 3324
Travelodge ☎ 0870 191 1674
Sheffield, Arena - Etap ☎ 0114 243 4109
Premier Travel Lodge ☎ 0870 238 3316
Sheffield, Meadowhall - Premier Travel Inn ☎ 0870 990 6440
Sheffield, Richmond - Travelodge ☎ 0870 191 1674
Skeeby - Travelodge ☎ 0870 191 1675
Skipton - Travelodge ☎ 0870 191 1676
Tadcaster - Travelodge ☎ 0870 191 1685
Wakefield - Premier Travel Inn ☎ 0870 197 7257
Travelodge (2) ☎ 0870 191 1764/1678
Wakefield North - Premier Travel Inn ☎ 0870 850 6302
Woodhall - Days Inn ☎ 0114 248 7992
York - Premier Travel Inn ☎ 0870 990 6594
Travelodge ☎ 0870 191 1686
York, North West - Premier Travel Inn ☎ 0870 197 7280
York, South West - Premier Travel Inn ☎ 0870 238 3317

SELF-CATERING ACCOMMODATION

BEAMSLEY, North Yorkshire

The Beamsley Project
Harrogate Road, Beamsley,
Skipton BD23 6JA.
☎ **01756 710255.**
www.beamsleyproject.org.uk
●●● E/I/G/H

Holiday centre in Yorkshire Dales for groups of disabled people and their companions. Entrance level, automatic doors. Dining room and kitchen ground floor. Lounge and recreation area 1st floor. Lift, inside 110x210cm. Ground floor has four twin and two 4 bedded rooms, two with adjustable beds; bathroom with hoist, changing table and Clos-o-mat toilet; two roll-in shower rooms with WCs. 1st floor two 4 bedded rooms with en suite shower rooms. Unisex WCs. Cot sides and other equipment available. Induction loop in recreation room. Braille signs. No alcohol on premises. Catering can be arranged. A cottage for families and small groups is also available, see below.

Ⓟ ⊘ ⓘ

Rates: from £15 per person per night (2007).

The Cottage

●●● E/I/G/H ★★★★

Purpose-equipped cottage beside Beamsley Project. Entrance level 83cm. Ground floor lounge and kitchen/dining room. Controls useable from wheelchair, adjustable worktops. Wheelchair lift to 1st floor. Three twin bedrooms, one with adjustable bed. Shower room 81cm, roll-in shower, shower chair, handrails, space for side transfer to WC. Clos-o-Mat WC on ground floor. Mobile hoist, pillow lift and other equipment available.

Apply: The Beamsley Project
☎ 01756 710255.
W www.beamsleyproject.org.uk
Rates: from £35 per night (2007).

BEDALE, North Yorkshire
Elmfield Cottages

Arrathorne, Bedale.

●● F/G ★★★★

Two purpose built cottages, each for up to 4 people in rural area. Entrance level, 31". Lounge/kitchen open plan, controls useable from wheelchair. Twin and double bedrooms. En suite bathrooms; one with roll-in shower and seat, handrails, space for side transfer to WC.

Apply: Mr Lillie, Elmfield Cottage, Arrathorne, Bedale DL8 1NE.
☎ 01677 450052.
W www.elmfieldcottages.co.uk
Rates: from £285-£445 per week (2007).

BEVERLEY, East Yorkshire

Rudstone Walk Country Cottages

South Cave, Brough,
Nr. Beverley HU15 2AH.
☎ **01430 422230.**
W **www.rudstone-walk.co.uk**

●● D/E/F/G ★★★★

Two cottages designed for disabled people overlooking The Wolds and Humber. One has 1 step on approach, bedroom with roll-in shower room. Entrances level. The other has three bedrooms. Bathroom, handrails, space for side transfer to bath and WC. Bed & breakfast also available, see page 281.

Rates: from £355-£570 per week (2007)

BRIDLINGTON, East Yorkshire
Mowbray Holiday Flats

8 The Crescent, Bridlington YO15 2NX.
☎ **01262 676218.**
W **www.mowbrayflats.co.uk**

● F/G ★★

Self catering flats by harbour. Permits available for street parking. 1 step or ramp to entrance. Two ground floor flats. Doors 36". Lounge/kitchen and double bedroom. Shower room, shower tray, no handrails. Wheelchair hire available.

Rates: from £85-£394 per week (2007).

COMMONDALE, North Yorkshire

Fowl Green Farm

Commondale, Whitby YO21 2HN.

●● I/F/G ★★★-★★★★★

Four cottages in courtyard on working farm in North York Moors. Entrances level 36". Open plan lounge/kitchen. Double bedroom ground floor ⟲. Bath/shower room ⟲, handrails; 3 cottages have roll-in shower with seat, the other a bath with drop-down side. Additional bedrooms upstairs. Teletext TV.

Apply: Susan Muir ☎ 01287 660742.
W www.fowlgreenfarm.com
Rates: from £160-£540 per week (2007).

FILEY, North Yorkshire

Blue Dolphin Holiday Park

Gristhorpe Bay, Filey YO14 9PU.
☎ 01723 515155.

●● I/F/G ★★★

Haven holiday park north of Filey with wide range of facilities and entertainment. Caravans for 5 people adapted for disabled guests. Entrance ramp. Lounge/kitchen open plan. Two bedrooms, sliding door 75cm, ⟲ in double. Shower room 75cm, handrails, restricted ⟲, no space by WC. Open mid March-October.

Apply: Haven Holidays Reservations
☎ 0870 2422222.
Rates: on application.

Muston Grange Farm

Muston Road, Filey YO14 0HU.

●● F/G ★★★

One cottage, of 5, designed for disabled people ⟲ mile from Filey. Entrance level 33". Lounge/kitchen open plan. Twin and family bedrooms level. Bathroom ⟲, roll-in shower with seat, handrails, space by WC.

Apply: David & Gillian Teet
☎ 01723 516620.
Rates: from £295-£585 per week (2008).

Primrose Valley Holiday Park

Primrose Valley, Filey YO14 9RF.
☎ 01723 513771.

●● I/F/G ★★★★

Haven holiday park south of Filey with wide range of facilities and entertainment. Caravans for 5 people adapted for disabled guests. Entrance ramp. Lounge/kitchen open plan. Two bedrooms, sliding door 75cm, ⟲ in double. Shower room 75cm, handrails, restricted ⟲, no space by WC. Open mid March-October.

Apply: Haven Holidays Reservations
☎ 0870 2422222.
Rates: on application.

Reighton Sands Holiday Park

Reighton Gap, Filey YO14 9SJ.
☎ 01723 890476.

●● I/F/G ★★★

Haven holiday park between Filey and Bridlington with range of facilities and entertainment. Caravans for 5 people adapted for disabled guests. Entrance ramp. Lounge/kitchen open plan. Two bedrooms, sliding door 75cm, ⟲ in double. Shower room 75cm, handrails, restricted ⟲, no space beside WC. Open late March-October.

Apply: Haven Holidays Reservations
☎ 0870 2422222.
Rates: on application.

GRASSINGTON, North Yorkshire

The Barn

Broughton Fold, Grassington, Nr. Skipton

● F/G ★★★★

Converted cottage for 4 people off village square. Entrance 1 step, portable ramp available. One step in lounge. Kitchen 69cm, no ⟲. Double & twin bedrooms, ⟲ in twin. Bathroom 72cm, rail by bath, separate shower cubicle, no space for side transfer to WC. Garage available. Patio level, steps to garden. Similar unit upstairs.

Apply: Mrs P G Evans, The Outpost, 8 Sedber Lane, Grassington BD23 5LQ. ☎ 01756 753390. @ gail@art-by-gail.co.uk

Rates: from £270-£495 per week (2008).

HARROGATE, North Yorkshire

Brimham Rocks Cottages

High North Farm, Fellbeck, Harrogate HG3 5EY.

☎ 01765 620284. W www.brimham.co.uk

●● I/F/G ★★★★

Three, of 10, cottages designed for disabled people north west of Harrogate. "Rowan", sleeps 2-4 people. Entrance level. Open plan lounge/kitchen with sofabed. Twin/double bedroom. Shower room, ⟲, roll-in shower with seat, handrails, space by WC. "Lilac", sleeping 2-3, and "Cherry", for 4-6 people, have similar provision but an entrance step and a small step into the shower room. Swimming pool with hoist.

Rates: on application.

Dinmore House

Burnt Yates, Nr. Harrogate HG3 3ET

●● F/G ★★★★

"Owls Barn" is one of four cottages, 7 miles north-west of Harrogate in Nidderdale. Entrance level. Lounge/kitchen open plan, worktops 34", controls reachable from wheelchair. Sofa bed in lounge and extra single bed if required. Double bed gallery upstairs. Shower room level, 33" sliding door, roll-in shower with seat, handrails, space for side transfer to WC. Premier Cottages member.

Apply: Alan Bottomley ☎ 01423 770860. W www.dinmore-cottages.co.uk

Rates: from £270-£480 per week (2007).

Helme Pasture Lodges

Old Spring Wood, Hartwith Bank, Summerbridge, Harrogate HG3 4DR.

●● I/F/G ★★★★

Lodges in woodland between Harrogate and Pateley Bridge. Two designed for disabled people. A step on approach to level entrance. Lounge/kitchen open plan with sofabed. Double bedroom ⟲. Bathroom ⟲, handrail by bath, space for side transfer. A large lodge designed for wheelchair users can sleep up to 10 people or be split into two separate units. Waterproof sheet available. Cottages unsuitable for disabled people also available.

Apply: Rosemary Helme ☎ 01423 780279. W www.helmepasture.co.uk

Rates: from £220-£710 per week (2007).

HARWOOD DALE, North Yorkshire

Hardwick House Country Cottages

Harwood Dale, Nr. Scarborough YO13 0LA.
☎ **01723 870682.**
W www.hardwickhousecottages.co.uk

●● F/G ★★★★

5 cottages located on edge of North York Moors. "Langdale" cottage designed for disabled guests. Ramp to entrance, 40". Open plan lounge/kitchen. Double and twin bedrooms ↺. Shower room 36", ↺, roll-in shower, handrails, adjustable basin, space for side transfer to WC. One other cottage has ground floor accommodation.

Rates: from £270-£600 per week (2007).

HAWORTH, West Yorkshire

Stable Cottage

West Field Farm, Haworth.
W www.BronteCountryCottages.co.uk

●● E/F/G ★★★

Single storey cottage for 2 people. Ramp to Entrance 32". Min. door width 31". Lounge/kitchen open plan. Double bedroom. Shower room with shower seat, space for side transfer to WC. 4 other cottages available.

Apply: Clare Pickles, West Field Farm, Tim Lane, Haworth BD22 7SA.
☎ 01535 644568.
Rates: from £250-£350 per week (2006).

HUTTON-LE-HOLE, North Yorkshire

Moorland & Heather Cottages

Hutton-le-Hole

●● F/G ★★★★

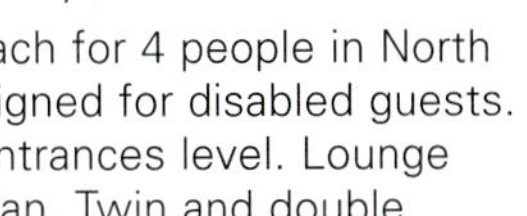

Two cottages each for 4 people in North York Moors designed for disabled guests. Ramp to one. Entrances level. Lounge /kitchen open plan. Twin and double bedrooms ↺, Bathroom sliding door, ↺, handrails, space for side transfer to bath and WC.

Apply: Mrs Susan Dussold, Byre Cottage, Hutton-le-Hole, York YO62 6UA.
☎ 01751 417743.
W www.moorlandcottages.com
Rates: on application.

INGLETON, North Yorkshire

Brentwood Farm Cottages

Barnoldswick Lane,
Burton in Lonsdale LA6 3LZ.

●● F/G ★★★★

Two cottages on farm between Yorkshire Dales and the Lake District. "Sycamores" designed for disabled guests. Paved path and ramp to entrance 75cm. Lounge/kitchen open plan. Ground floor twin bedroom. En suite shower room, 90cm, roll-in shower with seat, handrails, space by WC and under basin. Bedroom for 2-3 people and bathroom upstairs. Intercom between bedrooms. 2 steps to 2nd cottage.

Apply: Anita Taylor ☎ 015242 62155.
W www.brentwoodfarmcottages.co.uk
Rates: from £255-£500 per week (2008).

Self-catering accommodation

KEIGHLEY, West Yorkshire

The Mistal

Currer Laithe Farm, Nr. Keighley.
www.currerlaithe.co.uk

●● E/I/G

Specially adapted ground floor flat. Entrance ramp; Kitchen controls may be useable from wheelchair. Two bedrooms 33". Shower room 33", ⟲, shower chair, handrails, space for side transfer to WC. Car essential. Larger groups may book it farm guesthouse, which may also be available for self-catering at times, see page 286.

Apply: Miss J Brown, Currer Laithe Farm, Long Lee, Keighley BD21 4SL. ☎ 01535 604387.
Rates: from £380-£500 per week (2007).

LEEDS, West Yorkshire

Clarence Dock Apartments

●● G ★★

Student accommodation by Royal Armouries Museum. Seven apartments include a bedroom with en-suite bathroom designed for disabled people, 5 other bedrooms and a dining room/kitchen with lowered worktops. Refreshments and shop on site. Available July-September.

Ⓟ

Apply: Conference Office, University of Leeds LS2 9JT. ☎ 0113 233 6100.
confoffice@leeds.ac.uk
Rates: on application.

MASHAM, N. Yorkshire

Daleside

Swinburn Road, Masham, nr. Ripon.
www.self-catering-masham.co.uk

● F ★★★★★

Bungalow for up to 4 in quiet market town. Ramp or 2 steps at rear door; 1 step at front. Double door to open plan kitchen/dining area. Double and twin bedrooms, no ⟲. Shower room off double 100cm, handrails by seat and WC. Bathroom 84cm, raised WC, grabrail by bath. No children. Patio and private garden.

Ⓟ

Apply: Pam Usher. ☎ 01765 688277.
Rates: from £340-£555 per week (2007).

OSWALDKIRK, North Yorkshire

Angel Cottage

Wheatfield, Newton Grange, Oswaldkirk YO62 5YG.

●● F/G ★★★★

Holiday cottage 3 miles from Helmsley. Entrance 36", level. Accommodation ground floor except play gallery. Living room open plan. Dining room/kitchen 32". One bedroom adapted for desabled people, twin and family ⟲. Shower/toilet room 31" with grab rails, ⟲, roll-in shower with adjustable seat, toilet has movable support arms, space for side transfer to WC.

Apply: Jane Sweeney ☎ 01439 788493.
jane.sweeney@homecall.co.uk
Rates: from £400 per week (2008).

PICKERING, North Yorkshire

Cloth Fair Cottage

Rawcliffe House Farm, Stape,
Nr. Pickering YO18 8JA.
www.rawcliffehousefarm.co.uk
●● I/F ★★★★

One of 3 cottages on farm in North York Moors. Ramp with handrail to entrance 85cm. Lounge/kitchen open plan, controls useable from wheelchair. Twin bedroom 85cm, ↺. Bathroom 36", ↺, wheel-in shower with seat, handrails, space for side transfer to bath and WC. Raised WC seat and bed blocks available. Private patio. Short breaks and ground floor bed & breakfast suites available.

Apply: Jan & Duncan Allsopp.
☎ 01751 473292.
Rates: from £200-£475 per week (2008).

Keld Head Farm Holiday Cottages

Keld Head, Pickering YO18 8LL.
www.keldheadcottages.com
●● F/G 

Two, of 9, cottages sleeping up to 5 people on edge of National Park. Entrance 31", one step, portable ramp available. Internal doors 31". Lounge, kitchen/dining room ↺. Double and twin bedrooms. Bathroom ↺, handrail by bath and WC, no space for side transfer to WC. Raised WC seat available. Four other cottages have ground floor accommodation. Food supplies and meals service available. Premier Cottages member.

Apply: Mr & Mrs Fearn. ☎ 01751 473974.
Rates: from £286-£725 per week (2008).

Manor Farm Cottages

Newton-upon-Rawcliffe, Nr. Pickering.
www.members.aol.com/ManorfarmNewton
●● G ★★★★

"The Dairy House" is in a small group of cottages in North York Moors village. Ramp to front door from parking area. Internal doors 70cm. Lounge and kitchen ↺. Double and single bedrooms level. Ground floor shower room ↺, shower tray, space by WC, no handrails. Family bedroom and bathroom upstairs.

Apply: Mary Pennock. ☎ 01284 763568.
@ mpennock@ukonline.co.uk.
Rates: from £240-£489 per week (2007).

RICCALL, North Yorkshire

South Newlands Farm

Selby Road, Riccall, York YO19 6QR.
☎ **01757 248203.**
www.southnewlands.co.uk
●● I/F/G 

Two single storey cottages designed for disabled people on farm between Selby and York. Entrance level. Lounge with induction loop, and kitchen/dining room with lowered worktop. Double bedroom ↺ with roll-in shower room/WC. Also twin/double ↺ and twin/bunk room and Bathroom ↺, handrails bath transfer seat in one cottage. Toilet rails, shower seat, raised WC seat, vibrating alarm and some other equipment available or can be hired.

Rates: from £295-£495 per week (2007).

Self-catering accommodation

RIPON, North Yorkshire

Fountains Cottage

Fountains Abbey, Nr. Ripon.

● E/I/F/G

National Trust cottage for up to 7 people. One step from parking area. Rear door level, 30". Lounge, dining room with single bed on request, kitchen and shower room ground floor. Four bedrooms, bathroom and WC on 1st floor.

Ⓟ

Apply: National Trust Holiday Booking Office. ☎ 0870 4584422. See page 33.
Rates: from £350-£1136 per week (2007).

Sleningford Watermill Caravan & Camping Park

North Stainley, Ripon HG4 3HQ.
☎ 01765 635201.
www.ukparks.co.uk/sleningford

●● G

Level touring site north of Ripon on banks of River Ure. Tarred roads to hard standing pitches for up to 50 caravans and spaces for 30 tents. Unisex toilet unit designed for disabled people with level entrance, turning space, roll-in shower, handrails, space by WC. Shower chair available. Ramp to office and shop. Launderette level.

Ⓟ ⓘ

Rates: on application

SCARBOROUGH, North Yorkshire

Cayton Bay Holiday Park

Mill Ln, Cayton Bay, Scarborough YO11 3NJ.
☎ 01723 583111.

●● I/F/G ★★★★

Park Resorts holiday park 3 miles south of Scarborough with range of facilities and enter-tainment. Tree caravans for 5 people adapted for disabled guests. Entrance ramp. Lounge/kitchen open plan. Two bedrooms, sliding door 75cm, in double. Shower room 75cm, handrails, restricted. Open Easter-October.

Ⓟ

Apply: Park Resorts ☎ 0870 1299 299
Rates: on application.

SELBY, North Yorkshire

Cawood Holiday Park

Ryther Road, Cawood, Nr. Selby YO8 3TT.
☎ 01757 268450.
www.cawoodpark.com

●● G

Level site in Vale of York with self-catering units and pitches for touring caravans and tents. Three bungalows adapted for disabled people. Entrance level 39". Lounge 33" sliding door. Kitchen worktops 30", controls useable from wheelchair. Twin and single bedrooms 33", . Bathroom , handrails, space for side transfer to bath and WC. Shop and bar level. Unisex WC with basin for tourers.

Ⓟ

Rates: from £199 -£499 per week (2007).

SEWERBY, East Yorkshire

Field House Farm Cottages

Jewison Lane, Sewerby, Bridlington YO16 6YG.

☎ **01262 674932.**

W www.fieldhousefarmcottages.co.uk

 F/G 

"The Roost" and "Ostlers" are designed for disabled people on farm 1½ miles from coast. Ramp to entrance. Open plan lounge/kitchen. Each has two ground floor bedrooms with a roll-in shower room, with handrails and ↻, off the twin room. 5 other cottages available, one with ground floor accommodation.

Rates: from £300-£675 per week (2008).

SKIPSEA, East Yorkshire

Scout Holiday Homes Trust Caravan

Low Skirlington Leisure Park, Skipsea YO25 8SY

●● E/I/F/G

Unit for up to 6 people on family owned site near Driffield. Entrance ramp, 30". Open plan lounge/kitchen. Worktops 36". Double and single bedrooms 30", ↻. Shower room 30" sliding door, handrails, shower seat, space for side transfer to WC. Site has difficult access to the beach. Available April-October.

Apply: Scout Holiday Homes Trust. ☎ 020 8433 7290. See page 26.

Rates: from £125-£325 per week (2007).

SKIPTON, North Yorkshire

The Ghyll Holiday Cottages

Buckden, Nr, Skipton.

W www.dalegarth.co.uk

●● G

Three purpose-built single storey cottages in Upper Wharfdale. Entrances level. Wide doorways. Lounge/dining room. Kitchen ↻, controls not useable from wheelchair. One and two double/twin bedrooms. Bathrooms 84cm, ↻, handrails, roll-in shower, shower chair, space by bath and WC. Hoist, monkey pole, bed and chair raisers available. Other bedrooms and bathroom upstairs. Teletext TV. Sheltered garden with barbecue. Restaurant and swimming pool nearby.

Apply: Mr & Mrs Lusted, 4 Dalegarth, Buckden, Skipton BD23 5JU.

☎ 01756 760877. @ info@dalegarth.co.uk

Rates: from £387-£672 per week (2008).

THORPE BASSETT, North Yorkshire

The Old Post Office

Thorpe Bassett, Malton YO17 8LU.

● F ★★★★

Single storey cottage in village at edge of Wolds. Entrance step with handrail. Lounge and kitchen both ↻. Double and bunk bedrooms no ↻. Bathroom no ↻, grabrail by bath.

Apply: Mrs S D Simpson ☎ 01944 758047.

W www.ssimpsoncottages.co.uk

Rates: from £909-£330 per week (2008).

Rowgate Cottage

Rowgate Farm, Thorpe Bassett, Malton YO17 8LU

● I/F/G ★★★★

Cottage on farm for up to 5 people. Entrance level. Ground floor living room, kitchen and utility room/WC. Double handrail on stairs. Bedrooms on 1st floor. Bathroom with shower and handrails. raised WC seat and bathseat available. Teletext TV.

Apply: Janet Clarkson ☎ 01944 758 277
@ janet@rowgatecottage.fsnet.co.uk
Rates: on application

WHITBY, North Yorkshire

Bumbleby Cottage

Long Leas Farm, Hawkser, nr. Whitby YO22 4LA.

●● I/F/G ★★★★

Single storey cottage designed for disabled people off A171 a mile south of Whitby. Entrance level. Sliding door to open plan lounge/kitchen, controls useable from wheelchair. Two double bedrooms ⟲. One ensuite shower room ⟲, roll-in shower with seat, handrails, space by WC. Another cottage has entrance step, portable ramp available and a ground floor bedroom and bathroom with twin bedroom upstairs.

Apply: Brian McNeil ☎ 01947 603790.
W www.swallowcottages.co.uk
Rates: on application.

Millinder House Farm Cottages

Millinder House, Westerdale, Whitby YO21 2DE.
W www.millinderhouse.co.uk

●● I/F/G ★★★★

Two cottages, of 3, on North York Moors designed for disabled guests. Entrance level 87cm. Lounge/kitchen open plan, controls useable from a wheelchair. One unit has 3 bedrooms, ⟲ in double and twin. Bathroom with wheel-in shower, handrails, space for side transfer to bath and WC. The other has a twin/double bedroom and a roll-in shower room. Shower stool and raised WC seat available. Other equipment can be hired. Teletext TV. Baby sitting service.

Ⓟ

Apply: Joanna Hopkins. ☎ 01287 660053.
Rates: from £200-£505 per week (2008).

WRELTON, North Yorkshire

Beech Farm Cottages

wrelton, Nr Pickering YO18 8PG
☎ 01751 476612.
W www.beechfarm.com

● F ★★★★★

Group of cottages in village 3 miles from Pickering. two, sleeping 3 and 4 people, are single storey. entrances one and two steps. No specific fittings; toilet rail and bath seat available. Allergy free environment. Teletext TV. 2 other cottages have ground floor bedrooms. Regular disabled guests.

Ⓟ

Rates: from £355-£945 per week (2007).

YORK, North Yorkshire

York Lakeside Lodges

Moor Lane, York YO24 2QU.
☎ 01904 702346.
W www.yorklakesidelodges.co.uk

●● E/I/F/G ★★★★

Fourteen chalets for up to 7 people 2 miles from City centre. Some level with ground floor accommodation and bathroom with space for side transfer to WC. Minimum door width 34". One lodge is more specifically adapted for disabled guests.

Rates: from £220-£785 per week (2008).

This region comprises Cheshire, Cumbria, Greater Manchester, Lancashire and Merseyside. It includes the Lake District with the highest peaks in England, the western parts of the Pennines and the Peak District, coastal resorts, the great cities of Liverpool and Manchester and rolling countryside.

The leading resort in the area is Blackpool with miles of level promenade, piers, entertainment of all kinds and, of course, the Tower and the Pleasure Beach at which many rides can be enjoyed by disabled visitors. Other, quieter seaside resorts with level terrain include Southport and Morecambe, where the redeveloped promenade has views across to the Lake District.

Blackpool Pleasure Beach

Liverpool was the European Capital of Culture during 2008 and the city hosted a wide array of exhibitions, concerts and other events. The city is noted for its mercantile architecture and sporting heritage. Albert Dock near the city centre has been redeveloped and now houses a variety of shops, restaurants, museums and galleries including part of the Tate Gallery, the Customs & Excise Museum and the Beatles Museum.

Manchester offers all that can be expected of a metropolitan centre including top class theatre, music and sport with a wide range of shops and restaurants. In the redeveloped Castlefields area near the city centre, the Museum of Science & Industry is housed in the world's first passenger railway station. Away from the city centre, developments along the shores of the Manchester

Photo: www.britainonview.com

Manchester

Ship Canal include The Lowry and Imperial War Museum North at Salford Quays and the Trafford Centre for out-of-town shopping.

The historic towns of the region include Carlisle, Lancaster and Chester where the original city walls ring its picturesque shopping streets and cathedral. Advice on accessible sight-seeing routes can be obtained from the Tourist Information Centre.

The parks and gardens in the area include Liverpool University's Botanic gardens at Ness on the Wirral, the topiary gardens at Levens Hall near Kendal and Tatton Park near Knutsford in Cheshire. A large number of country parks have been established including the award winning Wyre Estuary Country Park in Lancashire. People interested in wildlife can choose from attractions including Chester Zoo and the Wildfowl & Wetlands Trust's Martin Mere near Ormskirk. In the Lake District a number of scenic paths have been developed for disabled people including the National Trust's Friars Crag Walk beside Derwentwater and the Ridding Wood Sculpture Trail in Grizedale Forest.

Throughout the area are displays of the local industrial heritage. Inland waterway transport is explored at the Boat Museum at Ellesmere Port and the silk industry at Macclesfield. The craft of glassmaking is on display at The World of Glass in St Helens. Small Pennine mill towns can be visited by the restored, award-winning East Lancashire Railway.

Photo: www.britainonview

USEFUL ADDRESSES

Visit Chester & Cheshire

Chester Railway Station, 1st Floor, West Wing Offices, Station Road, Chester CH1 3NT.
☎ **01244 405600** W **www.visitchester.com**

Information on the accessibility of about half of the places to stay, attractions and catering establishments in the county is given on the website by clicking the "Chester and Cheshire Welcomes All" button. The information is self-assessed but provided in a standard form.

Cumbria Tourism

Windermere Road, Staveley, Cumbria LA8 9PL.
☎ **01539 822222.**
@ **info@cumbriatourism.org**
W **www.golakes.co.uk**

Provides general information and a number of free publications about the county.

Lancashire & Blackpool Tourist Board

St Georges House, St Georges Street, Chorley PR7 2AA.
☎ **01257 226600.**
@ **info@visitlancashire.com**
W **www.lancashiretourism.com**

Marketing Manchester

Churchgate House, 56 Oxford Street, Manchester M1 6EU.
☎ **0161 237 1010.**
@ **touristinformation@marketing-manchester.co.uk**
W **www.visitmanchester.com**

Large print editions of the main tourist booklets are available from the Manchester Tourist Information Centre in St Peter's Square.

The Mersey Partnership

12 Princes Parade, Liverpool L3 1BG.
☎ **0151 227 2727.**
@ **info@visitliverpool.com**
W **www.merseyside.org**

Disabled Living

Redbank House, 4 St Chad's Street, Cheetham, Manchester M8 8QA.
☎ **0870 760 1580.**
@ **information@disabledliving.co.uk**
W **www.disabledliving.co.uk**

Have an information pack on holidays in print and on their website.

Disability Stockport

16 Meyer Street, Cale Green, Stockport SK3 8JE.
☎**/Textphone: 0161 480 7248.**
@ **disabilitystockport@btinternet.com**
W **www.disabilitystockport.org.uk**

Offers an information service to disabled people in Stockport.

Cheshire Centre for Independant Living

Oakwood Lane, Barnton, Cheshire CW8 4HE
☎ **01606 872760.**
@ **office@chesirecil.org**

A 'user-led' group of information providers in Cheshire providing information, training, information, practical help, direct payments and advocacy to assist disabled people throughout Cheshire.

North West England

DIAL

DIAL offers a free, impartial and confidential service of information and advice by telephone to disabled people, their relatives and professionals. The following DIAL UK members may be able to help disabled residents and visitors in their areas:

DI&S Blackpool, Fylde & Wyre
☎ 01253 625553

DIAL Chester ☎ 01244 345655
Textphone: 01244 342472

Halton Disability Services
☎ 01928 717222;
Textphone 01928 718999

DIS Hyndburn ☎ 01254 397979

Access Lancashire ☎ 01772 621633

Macclesfield DIB ☎ 01625 501759

Preston DISC ☎ 01772 558863

DIAL St Helens
☎/Textphone: 01744 453053

Vale Royal Disability Services
☎ 01606 888400

Warrington Disability Partnership
☎ 01925 240064;
Textphone: 01925 240853

West Lancashire Disability Helpline
☎ 0800 220676; Textphone: 01695 51512

Paveways, Wigan ☎ 01942 519909

USEFUL PUBLICATIONS & WEBSITES

The Access Guide to Blackpool - published by Blackpool Tourism. Available from Blackpool Tourism, Central Promenade, Blackpool FY1 1LY. ☎ 01253 478222.
@ tourism@blackpool.gov.uk
W www.visitblackpool.com

Miles Without Stiles is an on-line guide to 21 routes in the Lake District National Park that are considered accessible for people with limited mobility. They are classified into three standards of surface and gradient as well as the distance and other features of the area. Information of specific interest to disabled people such as the availability of parking and toilets is also given. There is also a link to a list of shorter paths and approaches to viewpoints that may be accessible to wheelchair users. This can be seen on their website W www.lake-district.gov.uk

Accessible Travel on Merseyside – a booklet giving information on public transport services for disabled people in the Merseyside PTA area is available, and updated on W www.merseytravel.gov.uk. Copies in alternative formats can be obtained from Merseytravel, 24 Hatton Garden, Liverpool L3 2AN ☎ 0151 227 5181 Textphone: 0151 330 1367.

www.disabledgo.org - this website includes detailed information on the accessibility of many premises in Blackpool, Liverpool, Salford and Stockport.

EQUIPMENT HIRE

Age Concern Bolton

72/74 Ashburner Street, Bolton BL1 1TN.
☎ **01204 382411.**
www.ageconcernbolton.org.uk

Manual wheelchairs can be supplied for periods of up to 3 weeks to Bolton residents and people visiting the area. People aged 50 upwards.

Blackpool Wheelchair Hire

183 Lytham Road, Blackpool FY1 6EU.
☎ **01253 408453.**
www.wheelchair-hire.com

Manual and electric wheelchairs and scooters are available for hire on daily or weekly rates. Delivery to hotels in the area can be arranged.

Care Ability

64/66 Bickerstaffe Street,
St Helens WA10 1DH.
☎/Textphone: 01744 451215.

Operates a loan service for manual wheelchairs.

Disability Services (Blackpool, Wyre & Fylde) Ltd

52 Clifton Street, Blackpool FY1 1PJ.
☎ **01253 476451.**

Can hire manual wheelchairs and scooters for use in and around Blackpool and operate a door-to-door community transport service available for outings in the area. NKS toilet keys are also available.

A list other organisations hiring equipment in the Blackpool area is given in The Access Guide to Blackpool, see above.

The Helpful Hand

6/8 Chester Road, Macclesfield SK11 8DG.
☎ **01625 424438.**
www.thehelpfulhand.co.uk

Manual and powered wheelchairs, scooters and a range of electric beds, chairs, stairlifts, commodes and incontinent equipment available for sale and hire.

Fred Walton Mobility Products

308 Mosley Common Road, Worsley,
Manchester M28 1DA.
www.fredwalton.co.uk

In addition to selling a wide range of equipment, manual wheelchairs are available to hire at weekly rates. Delivery can be arranged throughout the country.

Shopmobility Stockport

Level 2, Merseyway Car Park,
Stockport SK1 1PD.
☎ **0161 666 1100. @ admin@shopmobstockport.freeserve.co.uk**

Manual wheelchairs can be hired for up to 13 weeks for use within the UK. Temporary mermbership is available to visitors to the Stockport area.

The Wheelchair Centre

229 Droylsden Road, Audenshaw,
Manchester M34 5ZT.
☎ **0161 370 2661/5949.**
www.thewheelchaircentre.co.uk

Manual wheelchairs are available for hire on daily or weekly basis and lightweight scooters available by the week.

North West England

Shopmobility schemes provide wheelchairs and/or scooters for use in shopping centres in the following towns. For information on availability, etc. telephone in advance.

Accrington ☎ 01254 388388

Altrincham ☎/Textphone: 0161 929 1714

Ashton-under-Lyne ☎ 0161 399 9500

Barrow-in-Furness ☎ 01229 434039

Birkenhead ☎ 0151 647 6162

Blackpool ☎ 01253 349427

Bolton ☎ 01204 392946

Bury ☎ 0161 764 9966

Carlisle ☎ 01228 625950

Chester ☎ 01244 312626

Chorley ☎ 01257 260888

Crewe ☎ 01270 580031

Darwen ☎ 01254 262302

Kendal ☎ 01539 740933

Leigh ☎ 01942 777985;

Liverpool ☎ 0151 707 0877

Macclesfield ☎ 01625 613111

Manchester ☎ 0161 8394060

Manchester Wythenshawe ☎ 0161 437 3600

Nelson ☎ 01282 692502

Northwich ☎ 01606 353525

Oldham ☎ 0161 633 0040

Ormskirk ☎ 01695 570055

Preston ☎ 01772 204667

Rochdale ☎/Textphone: 01706 865986

Runcorn ☎ 01928 717445;

Southport ☎ 01704 546654

St Helens ☎ 01744 613388

Stockport ☎ 0161 666 1100

Trafford Centre ☎ 0161 747 8046

Wallasey ☎ 0151 606 4665

Warrington ☎ 01925 231941

Warrington, Birchwood ☎ 01925 822411

Wigan ☎ 01942 776070

Wilmslow ☎ 01625 522275

Winsford ☎ 01606 557550

Preston and Kendal Shopmobility have a mobiles unit visiting a number of towns in their area.

ACCOMMODATION WITH MEALS

AMBLESIDE, Cumbria

Rothay Manor Hotel

Rothay Bridge, Ambleside LA22 0EH.
☎ **015394 33605.**
W www.rothaymanor.co.uk
 D/G 

Country hotel. Main entrance 1 step, 40"; a level entrance is available. Public rooms level. Unisex WC. One ground floor bedroom with bathroom and shower. Also a 2-bedroomed suite with bathroom and shower both designed for disabled guests. Shower chairs available. Patio level and ramp with rail to garden. Special interest breaks offered.

Rates: from £80 per person BB (2008).

APPLEBY, Cumbria

Appleby Manor Hotel

Roman Road,
Appleby-in-Westmorland CA16 6JB.
☎ **017683 51571.**
W www.applebymanor.co.uk
●● D/E/F/G 

Hotel in country town. Reserved parking spaces. Side entrance level; main entrance 4 steps. Public rooms level except steps to leisure club. WCs level, not adapted. Two ground floor bedrooms 80cm, ⟲. Bathrooms ⟲, handrail by bath, space by WC. Raised WC seat and bathseat available. Other ground floor bedrooms level. A Best Western Hotel.

Rates: from £70 per person BB (2008).

BLACKPOOL, Lancashire

Bond Hotel

120 Bond Street, Blackpool FY4 1HG
☎ **01253 341218.**
W www.bondhotel.co.uk
 D/E/I/G/H ★★

Family run hotel catering for disabled guests. Entrance level, automatic doors. Restaurant, lounge and bar ground floor level. Sun roof. Two unisex WCs. Two lifts, largest 31", inside 48"x40". 50 bedrooms, including 10 on ground floor. All have bathrooms; ⟲ with space by WC in 44. Shared bathroom with hoist and roll-in shower room. Shower chairs and other equipment available. Special breaks and seasonal entertainment offered.

Rates: on application.

Century Hotel

406 North Promenade,
Blackpool FY1 2LB.
☎ **01253 354598.**
W www.centuryhotel.co.uk
●● D/E/I/F/G/H

Family owned hotel on seafront. Reserved parking bays. Ramp to entrance, automatic doors. Low reception desk. Public rooms on ground and 1st floors. Unisex WC ground floor. Lift 120cm, inside 110x90cm, floor announcements. 8 twin/double bedrooms designed for disabled guests. Shower rooms 85cm sliding door, ⟲, roll-in shower with seat, handrails, space by WC. Bed blocks and hoist available. Other bedrooms level. Vibrating alarms, induction loop and waterproof sheets available. Entertainment provided.

Rates: from £280-£315 per week BBE (2008).

De Vere Herons' Reach Blackpool

East Park Drive, Blackpool FY3 8LL.
☎ **01253 838866.**
●● D/E/F/G ★★★★

High class hotel in secluded grounds. Reserved parking bays. Entrance ramp or 8 steps, automatic door. Public rooms level. Unisex WCs ground floor and basement. Lift 31", inside 43"x55". Six bedrooms designed for disabled guests. Bathrooms sliding door, ↻, handrails, space by bath and WC. Other bedrooms level.

Ⓟ

Rates: on application.

Elizabeth Frankland Moore Home

539 Lytham Road, Blackpool FY4 1RA.
☎ **01253 343313.**
@ **blesma01@tiscali.co.uk**
●●●●●

BLESMA nursing and residential care home for ex-service men and women on southern edge of town. Six double and a single room are available for short stay respite care. 24 hour nursing cover.
Rates: on application.

Hilton Blackpool

North Promenade, Blackpool FY1 2JQ.
☎ **01253 623434.**
W **www.hilton.co.uk/blackpool**
●● D/E/I/F/G

Large hotel on seafront. Reserved parking bays. Car park entrance level; main entrance ramp or 2 steps. Public rooms 1st floor level. Swimming pool. Adapted WC cubicles. Lift 34½", inside 63"x51". Two double bedrooms and five twin rooms adapted for disabled guests. Roll-in shower rooms 30". Other bedrooms level. Waterproof sheets available. Special interest breaks arranged.

Ⓟ

Rates: on application.

Norbreck Castle Hotel

Queen's Promenade, Blackpool FY2 9AA.
☎ **01253 352341.**
@ **res722@britanniahotels.com**
●● D/E/I/F/G

Large seafront hotel north of town centre. Reserved parking bays. Ramp or 15 steps to front entrance, automatic doors; rear entrance level. Low reception desk. Public rooms ground floor. Unisex WC. Lifts to all floors 31", inside 56"x42", voice announce-ments. 23 bedrooms, double and twin, adapted for disabled guests. Shower rooms ↻, roll-in shower with seat, handrails, space for side transfer to WC. Other bedrooms level. Large button telephones and Teletext TV available. Entertainment offered.

Ⓟ

Rates: on application.

BOLTON, Greater Manchester

Express by Holiday Inn Bolton

3 Arena Approach, Horwich, Bolton BL6 6LB.
☎ **01204 469111.**
@ **ebhi-bolton@btconnect.com**
●● E/I/G

Limited service hotel 3 miles from Bolton and near M61, junction 5. Reserved parking bays. Entrance level. Low reception desk with induction loop. Breakfast room and unisex WC ground floor. Lift to upper floors. Four bedrooms with adaptations for disabled guests 84cm, ↻, no low clothes rail or curtain closer. Shower rooms 82cm, ↻, roll-in shower, handrails, space by WC. Mattress protectors. Vibrating alarms. Other bedrooms level.

Ⓟ

Rates: from £39-£69 per room BB (2008).

BORROWDALE, Cumbria

The Borrowdale Hotel

Borrowdale, Keswick CA12 5UY.

☎ **017687 77224.**

W theborrowdalehotel.co.uk

●● D/E/F/G ★★★

Traditional country hotel at southern end of Derwentwater. Reserved parking bays. Ramp or one step at entrance. Public rooms ground floor, min. door width 33". Unisex WC. Covered walkway to annexe which has 2 double/twin bedrooms designed for disabled guests. Bathrooms 33", ⟲, roll-in shower with seat, handrails, space by WC. Stairlift to 1st floor. Teletext TV. Wheelchair available. Guests attending the Cockermouth dialysis unit are accommodated.

Rates: on application.

BOWNESS-ON-WINDERMERE, Cumbria

Burn How Garden House Hotel

Back Belsfield Road, Bowness-on-Windermere LA23 3HH.

☎ **015394 46226.**

W www.burnhow.co.uk

●● D/E/G ★★★

Hotel near lake and shops. Reserved parking bays. Ramp to entrance 42". Public rooms level. Unisex WC. Four ground floor bedrooms in Rose Garden annexe ⟲, patio door to garden, portable ramp available. Bathrooms 31", ⟲, handrail by bath, space for side transfer to bath and WC one with roll-in shower. A Best Western Hotel.

Rates: from £50-£68 per person BB (2007).

The Burnside Hotel

Kendal Road, Bowness, Windermere LA23 3EP.

☎ **08700 468640.**

W www.burnsidehotel.com

●● D/E/I/F/G ★★★

Hotel overlooking Lake Windermere. Reserved parking bays. Entrance level. Public rooms level. Unisex WC. Lift to all floors. Family bedroom designed for disabled guests. Bathroom ⟲, roll-in shower, handrails, space for side transfer to bath and WC. Two twin rooms with bathrooms ⟲, no transfer to bath. Other bedrooms level. Waterproof sheets available. Steeply sloping garden.

Rates: from £60-£95 DBB per person (2007).

Fairfield Garden Guest House

Brantfield Road, Bowness Bay, Windermere LA23 3AE.

☎ **015394 46565.**

W www.the-fairfield.co.uk

● D/F/G ★★★★

Historic house above village. Garden entrance 1 step, portable ramp available; main entrance 4 steps. Dining room ramp or 1 step. One twin bedroom level, 30", ⟲, alarm call, can interconnect with adjoining room. Shower room 26", no ⟲, shower tray, handrails by WC. Accessible terrace overlooking garden. Access information on website. Car advisable.

Rates: from £30-£37 per person sharing BB (2007).

Lindeth Howe Country House Hotel

Lindeth Drive, Longtail Hill,
Windermere LA23 3JF.
☎ **015394 45759.**
www.lindeth-howe.co.uk
●● D/E/I/F/G 

Country house hotel overlooking Lake Windermere. Reserved parking bays. Ramp to entrance from car park; front entrance 1 step. Public rooms ground floor level. Unisex WC. Two bedrooms, double and twin, designed for disabled guests. Bathrooms 87cm, ⟲, handrails, space for side transfer to WC. Other bedrooms upstairs. Ramp to lawn and pond.

Rates: £120-160 per person (2008).

Windermere Manor

Rayrigg Road, Windermere LA23 1ES.
☎ **0845 603 0051.**
windermere.manor@actionforblindpeople.org.uk
● D/G

Hotel with adaptations and facilities for visually impaired people and their families and friends. Up to 51 guests can be accommodated in 27 bedrooms with own bathrooms. Full facilities for guide dogs. Outings, activities and entertainment arranged. Transfers from local stations. Volunteers can be arranged for some assistance. Self-catering also available. Run by Action for Blind People, see page 19.

Rates: from £44-£54 per night BBE (2007).

BRAMHALL, Greater Manchester

Legacy Bramhall County Hotel

Bramhall Lane South, Bramhall,
Stockport SK7 2EB.
☎ **0870 609 6148.**
●● D/E/F/G 

Modern hotel. Reserved parking bays. Entrance level, automatic door. Public rooms open plan. Unisex WC. Twin ground floor bedroom designed for disabled guests. Bathroom 36" sliding door, ⟲, handrails, space for side transfer to bath and WC. Other ground floor bedrooms level.

Rates: on application.

BROMBOROUGH, Merseyside

Village Hotel & Leisure Club Wirral

Pool Lane, Bromborough,
Wirral CH62 4UE.
☎ **0151 643 1616.**
village.wirral@village-hotels.com
●● D/E/I/F/G

Modern hotel. Reserved parking spaces. Entrance ramp or 8 steps. Public rooms level. Unisex WC. Lift, 60", inside 60"x72". Five twin bedrooms for disabled guests. Bathroom ⟲, space for side transfer to bath and WC. Other bedrooms level. Adapted changing room in Leisure Club.

Rates: on application.

BROUGHTON-IN-FURNESS, Cumbria

The Kepplewray Centre

Broughton-in-Furness LA20 6HE.

☎ **01229 716936.**

www.kepplewray.org.uk

●●● D/E/I/F/G/H

Activity centre in southern Lake District also open to people not taking part in organised programmes. Side entrance level; ramp at front door. Dining room and lounges level. Unisex WCs. Lift 85cm, inside 133x110cm, voice announcements, tactile signs. Bedrooms include 1 single and 1 twin rooms with roll-in shower rooms. Shared bathrooms and WCs equipped for a range of disabilities. Equipment includes Clos-o-Mat WC, adjustable height bed, shower chairs and electric hoist. "Wheels for All" cycle hire available.

Rates: on application.

CARLISLE, Cumbria

Ibis Carlisle

Portlands, Botchergate, Carlisle CA1 1RP.

☎ **01228 518000.** **H3443@accor.com**

●● G ★★

Hotel in centre of town. Entrance and public rooms level. Unisex WC. Lift to upper floors. Five bedrooms designed for disabled guests. Bathrooms ↺, handrails. Other 97 bedrooms level.

Rates: £49-£57 per room (2008).

CHESTER, Cheshire

Comfort Inn Chester

74 Hoole Road, Chester CH3 3NL.

☎ **01244 327542.**

www.comfortinnchester.com

●● D/E/G

Hotel near city centre and station. Reserved parking bays. Entrance level. Low reception desk. Breakfast room level. Two bedrooms designed for disabled guests 32", ↺. Bathroom 28" sliding door, handrails, space for side transfer to WC. Other ground floor bedrooms level.

Rates: from £52.50-£80 per room (2007).

The Dene Hotel

Hoole Road, Chester CH2 3ND.

☎ **01244 321165.** **www.denehotel.com**

● D/E/G ★★

Hotel in own grounds a mile from city centre. Entrance ramp or 3 steps. Public rooms level. One bedroom designed for disabled guests with bathroom with handrails and space by WC. Other ground floor bedrooms level. A circle hotel.

Rates: from £52.50 per person BB (2008).

Express by Holiday Inn Chester Racecourse

New Crane Street, Chester CH1 2LY.

☎ **0870 990 4065.**

hotel@chester-races.com

●● E/I/F/G

Limited service hotel at racecourse close to city centre. Reserved parking bays. Level entrance. Public rooms ground floor, open plan. Unisex WC. Lift to upper floors. 5 bedrooms designed for disabled guests. Shower rooms ↺, roll-in shower with seat, handrails, space by WC. Other bedrooms level.

Rates: £80-£85 per room BB (2008).

The Green Bough Hotel

60 Hoole Road, Chester CH2 3NL.
☎ **01244 326241.**
www.greenbough.co.uk
●● D/E/G ★★★★

Privately run hotel and restaurant on approach to city. Reserved parking bays. Entrance ramp or 2 steps. Public rooms level. WC level. Two bedrooms and a suite on ground floor with bathrooms ⟲, one has roll-in shower. Access statement available.

Rates: from £175 double BB (2008).

Holiday Inn Chester South

Wrexham Road, Chester CH4 9DL.
☎ **0870 400 9019.**
reservations-chester@ihg.com

●● D/F/G

Hotel 2 miles south of central Chester off A55. Reserved parking bays. Ramp to entrance, automatic doors. Bar and lounge open plan. Restaurant 1st floor. No lift, but full menu can be served in bar/lounge. Adapted cubicles in WCs. 2 bedrooms adapted for disabled people ⟲. Shower rooms ⟲, roll-in shower, handrails, space by WC. Other ground floor bedrooms level.

Rates: from £60-£155 per room (2008).

Ramada Chester

Whitchurch Road, Christleton, Chester CH3 5QL.
☎ **01244 332121.**
www.ramadachester.co.uk
●● D/E/I/F/G ★★★★

Hotel 1½ miles east of centre off A55. Reserved parking bays. Entrance level, automatic doors. Low reception desk. Public rooms level, open plan. Unisex WC. Three bedrooms designed for disabled guests. One has roll-in shower room with seat, ⟲, handrails, space by WC. The others have bathrooms. Other ground floor bedrooms level. Large print menu and telephone with large buttons.

Rates: from £69 BB (2008).

COCKERMOUTH, Cumbria

Shepherds Hotel

Egremont Road, Cockermouth CA13 0QX.
☎ **01900 822673.**
www.shepherdshotel.co.uk
●● D/E/F ★★★

Lodge at edge of town at the Lakeland Sheep & Wool Visitor Centre. Reserved parking bays. Ramp with handrails to entrance, or 11 steps. Public rooms open plan. Lift 80cm, inside 110x140cm. One twin room adapted for disabled guests on ground floor, ⟲. Bathroom 88cm, ⟲, handrails and drop seat by bath, space by WC. Also 4 double and 9 twin rooms level.

Rates: £69 per room BB (2007).

CREWE, Cheshire

The Hunter's Lodge

Sydney Road, Sydney, Crewe CW1 5LU.

☎ **01270 583440.**

www.hunterslodge.co.uk

●● D/E/I/F/G

Hotel in own grounds a mile from Crewe. Parking spaces can be reserved. Entrance level, double doors. Low reception desk. Public rooms level, mainly open plan. Unisex WC. Double bedroom designed for disabled guests with external entrance 79cm, ⟲. Bathroom ⟲, handrail by bath, space for side transfer to bath and WC. Other ground floor bedrooms level.

Rates: on application.

ECCLES, Greater Manchester

Monton House Hotel

116-118 Monton Road, Eccles M30 9HG.

☎ **0161 789 7811.**

www.montonhousehotel.co.uk

●● D/E/F/G ★★

Hotel in suburb 4 miles east of central Manchester near M602. Reserved parking bays. Entrance from car park level; 12 steps at main entrance. Lounge and bar ground floor, restaurant in basement. Lift to all floors. Double bedroom on ground floor adapted for disabled guests. Shower room ⟲ shower tray with seat, space by WC.

Rates: from £40 per night BB (2008).

ELLESMERE PORT, Cheshire

Holiday Inn Ellesmere Port/Cheshire Oaks

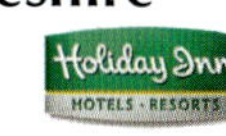

Centre Island, Lower Mersey Street, Ellesmere Port CH65 2AL.

☎ **0151 356 8111.**

sales@hiellesmereport.com

●● D/E/I/F/G

Waterfront hotel near Boat Museum. Reserved parking bays. Entrance level, automatic door. Low reception desk. Public rooms level, open plan. Unisex WC. Lift 80cm, inside 102x136cm. Four bedrooms designed for disabled guests, 76cm, ⟲, low switches and door viewer. Bathroom 81cm sliding door, ⟲, handrail by WC, space for side transfer. Waterproof sheets available. Other bedrooms level.

Rates: on application.

GILSLAND, Cumbria

The Hadrian's Wall Residential Study Centre

Birdoswald Roman Fort, Gilsland, Brampton CA8 7DD.

☎ **01697 747602**

●● D/E/I/F/G

Hostel accommodation for groups in converted farmhouse at archaeological site on Roman Wall. Reserved parking bay and drop-off point, main parking area 100m. Ramp to one entrance; main entrance 2 steps. Dining room, recreation room and other public areas level. Unisex WC. Family bedroom designed for disabled guests with roll-shower room, ⟲, shower seat, handrail by WC, space by WC. Waterproof mattresses. Other bedrooms upstairs. Advance booking only for groups of 10 or more.

Rates: on application.

GRANGE-OVER-SANDS, Cumbria

Netherwood Hotel

Grange-over-Sands LA11 6ET.

☎ 015395 32552.

www.netherwood-hotel.co.uk

●● D/E/F/G ★★★

Country house hotel overlooking Morecambe Bay. Courtyard entrance level 31"; main entrance 15 steps. Public rooms 1st floor level. Adapted WC cubicles. Unisex WC. Lift 31½", inside 35"x47". Double/twin bedroom designed for disabled guests. Bathroom, handrails, space for side transfer to bath and WC. Other bedrooms level.

 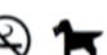  

Rates: from £75 BB per person (2008).

GRASMERE, Cumbria

Dale Lodge Hotel

Red Bank Road, Grasmere LA22 9SW.

☎ 01539 435300.

www.dalelodgehotel.co.uk

●● D/E/I/F/G ★★★

Hotel in own level grounds. Level entrance; front entrance one step, ramp available. Public rooms level. Unisex WC. Ground floor bedroom. Shower room with roll-in shower, handrails, space by WC. Other bedrooms upstairs.

Rates: from £100-£180 per room BB (2008).

HAYDOCK, Merseyside

Holiday Inn Haydock M6 J23

Lodge Lane, Newton-le-Willows WA12 0JG.

☎ 0870 400 9039.

reservations-haydock@ihg.com

●● D/E/I/F/G ★★★

Hotel off motorway beside racecourse. 4 reserved parking bays. Level entrance, automatic doors. Public rooms ground floor, level. Unisex WC. Lifts 80cm, inside 110x140cm. 4 bedrooms, double and twin, designed for disabled guests. Bathrooms. Other bedrooms level. Teletext TV. Leisure club ground floor.

Rates: on application.

Thistle Haydock Hotel

Penny Lane, Haydock, St Helens WA11 9SG.

☎ 0870 333 9136.

reservations.haydock@thistle.co.uk

●● D/E/I/F/G ★★★★

Modern hotel near M6 junction 23. Entrance ramp. Public rooms level. Unisex WC. Bedrooms designed for disabled guests with bathrooms. Other ground floor bedrooms level.

Rates: on application.

HETHERSGILL, Cumbria

New Pallyards

Hethersgill, Carlisle CA6 6HZ.

☎ 01228 577308.

www.newpallyards.freeserve.co.uk

● D/I/F/G ★★★★

Farmhouse bed & breakfast in north east Cumbria. Dining room level. Two ground floor bedrooms with bathrooms level. Evening meals by arrangement. Self-catering also available, see page 341.

Rates: from £30 per night BB (2008).

HOLMES CHAPEL, Cheshire

Ye Olde Vicarage Hotel

Knutsford Road, Cranage,
Holmes Chapel CW4 8EF.
☎ 01477 532041.
W www.cheshire-hotels.com

●● D/E/F/G ★★★

Hotel in central Cheshire countryside. Reserved parking bay. Both side and main entrances level. Low reception desk. Public rooms level. Ground floor bedroom adapted for disabled guests. Shower room 40", ↺, roll-in shower, handrails, space by WC. Shower chair and raised WC seat available. Other ground floor bedrooms level.

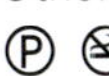

Rates: from £85 per night BB (2008).

KESWICK, Cumbria

Portland House

19 Leonard Street, Keswick CA12 4EL.
☎ 017687 74230. W www.portlandhouse.net

●● D/I/F/G

Guesthouse close to town centre. Parking spaces can be reserved. Entrance ramp or 1 step. Breakfast room level. Ground floor twin bedroom 100 cm, ↺. Shower room ↺, large shower tray with seat and handrail, space by WC. Toilet frame available. Teletext TV. Other bedrooms upstairs. Regular disabled guests.

Rates: from £35 per person BB (2007).

KIRKBY STEPHEN, Cumbria

Fat Lamb Hotel

Crossbank, Ravenstonedale,
Kirkby Stephen CA17 4LL.
☎ 015396 23242. W www.fatlamb.co.uk

●●● D/E/G ★★

Country inn between Lake District and Yorkshire Dales. Entrance level, 30". Public rooms level 30". WCs 30", ↺. Five double bedrooms level, 33". Bathrooms 34", ↺, handrails, bath seat. Some assistance can be given. Private nature reserve.

Rates: from £44 per person BB (2008).

KNOWSLEY, Merseyside

Express by Holiday Inn Liverpool - Knowsley

Ribblers Lane, Knowsley,
Prescot L34 9HA.
☎ 0151 549 2700.

●● D/E/F/G ★★★

Limited service hotel. Reserved parking bays. Entrance level, automatic door. Low reception desk. Public rooms open plan, level. Unisex WC. Lift to upper floors. One ground floor bedroom designed for disabled guests. Shower room ↺, roll-in shower with seat, handrails, space by WC. Vibrating pillow alarm.

Rates: from £49.95 per night (2008).

10 North West England

LANCASTER, Lancashire

Holiday Inn Lancaster

Waterside Park, Caton Road,
Lancaster LA1 3RA.

☎ **0870 400 9047.** @ **lancaster@ihg.com**

●● D/E/I/F/G ★★★

Hotel on northern edge of city, near M6 junction 34. Reserved parking bays. Entrance level, automatic doors. Restaurant level, large print menus. Platform lift or 3 steps to bar and lounge. Unisex WC. Lift 79.5cm, inside 156x138cm. 3 bedrooms, twin and doubles, adapted for disabled guests 88.5cm. Bathrooms ↺, handrails, space by bath and WC. Other bedrooms level. Waterproof sheet, vibrating alarms, portable induction loops available. 3 steps to leisure centre.

Rates: on application.

Thurnham Mill Hotel

Thurnham, Nr. Lancaster LA2 0BD.

☎ **01524 752852.**

W **www.thurnham-mill-hotel.co.uk**

●● D/E/F/G

Country hotel by canal south of Lancaster. Entrance from car park level. Main entrance 10 steps. Public rooms 1st floor level, ramp from bar to canal-side area. Unisex WC. Lift 72cm, inside 90cmx90cm. Bedroom, twin or double, designed for disabled guests ↺. Bathroom 72cm, ↺, no handrails. Other 14 bedrooms level.

Rates: on application.

LIVERPOOL, Merseyside

Campanile Liverpool

Chaloner Street, Queens Dock,
Liverpool L3 4AJ.

☎ **0151 709 8104.**

@ **liverpool@campanile-hotels.com**

●●

Hotel near Albert Dock. Reserved parking bays. Public rooms level. Unisex WC. 3 twin bedrooms designed for disabled guests. Bathroom ↺, handrails, space for side transfer. Other ground floor bedrooms level. See page 31.

Rates: on application.

Crowne Plaza Hotel Liverpool

St Nicholas Place, Pierhead,
Liverpool L3 1QW.

☎ **0151 243 8000.** W **www.cpliverpool.com**

●● D/E/I/F/G

High class hotel on historic waterfront. Reserved parking bays. Level entrance. Low reception desk. Public rooms ground floor level. Unisex WC. Lift 110cm, inside 156x136cm. 9 bedrooms designed for disabled guests 75cm, ↺. Bathrooms 77cm sliding door, ↺, space by bath and WC. Other bedrooms level.

Rates: on application.

Express by Holiday Inn Liverpool Albert Dock

Britannia Pavilion, Albert Dock, Liverpool L3 4AD.

☎ **0845 345 0000.**

@ **reservations@exliverpool.com**

 E/I/F/G

Limited service hotel in waterfront development. Reserved parking bays. Tarmac and cobbles on approach. 5 steps at main entrance with intercom; alternative level entrance available. Public rooms open plan. Unisex WC. Lift 31", inside 42"x55". Two family bedrooms designed for disabled guests. Shower room 31", ⟲, roll-in shower, handrails. Induction loop and vibrating pager. Other bedrooms level.

Rates: on application.

Greenbank Sports Academy

Greenbank Lane, Liverpool L17 1AG.

☎ **0151 280 2257.**

W www.greenbankacademy.co.uk

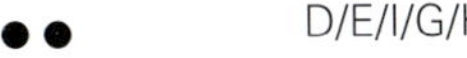 D/E/I/G/H

Accommodation at sports complex run by disabled people in Sefton Park area. Entrance level. Public rooms level. Unisex WC. Sleeps up to 24 people in 7 twin bedrooms and a dormitory.

Rates: from £20-£25 per person (2007).

Holiday Inn Liverpool City Centre

Lime Street, Liverpool L1 1NQ.

☎ **0151 709 7090.** **W www.hiliverpool.com**

●● D/E/I/F/G ★★★★

Hotel in city centre near station. 2 parking spaces can be booked in advance by disabled guests or neighbouring NCP car park. Entrance level, swing and revolving doors. Main public rooms 2nd floor, open plan. Unisex WCs 1st and 2nd floors. Lifts 90cm, inside 128x145cm. A bedroom adapted for disabled guests with bathroom 87cm, ⟲, handrails, space by bath and WC. Other bedrooms level. Disability awareness training for staff.

Rates: from £80-£150 per night (2008).

Ibis Liverpool

27 Wapping, Liverpool L1 8LY.

☎ **0151 706 9800.** @ **H3140@accor.com**

●● D/E/G ★★

Hotel in city centre near Albert Dock. Entrance level. Public rooms open plan. Unisex WC. Lifts to upper floors. Eight bedrooms with bathrooms designed for disabled guests. Other 119 bedrooms level.

Rates: from £59-£67 per room (2008).

YHA Liverpool

Tabley Street, Wapping, Liverpool L1 8EE.

☎ **0870 770 5924.** @ **liverpool@yha.org.uk**

●● D/E/I/F/G

Youth hostel in city centre. Slope to entrance, double doors. Low reception desk. Public rooms level. Unisex WC. Two bedrooms with twin and bunk beds adapted for disabled guests. Shower rooms ⟲, roll-in shower with seat, handrails, space for side transfer to WC. Waterproof sheet available by arrangement. For more information on Youth Hostels see page 34.

Rates: from £15.95 BB (2008).

LIVERPOOL AIRPORT, Merseyside

Express by Holiday Inn Liverpool John Lennon Airport

1 Speke Hall Avenue, Speke,
Liverpool L24 1UX.

☎ **0845 345 0000.**

W www.exliverpoolairport.com

●● D/E/I/F/G

Limited service hotel 1 mile from airport. Reserved parking bays. Entrance level, automatic door. Low reception desk. Public rooms open plan. Unisex WC and adapted cubicles. Lift 36", inside 43"x54", braille controls. 5 bedrooms ⟲. Shower rooms with shower tray. Other bedrooms level. Teletext TVs, vibrating alarm and portable induction loops. Shuttle bus to airport.

Rates: from £80 per room BB (2008).

LYTHAM ST ANNES, Lancashire

Chadwick Hotel

South Promenade,
Lytham St Annes FY8 1NP.

☎ **01253 720061.**

W www.thechadwickhotel.com

● D/E/F/G ★★★

Hotel overlooking Ribble estuary. Reserved parking bays. Entrance ramp, 42". Public rooms level. Unisex WC, NKS key available. Lift 20", inside 22"x42". One bedroom with bathroom adapted for wheelchair users. Other bedrooms level. Special breaks with entertainment.

Rates: from £55 single, £90 double BB (2008).

St Annes Hotel

69-71 South Promenade,
St Annes on Sea FY8 1LZ.

☎ **01253 713108.**

W www.st-annes-hotel.com

●●● D/E/I/F/G/H

Hotel on seafront designed for disabled guests. Reserved parking bays. Ramp with handrail to entrance, automatic door. Low reception desk. Public rooms level from reception or lift that serves 4 floors. 24, of 26, bedrooms accessible for wheelchair users in various formats of number of beds, connecting rooms and suites with cooking facilities. All have own bathrooms with features including roll-in showers and tracking hoists. Induction loops and toilet and mobility equipment available. Hydrotherapy pool and sensory room. Outings and entertainment organised. Transfers in accessible minibus can be arranged and care agencies employed if required.

Rates: on application

MACCLESFIELD, Cheshire

Common Barn Farm

Smith Lane, Rainrow,
Nr. Macclesfield SK10 5XJ.

☎ **01625 574878.**

W www.cottages-with-a-view.co.uk

●● D/G

Bed and breakfast in converted barn on Peak District working sheep farm. Designated parking spaces. Entrance level, double doors. Tea/breakfast room and lounge level. Unisex WC. Twin bedroom designed for disabled guests. Shower room 36", ⟲, roll-in shower with seat, handrails, space by WC. Other level bedrooms available and also self-catering cottages.

Rates: from £28 per person sharing BB (2007).

MANCHESTER & SALFORD, Greater Manchester

Campanile Manchester Salford

55 Ordsell Lane, Regent Road,
Salford M5 4RS.
☎ **0161 833 1845.**
@ **manchester@campanile-hotels.com**
●●

Hotel in renovated dock area. Reserved parking bays. Public rooms level. Unisex WC. 10 twin bedrooms designed for disabled guests. Bathroom ⟲, handrails, space for side transfer. Other ground floor bedrooms level. See page 31.

Rates: on application.

Castlefield Hotel

Liverpool Road, Castlefield,
Manchester M3 4JR.
☎ **0161 832 7073.**
W **www.castlefield-hotel.co.uk**
●● D/E/I/G ★★★

City centre hotel. Car park by lower level Y Club entrance. Restaurant, lounge and bar level. Unisex WC. Lift to all floors 37", inside 60"x63". Three twin bedrooms designed for disabled guests 35", high lighting levels. Bathrooms 35", ⟲, handrails, no space for side transfer to WC.

Rates: from £99 single,
£120 double midweek (2008).

Copthorne Manchester

Clippers Quay, Salford Quays,
Manchester M50 3SN.
☎ **0161 873 7321.**
W **www.copthorne.com/manchester**
●● D/E/I/G ★★★★

Modern hotel on waterfront. Designated parking bays. Ramp to entrance, automatic door. Public rooms level or ramp. Unisex WCs on 2nd and 3rd floors. Lift to all floors 80cm, inside 140x106cm. One double bedroom designed for disabled guests. Bathroom ⟲, handrails, space for side transfer to bath and WC. Other bedrooms level. Vibrating alarms, adapted telephones, induction loops and wheelchairs available.

Rates: on application.

Days Hotel Manchester City

Weston Building, Sackville Street,
Manchester M1 3BB.
☎ **0161 955 8062.**
W **www.meeting.co.uk/mcc**
● D/E/I/F/G ★★★

City centre hotel forming part of Manchester Conference Centre on University site. Street parking. Entrance level, automatic doors. Low reception desk. 5 steps to restaurant. Lounge and bar level. Unisex WC. Lift 32", inside 43"x56", Braille buttons. Two bedrooms designed for disabled people. Bathrooms 36", ⟲, space by bath and WC. Other bedrooms level.

Rates: on application.

Express by Holiday Inn Manchester East

Debdale Park, Hyde Road, Manchester M18 7LJ.

☎ **0870 720 1186**

@ **Manchester©morethanhotels.com**

●● E/F/G

Limited service hotel off A57, 3 miles from city centre. Reserved parking bays. Entrance level, automatic doors. Low reception desk. Public rooms open plan, level. 4 bedrooms designed for disabled guests. Shower room, roll-in shower with seat, handrails, space by WC. Other ground floor rooms level.

Rates: from £69 per night BB (2008).

Ibis Manchester Charles Street

Charles Street, Manchester M1 7DL.

☎ **0161 272 5000.** @ **H3143@accor.com**

●● D/E/G

Hotel near city centre and UMIST. Entrance level. Public rooms open plan. Lifts to upper floors. Seven bedrooms with bathrooms designed for disabled guests. Other bedrooms level.

Rates: from £65 per room (2008).

Ibis Manchester City Centre

96 Portland Street, Manchester M1 4GY.

☎ **0161 234 0600.** @ **H3142@accor.com**

●● D/E/G

City centre hotel near Conference Centre. Entrance level. Public rooms open plan. Lifts to upper floors. Seven bedrooms with bathrooms designed for disabled guests. Other 120 bedrooms level.

Rates: from £67 per room (2008).

Jurys Inn Manchester

56 Great Bridgewater Street, Manchester M1 5LE.

☎ **0161 953 8888.**

●● D/E/I/F/G ★★★

City centre hotel by Conference Centre. Ramp to entrance. Public rooms level. Unisex WC. Lift to all floors. 13 bedrooms designed for disabled guests. Shower rooms, Roll-in shower, handrails, space by WC. Other bedrooms level.

Rates: from £94 per room (2008).

Luther King House

Brighton Grove, Manchester M14 5JP.

☎ **0161 224 6404.** W **www.lkh.co.uk**

●● D/E/F/G ★★★

Conference centre with guest accommodation 2 miles from city centre. Reserved parking bays. Ramp to entrance 42". Restaurant and bar level. Unisex WC. Two twin bedrooms with bathrooms designed for disabled guests. Other ground floor bedrooms level. Braille signs and induction loops in meeting rooms.

Rates: from £42.50 single, £49.50 twin BB (2008).

The Midland Hotel

Peter Street, Manchester M60 2DS.

☎ **0161 236 3333.**

@ **midlandreservations@qhotels.co.uk**

●● D/G ★★★★

Luxury hotel in city centre. Main entrance ramp. Public rooms level. Unisex WCs on ground and 1st floors. Large lift. 10 bedrooms and bathrooms designed for disabled guests with handrails, space for side trans-fer to bath and WC. Other bedrooms level.

Rates: on application.

North West England

Novotel Manchester Centre

21 Dickinson Street, Manchester M1 4LX.
☎ **0161 235 2200.**
@ **h3145@accor.com**
●● D/E/F/G ★★★

Hotel in city centre between G-Mex and Piccadilly Station. Entrance level, 83cm. Low reception desk. Public rooms, ground floor, open plan. Unisex WC. Lift 85cm, inside 100x120cm, Braille keypad. Eight double bedrooms designed for disabled guests. Vibrating pillow and audible and visual alarms. Shower rooms 100cm sliding door, ⟲, roll-in shower, handrails and space by WC. Other bedrooms level.

Rates: from £55-£170 per room (2008).

Quality Hotel Manchester East/Sportcity

Hyde Road, Birch Street, West Gorton, Manchester M12 5NT.
☎ **0161 220 8700.**
W **www.qualityhotel-manchester.co.uk**
●● D/E/I/F/G ★★★

Hotel 1½ miles from city centre. Reserved parking bays. Kerb and then entrance level. Public rooms level. Unisex WC. Five double bedrooms designed for disabled guests. Bathrooms 90cm, ⟲, handrail, space for side transfer to WC. Other ground floor bedrooms level.

Rates: on application.

Renaissance Manchester Hotel

Blackfriars Street, Manchester M3 2EQ.
☎ **0161 835 2555.**
W **www.renaissancehotels.com/manbr**
●● D ★★★★

City centre hotel. Lift from basement car park. Entrance level, revolving and swing doors. Four steps with wheelchair lift to public rooms. Unisex WC and adapted cubicle in male toilet. Lifts to all floors. Tree bedrooms designed for disabled guests. Bathroom 48", ⟲, space for side transfer to bath and WC. Other bedrooms level, ⟲.

Rates: on application.

Stay Inn Hotel Manchester

55 Blackfriars Road, Salford M3 7DB.
☎ **0161 907 2277.** W **www.stayinn.co.uk**
●● I/G ★★★

Budget hotel. Reserved parking bays. Lip at entrance, 36". Public rooms ground floor open plan. Unisex WC. Three double bedrooms designed for disabled guests. Bathrooms 33", ⟲, handrails, space for side transfer to WC. Other ground floor bedrooms level, step to shower room. Accessible taxi service can be arranged.

Rates: £50 per room (2008).

Thistle Manchester

3-5 Portland Street, Piccadilly Gardens, Manchester M1 6DP.
☎ **0161 228 3400.**
@ **reservations.manchester@thistle.co.uk**
●● D/E/F/G ★★★★

City centre hotel. Valet parking. Entrance level. Public rooms level. Unisex WCs on ground and lower floors. Lift 78cm, inside 102x130cm. Double bedroom designed for disabled guests. Shower room 91cm, ⟲, roll-in shower, handrails, space by WC. Other bedrooms level. Induction loop in one room.

Rates: on application.

YHA Manchester

Potato Wharf, Castlefield, Manchester M3 4NB.

☎ **0870 770 5950.**

@ **manchester@yha.org.uk**

●● D/E/I/F/G 

Hostel in city centre. Reserved parking bays. Entrance ramp. Public rooms level. Unisex WCs. Lift to all floors 31", inside 43"x51". Two bedrooms designed for disabled people with shower rooms 35" sliding door, roll-in shower, handrails, space for side transfer to WC. Waterproof sheets available. Other bedrooms level. For more information on Youth Hostels see page 34.

Rates: on application.

MANCHESTER AIRPORT

Crowne Plaza Manchester Airport

Terminal 3, Ringway Road, Manchester Airport M90 3NS.

☎ **0870 400 9055.**

@ **reservations-manchesterairport@ihg.com**

●● D/E/I/FG

Hotel by airport. Reserved parking bays. Entrance level. Public rooms level, open plan. Unisex WC. Lift to all floors. Twin and double bedrooms, handrails, space for side transfer to bath and WC. Other rooms level.

Rates: on application.

Radisson SAS Hotel Manchester Airport

Chicago Avenue, Manchester M90 3RA.

☎ **0161 490 5000.** @ **sales.manchester.airport@radissonsas.com**

●● D/E/I/F/G 

Luxury hotel with walkways to rail station and air terminals. Ramp or small step at entrance. Public rooms 3rd floor open plan. Unisex WC. Lift to all floors. Several bedrooms with bathrooms designed for disabled guests, dimensions not supplied.

Rates: on application.

MUNGRISDALE, Cumbria

Brow Bottom

Bowscale, Mungrisdale, Penrith CA11 0XH.

☎ **017687 79371.**

@ **colin.smith2@ukonline.co.uk**

●● D/E/I/G

Bed & breakfast in north Lake District. Entrance level. Large lounge level. Double bedroom with roll-in shower room 33", handrails, space for side transfer to WC, raised WC seat. Shower chair and bed rail available. Also a second double bedroom.

Rates: from £35 per person BB (2007).

NANTWICH, Cheshire

Alvaston Hall Hotel

Middlewich Road, Nantwich CW5 6PD.

☎ **01270 624341.**

W **www.warnerbreaks.co.uk**

●● D/I/F/G 

Country hotel for adults with a range of activities and entertainment. Reserved parking bays. Small ramp to entrance. Most public rooms level. Lift to main bedroom floors 80cm, inside 110x135cm. 10 bedrooms adapted for disabled guests shower room 80cm, , shower tray, handrail, space by WC. Equipment can be ordered. Special interest breaks offered.

Rates: on application.

The Wingate Centre

Wrenbury Hall Drive, Wrenbury, Nantwich CW5 8ES.

☎ **01270 780456.**

www.wingatecentre.co.uk

●●● D/E/I/F/H

Group accommodation for children and adults owned by Wingate Special Children's Trust in rural area. Reserved parking bays. Entrance level. Public rooms level. Lifts to 1st floor. Nine ground floor twin bedrooms designed for disabled people and bedrooms for 32 people upstairs. Showers, WCs and bathrooms designed for wheelchair users. Hoists, shower chairs, waterproof sheets and other equipment and sluice rooms available. Fully equipped gymnasium available at extra cost. Advice on outings in the area provided.

Rates: on application.

NORTHWICH, Cheshire

Floatel Northwich

London Road, Northwich CW9 5HD.

☎ **01606 44443.**

www.hotels-northwich.com

●● D/E/G ★★★

Modern hotel floating on River Weaver. Reserved parking bays. Entrance ramp. Reception and lounge level. Restaurant and bar 1st floor. Lift. Other bedrooms level.

Rates: from £49 double BB (2008).

PENRITH, Cumbria

Penrith Campus

University of Central Lancashire, Newton Rigg, Penrith CA11 0AH.

☎ **01772 894080.**

kmorsman@uclan.ac.uk

●● D/E/I/F/G

Student accommodation 2 miles from Penrith. Reserved parking bays. Entrance level. Public rooms ground floor. Split level dining room with wheelchair lift. Unisex WC. Four ground floor bedrooms designed for disabled people. Roll-in shower rooms, handrails, space for side transfer to WC. Other ground floor bedrooms level. Available in vacations only.

Rates: on application.

PRESTON, Lancashire

Holiday Inn Preston

Ringway, Preston PR1 3AU.

☎ **0870 400 9066.** **www.hipreston.com**

●● D/E/I/F/G

Hotel in city centre. Reserved parking bays. Slope to entrance, automatic door. Main public rooms 1st floor, open plan. Unisex WC. Lift to all floors. Bedroom adapted for disabled guests. Bathroom, space by bath and WC. Other bedrooms level. Waterproof sheet can be supplied. Braille menus and information.

Rates: on application.

Ibis Preston North

Garstang Road, Broughton, Preston PR3 5JE.

☎ **01772 861800.** **H3162@accor.com**

●● D/E/G

Hotel off M55 junction 1. Entrance level. Public rooms open plan. Lifts to upper floors. Two bedrooms with bathroom designed for disabled guests. Other bedrooms level.

Rates: from 47-£51 per room (2008).

Novotel Preston

Reedfield Place, Walton Summit,
Preston PR5 6AB.
☎ **01772 313331.** @ **H0838@accor.com**
●● D/E/G ★★★

Hotel off M6 junction 29, 5 miles from Preston. Reserved parking bays. Entrance level. Public rooms level, open plan. Adapted WC cubicles. Lift. Two bedrooms designed for disabled guests. Bathroom ⭮, space for side transfer to bath and WC. Other bedrooms level.

Rates: on application.

RUNCORN, Cheshire

Campanile Runcorn

Lowlands Road, Runcorn WA7 5YP.
☎ **01928 581771.**
@ **runcorn@campanile-hotels.com**
●●

Hotel near railway station off A557. Reserved parking bays. Public rooms level. Unisex WC. 2 twin bedrooms designed for disabled guests. Bathroom ⭮, handrails, space for side transfer. Other ground floor bedrooms level. See page 31.

Rates: on application.

Holiday Inn Runcorn

Holiday Inn HOTELS · RESORTS

Wood Lane, Beechwood,
Runcorn WA7 3HA.
☎ **0870 400 9070.**
@ **reservations-runcorn@ihg.com**
●● D/E/I/F/G

Hotel off M56 J12, 2 miles from Frodsham. 5 reserved parking bays. Ramp to side entrance. Public rooms ground floor, open plan. Unisex WC. Lift 80cm, inside 140x150cm. Bedrooms adapted for disabled guests with bathroom ⭮, space by bath and WC, no handrails. Other bedrooms level. Room for carer. Induction loop. Large print menus.

Rates: from £35-£130 per night (2008).

ST HELENS, Merseyside

Hilton St Helens

Linkway West, St Helens WA10 1NG.
☎ **01744 453444.**
@ **reservations.sthelens@hilton.com**
●● D/E/I/F/G ★★★★

Modern hotel near town centre. Reserved parking bays. Induction loop at reception. Entrance level, automatic doors. Public rooms level, open plan. Unisex WC. Lifts 80cm, inside 106x137cm. Two double bedrooms designed for disabled guests. En suite bathrooms 83cm sliding door, ⭮, space for side transfer to bath and WC. Other bedrooms level. Some equipment available. Teletext TV. Hoist for pool.

Rates: on application.

SHAP, Cumbria

Shap Wells Hotel

Shap, Penrith CA10 3QU.
☎ **01931 716628.**
@ **manager@shapwells.com**
●● D/E/F/G ★★★

Large hotel in country near A6 and M6. Entrance threshold. Restaurant, lounge and bar level. Games room steps or external level route. Some adaptations in WCs. Lift to upper floors. One double and 3 twin ground floor bedrooms ramp, 39", ⭮ with bathrooms designed for disabled guests. Ramp to other ground floor bedrooms. Closed January and February.

Rates: on application.

SOUTHPORT, Merseyside

Salfordian Hotel

37 Park Crescent, Southport PR9 9LT.
W **www.salford.gov.uk/salfordian**
●● D/E/F/G

Hotel owned by a charity in own grounds. Ramp with handrails or 7 steps to entrance, double doors. Public rooms ground floor. Two unisex WCs. Lift 36", inside 54"x42". 26 bedrooms, all 34" ↻. Shower rooms 29", handrail in shower cubicle. Entertainment and outings arranged.

Apply: Salfordian Booking Office
☎ 0161 925 1233.
Rates: from £99-£120 per week FB (2008).

Vitalise Sandpipers

Fairway, Southport PR9 0AL.
☎ **01704 538388.**
●●●●● D/E/I/H

Centre on shore of Marine Lake, a mile from town centre. Purpose-built for breaks by disabled people and carers. Accommodation in 30 single and and four twin ensuite bedrooms. Facilities include bar and craft room. Special interest weeks arranged. 24-hour care on-call and personal support provided.

Apply: Vitalise ☎ 0845 345 1970 (see pg 27).
Rates: on application.

TEBAY, Cumbria

Primrose Cottage

Orton Road, Tebay CA10 3TL.
☎ **015396 24791.**
W **www.primrosecottagecumbria.co.uk**
● E/F/G ★★★★

Country guesthouse in village near M6 junction 38. Level entrance. Breakfast room upstairs. Ground floor double and twin bedrooms with own bathrooms. Pub/restaurant nearby. Self-catering also available, see page 345.

Rates: from £30 per person BB (2007).

WARRINGTON, Cheshire

Holiday Inn Warrington

Woolston Grange Avenue, Woolston, Warrington WA4 1PX.
☎ **0870 400 9087.**
W **www.warrington.holiday-inn.com**
●● D/E/I/F/G

Hotel east of town centre near M6 junction 21. Reserved parking bays. Entrance level, automatic door. Reception level, ramp or 2 steps to public rooms. Unisex WC. Lift 80cm. 2 bedrooms designed for disabled guests. Bathroom sliding door, ↻, low bath, space by bath and WC. Other bedrooms level. Vibrating alarms, sound amplifiers, induction loops and large print menus available.

Rates: on application.

Paddington House Hotel

514 Manchester Road, Warrington WA1 3TZ.
☎ **01925 816767.**
@ **hotel@paddingtonhouse.co.uk**
● D/E/F/G ★★

Hotel between town centre and M6 Junction 21. Reserved parking bays. Ramp to entrance. Public rooms ground floor, level. Unisex WC. Lift to upper floors. 2 steps to a ground floor bedroom ↻. Bathroom ↻, space by bath and WC. Other bedrooms level.

Rates: from £45 per night BB (2007).

Tall Trees Lodge

Tarporley Road, Lower Whitley, Warrington WA4 4EZ.
☎ **01928 790824.**
www.talltreeslodge.co.uk
●● E/I/F/G ★★★

Lodge accommodation in country. Reserved parking bays. Ramp to entrance. No public rooms, breakfast served in bedroom. One bedroom designed for disabled guests, large button telephone. Bathroom 36", handrails, space for side transfer to bath and WC. Waterproof sheet and bath board available.

Rates: £49.95 per room BB (2008).

WATERMILLOCK, Cumbria

Knotts Mill Country Lodge

Watermillock, Penrith CA11 0JN.
☎ **017684 86699.** **www.knottsmill.com**
●● D/E/G ★★★

Guest house in own grounds by Ullswater. Ramp to entrance. Dining Room and Lounge level. Ground floor bedroom 30". Shower room 33", seat in shower tray, handrail and space by WC. 3 other ground floor rooms.

Rates: from £35 per person BB (2007).

WIDNES, Cheshire

Everglades Park Hotel

Derby Road, Widnes WA8 3UJ.
☎ **0151 495 5500.**
www.evergladesparkhotel.com
●● D/E/I/F/G

Modern hotel in country near M62 junction 7. Parking bays can be reserved. Entrance level. Main public rooms level. Unisex WC. Four twin bedrooms designed for disabled guests. Bathrooms 76cm sliding door, handrails, space for side transfer to bath and WC. Waterproof sheets on request. Other ground floor bedrooms level.

Rates: from £75 twin BB (2008).

Hillcrest Hotel

Cronton Lane, Widnes WA8 9AR.
☎ **0151 424 1616.**
● D/E/I/G ★★★

Hotel near town centre. Reserved parking bays. Ramp to entrance, 33". Restaurant and lounge 2 steps. Bar level. WCs level, not adapted. Bedrooms level, 30". Bathrooms 30", no handrails. Waterproof sheet available.

Rates: from £49 per room (2008).

WIGAN, Greater Manchester

Quality Hotel Wigan

Riverway, Wigan WN1 3SS.
☎ **01942 826888.**
enquiries@hotels-wigan.com
●● D/E/F/G ★★★

Modern town centre hotel. Reserved parking bays. Entrance level, double doors. Ramp to open plan public rooms. Unisex WC. Lift 31", inside 43"x54". Ground floor bedroom designed for disabled guests. Bathroom 34", handrails, space for side transfer to bath and WC. Other bedrooms level.

Rates: from £79 double (2007).

WILMSLOW, Cheshire

Holiday Inn Manchester Airport

Altrincham Road, Wilmslow SK9 4LR.
☎ **0870 443 6961.**
●● D/E/I/F/G ★★★

Hotel 3 miles from airport by Styal Country Park. Reserved parking bays. Ramp or 10 steps to entrance. Low reception desk. Public rooms ground floor. Unisex WC. Lift to upper floors. Stairlift on 6 steps to two ground floor bedrooms designed for disabled guests. Bathrooms, roll-in shower with seat, handrails, space by WC.

Rates: on application.

WORSLEY, Greater Manchester

Novotel Manchester West

Worsley Brow, Worsley,
Manchester M28 2YA.
☎ **0161 799 3535.** @ **H0907@accor.com**

●● D/E/F/G ★★★

Hotel west of Manchester near M60 junction 13. Reserved parking bays. Slope to entrance, automatic doors. Low reception desk with induction loop. Public rooms level, open plan. Braille menus. Adapted cubicles in WCs. Lift to all floors. Two ground floor bedrooms designed for disabled guests. Bathrooms ⟲, handrails, space for side transfer. Other bedrooms level. Light alarms available.

Rates: from £59-£99 per night (2008).

LODGE ACCOMMODATION

There are Days Inn (see page 34) Formule 1 (see page 34), Premier Travel Inn (see page 38) and Travelodge (see page 38) properties in the following areas in this region:

Ashton-in-Makerfield	Premier Travel Inn	☎ 0870 990 6582
Ashton-under-Lyne	Travelodge	☎ 0870 191 1734
Barrow	Travelodge	☎ 0870 191 1781
Blackburn, North West	Premier Travel Inn	☎ 0870 990 6388
Blackburn, South	Premier Travel Inn	☎ 0870 197 7187
	Travelodge	☎ 0870 191 1622
Blackpool	Premier Travel Inn	☎ 0870 197 7032
	Travelodge	☎ 0870 085 0950
Blackpool Airport	Premier Travel Inn	☎ 0870 197 7034
Blackpool, Bispham	Premier Travel Inn	☎ 0870 197 7033
Bolton	Premier Travel Inn	☎ 0870 197 7282
Bolton, West	Travelodge	☎ 0870 444 8641
Burnley	Premier Travel Inn	☎ 0870 197 7045
	Travelodge	☎ 0870 191 1625
Bury	Travelodge	☎ 0870 191 1802
Carlisle	Premier Travel Inn	☎ 0870 197 7053
	Travelodge	☎ 0870 191 1627

Carlisle M6 - Premier Travel Inn ☎ 0870 850 6334
Travelodge ☎ 0870 191 1628
Carlisle North - Premier Travel Inn ☎ 0870 990 6502
Carlisle South - Premier Travel Inn ☎ 0870 197 7054
Carnforth M6 - Travelodge ☎ 0870 191 1626
Charnock Richard- Days Inn ☎ 01257 791 746
Cheadle - Premier Travel Inn ☎ 0870 197 7172
Chester, East - Premier Travel Inn ☎ 0870 197 7059
Chester, North - Premier Travel Inn ☎ 0870 990 6470
Chester, South East - Premier Travel Inn ☎ 0870 197 7058
Chorley - Premier Travel Inn ☎ 0870 990 6376
Travelodge ☎ 0870 191 1671
Chorley, South - Premier Travel Inn ☎ 0870 990 6604
Crewe - Premier Travel Inn ☎ 0870 197 7068
Travelodge ☎ 0870 191 1796
Crewe, Barthomley - Travelodge ☎ 0870 191 1571
Handforth - Premier Travel Inn ☎ 0870 990 6602
Haydock - Premier Travel Inn ☎ 0870 197 7131
Travelodge ☎ 0870 191 1645
Heywood - Travelodge ☎ 0870 191 1661/1763
Kendal - Travelodge ☎ 0870 191 1827
Killington Lake - Premier Travel Inn ☎ 0870 197 7145
Kirkham - Premier Travel Inn ☎ 0870 990 6636
Knutsford - Travelodge ☎ 0870 191 1652
Knutsford M6 - Travelodge ☎ 0870 191 1653
Knutsford, Mere - Premier Travel Inn ☎ 0870 990 6482
Lancaster - Premier Travel Inn ☎ 0870 197 7290
Travelodge ☎ 0870 191 1654
Liverpool - Formule 1 ☎ 0151 709 2040
Premier Travel Inn ☎ 0870 238 3323
Travelodge ☎ 0870 191 1656
Liverpool, Aintree - Premier Travel Inn ☎ 0870 197 7157
Liverpool, Albert Dock - Premier Travel Inn ☎ 0870 990 6432
Liverpool Docks - Travelodge ☎ 0870 191 1530
Liverpool, North - Premier Travel Inn ☎ 0870 197 7158
Liverpool Roby - Premier Travel Inn ☎ 0870 990 6596
Liverpool, Tarbock - Premier Travel Inn ☎ 0870 197 7159

North West England

Liverpool, West Derby - Premier Travel Inn ☎ 0870 197 7160
Lymm - Travelodge ☎ 0870 191 1657
Lytham- Premier Travel Inn ☎ 0870 990 6608
Macclesfield - Travelodge ☎ 0870 191 1658
Macclesfield, North - Premier Travel Inn ☎ 0870 197 7167
Macclesfield, South West - Premier Travel Inn ☎ 0870 990 6412
Manchester - Premier Travel Inn ☎ 0870 238 3315
Travelodge ☎ 0870 191 1659
Manchester, Ancoats - Travelodge ☎ 0870 191 1782
Manchester, Deansgate - Premier Travel Inn ☎ 0870 990 6504
Manchester, Denton - Premier Travel Inn ☎ 0870 197 7173
Manchester, Didsbury - Premier Travel Inn ☎ 0870 197 7309
Travelodge ☎ 0870 191 1662
Manchester, GMEX - Premier Travel Inn ☎ 0870 990 6444
Manchester, Heaton Park - Premier Travel Inn ☎ 0870 197 7174
Manchester, Hyde - Premier Travel Inn ☎ 0870 990 6334
Manchester, MEN Arena - Premier Travel Inn ☎ 0870 990 6366
Manchester, Middleton - Premier Travel Inn ☎ 0870 990 6406
Manchester Sportcity - Travelodge ☎ 061 220 8848
Manchester West - Premier Travel Inn ☎ 0870 990 6480
Manchester Airport - Premier Travel Inn ☎ 0870 197 7178
Travelodge ☎ 0870 191 1680
Middlewich - Travelodge ☎ 0870 191 1663
Nantwich - Premier Travel Inn ☎ 0870 990 6418
Northwich - Premier Travel Inn ☎ 0870 990 6494
Northwich South - Premier Travel Inn ☎ 0870 990 6362
Oldham - Premier Travel Inn ☎ 0870 197 7292
Travelodge ☎ 0870 191 1735
Oldham, Chadderton - Premier Travel Inn ☎ 0870 197 7203
Penrith - Travelodge ☎ 0870 191 1667
Preston - Travelodge ☎ 0870 191 1650
Preston, East - Premier Travel Inn ☎ 0870 197 7215
Preston, North - Premier Travel Inn ☎ 0870 990 6410
Preston, South - Premier Travel Inn ☎ 0870 990 6462
Preston, West - Premier Travel Inn ☎ 0870 197 7214
Prestwich - Premier Travel Inn ☎ 0870 197 7175
Rainhill - Premier Travel Inn ☎ 0870 990 6446

Rochdale - Premier Travel Inn ☎ 0870 197 7219
Runcorn - Premier Travel Inn ☎ 0870 197 7224
St Helens, North - Premier Travel Inn ☎ 0870 990 6374
St Helens, South - Premier Travel Inn ☎ 0870 197 7237
Sale - Premier Travel Inn ☎ 9879 197 7179
Salford Quays - Premier Travel Inn ☎ 0870 197 7176
Southport - Premier Travel Inn ☎ 0870 197 7071
Stockport, East - Premier Travel Inn ☎ 0870 990 6544
Stockport, South - Premier Travel Inn ☎ 0870 197 7242
Swinton - Premier Travel Inn ☎ 0870 990 6528
Trafford Centre - Premier Travel Inn ☎ 0870 197 7307
Trafford Centre North - Premier Travel Inn ☎ 0870 990 6310
Trafford Park - Travelodge ☎ 0870 191 1838
Warrington - Premier Travel Inn ☎ 0870 197 7259
Travelodge ☎ 0870 191 1679
Warrington, East - Premier Travel Inn ☎ 0870 990 6524
Warrington, N E - Premier Travel Inn ☎ 0870 990 6600
Warrington, N W - Premier Travel Inn ☎ 0870 197 7260
Warrington, South - Premier Travel Inn ☎ 0870 990 6526
Whitehaven - Premier Travel Inn ☎ 0870 197 7268
Widnes - Travelodge ☎ 0870 191 1682
Wigan, North - Premier Travel Inn ☎ 0870 990 6474
Wigan, South - Premier Travel Inn ☎ 0870 197 7270
Wigan, West - Premier Travel Inn ☎ 0870 197 7271
Wilmslow - Premier Travel Inn ☎ 0870 990 6506
Wirral, Bromborough - Premier Travel Inn ☎ 0870 197 7273
Wirral, Eastham - Travelodge ☎ 0870 191 1683
Wirral, Greasby - Premier Travel Inn ☎ 0870 990 6588
Wirral, Heswall - Premier Travel Inn ☎ 0870 197 7274
Wirral, South - Premier Travel Inn ☎ 0870 197 7275
Wirral, Two Mills - Premier Travel Inn ☎ 0870 990 6564

SELF-CATERING ACCOMMODATION

AINSTABLE, Cumbria

The Old Dairy Cottage

Rowfoot, Ainstable, Carlisle CA4 9PZ.

●● G ★★★★

Single storey cottage on smallholding with rare breeds in Eden Valley, 12 miles from both Carlisle and Penrith. Entrance level. Lounge/kitchen open plan. Controls useable from wheelchair. Twin/double bedroom ⟲. Bathroom 36", ⟲, roll-in shower, handrails, space by bath and WC. Level conservatory and garden.

Ⓟ

Apply: Mr & Mrs Moffat ☎ 01768 896409.
www.jackiemoffat.co.uk
Rates: from £250-£310 per week (2008).

AMBLESIDE, Cumbria

Nationwide

Borrans Road, Ambleside

●● E/I/H

Holiday bungalow specially adapted for disabled people close to Lake Windermere. Accommodation for up to 7 people in three bedrooms. Level throughout. Roll-in shower. Hoist and shower chair available.

Ⓟ

Apply: Grooms Holidays ☎ 08456 584478
selfcatering@johngrooms.org.uk
Rates: on application.

Restharrow

Far Sawrey, Ambleside

●● E/I/F/G

Adapted cottage on west shore of Lake Windermere. Entrance ramp. All accommodation level. Lounge and kitchen ⟲, no adaptations. Two twin bedrooms ⟲. Shower room with roll-in shower, seat, space for side transfer to WC.

Ⓟ

Apply: National Trust Holiday Booking Office. ☎ 0870 4584422. See page 33.
Rates: from £269-£723 per week (2008).

Stable Cottage

High Wray Farm,
Ambleside LA22 0JE.

www.highwrayfarm.co.uk

●● F/G ★★★★

Cottage designed for disabled guests on farm west of Lake Windermere between Ambleside and Hawkshead. Entrance level, 85cm. Open plan lounge/kitchen, controls useable from wheelchair, worktops 76.5cm and 92cm. Double and twin bedrooms 85cm, ⟲. Both have en-suite bathrooms, that from the double has 81cm sliding door, roll-in shower, handrails, space by WC. Shower chair available. Teletext TV. Bed & Breakfast available in farmhouse.

Ⓟ

Apply: Sheila Briggs ☎ 015394 32280.
Rates: £295-£545 per week (2007).

APPLEBY, Cumbria

Wild Rose Park

Ormside,
Appleby-in-Westmorland CA16 6EJ.
☎ **017683 51077.**
www.wildrose.co.uk

●● G ★★★★★

Touring site with pitches for 180 caravans and 25 tents. Two toilet blocks with unisex WC. Roll-in shower room. Restaurant, shop, games room and laundry level. Open all year, limited facilities in winter. Scooter available.

Ⓟ

Rates: on application.

BAILEY, Cumbria

Bailey Mill

Bailey, Nr, Newcastleton TD9 0TR.

www.holidaycottagescumbria.co.uk

●● E/I/F/G ★★

Converted mill near Scottish Border, 7 miles from Newcastleton. Two courtyard apartments, for 6 and 4 people, designed for disabled guests. Entrances level, Internal doors 33". Shower rooms, roll-in shower, space by WC. Meals, bar, Jacuzzi and sauna available.

Apply: Mrs Copeland ☎ 01697 748617.

Rates: from £148-£528 per week (2008).

BOWNESS-ON-WINDERMERE, Cumbria

Deloraine

Helm Road,
Bowness-on-Windermere LA23 2HS.

●● G ★★★

Accommodation in grounds of Edwardian house. "Birch Cottage" sleeps up to 6. Entrance level. Lounge/kitchen open plan. One bedroom. Shower room, handrails, shower chair, space for side transfer. chair, space for side transfer. Other units available. Access details on website. Available March-December.

Apply: Mr & Mrs Fanstone
☎ 015394 45557.
www.deloraine.demon.co.uk

Rates: from £220-£600 per week (2008).

Mitchelland Farm Bungalow

Crook, Nr. Bowness

●●● I/F/G/H ★★★★

Bungalow on small farm 3 miles from Lake Windermere. Ramp or 2 steps on approach. Entrance 33". Lounge 28", sofabed. Kitchen open plan, worktops 36", controls useable from wheelchair. Double and twin bedrooms 28". Twin room has en suite shower room, 44" double doors, roll-in shower with shower chair, handrails, space by WC. Separate bathroom, handrails, space by WC. Waterproof sheet available. Sitting service and help in getting up for disabled guests by arrangement. Wheelchair, raised WC seat, bedblocks and a hoist with a sling are available. Two purpose built log-cabins due for completion late 2007.

Apply: Jane & Stuart Higham, Mitchelland Farm, Crook, Nr. Bowness LA8 8LL.
☎ 015394 47421.
www.lakedistrictdisabledholidays.co.uk

Rates: from £320-£480 per week (2008).

CARNFORTH, Lancashire

Pine Lakes Resort

Dock Acres, Carnforth LA6 1JZ.

☎ 01524 736191.

www.pinelakelodges.co.uk

●● F ★★★★

Holiday park by wildlife and watersports lake. Two cabins, for up to 6, designed for disabled people, one with a step on approach. Entrances have 3" cill. Lounge /kitchen open plan. Double and twin bedrooms and double sofa bed in lounge. Bathroom 90cm, space by WC. Site facilities level or ramped.

Rates: on application.

COCKERMOUTH, Cumbria

Higham Hall Bungalow

Higham Hall, Bassenthwaite Lake, Cockermouth CA13 9SH.

●● G

Bungalow in grounds of adult education college available for holiday lets when not in use by course participants. Entrance level. Lounge and kitchen ⟲. Twin bedroom level. Shower room ⟲, roll-in shower, handrails, space for side transfer to WC.

Ⓟ

Apply: Higham Hall ☎ 017687 76276.
@ admin@highamhall.com
Rates: on application.

Irton House Farm

Isel, Cockermouth CA13 9ST.
☎ 017687 76380.
W www.disabled-holiday.net

●● F/G ★★★★

Four ground floor apartments designed for wheelchair users. Entrance 33". Lounge/kitchen open plan ⟲. Worktops 33", controls reachable from wheelchair. Twin bedroom 36", ⟲. Shower room 33", ⟲, roll-in shower, handrails, tilting mirror.

Rates: on application.

Simonscales Mill Cottage

Simonscales Mill, Simonscales Lane, Cockermouth CA13 9TG.
W www.simonscales.fsnet.co.uk

●● I/F/G/H

Cottage for up to 4 people by river, a mile from Cockermouth. Ramp to entrance 30". Lounge/kitchen open plan, controls useable from wheelchair. Twin bedroom 31½", sliding door, adjustable height beds. En suite bathroom ⟲, roll-in shower, handrails, space for side transfer to WC. Shower chair and waterproof sheet available. 2nd bedroom with double and bunk beds and en suite shower room. Convenient for Lakeland Dialysis Unit.

Apply: Mrs Sue Lowes. ☎ 01900 822594.
Rates: from £325-£400 per week (2008).

DALSTON, Cumbria

Green View Lodges

Welton, Nr. Dalston, Carlisle CA5 7ES.
W www.green-view-lodges.com

●● G 

Two pine lodges, each for up to 6 people. Entrance ramp. Lounge/kitchen open plan. Two double and a twin bedrooms. Bathroom and two WCs with space for side transfer, shower tray. Three other units on site. Pub/restaurant nearby.

Apply: Colin Oliver. ☎ 016974 76230.
Rates: from £395-£650 per week (2007).

HETHERSGILL, Cumbria

New Pallyards

Hethersgill, Carlisle CA6 6HZ.
☎ **01228 577308.**
www.4starsc.co.uk
newpallyard@btinternet.com

 I/F/G 

Four, of six, cottages on farm near Scottish border may be suitable for disabled guests. Entrances level. Step to lounge in one. One sleeps up to 8, three sleep 4 and the other is for 2 people. One has bathroom with space for side transfer to bath and WC. One has an en suite shower room and a bathroom. The other has a shower room. No adaptations. Evening meals available in farm house, see page 320.

Rates: from £127-£672 per week (2008).

KENDAL, Cumbria

Greenbank Cottage

Crosthwaite, Nr. Kendal LA8 8JD.

● I/F/G 

Cottage in Winster valley for up to 6 adults and baby. Entrance step. Lounge and kitchen level, no adaptations. One twin bedroom level. Shower room/WC 1 step, roll-in shower with seat, handrails. Other bedrooms, bathrooms and WC upstairs.

Ⓟ

Apply: Mr & Mrs Gaskell. ☎ 015395 68598.
www.greenbank-cumbria.co.uk
Rates: from £420-£750 per week (2007).

Top Thorn Farm

Whinfell, Kendal LA8 9EG.
☎ **01539 824252.**
www.topthornholidaycottagescumbria.co.uk

●● G

One, of two, cottages designed for disabled people on farm 4 miles north of Kendal. Ramp to patio door. Ground floor lounge and kitchen, controls useable from wheelchair, and twin/double bedroom. Shower room 890mm sliding door, roll-in shower, handrails. Accommodation for up to 8 people upstairs. Alarm and intercom systems. Induction loop and Teletext TV.

Ⓟ

Rates: £300-£700 per week (2008).

KESWICK, Cumbria

Calvert Trust

Keswick

●● I/F/G/H

Four fully accessible, self-catering units. On the outskirts of Keswick "The Grooms Cottage" and "The Shillies" sleep between 5-12 people and "The Coach House" sleeps up to 14 in bunks. "The Southbarn", 3 miles outside Keswick, sleeps 6.

Ⓟ ⓘ

Apply: Calvert Trust Keswick, Little Crosthwaite, Keswick CA12 4QD.
☎/Textphone: 01768 772255.
enquiries.calvert.keswick@dial.pipex.com
Rates: from £250-£545 per week (2008).

KIRKBY LONSDALE, Cumbria

Barkinbeck Cottage

Nr. Kirkby Lonsdale.

●● G ★★★

Flat for up to 4 people on farm between Kendal and Kirkby Lonsdale. Entrance level 35". Lounge/kitchen open plan. Worktops 31" and 35", controls useable from wheelchair. Bedrooms ⟲. Shower room 31", ⟲, roll-in shower, seat, handrails, space for side transfer to WC.

Apply: Ann Hamilton, Barkin House, Gatebeck, Kendal LA8 0HX. ☎ 015395 67122 (evenings).
W www.barkinbeck.co.uk
Rates: from £270-£370 per week (2008).

KIRKBY STEPHEN, Cumbria

Moss Cottages

Newbiggin-on-Lune, Nr. Kirkby Stephen.

●● G ★★★

Two cottages designed for disabled guests in converted barn. Each sleeps 4 people and has a ramped entrance. Each has open plan lounge/kitchen useable from wheelchair. Shower room ⟲, roll-in shower, shower chair, handrails, space for side transfer to WC, raised WC seat.

Apply: Doreen & George Moynihan, The Moss, Newbiggin-on-Lune, Kirkby Stephen CA17 4NB. ☎ 015396 23316.
W www.cumbrianholidaycottages.co.uk
Rates: from £280-£340 per week (2008).

Sykeside Farm

Soulby, Kirkby Stephen CA17 4PJ.

●● F/G

Two cottages in converted barn in upper Eden Valley. "Rainbow Cottage" sleeps up to 8. It has ramp to entrance and all accommodation on ground floor. Open plan kitchen/dining area, lounge and 3 bedrooms. Bathroom 83cm, ⟲, level shower, space by bath and WC. "Beck View" has entrance step, portable ramp available. Ground floor kitchen/dining area, two bedrooms and bathroom. Large lounge, bedroom and shower room on 1st floor.

Apply: Wendy Wharton ☎ 017683 71137
Rates: on application.

LANCASTER, Lancashire

Langthwaite Farm

Langthwaite Road, Lancaster LA2 9EB.
☎ **01524 62388.**
W **www.langthwaitefarmcottages.co.uk**

●● I/F/G

Two cottages designed for disabled people on farm 1 mile southeast of Lancaster. Ramp to entrance from carport; front entrance level. Open plan lounge/kitchen, controls useable from wheelchair in one. Two and three bedrooms on ground floor; stairlifts to lounge with balcony and single bedrooms on 1st floor. Bathrooms level, ⟲, roll-in showers, handrails in one, space by WC. Equipment can be hired locally. One cottage has teletext TV. Enclosed garden.

Apply: Mr & Mrs Deering.
Rates: on application.

LORTON, Cumbria

Southwaite Green

Lorton, Cockermouth CA13 0RF.

W www.southwaitegreen.co.uk

●● F/G

Four cottages in western Lake District with one designed for disabled people. Entrance level 85cm. Lounge/kitchen open plan, worktops 90 and 75cm. 2 double/twin bedrooms ⟲. Shower room 84cm, roll-in shower with seat, handrails. Space by WC. One other cottage has a ground floor bedroom and bathroom. Teletext TV. Shopping and meals can be ordered. Access statement on request.

Ⓟ

Apply: Marna McMillin ☎ 01900 821055.
Rates: £400-£850 per week (2008).

LOWICK GREEN, Cumbria

Bark Cottage

The Meadows, Lowick Green.

W www.tannerybarn.freeserve.co.uk

●● I/F/G ★★★

Ground floor flat designed for disabled people between Coniston Water and Ulverston. Sleeps 2-6. Ramp to entrance 90cm. Open plan lounge/kitchen. Double and family bedrooms ⟲, also futon sofabed. Shower room 90cm, ⟲, roll-in shower with seat, handrails, space for side transfer to WC. Also bathroom/WC. Waterproof sheet available.

Ⓟ

Apply: Joe Fairclough & Jenny Tancock, Tannery Barn, The Meadows, Lowick Green LA12 8DX. ☎ 01229 885416.
Rates: from £230-£450 per week (2007).

MACCLESFIELD, Cheshire

Lower House Cottage

Wildboarclough, Nr. Macclesfield.

●● I/F/G ★

Cottage in western Peak District for up to 6 people. Entrance level, 30". Lounge level. 6" step to kitchen/dining room ⟲, portable ramp available. Ground floor bedroom level. Shower room ⟲, roll-in shower with seat, handrails, space for side transfer to WC. Two bedrooms upstairs. Waterproof sheet and commode chair available.

Ⓟ

Apply: Mrs Waller, Blaze Farm, Wildboarclough Macclesfield SK11 0BL. ☎ 01260 227229.
Rates: on application.

The Old Byre

Pye Ash Farm, Leek Road, Bosley, Macclesfield SK11 0PN.

●● I/F

Two interconnecting cottages for up to 4 and 6 people on farm near village. Entrance level. Each cottage has open plan lounge/kitchen, level bedrooms and a roll-in shower room/WC with handrails, Small step between the two units when booked together.

Ⓟ

Apply: Dorothy Gilman ☎ 01260 223293.
@ dotgilman@hotmail.co.uk
Rates: from £250-£500 per week (2008).

10 North West England

Strawberry Duck Cottage

Bryher Cottage, Bullgate Lane,
Bosley, Macclesfield SK11 0PP.

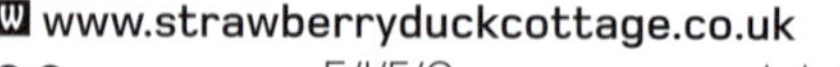
www.strawberryduckcottage.co.uk

●● E/I/F/G ★★★

Single storey cottage for up to 4 people on edge of Peak District. Entrance 31" level; ramp to patio door. Lounge with double sofa bed. Kitchen open plan, controls useable from wheelchair. Twin bedroom 31" ⟲. Shower room 30", roll-in shower with seat, handrails, space for side transfer to WC. Waterproof sheet available. Level access to summer house and pond.

Ⓟ

Apply: Emma Carter ☎ 01260 223591.
Rates: from £250 per week (2008).

MORECAMBE, Lancashire
Venture Caravan Park

Langridge Way, Westgate,
Morecambe LA4 4TQ.
☎ 01524 412986.
www.venturecaravanpark.co.uk

●● I/G ★★★★

One static caravan for 4 or 6 people designed for disabled people. Entrances ramped, 46". ⟲ in lounge and one bedroom. Kitchen worktops 36". Shower room ⟲, handrails, space for side transfer to WC. Other vans for hire. Ramp to office, club room and shop. WC/shower rooms on site.

Ⓟ

Rates: on application.

PENRITH, Cumbria
Crowdundle

Acorn Bank,Temple Sowerby, Nr. Penrith

●● F/G

Ground floor apartment in wing of National Trust house. Small kitchen. Double bedroom. Bathroom with some adaptations. Other apartments on site.

Ⓟ

Apply: National Trust Holiday Booking Office ☎ 0870 4584422. See page 33.
Rates: from £255-£654 per week (2008).

RIMINGTON, Lancashire
Lower Laithe

Higher Gills Farm, Rimington,
Clitheroe BB7 4DA.

●● I/F/G ★★★★

Ground floor flat on farm at the foot of Pendle Hill. Entrance level, 31". Portable ramp for threshold. Lounge/kitchen open plan ⟲. Twin and double bedrooms ⟲ and double sofa bed in lounge. Bathroom 31", ⟲, handrails, bath seat, space for side transfer to bath and WC, raised WC seat. Second flat available upstairs.

Ⓟ

Apply: Mrs Pilkington ☎ 01200 445370.
www.highergills.co.uk
Rates: from £250-£350 per week (2007).

ROWELTOWN, Cumbria
Low Luckens Organic Resource Centre

Low Luckens, Roweltown, Carlisle CA6 6LJ.
☎ 016977 48186.
www.lowluckensfarm.co.uk

●● G

Hostel for up to 9 people on organic beef farm north east of Carlisle. Entrance ramp. Lounge/kitchen open plan, cooker controls useable from wheelchair. One ground floor bedroom. Shower room ⟲ level shower, handrails, space by WC. Advance notice for guide dogs.

Ⓟ

Rates: £375 per night for Centre, £15 per night individual (2007).

TEBAY, Cumbria

Primrose Lodge

Primrose Cottage, Orton Road,
Tebay CA10 3TL.

☎ 015396 24791.

W www.primrosecottagecumbria.co.uk

●● E/F/G

Self-catering bungalows designed for disabled guests in grounds of country guesthouse. Entrance level. Lounge/kitchen open plan, controls useable from wheelchair. Double bedroom with own bathroom. Twin bedroom and sofa-bed in lounge. Shower room ⟲, roll-in shower with seat, handrails, space by WC. A ground floor flat without adaptations is also available. For information on bed & breakfast see page 332.

Rates: from £320-£500 per week (2007).

THURSTONFIELD, Cumbria

The Tranquil Otter

The Lough, Thurstonfield, Carlisle CA5 6HB.

☎ 01228 576661.

W www.thetranquilotter.co.uk

●● F/G ★★★★★

Six, of 7, lakeside lodges adapted for disabled people. Ramp to entrance ramp, 90cm. Lounge/kitchen open plan, controls may be useable from wheelchair. Two lodges have a bedroom for two people, two have 2 bedrooms for up to 4 people and the other has 3 bedrooms, all ⟲. Shower rooms 75cm, ⟲, handrails, roll-in shower, shower stool, space by WC. The 2 other lodges have ground floor accommodation. Accessible shop, bird hide and paths around lake. Use of wheely-boat on lake. Scooter available.

Rates: from £380-£984 per week (2008).

Inside Durham Cathedral

The North East region covers the area between the Tees Valley and the Scottish border including County Durham, Northumberland and Tyne & Wear. Within its boundaries are the natural wild areas of the northern Pennines, the dramatic Northumberland Coast, the Tyne valley and the extensive Northumberland National Park.

Much of Britain's history was moulded in the region. Hadrian's Wall, now a World Heritage Site, was for centuries the northern boundary of the Roman Empire. The Wall and its associated areas can be explored at many sites including Corbridge and Segedunum Fort in Wallsend. Britain's early Christian heritage is represented by Lindisfarne Priory on Holy Island near Berwick-on-Tweed, the majestic Durham Cathedral and Bede's World at Jarrow. Evidence of the turbulent Middle Ages can be seen at castles such as Bamburgh and Barnard Castle. A more peaceful feature of Barnard Castle is the Bowes Museum housing the North's greatest collection of fine and decorative art.

With its extensive coastline, the area has a long seafaring tradition. Captain Cook was born near Middlesbrough where his life and achievements are depicted at the Captain Cook Birthplace Museum. A replica of his ship, "Endeavour" can be seen at Stockton-on-Tees and an 1800s quayside has been reconstructed at Hartlepool.

Newcastle

The Industrial Revolution brought pioneering developments in mining, engineering, shipbuilding and other heavy industry to the region as depicted at the Discovery Museum in Newcastle. The world's first public railway ran between Stockton and Darlington and the railway heritage is widely displayed including at Locomotion, the National Railway Museum's new centre at Shildon in Co. Durham.

As to the present and future, the country's most prominent work of art, the Angel of the North, greets travellers approaching Gateshead where, on the southern bank of the Tyne, the Baltic Centre for Contemporary Art and the Sage music performance centre were built to mark the Millennium. Across the river in the lively regional capital of Newcastle-upon-Tyne, another Millennium project, the Life Centre focuses on the science of genetics. Holiday shoppers can choose between Newcastle's city centre shops around Eldon Square or the out-of-town MetroCentre in Gateshead.

There are many opportunities for countryside recreation and outdoor activities in the region. Kielder Forest, Europe's largest man-made woodland, has a visitor centre at Kielder Castle and a wide range of water sports are available on Kielder Water as well as trips on an accessible cruiser. The Wildfowl & Wetlands Trust has a centre at Washington near Sunderland. At Alnwick in Northumberland, the gardens of the castle are being recreated – try the accessible treetop walkway.

Photo: www.britainonview © Pawel Libera

USEFUL ADDRESSES

North East England Tourism

Tourism Enquiries, Stella House, Gold Crest Way, Newburn, Riverside, Newcastle upon Tyne NE15 8AY.

☎ **0870 160 1781.**

www.visitnortheastengland.org.uk

Publications include an annual guide to Holidays & Short Breaks in North East England.

Disability North

Castles Farm Road, Newcastle upon Tyne NE3 1PH.

☎ **0191 284 0480.**

@ **reception@disabilitynorth.org.uk**

The Information & Advisory Service can offer advice on holiday accommodation for people with a disability.

South Tyneside Council on Disabilities

25-27 Flagg Court, South Shields NE33 2LS.

☎ **0191 454 9707.**

@ **disabilities@btconnect.com**

Provide advice and information for disabled people and their carers.

DIAL

DIAL offers a free, impartial and confidential service of information and advice by telephone to disabled people, their relatives and professionals. The following DIAL UK members may be able to help disabled residents and visitors in their areas:

Blyth Valley Disabled Forum

☎ **01670 364657**

Darlington Assn on Disability

☎ **01325 489999; Textphone: 01325 245061**

Hartlepool Access Group

☎ **01429 861777**

BLISS-Ability, South Shields

☎**/Textphone: 0191 427 1666**

USEFUL PUBLICATIONS

Durham City Access for All (new edition planned for late 2007) gives information on the accessibility of premises and attractions in the city. Information on accessible attractions is available from Durham Tourist Information Centre, 2 Millennium Place, Durham DH1 1WA.

☎ 0191 384 3720.

@ touristinfo@durhamcity.gov.uk

County Durham Access Directory – A booklet, published regularly, giving information for people with disabilities about transport services in the county. Available in print, braille or on tape from Public Transport Group, Durham County Council, Environment & Technical Services, County Hall, Durham DH1 5UQ.

☎ 0191 383 3337.

EQUIPMENT HIRE

Adapt-ability
Sanderson Street, Coxhoe,
Durham DH6 4DF.
☎ **0800 0925092.**
@ **info@adapt-ability.co.uk**
W **www.adapt-ability.co.uk**

This company has manual and powered wheelchairs and scooters and a range of other equipment for hire from the above address and also from a branch in Hartlepool.

Middlesbrough Shopmobility
1st Floor Car Park, Hill Street,
Middlesbrough TS1 1TE.
☎ **01642 254545.**
@ **info@middlesbroughshopmobility.co.uk**

As well as regular Shopmobility services, Middlesbrough Shopmobility can provide wheelchairs to residents and visitors on a longer term basis for £10 per week with a £50 deposit.

Redcar Shopmobility
2 Pybus Place, Redcar TS10 3AE.
☎ **01642 498894.**
@ **redcarsmobility@btconnect.com**

Extended hire of manual wheelchairs and lightweight scooters is available to visitors to the area and to residents of Redcar for use elsewhere, except America.

South Shields Shopmobility
35 Mile End Road, South Shields NE33 1TA.
☎ **0191 454 6286.**
@ **info@ssshopmobility.wanadoo.co.uk**

Manual wheelchairs can be hired by members of South Shields Shopmobility on a long-term or holiday basis in UK at a cost of £7 per week with a deposit of £20.

Stockton-on-Tees Shopmobility
3-5 Bridge Road,
Stockton-on-Tees TS18 1BH.
☎ **01642 605676.**
@ **stocktonshop@aol.com**

Manual and powered wheelchairs and a limited number of scooters are available for hire both by residents going on holiday and visitors to the area. Some other mobility equipment is also available as are sales and repair and other services.

Shopmobility schemes provide wheelchairs and/or scooters for use in shopping centres in the following towns. For information on availability, etc. telephone in advance.

Durham ☎ **0191 386 8556**

Gateshead ☎ **0191 477 9888**

MetroCentre ☎ **0191 493 2386**

Middlesbrough ☎ **01642 254545**

Redcar ☎ **01642 498894**

South Shields ☎ **0191 454 6286**

Stockton-on-Tees ☎ **01642 605676**

Sunderland ☎ **0191 514 3337**

Wallsend ☎ **0191 263 5029**

ENJOY the unique experience of Hedley Hall, EXPLORE the beautiful counties of Durham and Northumberland and DISCOVER the culture of the cities of Newcastle Upon Tyne and Durham.

Hedley Hall, Hedley Lane, Nr, Sunniside,
Newcastle Tyne and Wear NE16 5EH

01207 231 835

brenda@hedleyhallcountrycottages.com
www.hedleyhallcountrycottages.com

www.teesactive.co.uk

Discover TEESDALE

an outstanding experience

- Outstanding Natural Beauty
- Rich Culture & Heritage
- Traditional Shopping & Markets
- Fine Food & Produce
- Ideal Landscape for Outdoor Pursuits

Tourist Information

Barnard Castle, Durham Dales

Tel: 01833 690 909 www.teesdale.gov.uk

E-mail: tourism@teesdale.gov.uk

17thC listed Dower house with spacious en-suite bedrooms. Unsurpassed hospitality in extremely comfortable surroundings.

Your home in the country.

The Coach House at Crookham
Cornhill-on-Tweed,
Northumberland TD12 4TD
Tel. **01890 820293**
email. **stay@coachhousecrookham.com**
web. **www.coachhousecrookham.com**

Three spacious 5★ M2 contemporary stone cottages, roll-in showers with roll-in wheel chair. Exceptionally light. Four further cottages with ramps, wide doors and space; Accessibility Grade 2. Beautiful farm; marvellous views to coast and hills; tranquil place of beauty. Indoor pool, sauna, steam, Jacuzzi, gym, beautician. games room, fly-fishing. (Sorry, facilities non-accessible.) England's Self Catering Holiday of the Year 2000

Contact Details: Alun Moore, Beacon Hill , Longhorsley, Morpeth. Northumberland NE65 8QW

Tel **01670 780 900**

alun@beaconhill.co.uk **www.beaconhill.co.uk**

Keep up to date with what's happening at RADAR

www.radar.org.uk

ACCOMMODATION WITH MEALS

BARDON MILL,
Montcoffer

Bardon Mill, Hexham NE47 7HZ.

☎ **01434 344138.**

www.montcoffer.co.uk

●● D/F ★★★★★

Bed & breakfast in village. Ramp to entrance 32". Dining room and lounge level. Ground floor twin/double and family bedrooms 33", ⟲. Bathrooms ⟲, one with roll-in shower and handrails. Fridges in all bedrooms. Nearby inn serves evening meals.

Rates: from £30-£45 single BB (2007).

BERWICK-ON-TWEED, Northumberland
Meadow Hill Guest House

Duns Road, Berwick-on-Tweed TD15 1UB.

☎ **01289 306325.**

www.meadow-hill.co.uk

●● D/E/F/G ★★★★

Licensed guest house. Entrance ramp, double doors. Dining room level, 80cm. Lounge/bar level 75cm. Two ground floor bedrooms for disabled guests, one with ramped entrance from car park. Shower rooms with wheel-in shower with seat, handrails, space for side transfer to WC. Other bedrooms with bathrooms upstairs.

Rates: from £30 per night BB (2008).

BOLDON, Tyne & Wear
Quality Hotel Sunderland

Witney Way, Boldon NE35 9PE.

☎ **0191 519 1999.**

www.hotels-sunderland.com

●● E/I/F/G ★★★

Modern hotel at A19/A184 junction. Reserved parking bays. Entrance level 90cm. Public rooms open plan. Unisex WC. Three bedrooms, double and twin, designed for disabled guests ⟲. Bathroom 90cm, handrails, space for side transfer to bath and WC. Other ground floor rooms level. Teletext TVs.

Rates: on application.

CRAMLINGTON, Northumberland
Innkeeper's Lodge Cramlington

Blagdon Lane, Cramlington NE23 8AU.

☎ **01670 736111.**

●● D/E/F/G

Lodge accommodation attached to Snowy Owl Vintage Inn on A1068. Reserved parking bays. Entrances level. Restaurant level. One bedroom designed for disabled guests. Shower room ⟲, space by WC. Other ground floor rooms level.

Rates: from £59.95-£62.95 per room BB (2008).

CROOKHAM, Northumberland

The Coach House

Crookham, Cornhill-on-Tweed TD12 4TD.

☎ **01890 820293.**

www.coachhousecrookham.com

●● D/E/I/F/G ★★★★

Guesthouse in village on A697. Entrance level 36". Public Rooms level. Unisex WC. Five ground floor bedrooms, beds can be raised. Bathrooms 28", shower with chair. Paved terrace. Evening meals available.

Rates: from £42-£72 per person BB (2008).

DARLINGTON, Co. Durham

Aston Hotel Darlington

Newton Park, Coatham Munderville, Darlington DL1 3NL.

☎ **01325 329600.**

www.astonhotels.co.uk

●● D/E/F/G

Hotel near A1(M) J 59 north of town. Reserved parking bays. Entrance level, automatic door. Low reception desk. Public rooms level. Unisex WC. Lift to all floors. 3 twin/double bedrooms designed for disabled guests. Shower room, roll-in shower, handrails, space by WC. Vibrating and visual alarm. Other bedrooms level.

Rates: from £89 room only midweek (2008).

DURHAM, Co. Durham

Durham Marriott Hotel Royal County

Old Elvet, Durham DH1 3JN.

☎ **0191 386 6821.**

www.astonhotels.co.uk

●● D/G ★★★★

City centre hotel. Reserved parking bays. Entrance level, automatic doors. Public rooms ground floor level. Adapted WC cubicles. Lift to all floors in new building. Bedroom and bathroom adapted for disabled guests. Other level bedrooms available.

Rates: on application.

GATESHEAD, Tyne & Wear

Express by Holiday Inn Newcastle MetroCentre

Clasper Way, Swallwell, Newcastle upon Tyne NE16 3BE.

☎ **0870 720 0951.**

Newcastle@morethanhotels.com

●● G

Limited service hotel near A1 and MetroCentre, 5 miles from city centre. Reserved parking bays. Entrance level, automatic door. Double bedrooms designed for disabled guests. Shower room 80cm, roll-in shower with seat, handrails, space by WC. Other level rooms available.

Rates: from £59-£100 per room BB (2008).

Hilton Newcastle Gateshead

Bottle Bank, Gateshead NE8 2AR.

☎ **0191 490 9700.**

@ **reservations.newcastle@hilton.com**

●● D/E/I/F/G

High class hotel on riverfront facing Tyne Bridge. Reserved parking bays. Entrance level. Public rooms on ground floor open plan. Unisex WCs ground floor and basement. Lift 111cm, inside 140x138cm. 12 bedrooms designed for disabled guests 76cm ↺, visual and tactile alarms. Bathrooms ↺, roll-in shower, with seat, handrails, space by bath and WC. Other bedrooms level. Braille menu. Teletext TV.

Rates: on application.

Tulip Inn Newcastle Gateshead

Maingate, Kingsway North, Team Valley Trading Estate, Gateshead NE11 0BE.

☎ **08704236454**

W **www.tulipinnnewcastlegateshead.co.uk**

●● D/E/I/F/G ★★★

Hotel 2 miles from city centre between the MetroCentre and the Angel of the North. Reserved parking bays. Slight ramp to level entrance, automatic doors. Restaurant, lounge and bar ground floor level. Unisex WC. Lift 80cm, inside 108x213cm. 6 rooms, double and twin, designed for disabled guests, vibrating alarm, large button phone. Shower rooms ↺, roll-in shower with seat, handrails, space by WC. Other bedrooms level. Teletext TV and induction loop.

Ⓟ

Rates: from £51.50 per room (2007).

HEXHAM, Northumberland

De Vere Slaley Hall

Slaley, Hexham NE47 0BY.

☎ **01434 673350.**

@ **slaley.hall@devere-hotels.com**

●● D/F/G ★★★★

High class country hotel. Reserved bays in Club House car park with buggy or valet parking from hotel. Ramp to entrance , 48" double doors. Public rooms ground floor, min. door width 53". Unisex WC. Lift 43", inside 61"x53". Three ground floor bedrooms designed for disabled guests 32". Bathroom 29" sliding door, ↺, handrails, space for side transfer to bath and WC. Other bedrooms level. Wheelchair available.

Rates: on application.

MIDDLESBROUGH

Express by Holiday Inn Middlesbrough

Marton Road, Middlesbrough TS4 3BS.

☎ **01642 814444.**

@ **ebhi-middlesboro@btconnect.com**

●● E/I/F/G

Limited service hotel in suburbs. Reserved parking bays. Level entrance, automatic doors. Low reception desk. Open plan public areas. Unisex WC. Lift to upper floors. Four bedrooms designed for disabled guests, low controls, vibrating alarm. Shower room ↺, roll-in shower with seat, space by WC. Toby Restaurant adjacent.

Ⓟ

Rates: from £55 per room BB (2008).

MORPETH, Northumberland

Linden Hall

Longhorsley, Morpeth NE65 8XF.

☎ **01670 500000.**

W www.macdonaldhotels.co.uk

●● D/E/G ★★★★

Country house hotel. Ramp to entrance, 43". Public rooms level. Unisex WC in basement. Lift to all floors. All bedrooms with bathrooms 30", three ⟲, one with handrails.

Rates: from £99 double per night BB (2008).

NEWCASTLE UPON TYNE, Tyne & Wear

Copthorne Hotel Newcastle

The Close, Quayside, Newcastle upon Tyne NE1 3RT.

☎ **0191 222 0333.**

W www.copthornenewcastle.co.uk

●● D/E/I/F/G ★★★★

City centre hotel. Reserved parking bays. Entrance level, automatic doors. Public rooms level. Unisex WC. Lift 42", inside 76"x54". One bedroom designed for disabled guests 32", ⟲. Bathroom 32", ⟲, handrails, space by to bath and WC. Other bedrooms level.

Rates: on application.

Holiday Inn Newcastle upon Tyne

Great North Road, Seaton Burn, Newcastle upon Tyne NE13 6BP.

☎ **0870 787 3291**

W www.newcastle.holiday-inn.com

●● D/E/I/F/G

Hotel 7 miles north of city centre. Entrance steep ramp or 1 step, 64" double doors. Public rooms ground floor. Platform lift to Restaurant and Conference rooms. Handrail in WCs. Two ground floor bedroom 29", handle over bed. Bathroom 30", handrails.

Rates: on application.

Innkeeper's Lodge Gosforth

Falcons Nest Vintage Inn, Rotary Way, Newcastle NE3 5EH.

☎ **0191 236 7078.**

●● D/E/F/G ★★★

Budget Hotel north of city by race course. Reserved parking bays. Ramp to entrance. Restaurant and bar level. Unisex WC. 3 bedrooms designed for disabled guests, vibrating and visual alarms. Shower rooms ⟲, roll-in shower with seat, space by WC. Interconnecting rooms available.

Ⓟ ⊗

Rates: from £59.95 per night (2008).

Jurys Inn Newcastle

St James' Gate, Scotswood Road, Newcastle upon Tyne NE4 7JH.

☎ **0191 201 4400.**

@ jurysinnnewcastle@jurysdoyle.com

●● D/E/I/F/G

City centre hotel. Public car park over road; 2 spaces in front of hotel can be arranged. Entrance ramp or 3 steps, automatic door. Low reception desk. Public rooms level, open plan. Unisex WCs on ground and 1st floors. Lift 89cm, inside 155x130cm. 14 bedrooms designed for disabled guests; 2 on 1st floor have automatic door openers. Bathrooms 70cm, ⟲, handrails, space by WC; 2 have roll-in showers. Other bedrooms level. Wheelchair available.

Ⓟ ⊗ 🚌

Rates: from £71 per room (2008).

Novotel Newcastle

Ponteland Road, Kenton,
Newcastle upon Tyne NE3 3HZ.

☎ **0191 214 0303.**

@ **H1118@accor.hotels.com**

●● D/E/I/F/G 

Hotel on city outskirts. Reserved parking bays. Entrance level, automatic door. Public rooms level, except 3 steps to bar. Unisex WC. Lift to all floors. Four bedrooms designed for disabled guests. Bathrooms ⟲, handrails, space for side transfer to bath and WC. Other rooms level.

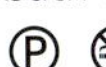

Rates: on application.

REDWORTH, Co. Durham

Paramount Redworth Hall Hotel

Redworth, Newton Aycliffe DL5 6NL.

☎ **01388 770600.**

@ **redworthhall@paramount-hotels.co.uk**

●● D/E/I/G ★★★★

Country house hotel in southern County Durham. Ramp to rear entrance; 2 steps to main entrance. Public rooms level on ground and 1st floors. Unisex WC. Lift 30", inside 42" x 55". Three bedrooms, double and twin, designed for disabled guests, recently refurbished up to high standards. Bathrooms 34" turning space, handrails, space for side transfer to bath and WC. All bedrooms level, teletext TV, some fitted for hearing impaired guests.

Rates: on application.

SOUTH SHIELDS, Tyne & Wear

Little Haven Hotel

River Drive, Littlehaven,
South Shields NE33 1LH.

☎ **0191 455 4455.**

W **www.littlehavenhotel.com**

●● D/E/F/G 

Modern hotel facing beach. Reserved parking bays. Entrance level 81cm. Low reception desk. Public rooms level. Unisex WCs on ground and 1st floors. Lift 80cm. Four bedrooms, double and twin, designed for disabled guests ⟲. Bathrooms 86cm, ⟲, space by bath and WC. Other bedrooms level.

Rates: from £64-£79.50 twin BB (2008).

STOCKTON-ON-TEES

Express by Holiday Inn Stockton-on-Tees

Wynyard Park Services, Coal Lane,
Wolviston, Stockton-on-Tees TS22 5PZ.

☎ **01740 644000.**

@ **ebhi-stockton@btconnect.com**

●● E/I/F/G

Limited service hotel at A19/A689 junction between Stockton and Hartlepool. Reserved parking bays. Entrance level, automatic doors. Low reception desk. Unisex WC. 2 double bedrooms designed for disabled guests. Shower room 80cm, ⟲, roll-in shower with seat, handrails, space by WC. Other level rooms available. Meals in adjoining Toby Carvery.

Rates: on application.

WARK, Northumberland

Battlesteads Hotel

Wark, Hexham NE48 3LS.

☎ **01434 230209.**

W **www.battlesteads.com**

●● D/E/F/G 

Inn and restaurant in village north of Hexham on North Tyne. 4 reserved parking bays. Entrance level. low reception desk. retaurant, bar and conservatory level. Unisex WC. 4 ground floor twin bedrooms designed for disabled guests. Shower room ↺ , roll-in shower with seat, handrails, space under basin and by WC. Closed February.

Rates: from £90 per twin room BB (2008).

WARKWORTH, Northumberland

Warkworth House Hotel

16 Bridge Street, Warkworth NE65 0XB.

☎ **01665 711276.**

W **www.warkworthhousehotel.co.uk**

●● D/E/I/F ★★★

Hotel in village. Reserved parking bays. Entrance from car park level; step at front entrance. Public rooms level, min. door width 32". Unisex WC to be provided during 2007. Two ground floor bedrooms designed for disabled guests. One has twin beds and a bathroom. The other has a double bed, roll-in shower and is non-smoking. 12 bedrooms upstairs.

Ⓟ

Rates: from £57.50 per person BB (2008).

WASHINGTON, Tyne & Wear

Campanile Washington

Emerson Road, Washington NE37 1LE

☎ **0191 416 5010.**

@ **washington@campanile-hotels.com**

●●

Hotel near A1(M) and A195. Reserved parking bays. Public rooms level. 2 twin bedrooms designed for disabled guests. Bathroom ↺, handrails, space for side transfer. Other ground floor bedrooms level. See page 31.

Ⓟ

Rates: on application.

Holiday Inn Washington

Emerson, Washington NE37 1LB.

☎ **0870 400 9084**

●● D/E/I/F/G

Hotel in suburb off A1(M) J64. Reserved parking bays. Entrance level, automatic door. Low reception desk. Public rooms level. Unisex WC. Lift 78cm. Four bedrooms designed for disabled guests ↺, low clothes rail and door viewer, alarm system. Bathroom 90cm, ↺, handrails, space by bath and WC, bathseat. Other bedrooms level. Flashing door bell and induction loop.

Ⓟ

Rates: on application.

LODGE ACCOMMODATION

There are Premier Travel Inn (see page 38) and Travelodge (see page 38) properties in the following areas in this region.

Berwick - Travelodge ☎ 0870 191 1779
Cramlington - Premier Travel Inn ☎ 0870 197 7188
Darlington - Premier Travel Inn ☎ 0870 197 7300
Durham - Travelodge ☎ 0870 191 1636
Durham, East - Premier Travel Inn ☎ 0870 197 7084
Durham, North - Premier Travel Inn ☎ 0870 197 7086
Durham, South - Premier Travel Inn ☎ 0870 197 7087
Gateshead - Premier Travel Inn ☎ 0870 197 7283
Travelodge ☎ 0870 191 1783
Gateshead, Whitemare Pool - Travelodge ☎ 0870 191 1665
Hartlepool - Premier Travel Inn ☎ 0870 197 7127
Middlesbrough, South - Premier Travel Inn ☎ 0870 990 6540
Newcastle upon Tyne - Premier Travel Inn ☎ 0870 238 3318
Travelodge ☎ 0870 191 1664
Newcastle Airport - Premier Travel Inn ☎ 0870 197 7190
Newcastle Airport South - Premier Travel Inn ☎ 0870 990 6338
Newcastle, Holystone - Premier Travel Inn ☎ 0870 197 7189
Newcastle, New Bridge St - Premier Travel Inn ☎ 0879 850 6336
Newcastle, North - Travelodge ☎ 0870 191 1666
Newcastle, Quayside - Premier Travel Inn ☎ 0870 990 6530
Newcastle, South - Premier Travel Inn ☎ 0870 990 6590
Newton Aycliffe - Premier Travel Inn ☎ 0870 197 7085
Sedgefield - Travelodge ☎ 0870 191 1673
Stockton-on-Tees Premier Travel Inn ☎ 0879 197 7243
Sunderland - Travelodge ☎ 0870 191 1550
Sunderland N W - Premier Travel Inn ☎ 0870 990 6514
Sunderland West - Premier Travel Inn ☎ 0870 197 7245
Thornaby - Premier Travel Inn ☎ 0870 197 7244
Washington - Travelodge (2) ☎ 0870 191 1771/2

SELF-CATERING ACCOMMODATION

ALNWICK, Northumberland

Bog Mill Holiday Cottages

Bog Mill, Alnwick NE66 3PA.

☎ 01665 604529. W www.bogmill.co.uk

●● I/F ★★★★

"Stable" cottage designed for disabled people 1 mile from Alnwick. Ramp to entrance 91cm. Lounge and dining room 83cm. Kitchen open plan, controls useable from wheelchair. Double bedroom level. Bathroom 83cm, ↺, roll-in shower with seat, handrails, space by bath and WC. Twin bedroom upstairs. Two other cottages are also available.

Ⓟ

Rates: from £180-£550 per week (2007).

BARDON MILL, Northumberland

Peel Bothy

Bardon Mill, Nr Hexham

●● G

Cottage for 2 people near Hadrian's Wall. Entrance to lounge. Kitchen. Double bedroom. Bathroom with adapted shower.

Ⓟ

Apply: National Trust Holiday Booking Office ☎ 0870 4584422. See page 33.

Rates: on application.

Springwell Cottage

Twice Brewed, Bardon Mill, Nr. Hexham

●● G

Adapted cottage on National Trust's Hadrian's Wall Estate. Entrance level 35". Lounge/kitchen open plan. Worktops 29" and 35". Twin bedroom ground floor ↺. Shower room level 35", ↺, handrails, shower chair, space for side transfer to WC. Stairlift to two 1st floor bedrooms. Travel cot available.

Ⓟ

Apply: National Trust Holiday Booking Office ☎ 0870 4584422. See page 33.

Rates: from £291-£848 per week (2008).

BARNARD CASTLE, Co. Durham

East Briscoe Farm Cottages

Baldersdale, Barnard Castle DL12 9UL.

☎ 01833 650087.

W www.eastbriscoe.co.uk

●● I/F/G ★★★★

Six cottages near village and 6 miles from Barnard Castle. "Low Barn Cottage" sleeps 4/5 people. Entrance ramp, 75cm. Lounge 75cm. Kitchen, ramp, open plan, ↺. Double bedroom level, ↺. Also twin and double bedrooms, level. Bathroom 75cm, ↺, handrails. No smoking or dogs in this cottage. Also ground floor "Studio Cottage" accommodates 2 people, no ↺.

Ⓟ ⓘ

Rates: from £195-£450 per week (2008).

BEALE, Northumberland

Haggerston Castle Holiday Park

Haggerston Castle, Beal, Nr. Berwick TD15 2PA.

☎ 01289 381333.

W www.haggerstoncastle-park.co.uk

●● I/G ★★★★★

Six caravans adapted for disabled people on Holiday Park near Northumberland coast. Ramp with handrails to entrance 29½". Lounge/kitchen open plan, controls useable from wheelchair. Two bedrooms 30" sliding door, hooks for ceiling hoist. Shower room 20½" sliding door, ↺, roll-in shower with seat, handrails, space by WC. Entertainment on site. Open March-November.

Ⓟ

Apply: Haven Holidays Reservations ☎ 0870 2422222.

Rates: on application.

BERWICK-ON-TWEED, Northumberland

Ord House Country Park

East Ord, Berwick-upon-Tweed TD15 2NS.
☎ **01289 305288.**
www.ordhouse.co.uk
●● I/F ★★★★★

Park for touring caravans in village near Berwick. Most site facilities level. Lift to clubhouse. Unisex WC/shower with NKS lock. Pitches for touring caravans and tents.

Rates: on application.

Scout Holiday Homes Trust Caravan

Berwick Holiday Centre, Magdalane Fields, Berwick-on-Tweed TD15 1NE
●● E/I/F/G

Adapted unit for 5 adults and a small child. Ramp to entrance 30". Open plan lounge/kitchen, worktops 36". Two bedrooms, turning space in double. Shower room/WC 30" sliding door, handrails, space for side transfer to WC and shower seat. Veranda and sea view. Activities and entertainment on site. Available April-October.

Apply: Scout Holiday Homes Trust
☎ 020 8433 7290. See page 26.
Rates: from £145-£420 per week (2007).

BINGFIELD, Northumberland

The Hytte

Bingfield, Hexham NE46 4HR.
☎ **01434 672321.**
www.thehytte.com
●●● I/F/G/H ★★★★★

Environmentally friendly cottage, to sleep up to 8, designed to be used by disabled people in country north of Corbridge and Hexham. Entrance level 83cm. Open plan lounge/kitchen, controls useable from wheelchair, lowered worktop. Four twin or double bedrooms, one with electric twin/double bed with most space, adjustable clothes rails. Bathroom has space by bath; also an accessible shower room. Electric hoist available. Garden, sauna and hot tub.

Apply: Sonja & Simon Gregory.
Rates: from £500-£850 per week (2008).

BOWES, Co. Durham

Mellwaters Barn

East Mellwaters Farm, Stainmore Road, Bowes, Barnard Castle DL12 9RH.
☎ **01833 628181.**
www.mellwatersbarn.co.uk
●●● I/F/G/H

Four units designed to be used by disabled people on farm in Upper Teesdale. Level entrance. Open plan lounge/kitchen, controls useable from wheelchair. Through or stair lifts to upper floor. Two units have one twin bedroom and the others have two, all with adjustable beds and clothes rails. Bathrooms 85cm, handrails, space by WC, hoist. One unit has a roll-in shower with seat. Induction loops. Waterproof sheets and some other equipment available. Units can be linked. A 5th cottage is planned.

Rates: £165-£300 per week (2008).

COCKFIELD, Co. Durham

Swallows Nest

Low Lands Farm, Cockfield,
Nr. Bishop Auckland.

●● G ★★★★

Cottage designed for disabled people on farm between Bishop Auckland and Barnard Castle in Teesdale. Entrance level. Internal doors 80cm. Kitchen controls useable from wheelchair. Double bedroom with roll-in shower room, ⟲, handrails, space by WC. Twin bedroom with 2 steps to bathroom. A 2nd cottage is also available. Farm largely level.

Ⓟ ⓘ

Apply: Mrs Tallentire, Low Lands Farm, Cockfield, Bishop Auckland DL13 5AW.
☎ 01388 718251.
W www.farmholidaysuk.com
Rates: from £160-£340 per week (2007).

COWSHILL-IN-WEARDALE, Co. Durham

Cornriggs Cottages

Low Cornriggs Farm, Cowshill,
Bishop Auckland DL13 1AQ.
W **www.britnett.net/lowcornriggsfarm**

●● F/G ★★★★★

Cornriggs Cottages are near to the beautiful village of Cowshill. Both cottages are fitted to a very high standard. Have a level entrance, wide door ways and large rooms and corridors, Lounge /kitchen open plan, controls useable from a wheel chair, Twin bedroom with roll in shower, hand rails and space buy WC.Double bed room with large bath room hand rails, Space WC, Twin bedroom, & Single. Garden and Patio area. Parking flat. Home baking and meals can be ordered. Weekly stays. Short breaks available. Open all year.

Ⓟ

Apply: Mr & Mrs Elliott ☎ 01388 537600.
@ cornriggsfarm@btconnect.com
Rates: from £320-£580 per week (2007/8).

CRASTER, Northumberland

Craster Pine Lodges

9 West End, Craster, Alnwick NE66 3TS.
☎ **01665 576286.**
W **www.crasterpinelodges.co.uk**

●● I/F/G ★★★★

Lodge designed for disabled people on edge of fishing village. Entrance ramp, double doors. Lounge/kitchen open plan, controls useable from wheelchair. Double and twin bedrooms ⟲, Also bunkroom. Shower room ⟲, roll-in shower with seat, space for side transfer to WC. A second lodge also available.

Ⓟ

Rates: from £220-£599 per week (2007).

EDMUNDBYERS, Co. Durham

YHA Edmundbyers

Low House, Edmundbyers,
Consett DH8 9NL.
☎ **01207 255651.**
@ **edmundbyers@yha.org.uk**

●● F/G ★★★★★

Self-catering hostel in North Pennine village near Derwent Reservoir. Entrance step, portable ramp available. 2" step to lounge/dining room. Kitchen not adapted. Ground floor bedroom for 5 people ⟲. Shower room 36", roll-in shower with seat, handrails, space by WC. Portable induction loop and Teletext TV. For further information on Youth Hostels see page 34.

Ⓟ

Rates: £13 adult per night (2007).

HEXHAM, Northumberland

The Old Byre

Rye Hill Farm, Slaley, Nr. Hexham NE47 0AH.

●● I/F/G ★★★★

Converted barn for up to 7 people south of Hexham. Entrance level 36". Lounge/kitchen open plan, controls not useable from wheelchair. Twin bedroom ground floor. En suite shower room 33", roll-in shower, handrails, no space for side transfer to WC. Other bedrooms and bathrooms upstairs. Waterproof sheets available. Evening meals can be supplied.

Apply: Mrs E Courage ☎ 01434 673259.

www.ryehillfarm.co.uk

Rates: from £350-£700 per week (2006).

KIELDER, Northumberland

Calvert Trust Kielder

Kielder Water, Hexham NE48 1BS.

☎ 01434 250232

●● I/G/H ★★★★

Ten purpose-built chalets. Entrance level 36". Lounge/kitchen open plan with height adjustable work surfaces. Three twin bedrooms. Bathroom, roll-in shower, shower chair, handrails, adjustable basin, side transfer to bath and WC. Second WC with basin. Meals and activities, including hydrotherapy pool may be booked in advance from Activity Centre, see page 499.

Rates: on application.

MORPETH, Northumberland

Beacon Hill Farm Holidays

Beacon Hill Farm, Longhorsley, Morpeth NE65 8QW.

www.beaconhill.co.uk

●● F/G ★★★★★

Seven, of 15, cottages adapted for disabled people. Entrance ramp. Lounge and kitchen level, no adaptations in kitchen. Three sleep 6 people and the others up to 4. Three cottages have a roll-in shower room. The others have a bathroom, handrails, space for side transfer to bath and WC. Shower chair available. TV with induction loop. Premier Cottages member.

Apply: Alun Moore ☎ 01670 780900.

Rates: from £245-£1455 per week (2007).

SEAHOUSES, Northumberland

St Omers Trust Caravan

Seafield Caravan Park, Seahouses

●● E/I/G

2 caravans adapted for disabled people and their families on coastal site. Entrance ramp. Lounge, kitchen and two bedrooms for up to 4 adults and two children. Shower room with shower chair, handrails and space for transfer to WC. Central heating. Available February-December.

Apply: St Omer's Trust ☎ 0870 242 0932.

Rates: from £35 per night (2007).

WOOLER, Northumberland

Riverside Holiday Park

Brewery Road, Wooler NE71 6QG

☎ 01668 281447.

riverside@btconnect.com

●● I/F/G ★★★★

Holiday Park on edge of Northumbria National Park with range of facilities and entertainment. Caravans for 5 people adapted for disabled guests. Entrance ramp. Lounge/kitchen open plan. Two bedrooms, sliding door 75cm, in double. Shower room 75cm, handrails, restricted. Open Easter-October.

Rates: on application.

Self-catering accommodation

Glenfinnan Monument, Loch Shiel

Scotland offers something for everyone - dramatic and attractive scenery both in the countryside and around the coast, historic towns, a well established arts scene, seaside resorts, wilderness areas for solitude, the bustle of major cities and many other attractions.

Edinburgh has all the amenities of a capital city. The historic core of the city either side of the Royal Mile running between the castle and the Palace of Holyroodhouse and the Scottish Parliament contrasts with the elegant Georgian terraces in the New Town, north of Prince's Street. Galleries and museums include the Museum of Scotland, the National Gallery of Scotland and the Scottish National Portrait Gallery. Other attractions include the Scotch Whisky Heritage Centre and Our Dynamic Earth, a Millennium project. In August the Edinburgh Festival attracts arts lovers to a wide range of performances and events held in a variety of venues, many of them accessible.

Photo: www.britainonview © Rod Edwards

Scotland's largest city, Glasgow had its major development in the 19th Century and has recently enjoyed a renaissance particularly in the city centre and on the waterfront. On the outskirts of the city can be found the Burrell Collection in its purpose built gallery.

Other attractions in central Scotland include Greenbank Gardens at Clarkston, owned by the National Trust for Scotland, the David Livingstone Centre at Blantyre, a wildlife park in Palacerigg Country Park near Cumbernauld and Flotterstone Glen in the Pentland Hills.

In the south east of the country there are the hills around the small towns of Peebles, Selkirk and Hawick and small fishing ports such as Eyemouth. The home of Sir Walter Scott can be visited at Abbotsford near Melrose. Further west is the picturesque south-facing coast and countryside of Dumfries and Galloway, while the resorts of Ayr and Largs can be found on the Ayrshire coast. Some attractions in the area include Burns Cottage at Alloway, Culzean Castle and Country Park near Maybole, Drumlanrig Castle in Dumfriesshire, the World Heritage Site of New Lanark and Vikingar! at Largs which displays the Viking history of the area.

Fountains outside Aberdeen art gallery

Photo: www.britainonview © Natalie Pecht

North of the Forth in eastern Scotland are the major centres of Dundee, Perth and Aberdeen. Each has its own attractions and can be used as a base for touring the surrounding countryside. Devotees of history can visit the Bannockburn Heritage Centre at Stirling, while country lovers can choose from many sites around the Perthshire towns of Pitlochry and Dunkeld, as well as in the Grampians. There are many opportunities to visit a whisky distillery in the area. Visitor centres displaying the historic life of the area include the Grampian Transport Museum at Alford, the North East Scotland Agricultural Heritage Centre in Aden Country Park, Aberdeenshire, the Angus Folk Museum and the Scottish Fisheries Museum at Anstruther in Fife.

Dunbeath Castle

Photo: www.britainonview © Glyn Satterley

The regional centre of much of the vast area covered by the Highlands and Islands is Inverness. Outside the city, Culloden Battlefield can be viewed from a Visitor Centre owned by the National Trust for Scotland. When travelling inland visitors soon reach Loch Ness in the Great Glen, although sightings of the monster cannot be guaranteed. While the area contains dramatic wilderness country, there are also many small towns and villages to provide a welcome. Inverewe Gardens at Poolewe in Wester Ross are world famous and there are displays of crafts and farming at the Highlands Folk Museum in Kingussie.

Islands have their own attractions for many visitors and some of those off the west coast can be reached by short ferry trips or, in the case of Skye, by bridge. Highland life 100 years ago is depicted at the Skye Cottage Museum. Visiting Orkney, Shetland and the Western Isles needs more planning but all have a distinctive lifestyle and many reminders of their Nordic past.

USEFUL ADDRESSES

VisitScotland

Quality & Standards, Thistle House, Beechwood Park North, Inverness IV2 3ED.
www.visitscotland.com

VisitScotland operate an Accessibility Scheme for places to stay and attractions that are inspected against specific criteria for three levels of impaired mobility. Information is given in **Accessible Scotland** (see below). Indications of access are included in other publications and on their website.

Orkney Disability Forum

Power Station Offices, Great Western Road, Kirkwall KW15 1AN.
☎ 01856 871515.

Offers a Dial-a-Bus and a Shopmobility service and can provide information on access in Orkney.

DIAL

DIAL offers a free, impartial and confidential service of information and advice by telephone to disabled people, their relatives and professionals. The following groups may be able to help disabled residents and visitors in their areas:

Contact Point in East Dunbartonshire

☎/Textphone: 0141 578 0183

Disability Resource Centre, Clydesdale

☎ 01555 770123

Three Eyes Project Glasgow

☎ 0141 954 8432

Wellbeing Glasgow

☎ 0141 248 1899
Textphone: 01983 525424

South Lanark Disability Forum

☎/Textphone: 01698 307733

CalMac Ferries

The Ferry Terminal, Gourock PA19 1QP.
☎ 08705 650000 (enquiries),
☎ 01475 650350 (brochures).
@ reservations@calmac.co.uk
www.calmac.co.uk

Operate a wide range of routes off the west coast of Scotland. Facilities for disabled passengers vary depending on the vessel used on the route, information is being included on the website under The Fleet. Anyone who may need assistance should notify the company when booking and checking in. Fare concessions for disabled drivers are available on production of appropriate documents.

NorthLink Ferries

Kiln Corner, Ayre Road, Kirkwall, Orkney KW15 1QX
☎ Reservations 0845 6000 449,
☎ Administration 01856 885500.
@ info@northlinkferries.co.uk
www.northlinkferries.co.uk

Operates ferry services to Orkney and Shetland from Aberdeen and between Scrabster in Caithness and Stromness on Orkney, using three modern vessels. Each has toilets for disabled passengers and lifts between decks. Those used for overnight sailings have 4 cabins designed for disabled people of which two have enhanced facilities including hoists. Concessionary rates and special boarding arrangements are available for disabled people. There are toilets for disabled people at each of Northlink's terminals. Advance notice of passengers requiring assistance is appreciated.

Pentland Ferries

Pier Road, St Margaret's Hope,
South Ronaldsay, Orkney KW17 2SW.
☎ **01856 831226.**
W **www.pentlandferries.co.uk**

Operate car ferries on the 1-hour crossing between Gill's Bay in Caithness and the southern Orkney island of South Ronaldsay. No specific facilities are available for disabled passengers.

The three largest airports in Scotland are operated by BAA Scotland. For information on the services at each contact:

Aberdeen Airport ☎ **0870 040 0006.**
W **www.aberdeenairport.com**

Edinburgh Airport ☎ **0870 040 0007.**
W **www.edinburghairport.com**

Glasgow Airport ☎ **0870 040 0008.**
W **www.glasgowairport.com**

They share a Textphone enquiry number on 0141 585 6161.

Highlands & Islands Airports Ltd

Inverness Airport, Inverness IV2 7JB.
☎ **01667 464000.** W **www.hial.co.uk**

HIAL operate 11 airports in northern Scotland providing commercial, tourist and emergency services. Facilities at some of the smaller airports are limited but all have basically accessible terminals and most have lifts for passengers who cannot use the steps into aircraft.

Highland Adventure Safaris

Drumdewan, Aberfeldy PH15 2JQ.
☎ **01887 820071.**
@ **info@highlandsafaris.net**
W **www.highlandsafaris.net**

From its base at an accessible visitor centre, between Aberfeldy and Tummel Bridge, Highland Adventure Safaris use a long wheelbase Land Rover to explore the Perthshire Highlands going to areas that would otherwise be inaccessible to many people. Assistance with getting on and off the vehicle can be provided.

Mobility Assist

113 Forest Road, Selkirk,
Scottish Borders TD7 5DD.
☎ **01750 23456.**
@ **colinmclaren@msn.com**

Mobility Assist operates a taxi service in the Scottish Borders area using vehicles with rear lifts. They also hire wheelchairs.

USEFUL PUBLICATIONS & WEBSITES

Accessible Scotland – gives information on places to stay and visitor attractions throughout Scotland that have been inspected for access criteria. Three levels of accessibility are indicated – access for those with mobility impairment, wheelchair access with assistance and wheelchair access without assistance. Additional information on accessibility is given for some attractions. The brochure can be obtained by calling 0845 2255 121 or on www.visitscotland.com

---

Historic Scotland: Access Guide - gives information on facilities, and difficulties, for disabled people at over 70 historic buildings and sites throughout Scotland. Available free from Historic Scotland, Longmore House, Salisbury Place, Edinburgh EH9 1SH. ☎ 0131 668 8800.
W www.historic-scotland.gov.uk

Countryside Visits: Places to visit in the Scottish Borders with some access for wheelchair users – A free booklet prepared in 2004 by the Scottish Borders Council Rangers Service with the Borders Disability Forum. It is available from the Rangers Service, Harestanes, Ancrum, Jedburgh TD8 6UQ. ☎ 01835 830281. Updated information can be found on
W www.bordersdisabilityforum/news.rangers

National Trust for Scotland: Access Guide – a booklet published in 2007 giving information on accessibility and facilities at NTS sites and premises throughout Scotland. Available from The National Trust for Scotland, Wemyss House, 28 Charlotte Square, Edinburgh EH2 4ET.
☎ 0844 493 2100. W www.nts.org.uk

Shetland Access Guide – Disability Shetland have detailed information on facilities for disabled people on inter-island ferries and some premises in Lerwick on their website – see
W www.shetlandcommunities.org /disability-shetland

Spey Access Guide - Where to Go in Badenoch & Strathspey - published 2004 by Badenoch & Strathspey Disabled Access Panel. Send A5 SAE to VABS, 1 Inverewe, Grampian Road, Aviemore PH22 1RH.
☎ 01479 810004.
W www.speyaccessguide.org

---

www.disabledgo.org - this website includes detailed information on the accessibility of many premises in Aberdeen, Angus, East Dumbartonshire, Edinburgh and Glasgow.

EQUIPMENT HIRE

Shopmobility Dundee

Overgate Centre, Dundee DD1 1UF.
☎ 01382 228525.
@ shopmobility-dun@btconnect.com

Visitors to the Dundee area can borrow a manual wheelchair, if available, for the duration of their stay. Proof of ID is required and donations and pre-booking are encouraged.

Shopmobility schemes provide wheelchairs and/or scooters for use in shopping centres in the following areas. For information on availability, etc. telephone in advance.

Ayr ☎ 01292 618086

Coatbridge ☎ 01236 605795

Dundee ☎ 01382 228525

East Kilbride ☎ 01355 571300

Edinburgh Gyle ☎ 0131 317 1460

Edinburgh Leith ☎ 0131 555 8888

Elgin ☎ 01343 552528

Falkirk ☎ 01324 630500

Fort William ☎ 01397 700051

Glasgow Braehead ☎ 0141 885 4630

Greenock ☎ 01475 732600,

Hamilton ☎ 01698 459955

Inverness ☎ 01463 717624

Kirkcaldy ☎ 01592 412199

Livingston ☎ 01506 442744

Motherwell ☎ 01698 303199

Oban ☎ 01631 567150

Paisley ☎ 0141 889 0441

Peterhead ☎ 07748 532242

Perth ☎ 01738 783960

Pitlochry ☎ 01796 473866

Stirling ☎ 01786 449606

Lothian Shopmobility operate a mobile unit that covers many major events in and around Edinburgh. For information ☎ 0131 225 9559.

Equipment hire

SCOTLAND - ACCOMMODATION

For ease of reference accommodation entries for Scotland are divided into four areas (see map, page 53). The localities covered by each of these areas are as follows

In Scotland each type of holiday accommodation (hotels, guest houses, bed & breakfast, self-catering, hostels, etc.) are graded for quality as indicated by one to five stars.

★ - Fair and acceptable
★★ - Good
★★★ - Very good
★★★★ - Excellent
★★★★★ - Exceptional

In the following section the star grading, where known, is given and the type of accommodation is referred to in the opening words of each entry.

Further information about gradings can be obtained from Tourist Information Centres or the Scottish Tourist Board Quality Assurance ☎ 01463 716996.

NOTE – In Scotland the original, pre 2002, criteria for the National Accessible Scheme are still in operation.

SOUTH EAST SCOTLAND
ACCOMMODATION WITH MEALS

EDINBURGH

Ardgarth Guest House

1 St Mary's Place, Portobello,
Edinburgh EH15 2QF.
☎ **0131 669 3021.**
W www.ardgarth.com
●● D/E/F/G ★★★

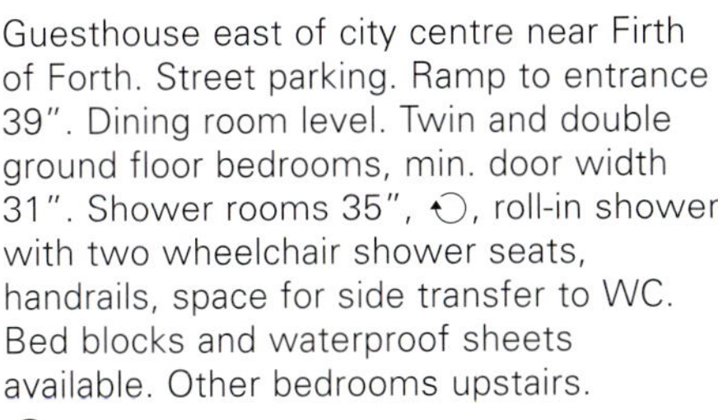

Guesthouse east of city centre near Firth of Forth. Street parking. Ramp to entrance 39". Dining room level. Twin and double ground floor bedrooms, min. door width 31". Shower rooms 35", ⟲, roll-in shower with two wheelchair shower seats, handrails, space for side transfer to WC. Bed blocks and waterproof sheets available. Other bedrooms upstairs.

Rates: from £25-£50 per person BB (2008).

Best Western Edinburgh City Hotel

79 Lauriston Place, Edinburgh EH3 9HZ.
☎ **0131 622 7979.**
W www.bestwesternedinburghcity.co.uk
●● D/E/I/F/G ★★★

City centre hotel. On-site parking for disabled motorists. Entrance level 86cm, automatic door. Public rooms level, open plan. Lift 75cm, inside 206x207cm. Three bedrooms, doubles and single, designed for disabled guests. Bathroom 75cm, ⟲, roll-in shower, handrails, space for side transfer to bath and WC, emergency call. Other bedrooms level. Nursing care can be arranged.

Rates: from £80 single, £140 per room (2007).

Best Western Kings Manor Hotel

100 Milton Road East, Edinburgh
EH15 2NP.
☎ **0131 468 8003.**
W www.kingsmanor.com
●● D/E/F/G ★★★

Hotel 4 miles east of city centre. Reserved parking bays. Ramp with handrails to entrance, automatic door. Low reception desk. Public rooms ground floor, level. Adapted cubicles in WCs. Lift 160cm, inside 240x220cm. Three ground floor bedrooms adapted for disabled guests. Bathrooms 140cm, ⟲, 2 have low level baths and the other a roll-in shower, handrails, space by WC. 13 other level; bedrooms. Regular disabled guests.

Rates: from £90-£140 per room (2007).

Caledonian Hilton

Princes Street, Edinburgh EH1 2AB.
☎ **0131 222 8888.**
W www.hilton.co.uk/caledonian
●● D/E/I/F/G ★★★★★

Luxury hotel in city centre. Reserved parking bays. Ramp or 3 steps at entrance. Public rooms ground floor, mainly open plan. Adapted cubicles on 1st floor WCs. Lift to all floors with braille buttons. Two bedrooms adapted for disabled guests. Bathrooms ⟲, space by bath and WC. Other bedrooms level.

Rates: on application.

Express by Holiday Inn Edinburgh – Waterfront

Britannia Way, Ocean Drive, Edinburgh EH6 6JJ.
☎ **0131 555 4422.**
www.expressedinburgh.co.uk

●● E/F/G ★★★

Limited service hotel in Ocean Terminal area north of city centre. Reserved parking bays. Entrance level, automatic doors. Low reception desk. Public rooms open plan. Unisex WC. Lift inside 130x130cm. 7 double bedrooms designed for disabled guests 88cm, ⟲, visual smoke alarm. Shower room 82cm, roll-in shower with seat, handrails, space by WC. Other bedrooms level.

Rates: on application.

Holiday Inn Edinburgh

132 Corstophine Road, Edinburgh EH12 6UA.
☎ **0870 400 9026.**
reservations-edinburgh@ihg.com

●● D/E/I/F/G ★★★

Hotel in suburb west of city centre. Reserved parking bays by level entrance, automatic door. Low reception desk. Wheelchair lift or 12 steps to open plan restaurant, lounge and bar. Unisex WC. Lift 68cm, inside 83x118cm. Five 2nd floor bedrooms adapted for disabled guests, more planned. Bathrooms 89cm sliding door, ⟲, handrails, space by WC and bath. Other rooms level.

 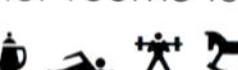

Rates: on application.

Holiday Inn Edinburgh North

107 Queensferry Road, Edinburgh EH4 3HL.
☎ **0870 400 9025.**

●● D/E/G ★★★

Hotel 1½ miles from city centre. Reserved parking bays. Entrance ramp or 3 steps, automatic door. Public rooms ground floor or level from lift. Unisex WC. Lift 29", inside 43"x50". 2 bedrooms on 1st floor designed for disabled guests 29". Bathroom 30", ⟲, handrails, space for side transfer to bath and WC. Other bedrooms level.

Rates: on application.

Ibis Edinburgh

6 Hunter Square, Edinburgh EH1 1QW.
☎ **0131 240 7000.** **H2039@accor.com**

●● G ★★

Hotel off Royal Mile. Car park 500m. Entrance level, automatic door. Public rooms level, open plan. Unisex WC in basement. Lifts 180cm, inside 190x190cm. Six bedrooms designed for disabled guests. Bathrooms ⟲, handrail by bath, space for side transfer to bath and WC. Other bedrooms level.

Rates: from £57-£89 per room (2008).

Jurys Inn Edinburgh

43 Jeffrey Street, Edinburgh EH1 1DH.

☎ 0131 200 3300.

@ jurysinnedinburgh@jurysdoyle.com

●● D/E/I/F/G ★★★

City centre hotel. Car park 250m. Main entrance ramp or 4 steps, automatic doors; steps from Royal Mile. Ramp or 4 steps from lobby to reception, low desk. Public rooms level, open plan. Unisex WC. Lift 90cm, inside 210x143cm. Bedroom with bathroom designed for disabled guests 93cm, ⟲, handrails, space for side transfer to bath and WC. 8 other bedrooms with some adaptations and all level. Wheelchair, waterproof sheets and teletext TVs available.

Rates: from £79 per room (2007).

Melville Guest House

2 Duddingston Crescent, Edinburgh EH15 3AS.

☎ 0131 258 2358.

W www.melvilleguesthouse.com

●● D/F ★★★

Guesthouse off A1, 3½ miles east of city centre. Steep drive from street to parking area. Ramp to entrance. Dining room and lounge level. Twin bedroom ground floor. Bathroom designed for disabled guests ⟲, handrails, roll-in shower, space for side transfer to bath and WC.

Rates: from £25-£37 per person BB (2007).

Novotel Edinburgh Centre

80 Lauriston Place, Edinburgh EH3 9DG.

☎ 0131 656 3500.

@ H3271@accor.com

●● D/E/F/G ★★★★

Modern hotel in Old Town. Reserved parking bays. Public rooms level, open plan. Unisex WC. Lifts to upper floors. Nine bedrooms with bathrooms designed for disabled guests. Other bedrooms level.

Rates: from £69-£199 per night (2007).

Parliament House Hotel

15 Calton Hill, Edinburgh EH1 3BJ.

☎ 0131 478 4000.

W www.parliamenthouse-hotel.co.uk

●● D/E/F/G ★★★

City centre town house hotel. Street parking or car park 250m. Slope to level entrance. Lounge and bar ground floor level. Stairs to restaurant; breakfast can be served in bedrooms or lounge. Lift 80cm, inside 134x100cm. Three bedrooms, family, double and twin, designed for disabled guests. Bathrooms ⟲, handrails, space for side transfer; family room has roll-in shower and shower chair. Other bedrooms level.

Rates: on application.

Radisson SAS Hotel Edinburgh

80 High Street, Royal Mile, Edinburgh EH1 1TH.

☎ 0131 557 9797.

W www.radissonsas.com

●● D/E/I/G ★★★★

Hotel in city centre. Entrance level. Public rooms ground floor or level from lift. Three bedrooms, double or twin, with bathrooms designed for disabled guests. Other bedrooms level.

Rates: on application.

Smart City Hostel

50 Blackfriars Street, Edinburgh EH1 1NE.
☎ **0131 524 1989.**
www.smartcityhostels.com
●● D/E/I/F/G

Newly built hostel in Old Town. Street and public car park. Sloping street. Entrance level, double doors. Stairlifts on 9 steps to café, lounge and bar. Accessible roof garden. Lift to upper floors 80cm, inside 110X140cm. One 2-person and two 8 person bedrooms designed for disabled guests with roll-in shower rooms. Other bedrooms level. Waterproof sheets available. Care Agency arrangements in place with advance notice.

Rates: from £16.50-£30.50 per person (2007/8).

GALASHIELS, Scottish Borders

Ettrickvale

33 Abbotsford Road,
Galashiels TD1 3HW.
☎ **01896 755224.**
www.ettrickvalebandb.co.uk
● D/G ★★★

Bed & breakfast bungalow on edge of town. 3 steps from parking area, portable ramp available. Entrance level, 32". Dining room level. Two bedrooms with own bathrooms. Double bedroom ⟲. Separate bathroom/WC ⟲, handrail by bath, sheet in shower tray, space by WC. Evening meals by arrangement.

Rates: from £20 per person BB (2007).

GOREBRIDGE, Midlothian

Ivory House

14 Vogrie Road, Gorebridge EH23 4HH.
☎ **01875 820755.**
www.ivory-house.co.uk
●● D/F ★★★★

Guesthouse in village 10 miles south east of Edinburgh. Entrance to Coach House level. Lounge and dining room level. Double bedroom ground floor ⟲. Bathroom ⟲, handrail, bath seat, space by bath and WC. Also available for self-catering.

Ⓟ

Rates: from £45-£60 per person BB (2007).

NORTH BERWICK, East Lothian

Leuchie House MS Respite Centre

North Berwick EH39 5NT
☎ **01620 892864.**
enquiries@leuchie.com
●●●●● D/E/I/F/G/H

Specially adapted holiday home for up to 20 guests. Ramp or step at entrance. 4 single and 8 twin rooms adapted for disabled guests. ⟲. Roll-in shower, handrails. 24hr nursing care. Equipment and physiotherapy available. Outings and activities arranged. Priority for guests with multiple sclerosis.

Ⓟ

Rates: on application.

PEEBLES, Scottish Borders

Cringletie House

Edinburgh Road, Peebles EH45 8PL.

☎ 01721 725750. W www.cringletie.com

●● D/I/F/G ★★★★

Country house hotel north of Peebles. Reserved parking bay. Platform lift or 4 steps at entrance, automatic door. Low reception desk. Lounge and bar ground floor open plan. Restaurant 1st floor. Unisex WC. Lift 92cm, inside 140x140cm. Twin and double bedrooms on ground floor, 110 cm, ↺. One with tilting bed and chairs, automatic door, touch lights and other features. Bathroom 100cm, ↺, handrails, roll-in shower with seat, space by bath and WC, low basin. Other bedrooms level. Portable induction loop. Accessible woodland paths in grounds.

Rates: from £90-£140 per person BB (2007).

WHITBURN, West Lothian

Best Western Hilcroft Hotel

East Main Street, Whitburn EH47 0JU.

☎ 01501 740818

W www.hilcroft.com

●● D/E/I/F/G ★★★

Hotel near M8 J4 midway between Edinburgh and Glasgow. Reserved parking bay. Entrance level, automatic door. Public rooms ground floor, min. door width 36". Unisex WC. One bedroom adapted for disabled guests on ground floor. Bathroom ↺, handrails, space by bath and WC. Other ground floor bedrooms level.

Rates: from £95 double, £80 single BB (2007).

LODGE ACCOMMODATION

There are Premier Travel Inn (see page 38) and Travelodge (see page 38) properties in the following areas in this region.

Edinburgh – Premier Travel Inn .... ☎ 0870 990 6610
Travelodge .... ☎ 0870 191 1637
Edinburgh, Dreghorn – Travelodge .... ☎ 0870 191 1639
Edinburgh, East – Premier Travel Inn .... ☎ 0870 197 7091
Edinburgh, Leith – Premier Travel Inn .... ☎ 0870 197 7093
Edinburgh, Morrison St. – Premier Travel Inn .... ☎ 0870 238 3319
Edinburgh, Newcraighall – Premier Travel Inn .... ☎ 0870 990 6336
Falkirk, East – Premier Travel Inn .... ☎ 0870 197 7098
Falkirk, North – Premier Travel Inn .... ☎ 0870 197 7099
Falkirk, West – Premier Travel Inn .... ☎ 0870 990 6550
Inveresk – Premier Travel Inn .... ☎ 0870 197 7092
Livingston – Premier Travel Inn .... ☎ 0870 197 7161
Travelodge .... ☎ 0870 191 1788
Musselburgh – Travelodge .... ☎ 0870 191 1638
Polmont – Premier Travel Inn .... ☎ 0870 197 7098
South Queensferry – Premier Travel Inn .... ☎ 0870 197 7094

National Key Scheme Toilets

Environmental and Consumer Services are responsible for Edinburgh's public toilets, and operate the National Key Scheme in all our toilets with disabled access. The list below details locations and opening times of these facilities.

Location	Opening Times
Ardmillan	24hr
Bath Street	10am - 8pm
Bruntsfield	24hr
Canaan Lane	10am - 6pm
Canonmills	24hr
Castle Terrace Car Park	8am - 8pm
Granton Square	24hr
Hamilton Place	10am - 6pm
Haymarket	8am - 8pm
High Street, South Queensferry	24hr
Hope Park	10am - 6pm
Joppa	24hr
Mound	24hr
Nicolson Square	24hr
Pipe Street	24hr summer only
Ross Band Stand	8am - 8pm summer only
St James	8am- 6pm
St John's Road	10am - 6pm
Taylor Gardens	24hr
Tollcross	10am - 8pm
West End	8am - dusk

Telephone: For further information please contact 0131 529 3030

SERVICES FOR COMMUNITIES

SELF-CATERING ACCOMMODATION

BONCHESTER BRIDGE, Scottish Borders

Cherry & Quince Cottages

Bonchester Bridge, Nr. Hawick TD9 9TD

●● I/F/G ★★★

Cottages, each for up to 6 people, 1½ miles from village. "Cherry Cottage", entrance level 30". Lounge and dining room 31". Kitchen 28", no ↻. Twin bedroom ground floor, monkey pole available. Bathroom 28", ↻, roll-in shower, handrails, space for side transfer to bath and WC. Twin and double bedrooms upstairs. "Quince Cottage" is similar but internal doors 27" and ground floor shower room with handrails and shower chair. Handrails to garden.

Apply: Mr N Morrison, Northern Cottage, Blacklee Square, Bonchester Bridge, Hawick TD9 9TD. ☎ 01450 860678.
W www.disabled-holidays-scotland.co.uk
Rates: from £150-£385 per week (2007).

COLDSTREAM, Scottish Borders

Cotoneaster Cottage

Little Swinton, Nr. Coldstream

●● F/G

Cottage for 7 people designed for disabled people on Borders farm. Entrance level. Lounge and kitchen ↻, controls useable from wheelchair. Twin, double and family bedrooms. Bathroom ↻, roll-in shower, handrails, space for side transfer to WC. Shower chair and raised WC seat available. Another cottage with ground floor accommodation available.

Apply: Sue Brewis, Leet Villa, Leet Street, Coldstream TD12 4BJ. ☎ 01890 882173.
W www.littleswinton.co.uk
Rates: from £200-£400 per week (2007).

DIRLETON, East Lothian

Denis Duncan House

Manse Road, Dirleton EH39 5EL.
W **www.thelinberwicktrust.org.uk**

●●● I/F/G/H

Purpose built cottage in village west of North Berwick to accommodate up to six people including 2 who are disabled. Entrance level, double doors. Internal doors minimum 90cm. Ground floor lounge, dining room and conservatory. Kitchen with adjustable height worktops and controls usable from wheelchair. Ground floor twin bedroom with adjustable beds. Ceiling hoist to bathroom, ↻ adjustable height bath and basin, Clos-o-Mat WC, roll-in shower with seat, handrails. Induction loop, vibrating alarm clock, angled cutlery and other equipment available. Two twin bedrooms and bathroom upstairs. Accessible garden.

Apply: The Lin Berwick Trust, Eastgate House, Upper East Street, Sudbury CO10 1UB. ☎ 01787 372343.
@ info@thelinberwicktrust.org.uk
Rates: from £370-£785 per week (2008).

ETTRICK, Scottish Borders

Elspinhope Cottage

Cossarshill Farm, Ettrick Valley, Nr. Selkirk.
W **www.ettrick-holidays.co.uk**

F/G

Purpose built cottage for disabled guests on farm in upper Ettrick Valley. Ramp to side entrance 83cm; 1 step at front door. Internal doors 83cm. ↻ in lounge and kitchen. Twin bedroom and en-suite roll-in shower room with seat, handrails and space by WC. Also double bedroom, bunkroom and separate bathroom/WC.

Apply: Mrs D Jackson, Ettrick Holidays, Cossarshill Farm, Ettrick Valley, Selkirk TD7 5JB. ☎ 01750 62259.
Rates: from £325-£500 per week (2007).

LONGNIDDRY, East Lothian

Seaton Sands Holiday Village

Longniddry EH32 0QF.

☎ **01875 813333.**

●● F/G

Holiday park on coast half hour east of Edinburgh with wide range of facilities and entertainment. Caravans for 5 people adapted for disabled guests. Entrance ramp. Lounge/kitchen open plan. Two bedrooms, sliding door 75cm, ⟲ in double. Shower room 75cm, handrails, restricted ⟲, no space by WC. Wheelchair hire available. Open Mid March-October.

Apply: Haven & British Holidays ☎ 0870 242222.

W www.havenholidays.com

Rates: on application.

MADDISTON, Falkirk

Avon Glen Chalet Park

Melons Place. Maddiston, Falkirk FK2 0BT.

☎ **01324 861166.**

@ **seatondorothy@aol.com**

●● F/G ★★★

One chalet, of 3, by River Avon between Falkirk and Bathgate. Ramp or 2 steps on approach. Entrance step, portable ramp available. Open plan lounge/kitchen, cooker controls useable from wheelchair. Twin and double bedrooms, ⟲ in one. Shower room 32", ⟲, roll-in shower, handrails, space by WC. Shower seat and raised WC seat available. Veranda overlooking river.

Rates: from £290-£430 per week (2007).

MELROSE, Scottish Borders

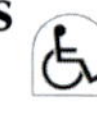

Eildon Holiday Cottages

Dingleton Mains, Melrose TD6 9HS.

W **www.eildon.co.uk**

@ **info@eildon.co.uk**

●●● I/F/G/H ★★★

Five of 6 cottages designed for disabled people, sleeping 2-6. Entrances level, min. door width 34". 3 cottages have roll-in showers and 2 have ground floor bathrooms; all have handrails and space for side transfer. Electric hoists in 2 cottages. Propad mattress, commode, raised WC seat and other equipment available. One cottage kept smoke and animal-free. Immediate surroundings level. Available April-November.

Apply: Jill Hart. ☎ 01896 823258.

Rates: from £290-£670 per week (2007).

WEST CALDER, West Lothian

Steading Cottage

Crosswoodhill Farm,
West Calder EH55 8LP.

W **www.crosswoodhill.co.uk**

●● I/F/G ★★★★

Cottage on farm 18 miles west of Edinburgh, north side of Pentland Hills. Entrance level, 35½". Lounge/kitchen open plan, no adaptations. Single and double ground floor bedrooms. Bathroom 32½", ⟲, roll-in shower, handrails, space for side transfer to WC. Raised WC seat available. Double bedroom also has en suite shower room. Family bedroom and WC upstairs. Another two cottages with ground floor accommodation available. Owner a nurse.

Apply: Geraldine Hamilton ☎ 01501 785205.

@ cottages@crosswoodhill.co.uk

Rates: from £350-£760 per week (2007).

SOUTH WEST SCOTLAND
ACCOMMODATION WITH MEALS

AYR, Ayrshire
Ramada Ayr

Dalblair Road, Ayr KA7 1UG.
☎ **01292 269331.**
@ **sales.ayr@ramadajarvis.co.uk**
●● D/E/I/F/G ★★★

Hotel in coastal town. Reserved parking bays. Entrance from car park level, 84cm; 6 steps at main entrance. Public rooms ground floor, open plan. Unisex WC 1st floor, adapted cubicles in ground and 1st floor toilets. Lift 76cm, inside 160x96cm. 3 bedrooms adapted for disabled guests with shower rooms 79cm, roll-in shower with seat and handrails, no ↺ or space by WC. Other bedrooms level.

Rates: on application.

BIGGAR, Lanarkshire
Glenholm Guesthouse

Broughton, by Biggar, Tweeddale ML12 6JF.
☎ **01899 830408.**
W **www.glenholm.co.uk**
●● D/E/I/F/G 

Farm guesthouse. Entrance level. Dining room and lounge level. Unisex WC. Twin bedroom designed for disabled guests. Shower room ↺, roll-in shower with seat, handrails, space by WC. Other bedrooms upstairs. Computer courses offered, training room accessible.

Rates: from £33-£35 single BB (2007).

CASTLE DOUGLAS, Dumfries & Galloway
Douglas House

63 Queen Street, Castle Douglas DG7 1HX.
☎ **01556 503262.**
W **www.douglas-house.com**
●● D/E/G

Bed & breakfast house near centre of market town. Street parking. Ramp available for entrance step. Dining room and lounge ground floor 79cm. Double/twin bedroom designed for disabled guests. Bathroom 72cm, ↺, handrails, space by bath and WC. Also single room on ground floor and twin and double upstairs. Teletext TV. Regular disabled guests.

Rates: from £35-£45 per person sharing (2007).

CLYDEBANK, Dunbartonshire
The Beardmore Hotel

Beardmore Street, Clydebank G81 4SA.
☎ **0141 951 6000.**
W **www.thebeardmore.com**
●● D/E/F/G ★★★★

High-class hotel. Parking bays can be reserved. Entrance level with slow revolving door and swing door. Public rooms ground floor, level. Unisex WC. Lift 110cm, inside 150x135cm. Six bedrooms designed for disabled guests. Bathrooms 92cm, ↺, handrails, seat at head of bath, space for side transfer to WC. The other 150 bedrooms level ↺.

Rates: on application.

DUMFRIES, Dumfries & Galloway

Aston Hotel Dumfries

Crichton Estate, Bankend Road, Dumfries DG1 4TA.

☎ 0845 634 0205.

W www.astonhotels.co.uk

●● D/E/F/G ★★★

Hotel south of town by Conference Centre. Reserved parking bays. Entrance automatic door. Low reception desk. Public rooms level. Unisex WC. Lift to upper floors. 3 bedrooms designed for disabled guests. Shower room, handrails, space by WC. Other bedrooms level.

Rates: from £89 per room midweek (2007).

GLASGOW

Campanile Glasgow

10 Tunnel Street, Glasgow G3 8HL.

☎ 0141 287 7701.

@ glasgow@campanile-hotels.com

●●

Hotel near Exhibition Centre and M8 Junction 19. Reserved parking bays. Public rooms level. Unisex WC. 6 bedrooms designed for disabled guests. Bathroom, handrails, space for side transfer. Other ground floor bedrooms level. See page 31.

Rates: on application.

Express by Holiday Inn Glasgow Theatreland

165 West Nile Street, Glasgow G1 2RL.

☎ 0141 331 6800.

@ info@hiexpressglasgow.co.uk

●● E/I/F/G 

Limited service hotel in city centre. Entrance level. Low reception desk. Open plan lounge/bar and unisex WC ground floor. Breakfast room 1st floor. Lift 80cm, inside 110x142cm. 2 double bedrooms designed for disabled guests. Shower rooms 84cm, roll-in shower and seat, handrails, space by WC. Other bedrooms level. Visual and vibrating alarms and induction loop available. Restaurant adjoining.

Rates: £79 per room BB (2007).

Hilton Glasgow

1 William Street, Glasgow G3 8HT.

☎ 0141 204 5555.

W www.hilton.co.uk/glasgow

●●  D/E/I/G 

Luxury city centre hotel. Reserved parking bays. Entrance level, revolving and swing doors. Public areas level. Unisex WC. Lifts 39", inside 40½"x67". Two twin bedrooms designed for disabled guests. Bathrooms, handrails, space for side transfer to bath and WC. Other bedrooms level; two with visual alarms. Vibrating pillow and wheelchair available.

Rates: on application.

Holiday Inn Glasgow City Centre Theatreland

161 West Nile Street, Glasgow G1 2RL.

☎ 0141 352 8300.  **www.higlasgow.com**

●● D/E/I/F/G ★★★

City centre hotel. Entrance level, automatic door. Open plan public rooms ground floor, level. Unisex WC. Lifts 80cm, inside 110x140cm. 5 double/twin bedrooms designed for disabled guests. Shower rooms 79cm, ⟲, roll-in shower with seat, handrails, space by WC. Other bedrooms level. Teletext TV, visual and vibrating alarms, induction loop and large print menus available.

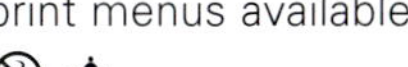

Rates: on application.

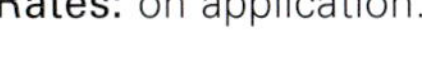

Ibis Hotel Glasgow

220 West Regent Street, Glasgow G2 4DQ.

☎ 0141 225 6000. @ H3139@accor.com

●● D/E/G ★★

Hotel in city centre. Entrance level. Public rooms open plan. Lifts to upper floors. Six bedrooms with bathrooms designed for disabled guests. Flashing and vibrating alarms. Other bedrooms level.

Rates: from £51-£53 per room (2008).

Jurys Inn Glasgow

80 Jamaica Street, Glasgow G1 4QE.

☎ 0141 314 4800.

@ jurysinnglasgow@jurysdoyle.com

●● D/E/I/F/G ★★★

Large modern hotel in city centre. NCP car park nearby. Level entrance, automatic doors. Low reception desk. Public rooms ground floor, open plan. Unisex WC. Lifts 89cm, inside 140x160cm. 20 twin and double bedrooms designed for disabled guests. Bathrooms 81cm, ⟲, handrails, space by bath and WC. Two rooms have roll-in shower with seat. Other 300 bedrooms level.

Rates: from £69 per room (2007).

Novotel Glasgow Centre

181 Pitt Street, Glasgow G2 4DT.

☎ 0141 222 2775.

@ H3136@accor.com

●● D/E/I/F/G ★★★

City centre hotel. Bays in basement car park can be reserved. Entrance level. Low reception desk. Public rooms ground floor open plan; 3 steps to restaurant, ramp available. Unisex WC. Lift to all floors. 8 bedrooms designed for disabled guests. Bathrooms have folding door, ⟲, handrails, space by bath and WC. Other bedrooms level. Vibrating alarms available.

Rates: on application.

GLASGOW AIRPORT, Renfrewshire

Express by Holiday Inn Glasgow Airport

St Andrews Drive, Glasgow Airport, Paisley PA3 2TJ.

☎ 0141 842 1100.

W www.expressglasgowairport.com

●● D/E/F/G

Limited service hotel with walkway to airport terminal. Reserved parking bays. Entrance level, automatic doors. Low reception desk. Public rooms open plan. Unisex WC. Lift inside 130x140cm. 7 double bedrooms designed for disabled guests 88cm, ⟲, visual smoke alarm. Shower room 82cm, roll-in shower with seat, handrails, space by WC. Other bedrooms level.

Rates: on application.

Holiday Inn Glasgow Airport

Abbotsinch, Paisley PA3 2TR.
☎ 0870 400 9031.
@ reservations-glasgow@ihg.com
●● D/E/I/F/G

Hotel facing airport terminal. Reserved parking bays. Entrance ramp or 2 steps, automatic door. Low reception desk. Open plan public rooms, level. Unisex WC. Lift 77cm, inside 120x180cm. Three 2-person bedrooms adapted for disabled guests 69cm, ⟲. Bathrooms 89cm, ⟲, handrails, space by bath and WC. Other bedrooms level.

Rates: from £80 room only (2007).

GREENOCK, Inverclyde

Express by Holiday Inn Greenock

Cartburn, Greenock PA15 1AE.
☎ 01475 786666.
W www.hiexpressgreenock.co.uk
●● D/I/F/G

Modern hotel in town centre. Reserved parking bays. Entrance level, automatic doors. Low reception desk. Public rooms level, open plan. Unisex WC. Lift 79.5cm, inside 107x139cm. Two twin bedrooms designed for disabled guests with wheel-in shower rooms ⟲, handrails, space by WC, alarm call. Also two double rooms accessible to wheelchair users. Other bedrooms level. Vibrating alarm pad available.

Rates: from £59.95 per night BB (2007).

IRVINE, Ayrshire

Menzies Hotel

46 Annick Road, Irvine KA11 4LD.
☎ 0870 3339156. @ irvine@thistle.co.uk
●● D/E/I/G ★★★

Modern hotel. Reserved parking bays. Entrance ramp, 64". Main public rooms open plan, level except 3 steps to part of bar. Unisex WC. One bedroom adapted for disabled guests. Bathroom 36", ⟲, handrails, space for side transfer to bath and WC. Other ground floor bedrooms level.

Rates: on application.

KILMARNOCK, Ayrshire

Best Western Fenwick Hotel

A77 Ayr Road, Fenwick,
By Kilmarnock KA3 6AU.
☎ 01560 600478.
W www.thefenwickhotel.co.uk
●● D/E/I/F/G ★★★

Hotel and country inn north of Kilmarnock. Reserved parking bays. Ramp with handrails to entrance 48". Public rooms ground floor, level. Braille menus. Unisex WC. 8 double or twin bedrooms on ground floor. Bathrooms 35½", ⟲, space by bath and WC.

Rates: from £70 double BB (2007).

LENNOXTOWN, Dunbartonshire

Glazert Country House Hotel

25 Milton Road, Lennoxtown,
Glasgow G65 7DJ.
☎ 01360 310790.
W www.glazert.co.uk
●● D/E/I/F/G

Family-run hotel north of Glasgow. Entrance double doors. Public rooms level. Unisex WC. Two ground floor bedrooms, twin and double, 79cm. Bathrooms 75cm, handrails, no ⟲. Regular disabled guests.

Rates: from £40 single, £55 double BB (2007).

South West Scotland – accommodation with meals

MOFFAT, Dumfries & Galloway

Lochhouse Farm Retreat Centre

Beattock, Moffat DG10 9SG.
☎/Textphone: 01683 300451.
W www.lochhousefarm.com

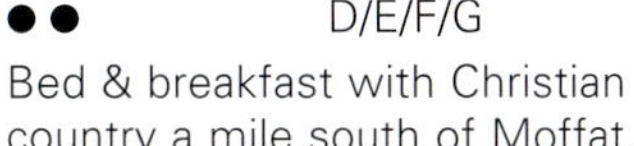

●● D/E/F/G ★★★

Bed & breakfast with Christian ethos in country a mile south of Moffat. Reserved parking spaces. Ramp to entrance, 84cm. Dining room and lounge level. Ground floor twin bedroom, level. Shower room with roll-in shower, ⟲, handrails. Other bedrooms upstairs. Self-catering cottages also available, see page 387.

Rates: from £25 per person BB (2007).

MOTHERWELL, Lanarkshire

Express by Holiday Inn Strathclyde M74

Strathclyde Country Park,
Hamilton Road, Motherwell ML1 3RB.
☎ 01698 858585. w www.hiexpress.co.uk

●● E/I/F/G ★★★

Limited service hotel near M74 junction 5. Reserved parking bays. Dropped kerb at entrance. Public rooms level, open plan. 6 double bedrooms designed for disabled guests. Shower rooms 30", ⟲, two with roll-in showers, 4 with shower tray with seat, handrails, space by WC. Waterproof sheets available. Other bedrooms level.

Rates: on application.

NEW LANARK, Lanarkshire

New Lanark Mill Hotel

Mill One, New Lanark Mills,
Lanark ML11 9DB.
☎ 01555 667200. W www.newlanark.org

●● D/E/I/F/G ★★★★

Hotel in converted mill at World Heritage Site. Entrance level. Low reception desk. Ground floor lounge, bar and unisex WC. Restaurant 3rd floor. Lift 32" to all floors. 5 twin bedrooms designed for disabled guests. Shower rooms 36", ⟲, roll-in shower, handrails, space for side transfer to WC. Other bedrooms level.

Rates: from £54.50 per person BB (2007).

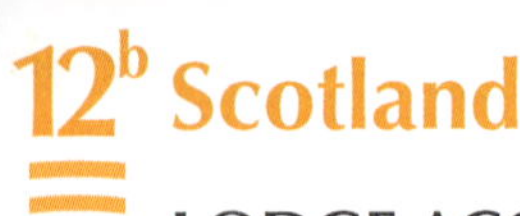

LODGE ACCOMMODATION

There are Days Inn (see page 34), Etap (see page 34), Premier Travel Inn (see page 38) and Travelodge (see page 38) properties in the following areas in this region.

Abington – Days Inn ☎ 01864 502782
Annandale Water – Premier Travel Inn ☎ 0870 197 7163
Ayr – Premier Travel Inn ☎ 0870 197 7020
Travelodge ☎ 0870 085 0950
Bearsden – Premier Travel Inn ☎ 0870 990 6532
Bellshill – Premier Travel Inn ☎ 0870 197 7106
Cambuslang – Premier Travel Inn ☎ 0870 197 7306
Cumbernauld – Premier Travel Inn ☎ 0870 197 7108
Dumbarton – Travelodge ☎ 0870 191 1633
Dumfries – Premier Travel Inn ☎ 0870 197 7078
Travelodge ☎ 0870 191 1634
East Kilbride – Premier Travel Inn ☎ 0870 197 7110
East Kilbride, Peel Park – Premier Travel Inn ☎ 0870 990 6542
Glasgow – Etap ☎ 0870 222 2288
Premier Travel Inn ☎ 0870 238 3320
Travelodge ☎ 0870 191 1641
Glasgow Airport – Premier Travel Inn ☎ 0870 238 3321
Travelodge ☎ 0141 889 1359
Glasgow, East – Premier Travel Inn ☎ 0870 197 7109
Glasgow, Paisley Road – Travelodge ☎ 0870 191 1642
Glasgow, Stepps – Premier Travel Inn ☎ 0870 197 7111
Greenock – Premier Travel Inn ☎ 0870 197 7120
Gretna – Days Inn ☎ 01461 337566
Hamilton – Premier Travel Inn ☎ 0870 197 7124
Kilmarnock – Premier Travel Inn ☎ 0870 197 7148
Travelodge ☎ 0870 191 1649
Milngavie – Premier Travel Inn ☎ 0870 197 7112
Motherwell – Premier Travel Inn ☎ 0870 197 7164
Paisley – Premier Travel Inn ☎ 0870 197 7113

SELF-CATERING ACCOMMODATION

AYR, Ayrshire

Craig Tara Holiday Park

Dunure Road, Ayr KA7 4LB.

☎ **01292 265141.**

●● F/G

Holiday park on coast 4 miles from Ayr with wide range of facilities and entertainment. Caravans for 5 people adapted for disabled guests. Entrance ramp. Lounge/kitchen open plan. Two bedrooms, sliding door 75cm, ⟲ in double. Shower room 75cm, handrails, restricted ⟲, no space by WC. Wheelchair hire available. Open Mid March-October.

Apply: Haven & British Holidays

☎ 0870 242222.

W www.havenholidays.com

Rates: on application.

Sundrum Castle Holiday Park

By Ayr KA6 5JH.

●● I/F/G ★★★★

Holiday park in countryside near Ayr with range of facilities. Caravans for 5 people adapted for disabled guests. Entrance ramp. Lounge/kitchen open plan. Two bedrooms, sliding door 75cm, ⟲ in double. Shower room 75cm, handrails, restricted ⟲. Open March-November.

Ⓟ

Apply: Parkdean Holidays

☎ 0871 641 2066.

W www.parkdeanscotland.co.uk

Rates: Holiday homes from £169 per week. Short breaks (3 or 4 nights) from £102

BIGGAR, Lanarkshire

Carmichael Country Cottages

Carmichael, by Biggar, Clydesdale.

●● I/G ★★-★★★★

Ten cottages, for 2-6 people, with ground floor accommodation. No special adaptations but rooms level and most doors 31". Some bathrooms ⟲, space for side transfer. Portable ramp available for cottages with entrance steps. Check requirements when booking. Ramp to farm shop and visitor centre with restaurant.

Ⓟ

Apply: Estate Office, Westmains, Carmichael, by Biggar ML12 6PG.

☎ 01899 308336.

W www.carmichael.co.uk

Rates: from £205-£555 per week (2007).

DUMFRIES, Dumfries & Galloway

Cairnyard Holiday Lodges

Nether Cairnyard, Beeswing, Dumfries DG2 8JE.

●● F/G ★★★

Four lodges, two for 2 and two for 4 people, in grounds of country house 5 miles from town. Entrances ramped. Lounge/kitchen open plan. Bedrooms 32", ⟲. Bath or shower rooms 32", ⟲.

Ⓟ

Apply: Mr Farnell ☎ 01387 730218.

W www.cairnyard.co.uk

Rates: from £220-£427 per week (2007).

Gubhill Farm

Ae Forest, Dumfries DG1 1RL.

●● I/F/G ★★★

"Stockmans Cottage" for 4 people on farm north of Dumfries. Ramp to entrance 80cm. Lounge/kitchen open plan, controls useable from wheelchair. Double and twin bedrooms 80cm. Shower room ↺, roll-in shower with seat, handrails, space for side transfer to, and ceiling hook over WC.

Apply: David & Gill Stewart
☎ 01387 860648. W www.gubhill.co.uk
Rates: from £217-£485 per week (2007).

Nunland Country Holidays

Lochfoot, Dumfries DG2 8PZ.
☎ 01387 730214. W www.nunland.co.uk

●● I/F/G ★★★★

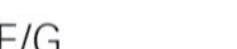

Self-catering cottages in grounds of country house 5 miles west of Dumfries. "Solway Lodge" designed for disabled people. Entrance level 80cm or French window 150cm. 78cm door to open plan lounge/kitchen, controls useable from wheelchair. Twin and double bedrooms, ↺ in double. Sliding door from double bedroom to shower room ↺, roll-in shower with seat, handrails, space by WC. Veranda level. Teletext TV.

Apply: Mr & Mrs Chambers.
Rates: from £259-£519 per week (2007).

GATEHOUSE OF FLEET, Dumfries & Galloway

Rusko Holidays

Gatehouse of Fleet, Casrtle Douglas DG7 2BS. **☎ 01557 814215.**
W www.ruskoholidays.co.uk

●● I/F/G ★★★★

Holiday cottages on edge of nature reserve and forest park, near coast. "Upper Rusko Cottage" designed for disabled people. Ramp to front door, back door by parking level. Door widths 85cm. Lounge/kitchen open plan, controls useable from wheelchair. Twin bedroom ↺ Own bathroom ↺, roll-in shower, handrails, space by bath and WC. Second twin bedroom and bunkroom. Separate shower room. Bed blocks and waterproof sheets if required. Large print brochures, colour contrasts and Teletext TV available. Another unit has ground floor accommodation with one step.

Rates: from £449-£677 (2007).

MAYBOLE, Ayrshire

Royal Artillery Cottage

Culzean Castle, Maybole.

●● ★★

Cottage adapted for disabled people in grounds of Culzean Castle near South Ayrshire coast. Lounge, kitchen with lowered units, two twin bedrooms and bathroom.

Apply: National Trust for Scotland
☎ 0844 493 2100
Rates: on application.

MOFFAT, Dumfries & Galloway

Lochhouse Farm Retreat Centre

Beattock, Moffat DG10 9SG.

☎/Textphone: 01683 300451.

www.lochhousefarm.com

 F/G 

2 holiday cottages attached to bed & breakfast a mile south of Moffat. Ramp to walkway. Entrance 83cm, level. Lounge/kitchen open plan with conservatory. Bedroom with double and single beds. Shower room with roll-in shower and handrails. For information on bed & breakfast see page 383.

Rates: from £200-£350 per week (2007).

SANDHEAD, Dumfries & Galloway

Culmorebridge Cottages

Sandhead, Stranraer DG9 9DX.

☎ 01776 830539.

www.culmorebridge.co.uk

●● I/F/G 

Four cottages designed for disabled people on woodland, coastal site. Entrance level. Doors 90cm. Open plan lounge/kitchen; controls useable from wheelchair. Twin and 2 double bedrooms. Bathroom and roll-in shower room. Level outside decking.

Rates: from £350-£550 per week (2007).

SOUTHERNESS, Dumfries & Galloway

Southerness Holiday Village

By Dumfries DG2 8AZ.

●● E/F/G 

On the Solway Firth, 18 miles south of Dumfries. 3 timber lodges adapted for disabled guests, sleeping 6. Bathrooms have roll-in shower with seat and handrails. Restaurant, shops and entertainment available. Open March-October.

Apply: Parkdean Holidays

☎ 0871 641 2066.

parkdeanscotland.co.uk

Rates: Holiday homes from £169 per week. Short breaks (3 or 4 nights) from £102

EASTERN SCOTLAND
ACCOMMODATION WITH MEALS

ABERDEEN

Aberdeen Marriott Hotel

Overton Circle, Dyce, Aberdeen AB21 7AZ.
☎ **01224 770011.**

●● D/E/G ★★★★

Hotel near airport. Entrance level. Lounge and bar level. Adapted WC cubicles. Four bedrooms designed for disabled guests. Bathroom with handrails and space by bath and WC. Other bedrooms level. Changing facilities for disabled people in Leisure Club.

Rates: on application.

Express By Holiday Inn Aberdeen City Centre

Chapel Street, Aberdeen AB10 1SQ.
☎ **01224 623500.**
www.hieaberdeen.co.uk

●● D/E/I/F/G ★★★

Limited service hotel in city centre. Reserved parking bays. Entrance level, semi-automatic door. Low reception desk. Open plan public rooms. Unisex WC. Lift 36", inside 42"x54". 8 double bedrooms designed for disabled guests. Shower rooms 35", ⟲, roll-in shower, handrails, space by WC. Other bedrooms level. Vibrating alarms and Teletext TV.

Rates: from £45-£99 per room BB (2007).

Holiday Inn Aberdeen

Claymore Drive, Bridge of Don, Aberdeen AB23 8BL.
☎ **0870 400 9046.**
@ **reservations@hiaberdeen.com**

●● D/E/I/F/G ★★★★

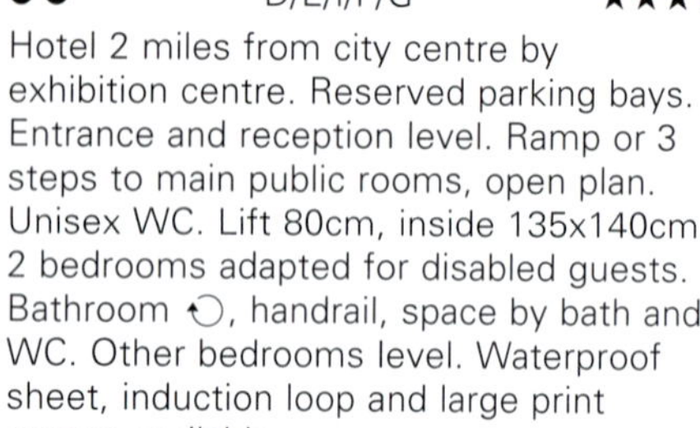

Hotel 2 miles from city centre by exhibition centre. Reserved parking bays. Entrance and reception level. Ramp or 3 steps to main public rooms, open plan. Unisex WC. Lift 80cm, inside 135x140cm. 2 bedrooms adapted for disabled guests. Bathroom ⟲, handrail, space by bath and WC. Other bedrooms level. Waterproof sheet, induction loop and large print menus available.

Rates: on application.

Holiday Inn Aberdeen West

Westhill Drive, Westhill, Aberdeenshire AB32 6TT.
☎ **01224 270300.**
@ **reservations@hiaberdeenwest.co.uk**

●● D/E/I/F/G ★★★★

Hotel west of city. Reserved parking bays. Entrance level, automatic door. Low reception desk. Public rooms ground floor. Unisex WC. Lift to all floors 90cm, inside 130x150cm. Bedrooms designed for disabled guests on each floor. Shower rooms ⟲, roll-in shower with seat, handrails, space by WC. Other bedrooms level. Vibrating alarms available and Teletext TV.

Rates: on application.

The Marcliffe Hotel & Spa

North Deeside Road, Aberdeen AB1 9YA.

☎ **01224 861000.** **www.marcliffe.com**

 D/E/F/G 

Luxury hotel in suburb. Reserved parking bay. Entrance level, automatic doors. Main public rooms level, open plan. Unisex WC. Lift 59″, inside 59″x78″. Twin bedroom designed for disabled guests. Bathroom ⟲, roll-in shower, handrails, space for side transfer to bath and WC. Other bedrooms level. Paved garden paths.

Rates: on application.

Thistle Aberdeen Airport

Argyll Road, Dyce, Aberdeen AB21 0AF.

☎ **01224 725252.**

Aberdeen.Airport@Thistle.co.uk

 D/E/F/G 

Hotel near airport. Reserved parking bays. Ramp or 3 steps to entrance 160cm. Public rooms level. Unisex WC. One bedroom designed for disabled guests. Shower room 87cm, ⟲, roll-in shower, handrails, space for side transfer to WC. Waterproof sheets available. Other ground floor rooms level.

Rates: on application.

ABERNETHY, Perthshire

Gattaway Farm

Abernethy PH2 9LQ.

☎ **01738 850746.**

www.smoothhound.co.uk/hotels/gattaway

●● D/E/I/F/G ★★★

Farmhouse bed & breakfast. Entrance from parking 1 step, ramp available; front entrance 3 steps. Dining room and lounge level. One twin bedroom level. Shower room ⟲, roll-in shower with seat, handrails, space for side transfer to WC. Waterproof sheets available. 2 double bedrooms upstairs. Terrace level; garden 3 steps. Evening meals by arrangement.

Rates: from £45 per room BB (2007).

BLAIRGOWRIE, Perthshire

Kinloch House Hotel

by Blairgowrie PH10 6SG.

☎ **01250 884237.**

www.kinlochhouse.com

●● D/F 

Country house hotel west of Blairgowrie. Ramp to entrance, 38″. Public rooms level. WCs not adapted. Four twin bedrooms level. Bathrooms ⟲, handrails, space for side transfer to bath and WC. Toilet frame available.

Rates: on application.

BROUGHTY FERRY, Angus

The Fort Hotel

58/60 Fort Street, Broughty Ferry, Dundee DD5 2AB.

☎ **01382 737999.** **www.fort-hotel.com**

●● D/E

Small hotel. Reserved parking bay. Entrance ramp. Restaurant level. Ramp to bar and lounge. Unisex WC. Ground floor bedroom designed for disabled guests. Shower room ⟲, roll-in shower, handrails, space for side transfer to WC.

Rates: from £60 twin per night BB (2007).

BUCHLYVIE, Stirlingshire

Upper Gartinstarry

Buchlyvie FK8 3PD.

☎ **01360 850309.**

@ **thegoldings@bigfoot.com**

●● D/E/I/F/G

Rural guesthouse between Stirling and Loch Lomond. Reserved parking bay. Entrance ramp or 2 steps. Dining room and lounge level. Family bedroom level 30", ⟲. Shower room 33", roll-in shower with seat, handrails, space for side transfer to WC. Also a level double bedroom.

Rates: from £25 per person BB (2007).

CALLANDER, Perthshire

Roman Camp Hotel

Callander FK17 8BG.

☎ **01877 330003.**

W **www.roman-camp-hotel.co.uk**

●● D/E/I/G ★★★★

Country house hotel. Entrance level, 48". Restaurant level. Step to lounge and bar. WCs with handrails. Ground floor twin bedroom. Bathroom 30", ⟲, handrails, shower seat, space by WC. 6 other ground floor bedrooms.

Rates: from £135 per night BB (2007).

CRIEFF, Perthshire

Ancaster BLESMA Home

Alligan Road, Crieff PH3 3JU.

☎ **01764 652480.**

@ **blesma.crieff@btconnect.com**

●●●●●

BLESMA nursing and residential home for disabled ex-servicemen and women. Respite and holiday care offered in twin bedrooms with their own bathrooms. 24 hour nursing cover. Outings and entertainment arranged.

Rates: on application.

DRYMEN, Stirlingshire

Rowardennan Youth Hostel

Rowardennan, by Drymen G63 0AR.

☎ **0870 004 1148.**

●● D/E/F/G ★★★★

Hostel by Loch Lomond. Ramp or 4 steps on approach. Entrance 48". Dining room level. Lounge 2 steps. 8 ground floor family rooms with bunks. Unisex WC. Roll-in shower room, ⟲, no handrails. For more information on youth hostels see page 34.

Rates: from £13-£14 adult per night (2007).

DUNDEE, Angus

Swallow Hotel Dundee

Kingsway West, Invergowrie, Dundee DD2 5JT.

☎ **01382 641122.**

@ **res.dundee@crermgmt.com**

●● D/E/F/G ★★★★

Hotel in country. Reserved parking space. Entrance level, automatic door. Public rooms level, open plan. Two twin bedrooms level, limited ⟲. Bathrooms ⟲, space for side transfer to bath and WC. Some other level bedrooms.

Rates: from £94 single weekdays (2007).

DUNFERMLINE, Fife

Express by Holiday Inn Dunfermline

Halbeath, Dunfermline KY11 8DY.

01383 748220.

www.hiexpressdunfermlibe.co.uk

●● E/I/F/G

Limited service hotel 1½ miles from city centre near M90 J3. Reserved parking bays. Entrance level, automatic doors. Low reception desk, Public rooms level, open plan. Unisex WC. Lift 90x140 cm. Five family bedrooms designed for disabled guests. Shower rooms 94cm, , roll-in shower, handrails, space by WC. Waterproof sheets available. Other bedrooms level.

Rates: from £49 per room (2007).

Pitbauchlie House Hotel

Aberdour Road, Dunfermline KY11 4PB.

01383 722282.

info@pitbauchlie.com

●● D/E/F/G ★★★

Hotel in own grounds south of town. Reserved parking bays. Entrance level, double doors. Public rooms level. Unisex WC. Double bedroom designed for disabled guests . Bathroom 95cm , space for side transfer to WC. Other ground floor bedrooms level.

Rates: on application.

DUNKELD, Perthshire

Hilton Dunkeld House Hotel

Dunkeld PH8 0HX.

01350 727771.

www.hilton.co.uk/dunkeld

●● D/E/F/G ★★★★

Country house hotel with grounds leading down to River Tay. Reserved parking bays by front and side doors. Ramps at main and side door. Main public rooms ground floor, level. Wheelchair lift to conference rooms and leisure club. Unisex WC. Lift to all floors 80cm, inside 95x1.65cm, manual doors. Two ground floor bedrooms adapted for disabled guests. Bathrooms 100cm, , roll-in shower with seat, handrails, space by bath and WC. Other level bedrooms available. Changing room and WC for disabled people in Leisure Club.

Rates: on application.

LUNDIN LINKS, Fife

Swallow Old Manor Hotel

Lundin Links, Nr. St Andrews KY8 6AJ.

01333 320368.

● D/E/F/G ★★★★

Country house hotel overlooking Largo Bay. Reserved parking bay. Main and car park entrances level. Public rooms level, min. door width 90cm. Unisex WC. 8 ground floor bedrooms . Bathrooms , no adaptations.

Rates: on application.

MONTROSE, Angus

Best Western Links Hotel

Mid Links, Montrose DD10 8RL.
☎ 01674 671000.
W www.bw-linkshotel.co.uk
●● D/E/F/G ★★★★

Hotel by park in coastal town. Reserved parking bays. Entrance level. Public rooms ground floor. Unisex WC. One ground floor bedroom ⟲. Bathroom 84cm, ⟲, space by bath and WC, shower/bath seat. Other bedrooms upstairs.

Rates: from £78-£109 double BB (2006).

PERTH, Perthshire

Express by Holiday Inn Perth

200 Dunkeld Road, Perth PH1 3AQ.
☎ 01738 636666.
W www.hiexressperth.co.uk
●● E/F/G

Hotel north of city near M90 junction 10. Reserved parking bays. Entrance level. Low reception desk. Public rooms open plan. Unisex WC ground floor. Lift inside 130x130cm. 5 double bedrooms on 1st floor designed for disabled guests 88cm, ⟲, visual smoke alarm. Shower room 82cm, roll-in shower with seat, handrails, space by WC. Other bedrooms level.

Ⓟ 🚭

Rates: on application.

Innkeepers Lodge Perth City Centre

18 Dundee Road, Perth PH2 7AB.
☎ 01738 624471.
●● D/E/I/F/G ★★

Hotel near city centre overlooking river. Reserved parking bays. Entrance ramp with handrails. Public rooms level or ramp. Unisex WCs. Lift 88cm. Two bedrooms designed for disabled guests. Shower room 80cm, ⟲, handrails, roll-in shower with seat, space by WC. Other bedrooms level.

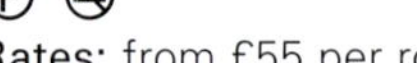

Rates: from £55 per room BB (2007).

Sunbank House Hotel

50 Dundee Road, Perth PH2 7BA.
☎ 01738 624882.
W www.sunbankhouse.com
●● ★★★★

Small hotel near city centre. Entrance level. Dining room and lounge level. One ground floor bedroom 32", ⟲. Bathroom 30" sliding door, ⟲, handrails, space for side transfer to bath and WC. Wet room also available.

Ⓟ 🚭

Rates: from £40 per person BB (2007).

ST ANDREWS, Fife

Rufflets Country House

Strathkinness Low Road,
St Andrews KY16 9TX.
☎ 01334 472594. W www.rufflets.co.uk
●● D/E/F/G ★★★★★

Country house hotel. Reserved parking bays. Entrance ramp, 37". Public rooms level. Adapted WC cubicles. 2 ground floor bedrooms, ⟲ in one. Bathrooms 33", ⟲, one has shower with seat, handrails, space for side transfer to WC. Formal gardens level.

Ⓟ 🚭

Rates: on application.

STIRLING, Stirlingshire

Express by Holiday Inn Stirling

Springkerse Business Park,
Stirling FK7 7XH.
☎ 01786 449922. W www.hiex-stirling.com
●● E/F/G ★★★

Limited service hotel in suburb near M9/M80 junction. Reserved parking bays. Entrance level. Low reception desk. Public rooms open plan. Unisex WC ground floor. Lift inside 130x130cm. 4 double bedrooms on 1st floor designed for disabled guests 88cm, ⟲, visual smoke alarm. Shower room 82cm, roll-in shower with seat, handrails, space by WC. Other bedrooms level.

Rates: on application.

Stirling Youth Hostel

St John Street, Stirling FK8 1EA.

☎ **0870 004 1149.** @

stirling@syha.org.uk

●● E/G ★★★★

Town centre hostel. Main entrance ramp, 48". Reception, dining room and members kitchen ground floor. No lift to 1st floor TV lounge, meeting room and laundry. Unisex WC. One twin bedroom with shower room/WC designed for disabled people. Other bedrooms upstairs. For more information on Youth Hostels see page 34.

Rates: from £15 adult overnight (2007).

LODGE ACCOMMODATION

There are Premier Travel Inn (see page 38) and Travelodge (see page 38) properties in the following areas in this region.

Aberdeen – Premier Travel Inn ☎ **0870 990 6300**
Travelodge ☎ **0870 191 1617**
Aberdeen Airport – Travelodge ☎ **0870 191 1809**
Aberdeen, Bucksburn – Travelodge ☎ **0870 191 1618**
Aberdeen, North – Premier Travel Inn ☎ **0870 197 7012**
Aberdeen, South – Premier Travel Inn ☎ **0870 197 7013**
Aberdeen, West – Premier Travel Inn ☎ **0870 990 6430**
Aberdeen, Westhill – Premier Travel Inn ☎ **0870 990 6348**
Dundee – Premier Travel Inn ☎ **0870 197 7079**
Travelodge ☎ **0870 191 1801**
Dundee, East – Premier Travel Inn ☎ **0870 990 6324**
Dundee, North – Premier Travel Inn ☎ **0870 990 6420**
Dundee, West – Premier Travel Inn ☎ **0870 197 7081**
Travelodge ☎ **0870 191 1635**
Dunfermline – Premier Travel Inn ☎ **0870 600 1486**
Travelodge ☎ **0870 191 1787**
Glenrothes – Premier Travel Inn ☎ **0870 197 7114**
Travelodge ☎ **0870 191 1778**

Scotland

Kinross – Travelodge .... ☎ 0870 191 1651
Monifieth – Premier Travel Inn .... ☎ 0870 197 7080
Perth – Travelodge .... ☎ 0870 191 1751
Stirling – Premier Travel Inn .... ☎ 0870 197 7241
Travelodge .... ☎ 0870 191 1677

SELF-CATERING ACCOMMODATION

ABERFELDY, Perthshire
Loch Tay Lodges
Acharn, Aberfeldy.
W www.lochtaylodge.co.uk
●● E/G ★★★
Six lodges in village include a ground floor unit for up to 6 people. Entrance level, 32". Two bedrooms, ceiling hook over one bed. Bathroom/WC 33", ↻. Bath lift available. Ramp to garden.

Apply: S & J Duncan Millar, Remony, Acharn, Aberfeldy PH15 2HR. ☎ 01887 830209.
Rates: from £215-£485 per week (2007).
Discount for disabled people may be available.

BALQUHIDDER, Perthshire

Lochside Cottages
Muirlaggan, Balquhidder, Lochearnhead FK19 8PB.
●● F/G ★★★★
Two cottages beside Loch Voil. "Stable Cottage" designed for wheelchair users. Entrance level, 43" double door. Internal doors 32". Lounge/kitchen open plan, worktop 36", cooker controls useable from wheelchair. Twin and double bedrooms, the latter more suitable for wheelchair users. Shower room with roll-in shower, handrails, space by WC. Shower chair and raised WC seat available.

Apply: Mrs Catriona Oldham ☎ 01877 384219.
W www.lochsidecottages.co.uk
Rates: from £180-£395 per week (2007/8).

BLAIR ATHOLL, Perthshire
Blair Castle Caravan Park
Blair Atholl, Pitlochry PH18 5SR.
☎ 01796 481263.
W www.blaircastlecaravanpark.co.uk
●● F/G ★★★★★
Country Park for touring caravans and camping. Ramp to reception centre, shop and other facilities. Unisex WC/bathroom for tourers. 27 holidays homes for hire.
Rates: on application.

BRAEMAR, Aberdeenshire

Derry
Mar Lodge, Braemar
●● ★★★★
Ground floor apartment adapted for disabled people. Lounge/kitchen open plan. Double and twin bedrooms ↻. Bathroom/WC and separate WC.
Apply: National Trust for Scotland
☎ 0844 493 2100.
Rates: on application.

CRATHIE, Aberdeenshire

Crathie Opportunity Holidays

The Manse Courtyard, Crathie, Ballater AB35 5UL.

☎ **01339 742100.**

www.crathieholidays.org.uk

●●● I/E/F/G/H ★★★★

4 cottages designed for disabled people in Deeside between Ballater and Braemar. Entrances level. Min. door width 80cm. Open plan lounge/kitchen. Controls useable from wheelchair. Twin bedroom ⟲, ceiling track & hoist. Two cottages also have a second smaller bedroom and 2 have a 1st floor gallery. Shower room ⟲, roll-in shower with seat, handrails, Clos-o-Mat WC, adjustable height basin. Mobile hoist, shower chair, scooter and some other equipment available. One cottage allergy free. Sensory adventure playground. Teletext TV. Braille and tape information pack.

Rates: from £289-£572 per week (2007).

CRIANLARICH, Perthshire

Crianlarich Youth Hostel

Station Road, Crianlarich FK20 8QN.

☎ **0870 155 3255.**

crianiarich@syha.org.uk

●● E/G ★★★

Self-catering hostel. Ramp and kerb from car park. Ramp to reception. Lounge and kitchen level, worktops 36". One bedroom with single and bunk beds with own shower room ⟲, roll-in shower with seat, handrails, space for side transfer to WC. Also 2 dormitories with 2 and 3 sets of bunks level, 27" ⟲. Unisex WC. Washrooms 28", step to shower, handrails. Vibrating alarm available. Advance booking required. For more information on Youth Hostels see page 34.

Rates: from £12-£14 adult per night (2007).

KELTY, Fife

Benarty Holiday Accommodation

Benarty House, Kelty KY4 0HT.

● I/F/G ★★

"The Steading" bungalow for up to 6 people on farm near Country Park. Step on approach. Entrance 30". Lounge and kitchen 36", no adaptations. Double bedroom 36", ⟲. 2 twin bedrooms limited ⟲. Bathroom 30", handrail by bath, no adaptations. Shower room. Step to garden. Another cottage and two caravans also available. 'The Horsemill' has 3 bedrooms, one with wet floor showeroom, wheelchair accessible. 2 rooms double/twin and one single.

Apply: Mrs B Constable ☎ 01383 830235.

Barbara@benartyholidaycottages.co.uk

Rates: from £200-£375 per week (2007).

KINLOCH RANNOCH, Perthshire

Dunalastair Holiday Houses

Dunalastair Estate, Kinloch Rannoch, By Pitlochry PH16 5PD.

☎ **0845 230 1491**

www.dunalastair.com

●● I/F/G ★★★★

"Old Laundry Cottage" for 2 guests in Central Highlands. Ramp with handrail to entrance. Level kitchen, dining room and lounge. Four poster bed in studio style bedroom/living area ⟲. Folding bed available. Bathroom with roll-in shower, ⟲, handrails by WC. Own garden. Other cottages available.

Rates: £303-£555 per week (2007).

KIRRIEMUIR, Angus

Westmuir Holidays

1 Netherton Gardens, Westmuir, Kirriemuir DD8 5LG.
www.westmuirholidays.co.uk
●● I/F/G

Bungalow with adaptations for disabled guests in village. Ramp from driveway to entrance. Lounge, dining room and kitchen level. Single and double bedrooms. Bed raisers and mobile electric hoist available. Shower room ⟲, Roll-in shower, handrails, space by WC. Battery re-charging facility. Accessible footpaths in the area.

Ⓟ

Apply: Gwen Wood. ☎ 01828 632568.
Rates: £100 per night (2007).

PITLOCHRY, Perthshire

Burnside Apartment Hotel

19 West Moulin Road, Pitlochry PH16 5EA.
☎ 01796 472203.
www.burnsideapartments.co.uk
●● G ★★★

Apartment hotel near town centre. One 4 person unit designed for accompanied disabled guests. Entrance 34". Lounge with pull-down bed. Kitchen open plan, worktops 34". Twin bedroom 32", ⟲. Bathroom 32", ⟲, handrails, space for side transfer to bath and WC. One other ground floor studio apartment. Coffee Shop/Bistro level. Reception service and daily housekeeping.

Ⓟ

Rates: from £75-£114 daily (2007).

The Lodge

Clunie Bridge Road, Pitlochry
●● F/G

Single storey cottage in own grounds short walk from town centre. Entrance level. Door widths 32½". Lounge/dining room with patio. Kitchen controls useable from wheelchair. Bedroom with double and single beds ⟲, en suite shower room, not adapted. Also double and twin bedrooms, one with en suite bathroom. Separate shower room ⟲, roll-in shower with seat, handrails, space by WC. No small children.

Ⓟ

Apply: Anne & Graham Brown, Kilbrannan Lodge, Clunie Bridge Road, Pitlochry PH16 5JX. ☎ 01796 473616.
kilbrannan@aol.com
Rates: on application.

Tummel Valley Holiday Park

Nr. Pitlochry PH16 5SA.
●● I/F/G ★★★★

Holiday park beside river with range of facilities. Caravan for 5 people adapted for disabled guests. Entrance ramp. Lounge/kitchen open plan. Two bedrooms, sliding door 75cm, ⟲ in double. Shower room 75cm, handrails, restricted ⟲. Open March-November.

Ⓟ

Apply: Parkdean Holidays ☎ 0871 641 2066.
www.parkdeanscotland.co.uk
Rates: Holiday homes from £189 per week. Short breaks (3 or 4 nights) from £114

STIRLING, Stirlingshire

Hawthorn Cottage

West Drip Farm, by Stirling FK9 4UJ.

W www.westdripfarm.com

●● F/G ★★★★

Bungalow designed for disabled people on farm north of Stirling and M9. Ramp or 1 step to entrance. Lounge and kitchen/dining room ↺, kitchen controls not useable from wheelchair. Three bedrooms for up to 6 people in total, ↺ in double and one twin. Bathroom 32", ↺, handrails, space by bath and WC. Also one bedroom has en suite shower room with no adaptations.

Apply: Mrs Eleanor Graham ☎ 01786 472523.
Rates: from £360-£610 per week (2007).

TURRIFF, Aberdeenshire

Elmwood

Delgatie Castle, Turriff.

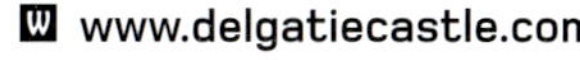

W www.delgatiecastle.com

●● I/G ★★★★

Cottage designed for disabled people in converted coach house. Entrance level. Ground floor lounge, kitchen, double bedroom and shower room with roll-in shower, handrails and space for side transfer. Waterproof sheet available. Three other bedrooms and a bathroom upstairs. Other cottages and apartments available in Castle.

Apply: Mrs Joan Johnson, Delgatie Castle, Turriff AB53 5TD. ☎ 01888 562750.
Rates: on application.

HIGHLANDS & ISLANDS

ACCOMMODATION WITH MEALS

ARDGOUR, Inverness-shire

The Inn at Ardgour

Ardgour, Fort William PH33 7AA.

☎ 01855 841225. W www.ardgour.biz

●● D/E/F/G ★★★

Inn in village on Loch Linnhe. Reserved parking bay. Entrance level. Slope to reception. Restaurant and bar ground floor. Unisex WC. One ground floor bedroom 33" ↺. Bathroom handrail by WC, space by bath and WC.

Rates: on application.

AVIEMORE, Inverness-shire

Hilton Coylumbridge

Aviemore PH22 1QN.

☎ 01479 810661.

@ reservations.coylumbridge@hilton.co.uk

●● D/E/F/G ★★★★

Country resort hotel in forested estate. Reserved parking bays. Entrance level, automatic door. Open-plan lounge/bar. Ramp to restaurant. Adapted cubicles in WCs. Two bedrooms adapted for disabled guests 84cm, ↺. Bathrooms 86cm, ↺, handrail by WC, space by bath and WC. Bath lift, raised WC seat and bedrails available. Other ground floor bedrooms level. Evening entertainment.

Rates: on application.

BALLACHULISH, Argyll

The Ballachulish Hotel

Ballachulish, Nr. Fort William PH49 4JY.

☎ **01855 811602.**

@ **reservations.ballachulish@foliohotels.com**

●● D/E/F/G 

Country house hotel. Reserved parking bays. Ramp to entrance 28½". Public rooms level. WCs not adapted. One bedroom adapted for disabled guests. Shower room 36", ↺, handrails. Six other level bedrooms, some with handrails in bathrooms.

Rates: on application.

Isles of Glencoe Hotel

Ballachulish PH49 4HL.

☎ **0871 222 3417.**

@ **reservations@freedomglen.co.uk**

●● D/E/G 

Hotel on Loch Leven. Reserved parking bays. Entrance level, 58". Public rooms level except step or steep ramp to Conservatory . Unisex WC. Double and twin bedrooms designed for disabled guests. Bathrooms ↺, handrails, space for side transfer to bath and WC. Other ground floor bedrooms level. French doors leading to lochside.

Rates: on application.

BEAULY, Inverness-shire

Priory Hotel

The Square, Beauly IV4 7BX.

☎ **01463 782309.**

W **www.priory-hotel.com**

●● D/G ★★★

Small hotel in village. Entrance step. Public rooms 2 steps, portable ramp available. Unisex WC. Lift 39", inside 96"x48". Two twin bedrooms designed for disabled guests. Bathroom ↺, handrails, space for side transfer. Other bedrooms level.

Ⓟ

Rates: from £45 per person BB (2007).

BRORA, Sutherland

Glenaveron

Golf Road, Brora, Sutherland KW8 6QS

☎ **01408 621601.**

W **www.glenaveron.co.uk**

●● D/F 

Guest house in coastal village on A9. Reserved parking bay. Ramp with handrails to entrance. Reception level. Dining room and lounge level. One twin room adapted for disabled guests on ground floor. Shower with seat, handrails by toilet. Other bedrooms upstairs. Raised toilet seat available. Garden level.

Ⓟ

Rates: £32-£34 per person per night (2007).

CARDROSS, Argyll

Kirkton House

Darleith Road, Cardoss G82 5EZ

☎ **01389 841951.**

W **www.kirktonhouse.co.uk**

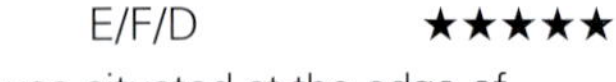

●●● E/F/D ★★★★★

Farm guesthouse situated at the edge of Cardross village with views over the Firth of Clyde. Entrance level. Dining room and lounge on ground floor level. One family bedroom on ground floor adapted for disabled guests ↺. Bathroom ↺, handrails. Easy access to garden. Personal assistance available on request. Closed December and January.

Rates: from £45 single, £70 double (2007).

CONTIN, Ross-shire

Coul House Hotel

Contin, by Strathpeffer IV14 9ES.

☎ **01997 421487.**

www.coulhousehotel.co.uk

 D/E/G ★★★

Country hotel 20 miles north west of Inverness. Entrance ramp. Public rooms level. WCs not adapted. Four ground floor bedrooms. Bathrooms 33", handrails.

Rates: on application.

DUFFTOWN, Moray

Braehead Villa

Braehead Terrace, Dufftown AB55 4AN.

☎ **01340 820461.**

www.visit-dufftown-scotland.co.uk

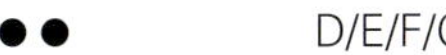

●● D/E/F/G ★★★

Small bed & breakfast house in middle of small town. Ramp to entrance, 84cm. Breakfast room level. Twin bedroom on ground floor, 84cm, ⟲. Shower room ⟲, roll-in shower with seat, handrails, space by WC. 2 other bedrooms upstairs.

Rates: £25-£35 per person BB (2007).

GRANTOWN-ON-SPEY, Moray

Culdearn House Hotel

Woodlands Terrace, Grantown-on-Spey, Morayshire PH26 3JU.

☎ **01479 872106.**

www.culdearn.com

● D/F/G ★★★★

Hotel on the A95 approach to the town. Side entrance level; 2 steps at main entrance. Restaurant and lounge ground floor. 1 twin bedroom on ground floor, no ⟲. Bathroom 60cm, ⟲, shower with tray, no handrails. Open March-December.

Rates: from £88 per person BBE (2007).

Holmhill House

Woodside Avenue, Grantown-on-Spey PH26 3JR.

☎ **01479 873977.**

www.holmhillhouse.co.uk

●● D/G ★★★★

Guesthouse on edge of town in Cairngorm National Park. Slope with handrail to entrance, 96cm, automatic door. Reception and public rooms level, min. door width 90cm. Unisex WC. Lift 80cm, inside 140x110cm. All bedrooms level. 4 bedrooms with own bathrooms. Two single rooms share a bathroom designed for disabled guests 87cm, ⟲, roll-in shower with seat, space by WC. Children's play room. Evening meals by arrangement.

Rates: from £30-£32 per night BB (2008).

INVERNESS, Inverness-shire

Glen Mhor Hotel

9-13 Ness Bank, Inverness IV2 4SG.

☎ **01463 234308.** **www.glen-mhor.com**

● D/F/G ★★★

Traditional hotel in quiet city centre area. 2 reserved parking bays. Ramp to entrance. Public rooms ground floor, min. door width 28" to lounge. Unisex WC in adjoining building. Bedrooms with bathrooms level.

Rates: from £47 per person BB (2007).

Kingsmills Hotel

Culcabock Road, Inverness IV2 3LP.

☎ **01463 237166.**

@ **sales.Inverness@marriotthotels.co.uk**

●● D/E/I/F/G ★★★★

Hotel south of city centre. Reserved parking bays. Entrance level, automatic doors. Public rooms level, except 4 steps to conservatory, portable ramp available. Unisex WC. Lift 32", inside 42"x60". Two ground floor bedrooms designed for disabled guests, one with door to adjoining room. Bathrooms ⟲, handrails, space for side transfer to bath and WC. Other bedrooms level.

Rates: on application.

Ramada Inverness

Church Street, Inverness IV1 1DX

☎ **01463 235181.**

@ **sales.inverness@ramadajarvis.co.uk**

●● D/E/I/G ★★★

Hotel in city centre. Ramp at main entrance. Public rooms level. Unisex WC/ Lift to upper floors. Double bedrooms adapted for disabled guests on 1st floor. Roll-in shower room ⟲, handrails. Other bedrooms level. Platform lift to pool.

Rates: on application.

ISLE OF MULL

The Tobermory Hotel

Main Street, Tobermory, Isle of Mull PA75 6NT.

☎ **01688 302091.**

W **www.thetobermoryhotel.com**

●● D/F/G ★★★

Family hotel facing bay. Street parking. Entrance level 34". Lounges level, ramp to restaurant. Ground floor twin bedroom, 34", ⟲ with shower room. Also ground floor single room.

Rates: from £38-£59 per person BB (2007).

ISLE OF SKYE, Inverness-shire

Shorefield House

Edinbane, Isle of Skye IV51 9PW.

☎ **01470 582444.** W **www.shorefield.com**

●● D/E ★★★★

Guesthouse between Portree and Dunvegan. Ramp with handrails to entrance. Dining room and lounge level. Twin bedroom designed for disabled guests. Shower room 82cm, roll-in shower with seat, handrails, space for side transfer to WC. 3 other bedrooms on ground floor.

Apply: Mrs Hillary Prall

Rates: from £30-£45 per night BB (2006).

KINTYRE, Argyll

Dunvalanree

Port Righ, Carradale, Kintyre PA28 6SE.

☎ **01583 431226.**

W **www.dunvalanree.com**

●● D/F/G ★★★★

Small hotel overlooking coast. Ramp to bedroom from car park, 3 steps to main entrance. Public rooms ground floor. One double bedroom on ground floor designed for disabled guests ⟲. Shower room ⟲, roll-in shower with seat, handrails, space by WC. Other bedrooms upstairs.

Rates: on application.

LOCHGILPHEAD, Argyll

Empire Travel Lodge

Union Street, Lochgilphead PA31 8JS.

☎ 01546 602381. W empirelodge.co.uk

●● ★★★

Lodge accommodation in town centre. Reserved parking bays. Ramp to entrance from car park; 3 steps at main entrance. Dining room 5 steps, breakfast can be served in bedroom. Twin bedroom designed for disabled guests. Bathroom 39", ⟲, handrails, space for side transfer to bath and WC. All ground floor bedrooms level.

Ⓟ

Rates: from £30 per person BB (2007).

NAIRN, Highland

Claymore House Hotel

Seabank Road, Nairn IV12 4EY.

☎ 01667 453731.

W www.claymorehousehotel.com

●● D/E/I/F/G ★★★★

Hotel outside town centre. 2 steps to main entrance; ramp to Garden Suite. Public rooms ground floor. Unisex WC. Garden suite double/twin bedroom ⟲. Shower room ⟲, roll-in shower, handrails, space by WC. Shower chair available. Other ground floor bedrooms level.

Ⓟ 

Rates: from £95 double BB (2007).

Covenanters Inn

Auldearn, Nairn IV12 5TG.

☎ 01667 452456.

W www.covenanters-inn.co.uk

●● D/E/F/G

Inn in village east of Nairn. Reserved parking bays. Ramp with handrails, or 4 steps, to entrance. Public rooms ground floor. Unisex WC. Twin bedroom designed for disabled guests. Shower room ⟲, roll-in shower with seat, handrails, space by WC. Other bedrooms level.

Rates: from £60 double BB (2007).

OBAN, Argyll

Falls of Lora Hotel

Connel Ferry, by Oban PA34 1PB.

☎ 01631 710483.

W www.fallsoflora.co.uk

●● D/E/I/F/H

Hotel facing Loch Etive, five miles from Oban. Reserved parking bay. Entrance level. Public rooms level. Adapted WC cubicles. Twin bedroom adapted for disabled guests. Bathroom 36", no ⟲ or handrails. Other ground floor bedrooms available. Closed Mid December to end of January. A Circle Hotel.

Rates: from £24.50-£65.50 per person BB (2007).

Oban Caledonian Hotel

Station Square, Oban PA34 5RT.

☎ 0871 222 3420.

@ reservations@freedomglen.co.uk

●● D/E/I/F/G ★★★★

High-class hotel in town centre. Ramp or 1 step to entrance, automatic door. Low reception desk. Lounge and restaurant level. 3 steps to Bar. Adapted cubicles in toilets. Lift to upper floors. Two bedrooms designed for disabled guests. Bathrooms have low bath and space by WC. Other bedrooms level.

Rates: on application.

ORKNEY

The Observatory Guest House

North Ronaldsay, Orkney KW17 2BE.
☎ 01857 633200.
W www.nrbo.f2s.com
●● D/E/I/F/G ★★★

Guesthouse attached to bird observatory and croft on north Orkney island. Ramp to entrance 86cm. Dining room, lounge and bar level. Unisex WC. Twin bedroom designed for disabled guests 84cm, ⟲. Shower room 82cm, roll-in shower, handrails, space by WC. Shower chair available. Other bedrooms and hostel annexe with 4-bed dormitories upstairs. Some paths with gentle gradients.

Rates: from £40 per person DBB (2007).

SHETLAND

Baltasound Hotel

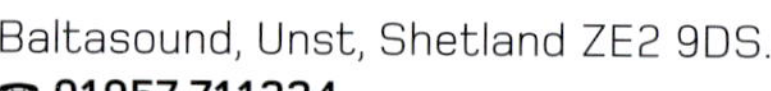

Baltasound, Unst, Shetland ZE2 9DS.
☎ 01957 711334.
W www.baltasound-hotel.shetland.co.uk
●● D/E/I/F/G ★★

Small hotel on northernmost island. Reserved parking bay. Entrance to dining room 1 step, 3"; main entrance 3 steps. Public rooms level, min. door width 31". Three bedrooms adapted for disabled guests, two in chalets in grounds, 35" ⟲. Bathrooms sliding door, ⟲. Bathseat and waterproof sheet available. Other level bedrooms available.

Rates: from £39-£49 per person BB (2007).

Lerwick Youth Hostel

Islesburgh House, King Harald Street, Lerwick ZE1 0EQ.

☎ 01595 692114.

@ receprion.islesburgh@shetland.gov.uk

●● E/I/F/G ★★★★★

Hostel in town centre. Slope to level entrance 30". Lounge and cafe ground floor. Dining room 1st floor. Lift 30", inside 53"x55". Two twin and 4 group bedrooms level, ⟲. Waterproof sheets available. Roll-in shower room and 2 unisex WCs designed for wheelchair users. Wheelchair available. Open April-September for individuals and for groups of 10 or more at other times. For more information on Youth Hostels see page 34.

Rates: from £15.50 adult per night (2007).

The Shetland Hotel

Holmsgarth Road, Lerwick ZE1 0PW.

☎ 01595 695515.

W www.shetlandhotels.com

 D/E/I/F/G

Hotel in town centre. Ramp to level entrance. Public rooms level. Unisex WC. Lift 60", inside 72"x60". Twin bedroom designed for disabled guests. Shower room with sliding door, ⟲, roll-in shower, space for side transfer to WC. Waterproof sheets available. Other bedrooms level. Wheelchair available.

Rates: £79 single, £99.50 twin BB (2007).

SPEAN BRIDGE, Inverness-shire

Old Pines Hotel & Restaurant

Spean Bridge, by Fort William PH34 4EG.

☎ 01397 712324. W www.oldpines.co.uk

●●● D/E/F/G ★★★★

Hotel with restaurant in large grounds. Entrance ramp or step. Three bedrooms with shower rooms ⟲, roll-in shower with seat, handrails, space for side transfer to WC. Assistance may be available.

Rates: from £82.50-£90 per person DBB (2007).

TAYNUILT, Argyll

Roineabhal

Kilchrenan, Taynuilt PA35 1HD.

☎ 01866 833207.

W www.roineabhal.com

●● D/E/I/F/G ★★★★

Country house by Loch Awe. Entrance ramp or 2 steps. Dining room and lounge level. One ground floor twin bedroom ⟲. Ramp to shower room 32", roll-in shower with seat, handrails, space by WC. Waterproof sheet available. 2 other bedrooms upstairs. Baby sitting arranged. Evening meals available.

Rates: from £45-£55 per person BB (2007).

ULLAPOOL, Ross-shire

Dromnan Guest House

Garve Road, Ullapool IV26 2SX.

☎ 01854 612333.

W www.dromnan.com

●● D/E/F ★★★★

Guesthouse overlooking Loch Broom. Entrance ramp. Dining room and lounge level. Twin bedroom level. Bathroom ⟲, shower with seat, space by WC. Other ground floor bedrooms available.

Rates: from £27-£30 per night BB (2007).

WESTERN ISLES

Dolly's Bed & Breakfast

33 Aignish, Isle of Lewis HS2 0PB.
☎ **012851 870755.**
@ **dollysbb@yahoo.co.uk**

 D/G 

Bed & breakfast overlooking bay a short drive from Stornaway and airport. Ramp available for step to entrance, 77cm. Dining room and lounge level. Internal doors 82cm. Ground floor family bedroom ⭯. Ground floor shower room ⭯, roll-in shower with seat, handrails, space by WC. Other bedrooms upstairs. Teletext TV. Evening meals by arrangement.

Rates: £25-£30 per person BB (2007).

Doune Braes Hotel

Carloway, Isle of Lewis HS2 9AA.
☎ **01851 643252.**
W **www.doune-braes.co.uk**

 D/E/F/G 

Small hotel with restaurant in country near west coast of Lewis. Reserved parking bays. Ramp or 2 steps to entrance, double doors. Low reception desk. Public rooms open plan. Unisex WC. Lift to upper floor. Tw o bedrooms for disabled people in annexe, entrance level, 36", ⭯. Shower rooms 30", ⭯, shower tray. Other bedrooms level. Petrol available.

Rates: from £45 per person BB (2007).

LODGE ACCOMMODATION

There are Travel Inn (see page 38) and Travelodge (see page 38) properties in the following areas in this region.

Elgin – Premier Travel Inn .... ☎ **0870 197 7095**
Fort William – Premier Travel Inn .... ☎ **0870 197 7104**
Inverness – Premier Travel Inn .... ☎ **0870 197 7141**
Travelodge .... ☎ **0870 191 1648**
Inverness, East – Premier Travel Inn .... ☎ **0870 197 7142**
Inverness, Fairways – Travelodge .... ☎ **0870 191 1785**

SELF-CATERING ACCOMMODATION

ACHILTIBUIE, Ross-shire
Polbain Cottage
Polbain, Achiltibuie, Ullapool IV26 2YW.

●● I/F/G ★★★

Self-catering extension to croft house on coast facing the Summer Isles originally provided for disabled family members. Entrance level 92cm. Dining room and kitchen open plan, cooker controls useable from wheelchair. Separate lounge, ⟲ with single bed, level. Ground floor bathroom 84cm, handrails, no space for side transfer to WC, bath board and raised WC seat available. Double and twin bedrooms upstairs.

Apply: Ken Lowndes ☎ 01854 622361.
Rates: from £250-£450 per week (2008).

APPIN, Argyll
Appin House Apartments & Lodges

Appin House, Appin PA38 4BN

●● I/F/G ★★-★★★★

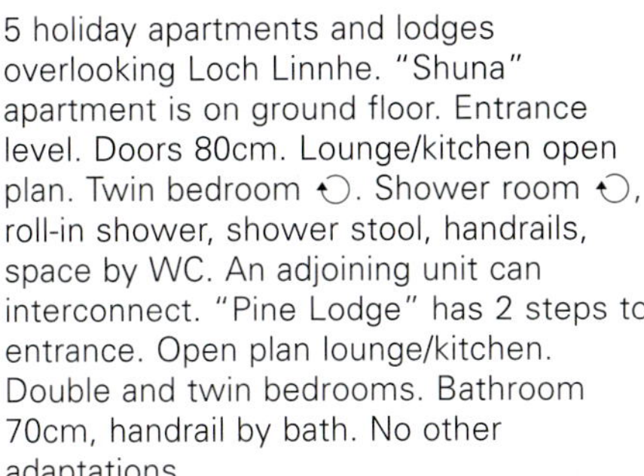

5 holiday apartments and lodges overlooking Loch Linnhe. "Shuna" apartment is on ground floor. Entrance level. Doors 80cm. Lounge/kitchen open plan. Twin bedroom ⟲. Shower room ⟲, roll-in shower, shower stool, handrails, space by WC. An adjoining unit can interconnect. "Pine Lodge" has 2 steps to entrance. Open plan lounge/kitchen. Double and twin bedrooms. Bathroom 70cm, handrail by bath. No other adaptations.

Apply: Mrs Denys Mathieson
☎ 01631 730207.
W www.appinhouse.co.uk
Rates: from £200-£1000 per week (2006).

ARDMADDY, Argyll

Caddleton Farm House
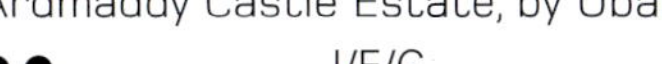

Ardmaddy Castle Estate, by Oban

●● I/F/G ★★★★

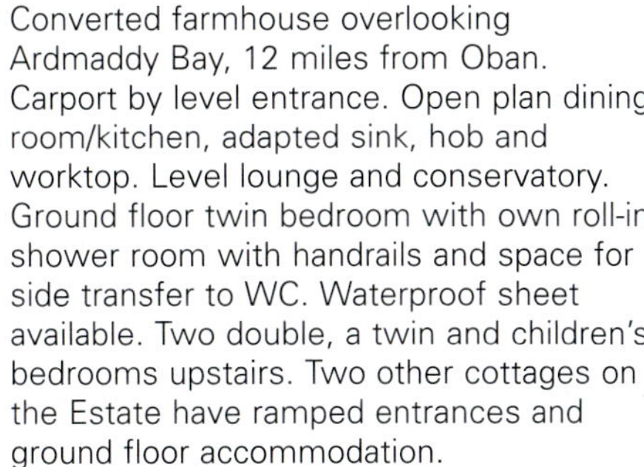

Converted farmhouse overlooking Ardmaddy Bay, 12 miles from Oban. Carport by level entrance. Open plan dining room/kitchen, adapted sink, hob and worktop. Level lounge and conservatory. Ground floor twin bedroom with own roll-in shower room with handrails and space for side transfer to WC. Waterproof sheet available. Two double, a twin and children's bedrooms upstairs. Two other cottages on the Estate have ramped entrances and ground floor accommodation.

Apply: Mrs Struthers, Ardmaddy Castle, by Oban PA34 4QY. ☎ 01852 300353.
@ ardmaddycastle@btopenworld.com
Rates: £315-£1918 per week (2007).

AVIEMORE, Inverness-shire
Benarty Holiday Accommodation

● G

"Aviemore Apartment" is a ground floor flat near rail and bus station. Entrance and doorways accessible for wheelchair users. Double bedroom with own bathroom, two twin bedrooms. Bathroom with no adaptations.

Apply: Mrs Constable, Benarty House, Kelty KY4 0HT. ☎ 01383 830 235.
@ barbara@benartyholidaycottages.co.uk
Rates: from £350-£450 per week (2007).

High Range Self-Catering Chalets

Grampian Road, Aviemore PH22 1PT.
☎ **01479 810636.**
www.highrange.co.uk

●● F/G ★★★★

Complex at south end of Aviemore. "Brae Riach" chalet is designed for disabled guests. Main entrance level. Internal doors 30". Lounge/kitchen open plan, controls useable from wheelchair. Single and double bedrooms and stowaway bed also available. Shower room, roll-in shower with seat, handrails, space by WC. 7 other chalets, touring park, motel, bar and restaurant on site.

Rates: from £430 per week (2006).

Shieling Apartment

Dalfaber Road, Aviemore

●● I/F/G ★★★★

Ground floor flat for 5 people in Victorian house. Entrance level, 95cm. Lounge /kitchen open plan. Two twin bedrooms. Bathroom, handrail by bath, space by WC. A two bedroom chalet, suitable for some disabled people, is also available.

Apply: Pine Bank Chalets, Dalfaber Road, Aviemore PH22 1PX. ☎ 01479 810000.
www.pinebankchalets.co.uk
Rates: from £490-£650 per week (2007).

DRUMNADROCHIT, Inverness-shire

Lochletter Lodges

Balnain, Drumnadrochit,
Inverness IV63 6TJ.
☎ **01456 476313.** **www.lochletter.com**

●●● I/G/H ★★★

Four chalets west of Loch Ness. One equipped for wheelchair users. Entrance level, 31". Lounge/kitchen open plan, controls useable from wheelchair. Two twin bedrooms and 2 stowaway beds. Shower room, roll-in shower, handrails, space for side transfer to WC. Shower chair, mobile hoist and other equipment available. Other chalets level. Indoor sports facilities.

Rates: £180-£420 per week (2007).

DULNAIN BRIDGE, Inverness-shire

Woodhead Cottage

Skye of Curr, Dulnain Bridge

●●● I/F/G/H ★★★

Cottage in Speyside for up to 6 people, purpose-built for disabled people. Ramp with handrail to entrance. Lounge/kitchen open plan, controls useable from wheelchair. Twin bedroom. Ceiling hoist to bathroom, handrails, roll-in shower, space by bath and WC. Shower chair available. Also double and bunk bedrooms and separate WC.

Apply: Ian & Catriona Shearer, Birch Cottage, Skye of Curr Road, Dulnain Bridge PH26 3PA. ☎ 01479 851298.
www.woodhead-cottage.co.uk
Rates: on application.

DUNOON, Argyll

Lyall Cliff Self Catering

141 Alexandra Parade, East Bay,
Dunoon PA23 8AW.
☎ **01369 702041.** **www.lyallcliff.co.uk**

●● D ★★★

Self catering units on promenade with sea views. Semi-detatched house for up to 8 with a twin bedroom on ground floor. Also one ground floor flat for 2-3 people. Both with ramp to entrance 30". Shower room 28", handrails, space by WC.

Rates: from £220-£675 per week (2007).

FORGIE, Moray
Garden Cottage

Forgie, Nr. Keith

●● I/F/G

Converted cottage for wheelchair users overlooking Spey Forest. Entrances level. Living room 90cm. Kitchen/dining room open plan, controls useable from wheelchair. Double and twin bedrooms ⟲. Hospital bed available. Bathroom ⟲, handrails, space for side transfer to WC. Separate roll-in shower room. Braille markings and safety flooring.

Apply: The Cobweb Foundation, 37-39 Bruce Street, Dunfermline KY11 7AG.
☎ 01358 724145.
W www.cobwebfoundation.org
Rates: on application.

FORRES, Moray

Tulloch Holiday Lodges

Rafford, Forres IV36 2RU.
☎ 01309 673311.
W www.tullochlodges.com

●● F/G ★★★★

Two, of 8, chalets for up to 6 people designed for disabled people on wooded lakeside site. Entrance ramp, 31". Living room and kitchen/dining rooms, no kitchen adaptations. Three bedrooms with double and twin beds. Bathroom 31", ⟲, handrails by bath and shower, shower seat, raised WC seat available.

Rates: from £385-£671 per week (2007).

GAIRLOCH, Ross-shire
Willow Croft

Big Sand, Gairloch, Wester Ross.

●● E/I/F/G ★★★

Specially designed bungalow in coastal crofting area. Entrance ramp, 33". Lounge 32". Kitchen 48", ⟲, some low worktops. Three bedrooms, ⟲ in 2. Shower room 32", ⟲, roll-in shower, shower chair, handrails, space for side transfer to WC. Also a bathroom with shower and a bathroom/sauna.

Apply: Mrs B Leslie, 40 Big Sand, Gairloch IV21 2DD. ☎ 01445 712448.
W sites.ecosse.net/iml
Rates: from £180-£475 per week (2006).

INVERNESS
Inverness Youth Hostel

15a Victoria Drive, Inverness IV2 3QB.
☎ 0871 330 8529.
@ Inverness@syha.org

●● G ★★★★★

Youth hostel in town centre. Entrance level. Public rooms level; kitchen ⟲, no adaptations. Two 3-bedded rooms ground floor ⟲. Own shower room 36", roll-in shower, handrails. For further information on youth hostels see page 34.

Ⓟ

Rates: £14-£15.75 adult overnight (2007).

ISLE OF SKYE

Greenbank

Halistra, Hallin, Isle of Skye IV55 8GL.
www.greenbankonskye.co.uk
●●● F/G

Bungalow designed for wheelchair users at north end of the island by sea loch. Entrance 80cm, threshold 1cm. Internal doors 75cm. Lounge and kitchen/dining room ⟲, controls may be useable from wheelchair. Double/twin bedroom ⟲ with en suite shower room ⟲, roll-in shower and seat, handrails, space for side transfer to WC and shower. Also twin bedroom with en-suite bathroom. Wheeled shower chair and monkey pole available. Some assistance is available from owners next door.

Apply: Hazel Wotton ☎ 01470 592369.
Rates: from £150-£460 per week (2008).

La Bergerie

Lochbay, Waternish.
www.la-bergerie-skye.co.uk
●● I/F/G

Cottage on shore for up to 8 designed for disabled people. Entrances level. Open plan lounge/kitchen, controls useable from wheelchair. Two ground floor bedrooms each with roll-in shower room with handrails and space by WC. Seat for shower available. Also twin and double bedrooms upstairs. Wheelchair available. A carer can be provided with advanced notice.

Apply: Mrs Chantal MacLeod, 33 Lochbay Waternish, Isle of Skye IV55 8GD. ☎ 01470 592282.
Rates: from £500-£960 per week (2008).

Whitewave – Skye's Outdoor Centre

No. 19 Linicro, Kilmuir, Isle of Skye IV51 9YN.
☎ **01470 542414.**
www.white-wave.co.uk
●● I/F/G

Accommodation attached to activity centre in crofting area of north Skye. Reserved parking bay. Ramp to entrance, 80cm. Public areas level. Unisex WC with roll-in shower. Ground floor bedroom with double and single beds 89cm, ⟲. One other ground floor bedroom, others upstairs. Activity and other courses, including Gaelic language, offered.

Apply: Anne Martin and John White
Rates: on application.

KEITH, Moray

Parkhead Croft

Drummuir, near Keith.
●● E/I/F/G ★★★

Single storey cottage designed for disabled people between Keith and Dufftown. Entrance level, 36". Open plan lounge/kitchen, controls useable from wheelchair. Double and twin bedrooms 36", ⟲, mattress protectors. Bathroom 36" sliding door, ⟲, handrails, roll-in shower, space for side transfer to bath and WC. Carpet or safety flooring throughout. Some other equipment can be provided. Pets by arrangement only.

Apply: The Cobweb Foundation, 37-39 Bruce Street, Dunfermline KY11 7AG.
☎ 01383 733849.
www.cobwebfoundation.org
Rates: on application.

KINCRAIG, Inverness-shire
Loch Insh Log Chalets

Kincraig PH21 1NU.
☎ 01540 651272. **W www.lochinsh.com**
●● I/F/G ★★★

Three chalets designed for disabled guests in wooded grounds of watersports and ski centre 6 miles from Kingussie and Aviemore. Entrance level 80cm. Lounge and open plan dining room kitchen, controls useable from wheelchair. Three ground floor bedrooms and loft bedroom for children. Waterproof sheet available. Shower room with roll-in shower and seat, handrails, space for side transfer to WC. Other units also available. Ramp to beach and on-site restaurant. Water sport and skiing facilities available.

Rates: on application.

LAIDE, Ross-shire
Rocklea

Little Gruinard, Laide, Wester Ross.
W www.heimdall-scot.co.uk/laide
●● F/G ★★★★

Log house for 5 people on coast north of Gairloch. Entrance ramp, 90cm. Lounge/kitchen open plan. Twin, double and single bedrooms, Bathroom, handrails, space for side transfer to bath and WC. Paved area overlooking sea.

Apply: Mr & Mrs Gilchrist, Grassvalley Cottage, 12 Woodhall Road, Edinburgh EH13 0DX. ☎ 0131 441 6053.
@ aandagilchrist@blueyonder.co.uk
Rates: from £220-£495 per week (2007).

MELFORT, Argyll
Melfort Pier & Harbour

Melfort Village, by Oban PA34 4XD.
☎ 01852 200333.
W www.mellowmelfort.com
●● I/F/G

Luxury houses overlooking Loch Melfort. Eight of 15 designed for disabled guests. Entrance ramp. Lounge, dining room and kitchen each 85cm. Kitchen controls not useable from wheelchair. Ground floor double or twin bedroom. En suite bathroom, roll-in shower with seat, handrails, space for side transfer to bath and WC. 1 or 2 bedrooms and bathroom upstairs. Teletext TV. Spabath, Sauna. Accessible restaurant on site.

Rates: from £90-£225 per night (2007).

NAIRN, Highland
Burnside & Mill Lodges

Raitloan, Geddes, Nairn IV12 5SA.
●● E/I/G ★★★★

Two single storey chalets adapted for disabled guests 4 miles from Nairn. Entrance ramp, 44". Wide Internal doors. Two twin bedrooms and bunkroom. Bathroom, shower, handrails.

Apply: Mr D Buchanan ☎ 01667 454635.
W www.geddesmill.co.uk
Rates: from £180-£420 per week (2007/8).

Hiddenglen Holidays

Laikenbuie, Grantown Road, Nairn IV12 5QN.
☎ **01667 454630.**
W **www.hiddenglen.co.uk**
●● I/F/G/H ★★★★

Two single storey lodges overlooking wildlife rich woods and loch, 4 miles from Nairn. Ramped approach. Entrance 76cm. Lounge/kitchen open plan, cooker controls useable from wheelchair. Double and twin bedrooms ⟲ and bunkroom. Bathroom 76cm, ⟲, handrails, space for side transfer to bath and WC. Mobile hoist available. Unadapted chalet also available.

Rates: from £140-£600 per week (2007).

Nairn Lochloy Holiday Park

East Beach, Nairn IV12 4PH.
●● I/F/G ★★★★

Holiday Park on Moray Firth with range of facilities. Caravan for 5 people adapted for disabled guests. Entrance ramp. Lounge/kitchen open plan. Two bedrooms, sliding door 75cm, ⟲ in double. Shower room 75cm, handrails, restricted ⟲. Open March-November

Apply: Parkdean Holidays
☎ 0871 641 2066.
W www.parkdeanscotland.co.uk
Rates: Holiday homes from £199 per week Short breaks (3 or 4 nights) from £120

NETHYBRIDGE, Inverness-shire

Fhuarain Forest Cottages

Badanfhuarain, Nethybridge PH25 3ED.
●●● I/F/G/H ★★★★

Two cottages designed for disabled people both sleeping 5 people in 3 bedrooms. Entrances level or ramped. Internal doors 75cm minimum and ⟲ in all rooms. Adapted bath or roll-in shower with seat and shower chair. Handrails and space by WCs. Hoist, monkey pole, raised WC seat, bed-blocks and wheelchair available. Detailed layouts and dimensions available.

Apply: Mrs Valery Dean ☎ 01479 821642.
W www.forestcottages.com
Rates: from £200-£475 per week (2007).

Lazy Duck Hostel

Badanfhuarain, Nethybridge PH25 3ED.
●● G

Bunkhouse acommodation for 6/8 people. Ramp to entrance. Doors 77cm. Lounge/kitchen open plan. Downstairs bunkroom for 4 with one curtained lower bunk accessible to wheelchair user. Shower room ⟲, roll-in shower with seat, handrails and space by WC. Covered garden.

Apply: David Dean ☎ 01479 821642.
W www.lazyduck.co.uk
Rates: from £10 per person per night (2007).

NEWTONMORE, Inverness-shire

Crubenbeg Farm Steading

Newtonmore, nr Aviemore PH20 1BE.
☎ **01540 673 566.**
W **www.crubenbeg.com**
●● I ★★★★

One single storey cottage, of 7, designed for disabled people 5 miles south of Newtonmore. Ramp to entrance 33½". Lounge and kitchen each 32". Twin bedroom ⟲, waterproof sheet available. Shower room ⟲, roll-in shower with chair, handrails, space for side transfer to WC. Games room.

Rates: from £280-£425 per week (2007).

NORTH KESSOCK, Inverness-shire

Bramble, Cherry & Willow Cottages

Drumsmittal, North Kessock, Nr. Inverness.

www.culbincrofthouse.co.uk

 F/G/H 

Three of 4 cottages designed for disabled people in country north of Inverness. Entrance level. Lounge/kitchen open plan, kitchen controls not useable from wheelchair. Two have 2 twin or double bedrooms, the third has 3 bedrooms. Shower room ⟲, roll-in shower, handrails, space by WC. Portable hoist and raised sockets in "Willow Cottage". The fourth unit has ground floor accommodation. Available May-September.

Apply: Elizabeth Ross, Culbin, Drumsmittal, North Kessock, Inverness IV1 3XF. ☎ 01463 731455.

Rates: from £350-£550 per week (2007).

OBAN, Argyll

Cologin Farm Holiday Chalets

Lerags Glen, by Oban PA34 4SE.

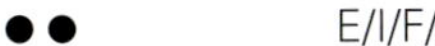 E/I/F/G ★★★★

Two lodges, each sleeping up to 6, designed for disabled people 3 miles from Oban. Ramp to entrance 79cm. Lounge with 2 sofabeds. Twin and double bedrooms. Bathroom 78cm sliding door, ⟲, handrails, space by bath and WC. Other units on site with level access. Farmhouse, sleeping up to 14. Entrance 79cm, lounge, dining room, kitchen and one bedroom with en suite bathroom ground floor and 4 bedrooms upstairs. Pub/restaurant on site.

Apply: Linda Battison. ☎ 01631 564501.

www.cologin.co.uk

Rates: from £60 per night, £265 per week (2007).

ORKNEY

Lochland Chalets & Hannabreck

Dounby, Orkney

●● F/G 

4 chalets north west of Kirkwall, one designed for disabled people. Entrance level, 33". Lounge/kitchen open plan, controls not useable from wheelchair. Twin and double bedrooms, restricted ⟲. Shower room 32", roll-in shower, shower chair, space for side transfer to WC. "Hannabreck" is a 2 bedroomed modernised cottage. Entrance level, 33". Lounge/kitchen open plan, controls not suitable for wheelchair users. Roll-in shower room with space for side transfer to WC.

Apply: Phyllis Norquoy, Bigging, Dounby, Orkney KW17 2HR. ☎ 01856 771340.

www.lochlandchalets.co.uk

Rates: £80-£400 per week (2007).

WESTERN ISLES

Cabhalan Cottage

Quidinish, Isle of Harris HS3 3JQ.

● I/F/G 

Secluded cottage on east coast for up to 6 people. Entrance level, 80cm. Lounge 65cm with double box-bed. Kitchen/dining room 65 cm, not adapted. Double and twin bedrooms. Shower room 65cm, ⟲, roll-in shower with seat and handrails, space for side transfer.

Apply: Mrs C A Macintyre, Struthmor, Quidinish, Isle of Harris HS3 3JD. ☎ 01859 530255. jsluty@hotmail.com

Rates: from £220-£400 per week (2007).

13 Wales

Barafundle Bay, Pembrokeshire

Wales has a tourist industry that is both well-established and rapidly modernising, providing opportunities for staying in traditional resorts, large cities, country towns or at more rural locations.

Well-established resorts with attractions for families and a largely level terrain are found around much of the coast. In the north these include Rhyl, Colwyn Bay and Llandudno. Aberdovey, Barmouth and Towyn are on the west coast and Tenby and Porthcawl in the south. The hillier sections of the coast have many historic towns, some with castles such as Harlech, Caernarfon and Conwy or with attractive harbours like New Quay.

Wales has three contrasting National Parks. The one covering the Pembrokeshire coast contains some of Britain's most dramatic coastal scenery and provides a thriving and varied wildlife habitat. The Snowdonia National Park in the north west includes impressive mountains. It is possible to get to the top of Wales' highest mountain on the Snowdon Mountain Railway with advance notice. The Brecon Beacons, stretching from the top of the once industrial valleys into mid-Wales, are not as high as Snowdonia but have a countryside which feels just as remote. Facilities for disabled visitors have been developed by each of the National Park Authorities.

Rural areas with attractive scenery can be found in other parts of Wales and there are many opportunities for countryside activities.

Photo: www.britainonview © Simon Kreiten

Water sports of all kinds are available on many reservoirs. The Wildfowl & Wetlands Trust has a centre near Llanelli and country parks have been developed in many areas including Ty Mawr near Wrexham and Caldicot Castle in Monmouthshire. The National Botanic Garden of Wales, including the spectacular Great Glasshouse, is at Llanarthe near Carmarthen.

Millennium Stadium, Cardiff

The early history and Celtic heritage of Wales is explored at Celtica in Machynlleth, which is also the home of the Centre for Alternative Technology. Elsewhere there are re-creations of local industrial heritage, be it slate mining in Snowdonia, quarrying in Anglesey, the National Woollen Museum near Newcastle Emlyn in Carmarthenshire or coal mining and heavy industry at the Rhondda Heritage Centre. Wales is notable for the number of preserved steam railways, several of which, including the Llanberis Lake Railway, can carry disabled passengers.

The facilities expected of a major modern city can be found in Cardiff - shops, music, sports including the Millennium Stadium, museums, night life and much more. The regenerated Cardiff Bay area is the home of the Welsh Assembly and the Wales Millennium Centre. A similarly wide range of attractions can be found in Swansea including the Dylan Thomas Centre and the National Waterfront Museum. Smaller towns worth visiting include the Victorian spa of Llandrindod Wells in mid-Wales, St David's with the country's smallest Cathedral, the university town of Aberystwyth on the west coast and the county towns of Cardigan, Carmarthen and Monmouth.

Photo: www.britainonview

USEFUL ADDRESSES

Visit Wales

PO Box 153, Bangor LL54 4WW.

☎ 0870 830 0306.

Textphone: 08701 211255.

@ info@visitwales.co.uk

W www.visitwales.co.uk

Produces a range of general tourist literature, which indicates accommodation suitable for disabled guests. Visit Wales does not carry out inspections under the National Accessible Scheme but does encourage providers to prepare and supply access statements on their properties.

Disability Wales/Anabledd Cymru

Bridge house, Caerphilly Business Park, Van Road, Caerphilly CF83 3GW.

☎ 029 2088 7325.

W www.disabilitywales.org

Can answer enquiries by letter or phone, Freephone Helpline: 0800 731 6282 (Monday-Friday 10am-1pm).

DIAL

DIAL offers a free, impartial and confidential service of information and advice by telephone to disabled people, their relatives and professionals. The following groups may be able to help disabled residents and visitors in their areas:

Taran Information Service, Anglesey

☎ 01248 750077; Textphone: 01248 750095

Disablement Welfare Rights, Bangor

☎ 01248 352227

Cerebra, Carmarthen

☎ 0800 328 1159

Denbighshire Disability Forum

☎ 01745 354445

Connect DRA, Pembrokeshire

☎ 01348 873884

DIAL Swansea, Neath, Port Talbot

☎ 01792 583322

DAP Torfaen

☎ 001495 763778

USEFUL PUBLICATIONS & WEBSITES

Places to Visit with Easier Access – a guide listing over 60 short trails, sites of historic, landscape or wildlife interest suitable for disabled people and anyone who just wants a nice and easy, hassle-free stroll in the Brecon Beacons. Available from National Park Information Centres, by post from Brecon Beacons National Park Authority, Plas y Ffynnon, Cambrian Way, Brecon LD3 7DP. ☎ 01874 624437 or view it online on W www.breconbeacons.org/visitus.

Enjoying Eryri: a guide for people with disabilities – published by the Snowdonia National Park Authority with assistance from Access Groups in the area. The booklet, in print or braille, and information on access to additional attractions in the area can be obtained from the Education & Communications Department, Snowdonia National Park Authority, Penrhyndeudraeth LL48 6LF. ☎ 01766 770274.
@ parc@eryri-npa.gov.uk or on the Snowdonia for All section on
W www.eryrf-npa.gov.uk

Easy Access Routes gives information on 20 paths in the Pembrokeshire Coast National Park. The paths range from 660 yards to 3 miles and aim to help disabled people enjoy the diverse natural and man-made heritage of the area. Information on viewpoints and some beaches is also included. The Guide, can be downloaded from the website or is available, price £3.83 including postage, from the Pembrokeshire Coast National Park Centre, Ruabon House, South Parade, Tenby SA70 7DL ☎ 01834 845040.
@ tenby.centre@pembrokeshirecoast.org.uk
W www.pembrokeshirecoast.org.uk

EQUIPMENT HIRE

British Red Cross

Red Cross House, North Wales Business Park, Cae Eithin, Abergele, LL22 8LJ
☎ **01745 828330.**

Provides wheelchairs and commodes for short-term loan from depots across North Wales. Transport and escort services are available in North West Wales only.

Bridgend Wheelchair Hire

43 Greenfields Avenue, Bridgend CF31 4SR
☎ **01656 661579.**
W www.bridgendwheelchairhire.co.uk

Manual and electric wheelchairs and scooters with a range of attachments and other equipment can be hired. A repair service is also offered.

CYMROD Clwb Teithio Dwyfor Travel Club

Sgwar yr Orsaf, PO Box 60,
Pwllheli LL53 5WT.
☎ **01758 614311.**

Wheelchairs and scooters are available for hire for disabled people on holiday in the area around Pwllheli on daily and weekly rates. They also have wheelchair accessible vehicles for use in the area that can be hired on a mileage basis. Advance enquiries requested.

Merthyr Tydfil Shopmobility

St Tydfil Square, Merthyr Tydfil CF47 8EW.
☎ **01685 373237.**
Textphone: 01685 373400.
@ shopmomerthyr@btconnect.com

As well as regular Shopmobility services, a range of manual and powered chairs are available for holiday hire at modest rates by both residents and visitors. Users are responsible for insurance if the vehicle is to be taken abroad. A hoist is also available. Training can be provided.

Mobility Freedom

105 North Road, Cardigan SA43 1DS.
☎ **01239 614674.**
W www.scootershed.net

Scooters and powered wheelchairs are available to hire with delivery available at additional cost.

Physically Impaired People of Pembrokeshire Association

The Coach House, Bridgend Square, Haverfordwest SA61 2ND.
☎ **01437 760999.**
@ pippapembs@btconnect.com

PIPPA offers a hire service for wheelchairs, scooters and bathroom equipment for visitors. Daily and weekly hire rates available. Advance bookings accepted in high season.

Shopmobility schemes exist to provide wheelchairs and/or scooters for use in shopping centres in the following towns. For information on availability, etc., telephone in advance.

Abergavenny ☎ **0800 298 3656**
Aberystwyth ☎ **01970 630060**
Bridgend ☎ **01656 667992**
Caldicot ☎ **01291 430230**
Cardiff ☎ **029 2039 9355**
Colwyn Bay ☎ **01492 533822**
Cwmbran ☎ **01633 874686.**
Merthyr Tydfil ☎ **01685 373237;**
Neath ☎ **01639 637372**
Newport ☎ **01633 673845**
Rhyl ☎ **01745 350665**
Swansea ☎ **01792 461785**
Wrexham ☎ **01978 312390**

WALES - ACCOMMODATION

For ease of reference accommodation entries for Wales are divided into three areas (see map, page 53). The localities covered by each of these areas are as follows

In Wales each type of holiday accommodation serving meals (hotels, guest houses, bed & breakfast, etc.) and also self-catering accommodation and holiday parks are graded for quality as indicated by one to five stars.

★ - Fair and acceptable
★★ - Good
★★★ - Very good
★★★★ - Excellent
★★★★★ - Exceptional

In the following section the star, where known, is given and the type of accommodation is referred to in the opening words of each entry.

Further information is available from Tourist Information Centres in Wales or Visit Wales.

NOTE – Visit Wales encourages premises to prepare an Access Statement and is not at present inspecting under the National Accessible Scheme.

NORTH WALES
ACCOMMODATION WITH MEALS

CONWY, Conwy
Conwy Youth Hostel

Larkhill, Sychnant Pass Road,
Conwy LL32 8AJ.
0870 770 5774.
conwy@yha.org.uk
●● D/E/I/F/G ★★★★

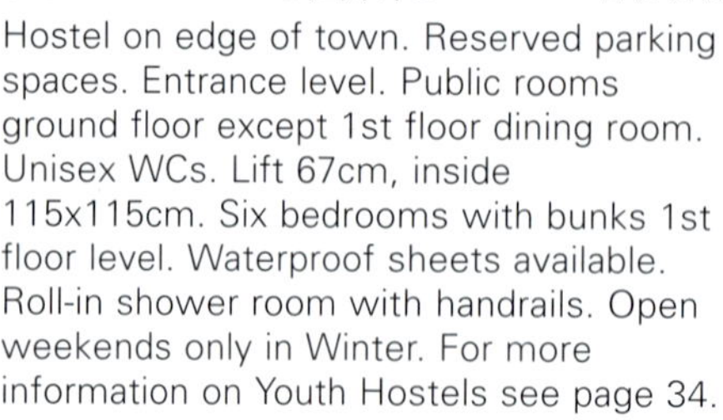

Hostel on edge of town. Reserved parking spaces. Entrance level. Public rooms ground floor except 1st floor dining room. Unisex WCs. Lift 67cm, inside 115x115cm. Six bedrooms with bunks 1st floor level. Waterproof sheets available. Roll-in shower room with handrails. Open weekends only in Winter. For more information on Youth Hostels see page 34.

Rates: from £15 adult overnight (2007).

DINAS DINLLE, Gwynedd
Bryn Mor Beach Hotel

Dinas Dinlle, Caernarfon Bay LL54 5TW.
01286 830314.
www.brynmorbeachhotel.com
●● D/E/F/G ★★★

Hotel facing beach near National Park. Reserved parking bays. Ramp with handrails to entrance. Low reception desk. Public rooms level. Unisex WC. Ground floor bedroom adapted for disabled guests. Bathroom, handrails, space by bath and WC. All bedrooms on ground floor.

Rates: on application.

DOLGELLAU, Gwynedd
Graig-Wen

Arthog, Nr. Dolgellau LL39 1BQ.
01341 250482.
graig-wen@supanet.com
●● D/E/F ★★

Country guesthouse overlooking Mawddach Estuary. 2 steps from car park, portable ramp available. Entrance level. Dining room, lounge and snooker room level. Double bedroom ground floor designed for disabled guests. Shower room, roll-in shower, handrails, space for side transfer to WC.

Rates: from £25 per person BB (2007).

HARLECH, Gwynedd
Estuary Lodge

Stryd Fawr, Talsarnau, Harlech LL47 6TA.
01766 771155.
www.estuarylodge.co.uk
●● D/E/F/G ★★★

Hotel in village between Harlech and Porthmadog. Level entrance. Low reception desk. Public rooms level, doors 32cm. One bedroom adapted for disabled guests. Shower room 83cm sliding door, roll-in shower with seat, handrails. Other bedrooms level.

Rates: from £50-£75 per room BB (2007).

LLANBEDR, Gwynedd

The Ranch Outdoor Discovery Centre

Bryn-y-Moel, Llanbedr, Gwynedd LL45 2HU.
☎ **01341 241358.**
●● D/E/I/F/G

Residential holiday/activity centre for groups of between 12 and 40 overlooking Cardigan Bay. Ground floor accommodation for up to 4 wheelchair users with roll-in showers/ WCs. Range of outdoor activities based on 11 acre site.

Rates: on application.

LLANDUDNO, Conwy

Bay Court Hotel

North Promenade, Llandudno LL30 2LP.
☎ **01492 877356.**
● D/E/G 

Hotel by seafront. Entrance level, 48" and 31". Public rooms level. Two ground floor bedrooms 29" with bathrooms, no adaptations. Open March-October.

Rates: from £39 per night DBB (2007).

Belmont Hotel

21 North Parade, Llandudno LL30 2LP.
☎ **01492 877770.**
belmont16@lineone.co.uk
 D/E/I/G 

Hotel owned by Royal Blind Society. Exterior and interior lifts. Most bedrooms have en-suite facilities. Some bedrooms with roll-in shower rooms designed for wheelchair users. Choice of either half or full board, short breaks available. Entertainment most nights. Guests needing personal care should be accompanied.

Rates: from £196-£294 BBE per person per week (2008).

Imperial Hotel

Promenade, Llandudno LL30 1AP.
☎ **01492 877466.**
www.theimperial.co.uk
●  F/G 

Hotel on seafront. Level entrance from car park to lift; 8 steps at front entrance. Public rooms level. Unisex WC on 2nd floor. Lifts min. 31½", inside 32"x84". 98 bedrooms level. Adapted WC on 2nd floor.

Rates: on application.

The Royal Hotel

Church Walks, Llandudno LL30 2HW.
☎ **01492 876476.**
www.royalhotelllandudno.com
●● D/E/F/G 

Traditional hotel. Parking space can be reserved. Entrance level. Public rooms level. WCs not adapted. Lift 85cm, inside 120x100cm. Six bedrooms level, 73cm, ⟲. Bathrooms 63cm, restricted ⟲, grabrails by bath and WC. Lift to rear garden.

Rates: from £40 per person BB (2007).

West Shore Hotel

West Parade, Llandudno LL30 2BB.
☎ **01492 876833.**
westshorehotel@johngrooms.org.uk
 D/E/I/G/H 

Grooms Holidays hotel specially adapted for disabled holiday makers. 17 bedrooms with roll-in shower rooms. Some equipment available including hoists but guests needing personal help should be accompanied or arrange care from a recommended local agency. Tail-lift bus for outings.

Rates: on application

LLANLLYFNI, Gwynedd

Ozanam Centre

Tyn-y-Pwll, Tan-yr-Allt, Llanllyfni, Caernarfon LL54 6RP.

☎ 01286 881568. W www.ozanamcentre.org

●● D/E/I/G ★★

Society of St Vincent de Paul centre for groups of up to 48. Entrance ramp, double doors. Two small steps in reception area. Dining room and lounges level. External ramp to activity room. Adapted WC cubicles. Lift 31½", inside 43"x57". Eight, of 19, bedrooms with en suite bathrooms. 1st floor bathroom and ground floor roll-in shower room designed for disabled people. Mountain activities can be arranged.

Ⓟ

Rates: on application.

MOLD, Flintshire

Beaufort Park Hotel

Mold CH7 6RQ. **☎ 01352 758646.**

W www.beaufortparkhotel.co.uk

● D/E/I/F/G ★★★

Country hotel. Parking spaces reserved. Ramp to entrance. Lounge and restaurant level. Ramp to bar. Unisex WC. 5 ground floor bedrooms 27", ⟲. Bathrooms 27", ⟲, handrail. 27 other ground floor bedrooms.

Ⓟ

Rates: on application.

Holiday Inn Chester West

A55 Northop Hall, Mold CH7 6HB.

☎ 01244 550011.

W www.holidayinn-chesterwest.co.uk

●● D/E/I/F/G

Hotel on A55. 8 reserved parking bays. Entrance level, automatic doors. Public rooms ground floor open plan. Large print menus. Unisex WC. Lift 90cm. Ground floor bedroom designed for disabled people. Bathroom 90cm, ⟲, handrails by bath, space by bath and WC. Other bedrooms level. Teletext TVs. Induction loop, portable fire alarms.

Ⓟ

Rates: on application.

NANT GWYNANT, Gwynedd

Pen-y-Pass Youth Hostel

Nant Gwynant, Caernarfon LL55 4NY.

☎ 01286 870428.

@ penypass@yha.org.uk

●● D/E/I/F/G ★★

Hostel in Snowdonia. Entrance 2" step. Public rooms level. Annexe with 4 bedrooms for up to 5 people. Unisex shower room/WC 32", ⟲, roll-in shower, handrails, space for side transfer to WC. For further information on youth hostels see page 34.

Ⓟ

Rates: from £14 adult over night (2007).

PANT GLAS, Gwynedd

The Old School Guest House

Bwlch Derwin, Pant Glas LL51 9EQ.

☎ 01286 660701.

W www.oldschool-henysgol.co.uk

●● D/F/G ★★★

Country guesthouse between Caernarfon and Porthmadog. Parking by entrance ramp. Dining room and lounge level. Family bedroom with shower room. Twin with bathroom ⟲. Double bedroom upstairs. Also ground floor suite in annexe with roll-in shower. Access statement on website.

Ⓟ

Rates: from £28 per person BB (2007).

PORTHMADOG, Gwynedd

Old Mill Farmhouse

From Oleu Farm, Trawsfynydd, Porthmadog LL41 4UN.
☎ **01766 540397.**
www.oldmillfarmhouse.co.uk
●● D/E/I/F/G ★★★

Farm guesthouse in Snowdonia. Public rooms in farmhouse level. Seven level bedrooms in adjoining building. One has roll-in shower room, ⟲, handrails, shower seat and space for side transfer to WC. Toilet frame and raised seat available. Ramp to garden and animal feeding area.

Rates: from £28-£30 per person BB (2007)

PWLLHELI, Gwynedd

Rhosydd

26 Glan Cymerau, Pwllheli LL53 5PU.
☎ **01758 612956.** @ **sewrhosydd@aol.com**
●● D/E/I/F/G ★

Guesthouse bungalow on edge of resort. Entrance level, 33". Dining room ⟲. Double bedroom with shower room ⟲, roll-in shower, handrails, space for side transfer to WC. Also twin bedroom and adjoining bathroom. Evening meals by arrangement. Child minding and some other assistance offered.

Apply: Mrs Sarah Williams.
Rates: on application.

RHYL, Denbighshire

Bodelwyddan Castle Hotel

Bodelwyddan LL18 5YA.
☎ **01745 585088.**
●● D/E/I/F/G ★★★

Country house hotel inland from Rhyl. Reserved parking bays. Ramp from car park and to entrance, 78cm. Public rooms ground floor, level or ramp from reception. Unisex WCs. Lift 82cm, inside 140x110cm. Nine bedrooms adapted for disabled guests. Bathrooms 100cm, ⟲, handrails, space for side transfer to bath and WC. Also 16 "easy access" bedrooms. Hoist in swimming pool. Entertainment and special interest breaks offered. A Warner hotel for adults only.

Rates: on application.

Brynteg Guest House

42 River Street, Rhyl LL18 1PT.
☎ **01745 338549.**
www.rhylguesthouse.co.uk
● D/E/I/F/G ★★★

Guesthouse near beach and town centre. Entrance level, 34". Public rooms level, min. door width 30". Ground floor twin/family bedroom ⟲ with bathroom. Waterproof sheet available. Other bedrooms upstairs.

Rates: from £15-£25 per person BB (2007).

LODGE ACCOMMODATION

There are Premier Travel Inn (see page 38) and Travelodge (see page 38) properties in the following areas in this Region.

Bangor - Premier Travel Inn .... ☎ 0870 197 7023
Travelodge .... ☎ 0870 191 1561
Halkyn - Travelodge .... ☎ 0870 191 1578
Holyhead - Travelodge .... ☎ 0870 085 0950
Northop Hall - Travelodge .... ☎ 0870 191 1591
Llandudno - Premier Travel Inn .... ☎ 0870 197 7162
Wrexham - Premier Travel Inn .... ☎ 0870197 7279
Travelodge .... ☎ 01978 365705

SELF-CATERING ACCOMMODATION

ABERDOVEY, Gwynedd

Wrekin

Corbett Avenue, Tywyn, Nr. Aberdovey.

Adapted 3 bedroom bungalow owned by Shropshire Scope. Applications through Scope affiliates, local authorities, etc. for disabled people not resident in Shropshire accepted from March.

Apply: Mr C Hayes, 21 Belvedere Walk, Shrewsbury SY2 5LT. ☎ 01743 240058.
Rates: on application.

ABERGELE, Conwy

Ty Mawr Holiday Park

Towyn Road, Towyn, Abergele LL22 9HG.
☎ 01745 832079.

●● I/F/G ★★★★

Park Resorts holiday park between Abergele and Rhyl with wide range of facilities and entertainment. Caravans for 5 people adapted for disabled guests. Entrance ramp. Lounge/kitchen open plan. Two bedrooms, sliding door 75cm, ↻ in double. Shower room 75cm, handrails, restricted ↻. Open Easter-October.

Ⓟ

Apply: Park Resorts Reservations
☎ 08701 299299.
W www.park-resorts.com
Rates: on application.

ABERSOCH, Gwynedd

Rhydolion

Llangian, Abersoch, Pwllheli LL53 7LR.
☎ **01758 712342.** **www.rhydolion.co.uk**

●● I/F/G ★★★★★

Ground floor cottage for up to 6 people. Ramp to entrance. Lounge/diner and kitchen. Double bedroom ⟲, low wardrobe rail. En-suite roll-in shower room with shower seat and handrails. Also twin and double bedrooms and bathroom. A second unit suitable for some disabled people is being developed.

Rates: from £180-£550 per week (2007).

ANGLESEY

Minfford Holidays

Lligwy, Dulas, Anglesey LL70 9HJ.
☎ **01248 410678.**
www.minffordd-holidays.com

●● F/G ★★★★

4 cottages and a small park of holiday caravans in country near Lligwy Bay on east of island. Two cottages designed for disabled people. Entrance level. Doors 90cm. Lounge. Open plan kitchen/dining room, most controls useable from wheelchair. One cottage has a ground floor bedroom with en-suite shower room with roll-in shower with mobile shower screen, handrails and space for transfer to WC. The 2nd has a daybed in lounge and two bedrooms upstairs. A 3rd cottage has ground floor accommodation but an entrance step and no adaptations. Two of the 10 caravans, for 4-6 people, have entrance ramp. Open plan lounge/kitchen. Double bedroom. Bathroom 30", small step to shower, handrails, no ⟲. Induction loop. Caravans closed November-March. Access statement on website.

Rates: on application.

COLWYN BAY, Conwy

Bron-Y-Wendon Caravan Park

Wern Road, Llanddulas,
Colwyn Bay LL22 8HG.
☎ **01492 512903.**
www.northwales-holidays.co.uk

●● G ★★★★★

Park for 130 touring caravans in small groups overlooking the sea. Unisex toilet with shower and seat, handrails, space for side transfer to WC. Office level. Open all year. Access statement available.

Rates: £18-£21 per pitch (2007).

DOLGELLAU, Gwynedd

Pen-y-Lon

Pentre Bach, Llwyngwril,
Nr. Dolgellau LL37 2JU.
www.pentrebach.com

●● F/G ★★★★

Cottage for up to 7 people overlooking Cardigan Bay. Front entrance level 78cm. Internal doors 75cm, except sun-lounge 74cm. Lounge, dining room and sun-lounge level. Kitchen ⟲. Double bedroom level, bedblocks available. WC level, ⟲, handrails. Downstairs accessible shower. Other bedrooms and bathroom upstairs. Two other cottages and organic produce available. Access statement on website.

Apply: Mr & Mrs Smyth ☎ 01341 250294.
Rates: from £375-£805 per week (2007).

HARLECH, Gwynedd

Ystumwern Hall Farm

Dyffryn Ardudwy, Nr. Harlech LL44 2DD.
☎ **01341 247249.**
W www.ystumgwern.co.uk
● ● F/G ★★★★★

Three cottages, for 2 to 8 people, with some adaptations for disabled guests on farm 5 miles from Harlech. Two have level entrance and a portable ramp is available for the 3rd. Internal doors 30". No specific adaptations in kitchens. In each unit one bedroom is designed for wheelchair user with a wheel-in shower room having handrails, shower seat, space by WC and under basin. Raised toilet seat available. Teletext TV. Other cottages available. Premier Cottages member.

Apply: Jane & John Williams.
Rates: from £220-£1250 (2007).

LLANFYNYDD, Flintshire

Clwyd Special Riding Centre

Llanfynydd, Wrexham LL11 5NH.
☎ **01352 770446.**
W www.clwydspecialridingcentre.org.uk
●● I/F/G

Accommodation designed for disabled people available for self-catering groups. Entrance 36". Lounge. 10 bedrooms, accommodating up to 18 in total. Two bathrooms and two roll-shower rooms, all with ⟲, handrails, space for side transfer to WC. Separate building with dining room and kitchen, controls useable from wheelchair. Long weekend bookings taken between April and November when not in use for RDA holidays.

Rates: on application.

PRESTATYN, Denbighshire

2 The Boulevard

Prestatyn, Denbighshire LL19 7EF

Adapted 3 bedroom bungalow owned by Shropshire Scope. Applications through Scope affiliates, local authorities, etc. for disabled people not resident in Shropshire accepted from March.

Apply: Mr C Hayes, 21 Belvedere Walk, Shrewsbury SY2 5LT. ☎ 01743 240058.
Rates: on application.

Presthaven Sands Holiday Park

Gronant, Prestatyn LL19 9TT.
☎ **01745 856471.**
●● I/F/G ★★★

Haven holiday park 3 miles east of Prestatyn with wide range of facilities and entertainment. Caravans for 5 people adapted for disabled guests. Entrance ramp. Lounge/kitchen open plan. Two bedrooms, sliding door 75cm, ⟲ in double. Shower room 75cm, handrails, restricted ⟲, no space by WC. Open Mid March-October.

Apply: Haven Holiday Reservations ☎ 0870 2422222.
Rates: on application.

Scout Holiday Homes Trust Caravan

●● E/I/F/G

Adapted unit for up to 6 people. Entrance ramp. 40". Open plan lounge/kitchen. Work surface 36". Two bedrooms, ⟲ in double. Shower room 30", handrails, space for side transfer to WC and shower seat. Available April-October.

Apply: Scout Holiday Homes Trust ☎ 020 8433 7290. See page 26.
Rates: from £155-£430 per week (2007).

PWLLHELI, Gwynedd

Afonwen Farm

Pwllheli LL53 6TX.

☎ **01766 810939.**

www.afonwenfarm.co.uk

●● I/F/G ★★★★

Seven cottages adapted for disabled guests. Entrance level. Lounge/kitchen open plan. All have ground floor bedrooms. One has en-suite bathroom, the others a roll-in shower room. Both ⟲, handrails, space for side transfer to WC. Also twin bedroom upstairs. Two other similar cottages but with no adaptations.

Rates: from £150-£460 per week (2007).

Hafan y Mor Holiday Park

Pwllhelli LL53 6HX.

☎ **01758 612112.**

●● I/F/G ★★★

Haven holiday park between Pwllhelli and Criccieth with wide range of facilities and entertainment. Caravans for 5 people adapted for disabled guests. Entrance ramp. Lounge/kitchen open plan. Two bedrooms, sliding door 75cm, ⟲ in double. Shower room 75cm, handrails, restricted ⟲, no space by WC. Open Late March-October.

Apply: Haven Holiday Reservations ☎ 0870 2422222.

Rates: on application.

RHOS-ON-SEA, Conwy

Beachmount Holiday Apartments

67 Colwyn Avenue, Rhos-on-Sea, Colwyn Bay LL28 4NN.

☎ **01492 549314.**

●● F

Two bedroomed bungalow for up to 4 people. Entrance ramp. Wide doors. Walk-in bath. Also a one bedroom ground floor flat said to be suitable for some wheelchair users. Near seafront. No small children.

Ⓟ 🚭

Rates: from £160-£470 per week (2007).

MID & WEST WALES ACCOMMODATION WITH MEALS

BRECON, Powys

The Beacons

16 Bridge Street, Brecon LD3 8AH.

☎ 01874 623339.

W www.thebreconbecons.co.uk

●● D/F/G ★★★

Guesthouse in country town. Rear entrance level 80cm. Dining room ½" step. Bar 2 steps. Family bedroom with own entrance level, 74cm. Bathroom 84cm, ⟲, handrails, space for side transfer to bath but not WC. One other ground floor bedroom level.

Ⓟ

Rates: from £36 per person BB (2007).

Brecon Castle Hotel

Castle Square, Brecon LD3 9DB.

☎ 01874 624611.

W www.breconcastle.co.uk

●● D/E/I/F/G ★★

Hotel on hill in town centre. Entrance level 48". Public rooms level, 26" door to lounge. Unisex WC. Twin bedroom adapted for disabled guests. Bathroom 30", ⟲, handrails, space for side transfer to bath and WC. Lift and other access improvements in 2008.

Ⓟ

Rates: on application.

BROAD HAVEN, Pembrokeshire

Broad Haven Youth Hostel

Broad Haven, Haverfordwest SA62 3JH.

☎ 01437 781688.

@ broadhaven@yha.org.uk

●● D/E/I/F/G ★★★

Single storey hostel near level beach. Entrance level, double doors. Min. door width 30". Two bedrooms have shared roll-in shower rooms. Adapted WC with basin and handrails. Shower room with handrails and seat. Wet rooms also available. Activity packages offered for groups with disabled people include riding and canoeing. Computer training suite available. Cafe bar also open all day. For more information on Youth Hostels see page 34.

Ⓟ U ⓘ

Rates: from £15 adult overnight (2007).

FELINGWM UCHAF, Carmarthenshire

Allt-y-golau Farmhouse

Allt-y-golau Uchaf,
Felingwm Uchaf SA32 7BB.

☎ 01267 290455. W www.alltygolau.com

● D/F/G ★★★★

Farm bed & breakfast in Tywi Valley. Entrance 2 steps. Dining room level 75cm. Lounge upstairs. Ground floor double and twin bedrooms. Private shower rooms; that for the twin room has ⟲, handrails. Raised WC seat and some bath equipment available. Access details on request or on website.

Ⓟ

Rates: from £30-£40 per person sharing BB (2007).

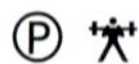

LLANDEILO, Carmarthenshire

Plough Inn

Rhosmaen, Llandeilo SA19 6NP.

☎ **01558 823431.**

W www.ploughrhosmaen.co.uk

●● D/E/F ★★★

Small country hotel. Reserved parking bays. Entrance level, 34". Public rooms level, min. door width 31". Adapted cubicle in ladies WC. Bedroom designed for disabled guests 32". Bathroom ⟲, roll-in shower, shower seat, handrails, space by bath and WC. 4 other ground floor bedrooms. Access statement on website.

Ⓟ

Rates: from £40-£60 per person BB (2007).

LLANDOVERY, Carmarthenshire

Llanerchindda Farm

Cynghordy, Llandovery SA20 0NB.

☎ **01550 750274.**

W www.cambrianway.com

●● D/E/F/G ★★

Farmhouse in the Cambrian Mountains. 1 step at entrance, ramp available. Public rooms level. One bedroom adapted for disabled users on ground floor, ⟲. Shower room ⟲, roll-in shower, handrails. Other ground floor bedrooms level. Garden with patio. Evening meals available.

Ⓟ

Rates: from £32-£35 BB (2008).

LLANDRINDOD WELLS, Powys

The Metropole

Temple Street, Llandrindod Wells LD1 5DY.

☎ **01597 823700.**

W www.metropole.co.uk

● D/E/I/G ★★★

Traditional hotel. Entrance ramp, double doors. Public rooms level. Unisex WC. Lift 31". 42 bedrooms level, two with adapted bathrooms.

Ⓟ

Rates: on application.

LLANGAMMARCH WELLS, Powys

Lake Country House Hotel

Llangammarch Wells LD4 4BS.

☎ **01591 620202.**

W www.lakecountryhouse.co.uk

● D/E/G ★★★★

Country house hotel west of Builth Wells. Small step at side entrance; main entrance 6 steps. Public rooms level. WCs large but not adapted. Ground floor bedrooms ⟲ with bathrooms. Extensive grounds which are difficult for wheelchair users.

Ⓟ

Rates: on application.

LLANWRTYD WELLS, Powys

New Hall Guest House

Victoria Road, Llanwrtyd Wells LD5 4SU.

☎ **01591 610265.**

W www.newhallguesthouse.co.uk

●● D/E/I/F/G ★★★★

Guesthouse in small town. Reserved parking bay. Entrance 1 step, ramp available. Dining room and lounge level. Ground floor twin/double bedroom, ⟲, adjustable clothes rails. Bathroom 80cm, ⟲, roll-in shower with seat, space by bath and WC. Other bedrooms upstairs. Evening meals available.

Ⓟ

Rates: from £30-£40 per person BB (2007).

PEMBROKE, Pembrokeshire

Rosedene

Hodgeston, Pembroke SA71 5JU.

☎ **01646 672586.**

W www.rosedeneguesthouse.co.uk

●● D/E/I/F/G ★★★★

Country licensed guesthouse. Entrance ramp 37". Public rooms level. Double/twin bedroom designed for disabled guests. Shower room ⟲, roll-in shower, handrails, space for side transfer to WC. Closed December and January.

Ⓟ ⓘ

Rates: from £32 per person BB (2007).

TENBY, Pembrokeshire

Greenhills Country House Hotel

St Florence, Nr. Tenby SA70 8NB.
☎ 01834 871291.
www.greenhillshotel.co.uk
●● D/E/I/F ★★

Country hotel, 3 miles from Tenby. Entrance level. Restaurant 1 step or ramp. Other public rooms level. WCs not adapted. Four ground floor twin or double bedrooms. Shower rooms no ⟲ or space for side transfer. Closed November-April.

Rates: from £35 per person BB (2007).

Manorbier Youth Hostel

Manorbier, Nr. Tenby SA70 7TT.
☎ 01834 871803.
@ manorbier@yha.org.uk
●● D/E/G ★★★

Hostel on coast. Entrance level 57". Public rooms level. 4, 6 and 8-bed dormitories level. Adapted WC and roll-in shower room. Open March-October and groups taken all year. For more information on Youth Hostels see page 34.

Rates: from £12.50 adult per night (2007).

LODGE ACCOMMODATION

There are Travelodge (see page 38) properties in the following areas in this Region.

Cross Hands - Travelodge .... ☎ 0870 191 1729
Pembroke Dock - Travelodge .... ☎ 0870 191 1799
St Clears - Travelodge .... ☎ 0870 191 1553

SELF-CATERING ACCOMMODATION

ABERAERON, Ceredigion

Abermydyr

Ciliau Aeron, nr. Aberaeron
●● F/G

National Trust cottage by River Aeron. Ground floor lounge, dining room, kitchen and twin bedroom with shower room designed for disabled people. Also double and twin bedrooms and bathroom upstairs. Ramps throughout ground floor.

Apply: National Trust Holiday Booking Office ☎ 0870 4584422. See page 33.
Rates: from £506-£1161 per week (2007)

Ty Glyn Holiday Centre

Ciliau Aeron, nr. Lampeter SA48 8DE.
●●● I/G/H ★★★

Purpose-built centre in country for self-catering groups of children and young people with disabilities. Large lounge/dining area with patio and well equipped kitchen. Accommodation for up to 16 people in 9 single and shared bedrooms. ⟲ in all rooms, one with adjustable height bed. Toilet facilities include 3 showers, one roll-in, and a specially equipped bathroom with electric hoist. Mobile hoist available. Walled garden with playground.

Apply: Louise Hutchins, Hafod, Llanarth, Ceredigion SA47 0QB. ☎ 01545 580708.
www.tyglyndavistrust.co.uk
Rates: from £600 per week per group (2007).

AMROTH, Pembrokeshire

Lower Pendeilo Farm

Amroth SA67 8PR.
www.lowerpendeilofarmholidays.com
●● I/F/G ★★★★

Smallholding 1½ miles from sea. "Sunflower", for 2-4 people was originally built for disabled family member. Entrance level, double doors. Internal doors 32½". Lounge and kitchen, controls useable from wheelchair. Twin bedroom ⟲. Folding bed in lounge. Shower room ⟲, shower has small lip and seat, handrails, space by WC and under basin. Teletext TV. A second cottage is also available. Access details in website.

Ⓟ

Apply: Mr & Mrs Jenkinson.
☎ 01834 831326.
Rates: from £345-£595 per week (2007).

BONCATH, Pembrokeshire

2 Bro-Iorwerth

Boncath SA37 0JL
●● F/G ★★★

Converted stable in village. Ramp to level entrance. Lounge open plan. Kitchen 31", controls useable from wheelchair. Ground floor bedroom with adjustable single bed and roll-in shower room with handrails and space by WC. Three double/twin bedrooms and bathroom upstairs. Patio and barbecue. Ramp for garden door from lounge. Pub serving meals nearby. A second cottage is available.

Ⓟ

Apply: Mrs M Jenkins, Rhosfach, Efailwen, Clunderwen SA66 7XG. ☎ 01994 419222.
pembscottages@aol.com
Rates: from £230 per week (2007).

Clynfyw Countryside Centre

Abercych, Boncath SA37 0HF.
☎ **01239 841236.**
www.clynfyw.co.uk
●● E/I/F/G/H ★★★-★★★★★

4 single storey cottages designed for disabled people on organic farm in North Pembrokeshire. Entrances level, doors 42". Lounge and kitchen level ⟲. Controls useable from wheelchair. 3 or 2 twin bedrooms level ⟲. Bathroom 33", ⟲, handrails, space for side transfer to bath and WC. Roll-in shower in some units. Fittings vary between units. Bed blocks, transfer boards, cotsides, shower chairs available. Care and meals can be provided with prior requests. Special interest courses offered. Accessible woodland farm trails, play areas, games room and dance performance space. Full access statement on website.

Ⓟ

Apply: Jim Bowen.
Rates: from £220-£650 per week (2007).

BORTH, Ceredigion

Brynowen Holiday Park

Borth, Aberystwyth SY24 5LS.
☎ **01970 871366.**
●● I/F/G ★★★

Park Resorts holiday park at south end of Borth seafront with range of facilities. Caravans for 5 people adapted for disabled guests. Entrance ramp. Lounge/kitchen open plan. Two bedrooms, sliding door 75cm, ⟲ in double. Shower room 75cm, handrails, restricted ⟲. Open Easter-October.

Ⓟ

Apply: Park Resorts Reservations
☎ 08701 299299. www.park-resorts.com
Rates: on application.

Mid & West Wales – self-catering accommodation

BRECON, Powys

Canal Barn Bunkhouse

Ty Camlas, Canal Bank, Brecon LD3 7HH.

W **www.canal-barn.co.uk**

●● F/G ★★★★

Single storey bunkhouse for groups on edge of town and Brecon Beacons. Ramp on approach. 2" sill at entrance, portable ramp available. Lounge/dining room and kitchen ⟲, standard height kitchen units. 6 bedrooms for up to 24 people in bunks. Two shower rooms 90cm, ⟲, roll-in shower with seat, handrails, space by WC. 3 other level bathrooms. Regularly used by disabled people.

Apply: Ralph Day ☎ 01874 625361.
Rates: from £12 per person (2007).

BROAD HAVEN, Pembrokeshire

Rocksdrift & Seaview Apartments

Broad Haven, Haverfordwest SA62 3JW.

☎ **01437 781507.**

W **www.broad-haven.com**

●● E/I/G ★★★★

Five flats 20 yards from beach. Two, for up to 6 people, designed for wheelchair users. Lounge/kitchen open plan, work tops 39". Twin and double bedrooms. Bathroom ⟲, handrails, space for side transfer to bath and WC. Bath seat and raised WC seat available.

Ⓟ

Rates: from £252-£819 per week (2007).

BUILTH WELLS, Powys

Penrheol Farm

Llanynis, Builth Wells LD2 3HH.

●● F/G ★★★★

Two ground floor suites on farm overlooking the Irfon Valley. "Wye Suite" designed for disabled people. Entrance level 91cm. Lounge/kitchen open plan. Double bedroom with shower room adjoining. 2 twin bedrooms with en suite shower rooms. All 36", ⟲, roll-in shower with seat, handrails, space for side transfer to WC. "Irfon Suite", sleeps 2 people, level, no adaptations.

Ⓟ

Apply: Anne & Tony Brooks.
☎ 01982 553853.
@ penrheol@btinternet.com
Rates: on application.

CARDIGAN, Ceredigion

Canllefaes Ganol Cottages

Penparc, Cardigan SA43 1SG.

W **www.canllefaes.com**

●● I/F/G ★★★★★

2 adapted cottages, of six, 3 miles from Cardigan. Slope to entrance 29½". Lounge/kitchen open plan, worktops 35½". One has a double bedroom with en suite shower room ⟲, roll-in shower with seat, handrails, space by WC. Also 2 twin bedrooms and bunkroom. The second cottage has double and twin bedrooms and shower room with roll-in shower and seat, handrails, space by WC. Waterproof sheet available. Owner can sign and lipspeak

Ⓟ

Apply: Lynne Mansfield ☎ 01239 613712.
Rates: from £200-570 per week (2007).

Gorslwyd Farm

Tan-y-Groes, Cardigan SA43 2HZ.

☎ **01239 810593.**

www.gorslwyd.co.uk

●●● E/I/F/G/H ★★★★

Eight purpose-built cottages for up to 6 people 2 miles from beaches. All entrances level, 33". Six units all ground floor, of which 2 can interconnect; 2 have some bedrooms upstairs. Lounges and kitchens 33". Ground floor bedrooms 33", ⟲, fittings include hoist. Bathrooms 33", ⟲, fittings vary and include roll-in showers, handrails, special baths, wheelchair-height basins. Accessible garden and games room. Access statement available.

Apply: Steve & Roni McKenzie

Rates: from £200-£600 per week (2007).

Trenewydd Farm Holiday Cottages

St Dogmaels, Cardigan SA43 3BJ.

☎ **01239 612370.**

www.cottages-wales.com

● F/G/P ★★★★★

Five cottages, for 2-9 people, on farm 3 miles from coast. One has entrance ramp and is single storey. Each has a ground floor bedroom and bathroom. No adaptations. Meals available.

Rates: from £200-£890 per week (2007).

CARMARTHEN, Carmarthenshire

Hamdden Llety Meiri

Llety Mieri, Golden Grove, Carmarthen SA32 8NL.

www.vacationcottageswales.com

●● E/I/F/G ★★★★

Three cottages for up to 4 people. Entrances level. All doors 31½". Kitchen units 35". Shower rooms ⟲, roll-in shower, handrails, space for side transfer to WC. Games room on site.

Ⓟ

Apply: Catherine McLoughlin

☎ 01558 823059.

Rates: from £210-£395 per week (2007).

CASTLEMARTIN. Pembrokeshire

Cornerstone Cottage

Castlemartin

●● F/G

Cottage for 3 people designed for disabled guests. Ramped entrances. Min. door width 84cm. Lounge/kitchen open plan. Controls useable from wheelchair. Double bedroom ⟲, and single bedroom. Shower room, roll-in shower, handrails, space by WC.

Ⓟ

Apply: Mrs Christine Neve, 2 Pound Cottages, Castlemartin, Pembroke SA71 5HN. ☎ 01646 661369.

Rates: on application.

FISHGUARD, Pembrokeshire

Gellifawr Hotel & Cottages

Pontfaen, Nr. Fishguard SA65 9TX.
☎ **01239 820343.** W **www.gellifawr.co.uk**

●● G ★★★★

Cottages adjoining country hotel near Newport and Fishguard. "Dove" and "Ty Nant Cottages" designed for disabled guests. Level entrance. Open plan lounge/kitchen. Twin and 2 double bedrooms. Shower room ⟲, roll-in shower with seat, handrail and space by WC. Meals and bar available in hotel.

Ⓟ

Rates: from £250-£640 per week (2007).

HAVERFORDWEST, Pembrokeshire

Ivy Court

Llys-y-Fran, Nr. Haverfordwest SA63 4RS.
☎ **01437 532473.** W **www.ivycourt.co.uk**

●● F/G ★★★★

"The Roses" is a single storey cottage, in a group of 10, in mid-Pembrokeshire by Country Park. Entrance threshold, 33". Lounge 30". Kitchen 33", ⟲, no adaptations. Twin and double bedrooms. Bathroom 30", ⟲, handrail by bath. Premier Cottages member.

Ⓟ

Apply: Rosemarie & Gareth Rees-Paton
Rates: from £280-£630 per week (2007).

Keeston Hill Cottage

Keeston, Nr. Haverfordwest SA62 6EJ.
W **www.keestonhillcottage.co.uk**

●● F/G ★★★★

Ground floor flat 4 miles from Haverfordwest. Entrance step, portable ramp available. Lounge 30". Kitchen open plan, controls may be useable from wheelchair. Double and twin bedrooms; rollaway bed also available. Ramp to bathroom 30", ⟲, handrails, space for side transfer to bath and WC. Bath board and raised WC seat available. 2nd flat upstairs. Step at neighbouring restaurant and bar.

Ⓟ

Rates: from £215-£395 per week (2007/8).

KIDWELLY, Carmarthenshire

Carmarthen Bay Holiday Park

Kidwelly SA17 5HQ. ☎ **01267 267511.**

●● I/F/G ★★★

Park Resorts holiday park 2 miles from Kidwelly with range of facilities and entertainment. Caravans for 5 people adapted for disabled guests. Entrance ramp. Lounge/kitchen open plan. Two bedrooms, sliding door 75cm, ⟲ in double. Shower room 75cm, handrails, restricted ⟲. Open Easter-October. See below for unit owned by voluntary organisation.

Ⓟ

Apply: Park Resorts Reservations
☎ 08701 299299. W www.park-resorts.com
Rates: on application.

Scout Holiday Homes Trust Chalet

●● E/I/F/G

Adapted unit for up to 6 people. Entrance ramp. Open plan lounge/kitchen. Three bedrooms. Shower room 30", handrails, space for side transfer to WC and shower seat. Available April-October.
Apply: Scout Holiday Homes Trust
☎ 020 8433 7290. See page 26.
Rates: from £130-£450 per week (2007).

LAMPETER, Ceredigion

Gaer Cottages

Cribyn, Lampeter SA48 7LZ.
☎ **01570 470275.**
www.selfcateringinwales.co.uk
●●● E/I/F/G/H ★★★★★

Cottages in country west of Lampeter. Six, of 9, with ground floor accommodation designed for disabled guests. Level entrance or portable ramp available. Open plan kitchens ⟲; controls and worktops useable from wheelchair in one. One has 3 bedrooms sleeping up to 7; the others sleep up to 4 in 2 bedrooms. Adjustable height beds. Bunk beds available for children. Bathrooms ⟲, space by WC, roll-in shower with seat in 3. Portable hoist and other equipment available. Hoist in heated pool. Access statement on request.

Ⓟ

Rates: from £200-£975 per week (2007).

LLANDEILO, Carmarthenshire

Maerdy Cottages

Taliaris, Nr. Llandeilo SA19 7DA
www.maerdyholidaycottages.co.uk
●● I/F/G ★★★★

Two cottages, of 6, adapted for disabled people on edge of Brecon Beacons. Both have entrance ramps and open plan lounge/kitchen. "The Stable" has 3 ground floor bedrooms ⟲. Bathroom ⟲, roll-in shower and shower chair, space for side transfer to bath and WC. "The Barn" has ground floor double/single bedroom with accessible basin and roll-in shower with seat and handrails. Three double bedrooms upstairs. Ramp to garden. Some other equipment available. One other unit has ground floor accommodation. Meals available.

Ⓟ

Apply: Mrs M E Jones, Dan-y-Cefn, Manordeilo, Llandeilo SA19 7BD.
☎ 01550 777448/01558 823874.
Rates: from £200-£750 per week (2007).

LLANFAIR CAEREINION, Powys

Madog's Wells

Llanfair Caereinion, Welshpool SY21 0DE.
www.madogswells.co.uk
●● F/G/H ★★★★★-★★★

Three bungalows designed for disabled people. Ramp to level entrances, 34". Lounge/kitchen open plan, controls in reach from wheelchair. Two units have three bedrooms and the other two, all ⟲. All have a shower room 32", ⟲, roll-in shower and seat, handrails, space for side transfer to WC. Towels in trolley. There are separate WCs in the larger units. Owner knows American sign language. Access Statement available

Ⓟ

Apply: Michael & Ann Reed ☎ 01938 810446.
Rates: from £200-£480 per week (2007).

MACHYNLLETH, Powys

Yr Hen Stablau

Pantlludw, Machynlleth SY20 9JR.
☎ **01654 703428.**
www.selfcateringcottagewales.co.uk
●● F/G/H ★★★★

Converted stables in southern Snowdonia, a mile from Machynlleth. Entrance level. Lounge and kitchen ground floor. Double bedroom level. Shower room 86cm, ⟲, roll-in shower with seat, handrails, space by WC. Two twin bedrooms and WC upstairs. Teletext TV. Terrace accessible.

Ⓟ

Rates: from £300-£640 per week.

MOYLGROVE, Pembrokeshire

Cwm Connell Coastal Cottages

Moylgrove, Nr. Cardigan SA43 3BX.

●● I/G

Cottages near coast. "Yr Ffald" designed for disabled people. Entrance level, 31½". Lounge/kitchen open plan, controls useable from wheelchair. Double and twin bedrooms, sliding door, ↺. Shower room 31½" sliding door, ↺, roll-in shower and seat, handrails, space for side transfer to WC. Waterproof sheet available. Two other units with ground floor accommodation. Closed December and February. Access Statement available. Premier Cottages member.

Apply: Susan Jenkins ☎ 01239 881691.
@ rtg@sa43.com
Rates: from £320-£559 per week (2007).

NARBERTH, Pembrokeshire

Caerwen

Jesse Road, Narberth SA67 7DP

Purpose designed and equipped house for families with disabled children with autism and other learning disabilities. Sleeps up to 6 plus a baby. Ground floor lounge/dining room, kitchen, breakfast room, utility room and soft playroom. 4 bedrooms, one with en suite bathroom, and also a family bathroom. Garden with secure fencing. A Family Helper available if required.

Apply: The Harriet Davis Trust, Tenby Observer Offices, Warren Street, Tenby SA70 7JY. ☎ 01834 845197.
@ helen@harriet-davis-trust.freeserve.co.uk
Rates: on application.

NEW QUAY, Ceredigion

Quay West Holiday Park

New Quay SA45 9SE.
☎ 01545 560477.

●● F/G

Holiday park on cliff-top overlooking New Quay harbour with wide range of facilities and entertainment. Caravans for 5 people adapted for disabled guests. Entrance ramp. Lounge/kitchen open plan. Two bedrooms, sliding door 75cm, ↺ in double. Shower room 75cm, handrails, restricted ↺, no space by WC. Open Mid March-October.

Apply: Haven & British Holidays ☎ 0870 242 2222. W www.havenholidays.com
Rates: on application

NEWPORT, Pembrokeshire

Trefdraeth Youth Hostel

Lower St Mary Street, Newport SA42 0TS.
☎ 0870 770 6072.

●● F/G ★★★

Self-catering hostel in small town. Entrance level. Kitchen/dining room level. Main lounge upstairs. Three ground floor bedrooms, two with 6 beds and one with 4 beds, restricted access to the latter. Unisex shower room/WC designed for wheelchair users, roll-in shower. For more information on Youth Hostels see page 34.

Rates: from £12.50 adult per night (2007).

PENALLY, Pembrokeshire

The Wheelabout

The Ridgeway, Penally, Nr. Tenby SA70 8DL

●●● I/H

Purpose designed and equipped house for families with disabled children, sleeps 10. Ground floor dining room, kitchen, laundry, 1 double and a 4-bed bedroom, bathroom, roll-in shower room and changing room. Lift to 1st floor with lounge, bedroom with overhead hoist, adjustable bed, en suite bathroom/WC with hydraulic bath and basin. Parents' bedroom with own toilet. Other equipment available. Part time assistance from Family Helper if required. Heated indoor pool with hoist. Available for disabled adults and carers outside main holiday season.

Apply: The Harriet Davis Trust, Tenby Observer Offices, Warren Street, Tenby SA70 7JY. ☎ 01834 845197.
@ helen@harriet-davis-trust.freeserve.co.uk
Rates: on application.

PENDINE SANDS, Carmarthenshire

Pendine Sands Holiday Park

Nr. Carmarthen SA33 4NZ.

●● I/F/G ★★★★

Holiday park on coast. Caravans for 5 people adapted for disabled guests. Entrance ramp. Lounge/kitchen open plan. Two bedrooms, sliding door 75cm,  in double. Shower room 75cm, handrails, restricted. Open March-November.

Apply: Parkdean Holidays ☎ 0871 641 2066.
W www.parkdeanwales.co.uk
Rates: Holiday homes £179 per week. Short breaks (3 or 4 nights) from £108.

STACKPOLE, Pembrokeshire

National Trust Stackpole Centre

The Old Home Farm Yard, Stackpole, Pembroke SA71 5DQ.
☎ 01646 661425.

●●●● F/I/G

Self-catering multi-purpose centre run by National Trust on south Pembrokeshire coast with 3 large group houses and 5 cottages designed to be used by disabled people. Other facilities include swimming pool, soft play area, art room and theatre. Accessible woodland walks and fishing.

Rates: on application.

TENBY, Pembrokeshire

Giltar View

Southcliffe Street, Tenby SA70 7EA

●●● I/H

House adapted for families with disabled children, sleeps 8. Ground floor lounge, kitchen and laundry. Wheelchair lift to bedroom with adjustable and single beds. En suite bathroom/WC with adjustable bath and basin, hoist, shower and shower chair. Four other bedrooms, bathroom/WC and cloakroom. Other equipment available. A Family Helper gives assistance if required. Available for disabled adults and carers outside main holiday season.

Apply: The Harriet Davis Trust, Tenby Observer Offices, Warren Street, Tenby SA70 7JY. ☎ 01834 845197.
@ helen@harriet-davis-trust.freeserve.co.uk
Rates: on application.

Harriet's House

Castle Square, Tenby SA70 7BW

●●● I/H

Flat adapted for families with disabled children, sleeps 7. Ground floor lounge, kitchen and laundry. Bedroom with adjustable and single beds. En suite bathroom/WC with adjustable bath and basin, shower, shower chair and hoist. Two other bedrooms, bathroom/WC and cloakroom. Other equipment available. A Family Helper gives assistance if required. Available for disabled adults and carers outside main holiday season.

Apply: The Harriet Davis Trust, Tenby Observer Offices, Warren Street, Tenby SA70 7JY. ☎ 01834 845197.
@ helen@harriet-davis-trust.freeserve.co.uk
Rates: on application.

Kiln Park Holiday Park

Marsh Road, Tenby SA70 7RB.
☎ **01834 844121.**

●● F/G

Holiday park on coast at western edge of Tenby with wide range of facilities and entertainment. Caravans for 5 people adapted for disabled guests. Entrance ramp. Lounge/kitchen open plan. Two bedrooms, sliding door 75cm, ⟲ in double. Shower room 75cm, handrails, restricted ⟲, no space by WC. Open Mid March-October. One caravan on hilly area.

Apply: Haven & British Holidays
☎ 0870 242 2222.
W www.havenholidays.com
Rates: on application

WALWYN'S CASTLE, Pembrokeshire

Rosemoor Country Cottages

Walwyn's Castle, Haverfordwest SA62 3ED.
☎ **01437 781326.**
W **www.rosemoor.com**

●● I/G ★★★★

Group of cottages by Nature Reserve in National Park. "Apple" has level entrance and lounge, kitchen and double bedroom on ground floor. En suite shower room ⟲, roll-in shower with seat, handrails, space for side transfer to raised WC. Also 2 bedrooms and bathroom on 1st floor. Waterproof sheets available. 3 other units have ground floor accommodation.

Rates: from £335-£835 per week (2007).

WHITLAND, Carmarthenshire

Homeleigh Country Cottages

Red Roses, Whitland SA34 0PN.

●●● I/F/G/H ★★★★

Three cottages designed for disabled people on smallholding on edge of National Park. Entrances level, 90cm. Lounge/kitchen open plan, low level worktops. Each has a ground floor shower room 90cm, ⟲, roll-in shower with seat, handrails, space for side transfer to WC. Cottage 1 has 3 double ground floor bedrooms; Cottage 2 has 1 ground floor double bedroom and 2 doubles and bathroom upstairs; Cottage 3 has 2 ground floor double bedrooms and 2 double bedrooms and bathroom upstairs. Hoist, some equipment and carer available. 3 additional units being provided.

Apply: Mrs Morfydd Turner
☎ 01834 831765. W www.homeleigh.org
Rates: from £230-£810 per week (2007).

Latchygors Cottage

Llanfallteg, Whitland SA34 0UJ.

●● F/G ★★★★★

Cottage designed for disabled people on smallholding 3 miles from Whitland. Entrance level. Lounge/kitchen open plan. Twin bedroom ⟲. Bathroom 82cm bifold door, ⟲, handrails, space by bath and WC, low mirror. Raised WC seat. External doors to lounge, kitchen and bedroom. Accessible path round lake and fishing platforms. Closed January & February. Access statement available

Apply: Marilyn & Peter Scholfield

☎ 01994 240460.

W latchygors.co.uk

Rates: from £150-£280 per week (2007).

SOUTH WALES ACCOMMODATION WITH MEALS

BRIDGEND, Glamorgan

Express by Holiday Inn Bridgend

The Derwen, Bridgend CF32 9SH.

☎ **01656 646200.**

@ **ebhi-bridgend@btconnect.com**

●● E/I/F/G

Limited service hotel near M4 junction 36 and Sarn Park Services. Reserved parking bays. Level entrance. Public area open plan. Unisex WC. Lift to upper floors. 4 ground floor family bedrooms designed for disabled guests. Shower rooms ⟲, roll-in shower with seat, handrails, space by WC. Other bedrooms level. Vibrating pillow alarms available. Harvester restaurant adjoining.

Rates: from £50-£60 per room BB (2006).

CARDIFF

The Big Sleep Hotel

Bute Terrace, Cardiff CF10 2FE.

☎ **029 2063 6363.**

W **www.thebigsleephotel.com**

●● D/E/I/F/G

Modern hotel in city centre. 1 reserved parking bay. Entrance from car park level; steps at main entrance. Reception and bar ground floor. Restaurant and unisex WC 2nd floor. Lift 78cm. Three bedrooms, twin, double and family, designed for disabled guests on 2nd floor. Bathrooms with no ⟲, space by bath and WC, alarm cord and handrail by WC.

Rates: from £45-£120 per room (2008).

Campanile Cardiff

Caxton Place Pentwyn, Cardiff CF23 7HA.

☎ **029 2054 9044.**

@ **cardiff@campanile-hotels.com**

●●

Hotel off A48 between M4 and city centre. Reserved parking bays. Public rooms level. Unisex WC. 2 twin bedrooms designed for disabled guests. Bathroom ⟲, handrails, space for side transfer. Other ground floor bedrooms level. See page 31.

Rates: on application.

Copthorne Hotel Cardiff

Copthorne Way, Culverhouse Cross, Cardiff CF5 6DH.

☎ **029 2059 9100.**

@ **sales.cardiff@mill-cop.com**

●● D/E/I/F/G ★★★★

Hotel by lake 4 miles west of city centre. Reserved parking bays. Entrance level. Public rooms level, open plan. Unisex WC. Lift to all floors. Two ground floor bedrooms with bathrooms designed for disabled guests. Other bedrooms level.

   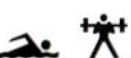

Rates: on application.

Express by Holiday Inn Cardiff Bay

Schooner Way, Atlantic Wharf, Cardiff CF10 4EE.

☎ **029 2044 9000.**

W **www.exhicardiff.co.uk**

●● E/I/G ★★★

City centre limited service hotel. Reserved parking bays. Entrance level. Low reception desk. Public rooms open plan. Unisex WC. Six bedrooms designed for disabled guests 83cm. Shower rooms ⟲, roll-in shower, handrail, space by WC. Other bedrooms level. Vibrating and flashing alarm.

Rates: on application.

Hilton Cardiff

Kingsway, Cardiff CF10 3HH.

☎ **029 2064 6314.**

W **www.hilton.co.uk/cardiff**

●● D/E/F/G 

City centre hotel. 200m to parking area, valet parking. Ramp or 5 steps to entrance, automatic and revolving doors. Public rooms ground floor. Unisex WC 1st floor. Lifts 90cm, inside 140x1200cm. 6 double bedrooms designed for disabled guests with adjoining rooms for carers if required. Shower rooms, ⟲, roll-in shower with seat, handrails, space for side transfer to WC. Other bedrooms level. Teletext TV. Vibrating alarms. Adapted changing rooms and pool hoist.

Rates: on application.

Holiday Inn Cardiff City

Castle Street, Cardiff CF10 1XD.

☎ **0870 400 8140.**

@ **reservations-cardiffcity@ihg.com**

● D/E/I/F/G 

City centre hotel. Reserved parking bays. Entrance level, automatic doors. Lounge and bar, open plan. Restaurant lower ground floor. Unisex WC. Lift 35", inside 40"x65". Four double bedrooms adapted for disabled guests 28". Bathrooms 23", ⟲, handrail by shower. Other rooms level. Induction loops and Teletext TV.

Rates: on application.

Ibis Hotel Cardiff City Centre

Churchill Way, Cardiff CF10 2HA.

☎ **029 2064 9250.** @ **H2936@accor.com**

●● D/E/G

Hotel in city centre. Entrance level. Public rooms open plan. Unisex WC. Lift to upper floors. Six bedrooms with bathrooms designed for disabled guests. Other bedrooms level.

Rates: £60-£65 per room (2008).

Ibis Hotel Cardiff Gate

Cardiff Gate Business Park, Pontprennau, Cardiff CF23 8RA.

☎ 029 2073 3222. @ H3159@accor.com

●● D/E/F

Hotel off M4 junction 30 east of Cardiff. Entrance level. Public rooms open plan. One bedroom with bathroom designed for disabled guests. Other bedrooms level.

Rates: from £42-£52 per room (2008).

Novotel Cardiff Central

Schooner Way, Atlantic Wharf, Cardiff CF10 4RT.

☎ 029 2047 5000. @ h5982@accor.com

●● D/E/G ★★★★

City centre hotel. 6 reserved parking bays. Entrance level, automatic doors. Low reception table. Public rooms level, open plan. Unisex WC. Lift to all floors. 6 rooms designed for disabled guests. Bathrooms ⭯, handrails, space by bath and WC. Other bedrooms level. Vibrating and light alarms, touch phone, large print information, portable induction loop available.

Rates: on application.

Park Inn Cardiff City Centre

Mary Ann Street, Cardiff CF10 2JH.

☎ 029 2034 1441.

W www.cardiff-city.parkinn.co.uk

●● D/E/I/F/G

City centre hotel. Entrance ramp, automatic doors. Public rooms level. Unisex WC. Lift to all floors. Eight bedrooms with bathrooms designed for disabled guests. Other 138 bedrooms level.

Rates: on application.

Park Inn Cardiff North

Circle Way East, Llanedeyrn, Cardiff CF23 9XF.

☎ 029 2058 9988.

W www.cardiff-city.parkinn.co.uk

●● D/E/F/G ★★★★

Hotel near M4 junction 29. Reserved parking bays. Entrance level, automatic door. Public rooms level. Unisex WC. Lift to all floors, 89cm. Two double bedrooms designed for disabled guests. Bathroom ⭯, handrails, space beside bath and WC. Other bedrooms level.

Rates: on application.

Park Plaza Hotel Cardiff

Greyfriars Road, Cardiff CF10 3AL.

☎ 029 201 1111.

W www.parkplazacardiff.com

●● D/E/F/G ★★★★

Modern city centre hotel. Reserved bay in NCP car park next to hotel. Ramp with handrail to entrance, revolving and swing doors. Public rooms, ground floor. Unisex WC. Lift 90cm, inside 130x130cm, brailled controls and voice announcements. 7 bedrooms designed for disabled guests. Shower rooms 90cm, ⭯, roll-in shower, space by WC. Vibrating alarm.

Rates: on application.

Welsh Institute of Sport

Sophia Gardens, Cardiff CF11 9SW.

☎ 0845 045 0902. @ wis@scw.co.uk

●● D/E/I/F/G

For information on accommodation that can be used by non-participants in the Institute's courses, see page 504.

Rates: on application.

COWBRIDGE, Glamorgan

Jane Hodge Respite Care & Holiday Centre

Trerhyngyll, Cowbridge CF71 7TN.

☎ **01446 772608.**

●●●●● D/E/I/G/H

Respite care centre, owned by John Grooms Charity, designed for disabled people with high dependency needs. Accommodation in 30 single, twin and family bedrooms with roll-in shower room or bathroom. Hoists and other equipment available. Physiotherapy, care and support packages provided. Outings and entertainment offered.

Rates: on application

MONMOUTH, Monmouthshire

Riverside Hotel

Cinderhill Street, Monmouth NP25 5EY.

☎ **01600 715577.**

www.riversidehotelmonmouth.co.uk

●● D/E/I/G ★★

Town centre hotel. Step at entrance from car park. Restaurant and lounge level. Bar 2 steps. WCs not adapted. Two bedrooms with external ramp entrance, 33". Shower rooms 33" sliding door, ⟲, handrails, space for side transfer to WC.

Rates: from £46-£59 per room (2007).

NEATH, Glamorgan

Cwmbach Cottages

Cadoxton, Neath SA10 8AH.

☎ **01639 639825.**

www.cwmbachcottages.co.uk

●● D/E/F/G 

Guesthouse 1½ miles north of Neath. Entrance step. Dining room and lounge level. Twin bedroom designed for disabled guests with own entrance ramp from car park. Bathroom ⟲, handrails, bathseat, space for side transfer to bath and WC. Other bedrooms level.

Ⓟ

Rates: from £32-£60 per room BB (2007).

NEWPORT, Monmouthshire

Express by Holiday Inn Newport

Lakeside Drive, Coed Kernew, Newport NP10 8BB.

☎ **0870 990 4083.**

www.hiexpressnewport.co.uk

●● E/I/F/G

Limited service hotel west of Newport. Reserved parking bays. Entrance level, automatic door. Low reception desk. Public areas open plan. Unisex WC. Lift 80cm, inside 135x138cm. 8 two-person rooms designed for disabled guests, low clothes rail, connect to neighbouring room. Shower rooms 76cm, ⟲, roll-in shower with seat, handrails, space by WC. Other bedrooms level. Vibrating pillow alarms.

Rates: from £40-£75 per room BB (2007).

Hilton Newport Hotel

Chepstow Road, Langstone, Newport NP18 2LX.

☎ **01633 413737.**

www.hilton.co.uk/newport

●● D/E/I/G

Hotel near M4 J24. Reserved parking bays. Entrance level. Public rooms level, open plan. Unisex WC. Four double bedrooms designed for disabled guests, door and curtain controls by bed, door to adjoining room, visual and vibrating alarm. Bathroom ⟲, handrails, space for side transfer to bath and WC. Other ground floor bedrooms level.

Rates: on application.

PONTYPOOL, Monmouthshire

Express by Holiday Inn Pontypool

Tyr'felin, Lower Mill Field, Pontypool NP4 0HR.

☎ **01495 755266.**

express-pontypool@btconnect.com

●● E/F/G

Limited service hotel at A472/A4042 junction near Pontypool. 3 reserved parking bays. Slight slope to level entrance. Low reception desk. Public rooms level, open plan. Unisex WC. Three double bedrooms designed for disabled guests, two with adjoining twin rooms. Shower rooms with turning space, roll-in shower with seat, handrails, space by WC. Other ground floor rooms level. Vibrating alarms. Harvester Restaurant adjacent.

Rates: from £50-£60 per room BB (2007).

PONTYPRIDD, Glamorgan

Glamorgan Court

University of Glamorgan, Pontypridd

●● D/E/F/G

Student accommodation. Reserved parking bays. Entrance ramp with handrails. Lift to restaurant. Bar accessible. Accommodation in flats with 6 bedrooms and shared kitchen. Four single bedrooms designed for wheelchair users with own roll-in shower room with handrails and space for side transfer. Other ground floor bedrooms level. Available Summer vacations.

Ⓟ

Apply: Conference Services, Glamorgan Business Centre, University of Glamorgan, Pontypridd CF37 1DL. ☎ 01443 482002.

www.glamorganconferenceservices.co.uk

Rates: from £35 per person BB (2007).

PORTHCAWL, Glamorgan

Glamorgan Holiday Hotel

The Square, Porthcawl CF36 3BW.

☎ **01656 785375.**

www.glamorganholidayhotel.com

●●●● D

Hotel by harbour, owned by a charity offering respite care and holiday breaks for elderly and disabled people. Public rooms include lounge, restaurant, sun-lounges and bar. Lift to upper floors. 14 twin and 25 single bedrooms, most with own bathrooms. Equipment and personal care available. Registered with Care Standards Inspectorate. Entertainment and outings in adapted coach offered. A self-catering unit is also available. Open March-December.

Rates: £214-£599 per week FB (2007).

The Rest Convalescent Hotel

Rest Bay, Porthcawl CF36 3UP.

☎ 01656 772066.

W www.theresthotel.co.uk

●●● D/E

Seaside hotel run by charitable trust. Public rooms level including lounges, shop, bar and billiard room. 25 ground floor bedrooms and 31 level from lift. Most have en suite bathrooms. Guests needing day-to-day care should be accompanied. Outings and entertainment arranged.

Rates: from £228 per week FB (2007).

SWANSEA

Express by Holiday Inn Swansea

Neath Road, Llandarcy, Swansea SA10 6JQ.

☎ 01792 818700.

W www.hiexpressswansea.co.uk

●● D/E/F/G ★★★

Limited service hotel near M4 Junction 43 east of Swansea. 4 reserved parking bays. Entrance level automatic door. Low reception desk. Public rooms level, open plan. Unisex WC. Slope to adjoining Harvester restaurant. Lift 34", inside 43"x56". 6 bedrooms designed for disabled guests. Shower rooms , handrails, roll-in shower with seat, space by WC. Other bedrooms level.

Rates: on application.

Ibis Swansea

Fabien Way, Swansea SA1 8LD.

☎ 01792 638800. @ h6653@accor.com

●● D/E/F

Hotel in waterfront area. Reserved parking bays. Entrance level. Public rooms open plan. Unisex WC. Lift to upper floors. 5 bedrooms with shower rooms designed for disabled guests. Other bedrooms level.

Rates: from £48-£53 per room (2008).

Swansea Marriott

Maritime Quarter, Swansea SA1 3SS.

☎ 01792 642 020.

●● G ★★★★

Hotel by beach and marina. Reserved parking bays. Entrance ramp or 3 steps, automatic doors. Public rooms level. Unisex WC. Lift to all floors. Double bedroom designed for disabled guests 30". Shower room 30", ⟲, roll-in shower, handrails, adjustable mirror, space for side transfer to WC. Other bedrooms level.

Rates: on application.

SWANSEA BAY, Glamorgan

Best Western Aberavon Beach Hotel

Port Talbot, Swansea Bay SA12 6QP.

☎ 01639 884949.

W www.aberavonbeach.com

●● D/E/I/G ★★★

Seafront hotel. Entrance ramp or 1 step. Public rooms level. Unisex WC. Lift 31" to all floors. One bedroom with bathroom designed for disabled guests. 51 other bedrooms level. Access statement on website.

Rates: from £72 single, £82 double BB (2007).

LODGE ACCOMMODATION

There are Days Inn (see page 34), Etap (see page 34) Premier Travel Inn (see page 38) and Travelodge (see page 38) properties in the following places in this area.

Bridgend - Days Inn ☎ 01656 659 718
Premier Travel Inn ☎ 0870 197 7041
Caerphilly, Crossways - Premier Travel Inn ☎ 0870 197 7046
Caerphilly, North - Premier Travel Inn ☎ 0870 990 6368
Cardiff - Etap ☎ 029 2045 8131
Travelodge ☎ 0870 191 1723
Cardiff Airport - Days Inn ☎ 01446 710787
Cardiff, East - Premier Travel Inn ☎ 0870 197 7051
Cardiff North - Premier Travel Inn ☎ 0870 850 6338
Cardiff, Ocean Park - Premier Travel Inn ☎ 0870 197 7050
Cardiff, Roath - Premier Travel Inn ☎ 0870 197 7049
Cardiff, West - Premier Travel Inn ☎ 0870 197 7052
Travelodge ☎ 0870 191 1725
Magor - Travelodge ☎ 0870 990 8815
Merthyr Tydfil - Premier Travel Inn ☎ 0870 197 7183
Monmouth - Travelodge ☎ 0870 191 1731
Newport - Premier Travel Inn ☎ 0870 197 7193
Pencoed - Travelodge ☎ 0870 191 1549
Port Talbot - Premier Travel Inn ☎ 0870 197 7211
Swansea - Premier Travel Inn ☎ 0870 990 6562
Swansea M4 - Travelodge ☎ 0870 191 1555
Swansea North - Premier Travel Inn ☎ 0870 197 7246

SELF-CATERING ACCOMMODATION

ABERGAVENNY, Monmouthshire

Lower Green Farm Cottages

Llanfair Green, Cross Ash,
Abergavenny NP7 8PA.
☎ 01873 821219.
W www.lower-green.fsnet.co.uk
●● F/G ★★★

Three cottages on farm east of Abergavenny. "Swallow Cottage" entrance step, portable ramp available. Lounge/kitchen open plan, controls not useable from wheelchair. Double bedroom level, ↻. Shower room 77cm sliding door, handrails, shower seat, no ↻. Family and twin bedrooms upstairs. "Ty Felin" has an entrance step and all rooms on the ground floor. Doors 78cm wide. The other cottage has 3 entrance steps and 3 steps inside.

Ⓟ

Apply: Mr & Mrs Pritchard.
Rates: from £160-£450 per week (2007).

CHEPSTOW, Monmouthshire

Byre Cottage

Cwrt-y-Gaer, Wolvesnewton,
Chepstow NP16 6PR.
W www.cwrt-y-gaer.co.uk
●● F/G ★★★

One of 3 cottages north of Chepstow. Covered parking. Entrance ramp. Open plan lounge/kitchen, pull-out worktops 24", controls useable from wheelchair. Twin bedroom, bedblocks available. Sofabed in lounge. Shower room ↻, handrails, shower seat, space for side transfer to WC. Access statement on website.

Ⓟ

Apply: Mr & Mrs Llewellyn. ☎ 01291 650700.
Rates: from £205-£335 per week (2007).

GOWER, Glamorgan

Gower Holiday Village

Scurlage, Nr. Port Eynon,
Swansea SA3 1AY.
☎ 01792 390431.
W www.gowerholidayvillagewales.co.uk
●● I/F/G ★★★

Holiday park with 63 bungalows. Paved paths. Entrances threshold or 1 step, portable ramp available. Lounge/kitchen open plan. Doors 30". No specific adaptations in bungalows but purpose designed unisex WC/shower by pool. Meals available April-October for group bookings. Closed January and February. Regular disabled guests.

Ⓟ

Rates: from £158-£558 per week (2008).

Penrice Castle Cottages

Penrice, Reynoldston, Nr. Swansea SA3 1LN.
☎ 01792 391212.
W www.penricecastle.co.uk
●● F/G ★★★★

"Estate Office Cottage" overlooks Penrice Park and Oxwich Bay and has been adapted for disabled guest. Approach and entrance level, 80cm. Internal doors 75cm. Lounge and Dining Room both ↻. Kitchen ↻, controls useable from wheelchair, door to patio. Twin and single bedrooms, adjustamatic bed in single, also folding bed for child. Shower room, ↻, roll-in shower with seat, handrails, raised WC seat. 11 other cottages available. Access statement available.

Ⓟ

Rates: from £345-£750 per week (2007).

PENDOYLAN, Glamorgan
Vineyard Cottages
Llanerch Vineyard, Hensol, Pendoylan CF72 8GG.
☎ **01443 225877.**
W www.llanerch-vineyard.co.uk
● F ★★★★★
Two cottages for up to 4 people in Vale of Glamorgan. Entrances level. Lounge/ kitchen open plan, controls useable from wheelchair. Shower room ⟲, shower seat, space for side transfer to WC. Two bedrooms and bathroom upstairs.
Ⓟ
Rates: from £350-£650 per week (2007).

PONTYPOOL, Torfaen
Elderberry Nook
Rhiw Ffranc Farm Holiday Apartments, Pentwyn, Abersychan, Nr. Pontypool NP4 7TJ.
W www.rhiwffrancfarmholidays apartments.co.uk
●● F/G ★★★★
Apartment designed for disabled people. Entrance level, 35". Lounge/kitchen open plan, controls not useable from wheelchair. Single fixed bed and roll-out single in lounge. Double bedroom 35½", ⟲. Shower room 36", roll-in shower with seat, handrails, space for side transfer to WC. Two other apartments available, one ground floor with ground floor accommodation. Large garden.
Ⓟ
Apply: Mrs Sargent ☎ 01495 775069.
Rates: on application.

PORTHCAWL, Glamorgan
Trecco Bay Holiday Park
Porthcawl CF36 5NG.
●● I/F/G ★★★★
Holiday park with wide range of facilities on coast. Caravans adapted for disabled guests for up to 5 people. Entrance ramp. Lounge/kitchen open plan. Two bedrooms, ⟲ in double. Shower room 75cm, handrails, restricted ⟲. Open March-October.
Ⓟ
Apply: Parkdean Holidays ☎ 0871 641 2066.
W www.parkdeanwales.co.uk
Rates: Holiday homes from £169 per week. Short breaks (3 or 4 nights) from £102.

RAGLAN, Monmouthshire
Harvest Home Holiday Accommodation
Bryngwyn, Raglan, Usk NP15 2JH.
☎ **01291 690007.**
W www.harvest-home.co.uk
●● I/F ★★★★★
Apartment designed for wheelchair user attached to farmhouse between Monmouth and Abergavenny. Entrance level except 2" sill, double doors, ramp available. Lounge/kitchen open plan. Controls useable from wheelchair. Double bedroom ⟲ and double sofa bed in living room. Adjustable wardrobe. Shower room ⟲, roll-in shower, handrails, space by WC and under basin. Shower stool and raised WC seat available. Breakfast can be served to apartment. Advanced booking only. Closed December.
Ⓟ
Apply: Barbara & Derek Jones.
Rates: on application.

ST BRIDES-SUPER-ELY, Glamorgan

Parc Coed Machen Country Cottages

St Brides-super-Ely, nr. Cardiff CF5 6EZ.

☎ **01446 760684/760612.**

www.parccoedmachen.co.uk

●● F ★★★★★

Two ground floor cottages, of 4, designed for disabled guests on organic farm in Vale of Glamorgan, a few miles from M4 junction 34. Step to entrance, portable ramp available. Lounge/kitchen open plan. Double and twin bedrooms, 30", ↻ in double. Bathroom 30", ↻, handrails, space by WC and bath.

Ⓟ

Rates: from £330-£425 per week (2008).

TALYGARN, Glamorgan

Vale Holiday Homes

Llwyn Nwydog Farm, Cowbridge Road, Talygarn, Pontyclun CF72 9JU.

☎ **01446 774144.**

www.valeholidayhomes.co.uk

●● F/G ★★★★

Group of 6 holiday cottages in Vale of Glamorgan north of Cowbridge. "Holly Cottage", for 4 people, designed for disabled guests. Entrance level, 33". Lounge/kitchen open plan. Double and twin bedrooms 30", ↻. Bathroom 30", ↻, space by bath and WC. Toilet frame and raised seat available. Bath board also available with grab rail in bath.

Ⓟ

Rates: £340-£400 per week (2007).

14 Channel Islands

Le Rocco Tower, Jersey

Photo: www.britainonview © Visit Guernsey

Air Services - there are flights to both Jersey and Guernsey from many airports and regular inter-Island flights. Consult your travel agent and request assistance in advance. Among the airlines offering scheduled services are:

Aer Arann
☎ **0800 587 2324** 🆆 **www.aerarann.com**

Aer Lingus
☎ **0870 876 5000** 🆆 **www.aerlingus.com**

Air Southwest
☎ **0870 241 82023**
🆆 **www.airsouthwest.com**

Aurigny Air Services
☎ **0871 871 0717.** 🆆 **www.aurigny.com**

Blue Islands
☎ **01481 727567.** 🆆 **www.blueislands.com**

BmiBaby
☎ **0871 224 0224.** 🆆 **www.bmibaby.com**

British Airways
☎ **0870 850 9850**
Textphone 0845 700 7706
🆆 **www.britishairways.com**

British Midland
☎ **0870 607 0555**
Textphone 01332 854015
🆆 **www.flybmi.com**

FlyBE
☎ **0871 700 0535.** 🆆 **www.flybe.com**

Thomsonfly
☎ **0870 1900 737.** 🆆 **www.thomsonfly.com**

Condor Ferries
Reservations, Ferry Terminal Building, Weymouth DT4 8DX.
☎ **0845 345 2001.**
@ **reservations@condorferries.co.uk**
🆆 **www.condorferries.co.uk**

Operate fast car ferry services to Guernsey, Jersey and France all year from Weymouth and from Poole from spring to October. A traditional ferry service is also operated all year from Portsmouth. Fast ferry services also operate between Jersey and Guernsey and to St Malo both from the Channel Islands and UK. There is lift between the car deck and the main passenger facilities. Disabled passengers should ask for any assistance that may be required when booking. For port enquiries contact Weymouth ☎ 01305 763003, Poole ☎ 01202 207215; Guernsey ☎ 01481 729666 or Jersey ☎ 01534 601000.

NOTE –

The **health services** in the Channel Islands are not part of the UK National Health Service. Although reciprocal agreements are in place for emergency treatment, visitors should have insurance including medical cover.

There are also reciprocal arrangements so that the Blue Badge is recognised for **parking concessions** in the Channel Islands.

ALDERNEY

Information on Alderney is available from the **Guernsey Tourist Board** (see below) or the **Alderney Tourism Office** ☎ 01481 822944 or see 🆆 www.alderney.gov.gg

Alderney Information Exchange
☎ **01481 824823**

A member of DIAL UK, offering a free, impartial and confidential service of information and advice by telephone to disabled people, their relatives and professionals.

ACCOMMODATION WITH MEALS

Simerock Guest House

Les Venelles, Alderney GY9 3TW.
☎ 01481 823645.
@ simerock.guests@virgin.net
● D/E/F

Guesthouse between town centre and cliffs. Entrance step, sliding door. Lounge and dining room level. Four ground floor bedrooms, 30", ⟲. Some with own shower room with shower tray. Shared bathroom and WC, ⟲. Level garden, slope to road.

Rates: from £30-£38 per person BB (2007).

GUERNSEY

USEFUL ADDRESSES

VisitGuernsey

Information & Accommodation Services, PO Box 23, St Peter Port, Guernsey GY1 3AN.
☎ 01481 723552.
@ enquiries@visitguernsey.com
W www.visitguernsey.com

Provides general information about Guernsey and also assists with finding accommodation suitable for disabled visitors.

St John Ambulance & Rescue Service

Healthcare Equipment Centre, Rohais, St Peter Port, Guernsey GY1 1YN.
☎ 01481 729268.

The centre has a range of equipment, including wheelchairs, for sale or hire. Early booking of hired equipment is recommended. Spare parts are stocked and repairs can be carried out.

Health Information Exchange

☎ 01481 707470

A member of DIAL UK, HIE offers a free, impartial and confidential service of information and advice by telephone to disabled people, their relatives and professionals.

Island Coachways

The Tramsheds, Les Banques, St Peter Port, Guernsey GY1 2HZ.
☎ 01481 720210. W www.icw.gg

This company operates bus services on Guernsey and is introducing new low floor vehicles with ramps and space for a wheelchair user. Contact the company for information on routes and schedules.

ACCOMMODATION WITH MEALS

Les Rocquettes Hotel

Les Gravées, St Peter Port, Guernsey GY1 1RN.
☎ 01481 722146.
www.lesrocquettesguernsey.com
●● D/F/G ★★★

Hotel in garden at edge of town. Atrium entrance level, 33"; main entrance 4 steps. Wheelchair lift from atrium to reception. Public rooms level except step to one bar. Unisex WC. Lift 31", inside 43"x55". Three twin bedrooms designed for disabled guests. Bathrooms ⟲, handrail, space for side transfer to bath and WC.

Rates: from £42-£61 per night BB (2007).

St Pierre Park Hotel

Rohais, St Peter Port, Guernsey GY1 1FD.
☎ 01481 728282.
www.stpierrepark.co.uk
●● D/E/G ★★★★

High class hotel in parkland. Reserved parking bays. Entrance level. Lounge and bar open plan. Restaurants on ground and lower floors. Unisex WC. Lifts 31" inside 48"x48" Two double bedrooms designed for disabled guests. Bathrooms 30" ⟲, handrails, space for side transfer to bath and WC. Other bedrooms level.

Rates: on application.

GUERNSEY
SELF-CATERING ACCOMMODATION

Red Cross Cottage

Les Buttes, St Saviours, Guernsey.
●● E/I/G ★★★

Ground floor cottage for up to 4 people. Entrance level, 28". Lounge/kitchen open plan. Two twin bedrooms 32", ⟲. Bathroom and 2 WCs with handrails and one with roll-in shower. Central heating. Car recommended.

Apply: Reservations Secretary, Red Cross Headquarters, Rohais, St Peter Port, Guernsey GY1 1YW. ☎ 01481 723088.
Rates: from £455 per week (2007).

JERSEY
USEFUL ADDRESSES

Jersey Tourism

Liberation Square,
St Helier, Jersey JE1 1BB.
☎ 01534 500777.
@ info@jersey.com W www.jersey.com

Jersey Tourism supplies general tourist material and can provide information on accessible accommodation, attractions, transport, equipment hire and other facilities.

Equipment can be hired from the following:

Channings Mobility
☎ 01534 631736
Toilet, walking and mobility equipment

Guardian Nursing Services
☎ 01534 852906
Wheelchairs and bathing equipment

The Hire Shop
☎ 01534 873699 – manual wheelchairs

Red Cross Jersey Branch
☎ 01534 864262
Wheelchairs and frames

Technicare
☎ 01534 888975
Scooters, hoists and other equipment

Shopmobility Jersey operates in the shopping precinct area of St Helier and Jersey Zoo. It can also arrange for a scooter to be delivered to a hotel. For details of hours and availability call ☎ 01534 739672.

Bus services on Jersey have been re-organised recently and low-floor vehicles that can carry passengers in wheelchairs are in use on most routes. For further information contact St Helier Bus Station Information Service ☎ 01534 877772.
W www.mybus.je

In addition to accessible taxis that can be hired from taxi ranks, the following have private hire cars that can carry wheelchair users:

Flying Dragon/Clarendon Cabs
☎ 01534 888333

Luxicabs ☎ 01534 887000

Citicabs ☎ 01534 499999

Andie Tague ☎ 01534 758476

The hydrotherapy pool and gymnasium at the Jersey Cheshire Home on the outskirts of St Helier may be booked by disabled visitors when not otherwise in use. Contact Jersey Cheshire Home, Rope Walk, St Helier JE2 4UU. ☎ 01534 285858.
@ jersey.cheshire@jerseymail.co.uk

Gentle Wanders: Access to Nature in Jersey, which gives details of 15 wildlife sites that can be accessed by wheelchair users is available from Jersey Tourism.

Sea fishing – a boat, "Theseus II", designed to carry wheelchair users can be chartered for fishing trips. ☎ 01534 858046 W www.tarkerseatrips.com

JERSEY

ACCOMMODATION WITH MEALS

Jersey Cheshire Home

Eric Young House, Rope Walk,
St Helier JE2 4UU.

☎ **01534 285858.**

W www.jerseycheshirehome.com

●●●●● D/E/I/H

The Leonard Matchan Suite is a respite unit attached to a purpose-built residential/ nursing home for disabled people. The suite has its own entrance, a single bedroom with a hoist and bathroom equipped for a disabled person and a lounge which can be used as a carers bedroom. The facilities of the Home are available if required, including hydrotherapy pool, outings and other activities. Rates depend on care required. Available to Jersey residents and disabled people visitors.

Rates: from £100 per night BB (2007).

Maison Des Landes Hotel

St Ouen, Jersey JE3 2AA.

☎ **01534 481683.**

W www.2000net.com/mdl

●●● D/E/I/H

Purpose-built hotel for disabled guests and their families. Accommodation for up to 45 in single, twin and family rooms with bathrooms. Hoists, wheelchairs and other equipment available. Personal care not provided. Adapted minibus for airport and ferry transfers and outings. Open March-November. Early booking recommended.

Rates: from £48-£60 per night FB (2007).

West View Hotel

La Grande Rue, St Mary, Jersey JE3 3BD.

☎ **01534 481643.**

W www.westviewhoteljersey.com

●● D/F/G ★★

Hotel in country in centre of island. Reserved parking bay. Level entrance. Public rooms ground floor, 2 steps to dining room, portable ramp available. Unisex WC. Bedroom adapted for disabled guests. Bathroom 39", no, handrails by WC, bathboard available. Other ground floor bedrooms level. Closed January-mid March.

Rates: from £31 per person BB (2008).

SELF-CATERING ACCOMMODATION

La Rocco Self-catering Apartments

La Pulente, St Brelade, Jersey JE3 8HG.

☎ **01534 743378.**

W www.laroccoapartments.com

●● F/G

Six apartments designed to be useable by disabled people overlooking bay on the west coast. Ramp to building; 3 ground floor units level and lift to 1st floor units. Each has open plan lounge/kitchen, controls useable from wheelchair. Four have one twin bedroom and bathroom, handrails, shower tray with seat, space for side transfer to WC. Two units have two bedrooms and bathrooms similarly equipped. Other units on site.

Rates: from £589-£1541 per week (2008).

15 Isle of Man

Peel

Photo: www.britainonview

USEFUL ADDRESSES

Isle of Man Department of Tourism & Leisure

Sea Terminal Buildings, Douglas IM1 2RG.

☎ 01624 686766.

☎ Brochures 08457 686868.

@ tourism@gov.im

W www.visitisleofman.com

The annual holiday guide to the Isle of Man gives details of accommodation, events and attractions. An accessible accommodation leaflet lists a number of serviced and self-catering places to stay meeting the criteria of the Isle of Man Accessible Scheme. A cassette tape is available for visually impaired visitors.

Manx Foundation for the Physically Disabled

Masham Court, Victoria Avenue, Douglas, Isle of Man IM2 4AW.

☎ 01624 628926.

@ mail@manxfoundation.co.uk

Isle of Man Steam Packet Co.

Imperial Buildings, Douglas, Isle of Man IM1 2BY.

☎ 08705 523523.

W www.steam-packet.com

Operate services to Douglas from Heysham and Liverpool all year and from Belfast and Dublin from late March to September. The 'Ben-my-Chree' ferry on the Heysham route has a lift to all decks and two cabins adapted for disabled passengers. The winter weekend service from Liverpool, which increase to a twice daily schedule in summer, and the seasonal Belfast and Dublin services use a fast Superseacat which is adapted for disabled passengers. When making a reservation notify the company of any assistance that may be required.

Air Services - there are flights to the Isle of Man from many mainland airports. Consult your travel agent and request assistance in advance. Among the airlines offering scheduled services are:

Aer Arann **☎ 0800 587 2324**
W www.aerarann.com

Blue Islands
☎ 0845 620 2122 W www.blueislands.com

Eastern Airw ays **☎ 01652 680600.**
W www.easternairways.com

FlyBE **☎ 0871 522 6100**
W www.flybe.com

Loganair **☎ 0870 850 9850**
W www.loganair.co.uk

VLM **☎ 0871 666 5050**
W www.flyvlm.com

Bus services run between the airport and Douglas and other major towns. Low floor buses are being introduced and information on these, and on arrangements for disabled passengers on their railways, can be obtained from **Isle of Man Transport**, Banks Circus, Douglas IM1 5PT.

☎ 01624 662525.

@ info@busandrail.dtl.gov.im

W www.iombusandrail.info

Disabled Go - information on the accessibility of many premises on the Isle of Man is available on W www.disabledgo.info

ACCOMMODATION WITH MEALS

Hilton Hotel & Casino Isle of Man

Central Promenade, Douglas,
Isle of Man IM2 4NA.
☎ **01624 662662.**
www.isleofman.hilton.com
●● D/E/F/G ★★★★

Hotel and entertainment complex on seafront. Reserved parking bays. Entrance level. Public rooms level. Unisex WC. Lift to all floors. Four bedrooms adapted for disabled guests. Other bedrooms level, in some. No adaptations in bathrooms.

Rates: on application.

Mount Murray Hotel & Country Club

Mount Murray, Santon,
Isle of Man IM4 2HT.
☎ **01624 661111**
www.mountmurray.com

●● D/E/I/F/G ★★★★

Country club hotel between Douglas and Castletown. Reserved parking bays. Steep slope to main entrance; other entrances have slight ramp. Restaurants and bars on ground and 1st floors. Unisex WC. Lift 32", inside 42"x82". 8 twin bedrooms designed for disabled guests 35", . Bathrooms , space for side transfer to bath and WC. Waterproof sheet available. Other bedrooms level.

Rates: on application.

Santon Motel

Santon, Isle of Man IM4 1EJ.
☎ **01624 822499.**
santonmotel@manx.net
● F/G ★★★

Motel between Ronaldsway Airport and Douglas. Reserved parking bays. One step at entrance to reception. One step to six ground floor bedrooms with bathrooms 30" minimum, no specific adaptations. Teletext TV. Breakfast served to room.

Rates: from £29.95-£39.95 per night (2007).

Sefton Hotel

Harris Promenade,
Douglas IM1 2RW.
☎ **01642 645500.**
www.seftonhotel.co.im
●● D/E/I/F/G ★★★★

High class seafront hotel. Reserved parking bays. Entrance ramp or 3 steps, automatic door. Low reception desk. Restaurant ramp or 1 step. Lounge and bar level. Breakfast room 1st floor. Unisex WCs on ground and 1st floors. Lift to all floors. Three bedrooms designed for disabled guests. Bathrooms , roll-in shower with seat, space by bath and WC. Other bedrooms level. Wheelchair available.

Rates: from £95 per room (2007).

SELF-CATERING ACCOMMODATION

Ballure Holiday Homes

Ballure, Maughold, Isle of Man.

●● F ★★★

Group of 6 cottages on hillside overlooking Ramsey Bay. One, for 6 people, adapted for disabled guests. Ramp to rear entrance. Internal doors 28½". Lounge and kitchen ⟲. Double and 2 twin bedrooms. Bathroom ⟲, space by WC and bath, raised WC seat, no handrails. Other cottages with ground floor accommodation but 2 steps to entrance.

Apply: David & Anne Craine, The Carrick, Port Lewaigue, Maughold IM7 1AG. ☎ 01624 813104. @ carrick@mcb.net

Rates: from £400-£450 per week (2007).

Close Chairn Cottages

St Judes Road, Sulby, Lezayre, Isle of Man IM7 2ES.

☎ 01624 897074.

 **www.closechairn.co.uk**

●● F/G ★★★★

"Beg Cottage" is one of 3 cottages at the edge of a village 4 miles from Ramsey. Entrance level. Internal doors 34". Lounge/kitchen open plan ⟲. Double bedroom. Shower room ⟲, roll-in shower with seat and handrail, space by WC. Can be booked with neighbouring cottages.

Rates: from £175-£300 per week (2007).

Dairy Cottage

Ballacregga Farm, Coast Road, Kirk Michael IM6 1AP.

●● I/F/G ★★★★

Cottage for up to 6 people on farm overlooking the west coast of the island. Ramp from parking to front door, 36". Internal doors 36". Lounge and kitchen ⟲. Double and 2 twin bedrooms, en suite bathroom with double. Bathroom ⟲, switches reachable from wheelchair. Toilet ⟲, space by WC, no handrails.

Apply: Mrs Carole Berry ☎ 01624 878892. W www.ballacregga.co.im

Rates: from £550 per week (2007).

Kionslieu Farm Cottages

Higher Foxdale, Isle of Man IM4 3HB.

● F/G ★★★★

5 cottages on farm courtyard in the centre of the island. "Redwheel Cottage" has 2 steps to entrance, portable ramp available. Open plan lounge/kitchen. Two bedrooms, one with bunks. Bathroom, grab rails by bath and WC, no space for side transfer. Raised WC seat available. A second cottage has ground floor accommodation.

Apply: Mrs F Barker. ☎ 01624 801349. W www.iomfarmholidays.com

Rates: from £410-£550 per week (2007).

16 Northern Ireland

Mount Stewart House, County Down

The six counties of Northern Ireland provide varied countryside, dramatic coastlines, historic towns and attractive villages.

Among the most notable landscapes are the Mourne Mountains on the southern coast of County Down, the Glens of Antrim on the north east coast and the Sperrin Mountains spanning counties Londonderry and Tyrone. However the most famous natural feature is the Giant's Causeway on the north Antrim coast. During the summer a bus fitted with a lift serves this World Heritage Site from nearby towns.

There are two major inland lakes, Lough Neagh and, in Co. Fermanagh, the extensive Lough Erne. Both offer many opportunities for angling and birdwatching. Boating is very popular on Lough Erne and there is the option of cruising south of the border along the re-opened Shannon-Erne waterway. The almost landlocked Strangford Lough in Co. Down is another mecca for birdwatchers. Near its mouth at Portaferry a modern accessible aquarium, Exploris, displays the natural history of both the Lough and the Irish Sea.

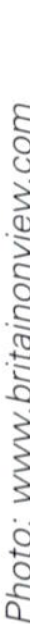

Belfast city centre has an array of facilities including theatres, shops, restaurants, bars and many other features including the Botanic Gardens, the Waterfront Concert Hall and W5 a state of the art centre to explore science. The Ulster Folk & Transport Museum, outside the city, has reconstructed buildings, collections of railway history and an exhibition about the Titanic, which was built in Belfast's shipyards. Other attractions on the outskirts of the city include Colin Glen Forest Park and Belfast Zoo.

Newcastle, County Down

Other historic towns include the walled City of Derry, Armagh with its two cathedrals, Georgian townscape and Palace Stables Heritage Centre, and Downpatrick which has many links with St Patrick. There are great castles at Enniskillen and Carrickfergus. Seaside resorts include Ballycastle and Portrush on the north coast and Bangor and Newcastle on the east. Tourists can learn about the linen industry at a visitor centre in Banbridge and visit the Ulster-American Folk Park near Omagh.

The National Trust owns several properties in Northern Ireland including Rowallane Gardens outside Belfast, Castle Ward overlooking Strangford Lough, the elegant Florence Court in County Fermanagh and the ornate Crown Bar in central Belfast. There are opportunities to enjoy and learn about the countryside at several of the country parks and countryside centres run by the Environment & Heritage Service including Roe Park near Limavady and Crawfordsburn outside Bangor.

Photo: www.britainonview.com

USEFUL ADDRESSES

Northern Ireland Tourist Board

St Anne's Court, 59 North Street, Belfast BT1 1NB.

☎ **028 9023 1221.**

Textphone: 028 9044 1522

@ **info@nitb.com**

W **www.discovernorthernireland.com**

All Northern Ireland Tourist Board publications, including guides to hotels, bed & breakfast, self-catering accommodation and attractions are available in alternative formats and can be downloaded from the website.

Disability Action

Portside Business Park, 189 Airport Road West, Belfast BT3 9ED.

☎ **028 9029 7880.**

Textphone: 028 9029 7882.

@ **hq@disabilityaction.org**

W **www.disabilityaction.org**

Disability Action can provide general information on holiday accommodation and transport in Northern Ireland.

Diabetes UK Northern Ireland

Bridgewood House, Newforge Lane, Belfast BT9 5NW.

☎ **028 9066 6646.**

@ **n.ireland@diabetes.org.uk**

An annual support holiday for children (8-11 years) and a youth support holiday (for ages 12-17) are arranged, aiming at assisting young people to manage their diabetes in a holiday environment at which there is an organised programme of events and activities. The holiday is staffed by volunteers including healthcare professionals. Weekends for adults and families are also arranged.

Translink

Central Station, Belfast BT1 3PB.

☎ **028 9066 6630.**

Textphone: 028 9035 4007.

W **www.translink.co.uk**

Translink can provide information on the accessibility of train and bus transport throughout Northern Ireland. Information on access at rail and bus stations is given on their website.

Norfolk Ferries

☎ **0870 600 4321.**

W **www.norfolkline-ferries.co.uk**

Victoria Business Park, West Bank Road, Belfast BT3 9JN.

12 Quays Terminal, Tower Road, Birkenhead CH41 1FE

Operate car ferries between Birkenhead and Belfast with both day and night services. The vessels have lifts, unisex toilets and cabins designed for disabled passengers. Advance notice of any special requirements is requested.

P&O Irish Sea

Larne Harbour, Larne BT40 1AW.

☎ **0870 2424777.**

Textphone: 01304 223090.

W **www.poirishsea.com**

Operate both fast craft and conventional ferries between Larne and Cairnryan and fast craft on a summer seasonal service between Larne and Troon. On board there are lifts between car and passenger decks and toilets for disabled passengers. A minibus is available at both terminals for foot passengers. Advice on the suitability of vessels is available when booking and at least 48 hours notice is requested for any assistance that may be required.

Stena Line

Stena House, Station Approach, Holyhead, Anglesey LL65 1DQ.
☎ **08705 707070.**
Textphone: 08795 421127.
W **www.stenaline.co.uk**

Operate traditional ferry and fast-ferry services between Stranraer and Belfast using vessels that are accessible to wheelchair users. Assistance can be provided at ports and on board although as much notice as possible is requested. Stena also operate a car ferry service between Fleetwood and Larne but no lifts between the vehicle and passenger decks are available.

EQUIPMENT HIRE

McElmeel Mobility Services

15 Ballyscandal Road, Armagh BT61 8BL.
☎ **028 3752 5333.**
@ **info@mobility-services.com**
W **www.mobility-services.com**

Vehicle adaption company that has for hire both cars fitted with hand controls and those that can carry passengers in wheelchairs.

Shopmobility Carrickfergus

10c High Street, Carrickfergus BT38 7AN.
☎ **028 9336 8415.**
@ **info@shopmobilitycarrickfergus.com**

In addition to a regular shopmobility service, a long-term hire scheme is available to members whether going on holiday elsewhere in Europe or visiting the area. Manual wheelchairs and lightweight scooters are available.

Shopmobility schemes exist to provide wheelchairs and/or scooters for use in the shopping centres of the following towns. For information on availability, etc. telephone in advance.

Ballymena ☎ **028 2563 8822**

Bangor ☎ **028 9145 6586**

Belfast ☎ **028 9080 8090**

Carrickfergus ☎ **028 9336 8415**

Derry ☎ **028 7136 8623**

Lisburn ☎ **028 9266 7557**

Magherafelt ☎ **028 7930 0414**

Newry ☎ **028 3025 6062**

Newtownards ☎ **028 9181 4952**

Omagh ☎ **028 8224 0772**

Belfast Shopmobility has satellite schemes at the Castle Court, Connswater and Forestside Shopping Centres.

ACCOMMODATION WITH MEALS

AGHADOWEY, Co. Londonderry

Brown Trout Golf & Country Inn 

209 Agivey Road, Aghadowey BT51 4AD.
☎ **028 7086 8209.**
www.browntroutinn.com
●● D/E/I/F/G ★★★

Country inn south of Coleraine and Ballymoney. Reserved parking bay. Entrance level, double doors. Lounge and bar level. Restaurant 1st floor but meals can be served in bar or breakfast in bedrooms. Unisex WC. Bedroom designed for disabled guests. Shower room ⟲, roll-in shower, handrails, space by WC. Other 14 bedrooms level ⟲. Cottage suites also available.

Ⓟ

Rates: from £40-£50 per person BB (2007).

ALDERGROVE, Co. Antrim

Park Plaza Belfast 

Belfast International Airport, Crumlin, Belfast BT29 4ZY.
☎ **028 9445 7000.**
www.parkplaza.com
●● E/I/G 

Hotel by airport. Reserved parking bays. Entrance level, automatic door. Public rooms level. Unisex WC. Lift 31", inside 42"x55". Three bedrooms designed for disabled guests. Bathrooms ⟲, handrails, space for side transfer to low-level bath and WC. Other bedrooms level.

Ⓟ

Rates: on application.

ARMAGH, Co. Armagh

Hillview Lodge

33 Newtownhamilton Road,
Armagh BT60 2PL.
☎ **028 3752 2000.**
www.hillviewlodge.com
●● D/E/F

Bed & breakfast a mile from Armagh City. Entrance level, 90cm. Dining room and lounge level. Two bedrooms designed for disabled guests. Shower room 90cm, roll-in shower, handrails, space for side transfer to WC. Other ground floor rooms available.

Rates: from £29-£38 per person BB (2007).

BALLYCASTLE, Co. Antrim

MS Centre at Dalriada

Coleraine Road, Ballycastle BT54 6BA.
☎ **028 2076 3793**
●●●●● D/I/H

Respite Care Centre with accommodation for 16 people with multiple sclerosis requiring full nursing care over 24-hour period.

Rates: on application.

BALLYMARTIN, Co. Down

Sharon Farm

6 Ballykeel Road, Ballymartin,
Kilkeel BT34 4PL.
☎ **028 4176 2521.**
●● D/E/I/F/G

Farmhouse bed & breakfast. Two separate shallow steps to entrance. Dining room and lounge level. Double, twin and family bedrooms level. Bathroom level, handrail. WC, space for wheelchair and helper, handrail. Waterproof sheet available. Regular disabled guests.

Rates: from £20-£23 per person BB (2007).

BANGOR, Co. Down

Clandeboye Lodge Hotel

10 Estate Road, Clandeboye,
Bangor BT19 1UR.
☎ **028 9185 2500.**
www.clandeboyelodge.com
●● D/E/I/F/G 

Country hotel. Reserved parking bays. Entrance level. Public rooms open plan, level. Two raised tables in award-winning restaurant. Unisex WC. Lift 48", inside 60"x84". Two double bedrooms, with extra sofa bed, designed for disabled guests. Shower rooms ↺, roll-in shower with seat, handrails, space for side transfer to WC. Waterproof sheet available. Other bedrooms level.

Rates: on application.

Marine Court Hotel

The Marina, Bangor BT20 5ED.
☎ **028 9145 1100.**
www.marinecourthotel.net
●● D/E/I/F/G 

Hotel overlooking marina. Reserved parking bays. Entrance level. Large lift to all floors. Public rooms 1st floor. Unisex WC. One bedroom designed for disabled guests. Bathroom with roll-in shower, handrails, space for side transfer to WC. Waterproof sheets available. Other bedrooms level.

Rates: on application.

BELFAST

Balmoral Hotel

Black's Road, Dunmurry, Belfast BT10 0ND.
☎ **028 9030 1234.**
www.balmoralhotelbelfast.com
●● D/E/I/F/G

Modernised hotel in south Belfast near M1. Reserved parking bays. Public rooms level. Eight twin/double bedrooms designed for disabled guests. Bathrooms ↺, handrails, some with roll-in showers.

Rates: on application.

Benedicts Hotel

7-21 Bradbury Place, Belfast BT7 1RQ.
☎ 028 9059 1999.
W www.benedictshotel.co.uk
●● D/E/I/F/G ★★★

Modern city centre hotel. Street parking. Level entrance. Open plan reception/ lounge, low desk. Bar ground floor. Restaurant and unisex WC 1st floor. Lift with braille buttons to all floors. Two bedrooms designed for disabled guests. Bathrooms ⟲, space by WC. Other rooms level.

Rates: £80 double per room BB (2007).

Europa Hotel

Great Victoria Street,
Belfast BT2 7AP.
☎ 028 9027 1066.
@ res@eur.hastingshotels.com
●● D/E/F/G ★★★★

City centre hotel. Car park adjacent. Entrance level, revolving and swing doors. Public rooms on ground and 1st floors. Unisex WC. Lift 54", inside 76"x56". Two twin bedrooms designed for disabled guests. Shower rooms 31", ⟲, roll-in shower and seat, handrails, space for side transfer to WC. Other bedrooms level.

Rates: on application.

Express by Holiday Inn Belfast

106A University Street, Belfast BT7 1HP.
☎ 028 9031 1909.
@ reservations@exhi-belfast.com
●● D/E/I/F/G

Hotel near city centre. Reserved parking bays. Entrance level, double doors. Low reception desk. Public rooms level, open plan. Unisex WC. Lift 79cm, inside 138x130cm. Six double bedrooms designed for disabled guests, door to adjoining room. Bath or shower rooms 90cm, ⟲, handrails, space for side transfer, roll-in shower with seat in some. Vibrating pillow alarms. Other bedrooms level.

Rates: from £75 per room BB (2007).

Hilton Belfast

4 Lanyon Place, Belfast BT1 3LP.
☎ 028 9027 7000.
W www.belfast.hilton.com
●● D/E/I/F/G ★★★★★

City centre riverside hotel. Reserved parking bays. Entrance ramp, slow revolving door and swing door. Public rooms level. Unisex WCs. Lift 110cm, inside 190x130cm. Nine bedrooms designed for disabled guests, 82cm, flashing light alarms, door to neighbouring room. Bathrooms 82cm, ⟲, handrails, space for side transfer to bath and WC. Other bedrooms level.

Rates: on application.

Jurys Inn Belfast

Fisherwick Place, Great Victoria Street, Belfast BT2 7AP.

☎ **028 9053 3500.**

●● D/E/F/G ★★★

City centre hotel. Public car park nearby, 2 spaces at rear of hotel can be made available in advance. Entrance ramp or 2 steps, automatic doors. Public rooms level, open plan. Unisex WC. Lift 78cm, inside 132x218cm. Five double/twin bedrooms designed for disabled guests 75cm, ↺. Bathrooms 78cm, ↺, handrails, space for side transfer to bath and WC, one has roll-in shower. Other bedrooms level. Teletext TV. Wheelchair and flashing alarm available.

Rates: from £70-£120 per room (2006).

Malmaison Belfast

34-38 Victoria Street, Belfast BT1 3GH.

☎ **028 9022 0200.**

W www.malmaison.com

●● D/E/F/G ★★★★

City centre hotel. Parking spaces can be reserved. Entrance level. Low reception desk. Restaurant and bar ground floor. Lounge 4th floor. Unisex WCs. Lift 32", inside 42"x54", braille controls. Three bedrooms designed for disabled guests, one double and two with double and single beds. Shower rooms 30", roll-in shower, with seat, handrails, space by WC. Other bedrooms level. Wheelchair available.

Rates: on application.

Park Avenue Hotel

158 Holywood Road, Belfast BT4 1PB.

☎ **028 9065 6520.**

W www.parkavenuehotel.co.uk

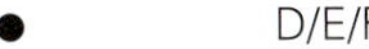

●● D/E/F/G ★★★

Modern hotel near Belfast City Airport. Reserved parking bay. Entrance level, double doors. Low reception desk. Public rooms level. One higher table in restaurant. Unisex WC. Bedroom with double and single beds designed for disabled guests. Shower room ↺, roll-in shower with seat, handrails, space by WC. Other bedrooms level.

Rates: From £99 double midweek BB (2007).

Radisson SAS Hotel Belfast

The Gasworks, 3 Cromac Place, Belfast BT7 2JB.

☎ **028 9043 4065.**

W www.belfast.radissonsas.com

●● D/E/I/F/G ★★★★

High class city centre hotel. Reserved parking bays. Small ramp to entrance, automatic revolving door. Main public rooms ground floor open plan. Unisex WC. Lifts to all floors 110cm, inside157x130cm. 6 double bedrooms designed for disabled guests, ↺, lowered work surfaces and controls. Bathrooms ↺, handrails, space by WC and bath. Interconnecting rooms available. Induction loop in public areas, Braille signs and Teletext TV.

Rates: on application.

Stormont Hotel

587 Upper Newtownards Road, Belfast BT4 3LP.

☎ **028 9065 1066.**

@ **res@stor.hastingshotels.com**

●● D/E/I/F/G ★★★★

High class hotel east of city centre. Reserved parking bays. Entrance ramp or 6 steps, automatic door. Public rooms level, except part of lounge. Unisex WC. Lift 43", inside 54"x64". One bedroom designed for disabled guests. Shower room 33", ⟲, roll-in shower, handrail, space for side transfer to WC. Waterproof sheet available. Other bedrooms level.

Rates: on application.

Tara Lodge

36 Cromwell Road, Belfast BT7 1JU.

☎ **028 9059 0900.**

W **www.taralodge.com**

●● D/E/G

Modern bed & breakfast near city centre. Front entrance level; ramp to rear entrance. Breakfast room and unisex WC on ground floor. Lounge 1st floor. Lift 78cm, inside 138x110cm. 2 bedrooms designed for disabled guests 81cm, ⟲. Wet rooms. Shower room ⟲, roll-in shower with seat, handrails, space by WC, low basin and mirror. Other bedrooms level.

Rates: from £70 single, £85 double weekdays BB (2007).

BUSHMILLS, Co. Antrim

Bushmills Inn Hotel

9 Dunluce Road, Bushmills BT57 8QG.

☎ **028 2073 3000.**

W **www.bushmillsinn.com**

●● D/E/F/G ★★★

Hotel in village beside historic distillery. Reserved parking bay. Entrance level, double doors. Restaurant, one lounge and bar ground floor level. Unisex WC. Double bedroom ground floor designed for disabled guests. Bathroom 80cm, ⟲, handrails, space by bath and WC. Some other ground floor bedrooms.

Rates: on application.

Valley View

6A Ballyclough Road, Bushmills BT57 8TU.

☎ **028 2074 1608/1319.**

W **www.valleyviewbushmills.com**

●● D/E/I/G

Rural bed & breakfast house 6 miles from Giant's Causeway. Ramp from parking area. Entrance level 33". Dining room and lounge level. Two ground floor bedrooms designed for disabled guests. Shower rooms 33", roll-in shower, handrails, space for side transfer to WC. Waterproof sheet available. Three other ground floor bedrooms.

Rates: from £27-£29 per person BB (2007).

CLOGHER, Co. Tyrone

Corick House Hotel

20 Corick Road, Clogher BT76 0BZ.

☎ **028 8554 8216.**

W www.corickcountryhouse.com

●● D/E/I/F/G ★★★

Country house hotel in Clogher Valley. Reserved parking bays. Ramp to entrance. Public rooms level including restaurant, conservatory and bar. Unisex WC. Ground floor bedroom adapted for disabled guests. Bathroom ⟲, handrail by WC. Space for side transfer to bath and WC. Waterproof sheet available. Other level bedrooms available.

Rates: from £50-£65 per person BB (2007).

COOKSTOWN, Co. Tyrone

Glenavon House Hotel

52 Drum Road, Cookstown BT80 8QJ.

☎ **028 8676 4949.**

W www.glenavonhotel.co.uk

●● D/E/I/F/G ★★★

Hotel on edge of town. Reserved parking bays. Entrance level. Public rooms level, basement and ground floor. Two WCs for wheelchair users. Lift 42", to all floors. Bedroom designed for disabled guests. Bathroom with roll-in shower. 58 other level bedrooms.

Rates: from £67.50 single. Double from £105. See website for offers.
Rates: £95 double BB (2007).

Tullylagan Country House Hotel

408 Tullylagan Road, Cookstown BT80 8UP.

☎ **028 8676 5100.**

W www.tulyagan.com

●● D/E/I/F ★★

Country house hotel between Cookstown and Dungannon. Reserved parking bays. Entrance level. Public rooms level. Unisex WC. Two bedrooms adapted for disabled guests. Shower rooms ⟲, roll-in shower with seat, handrails, space for side transfer to WC. Other bedrooms upstairs.

Rates: from £40-£60 per person BB (2007).

CRAWFORDSBURN, Co. Down

The Old Inn

15 Main Street, Crawfordsburn, Bangor BT19 1JH.

☎ **028 9185 3255.**

W www.theoldinn.com

●● D/G ★★★

Old established hotel in village between Bangor and Belfast. Reserved parking bay. Level entrance to right of main entrance. Restaurant, lounge and bar ground floor, level. Unisex WC. Bedroom for two people adapted for disabled guests, low-level fittings, push button door control. Shower room ⟲, roll-in shower, space by WC. Other ground floor bedrooms level. Northern Ireland Hotel of the Year 2007 award.

Rates: from £105.

CUSHENDALL, Co. Antrim

The Burn

63 Ballyeamon Road, Cushendall BT44 0SN.
☎ 028 2177 1733.
W www.theburn-guesthouse.com
●● D/E/F/G

Country house bed & breakfast. Entrance 2 steps, portable ramp available. Dining room and lounge level. Family, and two double /twin bedrooms level, 30". One with bathroom adapted for disabled guests.

Rates: from £20 per person sharing BB (2007).

Cullentra House

16 Cloughs Road,
Cushendall BT44 0SP.
☎ 028 2177 1762.
@ cullentra@hotmail.com
● E/F

Country guesthouse. Entrance 3 steps. Dining room and lounge both level, 30". Twin, double and family bedrooms level. Shower and bathrooms not adapted.

Rates: from £20 per person BB (2007).

DUNGANNON, Co. Tyrone

Cohannon Inn & Autolodge

212 Ballynakelly Road,
Dungannon BT71 6HJ.
☎ 028 8772 4488.
W www.cohannon-inn.com
●● D/E/G ★★

Hotel off M1 motorway. Reserved parking space. Entrance level. Public rooms level. Unisex WC. One bedroom designed for disabled guests. Shower room ⟲, handrails, shower tray, space by WC. Other ground floor rooms level.

Rates: from £49.95 per room (2007).

ENNISKILLEN, Co. Fermanagh

Killyhevlin Hotel

Killyhevlin, Enniskillen BT74 6RW.
☎ 028 6632 3481. W www.killyhevlin.com
●● D/E/I/G ★★★★

Country hotel on shore of Lough Erne. Reserved parking bays. Entrance ramp or 3 steps. Public rooms level. Unisex WC. Bedroom with double and single beds designed for disabled guests. Shower room ⟲, roll-in shower, handrails, space by WC. A suite is also available

Rates: from £52.50 per person BB (2006).

Lackaboy Farm Guest House

Old Tempo Road, Enniskillen BT74 4RL.
☎ 028 6632 2488.
● D/E/F/G ★★

Guesthouse 2 miles from Enniskillen. Entrance step. Dining room and lounge level. Twin and single ground floor bedrooms with en suite shower rooms, no adaptations. Shared bathroom.

Rates: from £25.50-£30 per person BB (2007).

The Olde Schoolhouse B&B

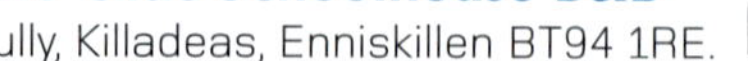

Tully, Killadeas, Enniskillen BT94 1RE.
☎ 028 6862 1688.
@ joanmoore@easy.com
●● D/E/F

Guesthouse in country east of Enniskillen. Entrance level 30½". Lounge level. Twin bedroom level 30". Shower room 30", ⟲, handrails, space for side transfer to shower seat and WC. Other bedrooms upstairs.

Rates: from £27.50 per night BB (2007).

KILKEEL, Co. Down
Mourne Activity Centre

42 Ballinran Road, Kilkeel BT34 4JA.
☎ **028 4176 5727.**
@ **tina.kenmuir@inclusionmatters.org**
●● E/I/F/G

Holiday & Conference Centre for groups of 10 or more near Mourne Mountains owned by Phab Northern Ireland and designed for use by disabled people. Reserved parking bays. Entrance level. Public rooms level, automatic door closers. One single, 7 twin and one 6-bed room ground floor. Bathrooms and WCs equipped for wheelchair users, roll-in showers. Also 2 bedrooms and bathroom on 1st floor.

Rates: from £12-£16 per night (2007).

LISBURN, Co. Antrim
Hilltop

60 Tullyard Road, Drumbo,
Lisburn BT27 5JN.
☎ **028 9082 6021.**
@ **mccarneypat@hotmail.com**
●● D/E/I/F/G

Bed & breakfast bungalow 1½ miles from village. Entrances ramped. Internal doors 31". Double bedroom with roll-in shower room, handrails, space by WC. Also a 2nd level bedroom with bathroom. Induction loops in bedrooms Waterproof sheet available.

Ⓟ

Rates: from £25-£40 per room BB (2007).

LISNASKEA, Co. Fermanagh
Share Holiday Village

Smith's Strand, Lisnaskea BT92 0EQ.
☎ **028 6772 2122.**
W **www.sharevillage.org**
●●● E/I/F/G ★★★

Holiday and Activity Centre designed for use by disabled people. Guesthouse accommodation with 6 ground floor bedrooms and 7 first floor bedrooms, all with own bathrooms with lift access. Also 17 self-catering chalets with open plan lounge/kitchen, two or three bedrooms and bathrooms. Restaurant and shop on site. Volunteers available to assist disabled guests. Water and land based activities with qualified instructors and equipment supplied. Ramp to indoor pool and leisure centre. Adapted vehicles for ferry/airport transfers.

Rates: from £60 per night FB, self catering £350 per week (2007).

MAGHERAFELT, Co. Londonderry
The Terrace Hotel

42-48 Church Street,
Magherafelt BT45 6AW.
☎ **028 7963 4040.**
W **www.theterracehotel.com**
●● D/F/G ★★★

Hotel in town centre. Reserved parking bays. Level entrance. Low reception desk. Lounge and bar ground floor. Restaurant in basement. Unisex WCs. Lift 90cm, inside 100x150cm to all floors. Two bedrooms designed for disabled guests. Shower rooms 100cm, ⟲, roll-in shower, handrails. Space by WC. Other bedrooms level.

Rates: on application.

Accommodation with meals

NEWCASTLE, Co. Down

Burrendale Hotel & Country Club

51 Castlewellan Road,
Newcastle BT33 0JY.
☎ **028 4372 2599.** **W** **www.burrendale.com**

●● D/P ★★★

Country hotel on edge of town. Reserved parking bays. Entrance 2 steps or ramp. Main public rooms level; chairlift to some function rooms. Unisex WC. Lift 29", inside 33"x53". Thirteen bedrooms designed for disabled guests. Bathrooms 33", ⟲, handrails, space for side transfer to bath and WC. Other bedrooms level.

Rates: from £120 double BB per night (2007).

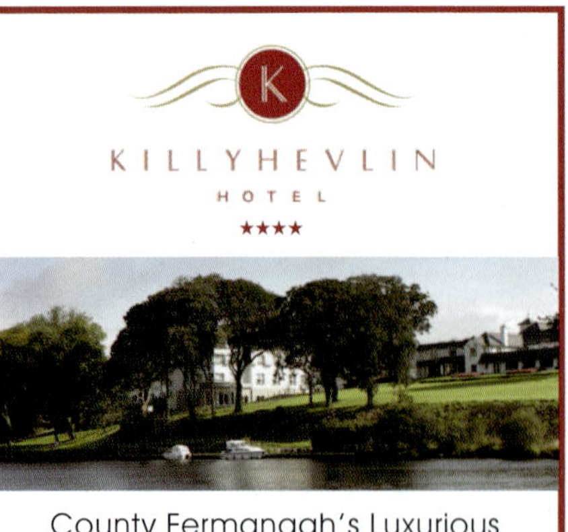

NEWRY, Co. Down

Canal Court Hotel

29 Merchants Quay, Newry BT35 8HF.
☎ **028 3025 1234.**
W **www.canalcourthotel.com**

●● D/E/I/F/G 

Modern city centre hotel. 5 reserved parking bays. Entrance level, double doors. Low reception desk. Lounge and bar ground floor open plan. Restaurant 1st floor. Lift to all floors. Unisex WCs. 2 standard and 6 deluxe bedrooms with bathrooms designed for disabled guests. Other bedrooms level.

Rates: from £80 single BB (2007).

NEWTOWNABBEY, Co. Antrim

Corrs Corner Hotel

315 Ballyclare Road,
Newtownabbey BT36 4TQ.
☎ **028 9084 9221.**
W **www.corrscorner.com**

●● D/I/G 

Hotel situated 7 miles outside central Belfast at the M2/A8 junction. Level entrance 33". Restaurant level. Unisex WC. 3 bedrooms adapted for disabled guests on ground floor. Shower rooms ⟲, roll-in shower and seat, handrails by WC. Weekend breaks available.

Rates: on application.

OMAGH, Co. Tyrone

Greenmount Lodge

58 Greenmount Road, Omagh BT79 0QU.

☎ **028 8284 1325.**

W www.greenmountlodge.com

●● D/E/F/G ★★★

Country guesthouse between Omagh and Ballygawley. Reserved parking bays. Ramp to entrance, 32". Dining room and lounge level. Unisex WC. Two bedrooms, single and double, level 34". Bathrooms 34", ⟲, roll-in shower with seat, handrails, space for side transfer to WC. Other bedrooms upstairs.

Rates: from £25.50 per person BB (2006).

Silverbirch Hotel

5 Gortin Road, Omagh BT79 7DH.

☎ **028 8224 2520.**

W www.silverbirchhotel.com

●● D/E/I/F/G ★★★

Hotel south of town centre. 5 reserved parking spaces. Entrance 3 steps or ramp with handrail. Public rooms ground floor level. Unisex WC. Lift to upper floors. 3 bedrooms designed for disabled guests. Bathrooms with roll-in shower and seat, space for side transfer to bath and WC. Other bedrooms level.

Rates: on application.

PORTAFERRY, Co. Down

The Narrows

8 Shore Road, Portaferry BT22 1JY.

☎ **028 4272 8148.**

W www.narrows.co.uk

●● D/E/F/G ★★★

Award-winning guest inn and restaurant designed to be used by disabled people facing Strangford Lough. Street parking and covered setting down point in courtyard. Restaurant ground floor. Lounge and meeting room 1st floor. Unisex WCs. Lift 32", inside 42"x55". Nine, of 13 bedrooms level. Bath or shower rooms ⟲, some with roll-in showers, some baths with handrails, space for side transfer to WC. Access to terraced garden from 1st floor. Town hilly.

Rates: from £50 per person BB (2007).

TEMPLEPATRICK, Co. Antrim

Hilton Templepatrick Hotel & Country Club

Castle Upton Estate,
Templepatrick BT39 0DD.

☎ **028 9443 5500.**

W templepatrick.hilton.com

●● D/E/I/F/G ★★★★

Hotel and leisure/golf resort. Reserved parking bays. Ramp to entrance, automatic door and revolving door with slow down control. Public rooms level. 3 unisex WCs on ground floor. Lift 34", braille buttons. Seven bedrooms designed for disabled guests 31", bedside curtain controls. Bathrooms ⟲, handrails by WC, space by bath and WC. Other bedrooms level. Wheelchair available.

Rates: on application.

LODGE ACCOMMODATION

There are Premier Travel Inn (see page 38) and Travelodge (see page 38) properties in the following localities:

Belfast - Travelodge .... ☎ 0870 191 1687

Carrickfergus - Premier Travel Inn .... ☎ 0870 850 6308

Derry - Travelodge .... ☎ 0870 191 1733

SELF-CATERING ACCOMMODATION

BELFAST

Queen's University Belfast Elms Village

78 Malone Road, Belfast BT9 5BW.

●● I/G

Student accommodation. Parking 75yds. Entrance ramp. 24 ground floor bedrooms adapted for disabled people. Shared lounge and kitchen. Shower room 31", ⟲, handrails, space for side transfer to WC and shower seat. Also separate WC designed for wheelchair users. Other bedrooms upstairs. Meals can be provided for groups of 25+ by arrangement. Available during Summer vacations.

Apply: The Conference Secretary ☎ 028 9097 5185.
Rates: on application.

BUSHMILLS, Co. Antrim

Ballylinny Holiday Cottages

Giants Causeway, Bushmills BT57 8SU.

●● I/F/G ★★★★

Six cottages near Giants Causeway with 1 designed for disabled people. Entrance level. Lounge/kitchen open plan, controls useable from wheelchair. Double/twin bedroom level, ⟲. Shower room, ⟲, roll-in shower with seat, handrails, space for side transfer to WC. Also 2 twin bedrooms and bathroom upstairs.

Ⓟ

Apply: Alan Laverty ☎ 0777 188 6516.
W www.giantscauseway.co.uk
Rates: on application.

CROM, Co. Fermanagh

Erne View

Crom Estate, Co. Fermanagh.

●● F/G

One cottage, of 7, on National Trust estate by Lough Erne. Rear entrance level. Ground floor kitchen, lounge with double sofabed and adapted WC. Four bedrooms. Bathroom and WC upstairs.

Ⓟ

Apply: National Trust Holiday Booking Office ☎ 0870 4584422. See page 33.
Rates: from £269-£723 per week (2007).

DUNDRUM, Co. Down

Murlough Cottage

Dundrum.

●● F/G

National Trust cottage on shore of Dundrum Inner Bay by Nature Reserve. One is single storey with adaptations for disabled guests. Adapted kitchen, lounge with double sofabed, twin bedroom and shower room/WC. A second cottage is also available.

Ⓟ

Apply: National Trust Holiday Booking Office ☎ 0870 4584422. See page 33.
Rates: from £228-£506 per week (2007).

ENNISKILLEN, Co. Fermanagh

The Bridges Youth Hostel

Belmore Street, Enniskillen BT74 6AA.

☎ **028 6634 0110.**

●● E/G

Modern self-catering hostel in town centre. Street parking. Level entrance. Café on ground floor. Lift to 1st floor reception, lounge, self-catering kitchen. and unisex WC. Two bedrooms designed for disabled people with roll-in shower room. Other bedrooms level. For further information on Youth Hostels see page 34.

Rates: from £15-£16 adult per night (2007).

Rose Cottage

Florence Court, Enniskillen.

●● F/G

Cottage adapted for disabled people at National Trust property. Ground floor has kitchen, lounge, dining room with sofabed, shower room and WC. Two bedrooms and bathroom upstairs.

Apply: National Trust Holiday Booking Office ☎ 0870 4584422. See page 33.

Rates: from £269-£723 per week (2007).

Tully Bay Holiday Homes

Blaney, Enniskillen BT93 7EQ.

●● F ★★★★★

Nine chalets for up to 6 people on shore of Lough Erne. Entrances level. Lounge and kitchen 33". Twin bedroom level. Other bedrooms upstairs. Two chalets have a ground floor shower room, roll-in shower, shower chair, space for side transfer to WC.

Apply: Helen Parke. ☎ 028 6864 1737.

www.tullybay.com

Rates: from £500-£650 per week (2007).

FEENY, Co. Londonderry

Drumcovitt Barn

704 Feeny Road, Feeny BT47 4SU.

www.drumcovitt.com

●● I/F/G ★★★★

Three cottages in grounds of country house in Sperrin Mountains. "Foyle Cottage" entrance level 34". Lounge /kitchen open plan, controls useable from wheelchair. Twin bedroom 34½". Shower room, roll-in shower with seat, handrails, space for side transfer to WC. Waterproof sheet can be provided. Also family bedroom and bathroom upstairs.

Apply: Mr & Mrs Sloan ☎ 028 7778 1224.

Rates: from £345-£425 per week (2007).

GREYABBEY, Co. Down

Barnwell Farm Cottages

Ballybryan Road, Greyabbey.

www.barnwellfarmcottages.co.uk

●● F/G ★★★★★

"Whin Cottage", one of a group of 7 cottages in the Ards Peninsula, is designed for disabled guests. Entrance level, 95cm. Internal doors 85cm. Lounge/kitchen open plan, controls useable from wheelchair. Single and family bedrooms. Shower room, roll-in shower with seat, handrails, space by WC, underfloor heating. Teletext TV. Shared games room.

Apply: Michael & Vi Calvert, Barnwell, 105 Mountstewart Road, Greyabbey BT22 2ES. ☎ 028 4278 8488.

Rates: from £222-£342 per week (2007).

LIMAVADY, Co. Londonderry

Ballyhenry House

172 Seacoast Road, Limavady BT49 9EF.
☎ 028 7772 2657. W ballyhenry.co.uk

●● I/F/G

Attached to bed & breakfast farmhouse near Lough Foyle coast, "Garden Apartment" designed for disabled guests. Entrance level, double patio doors. Lounge/kitchen open plan, controls usable from wheelchair. Double and double/twin bedrooms. Shower room ⟲, roll-in shower with seat, handrails, space by WC and under basin. Paved nature trails and farm tour. One other apartment. Meals may be available with advance notice.

Ⓟ

Rates: on application.

LISNASKEA, Co. Fermanagh

Share Holiday Village

Smiths Strand, Lisnaskea BT92 0EQ.
☎ 028 6772 2122.
W www.sharevillage.org

For information on this centre which has self-catering accommodation designed for disabled people see page 469.

Ⓟ

Rates: £350 per week (2007).

MACOSQUIN, Co. Londonderry

King's Country Cottages

66 Ringrash Road, Macosquin, Coleraine BT51 4LJ.
☎ 028 7035 1367.
@ patking@kingscottages.fsnet.co.uk

●● F/G ★★★

One cottage, of 6, designed for disabled people between Coleraine and Limavady. Entrance level 33". Lounge/kitchen open plan. Two bedrooms with double and single beds. Shower room 33", ⟲, roll-in shower with seat, handrails, space for side transfer to WC. Other units ground floor.

Ⓟ

Rates: from £260-£300 per week (2007).

MAGUIRESBRIDGE, Co. Fermanagh

Derryvree Farm Cottage

Belfast Road, Maguiresbridge

●● I/F/G ★★★

Cottage on farm 8 miles from Enniskillen. Patio entrance ramp, 34"; unpaved approach to front door, ramp 33". Lounge/kitchen open plan. Worktops 35" and kitchen table 29". Double bedroom ⟲. En suite shower room 31½", ⟲, roll-in shower with seat, handrails, space for side transfer to WC. Also separate bathroom and double sofabed in lounge. Bed & breakfast in farmhouse, not accessible, breakfast can be served to cottage.

Ⓟ

Apply: Mr & Mrs Bothwell, Derryvree House, 200 Belfast Road, Maguiresbridge BT94 4LD. ☎ 028 8953 1251.
@ wendy@derryvreehouse.com
Rates: from £170-£200 per week (2007).

NEWTOWNSTEWART, Co. Tyrone

Grange Court

21-27 Moyle Road, Newtownstewart, Omagh BT78 4AP.

☎ **028 8166 1877.**

grangecourt@dial.pipex.com

●● I/F/G ★★★★

One apartment, of 12, adapted for disabled people. Ramp to entrance, 33". Lounge, dining room and kitchen all ⟲. Cooker controls useable from wheelchair. Two twin bedrooms. Bathroom 33", ⟲, shower with handrails and seat, space by bath. WC 33", handrail, space by WC. Two other ground floor flats. Coffee shop on site.

Ⓟ

Rates: from £280-£380 per week (2007).

OMAGH, Co. Tyrone

Omagh Hostel

Glenhordial, 9a Waterworks Road, Omagh BT79 7JS.

☎ **028 8224 1973.**

www.omaghhostel.co.uk

●● E/I/G

Independent self-catering hostel 3 miles from town centre. Reserved parking bay. Entrance level. Dining room and lounge level. Two ground floor bedrooms designed for disabled guests. Unisex WC and roll-in shower designed for wheelchair users.

Ⓟ

Rates: from £10 adult per night (2007).

Trinity College, Dublin

Republic of Ireland

USEFUL ADDRESSES

Tourism Ireland Ltd

Head Office, 5th Floor, Bishop's Square, Redmond's Hill, Dublin 2.

☎ +353 (0)1 476 3400.

W www.tourismireland.com

UK Office: Nations House, 103 Wigmore Street, London W1U 1QS.

☎ 0800 039 7000.

@ info.gb@tourismireland.com

Tourism Ireland hold some information on accessible accommodation. Suitable properties are indicated in their annual Guide to Guest Accommodation and Guide to Self-Catering Accommodation and on their website although the information is not readily searchable.

Comhairle

7th Floor, Hume House, Ballsbridge, Dublin 4.

☎ +353 (0)1 605 9000.

W www.comhairle.ie.

Comhairle is a statutory body that provides information on the broad range of social services through a network of Citizens Information Centres, publications and on the internet at W www.oasis.gov.ie. It has developed an online resource on assistive technology at W www.assistireland.ie

Irish Wheelchair Association

Blackheath Drive, Clontarf, Dublin 3.

☎ +353 (0)1 818 6400.

@ info@iwa.ie W www.iwa.ie

The IWA is a voluntary organisation of people with physical disabilities. It operates an Information Resource Centre which has some information on accessible holidays in Ireland and elsewhere. It also has a holiday and respite centre in Roscommon, see page 485, a small holiday centre in Kilkenny, see page 494 and a respite centre in Dublin, page 481.

Irish Ferries

Contact Centre, PO Box 19, Alexandra Road, Ferryport, Dublin 1.

☎ 0818 300400.

@ info@irishferries.com

W www.irishferries.com

UK office: Corn Exchange, Brunswick Street, Liverpool L2 7TP.

☎ 08705 171717.

Operate car ferry services on the Holyhead-Dublin and Pembroke-Rosslare routes and also a fast ferry service between Holyhead and Dublin. All vessels have facilities for disabled passengers and at all 4 ports terminals have been built to be accessible. Advance notification at the time of booking is requested if passengers feel they have specific requirements. Much information for disabled passengers can be found on their website under 'More Information' and anyone with more specific information should contact the disability officers through the contact centre or on @ disabilityofficer@irishferries.com

Norfolk Line Ferries

☎ 0870 600 4321 (UK) or

☎ 01 819 2999 (Ireland).

W www.norfolkline-ferries.co.uk

12 Quays Terminal, Tower Road, Birkenhead CH41 1FE.

Alexandra Road Extension, Dublin Port, Dublin.

Operate a car ferry service between Birkenhead and Dublin 6 days a week. The vessels have lifts, unisex toilets and cabins designed for disabled passengers. Advance notice of any special requirements is requested.

P&O Irish Sea

Larne Harbour, Larne BT40 1AW.
☎ 0871 6644777.
Textphone: 01304 223090.
W www.poirishsea.com

Car ferry services are operated to Dublin from Liverpool however the vessels used do not have lifts between the car deck and the main passenger areas. Advice on the suitability of vessels is available when booking and at least 48 hours notice is requested for any assistance that may be required.

Stena Line

Stena House, Station Approach, Holyhead, Anglesey LL65 1DQ.
☎ 08705 707070.
Textphone: 08795 421127.
W www.stenaline.co.uk

Operate traditional and fast-ferry services between Holyhead and Dunlaogaire and Dublin and between Fishguard and Rosslare using vessels that are accessible to wheelchair users. Assistance can be provided at both port and on board although as much notice as possible is requested. There are toilets fitted with the NKS lock at the Fishgueard and Holyhead terminals.

Office of Public Works

Visitor Service, 6 Upper Ely Place, Dublin 2.
☎ +353 (0)1 647 6593.
@ info@heritageireland.ie
W www.heritageireland.ie

The OPW manages a wide range of heritage sites including monuments and historic buildings throughout the country. Their annual visitor information leaflets include an indication of the extent of access for disabled visitors.

Irish Railways – Iarnród Eireann – general information on access and services for disabled passengers as well and information on the accessibility of individual stations is available on W www.iarnrodeireann.ie - click on Your Journey. Requests for assistance should be made in advance, preferably at least 24 hours, to the station from which the journey is starting or to the Mobility Liaison Office, Iarnrod Eireann, Connolly Station, Dublin 1. ☎ +353 (0)1 703 2634.

Trident Holiday Homes

E8 Network Enterprise Park, Kilcoole, Co. Wicklow.
☎ +353 (0)1 201 8440.
@ reservations@tridentholidayhomes.ie.
W www.tridentholidayhomes.ie

Company representing a range of self-catering accommodation in many parts of Ireland. Their brochure indicates those that have some facilities for disabled people. Some of these are included in this guide.

EQUIPMENT HIRE

Advance Electrical Mobility

4 Crumlin Village, Dublin 12, Ireland.
☎ **+353 1 455 3168.**
@ **info@aemobility.com**
W **www.aemobility.com**

Supply and maintain a wide range of mobility and other equipment with powered scooters and wheelchairs being available for rent.

BOC Medispeed

Unit 19, Clondalkin Industrial Estate, Clondalkin, Dublin 22.
☎ **00 800 220 20202.**
@ **medispeed@bocgases.ie**

The major supplier of medical oxygen in Ireland can provide both domestic and ambulatory oxygen for tourists with advanced notice on arrival in the country or at their final destination.

MMS Medical Ltd

51 Eastgate Drive, Little Island, Cork, Ireland.
☎ **+353 21 461 8000.**
W **www.mmsmedical.ie**

Company, with additional centres in Dublin and Galway, that can hire and sell a wide range of mobility and other equipment.

Motability Ireland Ltd

The Irish Mobility Centre, Unit 21, Ashbourne Industrial Park, Ashbourne, Co Meath, Ireland
☎ **+353 1 835 9173.**
W **www.motabilityireland.com**

Family owned company with long experience of carrying out vehicle adaptations for disabled people. They have a fleet of hire cars including wheelchair accessible vehicles and automatic cars fitted with hand controls.

McElmeel Mobility Services

15 Ballyscandal Road, Armagh BT61 8BL.
☎ **028 3752 5333.**
@ **info@mobility-services.com**
W **www.mobility-services.com**

Vehicle adaption company that has for hire both cars fitted with hand controls and those that can carry passengers in wheelchairs.

Shopmobility Ireland (Dublin) provides wheelchairs and scooters for use in the Liffey Valley Shopping Centre, Clondalkin and Dundrum Town Centre near Dublin. Adapted toilets and designated parking bays also available. For information on availability, etc. contact in advance ☎ +353 (0)1 620 8731. @ ability@aol.ie

Shopmobility schemes also operates at the Mahon Point Shopping Centre, Cork. ☎ +353 (0)21 431 3033 and Whitewater Shopping Centre, Newbridge, Co Kildare.

REPUBLIC OF IRELAND ACCOMMODATION

For ease of reference accommodation entries for the Republic of Ireland are divided into four areas. The localities covered by each of these areas are as follows:

DUBLIN AREA
ACCOMMODATION WITH MEALS

DUBLIN

Berkeley Court Hotel

Lansdowne Road, Dublin 4.

☎ **+353 (0)1 665 3200.**

@ **berkeley-court@jurysdoyle.com**

●● D/E/I/F/G ★★★★★

High class hotel in central Dublin. Reserved parking spaces. Entrance level. Low reception desk. Public rooms ground floor, level. Unisex WC. Lift to all floors. Two bedrooms adapted for disabled guests with bathrooms ⟲. Other bedrooms level. A Jurys Doyle hotel.

Ⓟ

Rates: from €139 per night (2007).

Carmel Fallon Respite Centre

Blackheath Drive, Clontarf, Dublin 3.

☎ **+353 (0)1 818 6458.** W **www.iwa.ie**

●●●● D/E/I/F/G/H

Holiday and respite centre in grounds of Irish Wheelchair Association headquarters, near coast and public transport north of City Centre. Public rooms spacious. Six single bedrooms with own bath/shower rooms. Electric beds, overhead hoists, shower chairs and some other equipment available. Care provided. 5 and 10 night breaks offered. Sports centre and gym on site. Outings and activities arranged on arrival. For people aged 13-65.

Ⓟ

Rates: on application.

Conrad Dublin

Earlsfort Terrace, Dublin 2.
☎ +353 (0)1 602 8900.
www.ConradHotels.com
●● D/E/I ★★★★★

City centre hotel. Reserved parking bays. Entrance ramp, 42". Lounge and restaurant ground floor. Bar lower floor. Unisex WC. Lift 43", inside 60"x54". Bedroom designed for disabled guests 35", ↺. Bathroom 28", ↺, handrails, space for side transfer to bath and WC. Other bedrooms level.

Rates: on application.

Grafton Capital Hotel

Lower Stephen's Street, Dublin 2.
☎ +353 (0)1 648 1100.
www.capital-hotels.com
●● D/E/FG ★★★

Georgian townhouse hotel. Level entrance. Public rooms 1st floor. Unisex WC. Lift 80cm, inside 127x137cm. 4 double bedrooms designed for disabled guests ↺. Bathrooms 71cm, handrails, space by bath and WC. Bath seat available. Other bedrooms level. Teletext TV.

Rates: on application.

Ibis Hotel Dublin West

Red Cow Roundabout, Naas Road, Dublin 22.
☎ +353 (0)1 464 1480.
H0595@accor.com
●● D/G

Hotel near M50/N7 junction west of city. Reserved parking bays. Entrance level. Low reception desk with induction loop. Public rooms level, open plan. Unisex WCs. Lift 30", inside 42"x56". Seven ground floor bedrooms designed for disabled guests with double and single beds. Shower rooms 29", ↺, shower tray, handrails, handrails. Wheelchair, vibrating pillow and large dial telephone available. Other 143 bedrooms level.

Rates: from €72-€76 per room (2008).

Jurys Inn Christchurch

Christchurch Place, Dublin 8.
☎ +353 (0)1 454 0000.
●● D/E/I/G ★★★

Modern three star hotel in city centre. Entrance level. Public rooms open plan. Unisex WC. Lift 48", inside 60"x43". Two double bedrooms designed for disabled guests. Bathrooms 36", ↺, handrails, space for side transfer to bath and WC. Other bedrooms level.

Rates: from €97 per night (2007).

Jurys Inn Custom House

Custom House Quay, Dublin 1.
☎ +353 (0)1 607 5000.
●● D/E/I/G ★★★

Hotel in city centre. Limited parking spaces at rear can be reserved. Entrance level, automatic doors. Low reception desk. Public rooms level. Unisex WC. Lift inside 52"x55". Twelve double bedrooms designed for disabled guests. Shower rooms ↺, roll-in shower, handrails, space for side transfer to WC. Other bedrooms level.

Rates: on application.

Jurys Inn Parnell Street

Parnell Street, Dublin 1.
☎ +353 (0) 1 878 4900.
jurysinnparnellst@jurysinns.com
●● D/E/I/F/G

City centre hotel. No parking. Entrance level, automatic doors. Low reception desk. Public rooms 2nd floor, open plan. Unisex WC. Lift to all floors. 13 bedrooms, doubles & twins, designed for disabled guests, 2 with automatic door openers. Bathrooms, some with roll-in showers, ↺, handrails, space by WC. Other rooms level. Vibrating pillow alarms and wheelchair available.

Rates: from €95-€160 room only (2008).

Mespil Hotel

Mespil Road, Dublin 4.
☎ +353 (0)1 488 4600.
@ reservations@leehotels.com
●● D/E/I/G ★★★

Modern hotel by Grand Canal near city centre. Reserved parking bays. Entrance level, revolving and swing doors. Public rooms level. Adapted cubicle in WCs. Lift 105cm, inside 157x140cm. 15 bedrooms adapted for disabled guests, 93cm, ⟲. Bathrooms ⟲, handrails, space by bath and WC. Other bedrooms level.

Rates: from €115 per room (2007/8).

Trinity Capital Hotel

Pearce Street, Dublin 2.
☎ +353 (0) 1 648 1000.
@ info@trinitycapital-hotel.com
●● D/E/I/F/G ★★★

Modern hotel in central Dublin, by Trinity College. Reserved parking bays in basement car park. Level entrance. Lounge and bar ground floor open plan. Restaurant 1st floor. Lift 80cm, internal 127x137cm. Unisex WC 1st floor. 4 double/twin bedrooms designed for disabled guests. Bathrooms ⟲, handrails, space by bath and WC. Bathseat available. Other bedrooms level. Teletext TV.

Rates: on application.

DUBLIN AIRPORT

Hilton Dublin Airport

Northern Cross, Malahide Road, Dublin 17.
☎ +353 (0)1 866 1800.
@ reservations.dublinairport@hilton.com
●● D/E/I/F/G ★★★★

Hotel 8km from airport. Reserved parking bays. Entrance level. Public rooms level. Unisex WCs on ground and 1st floors. Lift to all floors. 8 double/twin bedrooms designed for disabled people. Shower rooms ⟲, roll-in shower with seat, space by WC. Other bedrooms level.

Rates: on application.

Holiday Inn Dublin Airport

Dublin Airport, Dublin.
☎ +353 (0)1 808 0500.
@ dublinairport@ihg.com
●● D/E/F/G ★★★★

Hotel by airport. Reserved parking bays. Entrance ramp, revolving or swing doors. Public rooms level, open plan. Unisex WC. Three bedrooms adapted for disabled guests. Bathrooms sliding door, ⟲, grabrail by bath, space for side transfer to bath and WC.

Rates: on application.

LODGE ACCOMMODATION

There are Travelodge (see page 38) properties in the following localities:

Dublin Airport ☎ +353 (0)1 807 9400
Dublin, Castleknock ☎ +353 (0)1 820 2626
Dublin, Rathmines ☎ +353 (0)1 491 1402

SELF-CATERING ACCOMMODATION

DUBLIN

302 Cowper Downs

Rathmines, Dublin 6.

●● I/F/G ★★

Ground floor flat in residential area 2 miles from city centre. One step to entrance. Living room with sofa bed. Kitchen controls useable from wheelchair. Double bedroom. Bathroom 36", ⟲, space by bath and WC. Wheelchair user in owner's family.

Ⓟ

Apply: John Kelly, Golf Links Road, Roscommon. ☎ +353 (0)90 662 5926.
@ kellyroscommon@eircom.net
Rates: €450 per week (2007).

WEST OF IRELAND
ACCOMMODATION WITH MEALS

BALLYVAUGHAN, Co. Clare
Gregans Castle Hotel

Ballyvaughan, Co. Clare.
☎ +353 (0)65 7077 005. W www.gregans.ie
● D/E/F ★★★★

Country house hotel in the Burren. Entrance level, 42". Public rooms level, min. door width 35". WCs not adapted. 7 large ground floor bedrooms with bathrooms. Open Easter-October.

Rates: from €150-€270 single per night BB (2007).

DONAMON, Co. Roscommon
Cuisle

Donamon, Co. Roscommon.
☎ +353 (0)90 666 2277. W www.cuisle.com
●●●● D/E/I/F/G/H

A fully accessible 35 bedroomed holiday centre owned by Irish Wheelchair Association. Restaurant, lounge and bar ground floor, open plan. Lift 36", inside 66"x58". 35 twin bedrooms with accessible bath/shower rooms. Adapted bathrooms and WCs on each floor. Adjustable height beds available that must be pre-booked. Hoists and some other equipment available. Personal and nursing care arranged with a month's advance notice. Adapted vehicles available.

Rates: on application.

DOOLIN, Co. Clare
Ballyvara House

Doolin, Co. Clare.
☎ +353 (0)65 707 4467.
W www.ballyvarahouse.ie
●● D/E/F/G ★★★★

Country guesthouse near village and west coast. Reserved parking bay. Slight slope to entrance, 30". Public rooms ground floor, min. door width 29". Unisex WC. Ground floor double bedroom designed for disabled guests. Shower room 30", roll-in shower with seat, handrails, space by WC. 5 other level bedrooms. Closed Nov-Feb.

Rates: €45-€75 per person BB (2007).

GALWAY, Co. Galway
Jurys Inn Galway

Quay Street, Galway.
☎ +353 (0)91 566444.
●● D/E/I/G ★★★

Hotel in town centre. Ramp from street to main entrance; 4 steps from car park. Public rooms level. Unisex WC. Lift 48", inside 72"x60". Ramp to 2 double bedrooms designed for disabled guests. Level entrance to 2 rooms. Bathrooms, handrails, space for side transfer to bath and WC. Other bedrooms level. Wheelchair available.

Rates: from €89-€125per room (2007).

Quality Hotel & Leisure Centre Galway

Oranmore, Galway.
☎ +353 (0)91 792244.
W www.qualityhotelgalway.com
●● D/E/I/F/G ★★★

Modern 3 star hotel in suburb on N6. Reserved parking bays. Entrance level. Public rooms level. Unisex WC. Lift 42", inside 48"x48". One bedroom and bathroom with adaptations for disabled guests, handrail by bath, space for side transfer to WC, no ⟲. Other bedrooms level.

Rates: from €89-€199 per room (2007).

Radisson SAS Hotel & Spa Galway

Lough Atalia Road, Galway.
☎ +353 (0)91 538300.
@ sales.galway@radissonsas.com
●● D/E/I/G ★★★★

Modern international hotel near city centre overlooking lough. Reserved parking bays. Ramp to entrance. Low reception desk. Lifts 104cm, inside 153x144cm. Public rooms ground floor or lift to leisure centre. Unisex WCs. 10 twin/double bedrooms designed for disabled guests. Shower rooms 29.5cm, ⟲, roll-in shower, handrails, space by WC. Other bedrooms level. Teletext TV. Regular disabled users.

Rates: on application.

KNOCK, Co. Mayo

The Belmont Hotel

Knock, Co. Mayo.
☎ +353 (0)94 93 88122.
W www.belmonthotel.ie
●● D/E/I/G ★★★

3 star hotel. Reserved parking bays. Entrance level. Carvery, lounge and bar open plan. Restaurant level, 27". Unisex WC. Three family bedrooms level, 30", ⟲. Shower rooms 30", ⟲, shower tray, handrail, space for side transfer to WC. Waterproof sheet and wheelchair available. Slope to garden.

Rates: on application.

Knock House Hotel

Ballyhaunis Road, Knock, Co. Mayo.
☎ +353 (0)94 93 88088.
W www.knockhousehotel.ie
●●● D/E/I/F/G/H ★★★

Modern hotel. Reserved parking spaces. Entrance level. Public rooms level. Unisex WC. Lift 80cm, inside 110x140cm. 3 and 2 double bedrooms designed for disabled guests. Shower rooms 75cm, roll-in shower with seat, handrails, space by WC. Also triple bedroom with adjustable bed and medical assessment unit. Other bedrooms level. Hoist, shower chair, waterproof sheet and wheelchair available.

Rates: from €55-€77 per person BB (2007).

LETTERKENNY, Co. Donegal

Fern House

Main Street, Kilmacrennan,
nr. Letterkenny, Co. Donegal.
☎ +353 (0)74 913 9218.
www.fern-house.com

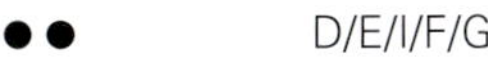 D/E/I/F/G

Bed & breakfast in centre of village, 9km from Letterkenney. Ramp from car park to entrance. Dining room ground floor. Twin bedroom designed for disabled guests. Shower room 36", roll-in shower, handrail, space by WC, no ↺. Other ground floor bedroom level. Regular disabled guests.

Ⓟ

Rates: on application.

WESTPORT, Co. Mayo

Hotel Westport Leisure Spa

Newport Road, Westport, Co. Mayo.
☎ +353 (0)98 25122.
www.hotelwestport.ie

●● D/E/I/F/G ★★★

High class hotel in parkland near town centre. Reserved parking bays. Entrance level, automatic door. Public rooms level. Unisex WC. Lift to upper floors. 7 bedrooms designed for disabled guests. Bathrooms ↺, handrails, space by WC and bath. Walk in shower. Other bedrooms level. Accessible leisure facilities. Special interest breaks arranged.

Rates: from €55 per person (2007).

LODGE ACCOMMODATION

There is a Travelodge (see page 38) property in the following locality:

Galway .... ☎ +353 (0)9 178 1400

SELF-CATERING ACCOMMODATION

BALLINROBE, Co. Mayo
Western Pride Holiday Homes

Lough Mask, Ballinrobe.

●● E/G ★★★

One cottage, sleeping 7/8 people, purpose designed for wheelchair users. Entrance level. Lounge, kitchen with fittings usable from wheelchair. One bedroom with en-suite bathroom equipped for disabled guests. 2 other level bedrooms and bathroom. 4th bedroom and shower room upstairs. Portable ramp available for other 8 units.

Apply: Mrs Keady, Western Pride Holiday Homes, Creagh, Lough Mask, Ballinrobe, Co. Mayo. ☎ +353 (0)94 9541671/41074. @ nelliekeady@eircom.net

Rates: from €200-€595 per week (2007).

BALLYSHANNON, Co. Donegal

Big Jimmy's Cottage

Creevy, nr. Ballyshannon.

●● F/G ★★★★

Single storey traditional cottage designed for disabled people in rural area between Rossnowlagh and Ballyshannon, near Donegal Town. Ramp to entrance, 91cm. Open plan lounge/kitchen, controls useable from wheelchair. Three twin /double bedrooms which can be arranged to suit needs. Shower room 91cm, ⟲, roll-in shower with seat, handrails, space by WC, low mirror. Teletext TV. Two other cottages have ground floor accommodation and can accommodate many wheelchair users. Accredited environmentally friendly accommodation.

Apply: Molly Reynolds, Creevy Co-op, Ballyshannon, Co. Donegal. ☎ +353 (0)71 985 2896. W www.creevyexperience.ie

Rates: from €525-€899 per week (2007).

SOUTH WEST IRELAND
ACCOMMODATION WITH MEALS

BLARNEY, Co. Cork
Ashlee Lodge

Tower, Blarney, Co. Cork.

☎ **+353 (0)21 438 5346.**

W **www.ashleelodge.com**

●● D/E/F/G ★★★★★

High class modern country hotel. Reserved parking bay. Ramp to entrance. Low reception desk. Public rooms open plan. Double bedroom designed for disabled guests. Shower room ⟲, roll-in shower with seat, handrails, space by WC.

Rates: from €80 per person BB (2007).

CORK, Co. Cork
Jurys Cork Hotel

Western Road, Cork.

☎ **+353 (0)21 425 2700.**

@ **cork@jurysdoyle.com**

●● D/E/I/G ★★★★

Re-built high class hotel by river in city centre. Reserved parking bays. Public rooms level. Unisex WC. Lift to all floors. Two bedrooms adapted for disabled guests with handrails in bathrooms. Other bedrooms level, ⟲ in most. Wheelchair available.

Rates: from €129 per night (2007).

Jurys Inn Cork
Anderson's Quay, Cork.
☎ **+353 (0)21 492 3000.**
@ **jurysinncork@jurysdoyle.com**
●● D/E/I/G ★★★
City centre hotel. Entrance level. Public rooms ground floor. Unisex WC. Lift 48", inside 72"x60". Seven bedrooms designed for disabled guests. Bathrooms ↺, handrails, space for side transfer to bath and WC, some with roll-in showers. Other bedrooms level.

Rates: from €85 per night (2007).

DINGLE, Co. Kerry
Smerwick Harbour Hotel
Gallarus Cross, Ballyferriter, Dingle, Co. Kerry.
☎ **+353 (0)66 915 6470.**
W **www.smerwickhotel.ie**
●● D/E/I/F/G ★★★
Hotel on coast 3 miles from Dingle. Reserved parking bays. Level entrance. Public rooms level. Unisex WC. Lift to upper floor. Ground floor bedrooms designed for disabled guests 80cm ↺. Bathrooms ↺, handrails, space by WC. Other bedrooms level. Occasional bar entertainment.

Rates: from €40-€90 per person BB (2007).

INNISHANNON, Co. Cork
Ceol na nEan
Innishannon, Co. Cork.
☎ **+353 (0)21 477 6147.**
W **www.ceol-na-nean.com**
●●● D/E/I/F/G/H
Bed & breakfast house on edge of village off N71 west of Cork and near Kinsale. Reserved parking bays. Entrance level. Dining room and unisex WC on ground floor. Lounge 1st floor. Lift 100cm, inside 93x148cm. Double bedroom designed for disabled guests 100cm, ↺, touch lamps, access to dressing table. Shower room ↺, roll-in shower with seat, handrails. One other level bedroom. Hoist, waterproof sheet, and some other equipment available and also a power chair. Hot tub with hoist.

Rates: €40 per person per night (2007).

KILLARNEY, Co. Kerry

Fairview Guest House
College Street, Killarney, Co. Kerry.
☎ **+353 (0)64 34164.**
W **www.fairviewkillarney.com**
●● D/E/I/G ★★★★
Modern guesthouse near town centre. Level entrance, double doors. Low reception desk. Public rooms level. Unisex WC. Lift to upper floors. 2 bedroom and bathroom designed for disabled guests. Other bedrooms level. Teletext TV.

Rates: from €40-€79 per person BB (2007).

Holiday Inn Killarney

Muckross Road, Killarney, Co Kerry.
☎ **+353 (0)64 33000.**
W www.holidayinnkillarney.com
●● D/E/I/G ★★★

Hotel near town centre. Reserved parking bays. Level entrance. Low reception desk. Open plan lounge and bar ground floor, also unisex WC. Restaurant 2nd floor. Lift to all floors. Six bedrooms designed for disabled people, twin, double and family. Bathrooms ↺, space by bath and WC. Other bedrooms level.

Rates: on application.

The Lake Hotel

Muckross Road, Killarney, Co. Kerry.
☎ **+353 (0)64 31035.**
W www.lakehotel.com

Country house hotel on lakeshore outside town. Reserved parking bays. Entrance level, double doors. Public rooms level. Unisex WC. Lift. 13 ground floor bedrooms level. Bathrooms ↺, space by bath and WC. Three rooms designed for disabled guests. Closed Mid-December to mid-February.

Rates: on application.

KINSALE, Co. Cork

Captain's Quarters Guesthouse

5 Denis Quay, Kinsale, Co. Cork.
☎ **+353 (0)21 477 4549.**
W www.captains-kinsale.com
●● F/G

Guesthouse in coastal town. Street parking. Entrance ramp, 90cm, doorphone for assistance. Dining room level. Lounge 1st floor. Single and twin bedrooms level, ↺. Adjoining shower room 75cm sliding door, roll-in shower with seat, handrails, space for side transfer to WC. Other bedrooms upstairs.

Rates: from €27-€46 per person BB (2007).

LIMERICK, Co. Limerick

Jurys Inn Limerick

Lower Mallow Street, Limerick.
☎ **+353 (0)61 207000.**
●● D/E/I/G ★★★

Hotel in city centre. Entrance level. Public rooms level. Unisex WC. Lift to all floors. Eight bedrooms designed for disabled guests, ↺. Bathrooms ↺, roll-in shower in some, handrails, space for side transfer to bath and WC. Other bedrooms level.

Rates: from €59-€125 per night (2007).

LODGE ACCOMMODATION

There are Travelodge (see page 38) properties in the following localities

Cork Airport .... ☎ +353 (0)21 431 0722

Limerick .... ☎ +353 (0)61 457000

SELF-CATERING ACCOMMODATION

KENMARE, Co. Kerry

Gortamullen Holiday Cottages

Kenmare, Co. Kerry.

●● I/G ★★★★

Group of self-catering cottages on edge of heritage town. Two single storey units designed for disabled guests. Ramp to entrance. Open plan lounge/kitchen, kitchen controls not useable from wheelchair. Double and twin bedrooms. Shower room ⟲, roll-in shower with seat and handrails, space by WC and under basin.

Ⓟ

Apply: Trident Holiday Homes, E8 Network, Enterprise Park, Kilcoole, Co. Wicklow ☎ +353 (0)1 607 7200.

www.tridentholidayhomes.ie

Rates: from €275-€710 per week (2007).

KILFINANE, Co. Limerick

Ballyhoura Forest Homes

Ballyorgan, Kilfinane, Co. Limerick.

●● F/G 

Group of 10 timber clad cottages in woodland, 3 miles from Kilfinane between Mallow and Tipperary. All sleep up to 6 and have level entrance. Open plan lounge/kitchen, controls may be useable from wheelchair. Twin bedroom with roll-in shower room with seat and space by WC. Two other bedrooms and bathroom.

Ⓟ

Apply: Trident Holiday Homes, E8 Network, Enterprise Park, Kilcoole, Co. Wicklow

☎ +353 (0)1 607 7200.

www.tridentholidayhomes.ie

Rates: from €290-€730 per week (2006).

KILLARNEY, Co. Kerry

Glenview Cottage

Brennans Glen, Tralee Road, Killarney, Co. Kerry.

☎ + 352 (0)66 976 4359.

www.glenviewcottage.com

I/F/G 

Cottage designed for disabled people in country near Killarney. Entrance level 36". Lounge/kitchen open plan with controls useable from wheelchair. Two double bedrooms ground floor, ⟲. Shower room 36", ⟲, roll-in shower with seat, handrails, space by WC. Twin bedroom upstairs. Owners live next door.

Ⓟ

Rates: from €230-€500 per week (2006).

KILMALLOCK, Co. Limerick

Bohernagore Self Catering

Ardpatrick, Kilmallock, Co. Limerick.

www.bohernagore.com

●● I/F/G

Single storey farmhouse between Kilmallock and Kilfinnane. Ramp with handrail to entrance 32". Lounge, dining room and kitchen ⟲. Controls useable from wheelchair. Four bedrooms, 2 doubles with en suite shower rooms, twin and single. Shower room ⟲, roll-in shower with seat, handrails. WC with handrails and space for side transfer. Food can be delivered.

Apply: Mary Flynn, Cuilmhoin, Tobernea West, Kilmallock, Co. Limerick.

☎ +353 (0)63 71206.

Rates: from €250-€450 per week (2007).

LAURAGH, Co. Kerry
The Pound House

Glentrasna, Lauragh,
nr. Kenmare, Co. Kerry.
www.thepoundhouse.com

 I/F/G ★★★★

Large cottage in Glentrasna valley south west of Kenmare. Entrance level, double doors. Lounge, dining room and kitchen ground floor. Two double or twin bedrooms ground floor ⟲. Shower room 80cm, roll-in shower, handrails. Shower chair available. Three other bedrooms upstairs. Teletext TV. Large garden. Evening meals can be ordered. Access details on website.

Apply: Lorna & David Ramshaw.
☎ +353 (0)64 83946.
Rates: from €550-€1300 per week (2007).

MIDLETON, Co. Cork
Trabolgan Holiday Village

Midleton, Co. Cork.
☎ **+353 (0)21 466 1551.**
www.trabolgan.com

 ★★★★

Holiday centre on East Cork coast with wide range of activities, catering and entertainment. Two holiday homes designed for disabled guests. Open plan lounge /kitchen, twin bedroom and bunk room, shower room with space for side transfer to WC. Some other accommodation may also be suitable for disabled people. Accessible airport transfers and hire of equipment can be arranged.

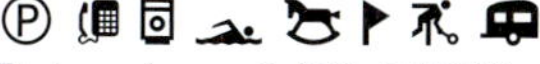

Rates: from €430-€1310 per week (2007).

CENTRAL, EAST & SOUTH EAST IRELAND
ACCOMMODATION WITH MEALS

CASHEL, Co. Tipperary
Aulber House

Golden Road, Cashel, Co. Tipperary.
☎ **+353 (0) 62 63713.**
www.aulberhouse.com

 D/G  ★★★

Guesthouse on edge of town. Reserved parking bay. Entrance 2 steps, portable ramp available. Restaurant and lounge level. One bedroom designed for disabled guests with shower room ⟲, roll-in shower with seat, space by WC. Other ground floor rooms level.

Rates: on application.

Watties B&B

Dominic Street, Cashel, Co. Tipperary.
☎ **+353 (0)62 61923.**
www.wattiesbandb.ie

●● D/F

Bed and breakfast in historic town. Reserved parking bay. Entrance level. Lounge and breakfast room ground floor. One bedroom and roll-in shower room designed for disabled guests. Other bedrooms upstairs.

Rates: from €38-€55 per night BB (2007).

GRAIGUENAMANAGH, Co. Kilkenny

Westend

Old Grange, Graiguenamanagh,
Co. Kilkenny.

☎ **+353 (0)59 972 4868.**

@ **westend@ireland.com**

●● D/E/I/F/G

Country guest house designed to be used by disabled guests between Graiguenamanagh and Thomastown. Level entrance 36". Dining room, lounges and patio level. 3 twin and 1 double bedrooms. Shower rooms 32", ⟲, roll-in shower, handrails, space by WC. Waterproof sheets available. Level garden. Evening meals available.

Rates: from €30 per night BB (2007).

KILKENNY, Co. Kilkenny

Claddagh Court Holiday Centre

College Road, Kilkenny.

☎ **+353 (0)56 776 2775.**

●●●● D/E/I/H

Purpose build 4 bedded holiday centre in grounds of Irish Wheelchair Association complex for people up to the age of 65. Equipment available including hoists, shower chairs and adjustable beds. Nursing care can be organised if required. Special interest breaks organised.

Rates: on application.

NEWBRIDGE, Co. Kildare

Keadeen Hotel

Curragh Road, Newbridge, Co. Kildare.

☎ **+353 (0)45 431666.**

W **www.keadeenhotel.kildare.ie**

●● D/E/I/F/G ★★★★

Country hotel near The Curragh Racecourse. Reserved parking bay. Entrance level. Public rooms ground floor. Unisex WC. Three ground floor bedrooms designed for disabled guests. Bathroom ⟲. Other ground floor bedrooms level. Waterproof sheet and wheelchair available. Gardens level.

Rates: on application.

NEWTOWNMOUNTKENNEDY, Co Wicklow

Marriott Druids Glen Hotel & Country Club,

Newtownmountkennedy,
Co. Wicklow.

☎ **+325 (0)1287 0800.**

W **www.marriottdruidsglen.com**

●● D/F/G ★★★★★

Country hotel near Wicklow Mountains, 25 miles south of Dublin. Reserved parking bays. Entrance level, automatic double door. Main public rooms ground floor, level. Unisex WCs. Lift 110cm, inside 180x110cm. Six bedrooms designed for disabled guests. Bathrooms ⟲, space by bath and WC. Other bedrooms level.

Rates: on application.

ROSSLARE, Co. Wexford

Kelly's Resort Hotel

Rosslare, Co. Wexford.

☎ +353 (0)53 913 2114. W www.kellys.ie

●● D/E ★★★★

4 star hotel by beach. Reserved parking bays. Entrance level. Public rooms level. Lift. Two bedrooms with roll-in shower room designed for disabled guests. Also 20 ground floor bedrooms. Special interest breaks offered. Closed December-February.

Rates: on application.

WATERFORD, Co. Waterford

Tower Hotel Waterford

The Mall, Waterford.

☎ +325 (0)51 862300.

W towerhotelwaterford.com

●● D/E/I/F/G ★★★

3 star city centre hotel. Reserved parking bays. Entrance ramp. Public rooms level. Unisex WC. Lift 32", inside 44"x54". Three double bedrooms designed for disabled guests 32". Shower rooms 32", roll-in shower, handrails, space for side transfer to WC. Other bedrooms level.

Rates: on application.

LODGE ACCOMMODATION

There is a Travelodge (see page 38) property in the following locality:

Waterford .... **☎ +353 (0)513 58885**

SELF-CATERING ACCOMMODATION

BANAGHER, Co. Offaly

Lime Kiln Cottages

Cosgrave South, Lusmagh,
Banagher, Co. Offaly.

☎ +353 (0)57 915 1224.

W banagherselfcatering.com

●● F/G

Two cottages designed for disabled guests in central Ireland countryside near River Shannon. Entrance level. All doors 85cm. Lounge and kitchen ⟲, controls useable from wheelchair. Two bedrooms, one double and the other with 3 single beds. Bathroom ⟲, handrails, space for side transfer to bath and WC. Bath seat available.

Rates: from €300-€400 per week (2007).

DROGHEDA, Co. Louth

The Sanctuary

An Grianan, Termonfechin,
Drogheda, Co. Louth.

☎ +353 (0)41 982 2119.

@ admin@an-grianan.ie

●● F ★★★★

Six bungalows in grounds of adult education college near coast east of Drogheda. 1 step at entrance. Door widths 30". Each has lounge/diner, kitchen and 4 twin bedrooms. Two bedrooms have private bathrooms, ⟲ and handrails in one. Also a shared bathroom/WC.

Rates: from €650-€895 per week (2007).

GLENDALOUGH, Co. Wicklow

Glendaloch International Youth Hostel

The Lodge, Glendalough, Co. Wicklow.
☎ **+353 (0)404 45342.**
@ **glendaloughyh@ireland.com**
●● I/F/G

Modernised hostel in scenic valley. Entrance ramp, double doors. Public rooms ground floor level. Kitchen controls not useable from wheelchair. Internal doors 36". Twin bedroom designed for wheelchair users. Shower room ⟲, roll-in shower with seat, handrails, space by WC. Other ground floor bedrooms available. Meals available. For further information on Youth Hostels, see page 34.

Rates: €18-€24 per night (2007).

KILMORE, Co. Wexford

Kilmore House

Ballask, Kilmore, Co. Wexford.
W **www.kilmorecottage.com**
●● F/G ★★★★

Three cottages designed for disabled people on farm near south Irish coast. "Teach Eile" and "Teach a Tri" for 4-5 people have level entrance. Open plan lounge/kitchen, controls useable from wheelchair. Double and twin bedrooms. Bathroom 82cm, ⟲, roll-in shower with seat, handrails, space by WC. Raised WC seat. Teletext TV. "Kilmore Cottage" has ramp or 2 steps to entrance, 81cm. Lounge/kitchen open plan. Double bedroom ground floor ⟲. Bathroom 80cm, roll-in shower with seat, handrails, space by bath and WC. 2 twin bedrooms and shower room upstairs.

Apply: Helen & John Cousins
☎ +353 (0)5391 35487.
@ info@kilmorecottage.com
Rates: €280-€725 per week (2007).

MULLINGAR, Co. Westmeath

6 The Jetty

Patrick Street, Mullingar, Co. Westmeath.
●● I/F/G

New flat in centre of town. Kitchen controls useable from wheelchair. Three double bedrooms one with en suite bathroom designed for disabled people.

Apply: John Kelly, Golf Links Road, Roscommon. ☎ +353 (0)90 662 5926.
@ kellyroscommon@eircom.net
Rates: from €400 per week.

ROSCREA, Co. Tipperary

Fairymount Farm

Ballingarry, Roscrea, Co. Tipperary.
☎ **+353 (0)67 21139.**
W **www.fairymountfarm.com**
●● I/F/G ★★★★

Two cottages designed for disabled people on farm on Knockshegowna Hill between Roscrea and Portumna. "Oakwood" has all entrances level. 29" door to open plan lounge/kitchen, controls useable from wheelchair. Two single and 2 double bedrooms ⟲, one with en-suite bathroom. Shower room ⟲, roll-in shower with seat, handrails, space by WC. "Fairymount" has a level entrance to the conservatory; steps at other entrances. 55" double door to open plan lounge /kitchen, controls useable from wheelchair. 3 twin bedrooms. One with en-suite shower room ⟲, roll-in shower, handrails. Also separate shower room. A 3rd cottage is also available.

Apply: Linda Kenny
Rates: from €320-€520 per week (2007).

ACTIVITY HOLIDAYS CONTENTS

OUTDOOR ACTIVITY CENTRES

The following centres can cater either for individuals or groups on organised programmes of outdoor activities. Some also offer facilities for self-programming groups, although centres that only operate in this way are found in the regional sections of this guide.

Activenture Holidays

Hindleap Warren, Wych Cross, Forest Row, Sussex RH18 5JS. ☎ **01342 828215.**

●●●

Run week-long activity holidays for young people with disabilities or special needs aged 8-18 during school holidays, and a weekend for over 18s, at Hindleap Warren Outdoor Centre. The Centre, owned by Federation of London Youth Clubs, has a 300-acre site in Ashdown Forest. Activities available with trained instructors include abseiling, canoeing, archery and obstacle courses. 30 people are accommodated on each holiday with young and adult staff as companions. Nurse in attendance. Early booking essential.

Avon Tyrrell

Bransgore, Hampshire BH23 8EE.
☎ **01425 672347.**
W **www.avontyrrell.org.uk**

●● D/E/I/G

Activity centre on 60 acre site in New Forest for groups of all ages offering a wide range of activities with qualified instructors including climbing, canoeing, archery, zip wire, high and low rope and environmental studies. Accessible accommodation on either full board or self-catering basis.

Activity Holidays

Badaguish Centre

Aviemore, Inverness-shire PH22 1QU.
☎ **01479 861285.**
@ **info@badaguish.org**
W **www.badaguish.org**
●●●● D/E/I/G

Centre providing activity holidays with support for people with disabilities. Offers a wide range of activities in an area that includes the Cairngorm Funicular Railway and Morlich Water Sports Centre. Respite care activity holidays with 24-hour care arranged for unaccompanied disabled people. For groups there is also accommodation in fully accessible log cabins or under canvas.

Bendrigg Trust

Bendrigg Lodge, Old Hutton, Kendal, Cumbria LA8 0NR.
☎ **01539 723766.**
@ **office@bendrigg.org.uk**
W **www.bendrigg.org.uk**
●●● D/E/I/F/G

Residential activity centre specialising in courses for disabled and disadvantaged people. A wide range of outdoor and indoor activities available with qualified, experienced staff. Individual programmes are planned for each group. Open weeks are available for individuals and carers. Accommodation for up to 40 people in small dormitories. Lift and ramp to 1st floor. Adapted showers, washrooms and WCs.

Bowles

Eridge Green, Tunbridge Wells TN3 9LW.

☎ **01892 665665.**

@ **admin@bowles.ac**

W **www.bowles.ac**

●● D/E/F/G

Offers activity courses for groups of young people and adults including disabled people. Modern accommodation includes 2 twin bedrooms with en-suite shower rooms designed for wheelchair users. 14 other bedrooms and dormitory accommodation for 70 available. Activities include ski slopes, rock climbing and water sports. Some specialist equipment available.

Calvert Trust Exmoor

Wistlandpound, Kentisbury, Barnstaple, Devon EX31 4SJ.

☎ **/Textphone 01598 763221.**

@ **exmoor@calvert-trust.org.uk**

●●● D/E/I/F/G

Activity centre near coast and Exmoor, designed for disabled people and their companions. All bedrooms have shower rooms accessible to wheelchair users. Indoor swimming pool, jacuzzi and steam room. Riding facility on site. Activities offered include climbing, sailing, canoeing, fishing and archery. High ropes course, challenge course, hand crank cycles, orienteering. Self-catering units also available, see page 175.

Calvert Trust Keswick

Little Crosthwaite, Keswick, Cumbria CA12 4QD.

☎ **/Textphone 01768 772255.**

@ **enquiries.calvert.keswick@dial.pipex.com**

●●● D/E/I/F/G

Outdoor activity holidays and educational or personal development courses designed for individual group requirements. Accommodation in converted farmhouse with wheelchair access throughout. Bedrooms with en suite shower rooms. Facilities include sports hall, climbing wall, indoor pool, games room, TV lounge and library. Activities include rock climbing, abseiling, riding, water sports, fell walking, orienteering, archery and hockey. Specialist courses offered. Standard and adapted equipment. Qualified staff. Self-catering accommodation also available, see page 341.

Calvert Trust Kielder

Kielder Water, Hexham, Northumberland NE48 1BS.

☎ **01434 250232.**

@ **enquiries@calvert-kielder.com**

●●● D/E/I/G

Purpose-built holiday centre by Northumberland National Park for disabled people and their families and friends. Activities include water sports, climbing, abseiling archery and zipwire with king swing and low ropes course. Instruction and equipment available. There is a hydrotherapy pool and recreation hall. Care packages available. For self-catering accommodation see page 361.

Activity Holidays

Clyne Farm Centre

Westport Avenue, Mayals,
Swansea SA3 5AR.

☎ **01792 403333.**

@ **info@clynefarm.com**

W **www.clynefarm.com**

●● D/E/F/G

Accredited Activity Centre, 3 miles from central Swansea. Offers a range of activities including riding, canoeing and an assault course and also special interest courses to groups and individuals. Entrance level. Dining room/lounge level. Ramp or one step to other rooms. Nine self-catering cottages sleeping 4-16 people, up to 51 in total. Some are ground floor and some suitable for wheelchair users. Some adaptations for disabled people.

Apply: Geoff Haden.

Coldwell Activity Centre

Back Lane, Southfield,
Burnley BB10 3RD.

☎ **01282 601819.**

@ **bookings@coldwell.org.uk**

W **www.coldwell.org.uk**

●● D/E/I/F/G

Group holiday accommodation in the Pennines by Coldwell Reservoir. Outdoor activity programme available. Reserved parking bay. Entrance ramp. Public rooms level. Unisex WC. Lift to 1st floor. Adapted shower room. Accommodation for up to 24 in 11 bedrooms. Minimum group size 12.

The Kepplewray Centre

Broughton-in-Furness,
Cumbria LA20 6HE.

☎ **01229 716936.**

W **www.kepplewray.org.uk**

●● D/E/I/F/G/H

Activity & holiday centre in southern Lake District designed for groups including disabled people. Accommodation for up to 45. Ramp to side door. Lift to upper floor. Variety of bedrooms, bathrooms and toilets fitted for a range of disabilities. Equipment includes Clos-o-Mat WC, adjustable height bed, shower chair and electric hoist. A wide variety of outside and indoor activities are available. Programmes offered for families, schools and organisations. See also page 319.

Loch Insh Watersports

Insh Hall, Kincraig,
Inverness-shire. PH21 1NU.

☎ **01540 651272.**

W **www.lochinsh.com**

Privately run watersport centre in Cairngorm National Park between Aviemore and Kingussie offering courses for families and groups. The jetty is accessible for wheelchair users from the car park and boathouse/restaurant. Adapted canoes and a catamaran are available. Advance booking required. For information on self-catering accommodation designed for disabled guests see page 409.

Medina Valley Centre

Dodnor Lane, Newport,
Isle of Wight PO30 5TE.
☎ **01983 522195.**
W www.medinavalleycentre.org.uk
●● D/E/F/G

Centre offering RYA sailing courses, including 2-day "taster" sessions for people aged from 8 upwards. Two adapted Challenger trimarans are available. Accommodation entrance level. Public rooms level. WC and shower for wheelchair users. Two bedrooms with en-suite bedrooms have been designed for disabled people and 5 others have level access. **Apply:** Peter Savory.

Mersea Island Festival

East Mersea Youth Camp, Rewsalls Lane, East Mersea, Colchester CO5 8SX.
☎ **01206 383226.**
W www.merseafestival.org.uk

Two activity breaks of 5 and 3 days are offered in August each year comprising sport, music and art. The programme is designed to be accessible to everyone and includes water-sports, climbing, paintballing, archery, circus skills and workshops in music, dance, arts and crafts all with qualified instructors. The 70-acre site on coast has camping accommodation and associated facilities for up to 350 people.

Plas Menai National Watersports Centre

Llanfairisgaer, Caernarfon,
Gwynedd LL55 1UE.
☎ **01248 670964. W www.plasmenai.co.uk**
●● D/E

Centre owned by Sports Council for Wales offering watersports courses for individuals and groups including disabled people. Accommodation entrance level. Public rooms level. Adapted WCs. 43 bedrooms in separate blocks with bathroom, shower room and WC designed for disabled people.

Queen Elizabeth II Silver Jubilee Activities Centre

Manor Farm Country Park, Pylands Lane, Bursledon, Hampshire SO31 1BH.
☎ **023 8040 4844.**
W www.qe2activitycentre.co.uk
●●

Residential activity centre in Country Park by Hamble River near Southampton. Accommodation is in 6 self-catering cabins each for up to 8 people. Adapted cooking facilities, showers and toilets are available for participants with disabilities. Activities offered include canoeing, riding, orienteering and indoor sports. Facilities adapted for disabled people include a motor boat and a climbing wall.

Vitalise Churchtown Outdoor Adventure Centre

Lanlivery, Bodmin, Cornwall PL30 5BT.
☎ **01208 872148.**
●●●● D/E/I/G/H

Provides outdoor activity, adventure and environmental breaks with qualified instructors for adults and children with physical, sensory and learning disabilities. The centre is a converted farm with 5 twin and ten single and and five twin ensuite bedrooms. Dormitory accommodation is also available for school and large groups. Facilities include indoor swimming pool, climbing wall, zipwire, nature reserve and extensive grounds. Minibuses and all equipment adapted for use by disabled people. Registered for personal care. A carer must accompany any child aged between 6 and 12. Two accessible self-catering lodges are available in the grounds. Owned by Vitalise, see page 27.

Activity Holidays

Whitewave - Skye's Outdoor Centre

No. 19 Lincro, Kilmuir, Isle of Skye IV51 9YN.

☎ **01470 542414.**

@ **info@whitewave.co.uk**

W **www.white-wave.co.uk**

●● D/E/I/F/G

Family run centre in north Skye offering activities including canoeing, archery, Gaelic language courses and informal break.

Apply: Anne Martin and John White.

Woodlarks Camp Site Trust

Tilford Road, Lower Bourne, Farnham GU10 3RN.

☎ **01252 716279.**

@ **woodlarks103@btinternet.com**

W **www.woodlarks.org.uk**

●●

A woodland site for tented camping with some indoor accommodation including toilets and washing facilities. Tents and beds provided. Totally accessible and equipped for wheelchair users. Heated swimming pool, aerial runway and barbeque sites. Available for group bookings with seven weeks are open to individuals as disabled participants and volunteer helpers.

SPECIAL INTEREST CENTRES/COURSES

The following establishments and organisations offer a variety of courses in non-vocational subjects and other topics. Special interest breaks are also held at a number of the hotels and holiday centres listed in the regional sections of this guide.

Ammerdown Centre

Ammerdown Park, Radstock, Bath BA3 5SW.

☎ **01761 433709.**

W **www.ammerdown.org**

●● D/E/F/G

Conference & retreat centre. Entrance level. Public and lecture rooms ground floor. Lift to 1st floor. One twin and 2 single bedrooms with bathrooms designed for disabled guests. Programme of events and further information available on request.

Burton Manor

Burton, Neston, Cheshire CH64 5SJ.

☎ **0151 336 5172.**

W **www.burtonmanor.com**

●● D/E/G

Short residential courses offered all year. Parking near entrance. Ramp to main house entrance. Bedroom annexe level. Public and some teaching rooms ground floor. Ramp from dining room to terrace. Induction loop in main lecture room. Unisex WC. Two twin bedrooms designed for disabled guests. En suite bathrooms ⟲, handrails, space for side transfer to bath and WC.

Claridge House Centre for Healing

Dormans Road, Lingfield, Surrey RH7 6QH.

☎ **01342 832150.**

W **www.claridgehouse.quaker.eu.org**

●● D/E/F/G

Centre for rest, healing and renewal in large garden run by Friends (Quakers) Fellowship of Healing offering weekend courses on a variety of subjects with a healing focus and midweek breaks. Rear entrance level; main entrance 5 steps. Dining room and lounges level. Two bedrooms adapted for wheelchair users sharing shower room ⟲, roll-in shower with seat, handrails, space for side transfer to WC. Guests can be met from station. Winner of the 2008 Catey Award for accessibility.

Apply: The Warden.

Dillington House

Ilminster, Somerset TA19 9DT.

☎ **01460 52427. Textphone 01460 258640.**

W **www.dillington.com**

●● D/E/G ★★★★

Offers a range of residential courses throughout the year. Main entrance ramp. Automatic doors. Public rooms ground floor. Some lecture rooms have an entrance step. Induction loop at reception and main teaching rooms and portable one for use elsewhere. Unisex WCs. One bedroom with adapted bathroom designed for disabled people. Individual requirements should be checked on booking. Additional 16 fully accessible bedrooms from January 2009.

The Earnley Concourse

Earnley, Chichester PO20 7JL.

☎ **01243 670392.**

W **www.earnley.co.uk**

●● D/E/F

Centre offering a range of short courses. Reserved parking bays. Entrance ramp. Public and most lecture rooms level, portable ramp available. Unisex WC. One bedroom with bathroom designed for disabled people. Other ground floor bedrooms level.

Apply: Owain Roberts, Administrator.

Higham Hall

Bassenthwaite Lake,
Cockermouth, Cumbria CA13 9SH.

☎ **01768 776276.**

@ **admin@highamhall.com**

W **www.highamhall.com**

●● D/G

Residential adult education college in northern Lake District offering a varied programme of short courses all year. Main public areas accessible to disabled people. Stairlift on main staircase. Induction loop in the lecture room and also a portable loop. Bungalow in the grounds adapted for wheelchair user and companions. For further information on this see page 340.

Holton Lee

East Holton, Poole BH16 6JN.

☎ **01202 631063.**

@ **info@holtonlee.co.uk**

W **www.holtonlee.co.uk**

●●● D/E/I/F/G/H

Purpose built centre for disabled people and carers in 350-acre estate overlooking Poole Harbour. Offers a range of residential and day courses on the environment, creative arts and personal development. The Barn has accommodation for up to nine people with adjustamatic beds, ceiling hoists and roll-in showers. There are also 3 self-catering cottages sleeping from 4 to 10 people. Powered wheelchairs/all-terrain vehicles are available.

Apply: The Administrator.

Rates: on application.

The Kingcombe Centre

Toller Porcorum, Dorchester, Dorset DT2 0EQ.

☎ 01300 320684.

W www.kingcombe-centre.demon.co.uk

●● D/E/I/F/G

Study centre in converted farm buildings surrounded by nature reserve. A variety of residential and day courses are organised throughout the year, many drawing on the natural history of the surrounding area. Small step to main building, ramp available. Main public rooms on ground floor, level or ramped. Unisex WC. Two bedrooms in annexe, single and twin, designed for disabled people. Roll-in shower room opposite, ⟲, handrails, space by WC, shower chair available. Accessible paths and boardwalks and all-terrain buggy. Escorts for visually impaired participants provided on some courses. Accommodation may also be available for self-programming groups.

Knuston Hall Residential College

Irchester, Wellingborough NN29 7EU.

☎ 01933 312104.

W www.knustonhall.org.uk

●● D/E/G

Offers short residential courses on literature, arts, crafts and music. Reserved parking bays. Entrance level, automatic doors. Main public rooms level. Most teaching rooms level and fitted with induction loop. Platform lift to lower teaching rooms and carpark. Ramp to 6 ground floor bedrooms with en suite bathrooms, one adapted for disabled people. Stair lift to 1st floor bedrooms. Individual requirements should be checked when enquiring about a course.

Pendrell Hall College

Codsall Wood, Nr. Wolverhampton WV8 1QP.

☎ 01902 434112.

W www.pendrell-hall.org.uk

●● D/E/I/F/G

Adult residential college offering non-vocational courses in a range of subjects. Reserved parking bay. Entrance ramp. Public rooms ground floor or in a separate building with ramp. Wheelchair lift to dining room. Lift to the 1st floor of the main building. Portable induction loop available. Unisex WC. In separate building 2 bedrooms with en suite bathrooms adapted for disabled people and 9 other ground floor bedrooms.

Welsh Institute of Sport

Sophia Gardens, Cardiff CF11 9SW.

☎ 0845 045 0902.

@ wis@scw.co.uk

W www.welsh-institute-sport.co.uk

●● D/E/I/F/G

Sports centre offering residential accommodation for courses and for non-participants. Entrance ramp, automatic doors. Lift 100cm, inside 120x120cm. Two twin bedrooms designed for disabled guests. Shower rooms with sliding door, ⟲, handrails, shower tray, space for side transfer to WC. Waterproof sheets available. Tactile signs and braille plan of premises.

HOLIDAYS AFLOAT

Accessible Boating

c/o Peter Bridle, 31 Burns Avenue, Church Crookham, Fleet, Hampshire GU52 6BN.

☎ **01252 622520.**

W **www.accessibleboating.org.uk**

"Madam Butterfly" is a purpose-built, 7-berth canal boat for disabled people and their companions based at Odiham on the Basingstoke Canal. It is equipped with hydraulic lifts at prow and stern, power-assisted steering and hoists for a shower/WC and over one bed. A day boat for groups is also available.

The Bruce Trust

PO Box 21, Hungerford, Berkshire RG17 9YY.

☎ **01672 515498.**

W **www.brucetrust.org.uk**

Operates 4 specially designed boats, two 12 berth, one 10 berth and one 6 berth, on the Kennet & Avon Canal. These are based at Great Bedwyn, for cruising between Reading and Devizes, and below Devizes Locks from where return cruises to Bath are possible. Each boat is equipped with a hydraulic lift and specially designed toilet. Full training can be given to group leaders.

The Bruce Wake Charitable Trust

Ayston, Oakham, Rutland LE15 9AE.

☎ **01572 822183.**

W **www.brucewaketrust.co.uk**

Operates three boats designed for use by disabled people, based at Upton-on-Severn between Tewkesbury and Worcester. Two narrowboats designed for a wheelchair user and family with berths for 6-7 people for holidays on the rivers and canals of the south west Midlands. They have two hydraulic lifts, a hoist over a bed and a specially designed WC/shower. Plus a wide-beamed boat is available for use on the rivers Severn and Avon and the Gloucester-Sharpness Canal.

The Canal Boat Project

PO Box 5768, Harlow CM20 2XB.

☎ **01279 424444.**

W **www.canalboat.org.uk**

The Canal Boat Project has a small fleet of purpose built or specially adapted accessible boats for hire to disabled people and community groups on the rivers Lee and Stort. A wide-beam residential boat sleeps up to 12 and day boats are also available. Each has a lift giving access most parts of the boats and some also have specialist control equipment to enable disabled people with disabilities to steer. Boats can be hired for self steering or with the services of a skipper.

Coventry Rainbow Canal Boat Trust

The "Lady Godiva" is a purpose built narrow boat that can carry up to six people for holidays and 12 on day trips on Midlands canals from its base at Sutton Stop north of Coventry. It has a ramp for boarding and a lift between the fore deck and the cabin. A skipper is provided. **Apply:** Bruce or Jill Pettigrew, 75 Wyke Road, Wyken, Coventry CV2 3DT.

☎ 024 7645 9621.

Docklands Canal Boat Trust

8 Lloyd Villas, Roman Road, East Ham, London E6 3SW.

☎ **020 7511 2911.**

W **www.dcbt.org.uk**

"Challenge" is a 70' narrowboat based on the Lee & Stort Canal on the Hertfordshire/Essex border. There are berths for up to 10 people. It has a lift between decks and other features for disabled people. A skipper is provided. Bookings are taken for one, two and five days from May to the end of September.

Ethel Trust Community Barge

Volserve House, West Bar Green,
Sheffield S1 2DA.
☎ **0114 278 6338.**
@ **etheltrust@tiscali.co.uk**
W **www.etheltrustcommunitybarge.co.uk**

"Ethel" is a purpose-built barge offering day and residential trips on the inland waterways of South Yorkshire for community groups including disabled people. It is based at Thorne, near Doncaster and has berths for up to 10 people. Access is by ramp and there are hydraulic lifts at the bow and the stern. There are two toilets, one with a shower, designed for disabled people. A skipper and crew member are supplied.

Jubilee Sailing Trust

Hazel Road, Woolston,
Southampton SO19 7GB.
☎ **02380 449138.**
W **www.jst.org.uk**

The JST offers adventure holidays as crew members of "Lord Nelson" and "Tenacious", purpose-built square-rigged tall sailing ships. Voyages last 4-10 days running around the UK, off the Canary Islands and sometimes further afield. Applications are taken from anyone aged over 16. People with disabilities, including wheelchair users, work alongside an equal number of able-bodied people. Special equipment includes flat wide decks, audio compasses, lifts between decks and an adjustable seat at the helm. The 10 person permanent crew on each ship includes medical pursers.

The Lyneal Trust

Lyneal Wharf, Ellesmere, Shropshire.
W **www.lyneal-trust.org.uk**

Charity providing water-based holidays for disabled people on the Llangollen Canal in north Shropshire. The "Shropshire Lass II" is a newly-built canal boat with berths for 8 people. It has a specially designed WC and shower, lift and hydraulic steering and all areas are accessible to wheelchair users. A second boat is available for day trips. At Lyneal Wharf there is a games room, kitchen and showers and two chalets and a bungalow which can accom-modate up to 16 people. The boats and land accommodation can be used for groups of different sizes.
Apply: Pushkar Trivedi, The Lyneal Trust, The Shirehall, Abbey Foregate, Shrewsbury SY2 6ND. ☎ 01743 252728.
@ pushkar.trivedi@shropshire-cc.gov.uk.

Peter Le Marchant Trust

Canalside Moorings, Beeches Road,
Loughborough LE11 2NS.
☎ **01509 265590.**
W **www.peterlemarchanttrust.co.uk**

The Trust has three boats designed for disabled and seriously ill people. "Seranade" takes up to 10 people on 4-5 day holidays, "Melody" is available for weekly hire by families and similar sized groups and "Symphony" takes up to 26 people on day trips. All have hydraulic lifts, toilets and showers designed for wheelchair users, central heating and resuscitation equipment.
Apply: Mrs Lynn Smith,
Trust Administrator.

Reach Out Projects

Holywell Lodge, 41 Holywell Hill,
St Albans AL1 1HE.

☎ **01727 818168.**

🆆 **www.reachoutprojects.org.uk**

ROP has a self-steered narrowboat with 12 berths and 2 wide-beamed boats with skippers for hire for day, weekend or longer periods. These are based on the Grand Union Canal at Hemel Hempstead. Two boats have access for disabled people. Available for hire by groups working with young people and others with special needs. Training is provided for self steerers.

The '72 Club

"The 72 Club" canal boat is owned by Queen Elizabeth's Foundation and based at Aldermaston Wharf near Reading. It can be used to cruise the Kennet & Avon Canal or the upper Thames, although an additional licence will have to be bought for the latter. It has accommodation for up to 7 people including 3 wheelchair users. Fittings include ceiling hoist tracking, adapted shower and toilet, microwave, central heating and low level windows. It is available for hire by the week or for short breaks.

Apply: Hoseasons ☎ 0870 543 4434

🆆 www.hoseasons.co.uk

Vale of Llangollen Canal Boat Trust

The Old Armour, Berwyn Street,
Llangollen LL20 8NF.

🆆 **www.canalboattrust.org.uk**

The Trust has two narrowboats adapted for disabled people based at Trevor on the Llangollen Canal. The "Millie" is available for holidays for up to 6 people. The "Glas y Dorlan" is used for day trips by groups of up to 12. Skipper provided.

Apply: Phil Davies ☎ 01978 861450.

@ office@canalboattrust.org.uk

Yorkshire Waterways Museum

Dutch River Side, Goole DN14 5TB.

☎ **01405 768730.**

🆆 **www.waterwaysmuseum.org.uk**

The "Sobriety" is a converted barge used for groups of up to 12 people for residential trips on the Aire & Calder canal and other waterways in Yorkshire and Lincolnshire. A lift is provided between the cabin and the deck level. A skipper is provided. Week-long, weekend and day bookings are taken. The museum also has a number of day boats adapted to carry disabled passengers.

WORKING HOLIDAYS

British Trust for Conversation Volunteers

SEDUM House, Mallard Way, Potterik Carr,
Doncaster DN4 8DB.

☎ **01302 388888.**

🆆 **www.btcv.org.**

BTCV's extensive conservation holidays programme includes projects that may be suitable for some disabled people. Full details of BTCV activities and contact details for regional offices is given on their website.

Index to advertisers

A

C

D

E

F

H

Index to advertisers

L

M

N

O

P

R

S

T

V

W

Y

Index to places – Accommodation entries

Index to places – Accommodation entries

C

Index to places – Accommodation entries

D

E

Index to places – Accommodation entries

Index to places – Accommodation entries

Index to places – Accommodation entries

N

Index to places – Accommodation entries

Index to places – Accommodation entries

S

T

Index to places – Accommodation entries

COMMENTS ON ACCOMMODATION MENTIONED IN THE 2009 GUIDE

RADAR would greatly appreciate hearing of readers' experiences at accommodation listed in this edition of the guide. Alternatively, please use this form to make us aware of establishments not currently listed but which are believed to be suitable

Name ....

Address ....

....

Name of accommodation..

Address ....

....

Listed in RADAR Guide Yes/No

If 'yes', please give page number:...

Your comments (please continue on a separate sheet if necessary): ....

....

....

....

....

Date of stay ....

Your disability...

Are you a wheelchair user? Full time/Sometimes/Not at all

Are you able to climb steps? ....

Please return to:
RADAR, 12 City Forum, 250 City Road, London EC1V 8AF